A USER GUIDE TO THE

UNIX™

S Y S T E M

Rebecca Thomas, Ph.D.
Jean Yates

Osborne **McGraw-Hill**
Berkeley, California

A USER GUIDE TO THE UNIX SYSTEM
INTERNATIONAL EDITION

3rd Printing 1987.

ISBN 0-07-099182-0

Printed and Bound in Singapore by Fong & Sons Printers Pte Ltd

TABLE OF CONTENTS

DEDICATION

To Fran, Tink, and Linda, without whose support and understanding throughout the years this book would not have been possible.

ACKNOWLEDGMENTS

With so many people to thank, it is impossible to thank them all. A few, however, stand out for us as we go to press with this book.

Several key people at Osborne/McGraw-Hill helped make this second edition what it is. First and foremost, Dr. Thomas thanks Geta Carlson for her excellent work in developing and editing this second edition. Her suggestions for change and her editorial assistance throughout the project helped to make this edition both a simpler and more complete guide to the UNIX system. Karen Hanson did an admirable job of coordinating the manuscript through the different editorial phases. Jean Yates thanks Kevin Gleason for editing her chapter, Chapter 1 ("Understanding the UNIX System"), and Becca Thomas thanks him for editing Chapter 2. Thanks should go to Denise Penrose for being there when she was needed, and to Brad Hellman and Sue Clupper for their assistance with the appendices. Last but not least, Becca expresses her appreciation of the fine work done by the art and production departments at Osborne. Keeping a book of this size on schedule required the coordinated assistance of many professionals.

Among those outside of Osborne who helped influence the direction of this book, Becca Thomas recalls in particular the comments and suggestions provided by Beth Howell, Joe Campbell, and Ric Farrow. Thanks also to Irene Pasternack for her suggestion of a way of using a personal dictionary to check the spelling of a document.

Several people outside of Osborne have also helped with this book. First, Becca Thomas would like to thank Gene Dronek, Armando Stettner, Bill Tuthill, and others for answering her numerous questions about the UNIX system. This book would not have been possible without access to the many different UNIX versions documented here. Dr. Thomas acknowledges the cooperation of the University of California for providing access to the latest Berkeley releases; Dynabyte Business Computers for a loan of a Monarch with a vanilla System III port; and both AT&T and Opus Systems for access to System V. Thanks also to Uni-Ops for many of the items in our appendix of resources.

Thanks to all those readers of the first edition who provided suggestions for this new edition. We welcome your further comments and encourage you to send them along c/o Osborne/McGraw-Hill.

Last but not least, Becca Thomas acknowledges the fine work performed by her three cats, Beetle Bailey, Grey Matter, and Nubbins, who acted as cheerleaders and paperweights throughout the rewriting process.

INTRODUCTION

For several reasons, anyone using the UNIX operating system needs a clear and comprehensive tutorial and reference guide. While Bell Laboratories has documented the UNIX system, the documentation was written largely by and for system programmers: it is too technical for most users in the growing UNIX marketplace. Furthermore, the UNIX system is much larger than microcomputer operating systems like CP/M or MS-DOS. The power and capabilities of the UNIX system can easily become overwhelming.

Whether you are familiar with the UNIX operating system or not, the revised **User Guide to the UNIX™ System** has been written for you. For beginning users, this guide offers step-by-step development of basic UNIX concepts and procedures. Like the first edition, the second edition uses a learn-by-doing approach with extensive computer-side tutorials for immediate, practical fluency. What is new in the second edition is the greatly expanded presentation of the concepts that underlie the UNIX system and an emphasis on the character of the system as a whole. This book isolates a core of information that everyone needs to know in order to use the UNIX system effectively.

If you already have some experience with UNIX, you will find that the broad base of information in this book makes it an excellent reference as well as a stepping-stone for more advanced study. We discuss over 75 commonly used UNIX command programs, documenting 44 of those in great depth. For each of the 44 commands explained in depth, you will find summaries of all available command options and extensive lists explaining error and informational messages for Bell Version 7, and System III and System V, as well as the Berkeley version of the UNIX system.

To make the different kinds of information in this book easier to access, we have divided the book into four parts. Part One gives you an overview of the UNIX system and its constituent programs and describes the application of these programs to business and science. In the 12 tutorial sessions that make up Part Two, you actually work with the system, learning fundamental concepts and procedures and mastering the special features of the system. Part Three explains 44 of the more useful command programs in detail. Finally, Part Four presents additional information in seven appendices.

Here is an overview of what you will find in each chapter and appendix:

In Chapter 1, "Understanding the UNIX System," you are introduced to the major features and facilities provided by the UNIX system. The last part of this chapter chronicles the development of the UNIX system by Bell Laboratories, the business community's discovery of the system, and the reasons that UNIX is becoming a major player in the microcomputer revolution.

Chapter 2, "UNIX in the Workplace," discusses the UNIX system as a support base for running applications. The first part of this chapter explains why the major features of this operating system constitute an especially useful and efficient applications environment. The chapter outlines the types of application software available today for the UNIX system.

In Chapter 3, "Fundamentals of Using the UNIX System," you begin actually working with the UNIX system. This chapter consists of five tutorial sessions that lead you from the basics of logging on the system to organizing your data into an electronic filing cabinet.

In Chapter 4, "Mastering the Special Features of the UNIX System," you will learn more about interacting with the popular UNIX command interpreters, the Bourne Shell and the C Shell. You will also learn how to control the execution of commands that you invoke.

"Text Processing with UNIX" is the topic of Chapter 5. Chapter 5 explains not only the **ed** and **ex** line-oriented editors but also the **vi** screen-oriented editor. In addition, you will learn how to use the **nroff** text formatter for producing paginated documents.

Chapter 6, "Commonly Used UNIX System Commands," covers 44 of the most commonly used UNIX command programs in detail. In addition to the summaries of available command options and the explanations of error and informational messages for Bell Version 7, System III, System V, and the Berkeley versions of these commands, Chapter 6 discusses each command's operation in detail and follows this up with extensive tutorial examples.

Appendix A, "Resources," continues this book's tradition of presenting information on computers that run UNIX, software that runs under UNIX, and user support of the UNIX system.

Appendix B, "Summary of UNIX System V," presents two extensive lists: the command programs included in Bell System V and commands available only with Bell System III or Version 7.

Appendix C, "Interacting With Your UNIX System," discusses communicating with your UNIX system in a broad sense. First of all, Appendix C explains the steps for setting up your terminal or modem to a UNIX computer. Next, Appendix C explains how users of non-UNIX microcomputers can access the UNIX system and discusses the communication software required to access text files and to transfer them between UNIX and the non-UNIX microcomputer system. In addition, Appendix C explains how to customize your working environment with shell variables. The general terminal interface is discussed, and finally the terminal mode settings for Bell Version 7, System III, System V, and Berkeley are tabulated.

Appendix D, "Essentials of System Administration," covers the basic steps for bringing a UNIX system up and shutting it down gracefully. This appendix explains how to create and maintain a file system and how to manage its disk space. The important topic of backing up your data is covered extensively. The procedures involved in disabling and enabling the terminal lines to the central computer are outlined. Finally, the appendix tells you how to add and delete user accounts.

Appendix E, "Octal Equivalents of ASCII," contains a useful chart of the ASCII character set along with the octal values of these characters.

Appendix F, "Quick Reference to UNIX System Commands," is a compendium of all the invocation options for the commands presented in Chapter 6.

Appendix G, "Selected Bibliography," provides an excellent reference to a wide range of literature, from introductory material to specific technical papers describing the UNIX System.

Finally, our extensive and detailed cross-referenced index will help you locate topics quickly and efficiently.

PART ONE

CHAPTER 1

UNDERSTANDING THE UNIX SYSTEM

By common estimates, half a million people use the UNIX operating system, which was developed by Bell Laboratories and is sold on over a hundred different computers. Like all operating systems, UNIX controls the activities and resources of your computer, interpreting the commands you enter at the keyboard and translating them into actions directed at some part of your computer system, such as its disk drive, memory, or printer. UNIX coordinates many activities of the computer at once, allowing one person to print a document while another person runs a spelling checker program, and while still another person is entering accounting data, and so on. The operating system channels all of the commands typed at different keyboards by different users and all of the streams of information generated by the running of various programs. The operating system keeps the computer organized, preventing the commands of one user or program from interfering with those of another. To keep your coworker's memo from appearing in your letter, for example, UNIX must organize the memory storage of your computer, effectively partitioning your work from anyone else's.

Designed in 1969, the UNIX system was originally intended to provide an environment in which programmers could create programs. It soon became apparent that UNIX also provided an environment in which business, scientific, and industrial users could run programs to help them in their work. The UNIX system was originally developed for medium-sized minicomputers (specifically the DEC PDP series) and later moved to large, powerful mainframe computers as well as microcomputers. Bell Laboratories has consistently introduced new versions of UNIX every few years. Each time another version has been released, it has included more new features both for programmers and for business users. There are, consequently, many versions of UNIX. They are shown in Table 1-1. Each version corresponds to a standard release from AT&T.

The UNIX system runs on so many computers and is used in so many different ways that the basic operating system has spawned dozens of implementations. An *implementation* is a customized UNIX version, usually for a specific computer. An implementation of UNIX is always based on one of the versions of UNIX shown in Table 1-1. Examples include Zeus, an implementation for Zilog computers, based on System V; Xenix, from Microsoft, a software company, based on System III and running on over 20 microcomputers; and PC/IX, an implementation for the IBM PC, also based on System III.

How the UNIX System Differs From Other Operating Systems

The purpose of all operating systems is much the same: to control a computer's activities. Operating systems differ in how they do their job and in what additional features they offer. UNIX is unique in its modular design, which allows

Table 1-1.   *The AT&T Versions of UNIX*

Version	Year Released	Comments
Version 6	1975	For use by universities only
Version 7	1978	First version sold commercially, but used mostly by universities
System III	1981	Change in numbering indicated change to commercial orientation
System V, Release 1	1983	Many enhancements of System III to improve commercial appeal
System V, Release 2	1984	Enhancements of Release 1 and performance improvements

users to add or remove parts to fit their precise needs, as seen in Figure 1-1. UNIX programs are like puzzle pieces; the modules fit together with standard connections. You can remove one and replace it with another or expand the whole system by adding many modules. In a way, every person's UNIX system is unique. Most users add or delete modules as needed, tailoring their implementation to their precise purposes. If you don't need a module, you can usually remove it without impairing the operation of the rest of the system. This feature is especially useful in microcomputer implementations, where disk drives have limited

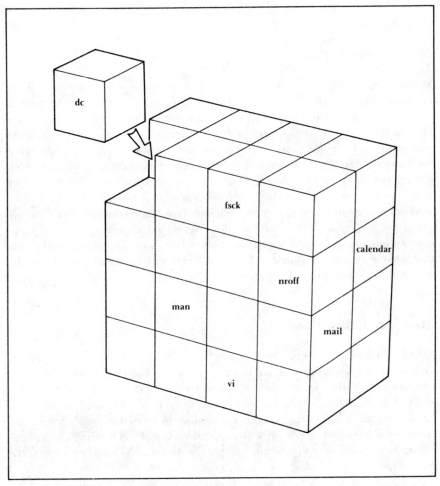

Figure 1-1. *The modular structure of the UNIX system*

capacity; removing unneeded programs makes room for more data files.

The UNIX system has many useful features, the most important of which are its

- Multitasking capability
- Multiuser capability
- Transportability
- Large selection of powerful UNIX-supplied programs
- Communications and electronic mail
- Library of applications software.

Multitasking Capabilities

Multitasking is performing more than one task at a time—for example, talking on the telephone and, at the same time, taking notes. You may even be using a calculator, which would be doing three things at once. Doing more than one thing at the same time on a computer is also multitasking. When you print a file and, while it is printing, start editing another document, you are performing multitasking operations. When you run two programs at the same time, such as sorting a mailing list in alphabetical order while word processing the letter to be sent to those on the mailing list, the computer is multitasking.

Multitasking with a computer lets you simultaneously perform tasks formerly performed sequentially. Not only is the original set of tasks performed more quickly, but you and the computer are also free to do still other things in the time that you have saved. In Chapters 3, 4, and 5 you will see many ways to use the multitasking capabilities of UNIX to speed up your work.

Multiuser Capabilities

UNIX is not only a multitasking system, it is a multiuser system. A multiuser system permits several users to use the same computer simultaneously. More than one terminal (keyboard plus display) can be connected to one computer, and the users of the terminals can all run programs, access files, and print documents at once. The operating system manages the requests made to the computer by many users, sorts them out, keeps them from interfering with each other, and assigns priorities when two or more people want to use the same data file or printer at the same time.

Multiuser capability saves time by allowing more than one person to work on a set of information at a time. A credit card company's telephone credit-checking department, for example, requires that many people access the same data more or less at the same time. When you buy something in a department store, a salesperson calls the credit card company. A clerk answers the telephone, takes the number of the credit card over the phone, and enters it at a computer terminal. A program then checks your number against a large data file on the computer containing the records of all credit cards. The record for your card number is shown to the clerk, and if your credit standing is good, the clerk gives approval, and off you go with your purchase. Multiply your clerk by ten, or by fifty, and you can see the enormous advantage of a multiuser system, where all can access the same file of data at the same time. Imagine how long it would take for you to get your purchase approved if the clerk had to wait in line for access to the data file, instead of being one of many looking at it simultaneously.

Another important part of this credit card company's system is its ability to maintain current data. If your credit card is stolen, for example, you want the number flagged immediately so that no one can use it. Multiuser operating systems allow someone to update the one central file that everyone is accessing and immediately change the data base that is available to all users. If each clerk at the credit card company had a single-user system with his or her own copy of the data file, every system would have to be updated—a time-consuming process. Your card could have been used several times before everyone's computer gave instructions to reject the card.

Not all implementations of the multiuser capability are quite as dramatic, but even in everyday computing for a small business, the gains are significant. The ability of two or more persons to simultaneously enter new accounts payable records or to print invoices or to do word processing, all on the same computer, saves time and frees people for more productive work.

A multiuser system generally costs less than the equivalent number of single-user systems. For instance, a high-performance four-user UNIX microcomputer costs about $12-15,000 today, which is a savings of $5-8,000 over the purchase of four $5,000 single-user systems.

UNIX System Portability

The UNIX system itself is very portable. That is, it is easier to modify the UNIX system code for installation on a new computer than to rewrite another operation system from scratch for the new computer. The ability to transport (or simply "port") the UNIX system from one brand of computer to another has been a major reason for the acceptance of this system.

The UNIX system runs on more brands and types of computers, small to large, than any other operating system. When you buy a UNIX-based computer, you can later change to a different one without learning a new computer operating system. This saves money and time. Having purchased a new copy of your old applications setup for the new computer, all you have to do is move your data to your new computer. You don't have to learn to use a new program, and you don't have

Table 1-2. *Programs in the UNIX System*

Application	Program or Data File on UNIX System
Spelling dictionary	spell, /usr/dict/words
Desk calculator	dc, bc
Text editing	ed, [ex and vi (University of California, Berkeley)]
Text print formatting	roff, nroff
Typesetting	troff
Accounting and invoicing system users	ac, sa, accton
Electronic mail	mail
Computer-aided instruction	learn
On-line manual for UNIX system	man
Formatting	tbl
Typeset mathematical equations	eqn
Interactive program debugger	adb
Assembler	as
Pattern scanning and processing language	awk
BASIC language interpreter	bas
Reminder service	calendar
C language compiler	cc, pcc
FORTRAN compiler (compatible with C)	f77
Relocating program loader	ld
Line printer spooler	lpr
Maintain program groups	make
Structured FORTRAN preprocessor	ratfor
Find and insert literature references in documents	refer, lookbib
Stream editor	sed
Command processing	sh, [csh (University of California, Berkeley)]
UNIX intersystem communication	uucp, unlog, uux
On-line communication	write, wall
Compiler generators	lex, yacc
File management	ar, cat, cd, chgrp, chmod, chown, cmp, comm, cp, diff, find, ln, ls, mkdir, mv, pr, rm, rmdir, tail, tar, touch
System status information	date, du, file, ps, pwd, stty, tty, who
System maintenance	clri, dcheck, df, dump, icheck, iostat, mkfs, mknod, mount, ncheck, quot, restore, sa, umount
Running program support	at, cron, echo, expr, kill, nice, sleep, tee, wait
Text processing (not including editors)	crypt, grep, look, sort, uniq, wc

to reenter your data. UNIX contains a set of programs that will let you connect your old computer to your new one and transfer the data from the old system to the new one easily (with the help of an experienced computer person). Retraining computer users is unnecessary because they use the same programs; the only difference, insignificant to them, is the computer hardware. Because neither rekeying of data nor retraining of personnel is required, you become productive on your new computer immediately.

UNIX System-Supplied Tools

The UNIX system comes with several hundred supplied programs (see Table 1-2). These programs can be divided into two classes:

- Integral utilities
- Tools

Integral utilities are parts of the UNIX system that provide such assistance to the operating system that they are absolutely necessary for the practical operation of a computer with UNIX. One example is the UNIX system command interpreter, or shell program. Without this program, you could not request (or command) your UNIX system to perform any work for you. Tools, on the other hand, are programs that are not necessary to the computer's basic operation, but provide significant additional value to UNIX. These tools include many applications programs, some of which may be purchased separately, such as electronic spreadsheet and sophisticated word processing packages.

Integral utilities are utilities that let you set up sophisticated automatic procedures to perform a series of tasks that would otherwise have to be performed as many separate actions. For example, you can set up a system so that typing one word at the computer terminal causes a mailing list to be sorted and the result merged with a letter, letters to all those on the list printed out, and a message sent to you at your terminal telling you that the task is complete.

UNIX system tools include an extensive "electronic filing cabinet" system, word processing, typesetting capabilities, an "electronic mail" system, and many other programs.

UNIX Communications

Communication software is part of the UNIX system. UNIX communications capabilities include the following options.

- Communicating between different terminals hooked into the same computer.
- Communicating between users of one computer in your office with users of another computer in your office. (This second computer may be a different brand or size.)
- Communicating between computers of different sizes and types in different locations—as far away as other countries.

The simplest form of electronic communication is between people using terminals hooked into the same computer. Using electronic mail or a direct terminal writing program, they can send messages reminding each other of meetings or requesting information. If two different UNIX computers, even of different brands, have been connected together with UNIX utilities, users of these different computers can send mail and exchange files as though they are on the same computer. The UNIX system can also use telephone lines to accomplish communication between computers in different locations. There are several large networks of UNIX-based computers across the United States that routinely send messages and data to each other.

Third-Party Applications Programs

In addition to the applications programs supplied by Bell, a library of over 500 UNIX applications programs has been developed and is sold by "third parties"—computer manufacturers and software companies. These programs are not part of the basic UNIX system, but can be purchased separately and then run by the system according to your particular needs. UNIX applications programs take advantage of UNIX's multiuser and multitasking capabilities and can typically be used by more than one person at a time. For example, most accounting programs let you and your assistants enter records in the payables file as well as print out checks at the same time.

Other UNIX applications programs were first developed for expensive mini-computers (those costing $100,000 and more) and later were adapted to the less expensive UNIX systems. These minicomputer programs generally are more useful than their microcomputer equivalents. For example, a minicomputer-based general ledger program might offer unlimited subledgers, integral cost accounting, integral manufacturing resources planning, and cost center analysis. A minicomputer word processing program might permit many word processors to work on the same very large document (a book or even an encyclopedia) at the same time, provide many automatic management features enabling the tracking of large numbers of documents in progress, and display the document on the screen the way it would actually look when typeset. Because of competition and generally lower prices for UNIX computer systems, the microcomputer version of the minicomputer-derived program costs less.

The Structure of the UNIX System

The UNIX system's parts may be functionally categorized as three levels: the kernel, the shell, and the tools and applications (see Figure 1-2).

- The kernel schedules tasks and manages data storage.
- The shell is a program that connects and interprets the commands typed by a user. It interprets user requests, calls programs from memory, and executes them one at a time or in a series called a "pipe."
- The supplied tools and applications add special capabilities to the operating system.

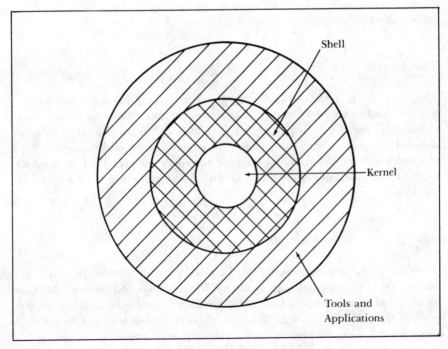

Figure 1-2.　*The parts of the UNIX system*

A description of the hierarchical file and directory system is also included here. It will let you set up useful filing systems in your computer for documents and data.

The UNIX hierarchical file system lets you set up electronic indexes for the large numbers of data files that collect on everyone's computer. It also functions as the basic structure through which you move from work area to work area.

The UNIX file system looks like the branches of an upside-down tree (see Figure 1-3). At the top is the root, or first directory from which a second level of directories descends. This initial level of directories is standard to most UNIX systems and is described in Figure 1-3. Each of these directories contains a major functional segment of the UNIX operating system.

Within your directory, you can set up efficient, timesaving filing systems. You can divide your work space into more subdirectories and move information around in them as needed. In Figure 1-4, a typical user has set up a system to separate the word processing files for different books into different subdirectories of the system. Accounting data and memos from other people on the system are saved in still other subdirectories.

Think about the way that you set up an organizational scheme for a filing cabinet. UNIX lets you build an electronic equivalent with the hierarchical file and directory system as the matrix.

The Kernel

The kernel is the heart of the operating system, controlling the hardware and actually turning parts of the computer system on and off at a program's commands. All operating systems have a kernel, although it may be called by other names. For instance, when you type in the command "ls" (to list the names of the files and subdirectories contained in your directory), the kernel directs the computer to read the names of the files from disk and to place them on the screen for you to see.

The Shell

There are several shells available to UNIX users. Typically, the Bourne Shell, and perhaps the C Shell as well, comes with a UNIX system. Other "menu" shells are usually sold as add-on packages. Menu shells are easy-to-use, "pick what you want off the menu list" systems. Many UNIX users take advantage of the different shells for different jobs. Beginners use the easy menu shells, while more experienced users prefer the command-driven C or Bourne Shells.

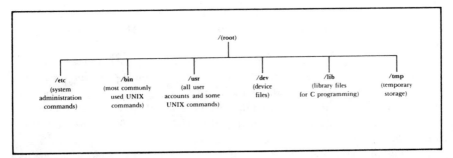

Figure 1-3. The UNIX file system

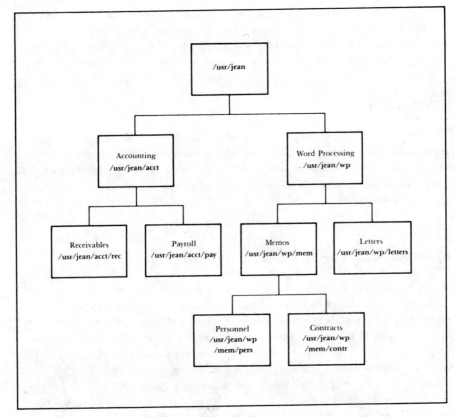

Figure 1-4. A typical UNIX directory system

The shell provides an easy connection between you and the computer. Like human interpreters who stand between two people who speak different languages and translate the spoken words of one into the language of the other, the shell stands between you and the kernel. It "speaks" both your language and the machine language understood by the computer. The shell program interprets commands that you type when you work with the operating system and translates them into commands that the kernel understands. The shell tells the kernel to do the work you have requested, eliminating the need for you to talk to the kernel directly in a way that the kernel could understand.

The shell also contains a facility for chaining, or "pipelining," commands. As seen in Figure 1-5, a file of data can be sent down a "pipeline" with stops along the way where different programs perform actions on the file. A single piping command can cause a data file to be processed by several programs sequentially down the pipeline. The output of one program flows down the pipe and becomes input to the next program. For example, a mailing list file could be started down a pipeline, sorted at the first stop by ZIP code, merged into a form letter at the next stop, copied and that copy sent to a storage location at the next, and printed out at the last stop.

UNIX Tools

The third, "outer" layer of the UNIX system contains the UNIX tools. The actual tools vary from implementation to implementation. Some implementations include all of the more than 400 UNIX tools. Some, however, only package a subset appropriate to one kind of user — word processors, business people, programmers, and so on.

Who Should Use the UNIX System?

When considering UNIX for your computer implementation, you should first weigh the constraints of its resource requirements. The UNIX system is physically larger than most microcomputer operating systems. A typical system requires up to 8 megabytes of space, and because of its multiuser capabilities and large set of programs, requires a computer with at least a 10-megabyte hard disk, a 16-bit processor, and a human manager, called a system administrator.

Unlike personal computers, where one person is responsible for his or her personal system, UNIX systems are often used by several people, few of whom want to spend the time maintaining or administering their system. System administration involves managing operation of the computer, saving data on backup disks

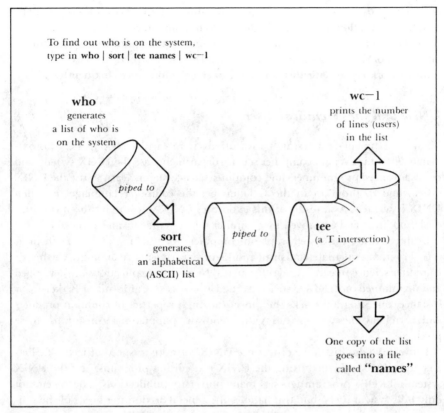

To find out who is on the system,
type in **who** | **sort** | **tee names** | **wc−1**

who
generates
a list of who is
on the system

piped to

sort
generates
an alphabetical
(ASCII) list

piped to

tee
(a T intersection)

wc−1
prints the number
of lines (users)
in the list

One copy of the list
goes into a file
called **"names"**

Figure 1-5. *A UNIX pipeline*

for storage, assigning passwords for new users, contacting the computer manufacturer when something goes wrong, and generally being an in-house question answerer. This last function can often be time-consuming, as UNIX is a large system with many different programs.

UNIX is ideal for offices that want to put everyone in electronic communication with each other and set up an office automation effort that requires more communication and more sharing of data files than is permitted by individual computers. UNIX-based computers offer a lower-cost alternative to the fabulous but very expensive mini- and mainframe-based systems of IBM, Wang, and Xerox. Larger UNIX systems can connect some 50 people together for easy exchange of electronic memos, mail, and data files. They can share common files of information, use large data bases together, and build a file system that places all of an office's records in one cohesive electronic filing system accessible to all users. UNIX systems allow very large single files to be maintained, so you could have an entire book, or even sets of books, in the computer at the same time and manipulate pieces of them at will. In summary, UNIX systems interconnect people who want to work closely together and need to share information frequently.

UNIX and the Technical User

Many government and research institutions were early UNIX users. Approximately 90% of university computer science departments use the UNIX system, and many advanced programmers and computer science majors learn to use the UNIX system and to program in the C language, the computer language in which UNIX is written. As a result of this exposure, UNIX software has been continuously modified and improved by computer science students and professors.

In universities, the system runs on computers for teaching and research projects. Programs calculate statistical results of experiments in biology, chemistry, computer science research, and other fields. Numerous applications are developed and maintained on UNIX systems. At the University of California at Berkeley, for instance, one program tracks the cancer-causing properties of common products and correlates these properties with trends in populations consuming these products.

University administrative offices use UNIX software to speed office tasks. Letters and papers are typed using the UNIX text-editing programs, and the UNIX system's TROFF program typesets many university publications. The system not only bills system users, but also handles the general accounting needs of the university. Research institutions and the government use UNIX systems for many of the same functions universities do.

UNIX Business Users

The UNIX system is the most popular operating system for multiuser microcomputers used in business. It lets several people use the same program at the same time. It is ideal when many users continually look at and change information in the same file, such as a payroll or accounts receivable file. It also lets several people each do more than one thing at a time.

Business UNIX users adapt and employ UNIX systems to fulfill their specific needs, including

* Text preparation and document storage
* Electronic mail
* Data base management.

Almost all business users need text-processing capabilities. Many companies produce their own documentation, books, newsletters, and reports. The UNIX system offers text-editing and text-formatting software. The text-formatting software interfaces with printers and typesetting equipment. The UNIX system has equation, table, and text-preparation software that supports total in-house production of journals and books.

In business, memos and letters are constantly exchanged. Electronic mail is an integral part of the UNIX system. Business users can send messages to other users on the same computer system and, by connecting a computer to telephone lines, to computers at distant locations. In many UNIX system installations, daily phone messages, departmental memos, reports, and accounting data are sent from person to person via their desk-top terminals.

Data bases are collections of information stored in the computer that you can access and manipulate quickly. UNIX users take advantage of the system's "electronic file cabinet" capabilities to arrange the information they store in specific filing compartments. Just as a file cabinet has drawers, file folders, and information within folders, so UNIX tools let you build electronic file cabinet drawers (directories) that hold folders (subdirectories) containing information (files). You can build your own custom filing systems, calendars, and reminder systems using basic UNIX tools.

The History of the UNIX System

Bell Laboratories is the research and development arm of AT&T. Established in 1925, it is one of the largest research groups in the world.

Bell Laboratories serves several dynamic functions in the Bell system. As a basic research organization, Bell Laboratories investigates scientific fields relevant to communications, including mathematics and physical sciences. At the forefront of applied research in communications technologies, it also designs and develops products and provides systems engineering. All of the Bell System's facilities, as well as many independent telephone companies, use the UNIX system internally.

The Origins of the UNIX System

For a brief period in 1969, the Computing Science Research Department of Bell Laboratories used a large General Electric 645 mainframe computer with an operating system called Multics. Multics was an early interactive multiuser operating system and a forerunner of modern operating systems. Interactive refers to the computer's almost immediate response to a typed-in command.

Previously, only batch-oriented operating systems were available. In a batch-oriented system, codes were punched onto rectangular cards. These codes were requests for information, data, or commands. A set of the cards was subsequently processed (read) by the computer in large batches. This usually required several minutes to several hours for the printed results confirming or fulfilling a request. This method was too slow for programmers who needed an immediate response from the system.

Although interactive, Multics still lacked capabilities that were essential to programmers. It retained certain batch mode characteristics that once preserved the privacy and security of each user's data, but now served to isolate the programmer's work. In 1969, Ken Thompson developed an operating system that would support coordinated teams of programmers in the development of programs and simplify the dialogue between human and machine, thus making computers more accessible to beginners and programmers alike. The result, the UNIX system, was not written all at once. It evolved in response to the programming requirements of specific projects and continues to evolve today.

The Development of the System

One such specific project was a program Ken Thompson developed called "Space Travel." It simulated the movement of the major celestial bodies in the solar system. Finding the cost of single-user interaction with a mainframe computer prohibitive, Thompson rewrote "Space Travel" for a lower-cost, less powerful minicomputer, a Digital Equipment Corporation (DEC) PDP-7.

Minicomputers were the first computers inexpensive enough for a single university department or small company and small enough for single-user interaction. However, the software available for the PDP-7 was limited, and it did not have the memory capability to handle continuous development. While it was less expensive to run "Space Travel" on the minicomputer, any program changes had to be written on the GE mainframe before execution by the PDP-7. Continuous loading of the paper tape was a slow and vulnerable process. Before Thompson could write programs on the minicomputer as well as run them, he had to develop the necessary software. Thompson wrote an operating system, a PDP-7 assembler (a program that translates code a programmer writes into instructions the computer can understand), and several utility programs (programs that perform standard tasks)—all in the assembly language specific to the PDP-7. The operating system was christened the UNIX system, a pun on the earlier Multics system on which some of its concepts are based.

The Evolution of the C Language

An operating system based on assembly language is "machine dependent" because each computer has its own assembly language. The program runs on one particular type or brand of computer and cannot be easily "transported" to a different computer. Because of the problems nontransportability posed, Thompson developed the transportable language, B. The B language was subsequently modified by Dennis Ritchie and renamed the C language. Ritchie, Thompson, and others then rewrote UNIX software in C. The UNIX system, based on Multics and originally written in assembly language for the PDP-7, had by 1980 been almost completely rewritten in C and could be moved to virtually any computer.

Not only are the UNIX system and most of its many supplied programs written in C, but many applications programs for UNIX and other operating systems are C-based as well. Popular programs like VisiCalc and WordStar are now written in C, instead of the assembly language in which they were first written.

The University of California at Berkeley And the UNIX System

Not long after the UNIX system was rewritten in the C language, Ken Thompson spent a year as a visiting professor at the University of California at Berkeley in 1976-77. He introduced the Berkeley Computer Science Department to the UNIX system and there developed much of the UNIX version eventually released as Version 6.

After Thompson left, Berkeley professors and students continued to develop UNIX enhancements, and many of them are now incorporated in System V. As a variation of the standard system, many computers run Berkeley Software Distribution (BSD) Version 4.2, available from the university. Universities, in particular, often buy Berkeley UNIX-based systems, and several computer manufacturers offer Berkeley UNIX systems.

Ken Thompson returned to Bell Laboratories in 1977, and the development of UNIX software continued. Demand for UNIX software grew rapidly. As graduates from universities, members of the Bell Laboratories organization, and government employees using the UNIX system filtered into the business world, the demand for UNIX in business and industry grew.

UNIX-based minicomputers were first widely employed inside the Bell System and by government research organizations to control laboratory experiments, support machine-aided design, supervise telecommunications networks, and perform business functions. Developing software to fulfill these specific applications presented programmers with a new challenge, and the UNIX system offered effective tools to meet it. By 1979, there were over 3000 UNIX system users, almost entirely inside the Bell System, universities, and a few government agencies that negotiated with AT&T for access to UNIX software.

The Business Community Discovers UNIX

Throughout the mid-1970s, as companies that worked with AT&T or that hired people who had used UNIX in their jobs started hearing about UNIX, AT&T experienced a growing number of requests for access to the UNIX system. In 1979, demand from the commercial world led AT&T to release UNIX Version 7 to the public and to decrease the price dramatically. Computer manufacturers responded by developing UNIX software for business computer systems. For the first time, small businesses could afford to use the UNIX system on their small computers. Interactive Systems, a software company in the Los Angeles area and the first to add enhancements to make UNIX easier to use, began selling UNIX to businesses in 1979, still only for use on large minicomputers. At the same time, Microsoft began development of Xenix, their version of UNIX for microcomputers.

Version 7's lower price was good, but the system was not a commercial product. It lacked features like the ability to protect confidential data, and it needed easier programs. In November of 1981, Bell released System III as the first "commercial" UNIX system. It solved a lot of the problems of Version 7 and cost less. By 1983, over 100 manufacturers sold UNIX-based micro-, mini-, and mainframe computers, and there were over 100,000 users.

The year 1983 marked a major change in the use of the UNIX system. The dominant type of UNIX user shifted from the traditional, minicomputer programmer/user to the business microcomputer user. This was made possible by the advent of a new, more powerful generation of microcomputers containing a more powerful central processing unit (CPU), or computer "brain."

Microcomputer CPUs are called microprocessors. The first microprocessors were 8-bit and ran CP/M, Apple DOS, and other single-user operating systems. A bit is the smallest unit of information a computer can manipulate. "Eight-bit" means a microprocessor can manipulate 8 bits at a time. People refer to 8-, 16-, or 32-bit microprocessors as least to most powerful. Roughly, the more bits, the more powerful the microprocessor. New 16- and 32-bit microprocessors have enough power to run the UNIX system. Some of them even have more power than the minicomputers on which UNIX software was originally developed.

As the interest in UNIX software for microcomputers grew, AT&T responded. System V was introduced in 1983. It was created in response to the clamor from the business community for an easier system for nonprogrammers. There is still a core of UNIX information that must be grasped, but friendly "menu" shells can be used to hide the system from users who only use UNIX occasionally or who have very little time to learn UNIX.

In 1983, AT&T introduced a new implementation of System V for microcomputers, and this system is gaining in popularity. At the same time, AT&T authorized Intel, Motorola, Zilog, and National Semiconductor to move UNIX to their company's microprocessors and to sell "System V microcomputer UNIX" to manufacturers of computers using the microprocessors each company sells.

AT&T is now selling applications packages, languages, and support for UNIX System V systems and encouraging current users to convert their System III, Version 7, or UNIX look-alike systems to new System V. AT&T does not yet dominate the UNIX world with its "standard" System V, but System V will grow in popularity as AT&T ceases to offer applications, languages, and support for earlier versions.

The Many UNIX Implementations And Versions

It should be obvious by now that there is no such thing as one standard UNIX system. Currently, most microcomputers run an enhanced implementation, Microsoft's Xenix. The Xenix implementation of the UNIX operating system runs on computers like the Tandy System 16, the Fortune 32:16, and Apple's Lisa. The different *implementations* of UNIX should be distinguished from the *versions* of UNIX that AT&T has released.

The UNIX system continues to evolve. As the needs of users change, this powerful system will change to accommodate them. AT&T is one of the largest companies in the world, and its UNIX System V will be a major factor in the software world for many years.

CHAPTER 2

UNIX IN THE WORKPLACE

The first part of this chapter discusses the UNIX system as an environment for running applications programs. The second part discusses the classes of applications programs available for the UNIX system that are of use in the business world. Some of these applications are supplied by the Bell UNIX system itself, but most must be purchased from other vendors.

The UNIX System Applications Environment

To describe how the UNIX system supports applications in a business environment, we discuss at greater length some characteristics identified in Chapter 1, such as portability, multiuser and multitasking capabilities, and the use of modular utility programs; we also discuss the hierarchical file system, the user interface, record/file locking, and system security.

Until the early 1980s the UNIX system was not available on microcomputers, so there was little development of business applications for this system. Now, as the UNIX system becomes increasingly available on microcomputers costing less than

$10,000, such as the IBM PC XT, an increasing number of business applications are being developed for the system. Several versions of the COBOL and BASIC languages are available for the UNIX system. Thus, many existing applications that have been written in these languages can be transported to the UNIX environment.

Portability

Portability is the ability of software that operates on one machine to operate on another, different machine. There are two types of portability to consider: the portability of the UNIX operating system itself (the kernel program described in Chapter 1) and of the applications programs. These programs are portable largely because the language they are written in, the C language, is portable. Generally only minor adjustments must be made to allow for differences between the computer systems.

More than 90% of the kernel program is written in C and less than 10% in machine-specific language. Thus, even the machine-specific UNIX kernel can be transported easily to a new computer system. At worst, only about 10% of the kernel program must be rewritten to move the kernel to an entirely new machine architecture. Compare this to the enormous effort required to transport even simple microcomputer operating systems, such as CP/M or MS-DOS. These systems have to be completely rewritten for a new architecture. (In fact, these operating systems are being rewritten in C for easier portability.)

Applications programs written in a higher-level language, such as C, Pascal, COBOL, or BASIC, are easily transported across UNIX systems. So business applications written in these languages may be easily transported.

Portable applications programs decrease programming costs. For instance, if your company outgrows its present UNIX-based system and purchases a more powerful computer, the applications software can be moved inexpensively to this new, larger UNIX system. Also, more software choices are afforded the vendor and end user, since more applications can be moved from different sources of UNIX programs.

Multiuser Capability

The UNIX multiuser capability means that more than one system user can access the same data at the same time. For instance, several people involved in a common project can all conveniently access one another's data.

As discussed in Chapter 1, a computer system that can support multiple users is generally less expensive than the equivalent number of single-user machines. Moreover, while in theory networks of single-user machines can access the same data, there are still few network implementations. And because there are no universal standard networks, users are locked into a proprietary, or vendor-specific, networking scheme. Communication between different proprietary networks is extremely difficult.

Multitasking Capability

Multitasking means that a given user can do more than one task at the same time. For instance, you could be updating your client database while printing your monthly sales report. You can easily execute more than one task at a time by placing some tasks in the "background" while you work on a task in the "foreground." Background tasks are those that can be executed without your intervention, such as sorting a large mailing list by ZIP code; foreground tasks are those that can be executed only with your intervention, such as creating a document with a word processor.

There is a limit to the number of simultaneous tasks that you can start in the background—generally a limit per user of some 20 simultaneous tasks and, depending on the computer system, a system-wide limit of some 50 or more tasks. Practically speaking, the more background tasks you start, the slower the overall system response. Each task takes longer to complete if it has more competition for the use of the CPU.

The progress of your background tasks can be seen directly with some window-based UNIX systems. The output of each task can be placed in a small portion (or window) of your terminal screen. This windowing ability will become increasingly available in the next few years.

The UNIX File System

A *file* is a unit of data that is stored on a magnetic disk (or tape). A name, the *filename*, identifies the file uniquely. A collection of files on the disk is called a file system. A *directory* is a special type of file that contains lists of filenames. All the files listed in a given directory are grouped together for convenient access. You will learn more about files and file systems in tutorial Chapters 3 and 4.

The simpler single-user microcomputer operating systems, such as CP/M and MS-DOS 1.1, use a so-called "flat," or one-dimensional, file system. In these systems all files reside in a single directory. When there are many files, as can be the case when you are using a fixed disk, working with all the files in a single directory becomes cumbersome.

The UNIX file system allows a hierarchical structure. The programs and data can be organized conveniently since the files can be grouped according to usage. You saw one example of such a scheme in the last chapter, in Figure 1-4, a typical UNIX directory system. You can create directories at will, so you can group your programs and data into the appropriate directories. For instance, you might have one directory for financial accounting data, another for text documents, and so forth. You will learn how to create and use an "electronic filing cabinet" for organizing the information stored as files in Chapter 3.

The UNIX file system allows you flexible control over access to your programs and data. Access by yourself, by defined groups of users, and by all system users can be controlled independently for each file that you have created. For instance, you might allow all members of a project group to access your data, but disallow access to system users not in your project group.

In the early days the UNIX system gained a reputation for destroying data and programs. Generally this problem occurred when the computer system was shut down improperly, say because of a power failure. The reason for this vulnerability was that data destined for a file is kept in main memory and is written to disk only when the memory space is needed for something else. System performance is improved by this "write behind" approach, since data is not written to disk every time that a write request is made. However, interrupting the power loses the data in main memory.

Recent improvements have helped make the UNIX file system as robust as any other file system: (1) The disk hardware is more reliable. (2) Periodic execution of the **sync** program forces the data in memory to be written to disk. (3) An easy-to-use file system check and repair program, **fsck**, has been added.

Modular UNIX Programs

First let's distinguish between a simple UNIX utility (or command) and an applications program. Utilities are simple programs that do simple tasks, such as telling you the current date and time. They are generally noninteractive; that is, after you start them executing they complete your request without further interaction.

Applications programs are more complex and can usually do several different tasks. Generally they are designed to be used interactively; that is, you continue to interact with the program after you start it running. Generally you enter a command mode where you type a command and the applications program responds by servicing your command request and awaiting your next command. You continue this dialogue until you exit the applications program.

As an example, you interact with the UNIX **mail** program in a dialogue as you read your mail: you read your mail messages one at a time, and after reading each message, you give a command instructing the **mail** program how to dispose of the message. You might save the message on disk, delete it, or send a reply.

Hundreds of utility programs (or commands) are supplied with most UNIX systems. They are designed to work together under direction of the UNIX shell. For instance, the shell can direct data to pass from one program to the next in a series called a *pipeline*, or simply *pipe* (recall Figure 1-5). You will learn how to use the shell to combine the UNIX programs to perform tasks beginning with Chapter 4.

Each utility program is designed to do one job well. If a different task must be done, a programmer writes a new program. This design philosophy gives the UNIX system user a large, flexible set of programs that work well together. And because the programs are independent, you can change your working environment easily, deleting some programs, adding new ones, or changing existing programs to suit your particular needs.

The User Interface

Originally the UNIX operating system was not intended to be used by the business community. It was designed for the computer programmer, who prefers a terse command syntax that uses few keystrokes. However, now the UNIX system is being used increasingly by business and casual users, who require a more explanatory interface. Also, the documentation supplied by Bell Laboratories is notorious for being dense and highly technical, having few if any examples and being often poorly written.

Bell Labs is currently taking steps to make the user interface and documentation more suitable for the commercial environment. A syntax standard for any new commands and existing commands alike will provide a more consistent and more easily remembered command syntax. The standard is appropriate for use with either the popular Bourne or C Shell command interpreters.

Bell Labs recognizes that beginning and infrequent users would be even better served by a more helpful interface, such as a menu-driven shell that would spare them the need to remember all operational details from one session to the next. A menu shell can easily replace the standard UNIX shell. A menu system displays the command options in plain English. The user types a key corresponding to a menu option; then either an applications program is started up to service the request or another menu or submenu is displayed. Examples of this menu shell are found in Fortune and Altos systems.

However, as the user becomes experienced with the system, menus can get in the way. Some menu systems also provide a command-driven interface. If the commands are simple and consistent, any user can quickly learn to operate the command interface.

Another possibility would be a user interface that is a fully integrated environment. This would provide guidance with help messages, supply consistent and readable documentation, and use common data and command structures across the various applications. A good example of this type of interface can be seen on the Apple Lisa (a non-UNIX machine).

The Lisa interface uses *icons*, pictorial representations of commands or items of data. The user employs a mouse to move the cursor among the icons and then selects one. This interface divides the CRT screen into windows so the user can display the output from several different programs at the same time. Although a Lisa-type interface is not available for the UNIX system at this writing, it or a similar interface won't be long in coming.

Integrated interfaces are becoming available that provide an umbrella for more than one applications program. Such interfaces are designed to give all the different applications programs a similar command syntax. Then you only have to learn one set of commands for all the different applications instead of a different command set for each application. For instance, word processing, file management, and spreadsheets might be "driven" by a common, easy-to-use menu shell. One disadvantage of many integrated interfaces is that if you need an application not provided in the integrated package, you must purchase it separately. And this separate application probably wouldn't interface with the integrated package.

A few vendors do provide a "generic" integrated user interface; that is, one that allows you to integrate applications from different third-party vendors so they can be accessed through this common user interface. Such an interface can be tailored to your specific requirements either by the system administrator or by yourself. Some integrated packages even let you pass data between the applications programs.

File and Record Locking

UNIX allows more than one user to update the same file at virtually the same time. But if two users update the same file at *exactly* the same time, problems can occur. The data shared between users could be compromised or even lost; the write operation of one user can undo the one just performed by the other user.

There still is no universal way to prevent two or more users from updating or writing to the same file at the same time. Data locks allow only one user at a time to update a shared database; they can operate on entire files or on records. A *file* lock prevents other users from writing to the file at all. A *record* lock prevents users from updating the same part of the data file but allows updating of different parts of the same file.

Several different UNIX system suppliers have provided one data locking scheme or another to prevent such data corruption. However, different vendors use different approaches. Thus, applications programs from one vendor may not be able to use the data locking scheme from another vendor. A good solution would be for a major supplier to select a file/record locking scheme at the kernel level that is adopted as the "standard" by all interested UNIX system vendors.

System Security

Computer system security means protecting computer hardware and the information contained within the system. Threats to system security come not only from *outside* the computer system but from *inside* the community of system users as well.

Outside threats to system security include (1) unauthorized access to the computer system; (2) unauthorized examination of the computer system's output, whether hard copy or magnetic media; (3) unauthorized tapping of data being transferred between computer systems over phone lines, microwave links, and the like; and (4) damage because of fire, electrical power surges and outages, and natural disasters. Some ways to minimize these problems are (1) isolating the computer system — that is, using a stand-alone system, one not connected to a network; (2) properly disposing of printed output and archiving magnetic media in a vault; (3) encrypting sensitive data — that is, putting it into a code indecipherable to others; and (4) protecting the system with fire alarms, electrical surge protectors, and the like.

Inside threats are more insidious. They might include destruction of software data by mistake or on purpose, examination of sensitive data by unauthorized users, and alteration of sensitive data without detection. Some ways to minimize these problems include education of personnel on proper backup procedures, restricting the scope of an irreversible action such as file deletion, preventing access to parts of the system containing sensitive data except by individuals with the "need to know," and the encryption of sensitive data that is accessible system-wide.

The Bell UNIX system provides several safeguards for system security, including (1) password protection for system access, (2) control of access to individual files, (3) encryption of data files, and (4) system accounting functions useful for analysis of which users did what. If these safeguards are not sufficient, consult a security specialist for your particular needs.

Applications for the UNIX System

The growing number of applications prorams are making UNIX-based systems increasingly useful in the business environment. Applications for UNIX-based systems generally fall into several areas:

* Word processing
* Financial accounting and spreadsheets
* Database management
* Communications
* Computer graphics
* Program development.

Many of the programs supplied with the UNIX system itself may be used to do tasks such as these. Some of these programs are self-contained in that a single program can do the task. For instance, the UNIX text editors and formatters may be used for text processing applications.

In other cases where a single program won't do the job, two or more UNIX programs may be combined. For instance, some database operations may be done by combining the appropriate UNIX programs. Combining these programs does require some expertise. Beginning users must be satisfied either with a single program solution or must get assistance from an experienced person. You will learn how to combine the UNIX programs in the tutorial chapters that follow.

The programs supplied with the UNIX system are totally inadequate for performing certain tasks. A good example would be trying to use the UNIX tools to do financial accounting functions. In such cases you must purchase a third-party applications program.

Independent vendors have developed fewer applications for the UNIX environment than for other popular operating systems like CP/M and MS-DOS. For one thing, the market penetration of UNIX-based systems hasn't been enough to warrant the development of many new applications or for transporting existing ones to the UNIX environment. However, now UNIX computer systems are making a larger penetration so applications are becoming increasingly available.

Word Processing

The UNIX system is well known for its extensive word processing or text production facilities. Here we are using the term word processing as well as text processing or production to mean the production of text on a monitor screen, a printer, or a typesetter. Much early UNIX system development involved writing software that could produce text documents.

Editors and Formatter Programs   Editor programs were developed that could create and change text. Text formatting programs were also designed to produce high-quality paginated documents suitable for publication.

The editors and formatters supplied by Bell Labs are separate programs. One reason for this approach is that when the UNIX text processing system was designed, CRT terminals were expensive and scarce. Thus, there was little demand for a combined editor/formatter with "on-screen" formatting ability.

When you are creating text with the UNIX system, you use an editor program to embed directives (or commands) within your document for the text formatter program. This text becomes the input data for the formatter program. The appearance of the final document depends on what format directives were embedded in the document. You will learn more about this process in Chapter 5 Section 12, "The **nroff** Text Formatter."

The use of separate programs for editing and print formatting has several advantages over combined programs: generally larger document files can be handled more conveniently; automatic chapter and section numbering as well as footnotes can be provided; and it is generally easier and quicker to change globally the appearance of the final document. You only need to change a few embedded formatting directives, rather than reformatting the entire document on the screen as combined programs require.

The main disadvantage of using separate programs is that you can't tell exactly what the final document will look like until you print it. In contrast, most integrated editor and print formatter packages can simulate the appearance of the printed document on the monitor screen. Thus, with UNIX you may have to experiment with the formatting commands until you achieve the desired result.

The **vi** (visual) screen-oriented text editor (developed at the University of California at Berkeley) was added to the text processing tool arsenal in System V. Previously Bell Labs supplied only a line-oriented editor, **ed**. The **vi** editor also has a powerful line-oriented counterpart, **ex**, which is an extension of the Bell **ed** editor.

There are two primary Bell UNIX text formatting programs, **nroff** and **troff**. **nroff** formats text for conventional ASCII hard-copy or CRT display terminals. **troff** formats text for a typesetting system. The UNIX text processing system also has other formatting programs that are used in conjunction with **nroff** or **troff**. The **tbl** program produces complex tables and **eqn** formats mathematical expressions. Recently, **pic** and **ideal** were introduced to provide simple graphics capabilities.

Typesetting Tools   The current **troff** program can drive phototypesetters, video-typesetters, and laser printers. A phototypesetter creates an image by projecting light through a stencil onto photographic paper. The paper is then developed in a separate step. These machines have high resolution and cost as much as $50,000. Videotypesetters are high-resolution devices. They have a resolution of some 750 to 3000 dots per inch and cost about $60,000. Laser printers use a lower-resolution process whereby a laser beam exposes the light-sensitive paper. These machines, such as the Canon LBP-10 (240 dots per inch) or Xerox (300 dots per inch) cost about $20,000. Recent advances have made it possible for the prices of laser printers to come down to less than $5000. Thus typesetting with laser printers could rival printing with letter quality printers in the near future.

Early versions of the UNIX **troff** program could only drive a Graphics Systems (later Wang) CAT/4 phototypesetter. Later the original **troff** program was rewritten to be "device-independent" (dvi). The dvi **troff** program produces intermediate ASCII code that can be converted to the necessary binary codes for driving several different phototypesetters. These include the Mergenthaler, Linotron 202, Autologic APS-5, and Compugraphic 8400 phototypesetters and the Imagen Canon LBP-10 laser printer. The dvi **troff** is now sold separately from the rest of the UNIX system. The **pic** and **ideal** graphics-drawing programs are also included.

The new dvi **troff** program can produce 256 different fonts with 128 point sizes compared to the 4 fonts and 15 point sizes for the previous version. The graphics programs provide basic shapes (such as arcs, circles, ellipses, diagonal lines, and spline curves) for including diagrams within a document.

One common criticism of **troff** (and **nroff**) is directed against the terse and unnatural syntax of its primitive format directives. However, its macro formatting directives are easier to use and remember. (Primitive and macro directives are discussed in Chapter 5.) Users also complain that **troff** consumes many system resources, especially when certain other programs are used as well. The symptom is that system response can slow down when these formatters are running. It's simply a fact that text formatting requires much processing power, and large amounts of memory are required to hold the textual data.

The main advantages to do-it-yourself typesetting with **troff** include (1) more control over document appearance, (2) decreased cost, and (3) faster turnaround time. The primary disadvantage is that you must learn to use **troff**. This is easier said than done since the Bell Labs documentation for these formatting programs is hard to comprehend. However, this book does cover the related **nroff** program. The **troff** program is simply an extension to **nroff**.

Writer's Workbench   Bell Labs has released a set of text processing tools known collectively as Writer's Workbench, or WWB. This suite of programs was designed to improve your writing. They point out stylistic as well as grammatical problems in your prose. You can use the WWB programs with almost any type of document from personal letters to technical dissertations. Note that these programs don't change your text; they simply make suggestions. You have to decide what changes to make and then edit your text manually.

Some of the WWB programs can assist you while you are composing your document. For instance, one program can help you determine the spelling of words you are unsure of. In fact you only need to know how to spell part of the word and the program will report all words (in its database) that match your word fragment. Another program explains word usage for over 700 commonly misused words — "that" versus "which," for example.

After composing your text you can proofread it with a WWB program that checks spelling and punctuation. It can locate unpaired parentheses or quotation marks as well as flag incorrect placement of punctuation within quotation marks. Another program locates all awkward and wordy phrases and suggests alternatives. Other programs note adjacent repeated words (such as "... and and ...") and split infinitives.

Another group of WWB programs analyzes your writing style by gathering statistics and comparing them to a prose standard. They report the reading grade level of your document, the sentence variation, number or percentage of occurrences of parts of speech and verb characteristics (infinitives, auxiliaries), sentence openings, overuse of long words, passive voice, expletives, and nominalizations. Another program can check your flow of ideas by listing section headings and the first and last sentence of each paragraph.

Other Text Processing Tools In addition to editors and text formatters, the UNIX system contains numerous other utilities that process text. One set of utilities (not part of WWB) checks the document for spelling errors. Other programs can sort textual data, locate text based on pattern recognition, and more. You will learn about these and other text processing tools beginning in Chapter 4.

Financial Accounting and Spreadsheets

Accountants, bookkeepers, and people with related jobs use financial accounting software. The Bell UNIX system doesn't provide such software so you must obtain it from third-party vendors. Most financial accounting systems now combine and integrate the basic four modules: payroll, accounts receivable, accounts payable, and general ledger.

The "basic four" and other general applications are often customized to meet the particular needs of a specialized application area. For instance, manufacturing, the retail/wholesale industry, and stock brokerage houses require specialized software. Examples of uses are inventory management of automobile parts, mail-order management, construction site job costing, financial report writing, payroll and bank reconciliation, project cost estimation, fixed assets, order status, whole-sale distribution, medical or legal time billing, and point of sale transaction processing. We document several such packages in Appendix A.

Do not confuse the so-called accounting software distributed with the Bell UNIX system with financial accounting software. The Bell accounting utilities are for accounting the use of the UNIX system resources, such as time spent running a program.

Unlike much of the sophisticated software that runs under the UNIX system, spreadsheet programs weren't developed on mainframes or minicomputers. The first successful spreadsheet program, VisiCalc (from VisiCorp), was written for the 8-bit Apple II personal microcomputer. In the early 1980s VisiCalc and related spreadsheets played a large part in popularizing personal microcomputers. Now spreadsheets are available for practically all processor types, including 16- and 32-bit, and run under many different operating systems.

Owing to hardware memory constraints, early spreadsheets were limited in capacity to some 200 rows and 20 columns or fewer. These limitations have been largely overcome with 16-bit and especially 32-bit processors. These machines can address enough physical memory so large spreadsheets can fit entirely in memory. Alternatively, some machines and software use a virtual memory approach to accommodate larger spreadsheets. With this approach there is no practical limit on the number of rows and columns since the portion that cannot fit into memory overflows onto the disk.

Some packages allow one spreadsheet to reference or link to data from a different spreadsheet. For instance, you might have one spreadsheet for your Eastern seaboard accounts and another for your Western accounts, and both would be linked to your national account summary spreadsheet. Some of the new larger capacity spreadsheets allow either "virtual" or "linking" spreadsheets to accommodate larger data bases. Another trend is the integration of the spreadsheet with other business functions such as database management and graphics display systems.

Database Management

The storage and retrieval of information is central to running a business successfully. Thus, database management systems (DBMS), also called computer information management systems (IMS), are key software components for the business user. Any DBMS must work with files for storing information, search to retrieve data, sort to reorganize data, and generate reports for displaying results. The IMS should interface with — or better still, be integrated with — other business applications such as spreadsheet, numerical data processing, word processing, and graphics software.

DBMS have three main parts: a data management system, a filing system, and a user interface. The data management system, the heart of the DBMS, provides storage, data reorganization, and retrieval of the information. The filing system contains the files holding the information. The DBMS frequently enhances the built-in UNIX file system. The user interface interacts directly with the user of the DBMS. Historically the weakest link in most database systems, these interfaces have been significantly improved by recent innovations, particularly in the use of plain English for queries between person and machine.

DBMS have been available for almost 20 years. They were first developed on large mainframe computers, later migrated to minicomputers, and within the last few years moved to personal microcomputers. In the early days the data was stored in either a rigid hierarchical or network structure. These inflexible structures made it difficult to change the relationships between the data items. In fact, for changes to be made, a new structure had to be created and all the data items reentered. These early systems also limited the number of possible relationships among the data items.

Today the most popular systems use a relational structure for the data. The basic element of a relational DBMS (or rDBMS) is the *relation*. The relation between the pieces of data can be represented by a two-dimensional table in which the related data items are entered into corresponding columns. The relationships are completely flexible — all combinations are possible at any time. Furthermore, the relational structure is simple to use and understand. A simple example would be a mailing list, as illustrated in Figure 2-1.

Each row in Figure 2-1 represents a *record* and contains all the information necessary to generate a mailing label. Each column contains data that is related to data in the other columns by virtue of being in the same record (or row). At least one column functions as a *key* for indexing (and perhaps sorting) the records (rows) of the database. For example, in Figure 2-1, the record number could represent a *unique key*.

The information in an rDBMS is the data values themselves, with no visible structural or linkage information. The user interface employs a high-level language that allows requests to be formulated simply. Thus, complex queries can be specified without writing a complex program. This facility enables business and casual users to use the rDBMS more easily.

The Bell UNIX system does not provide a complete, self-sufficient database management system. However, most UNIX systems contain the necessary program tools and routines for performing database-type manipulation. One commercial DBMS, **/rdb**, combines existing UNIX tools to create and manipulate a

Record number	Company name	Street address	City	State	ZIP code
1	Thomas Ventures	1839 Tenth Ave.	San Francisco	CA	94122
2	UNIX/WORLD Magazine	444 Castro St.	Mountain View	CA	94040
3	OSBORNE/McGraw-Hill	2600 Tenth St.	Berkeley	CA	94710

Figure 2-1.   *A simple relational database*

relational database. And as mentioned earlier, a DBMS can enhance the UNIX system's built-in file system.

What about data compatibility between the DBMS and other applications? There is a strong trend toward such compatibility. One recent step in this direction has been the formation of an Independent Software Information Standard group (ISIS). ISIS is a group of third-party software vendors formed to develop a standard format for data interchange. Data can easily go between UNIX applications that use this standard data format. For instance, the business user could use a financial accounting package, a word processing package, spreadsheet program, and graphics software to process the same data.

Communications

The UNIX system has several communication programs. The **mail** program is used to send and receive electronic mail, enabling users on your computer system or other computer systems to transfer messages. Messages sent from other users are placed in your mailbox (that is, a file on disk), and you may read them one at a time at your leisure.

The **write** program can communicate directly with another user currently logged on to your UNIX system. After starting this program, whatever you type will appear on the recipient's terminal. If the recipient also invokes **write**, a two-way communication is established. Whatever is typed on one keyboard is displayed directly on the terminal screen of the other user.

The UNIX **cu** program can be employed to call up (by modem or a direct wire connection) another UNIX system, a terminal, or even a non-UNIX system. It manages an interactive conversation and allows transfer of files between the connected devices. One disadvantage to **cu** is that transmission errors are not caught and signaled, enabling data integrity to be lost.

Although more difficult to use than **cu**, the UNIX **uucp** program can also transfer files between UNIX systems. Unlike **cu**, **uucp** can catch transmission errors and can recover from errors by retransmitting the data. Either dial-up (usually lower speed, 300 or 1200 baud modem-connected) or hard-wired (usually high-speed, 9600 baud) communication lines are used by **uucp**. This program can execute commands on a remote UNIX system as well.

Bell Labs began using the **uucp** program to set up a network, **UUCPNET**, between UNIX systems. This network was first used to distribute software and electronic mail between Bell UNIX installations. The original network has grown and now extends across the United States into Canada and even has a European branch. Related to **UUCPNET** is **USENET**, a set of sites that allow messages to be posted on an electronic bulletin board. Anyone with a UNIX system can subscribe to **USENET** services.

Local area networks (LAN) between UNIX machines are becoming increasingly popular. A LAN allows one stand-alone computer to communicate with another one. Most users use a LAN to log on to a remote machine or transfer data between machines. Such networks allow more flexibility in how users make connections between their machines and resources; for example, a central minicomputer with a large disk and tape could service several micros.

Today local area networks use proprietary hardware and software supplied by the LAN vendor. A network from one vendor may not be compatible with a network from a different vendor. This situation will change eventually when networks become standardized. The development of networking standards is still in progress.

Computer Graphics

Computer graphics is used primarily for presentation of results or as a decision-support tool. You generally use presentation graphics for instructional purposes so it should represent data in a simple straightforward way to be most effective. You would use analytical graphics to support decisions by discovering relationships in complex high-density data. Then you might use classical statistical techniques to verify and quantify the results.

Presentation graphics emphasizes versatility of pictorial representation. Typically it allows a user to represent data visually on a monitor screen, plotter (a printer for graphics), or conventional printer. Horizontal, vertical, clustered, or stacked line and bar charts, pie and exploded pie charts, scattergrams, surface contour plots, and even geographical maps are commonly displayed.

Analytical graphics generally requires sophisticated mainframe-developed software and expensive high-resolution graphics terminals. Presentation graphics requirements are less demanding. However, it still requires large amounts of processing power, memory, and either graphics boards for conventional terminals or high-resolution displays. Most computer graphics is for presentation and will remain so for the immediate future. Eventually when the hardware and software become less costly, analytical graphics will have a larger market share.

Business presentation graphics for the UNIX system is lagging behind other application areas. Business users would like to see integrated applications packages that combine word processing, database management, and spreadsheet analysis with presentation graphics. However, integrated business application packages generally supply everything except the graphics.

Application software for UNIX systems has lagged behind that for other more popular microcomputer operating systems, such as CP/M or MS-DOS. And graphics applications seem to be developed last since they are most complicated.

Business graphics development for multiuser systems is limited by expensive hardware requirements. Each user requires an expensive color high-resolution terminal with a dedicated microprocessor. In a multiuser environment this configuration quickly becomes cost prohibitive. Thus single-user operating systems, such as MS-DOS, are more likely targets for presentation graphics development. Witness the attractive market for IBM PC graphics packages available under PC-DOS.

Lack of standards for computer graphics has also hampered growth. Some reasons include: (1) Users don't want to be locked into a specific vendor and lose the ability to integrate other applications into their graphical environment. (2) Users as well as vendors are uncertain about what system to adopt especially since existing "standards" are still being considered and new ones are still being proposed. In the meantime each graphics vendor will invent its own proprietary scheme, which severely limits portability of applications. However, in time the various standards committees will decide on a standard, so this situation should improve.

The UNIX system as supplied from Bell provides some graphics functionality. Systems III and V contain the graphical commands formerly in Programmer's Workbench. They fall into four categories: (1) commands that manipulate and plot numerical data, (2) commands that generate tables of contents, (3) commands that interact with graphical devices, and (4) a collection of graphical utility commands (which translate graphical command requests into data that can be displayed on a graphical device such as a plotter). However, usually these primitive routines are not easily employed by the business user.

Program Development

System programmers developed the UNIX system for writing programs. Consequently, many powerful UNIX tools are available for both system and applications programming. Most of the tools are applicable for programming in the C language, although many of the tools are useful with other programming languages, too.

The Bourne Shell from Bell Labs and the C Shell from the University of California at Berkeley not only function interactively as command interpreters, but also as general purpose programming languages in their own right. You can create a file of UNIX commands, including variables and flow control constructions, known as a *shell script*. The shell can execute this file just as a BASIC interpreter can execute a BASIC program. Often algorithms are coded with shell scripts, debugged, and then rewritten in a more conventional programming language, such as C or Pascal.

Besides C, the Bell system provides FORTRAN 77, Rational FORTRAN, Snobol, a general-purpose macroprocessor (which translates one language — say, English — into C code for execution), and two facilities for writing compilers (a lexical analyzer and an LR(1)-based compiler-compiler), and a primitive BASIC language. Third-party suppliers have been busy transporting other language compilers and interpreters as well as cross-development tools to the UNIX system. So now you will find Ada, COBOL and variations, CBASIC, APL, Lisp, Franz Lisp, as well as assembly language for every major processor architecture.

The Bell System provides several different C language compilers: a general-purpose compiler, a portable compiler, and a compiler for producing stand-alone programs (that is, that can run without a resident kernel). In addition, a useful C syntax verifier produces more informative messages about problems with a C program. Some related utilities include a source code formatter for correctly spacing and indenting a C program so its structure can be easily discerned. Another program generates a C flow graph charting external references. And another utility produces a cross-reference listing.

The Bell system has always provided a general-purpose interactive debugger program. A symbolic debugger for C and FORTRAN programs was introduced starting with System III. Object code libraries and archives can be created and maintained with another program. Starting with System V, program fragments written in C, FORTRAN, and some other languages may be combined to give a functioning applications program. Some of the other tools include a dump program for displaying the contents of any file, including object code. Another program will generate a symbol table listing from an executable program. You can build a profile of time spent per routine with the profiler program tool. Another program allows you to maintain, update, and regenerate groups of programs automatically from a description file.

Programmer's Workbench Programmer's Workbench (PWB) is a collection of programs that was originally distributed with the Bell System 32V UNIX release for the VAX-11 processor. These programs were finally made generally available for all UNIX licensees in the System III release.

PWB consists of four major components: Remote Job Entry (RJE), the Source Code Control System (SCCS), document preparation, and statistical/graphics facilities. The document preparation facilities are largely the same as those discussed in the "Text Processing" section with the addition of the **mm** memorandum macro package. The statistical/graphics facilities were mentioned in the "Graphics" section. This leaves RJE and SCCS for discussion.

The Remote Job Entry system allows communication between a UNIX development system and a non-UNIX target system. Thus programs can be developed in a UNIX environment and then easily transported to a different target environment for testing. Originally the RJE system provided for submission of programs (or jobs) developed on a VAX-11 processor running PWB/UNIX to an IBM 370 or Univac 1100 mainframe test system running some other operating system.

The Source Code Control System is a collection of UNIX programs used to manage program and text development. They keep track of all changes made to text during a project and help coordinate the activities of the project team. More specifically, SCCS (1) manages the retrieval, updating, and storage of any version of a text module, (2) restricts access for updating text modules, (3) records changes made to a module, including where (which lines of text) and why the change was made, and (4) saves disk storage space. Only a single file containing the original version and a description of each change need be stored to reproduce any intermediate version of the text.

PART *TWO*

CHAPTER *4*

MASTERING THE SPECIAL FEATURES OF THE UNIX SYSTEM

CHAPTER **5**

TEXT PROCESSING

CHAPTER 3

FUNDAMENTALS
OF USING
THE UNIX SYSTEM

The best way to learn about the UNIX system is to use it. In Chapters 3 through 5 we present a series of hands-on tutorials to teach you the concepts and skills you will need to use the UNIX operating system effectively. If you have access to a computer with UNIX software, study these chapters while seated at the terminal. Enter the examples and compare the screen displays on your terminal with the illustrations in this book. If you don't have access to a system, study the examples as you read the text.

Here is a session by session overview of this chapter:

In Session 1, you will learn how to access your UNIX system and how to control system access by using a password.

In Session 2, you will actually begin using the system. First you will learn how the major parts of the system software are related to the computer hardware and to you as a system user. Then you will learn how to ask the UNIX system to perform simple tasks.

Session 3 is where you first learn how to communicate with system users via electronic mail. Then you will see how the UNIX system stores information, such as your mail messages. In this session you will also begin learning basic UNIX text processing so that you can create your own documents: memos, messages, letters, reports, or whatever.

In Session 4, you will learn more about data storage in the UNIX system and also how to use several tools for manipulating this data.

Finally, in Session 5 you will learn how the data stored in the UNIX system is organized. You will also learn how to use several tools for organizing your own data most effectively.

Some Basic Definitions

Before you begin working with the UNIX system, there are some definitions of terms and features that you should know about.

During much of your work with the UNIX system, you will be interacting with a program known as the *shell*. The shell is a program that interprets the commands you type. If the command is valid, the shell directs the UNIX system to carry out your request. If the command you type is invalid, you will see an error message, and then the shell will give you another chance to type a valid command. This dialogue of typing a command and getting a response continues until you sign off the system.

To let you know that it is ready for you to type a command, the shell will display a special symbol known as a *prompt*. There are two commonly used shells: the Bourne Shell developed at Bell Laboratories and the C Shell developed at U.C. Berkeley. Generally, the Bourne Shell uses a dollar sign ($) for its prompt while the C Shell uses a percent sign (%). Most of the screen displays in this book show the Bourne Shell prompt. Occasionally, you may find that your system administrator has changed the prompt for your shell. In any case some combination of characters making up a prompt will be displayed when the shell is ready to accept your command request.

Your terminal displays a *cursor* showing you where the text you type will be entered. Generally the cursor looks either like a shaded box (▓) or perhaps like an underscore character (__).

A UNIX system *command* is a program that performs some desired function. For instance, **date** is a program that displays the current date and time of day. The names for commands are shown in boldface type in the text of this book.

The UNIX command programs are either simple *utilities* that perform simple operations or complex *interactive programs* that perform one of several possible actions based on responses given by the user. The **date** command is an example of a simple utility: its only action is to display the current date and time. Interactive programs, in contrast, are generally capable of performing many operations. You actually interact with such a program in a dialogue fashion, typing commands and observing responses. You will be working with several interactive programs in your UNIX system. Some examples of interactive programs are the editors used to create and modify text documents, the UNIX electronic mail program, and perhaps most importantly the shell program itself.

A *command line* includes all the characters you type following the shell prompt until you press the RETURN key to terminate the line. A command line is made up of one or more distinct *elements*. Each element is a sequence of non-blank characters separated from other elements by one or more *blanks*. Here the term *blank* means either a space or a tab character. These characters are also called *whitespace characters* or simply *whitespace* since they appear "white" on printed paper.

The first command line element, which is typed immediately after the shell prompt, is always the name of the command program. For a simple command like **date**, you type the command name and then immediately terminate the command line with RETURN. Thus, an example of a simple shell command line is

$$\$ \text{ date}$$

where $ is the shell prompt and **date** the command name.

For a more complex command, you type the command name and then one or more blanks followed by one or more elements that specify additional information to the command. These additional elements are called *arguments* or *parameters*. For example, in the complex command line

$$\$ \text{ cp temp /usr/username}$$

$ is the shell prompt, **cp** is the command name, and **temp** and **/usr/username** are arguments.

A special class of command line arguments is called *options*. In the UNIX system, options look like arguments. They appear immediately after the command name and usually consist of a leading minus sign ($-$) or sometimes a plus sign ($+$), followed by one or more characters (generally letters and numbers). The purpose of an option is to specify a modification to the normal operation of the command. Some commands take no options while others may have several possible options. An example of a command line with an option argument would be

$$\$ \text{ du } -a$$

where the command name is **du** and the option argument is $-$**a**.

The option argument may consist of more than one letter or number or both. Each character may represent a different modifying option. For example, both the **t** and the **r** in the following command line are option letters:

$$\text{\$ ls } -\text{tr}$$

Here the **t** and the **r** each cause a different modifying action of the **ls** command. Sometimes the option letters must be separated from each other, as in **−t −r**, and at other times the option letters must be joined together, as in **−tr**, in order for the command to recognize them properly.

Occasionally several characters are combined to form a single modifying option. For instance, in this next command line,

$$\text{\$ pr } -\text{w80}$$

the characters **−w80** make up a single option.

Additional command line arguments may be present. Whitespace characters separate arguments from the preceding command name, from option letters, or from each other. These arguments are generally the names of the data items that the command operates on. For example, in the command line

$$\text{\$ cat } -\text{n fileA fileB}$$

cat is the command name, **−n** is an option, and **fileA** and **fileB** are additional arguments referring to two particular files named **fileA** and **fileB**.

Throughout the text we present something called a *command line format* statement. The format statement specifies a shell command line in general terms. For instance, in the last example, the general format of that particular command line would be

$$\text{\$ } command \; option \; argument1 \; argument2$$

Because in the UNIX system there are several possible options and arguments for most commands, the command line format statement allows us to describe all possible command lines in general terms. The use of brackets ([ ]) around an argument indicates that the argument is optional. Ellipses (...) that follow an argument indicate that the argument may be repeated. Thus, the preceding command line format statement could be completely generalized as shown here:

$$\text{\$ } command \; [\; option... \;] \; [\; argument... \;]$$

Here *option...* and *argument...* indicate that there may be more than one option or argument; and since each of these expressions is enclosed in square brackets, they are both optional — that is, the command may be used with no actual options or arguments at all.

Most command names are entered using lowercase letters. The UNIX system distinguishes between uppercase and lowercase letters; an uppercase character is interpreted differently from the lowercase version. Thus, you would type **date** to invoke the **date** command, whereas typing either **Date** or **DATE** would give an error message: neither is a valid name for **date**. Unless specified otherwise, you should always enter the command name in lowercase to ensure that the system interprets the command correctly. It's also important to use the proper case for option letters and command line arguments.

The space character, typed by pressing the space bar, is frequently required when entering commands. Spaces are used as *delimiters*, or separators between command line elements. In general, whenever one space is appropriate, more than one space or a tab character may be used as well. The space and tab characters are known collectively as the *whitespace characters*. It's important to emphasize that even though it appears to be nothing or blank space, a whitespace character is just as important as any other character. In fact, your computer and the UNIX operating system are quite finicky about the use of whitespace. Be sure to imitate our examples exactly.

There is a class of characters known as *control characters*, which are characters subject to special interpretation by the computer. Just as you hold down the SHIFT key to type a capital letter on a typewriter, you hold down the CONTROL key to type a control character. Thus you would type a CTRL-D by holding down the CONTROL key, pressing the D key, and then releasing the CONTROL key. The CONTROL key is often abbreviated CTRL or CTL; it is most often found in the lower left-hand corner of the keyboard, usually near the SHIFT key.

The characters used by the UNIX system are either visible printing characters, such as letters, numbers, and punctuation, or invisible, nonprinting control characters. Control characters are not generally displayed on a terminal screen or on paper unless special arrangements have been made to represent them as printing characters. The most common representation is to use a circumflex (^) followed by the control letter name, as in ^D for a CTRL-D.

Some Conventions

We use the following conventions in the text of this book:

Throughout the text, the command, option, file, and directory names appear in boldface type. In addition, any specific element in a command line that you are meant to enter into the computer will appear in boldface type. Thus, we would say, "Enter the command **ls −1 poem**." In contrast, general command line elements that are placeholders for specific names appear in italic type. Thus we might say, for example, "The command line format is *command option argument*."

Unless otherwise instructed, you should assume that every command line is to be completed with a press of the RETURN key. Instead of telling you to press RETURN explicitly, we will use the expression "enter the command," meaning that you should type the command and then press RETURN to make the system register what you have typed.

We use the following conventions in the screen simulation displays:

Generally your terminal displays both what you type and the computer's response. We differentiate between output from the computer and data typed at the keyboard: operator input appears in boldface type, while computer-generated characters do not. For example, consider this screen simulation:

$ date
Thu Nov 1 08:04:56 PST 1984
$ ▓

Here we first show the shell prompt, denoted by $, on the terminal screen. Next, since the word **date** is in boldface, we know that the operator entered this command. Although we do not show RETURN explicitly, the operator has pressed the RETURN key to end the command request. Next, the computer's response to the **date** command, which is used to display the current date and time of day, is shown in regular type. Once UNIX has responded to what the user has entered, another shell prompt appears; this indicates that the system is ready for your next request. Finally, the *cursor* (▓) shows you where the next input character you press will be displayed.

The results displayed on your terminal screen may differ somewhat from our presentation. UNIX software is often modified for specific purposes, and your displays may reflect such changes. For instance, some systems have been modified so the time of day does not show the seconds past the minute, so that in the last example, the seconds would not have been displayed.

In screen displays we indicate control characters using the circumflex (^) control letter notation. However, we place the representation in square brackets to indicate that the control sequence doesn't actually appear on the terminal screen. For instance, this screen

$ [^D]
(YOUR UNIX SYSTEM BANNER)
login: ▓

shows that a CTRL-D, indicated by [^D], was typed after the shell prompt. Because typing ^D will log you off the system, we have showed the sign-on banner followed by the login prompt "login:" and the cursor on the next line. The "login:" prompt indicates that the system is once again ready for you to initiate the login sequence.

SESSION 1

This first tutorial session discusses the steps for entering and leaving a typical UNIX system. We assume you already have an established account and have been assigned a user name and perhaps a password. Your user name, also called a login name or account name, is a one-word name that identifies you to the computer and to anyone else using the system. Most users employ some variation on their personal name as their user name. Most system implementations require a password for system access.

An important feature of UNIX is that you can have more than one account, each with a distinct user name. Each account might be established for a different reason. For instance, you might access one account to perform system maintenance, another to use an accounting package, and your personal account for everything else.

There is a special privileged account with the name **root** *for the person who must administer and maintain your UNIX system. The user of this account is also known as the* superuser, *since the ordinary access and protection features are not enforced for this privileged user.*

In the following sections, we will show you how to log on and log out of your UNIX system. We will also discuss how to install a new password or change an existing password. Your terminal displays may be somewhat different from those we present here because there are slight variations in command operations in different implementations of UNIX. The basic steps you need to perform, however, will be essentially the same as those we describe.

Logging In

The process of entering your UNIX system may be called either *logging in, logging on,* or perhaps *signing on.* The complementary process of leaving may be called *logging out, logging off,* or *signing off.*

The UNIX system is capable of communicating with many different types of terminals. The terminal may be a hard-copy device, such as a send-receive printer with a keyboard, or it may be a CRT display/keyboard combination (the latter is most common today). In addition to the commonly used asynchronous terminal, synchronous communication terminals are now supported in the latest Bell

UNIX release, System V. You may need to configure your terminal for communicating with the central computer, and if you are communicating via modem, you may have to set the modem device as well. See the section in Appendix C called "Setting Terminal Communication Options" for further information on setting the terminal and modem device for communication with the central computer.

The remainder of this tutorial assumes that your terminal is properly set up for communicating with your UNIX system. To get the computer's attention, press RETURN. (You may need to press LINE FEED, BREAK, ESCAPE, or some similar key on your system.) If a garbled display appears, press the BREAK key until the sign-on message is recognizable. (Some UNIX systems can change their communication speed to match your terminal. The BREAK key signals the computer to try another speed.) If after several tries the display is still unreadable, ask your system administrator for assistance.

When you have the system's attention, a UNIX system *banner line* may appear. The banner line identifies your system and tells you the system is running and ready to receive input. We show the banner line in parentheses to indicate that some systems don't display an identifying banner. The banner line is followed by a prompt requesting your login or user name. Your login prompt may appear as "login:", "user:", or some other variation. Here is an example:

```
(YOUR UNIX SYSTEM BANNER)
login:
```

Now type your user name and press RETURN. Remember to type in lowercase; if you type in uppercase, the system will use all uppercase characters until you log out and log in again. If you make a mistake, press RETURN several times, waiting a few seconds between each RETURN, and you will eventually get another login prompt.

After the UNIX system reads your user name, it will usually prompt you for a password, as shown in the following example. In this and subsequent examples, **username** stands for your user name. Of course, to run these examples on your system you should substitute your actual account name.

```
(YOUR UNIX SYSTEM BANNER)
login: username
Password:
```

Some systems may not require that you specify a password. If required, enter your password and press RETURN. The password you type is not echoed back to your screen for security reasons. After the system accepts your password, you are officially logged on.

If you make a typing mistake or enter your user name or password incorrectly, the UNIX system will display a message, such as "Login incorrect", prompting you for your user name again:

```
(YOUR UNIX SYSTEM BANNER)
login: username
Password:
Login incorrect
login:
```

When you reenter your user name, the system will ask you for your password again (if a password is required). You will be given another chance until you type both your user name and password correctly. If you are still unable to log on, consult the administrator of your UNIX system for assistance.

If you do not complete the login sequence successfully within a certain period (usually a minute), you may be disconnected if you are using a modem. Some systems may disconnect you after a number of unsuccessful attempts at logging in. These features help prevent unauthorized access to your UNIX system.

In addition, some UNIX installations may require a second dial-up password if you are accessing them by modem. This feature provides additional password security for some publicly accessible UNIX systems.

Beginning with Bell System III, the UNIX system has a feature to restrict users to a certain portion of the system. If you get a message starting with "subsystem root:", your UNIX system has such a restriction feature. To log on to such a system, simply repeat the login sequence we have just described when you get the "subsystem root:" message.

If your system implements the password aging feature, there will be a maximum number of weeks for which your password is valid. If you attempt to log on after your password has expired, the system will force you to supply a new one. There may also be a minimum number of weeks that must elapse before you can change your password.

Once you are logged on, the UNIX system may display a variety of messages beneath the password prompt. As with the banner line, we enclose the message line in parentheses in the following screen to emphasize that messages may or may not be displayed on your particular system:

```
(YOUR UNIX SYSTEM BANNER)
login: username
Password:
(YOUR UNIX SYSTEM MESSAGES)
```

Most systems display the last time your account was accessed (unless, of course, this is the very first time your account has been accessed). It is a good idea always to check the message indicating your last login time to be sure that it is in accord with your idea of when you logged in last. A discrepancy would suggest that someone else has been using your account.

In addition to the last login time, the system may display messages of the day, which are the latest messages for system users. Typically, the system's maintenance schedule (when the system will be down and therefore unavailable for users), warning messages (such as "low on disk space"), and perhaps a description of features added recently to your UNIX system are displayed at this time.

Another message you might see, "You have mail", would indicate that someone has sent you electronic mail. If this is the case, you may elect to read your mail now. If so, refer to the section "Receiving Electronic Mail" in Session 3 to learn how to read the contents of your mailbox file, which is a file that UNIX automatically sets up for you when you first receive mail.

Finally, after all your messages have been displayed, the system indicates that it is ready for your commands by displaying a shell prompt like $ or %. The shell prompt in the following screen is the $:

```
(YOUR UNIX SYSTEM BANNER)
login: username
Password:
(YOUR UNIX SYSTEM MESSAGES)
$ ▓
```

For more information on error conditions that may occur when you sign on to your UNIX system as well as how to use the **login** command to change from one account to another after you have initially signed on to your system, see the description of **login** in Chapter 6.

Installing or Changing Your Password

Whether or not a password is required for account access is really a matter of system administration policy. If you are the sole user of a single-user system, a password is superfluous. If you share a system with other users, however, you may wish to use a password to help prevent unauthorized users from accessing your account. In addition, you should change your password from time to time in case another system user has discovered your old password.

You would use the **passwd** command to install a password for the first time or to change an existing password. The **passwd** command is an example of an interactive program; that is, you change your password by conducting a dialogue with the **passwd** program. We will install or change your password now. After the shell prompt, enter **passwd**:

```
$ passwd
Changing password for username
Old password:
```

Of course, **passwd** would display your actual account name instead of "username". If you are installing your password for the first time, the prompt "Old password:" would not appear.

Now type in your old password (if requested). It will not appear on the screen for security reasons. Remember to press RETURN after your password. If you don't type in your old password correctly, **passwd** will respond with "Sorry." and exit. If so, simply enter **passwd** and try again.

The system will ask for your new password if your old password was specified correctly:

```
$ passwd
Changing password for username
Old password:
New password:
```

After you type your new password and press RETURN, the system asks you to repeat the entry to minimize the chance that you actually made a typing error, since you can't see what you typed.

```
$ passwd
Changing password for username
Old password:
New password:
Re-enter new password:
```

Finally, if both new password entries match, the system will store your new password in place of the old one. If they don't match, **passwd** may give you another chance to match them.

See the description of the **passwd** command in Chapter 6 for some hints on how to choose a password and for a listing of other error messages you may see when installing or changing your password.

Remember your password! You cannot log in to the system without it. If you do forget it, you will have to ask the person in charge of your system to delete your old password so that you can log in and reset it.

Logging Out

To conclude your first session, you must officially log out (sign off) of the UNIX system. Generally you log out by typing a ^D immediately after your shell prompt. If you are using the C Shell, you may have to enter **logout** instead of typing a ^D to sign off your system. In any case, you will know within a few seconds that you have successfully logged out of your system either when your terminal displays a message to log in again, as it does in the next screen, or when you are disconnected from a modem connection:

```
$ [ ^D ]
(YOUR UNIX SYSTEM BANNER)
login:
```

The symbol [^D] in this screen means that you typed a CTRL-D, which is not displayed (because it is a nonprinting control character). If you are using a dial-up (modem) line and were disconnected when you logged off, you must redial to log in again.

Do not just turn off your terminal. You must log out or else your terminal will remain on-line and another user could begin using your account. However, some systems have an auto logout feature that logs you off when you turn off the terminal. If you are connected by modem, the system will usually log you off automatically when you hang up, but you should check with your system administrator to be sure that this is the case.

SESSION 2

In this session you will learn about the different types of UNIX system software and their relationship to the system user and system hardware. Then you will see how to enter some simple commands. We also show you how to correct typing mistakes when entering a command request. You will learn how to suspend output from a command temporarily so that you can catch up on reading the display. In case you wish to abort a command, we show you how to terminate command execution. Finally, you will see that you may go ahead and enter the next command request before the last command has finished executing.

The UNIX System Software

In this section we describe the major UNIX system software components and their interrelation. The vast majority of computers on which the UNIX system runs have only one CPU, or processor. This processor can execute only one program at a time. Either the CPU is executing the kernel program, a shell program, or another command program.

The kernel program manages the resources of the computer system. These resources include the computer memory, disks, tape drives, terminals, printers, and other hardware components. The *file system*, which resides on the disk and provides an organization for all the UNIX system data, is also considered a resource and is managed directly by the kernel. The kernel program is always resident in the computer memory so that it is ready for execution with minimal delay.

Users of the UNIX system do not deal with the kernel program directly. Instead, UNIX users interact with an intermediary program, which may be either a shell or a command program. This intermediary program in turn accesses the kernel program. Thus, the user sees a shell or command program when she or he looks "down" into the UNIX system. The kernel also sees a shell or command program when it looks "up" toward the user. Figure 3-1 shows these relationships diagrammatically. Note that the "command program" shown in the figure can be either a simple UNIX *utility* program or a complex *interactive program.*

The UNIX shell is the most important component of the system software for you to understand at this point. The shell is a program that aids communication between you and the UNIX operating system. The shell is also called a *command interpreter* since it reads the command lines you type on the keyboard and interprets them as requests to run or execute command programs.

The shell finds the program requested by your command, brings it into memory, and executes it. When the shell performs this procedure, we say that it is *invoking* a program. After the command is completed, the shell prompt reappears, indicating that the shell is ready to respond to your next command request.

If the shell cannot locate the command program you specify, no harm is done. The shell simply issues a warning message and displays another prompt, indicating that you may try again. For example:

```
$ xyz
xyz: not found
$ 
```

The particular text of the "command not found" message depends on your particular shell.

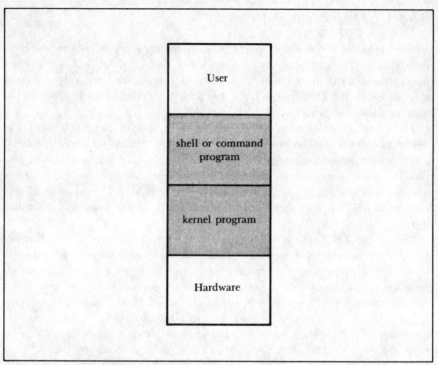

Figure 3-1.   *UNIX system software layers*

An executing program is known as a *process.* Thus an executing shell is sometimes called a *shell process,* and an executing command program, a *command process.* The UNIX system is a multitasking operating system, which means that you can schedule more than one process or task to run at the same time. Of course, if the system has only one CPU, then only one process can in actuality be executed at any given instant. However, the UNIX kernel is able to handle the processes in such a way that it can drop the execution of one process in order to execute a second and then return to the correct point in the first process. Thus, since the UNIX system is able to switch between processes very quickly, all the processes appear to be running simultaneously, even though the CPU's time is actually being shared. For this reason, UNIX is said to be a *time-sharing system.*

An important feature of UNIX shells is that they are interchangeable; that is, you can invoke one shell from another simply by typing the name of the desired shell as you would any command program. This is possible because, unlike some less flexible operating systems, the UNIX system command interpreter—that is, the shell—is not part of the kernel program; instead, the shell executes independently of the kernel just as any other command program would. The shell provides an environment for executing command programs, and since a programmer can write a new shell program, the environment in which commands execute may be changed easily by changing shells.

With this general sense of how UNIX software works, let's get some practice running command programs. Remember that all commands in the UNIX system are actually programs themselves.

Using Some Simple Command Programs

We will now introduce the **date** and **who** commands as a means of showing you how to manage the execution of a program.

Log in to your UNIX system as you did in the first session. The system may report the last time you logged in, any messages of general interest to users of the system, and so forth. Ultimately the cursor appears to the right of the shell prompt symbol, which is usually a $ or %.

Now type **date**. When you press RETURN to indicate that the command is complete, the shell will look on the disk for the program called **date**, read it into memory, and direct it to run, or *execute*. The result of **date**'s execution will be displayed immediately, and the shell will issue another prompt and wait for your next command request:

```
$ date
Thu Nov  1 09:34:50 PST 1984
$
```

Try mistyping the word **date** as **datte** and press RETURN. The system will inform you that the command **datte** is invalid:

```
$ datte
datte: not found
$
```

The shell informed you it could not find the command **datte** and then prompted you to enter another command.

To see who is currently logged into the system, use the **who** command. Here is an example of a response to the **who** command:

```
$ who
veronica    bx066    Oct 31 13:28
rathomas    dz24     Nov 1 07:42
spilchuk    tty5     Nov 1 07:39
$
```

The user names appear in the left-hand column, the names of the terminal devices that users are logged in to are listed in the next column, and the date and time of logging in appear in the last column. The output of the **who** utility is sorted by the second field, the login terminal designation.

Correcting Typing Errors

The only way to correct typing mistakes is to do so before you press RETURN in order to enter the command line. Once you press RETURN, the shell tries to invoke the command program using any arguments that you have requested. If you mistype the command name, the shell will respond with a "command not found" message, since the erroneous command program would not be found on the system. If you type the command name correctly but mistype one or more arguments for the command, either the command program itself will issue an error message and perhaps abort or else it will simply not work as desired.

Before you press RETURN, you have two options for correcting mistakes. The first is to use the default UNIX erase and line-kill editing characters to correct the command line. The second and preferable one is to assign your own erase and line-kill characters and employ these to correct the command line. First let's take a look at using the default command line editing characters.

You can correct typing mistakes as you go by using a special editing character called the *character-erase character* or simply the *erase character*. The default erase character is the #. When you type this character, the previous character on the command line is erased even though on many systems both the previous character and the # remain on the terminal display. On some systems, the # does not appear on the display in the correction process, and the previous character is erased.

As an example, after the shell prompt, enter **datte**. If you press RETURN, the shell responds with a "command not found" message. To correct the entry before pressing RETURN, press one erase character for each character you wish to erase. Then type the correct characters. Now when you press RETURN, the shell will correctly interpret your command as **date**. As a second example, mistype the **date** command to show that the erase character doesn't necessarily have to be entered at the end of the command name. Both examples are shown here:

```
$ datte
datte: not found
$ datte##e
Thu Nov  1 09:44:03 PST 1984
$ daa#tt#e
Thu Nov 1  09:44:06 PST 1984
$ 
```

Note that in **datte##e**, the first # erases the **e** and the second # erases the second **t** to give **dat**. Then the **e** is typed to complete the command name. In **daa#tt#e**, the first # erases the second **a** to give **da**, the second # erases the second **t** to give **dat**, and finally the **e** is typed to give **date**.

Alternatively, you can start over, effectively erasing all characters typed so far on the input line, by pressing the *line-kill character*. The default line-kill character is the at sign (@). When you type this line-kill character, the UNIX system will ignore what you have typed since the start of the command line. On most systems the cursor will jump to the beginning of the next line when you press the line-kill character.

As an example, type **datte** as before, only now press your line-kill character; the cursor may jump to the next line signaling you to continue. Now type **date** and press RETURN.

```
$ datte@
date
Thu Nov  1 09:45:37 PST 1984
$ 
```

It's interesting to note that the # and @ characters were originally adopted because they had been used in Multics, an operating system that had a significant influence on the development of the UNIX system. Because the terminals used with the Multics system could not generate control character codes, printing characters were commonly employed for control functions.

The main disadvantage in using # and @ as correction codes is that these printing characters are then unavailable for other uses. For this reason we recommend that you reassign the editing codes to be nonprinting control characters.

Terminal devices with a CRT display use the ^H, also known as a backspace character, to cause the cursor to back up one position and erase the character under it. Thus, you should employ this backspace character instead of the default erase character, #, as the UNIX erase character when you use a CRT display terminal.

While you are at it, assign a control character to be the line-kill character. We recommend using a ^X (or ^U, if desired) since these are frequently employed in various system implementations for this purpose. You may employ the **stty** (for "set teletype") command to do this reassignment. Simply type the command line exactly as shown in the following screen to reassign the erase character to be a ^H and the line-kill character to be a ^X:

```
$ stty erase '^h' kill '^x'
$
```

For further discussion of the **stty** command, see Chapter 6.

The next screen shows these reassigned editing characters being used. In the first case we typed **datte**, followed by two ^H characters, which moved the cursor back, erasing the trailing **te**. Then an **e** was pressed followed by a RETURN to end the command line. Note that the screen display appears as if **date** had been entered correctly to begin with. In the second case we also typed **datte**, but then we pressed the ^X line-kill character. The cursor jumped to the beginning of the next line, and we entered **date**.

```
$ date
Thu Nov  1 09:47:55 PST 1984
$ datte
date
Thu Nov  1 09:48:04 PST 1984
$
```

Some UNIX implementations can be set to display control characters as a caret (^) followed by the appropriate alphabetical character. As a general practice, however, we don't recommend making control characters visible because the terminal displays become very confusing when control characters are intermixed with printing characters.

If you are using # or @ or other printing characters as your correction codes, you may temporarily remove their special significance as correction characters so that they will be interpreted as ordinary printing characters. To do this, type an *escape character* immediately before the special character. The UNIX system generally employs the backslash (\ ) as this escape character. Thus to enter a # literally, type \#, and to enter an @ literally, type \@.

It's important to note that the same correction codes may be used to correct your input to *any* command level program as well as your shell. This is because these codes are interpreted at the level of the kernel program before they would be "seen" by the command program. When signing on most UNIX systems, you *must* use the default erase and line-kill characters to correct your user name or password. This is because the correction characters cannot be changed from their default values until the sign-on procedure has been completed.

Interrupting Program Execution

You can terminate the execution of most commands and return to the shell by pressing your *interrupt character* code. This character code tells the kernel program to send an *interrupt signal* to the command program. The default interrupt character is the ASCII delete character. The delete character is produced by pressing a special purpose key, which may be labeled RUB (for rubout) or DEL (for delete).

As an example, let's say you entered **who**, and after the command began execution, you decided that you didn't want to view the entire listing, which can be quite long on some heavily used larger systems. In this case, simply press your interrupt character and the shell prompt will reappear immediately:

```
$ who
veronica    bx066   Oct 31 [ Interrupt ]
$
```

Note that we indicate the interrupt signal by "[Interrupt]" on the screen displays. However, you will not see this on your screen.

Sometimes the shell prompt may not appear on a line by itself after an interrupt. This happens when the command is terminated before it prints the next new line character. (The new line character causes the cursor to jump to a new line.) If this is the case, simply press RETURN before typing your next command if you wish to start with a new line.

Like the line-editing codes, the interrupt character code may be reassigned to a different value. Here we recommend using the ^C for producing an interrupt signal because the delete character is frequently generated at random over noisy dial-up (modem) connections. If this happened while you were running a command, for example, the command would be terminated when a random delete character was received by your UNIX system. (Your shell is not affected by an interrupt signal.) To keep this from happening, you can employ the **stty** command to reassign the interrupt code, as shown here:

```
$ stty intr '^c'
$
```

Like the line-editing codes, the interrupt code is processed by the kernel program, which means that when you use the interrupt character, an interrupt signal will be sent to any command level program. Utilities are usually designed to respond to the signal differently than interactive programs, however. While an interrupt signal will usually terminate a utility program, interactive programs—such as the electronic mail program or the shell itself—are designed to simply stop executing the particular interactive request but will not terminate altogether. Such differences in the effect of interrupt signals on utilities and interactive programs will become clearer as you proceed through these tutorial sessions.

Suspending Program Display

You may temporarily suspend the display on your terminal without terminating the command producing the display. Freezing the display in this way is especially useful when you want to read at a slower pace than the normal scrolling speed of the terminal. Type the *stop character* code and the display will halt. To restart the display, type the *start character* code. The default stop character is a ^S, and the default start character is the ^Q. Some systems can be set up so that typing any character will restart the display.

The Berkeley UNIX system allows you to reassign the stop and start character codes to other values using the **stty** command. For instance, you may wish to assign them to the same character to get a "toggle" effect, whereby alternate pressing of the same character would stop and then start the display.

To do this now, let's assign the start character to be a ^S so that the start character will be the same as the default stop character.

```
$ stty start '^s'
$
```

Now whenever you press a ^S, the display will stop; the next time you press a ^S, the display will start, and so on.

The stop and start codes will stop and start the display produced by any command program, whether this program is a utility or an interactive program.

The Type-Ahead Buffer

A *buffer* is a temporary storage location for data. The characters you type at the keyboard are constantly being stored in a system input buffer known as a *type-ahead buffer*. In this way the characters you type will not be lost no matter how slow or fast the system response is. The one exception is when the buffer becomes full, in which case the UNIX system discards all the characters in the buffer and starts over.

There are at least three situations in which the type-ahead buffer comes into play. First, when one command may take longer to execute than another, the type-ahead buffer allows you to type in the next command request while the last command is still executing. Second, since UNIX is operating in a time-sharing environment and thus may be serving many terminals in rotation, it may not always be able to pay attention to your individual request, but the type-ahead buffer stores each command you type until UNIX can return to attend to it. In this case, your display freezes until the system can process the request. Third, since the terminal and the central computer are operating at different speeds, the type-ahead buffer helps make the interface between the terminal and the central computer possible.

If you have a terminal with a slow display rate (1200 baud or less), you can demonstrate the first use of the type-ahead buffer by typing two commands in rapid succession:

```
$ who
veronica    bx066      Oct 31 13:28
rathomas    dzdate24   Nov 1 07:42
spilchuk    tty5       Nov 1 07:39
Thu Nov  1 09:55:34 PST 1984
$ 
```

To illustrate how the type-ahead buffer functions with a faster terminal, you would have to type a command that requires even more time than **who** to execute and enter **date** for the second command.

This is the end of your second tutorial session. Don't forget to log off: press a ^D after your shell prompt. If you are using the C Shell and ^D doesn't work, type **logout** and press RETURN.

SESSION 3

This tutorial session covers the topics of sending and receiving electronic mail, the basic unit of organization for data called a file, *and two of UNIX's vehicles for word processing, the* **ed** *and* **ex** *editors.*

You will be creating several different data files in this and the following tutorial sessions. Immediately after logging on to your UNIX system and before creating any files, you must set your file creation mask value, or **umask** *value, to zero. This is important so that the results you get will be like those we depict in the screen examples. You may set the value to zero by entering* **umask 0**. *Then to verify that the value was set correctly, enter* **umask**. *The result should be the number zero, as shown here:*

```
$ umask 0
$ umask
0
$
```

Now you are ready to begin this tutorial session.

Sending Electronic Mail

The **mail** command is used to send electronic mail to users on your system. There are many different versions of the UNIX electronic mail programs available. We document the version from the Bell UNIX system. If your version is derived from the Bell version, it should behave as described here, although some of the operational details may differ.

Our first example will show you how to send mail to yourself. The **mail** command provides a convenient way to leave yourself a reminder. Type **mail**, a space, and then your own user name, which we indicate on the screen display as **username**, and end the command line with a RETURN. (Of course, you must substitute your actual user name for **username**.) Then enter a short reminder message, such as "Board meeting this Monday evening." If you make a typing mistake, you may use your erase and line-kill editing codes to correct the line before you press RETURN. (There is, as you recall from the last session, no way to correct the line after you press RETURN.) When you are satisfied that the text is correct, press RETURN. Now end the message by typing as the *first and only character* on the next line either a period or a ^D. (Because some versions of **mail** do not recognize the period, you may have to use a ^D.) In the past, we used ^D to log out. Here we are using ^D to indicate that we are finished with the **mail** program and want to send the message. If you do use a ^D, be careful to type only one ^D, since typing more than one may log you out of the system, and once you have logged out, you must repeat the login sequence.

$ mail username
Board meeting this Monday evening.

$

Before sending a mail message to another system user, you need to know the account name for that user. Of course, the easiest way is just to ask the person. If the recipient were currently using the system, however, you could determine the account name by using the **who** command as shown in the last tutorial session.

Once you have determined the recipient's user name, invoke the **mail** program by typing **mail**, a space, and the recipient's user name; end the command line with a RETURN. The cursor will then be positioned on the next line, waiting for your input.

For instance, to send mail to the user with account name **friend**, enter **mail friend**, as shown here:

$ mail friend

Now you may type your message. Remember to press RETURN at the end of each line. Whatever you type will be placed in computer memory to be sent when you exit **mail**. You may edit each line of text before pressing RETURN by using your UNIX erase and line-kill characters. However, after pressing RETURN there is no way to edit the previous line. If you decide not to send the message, you may abort the **mail** command by typing your interrupt code. (Recall that the default interrupt code is a delete character, but the code may have been reassigned to some other character, as explained in the last tutorial session.)

To exit the **mail** program and also send your message, either press ^D or type a period as the first and only character on a line, followed immediately by a RETURN, just as you did when you sent mail to yourself. Although we show a ^D being used in the following example, neither the ^D nor the blank line on which we depict it would actually appear on your terminal display:

$ mail friend
YOUR MESSAGE TEXT
[^D]
$

Since it is relatively easy to type too many ^D's and then log yourself out, we recommend ending your messages with a period if your version of **mail** recognizes the period as a terminator.

Receiving Electronic Mail

If you have messages in your mailbox, most UNIX systems will display a message like "You have mail" immediately after you log on and before you get your shell prompt. Let's see if this is the case for your system. Log off your system now either by pressing ^D after your shell prompt or perhaps by entering **logout** if you are using the C Shell.

```
$ [ ^D ]
(YOUR UNIX SYSTEM BANNER)
login: username
Password:
(YOUR UNIX SYSTEM MESSAGES)
You have mail.
$
```

The BANNER and MESSAGES lines were enclosed in parentheses to indicate that they may or may not actually appear on your terminal display.

To read your mail, simply enter **mail**. The **mail** program will display the sender's postmark on the first line. Following the "From" is the user name of the sender and the date and time the message was received in your mailbox. Next the message text is displayed. After printing the message, **mail** displays its own prompt, which is usually a question mark (?), and waits for further instructions as shown:

```
$ mail
From username Thu Nov  1 12:32:07 PST 1984
Board meeting this Monday evening.

?
```

mail is an *interactive program;* that is, you interact with the program by giving commands and receiving responses. We will describe all the possible interactive commands for the **mail** program in Chapter 6. For now simply enter **s reminder** after the **mail** prompt and your mail message will be saved in your workspace.

(We will show you how to find and examine this message again in the next tutorial session.) Since all messages in your mailbox have now been read and disposed of, the act of saving the message causes you to exit from the **mail** program and return to your shell.

? s reminder

$ ▓

The Ordinary File and Filenames

A *file* is a collection of information that is assigned a name and is stored on a secondary storage medium like a disk or magnetic tape. The mail message that you saved in the last section was written to disk as a file. The text we will create with an editor later in this tutorial session will also be handled by the UNIX system as a file. Files are discrete entities stored in the UNIX file storage system; they may be accessed at any time and manipulated in a number of different ways. Files are, in fact, the computer's way of organizing data so that it can be stored permanently and manipulated later.

There are several types of UNIX files; however, at this time we shall only concern ourselves with the type called *ordinary files,* which contain information like textual data or executable programs.

Once you create a file, it stays in the system until you explicitly remove it. Files can be created during any UNIX system session and can be accessed, if you have permission, at any time later. File access permission will be discussed in a later tutorial session.

Every file is identified by a *filename.* You might think of a file as a receptacle for data and of the filename as the way to reference that receptacle. When you refer to a file by its filename, however, you are also referring to the body of data contained within the file.

Figure 3-2 helps illustrate this concept. This figure shows that a filename names both a file and the contents of a file. For instance, in the last section you saved your mail message on disk as a file with the name **reminder**. Now whenever you refer to **reminder**, you are also referring to the contents of this file, which is the message "Board meeting this Monday evening."

Choosing a filename deserves some consideration. Here are some guidelines:

First, the majority of UNIX implementations allow a filename of as many as 14 characters. Some implementations may allow longer filenames. We recommend restricting your filenames to 14 characters or less for compatibility across UNIX systems.

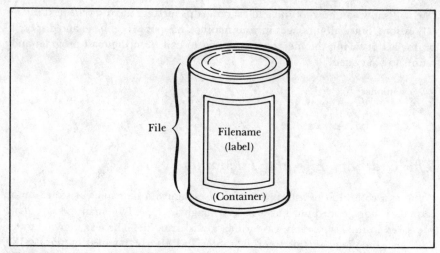

File { Filename (label)

(Container)

Figure 3-2.   *The relationship between files and filenames*

Second, choose a filename that gives you a clue to the contents or purpose of the file. For instance, for the **mail** message you saved earlier, the name "reminder" suggests the purpose of the file more than, for example, the name "mail" would.

Third, filenames are generally constructed using lowercase letters, numbers, and several other ASCII characters. Since many of the other ASCII characters have special meaning to the system, we recommend that you restrict the characters in the "other" category to the dot (.), the minus or dash (−), and the underscore (__). In particular, *don't* use the slash (/) in a filename if, for example, you are including a date in a filename. In addition, a filename should not begin with a dash or minus sign, as the system may confuse such a name with the minus sign that signals a command option argument. Some examples of valid filenames using these characters would be **reminder.11.01**, **becca7−13.let**, and **account__data**.

Related files are sometimes named with a common suffix or prefix, which might also serve to indicate the type or contents of the file. For instance, the file **becca7−13.let** might name a letter addressed to user **becca** and postmarked July 13th; similarly, **johnk8−12.let** would be the name of a letter to John K. postmarked August 8th. In these cases, the suffix or *extension* ".let" indicates a business or personal letter. Later we shall see that naming files with some characters in common enables these related files to be processed as a group.

The Line-Oriented Editors: ed and ex

Before we discuss the UNIX system commands that manipulate files, you need to learn how to create files and enter text into them. You have already created a file through the **mail** program. Now we will show you how to create files with the **ed** and **ex** *text editors*. If you have access to another, more sophisticated editor on your system and wish to use it, do so. In any case, read the following discussion to be sure you understand the concepts related to text editing as a whole that we cover here.

We discuss the **ed** editor because it is available on all UNIX systems. In fact, you may be working on a system where **ed** is the only text editor available. In either case, you should know how to use this program. The **ex** editor, developed at U.C. Berkeley, is more powerful than **ed**, having several more useful features. Now the **ex** editor is becoming increasingly available, especially since it is being distributed with the Bell System V UNIX system.

You will find **ex** to be very similar to **ed** because **ex** was designed so that its command set would include the **ed** commands. This is why we can document both **ed** and **ex** in parallel. Generally, **ex** differs from **ed** in that it has several additional commands, sometimes allows a somewhat shorter editor command line, and usually displays the changes to the text "automatically" after operations that alter the text. In most cases, you must make an explicit request for **ed** to display the modified text.

The remainder of this session examines how the **ed** and **ex** editors create, modify, and display a text file. Although this book does not cover everything about the **ed** and **ex** line editors, we document enough of the features for most needs. You should then be able to read the documentation supplied by Bell or Berkeley if you wish to use some of the more esoteric features of **ed** and **ex**.

The **ed** and **ex** editors manipulate text on a line-by-line basis; that is, the smallest unit of text you work with is an entire line. You display, change, delete, move, and copy text a line at a time. In contrast, with *screen-oriented editors* you move the cursor randomly through a screenful of text in a file to create or modify the text by as little as a character at a time. The **ex** editor has a screen-oriented counterpart, named **vi**, which we will discuss in Chapter 5.

We prefer to use line-oriented editors if access to the UNIX system is at a 1200-baud (or slower) communication rate. At such slow communication speeds the time it takes for the CRT display to be updated makes using a screen-oriented editor impractical. When you use a screen-oriented editor, the whole screen must be refreshed each time you make a change. On the other hand, at higher communication speeds a screen-oriented editor is preferable since it allows you to move around a screen of text freely, without line specifications, while you edit.

Before we create a file with **ed** and **ex**, there is some preliminary information about the editing process that you should know about.

The Edit Buffer

As you will recall from the discussion of the UNIX system's type-ahead buffer, a *buffer* is a temporary storage location for data. In text editing, the *edit buffer* serves as the temporary work space used during the editing session for creating and changing the text file. Both the **ed** and **ex** editors allocate such transient work areas or edit buffers. Text created with the editor is first placed in this buffer and can then be displayed and modified within the buffer before it is saved as a file. All the work that you do in an editing session is, in effect, done within the edit buffer.

Figure 3-3 shows some features of text as it exists within the edit buffer. As you can see from this figure, the text in the edit buffer is referenced by lines that are numbered consecutively. The editors renumber the lines automatically as text lines are added to or deleted from the buffer. At any one time the editor will be referencing one of the lines in the buffer, known as the *current line* (number 5 in this example). The last line may be referenced by the dollar sign ($) as well as an actual number. Similarly, the current line may also be indicated by the dot (.) as well as by a line number.

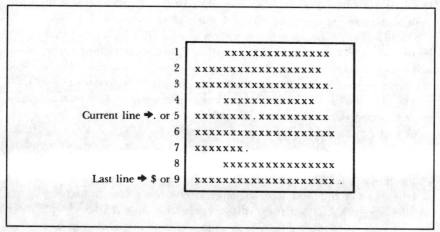

Figure 3-3.   Text in the edit buffer

The contents of the edit buffer are temporary; when you leave the editor program, any text remaining in the buffer is lost. If you wish to access that text in the future, you must make a copy of the buffer contents on disk as a file before leaving the editor.

Command Mode and Text Entry Mode

Most editors, including the ones we document here, operate in one of two modes: a *command mode* and a *text entry mode*. In command mode, whatever you type is interpreted by the editor as a command. In text entry mode, the editor adds whatever you type to the edit buffer.

After invoking an editor, you will be placed in either command or text entry mode. The UNIX editors we document in this book all start you in command mode. However, there are other UNIX editors that may begin in text entry mode.

It is easy to switch between modes. For the line-oriented editors we are discussing here, you would enter text entry mode from command mode by issuing either the append (**a**), insert (**i**), or change (**c**) commands. (We will discuss these commands in a moment.) Then whatever you type would be placed in the edit buffer. You may exit text entry mode and return to command mode by typing a period as the *first and only character* on an otherwise blank line, followed *immediately* by a RETURN.

Editing commands like append or insert may be entered as complete words or as abbreviations, which may be either the first or first and second letters of the word. Typing the entire word increases the chance for a typing mistake.

Editor Command Structure

The editing commands you will use have a simple and consistent structure: zero or more *line addresses* (or line numbers) followed by a *command*, which may be abbreviated as one or two characters, optionally followed by *parameters* to the command. Entering one or more spaces between the address, the command, and the parameters is optional but improves readability. We generally separate these elements by one space in our examples.

Thus, the command format for the **ed** and **ex** editors can be represented as follows:

line address range   commandletter [*parameter...*]

The *address range* indicates which lines in the edit buffer a command will affect. One number refers to a single line only, while two numbers separated by a comma indicate an inclusive range of lines. If no line number is specified, the current line is assumed.

The line address range can usually be constructed in several different ways. Often you may shorten the address range by choosing a default case for address range, which is the current line. The print command (**p**) can be omitted if the current line is to be displayed. Some examples of line address ranges with the print command are

1p	Print line number 1.
1,3p	Print lines 1 through 3.
.p	Print the current line.
p	Print the current line ("." assumed).
.	Print the current line ("**p**" assumed).
.,$p	Print from the current line through the end of the buffer.
1,$p	Print all lines in the buffer.

Starting the Editor to Create a File

Before starting up the editors, let's make sure your erase and line-kill correction characters are set to the default values: namely, **#** and **@**. The reason for this will become clear later on in the session. Simply enter **stty ek** to reset the erase (**e**) and kill (**k**) characters to these default values.

With these preliminaries out of the way, let's invoke the editors. After your shell prompt appears, type either **ed** or **ex**, followed by one or more spaces, and then the name for the file to contain the text you will create.

For your first example, enter **ed poem** or **ex poem**. In most of our examples the **ed** and **ex** editors will be shown operating side by side, as they are here:

```
$ ed poem                        $ ex poem
?poem                            "poem" [New file]
▮                                : ▮
```

Since you named the file **poem** and that file does not yet exist in your current workspace, both editors respond with a warning indication: **ed** displays "?poem" and **ex** "poem [New file]". These warning messages are normal; they indicate that you are creating **poem** in this session.

Interactive programs, such as editors, that have more than one operating mode generally display a prompt to indicate that they are in command mode. In this mode, whatever you type is interpreted as a command for the program. The **ex** editor always displays a colon (:) as its prompt. Older versions of **ed** did not display a prompt, but you can turn on a prompt with newer versions. The prompt, an asterisk (*) in this case, may be enabled by typing a capital **P** and then pressing RETURN after you have entered the editor. This capital **P** is not to be confused with the lowercase **p** of the print command. Here we show the **ed** prompt being turned on:

```
$ ed poem
?poem
P
*
```

Versions of **ed** earlier than the Bell System III release do not provide any prompt in command mode. With these versions, you have to determine whether you are in command or text entry mode by typing a period (.) as the *first and only character* on a line followed *immediately* by a RETURN and by then observing the response. Do this now. If you are in text entry mode, you will harmlessly exit this mode and return to command mode. If you have some text in the edit buffer and enter a period and then press RETURN while in command mode, the current line will be displayed. If there is no text in the edit buffer and you type a period as the first character, **ed** displays a question mark. The reason for this is that a period typed in command mode requests that the current line be displayed, but the edit buffer has no current line since no text has been entered yet. **ed**'s response — the question mark — indicates an error condition.

Getting Help

Recent versions of **ed** have a help function. When you enter **h** in command mode, a short diagnostic message is displayed. This message explains the reason for the last question mark diagnostic. Alternatively, if you enter **H**, throughout the editing session the **ed** editor will provide explanatory messages instead of just the cryptic question mark diagnostic. The **H** command is a toggle command; in other words, entering a subsequent **H** in command mode turns off the explanatory messages.

If you type **H** at this point, your interaction with the **ed** editor would look as shown.

$ ed poem

?poem

P

*.

?

*H

line out of range

*

Here the last question mark refers to an error condition described as "line out of range". The current line is "out of range" at this point since there is no current line until some text is entered in the buffer.

Entering Text

At this point we can begin entering text. Recall that when you first invoke the UNIX editors you are in command mode. To add text to the edit buffer, you must be in text entry mode. We shall use the editor's append command (a) to change modes. Enter a, and notice that the cursor is positioned at the beginning of the next line and that the command mode prompt (if it exists) disappears:

*a   :a

Once again, **ed** is shown on the left and **ex** is shown on the right. At this point, whatever text you type will be entered into the edit buffer. Type the text exactly as shown on the following screen (including the errors), correcting the errors as you go using the default erase (#) and line-kill (@) characters. End each line with RETURN:

*a   :a

Roses are Red.#   Roses are Red

Vil#olets are Blue   Vilets are@

Sugar is Sweet   Violets are Blue

Ans so are You.@   Sugar is Sweet

And so are You.   And so are Yopu.###u.

Finally, to leave test entry mode, type a period as the first and only character on the last line, followed immediately by RETURN:

*a	**:a**
Roses are Red.#	**Roses are Red**
Vil#olets are Blue	**Vilets are@**
Sugar is Sweet	**Violets are Blue**
Ans so are You.@	**Sugar is Sweet**
And so are You.	**And so are Yopu.###u.**
.	**.**
*	**:**

Are you back in command mode? Yes, if you see the command mode prompt (***** for **ed**, **:** for **ex**). However, with versions of **ed** that do not display a prompt, enter a period as the first character of the line. If you see the current line — "And so are You." — displayed, you have returned to command mode. If not, you were still in text entry mode, but now you have returned to command mode.

You may use either your erase or line-kill correction character to correct a typing error on a line before you press RETURN. (You will learn how to correct mistakes after you have pressed RETURN in a later session.) If you are using printing characters for your correction codes, your screen may get cluttered with these characters. However, these characters are not entered into the edit buffer, as you will see in a moment.

Displaying the Text

When you have returned to command mode, you can display the text you just entered into the edit buffer with the print (**p**) command. To display the entire buffer, enter **1,$p**. Here the numeral 1 denotes the first line of the buffer, the special character $ denotes the last line, and the construction **1,$p** means "display the contents of the edit buffer from line 1 through the last line inclusive." For the **ex** editor, you may enter the shorthand **%** instead of **1,$p** to display the entire buffer.

*1,$p	**:%**
Roses are Red	**Roses are Red**
Violets are Blue	**Violets are Blue**
Sugar is Sweet	**Sugar is Sweet**
And so are You.	**And so are You.**
*	**:**

Note that neither your character-erase code nor your line-kill code was displayed, since they were not entered into the edit buffer.

Saving the Text and Exiting the Editor

In order to exit the editor and save your text, you must do two things: first, save the contents of the edit buffer to the disk with the write (w) command, and second, leave the editor with the quit (q) command. If you do try to exit the editor without saving your work, both ed and ex will issue a warning. In fact, if you make any change at all to the edit buffer and try to exit without writing the buffer to disk, the editors will complain.

Let's see how the editors respond to a request to exit without saving the text. The older version of the ed editor would reply with a cryptic question mark and then ignore your request, thus giving you a second chance. If you asked to exit a second time, ed would let you leave; however, in this case the contents of the edit buffer would be lost. The ex editor complains even more verbosely and will not let you exit unless you change the form of the quit request in the way indicated by the warning message:

```
*q                                      :q
?                                       No write since last change (:quit! overrides)
warning: expecting 'w'                  :
*
```

If you were to enter another q at this point, you would exit ed. The ex editor won't let you exit until either you save your text with the write command or override the quit command by entering q! or quit!.

To save your work at any time from command mode, simply enter w. Since it is so easy to save your work, you should do so from time to time while editing. In fact, we recommend doing so every five or ten minutes. In this way, a problem, such as a power failure, would cause you to lose at most the last five or ten minutes of your work. In addition, if you make a mistake while editing and perhaps lose all the text stored in the buffer, you will still have a recent copy of your text safely stored on the disk file.

Enter w now:

```
*w                                      :w
62                                      "poem" [New file] 4 lines, 62 characters
*                                       :
```

Both editors display the number of characters just written to disk as the file named **poem**. Note that the character count (62 here) includes the space characters between words and the new line character at the end of each sentence. The text in the edit buffer remains intact; only a copy of it is saved. You may continue to add or change the text in the edit buffer if you wish since the contents of the file named **poem** on the disk will not be changed further until you write to that disk file again. Figure 3-4 illustrates this *write operation.*

Now you may leave the editor. Simply enter **q** and you should return to your shell:

```
*q                              :q
$                               $
```

The shell prompt here ($) indicates that you have indeed returned to the shell. As a shortcut, you may enter **x** from command mode of **ex** to save the text and exit the editor in one step.

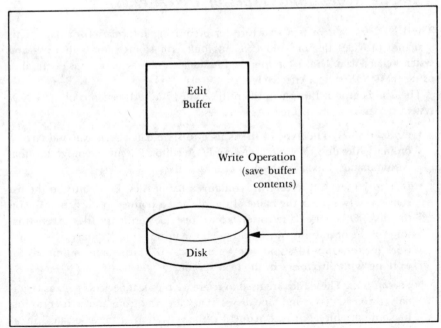

Figure 3-4. *Saving contents of the edit buffer*

For further practice, you should invoke your editor program with a different filename: for example, **letter**. Then add some text to the edit buffer: for example, "This letter was created in session 3." Write the buffer to disk with **w**, and exit from the editor with **q**. If you are using **ex**, this time enter **x** to save the text and leave the editor with one command.

At this point, we will suspend our exploration of **ed** and **ex** in order to examine some other features of the UNIX system. Our study of the line-oriented editors will resume in Sessions 9 and 10 of Chapter 5.

SESSION 4

Now that you know how to use an editor to create ordinary files, you are ready to learn some of the basic UNIX system commands that treat files. But first, let's take a general look at what the file system is and what types of files it consists of.

The File System and Types of UNIX Files

The UNIX *file system* is a structure for organizing information or data. This structure provides flexible and efficient long-term storage for both user- and system-related data. Understanding the file system and how to use it is essential to using the UNIX system effectively.

The data is grouped into named entities called *files*. All versions of the UNIX system recognize at least three types of files:

* *Ordinary files.* This type of file is used to store data. Users can add data to ordinary files directly with, for example, an editor. Executable programs (that is, commands) are also stored as ordinary files.

* *Directory files.* A directory file contains a list of files. Each entry in the list consists of two parts: the name of the file and a pointer to the actual file on the disk. Otherwise, directories behave just like ordinary files except that some of the operations you would use for manipulating ordinary files do not work for directory files and vice versa. You will learn some commands for working with directories in the next session.

* *Special files.* These files are used to reference physical devices, such as terminals, printers, disks, and tape drives. They are read from and written to just like ordinary files, but such requests cause activation of the associated physical device.

Since you already have some sense of what an ordinary file is, let's take a closer look at directory files for a moment. Just as a file is a structure for organizing data, so a directory is a structure for organizing files. In the list of filenames that a directory contains, the names may refer to ordinary files, special files, or to other directory files. Since directories may be listed inside of other directories, complex hierarchical structures of ordinary, special, and directory files result.

Directories provide the major tool within the UNIX file system for organizing files and thus the data contained within files. For instance, you may use directories to organize your work by projects or by classes of information. In the next session we provide an actual example for creating an "electronic filing cabinet" using directories to organize your electronic mail messages by date and sender. Before we work with several directories, however, you should learn how to manipulate ordinary files within a single directory.

Some Basic Commands for File Manipulation

In the following sections, you will learn how to manipulate ordinary files using several new UNIX commands. First you learn how to list the filenames in a directory since you need to know the name of a file in order to manipulate it. Next you will learn how to make a copy of a file in case you need a duplicate and how to remove a file in case you no longer need it. Finally, you will learn how to change the name of a file and how to create more than one name for the same file.

ls: List the Contents of a Directory

This tutorial session assumes that you are situated in your initial login or *home directory*. This would be the case immediately after you sign on to your UNIX system.

Your home directory now includes the names of several files. To display the names of those files, use the ls command. Enter ls and an alphabetically ordered listing of the filenames will appear. After the command is executed, you are returned to your shell, as indicated by your shell prompt.

```
$ ls
letter
poem
reminder
$
```

Note that our display of the format and content of the directory listing may differ from your UNIX system implementation. For instance, the filenames in your directory might be listed in rows, which is characteristic of the U.C. Berkeley version of the **ls** command:

```
$ ls
letter        poem        reminder
$ 
```

However your screen is formatted, it should now show that your directory contains three files named **letter, poem,** and **reminder.** Recall that you used an editor to create the ordinary files **letter** and **poem** and that you used the save command (**s**) from the **mail** program to create **reminder.**

cat: Concatenate and Print a File

cat is short for concatenate, which means to join together. This utility is used most often to display the contents of a single file, although you may use **cat** to display the contents of several files in succession. You might think of this command as, in effect, joining the file or files to the terminal screen for display.

You can display the contents of a file from an editor (by, for example, using the **1,$p** command with **ed**), but if you are interacting with the shell, using **cat** will be more direct. That is, if you use **cat**, you save having to invoke an editor, read the file into the edit buffer, print the contents of the edit buffer, and then exit the editor.

To use **cat** to display the contents of a single file named *filename,* use the following command line format:

$ cat *filename*

If you don't remember the name of the file you wish to **cat,** you can get the name from an **ls** listing.

As an example of using **cat,** let's look at the contents of **poem:**

```
$ cat poem
Roses are Red
Violets are Blue
Sugar is Sweet
And so are You.
$ 
```

To display the contents of more than one file, use a similar command line format:

$ **cat** *filename...*

The ellipses here indicate that you can repeat *filename;* that is, you can list the names of all the files you wish to access on the command line right after the command name **cat**. The names must be separated from each other and also from the command name by a space. For instance, to display the three files **letter**, **reminder**, and **poem** one right after the other, enter **cat letter reminder poem**.

```
$ cat letter reminder poem
This "letter" was created in session 3.
From username Thu Nov  1 12:32:07 PST 1984
Board meeting this Monday evening.

Roses are Red
Violets are Blue
Sugar is Sweet
And so are You.
$
```

If you mistype one of the filenames or request a file that isn't in your current directory, the **cat** utility displays an error message. To illustrate, enter **cat letters**.

```
$ cat letters
cat: cannot open letters
$
```

Because the filename **letters**, as distinct from **letter**, doesn't exist in your directory, **cat** cannot open it for reading into memory and subsequent display on your terminal. The "cat:" portion of the preceding error message means that the **cat** program, rather than some other program, issued the error message. Error messages frequently begin with the name of the command in order to help you identify the source of the error. By contrast, the shell generally doesn't identify itself when displaying an error message.

cp: Copy an Ordinary File

The **cp** command allows you to create a duplicate copy of an ordinary file. The command line format for using **cp** is

$ **cp** *srcfile destfile*

Here *srcfile* is the original or source filename and *destfile* (for "destination") is the name of the copy to be created. Note that the filename *destfile* must be different from *srcfile*.

One application for the **cp** (for "copy") command is to create a *backup* copy of an important file. Having a backup copy allows you to modify the original file without worrying that all will be lost if you make substantial errors or destroy the original file completely.

Our next example illustrates such a situation. Let's say you wish to edit **poem**, but first you make a copy named **poem.bak** by entering **cp poem poem.bak**. We use the **cat** command here to verify that **poem** and **poem.bak** are identical:

```
$ cp poem poem.bak
$ cat poem
Roses are Red
Violets are Blue
Sugar is Sweet
And so are You.
$ cat poem.bak
Roses are Red
Violets are Blue
Sugar is Sweet
And so are You.
$
```

Now let's say that after you invoked an editor to change **poem**, you accidentally erased the contents of the edit buffer and then issued the editor command to write the buffer to disk without catching your mistake until it was too late. Since the disk copy was just updated by the empty buffer, this disk copy is now empty as well. You have not lost the file entirely, however, since you still have a duplicate of the original copy, named **poem.bak**. Now you can make a copy of **poem.bak** using **cp** and call it **poem**. At this point you are ready to try editing **poem** again.

As you can see, this approach of first creating a backup file gives you a second chance. The previous example may seem trivial, since a file as short as **poem** can be produced quickly with an editor. But if you had a large file consisting of many pages of text or of original work and you accidentally destroyed it, you would be very grateful for the duplicate.

rm: Remove an Ordinary File

This command removes one or more ordinary files from a directory, effectively erasing the file. The **rm** (for "remove") utility removes a file by deleting its pointer in the appropriate directory. In this way, the *link* between that filename and the physical file is severed, so the file can no longer be accessed (at least under that filename). The command line format for using **rm** to remove one or more files is

$ **rm** *filename...*

where each *filename* is separated from the next and from the command name (**rm**) by white space.

Let's say that you have a backup copy of **poem** with the filename **poem.bak** and that you wish to remove the original file named **poem**. First list your directory, entering **ls**, and then remove the file, entering **rm poem**. Then list the directory again to verify that you have removed the file. This procedure is shown in the following screen:

```
$ ls
letter
poem
poem.bak
reminder
$ rm poem
$ ls
letter
poem.bak
reminder
$ 
```

mv: Move (Rename) a File

The **mv** (for "move") command changes the name associated with a file by associating a new filename with the pointer (or link) to the physical file in the directory entry and then removing the link to the old filename. The command line format for using **mv** is

$ **mv** *oldname newname*

This command line changes the name of the file from *oldname* to *newname*.

As an example, let's change the name of **poem.bak** to **poem**. Recall that we just removed **poem** with the **rm** command after we had made a copy of it with **cp** named **poem.bak**. First list the directory before the rename operation by entering **ls**. Now enter **mv poem.bak poem**. Finally, examine the directory to verify the results of the rename operation.

```
$ ls
letter
poem.bak
reminder
$ mv poem.bak poem
$ ls
letter
poem
reminder
$
```

ln: Creating Filename Aliases

The UNIX file system allows more than one filename for the same physical file, which means that it is possible to have aliases for any given file. For instance, the names **poem** and **verse** could *both* refer to the same file containing the text "Roses are Red...". Each new filename must be "linked" to the physical file.

The **ln** command (for "make link") may be used for establishing additional links. The operation involved in **ln** is similar to that in **mv**, as is clear from the command line format:

$ **ln** *oldname newname*

The difference here is that after the **ln** linking, both *newname* and *oldname* refer to the same file.

For example, let's create a filename alias for **poem** named **verse**. Simply enter **ln poem verse** and verify the additional name with an **ls** directory listing. Then if you display the contents of **verse** using **cat**, you see that they are the same as the contents of **poem**.

```
$ ln poem verse
$ ls
letter
poem
reminder
verse
$ cat verse
Roses are Red
Violets are Blue
Sugar is Sweet
And so are You.
$ cat poem
Roses are Red
Violets are Blue
Sugar is Sweet
And so are You.
$
```

We can see here that the **ln** operation worked because the directory listing does reveal the additional filename, **verse**. The contents of **verse** are the same as that of **poem** because they refer to the *same* file. If you were to change the contents of **verse**, you would alter the contents of **poem**. Although the names **poem** and **verse** are different, they both refer to the same contents — that is, to the same file.

Recall that you remove (or erase) a file by breaking the link between the filename (in the directory) and the physical file on disk. Thus to remove a file with more than one link from the file system, you must sever *all* the links. To prove this, enter **rm poem**. The physical file containing "Roses are Red..." is still accessible if you use the alternative name **verse**, as you can see if you enter **cat verse**. To eliminate the "Roses are Red..." text altogether, you must now erase **verse** by entering **rm verse**. All of these steps are shown here:

```
$ ls
letter
poem
reminder
verse
$ rm poem
$ cat verse
```

```
Roses are Red
Violets are Blue
Sugar is Sweet
And so are You.
$ rm verse
$ ls
letter
reminder
$ ▮
```

File Access Permissions

As you know, the data in your UNIX system is contained in files. You may restrict or permit access to this data by restricting or permitting access to the files containing the data. The UNIX system provides an easy means of controlling the file access that system users, including yourself, may have to all three types of UNIX files (that is, ordinary, directory, and special files).

Even if you are the sole user of a single-user UNIX system, you may wish to restrict access to certain important files to help prevent accidental damage of their contents. For instance, you might wish to retain the ability to read certain files while restricting your ability to write on them. If you are one of several users on a larger, multiuser system, restricting access to files will probably be more important. You may not wish other system users even to read your files, much less be able to modify them by writing to them. In general, the file access permission system allows you to control the fate of your files.

Types of File Access Permissions

The first step in learning to use file access permissions is to understand the three different classes of file users and the three modes of file access. These three classes of users and modes of access give rise to the nine different kinds of access permission allowed within the UNIX file system.

There are three classes of system users. First, every file has an owner. The owner is usually the system user who created the file. The superuser can change the individual ownership of a file if necessary. The owner has full control over restricting or permitting access to the file at any time. In addition to individual file ownership, it is possible to have one or more system users own the file collectively in a kind of group ownership. A system user who is not the file owner may access the file if this user belongs to the group of system users who are allowed to access the file. However, this user cannot restrict or permit access to the file; only the owner may do that. System users who are neither the individual nor group owners of the file form the last category, known simply as "other" users. To sum up, then, the three classes of system users who might access a given file are

- *Owner* (denoted by **u**, for user). The owner is the system user who created the file.
- *Group* (denoted by **g**). The group is one or more users who may access the file as a group.
- *Other* (denoted by **o**). The "other" category refers to any other user of the system.

The UNIX file system allows each user class to access the file independently of the other classes. That is, the access rights for the file owner, for the group owner, and for the "other" user category may be the same or different.

In addition to classes of file users, there are three ways of accessing a file. The meaning of these *access modes* is somewhat different for ordinary files than it is for directories. These modes and their meanings are summarized in Table 3-1.

The meaning of the three access modes for ordinary files is relatively straight-forward. System users with *read permission* may read (examine) the contents of an ordinary file (for example, by using **cat**). System users with *write permission* may write to a file and change its contents (for example, by using an editor). Write permission is also required to delete the file using the **rm** command. Even if write permission is not enabled, the file owner may always delete the file by first enabling write permission and then removing the file.

Table 3-1. *File Access Modes and Their Meanings*

Access Mode	Ordinary File	Directory File
Read	Allows examination of file contents	Allows listing of files within directory
Write	Allows changing contents of file	Allows creating new files and removing old ones
Execute	Allows executing file as command	Allows searching directory

Finally, system users with *execute permission* for ordinary files may execute the file as a command. Generally, an ordinary file is not given execute permission when it is created. Executing a file only makes sense if the file is actually a program (command) or a *shell script*. A shell script is a file that contains a list of one or more commands that can be executed by the shell.

The meaning of these same access modes is different for a directory file. The system user with read permission may read (by listing) the contents of the directory (for example, using the **ls** command). The system user with write permission, on the other hand, may use certain privileged programs to write on a directory. Write permission is necessary in order to create files (a process that writes an additional directory entry) or to remove files (a process that also modifies the directory entry). Recall that you may create a file either using an editor or **cp** to duplicate an existing file and that you may remove a file with **mv**.

Execute permission for a directory file is sometimes called *search permission*, which is a better term since directories may be searched but can't be executed like a command. A user must have execute permission for a directory in order to access the files named in that directory. Thus, even if you had read and write permission for an ordinary file that was listed in a directory, unless you also had execute permission for the directory containing the ordinary file, the UNIX system wouldn't let you read or write the contents of the ordinary file.

Determining File Access Permissions

The three classes of file users (owners, group, and others) may be combined with the three types of access (read, write, and execute) to give nine possible sets of permissions, as shown here:

The presence of a permission is indicated by the appropriate letter being in its correct location. The absence of a permission is indicated by a dash (−) in the same place. For instance, some common permission patterns for ordinary files and their meanings are

r − − r − − r − −

This ordinary file can be read (or examined) by all three user classes, but it cannot be written to (changed) or executed by anyone. A file with this set of permissions is known as *read-only* or *write-protected*. Generally, sensitive data files that must be publicly accessible (readable), such as the password file, may have this pattern of permissions.

- - x - - x - - x

This ordinary file can be executed like any command program file by all system user classes. That is, any user can type the name of the file after the shell prompt, and the file will be read into memory by the shell and run as a command program. This file is also write-protected and read-protected. Generally, executable programs (commands), such as **cat**, **ls**, and the like, that are installed in publicly accessible directories are given this set of permissions.

r w - - - - - -

This ordinary file is readable and writable only by the file owner. Generally, a file that the owner wishes to keep private from all other users has this set of permissions.

Some commonly seen permission patterns for directory files and their meanings are

r w x r w x r w x

This directory is completely accessible by all system users. In general, public directories that must be readable and writable by all users would have this set of permissions.

r w x - - - - - -

This directory is only accessible by its owner; other users cannot search it or read or write to any files contained in it. In general, users on a multi-user time-sharing system would establish this pattern of permissions for their home directory workspace.

You can easily determine what type a file is—whether ordinary, directory, or special—and what set of access permissions it has, as well as other information about the file, by using the long listing option (−1) with the **ls** (directory listing) command. The particular format and contents of your long listing may vary somewhat from what we show here, but the format is generally similar to the following:

```
$ ls −l letter
−rw−rw−rw−      1 becca        docum         40 Nov  1 13:23 letter
$
```

Here we have requested the long directory listing for the ordinary file called **letter**.

There is only one restriction on use of the long listing option: the user requesting a long directory listing must have execute (search) permission in addition to read permission for the directory that contains the file.

Because the long listing is especially helpful for working with files, it's important to know how to read it. Here is an explanation of what the various segments or *fields* in the long listing mean:

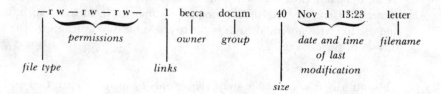

Reading from left to right, we see that the dash (−) in the file type field indicates that the file is an ordinary file. Next, the access permissions field tells us that the access permissions are all enabled. Next, the "1" indicates that there is only one link for this file from the directory, which means that this file only has one name associated with it. The word "becca" indicates that the file owner has the user name "becca"; the group that has access to this file is referred to as "docum." Moving to the next slot, we see that the file's size is 40 characters. The date and time, "Nov 1 13:23," show when the file was last modified. And last of all, the filename is listed; the filename is, of course, "letter."

While there are actually four types of files that may be indicated in the first field, the ones that are important for you to know are the dash (−), which indicates an ordinary file, and **d**, which indicates a directory file.

Changing File Access Permissions

Now that you understand what kinds of file access permissions are possible in UNIX, you are ready to learn how to control access permission. The **chmod** command (for "change mode") allows you to alter the permission modes of one or more files or directories. Because the command line format for **chmod** is somewhat more complicated than the format for other commands you've seen so far, we'll lead you through the details one by one:

$ **chmod** [*who*] *op-code permission... file...*

The *who* argument tells **chmod** the user class and may be any of the following:

* **u** User (individual file owner)
* **g** Group file owner
* **o** Users classified as "other"
* **a** All system users (file owner, group owner, and the "other" category).

The *op-codes* argument represents the operation to be performed by **chmod**:

* **+** Add the specified permissions to the existing permissions.
* **−** Remove the indicated permissions from the existing permissions.
* **=** Assign the indicated permissions.

The *permission* argument uses the same abbreviations as you saw earlier in the discussion of types of file access:

* **r** Read permission
* **w** Write permission
* **x** Execute permission.

To practice using **chmod**, let's restrict permissions for the file **letter** so that neither "group" nor "other" users can access it. First examine the directory listing for **letter** by entering **ls −l letter**. Next enter **chmod go−rw letter** to remove (−) read (**r**) and write (**w**) permission for the group (**g**) and other (**o**) user categories. Finally, verify the change by another long directory listing. The result should be similar to that shown here:

```
$ ls −l letter
−rw−rw−rw−    1 becca        docum              40 Nov  1 13:23 letter
$ chmod go−rw letter
$ ls −l letter
−rw−−−−−−−− 1 becca          docum              40 Nov  1 13:23 letter
$ 
```

As another example, let's remove write permission for the file owner to make **letter** "read-only" or "write-protected." To do this, enter **chmod u−w letter**. As before, verify the change with a long directory listing.

```
$ chmod u−w letter
$ ls −l letter
−r−−−−−−−−− 1 becca          docum              40 Nov  1 13:23 letter
$ 
```

Note that instead of using two steps as we did in the two preceding examples, you could have changed the permissions in one step by combining the requests on the same command line. To do this, you would separate each complete set of **chmod** arguments (*who op-code permission*) by a comma without any intervening whitespace. Thus, you could have entered the command line **chmod go−rw,u−w letter** to restrict "group" and "other" users and to write-protect **letter** all in one step.

Protecting Files

To get a sense of the usefulness of file permissions, let's see what can happen to unprotected files. Previously, we saw that the **rm** command could be used to remove a file by severing the link between the physical file on disk and the file-name in the directory. This is one way that the contents of a file might become lost.

Another common way to compromise the integrity of a file is to overwrite its contents with the contents of a different file. To exemplify this, we will use the **cp** command to copy a *source file* to a *destination file*, where the destination file already exists. The contents of this destination file will then be replaced by the contents of the source file.

Before proceeding, you will need to recreate the file **poem** since we erased its last link to the file system earlier. Enter your favorite line editor, either **ed** or **ex**, and then enter in the usual text for **poem**, save the text to disk, and exit the editor.

Now let's use **reminder** as our source file and **poem** as the destination. First make a backup copy of **poem** named **poem.bak** so that we may restore the contents of **poem** later. Then list the directory to verify that **poem.bak** was created:

```
$ cp poem poem.bak
$ ls
letter
poem
poem.bak
reminder
$
```

For comparison's sake, before you overwrite **poem**, display its contents using **cat**. Then overwrite **poem** by copying **reminder** to **poem**. Now examine the contents of **poem** again: **poem** contains the text from **reminder**.

```
$ cat poem
Roses are Red
Violets are Blue
Sugar is Sweet
And so are You.
$ cp reminder poem
$ cat poem
From username Thu Nov   1 12:32:07 PST 1984
Board meeting this Monday evening.

$
```

Now restore the correct contents of **poem** from the backup copy **poem.bak** by using **cp** to purposefully overwrite the incorrect contents, as shown here:

```
$ cp poem.bak poem
$ cat poem
Roses are Red
Violets are Blue
Sugar is Sweet
And so are You.
$
```

Like the **cp** command, the **mv** command overwrites the contents of a destination file if the latter already exists, as the next example illustrates. First enter **mv reminder poem**, and then list the directory to see that **reminder** is gone. Now use **cat** to examine **poem** and verify that the contents of **poem** were replaced by the contents of **reminder**.

```
$ mv reminder poem
$ ls
letter
poem
poem.bak
$ cat poem
From username Thu Nov   1 12:32:07 PST 1984
Board meeting this Monday evening.

$
```

Before proceeding, let's restore the files to their original condition. Since **poem** contains the former contents of **reminder**, simply rename **poem** to be **reminder** and restore the correct contents of **poem** using **poem**'s backup copy, as shown here:

```
$ mv poem reminder
$ mv poem.bak poem
$
```

At this point, having overwritten the contents of the file **poem** in two different ways, let's use **chmod** to write-protect **poem** so that it can't be overwritten. First remove read and write permission for the group owner (**g**) and other category (**o**), and remove write permission for yourself as well. As you did earlier, verify the changes by a long directory listing before and after using the change mode command:

```
$ ls -l poem
-rw-rw-rw-      1 becca        docum        62 Nov  1 09:26 poem
$ chmod go-rw,u-w poem
$ ls -l poem
-r---------  1 becca        docum        62 Nov  1 09:26 poem
$
```

Now if you try to overwrite **poem** with **reminder** using either **cp** or **mv**, both the **cp** and the **mv** commands issue complaints, as shown here:

```
$ cp reminder poem
cp: cannot create poem
$ mv reminder poem
mv: poem: mode 400
```

In the first case, since the file **poem** exists and write permission is denied, the **cp** command could not create another instance of **poem** and so **cp** exited. In the second case, the message "mode 400" from the **mv** command means that the destination file **poem** is read-only (or write-protected), but **mv** is waiting for you to type a response. Now if you were to enter a line beginning with a **y**, the rename operation would take place and **poem** would be overwritten. If you use any other character to begin the line, the **mv** program will exit without renaming **reminder**. This way you are given another chance to consider whether you wish to override the write-protection and thus overwrite the file's contents. Let's simply press RETURN to avoid overwriting **poem**.

Before leaving this session, reenable write permission for **poem**. Enter **chmod u + w poem**.

This concludes our discussion of the basic concepts and commands related to manipulating ordinary files. In the next tutorial session, we will introduce additional concepts and commands for working with directory files.

This would be a good time to log off unless you wish to continue with the next session right away.

SESSION 5

Whenever you perform work in the UNIX system, you are working within a directory. In the preceding session, you worked with ordinary files inside a single directory. In this session, you will move outside of this single directory and become acquainted with the large, tree-like structure of directories that orders the UNIX file system.

The File System Hierarchy

So far you have seen directories containing entries referring to ordinary files. In addition, directory entries can refer to other directories. This arrangement gives rise to the tree-like branching structure of the file system. Figure 3-5 shows the branching of our sample file system diagrammatically. You will create part of this sample file system in this tutorial session. This same file system will then be used in examples throughout the remainder of this book.

The UNIX file system always begins with a directory called the **root**; the **root** directory is designated by a slash (/). Branching from the **root** directory are several other directories (named **bin, etc, usr, lib**, and **tmp**) and an ordinary file (here named **unix**, which is the kernel program itself). These directories are considered *subdirectories* of the **root** directory, and conversely the **root** directory is considered the *parent directory* to these subdirectories. Each subdirectory can point to other directories (and to ordinary files), which gives rise to the branching, upside-down tree arrangement shown in Figure 3-5.

The main reason for having different directories is to keep some files at once together and separated from other files. For instance, files that are used by the system might be kept in certain directories, such as **bin, etc**, and **lib**, while files created by the system users might be kept in other directories, for example in **tmp** and in the subdirectories of **usr**.

To keep the diagram simple, we only show some of the possible branching

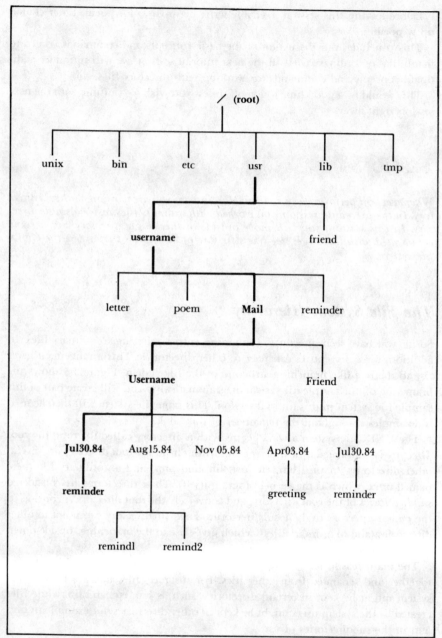

Figure 3-5. *Our sample file system*

detail in Figure 3-5. In an actual file system, however, there would probably be multiple branching from most directories. The directories **username** and **friend** correspond to the initial working directories or *home directories* of accounts with the same name. In other words, **username** is used both as an account name and a directory name. In the last session you were working in your home directory **username** (you substituted your actual name, of course, for **username** when you first logged on). We will show you how to move to other directories later in this session.

Branching from the home directory **username**, Figure 3-5 shows three ordinary files that you created in earlier tutorial sessions: **letter, poem,** and **reminder.** In this session you will create the directory named **Mail,** which will be the directory parent to an entire subtree of the file system. This subtree will be used for storage of your electronic mail messages.

Note that there is no connection between the directories named **Username** and **Friend** and **username** and **friend** as far as the file system structure is concerned. The capitalized names were chosen for organizing electronic mail messages received from accounts **username** and **friend,** as we shall see later in this tutorial.

You may use the same filename for different files if they occur in different directories. For instance, in Figure 3-5 three different files have the same name, **reminder.** One file occurs in the home directory, **username,** another in the subdirectory in the bottom-right corner of the figure, and the third in a subdirectory in the bottom-right corner.

Conventionally, in the UNIX system the names of both ordinary files and directories begin with a lowercase letter. We have adopted the policy of capitalizing the names of directories that we create in order to make it easier to distinguish them from the names of ordinary files, which we don't capitalize. You will probably find that most directory filenames not associated with your personal account begin with a lowercase letter.*

Of course, you can always tell a directory from an ordinary file by examining the file type (the first field) in a long directory listing. (Recall that an ordinary file is indicated by a dash (—) in this field and a directory by a **d.**) Our naming convention, however, enables you to make the distinction by simply inspecting the filenames with the short form of the **ls** command (without the **−l** option).

It is important to note that, strictly speaking, directories don't contain files; rather, they contain the names of the files. Thus, even though we may loosely

---

* It's of historical interest that the keyboard on the terminals available when the UNIX system was first being developed could only generate uppercase alphabetical characters. The UNIX input/output system was designed to translate all uppercase characters on input to the corresponding lowercase characters inside the system. Thus, in those early UNIX implementations, only lowercase filenames were possible.

speak of "files contained in a directory," we actually mean that the filenames are contained in the directory file. In fact, the directory file contains entries consisting of only two fields: a filename and a pointer to the disk file with that name. The pointer is simply a number that is used to find the place on the disk where the actual file is located.

Figure 3-6 shows a representation of the entries for the directory file **username**. The filenames in the directory entry are shown as the right-hand field or side of the box, and pointers to the disk files and to other directories are shown as arrows coming from the left-hand field or side of the box. The box itself represents the directory **username**.

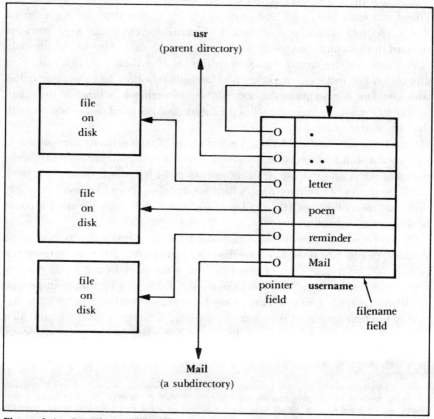

Figure 3-6. Detail of directory structure for **username**

In addition, this figure shows two directory entries that we haven't discussed yet. These entries are automatically created by the system whenever a directory file is created. The entry with the name dot (.) refers to the directory itself; that is, the pointer field for dot points to the directory itself. The entry named dot dot (..) refers to the parent directory; thus the pointer field of this entry points to the parent directory.

Now let's examine the **username** directory more closely. We show the pointers associated with the names of the files (**letter, poem,** and **reminder**) pointing to the actual files on disk. The pointer for **Mail** entry in this directory points to the subdirectory named **Mail** (only the name of this subdirectory is shown in the figure). The pointer for dot dot (..) points to the parent directory, **usr** in this case.

Actually, each directory is connected to its parent directory or any of its subdirectories by a pair of pointers that point in opposite directions, one up and one down the file system tree structure. This nexus of upward and downward pointers is like the glue that holds the file system hierarchy together. For instance, looking again at Figure 3-6, we see that not only does the pointer for the dot dot (..) entry point upward to the parent directory **usr**, but the **usr** directory (not shown) contains an entry named **username** whose pointer field points downward to the **username** directory. Similarly, the pointer entry for **Mail** in **username** points down to the **Mail** subdirectory, while the pointer for the dot dot (..) entry of the **Mail** directory (not shown) points up to its parent directory, **username**.

Working Directories and Pathnames

Before learning about the commands used for working with directory files, you need to be familiar with a few other terms used when referring to files and directories.

When you first sign on to your UNIX system, you begin work in a particular directory known as your *home directory*. Your home directory is a unique, fixed directory that is assigned when your system administrator establishes your account.

The directory in which you are working at any time is known as your *working directory* or *current directory*. Your working directory is not fixed and may be changed by use of the **cd** (change directory) command, as you will see later. Immediately after you log on to your UNIX system, your working or current directory will be your home directory.

Every file in the UNIX file system has one *absolute pathname* that serves to identify it uniquely. The absolute or *full pathname* begins with the **root** directory and describes a unique "path" of directories that descends through the file system tree and eventually points to the file in question, which may be an ordinary, directory, or special device file. You construct the pathname starting with a slash (denoting the **root** directory) and append the intermediate directory names in the path each separated from the next by a slash. You end with the *basename* of the target file. The basename is the portion of the pathname that remains when the directory prefixes are removed.

For instance, in the sample file system in Figure 3-5, the file depicted in the lower-left corner has **/usr/username/Mail/Username/July30.84/reminder** as its full pathname and **reminder** as its basename. To verify this, start at the **root** directory (denoted by **/**) and trace the boldface path down through the directories **usr, username, Mail, Username, July30.84,** finally reaching the ordinary file **reminder.** As another example, the home directory for the account **username** has the absolute pathname **/usr/username** and the basename **username.**

All files in the UNIX file system are referenced by a pathname. These files can always be uniquely identified by their absolute pathname. In many cases, however, the files can be referenced by a shorter *relative pathname.* The relative pathname, or *partial pathname,* begins with your current directory—the directory you are currently working in—and describes the path of directories to the target file. The easiest way to distinguish an absolute from a relative pathname is to note that absolute pathnames *always* begin with the **root** directory (**/**), but that relative pathnames do not.

For example, if you were located in your home directory **/usr/username** when you decided to access **reminder,** you could use a partial pathname to access **reminder,** and that partial pathname would be **Mail/Username/Jul30.84/reminder.** As another example, consider the fact that the filenames contained in your home directory, **letter, poem,** and **reminder,** are actually all partial pathnames relative to your home directory **/usr/username.** (They are also basenames since there are no directory prefixes to these pathnames.) Thus, in accessing these files from your home directory, you are actually using the partial pathname to these files.

When you reference files in the UNIX file system hierarchy, you must remember to use the proper pathway and never attempt to specify a pathname that leaps from one branch of the file system to another without first ascending the connective trunk between two branches. For instance, if your current directory were **friend,** the relative pathname to the example file **reminder** (in the lower left-hand corner of Figure 3-5) would be **../username/Mail/Username/Jul30.84/reminder.** The **..** moves up the file system hierarchy to the parent directory of **friend,** which is **/usr,** and then descends down through **username, Mail, Username,** and **Jul30.84** to the target file, **reminder.** Recall that dot dot (**..**) refers to the parent directory of your working directory. You must use dot dot when specifying a relative pathname that ascends the file system tree. As another example, the relative pathname from **friend** to the other file with the basename **reminder** (on the right side of Figure 3-5) would be **../username/reminder.**

Using a relative or partial pathname to access a file from your working directory constitutes a convenient shorthand method for referencing files. When you specify a file argument for a UNIX command, you may always use the absolute pathname for naming the file. The full pathname, however, is generally long and thus entails more chance of making typographical errors. What is more, the shell will always "fill in the gaps," so to speak, if you use relative pathnames properly. Thus, if the filename you specify doesn't begin with a slash (/), the shell assumes that it is a partial pathname relative to your working directory. The shell therefore converts the name you specify to the absolute pathname internally by adding the full pathname of the current working directory as a prefix.

As an example of the shell's role in interpreting partial pathnames, let's say you wish to use **cat** to display the contents of **poem**, which is located in your working directory, **/usr/username.** You could always specify the full pathname as the file argument as follows:

$ **cat /usr/username/poem**

Since the shell knows the working directory is **/usr/username,** however, you simply need to type

$ **cat poem**

The shell will automatically add the **/usr/username** directory prefix internally to generate the full pathname, **/usr/username/poem.**

Basic Commands for Working With Directories

With a sense of how the file system is structured and of the function of directories and pathnames within the file system, you are ready to learn the major commands for actually working with directories. The first command we will discuss may be used to display the full pathname of your working directory, which is sometimes a must for finding your location in the complex file system tree. You will also learn the command for creating a new directory file and the complementary command for removing a directory file from the file system. Finally, you will learn how to change your working directory in order to move around the file system tree to any directory for which you have access permission.

pwd: Print Working Directory

The **pwd** command displays the absolute pathname of your working directory. The command line format is simply

$ **pwd**

As an example, suppose you are in your home directory and you enter **pwd**. You will display the full pathname for this directory, as shown:

```
$ pwd
/usr/username
$
```

Of course, the response you get when you run this command will depend on where your particular home directory is actually located in your UNIX system implementation.

You will find **pwd** to be a valuable utility when you are moving around in the file system hierarchy. It is not uncommon to get lost in the UNIX file system, but you can use the **pwd** command to learn where you are, at any time, from any directory.

mkdir: Create a Directory File

You may wish to store files in a particular directory of your own creation. The **mkdir** command (for "make directory") allows you to create one or more new directories. The **mkdir** command has the following command line format:

$ **mkdir** *dirname...*

The argument *dirname* may be either an absolute or relative pathname. The ellipses indicate that you may specify more than one directory name on a single command line. Note that if *dirname* already exists, the **mkdir** command aborts and does not overwrite the existing directory. By contrast, it is possible to overwrite a preexisting ordinary file when attempting to create an ordinary file with the same name.

As an example, let's create a directory with the partial pathname **Mail** relative to your home directory. Simply enter **mkdir Mail**, and then list your home directory to verify.

```
$ mkdir Mail
$ ls
Mail
letter
poem
reminder
$ ▓
```

Notice that we have capitalized **Mail** so that, as the name of a directory, **Mail** can be distinguished at a glance from the name of an ordinary file. Also notice that in the alphabetically ordered **ls** listing, capitalized directory names are listed before lowercase ordinary filenames. It is not necessary, however, to capitalize a directory name when using **mkdir**.

Figure 3-7 shows the portion of the file system tree associated with the home directory, **/usr/username**, before and after **Mail** has been created.

cd: Change Working Directory

To change to any directory in the file system, use the **cd** command (for "change directory"). The command format is simply

$$\text{\$ cd } pathname$$

where *pathname* is either an absolute or relative pathname to the desired target directory.

To practice using **cd**, let's change to the **Mail** directory you created in the last section. First determine your current working directory by entering **pwd**. Then enter the command **cd Mail** to change directories. Finally, verify your new location with **pwd**.

```
$ pwd
/usr/username
$ cd Mail
$ pwd
/usr/username/Mail
$ ▓
```

Notice here that the pathname argument for **cd** is a partial pathname relative to

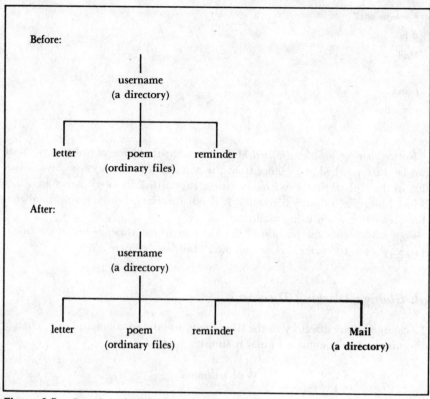

Figure 3-7.   Creating the Mail subdirectory

the original working directory, **/usr/username**. Alternatively, you could have moved to the same subdirectory by specifying its full pathname; that is, you could have entered the command line **cd /usr/username/Mail**.

Unless you do use a full pathname, any filename you specify as long as your working directory is **/usr/username/Mail** will be taken to mean a file relative to that directory. Thus, if you enter **cat poem,** you would observe an error message like the following:

```
$ cat poem
cat: cannot open poem
$
```

This error message means that the **cat** command cannot find the file **poem** in the working directory, **/usr/username/Mail**. Recall that **poem** was created within your home directory **/usr/username**.

You could display the contents of **poem** from the **Mail** working directory by specifying the relative pathname to **poem** from **Mail**. **Mail** is a subdirectory of your home directory, so your home directory is the parent of the **Mail** directory. Since a parent directory is denoted by dot dot (**..**), the partial pathname to the desired file from **Mail** is **../poem**, so you would enter **cat ../poem** to display the contents of **poem** while remaining in the **Mail** subdirectory:

```
$ cat ../poem
Roses are Red
Violets are Blue
Sugar is Sweet
And so are You.
$
```

The command line **cat ../poem** is interpreted by the system as "display the file obtained by moving to the parent directory (**..**) and selecting the file **poem** (**/poem**)."

This last example shows you one reason for changing your working directory so that it is the directory containing the file you are referencing. In this way, you can refer to the file by a simple basename instead of by the more complex pathname.

You can always return to your home directory from any other directory by simply typing the **cd** command without an argument. Enter **cd** now, and verify that you are back in your home directory by entering **pwd**. You don't need to specify your home directory as an argument to the **cd** command in this case because your shell always knows the name of your home directory.

```
$ cd
$ pwd
/usr/username
$
```

Now we will show you how to move around in your part of the file system hierarchy. First we need to create another subdirectory. Type the commands shown in boldface here:

```
$ mkdir Sample
$ ls
Mail
Sample
letter
poem
reminder
$ ▓
```

You may visualize the parent directory as a kind of bridge to another directory at the same level of the directory hierarchy. Consider the diagram of part of your practice file system shown in Figure 3-8. For instance, to get to the **Mail** directory from the **Sample** directory, you would enter **cd ../Mail** in order to move up one level to your parent directory (..), which in this case is **/usr/username**, and then to descend one level to the subdirectory **Mail**. Try this now by entering the commands in the following screen:

```
$ cd Sample
$ pwd
/usr/username/Sample
$ cd ../Mail
$ pwd
/usr/username/Mail
$ ▓
```

Now move back up to your home directory again by entering either the command **cd**, which always returns you to your home directory from anywhere in the file system, or **cd ..**, which returns you to your home directory *in this instance*, because your home directory happens to be the parent directory of **Mail**. Verify again with **pwd**.

```
$ cd ..
$ pwd
/usr/username
$ ▓
```

While remaining in your home directory, move a copy of the file **poem** to the subdirectory **Sample**, and then verify its location by listing the **Sample** directory contents with **ls**. Note that when the destination file argument for the **cp** com-

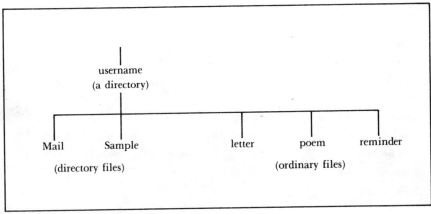

Figure 3-8. *Your personal file system*

mand is a directory, the ordinary file will be copied to that directory and will assume the same basename as in the source directory.

```
$ cp poem Sample
$ ls Sample
poem
$
```

If you wished to change the filename, you could specify the new basename in the destination pathname argument. For instance, to change the name of the file **poem** to **dumbpoem** as you move it, you could have entered the command line **cp poem Sample/dumbpoem.**

rmdir: Remove a Directory File

If you decide you no longer need a directory, you can use a special form of the **rm** command, **rmdir**, to remove it. To remove one or more directories, use the following command line format:

$ **rmdir** *pathname...*

For example, from your home directory **/usr/username**, enter **rmdir Sample**:

```
$ rmdir Sample
rmdir: Sample not empty
$ ls
Mail
Sample
letter
poem
reminder
$ ls Sample
poem
$
```

This last result illustrates that the **rmdir** command cannot remove a directory until it is "empty"—that is, until the directory contains no ordinary file or directory entries. This feature helps prevent you from accidentally removing files you wish to keep.

Now remove **poem** by entering the command **rm poem**, and then try to remove **Sample** again, as shown here:

```
$ rm poem
$ rmdir Sample
rmdir: Sample not empty
$ ls Sample
poem
$
```

The directory is still not empty, even though you just removed **poem**. This is because you removed **poem** from the wrong directory. Remember that in this last example, your working directory was your home directory, and you specified the basename **poem**, so that the shell prefixed the directory **/usr/username** to effectively give the command **rm /usr/username/poem**. Because you actually wished to remove the file **poem** from the **Sample** subdirectory, however, you should have entered **rm Sample/poem**. This command would have specified that **poem** is in the **Sample** directory, and the shell would have supplied **/usr/username** to correctly give the full pathname to **poem**: **/usr/username/Sample/poem**.

Instead of entering **rm Sample/poem** at this point, however, let's correct this mistake in another way. In the following screen, we move to the **Sample** directory and "remove" **poem** by moving it to your home directory with **mv**. By entering **mv poem ..**, we move **poem** back to our home directory, which is dot dot in this case, under the same name (**poem**). The **Sample** directory is now empty, as shown by the **ls** command. But now we try to remove **Sample** by entering **rmdir .**, where dot (**.**) stands for your current working directory, which is **Sample**. The result is probably not what you would have expected:

```
$ cd Sample
$ pwd
/usr/username/Sample
$ ls
poem
$ mv poem ..
$ ls
$ rmdir .
rmdir: cannot remove current directory
$ ▮
```

The moral is that you cannot use **rmdir** to remove either your current working directory (or your parent directory). The reason for this is fairly obvious: if you could remove your working directory, you would be removing the work space in which you yourself exist. Thus, if you wished to remove your working directory, you would have to change to its parent so that the directory you wished to remove had become a subdirectory. Then you could use **rmdir** to remove it.

To try this now, change to the parent directory of **Sample** by entering **cd ..** and verify with **pwd**. Then remove what is now the subdirectory **Sample** and verify with **ls**.

```
$ cd ..
$ pwd
/usr/username
$ rmdir Sample
$ ls
Mail
letter
poem
reminder
$ ▮
```

Sample has been eliminated at last!

An Electronic Filing Cabinet

Having practiced using the major commands for working with directories, you are probably eager to put directories to work as an organizing tool. In this section, we sketch a paradigm of how you might use directories to form an electronic filing cabinet, and in the process, we complete the leftmost branch of the sample file system (Figure 3-5) that we have been referring to throughout this session.

Suppose, for example, that you wish to organize and store the electronic mail messages you have received for easy retrieval. The first step is to devise a scheme to organize your message files. You might group messages by

* User name of sender
* Date of postmark.

Let's make the analogy that you are using one drawer of an office filing cabinet for all your mail messages. There are hanging folders in this drawer, one folder for each different system user who has sent you a message. Within each hanging folder, you might have a number of manila file folders, one for each date the message was postmarked. Finally, the mail messages themselves would be like the documents (sheets of paper) contained in the manila file folders.

The messages are the ordinary files of text stored in the directory corresponding to the postmark date. The "postmark date" directories are contained within and are subdirectories of the directory corresponding to the sender of the message. We show this scheme in Figure 3-9.

One way to create such a filing system would be to make a subdirectory and then change to that subdirectory and make another subdirectory and then change to that subdirectory and so forth until you have created the required directory structure. We illustrate this approach and in the process create the remainder of the left branch of our example file system (Figure 3-5) here:

```
$ cd
$ pwd
/usr/username
$ cd Mail
$ pwd
/usr/username/Mail
$ mkdir Username
$ ls
Username
$ cd Username
```

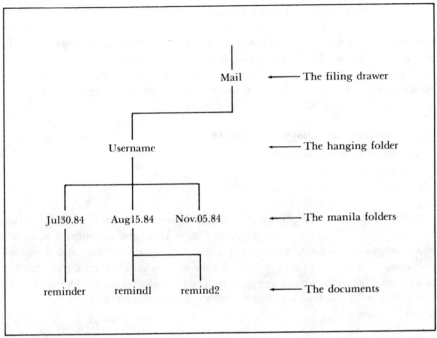

Mail ←———— The filing drawer

Username ←———— The hanging folder

Jul30.84   Aug15.84   Nov.05.84 ←———— The manila folders

reminder   remindl   remind2 ←———— The documents

Figure 3-9. *An organizational scheme for electronic mail messages*

```
$ pwd
/usr/username/Mail/Username
$ mkdir Jul30.84
$ ls
Jul30.84
$ cd
$ pwd
/usr/username
$
```

First we entered **cd** and then verified with **pwd** to make sure that we began in our home directory. Next we changed to the **Mail** subdirectory with **cd Mail** and verified with **pwd**. Then we created a subdirectory of **Mail** named **Username** by entering **mkdir Username**, and we verified that **Username** was created with **ls**.

Next we changed to the **Username** subdirectory, verified our location with **pwd**, and then created the **Jul30.84** subdirectory by entering **mkdir Jul30.84** and verified this step with **ls**. Finally, we returned to our home directory in one step with **cd** and verified that we had returned to our home directory with **pwd**.

To make use of the structure we just created, let's "move" the electronic mail message named **reminder**, which we stored in your home directory during Session 4, to the subdirectory **Mail/Username/Jul30.84**.

```
$ mv reminder Mail/Username/Jul30.84
$ ls Mail/Username/Jul30.84
reminder
$
```

You can organize your electronic mail files in a variety of ways. For instance, you might wish to have separate directories for received and transmitted mail, or you might prefer to group messages first under the postmark date and then the user name of the sender rather than under the user name and then the postmark, as we have done in the preceding example. The flexibility of the UNIX file system means that it is equally easy to implement an almost unlimited number of organizational schemes.

UNIX System On-Line Documentation

Most UNIX systems maintain on-line documentation about each command, but you may not find this documentation on smaller microcomputer implementations with limited disk space (for example, with 10 megabytes or less of disk space). If your system does have on-line documentation, you can get more information about a command by using the **man** (for "manual") command, which has the following command line format:

$ **man** *commandname*

Here you would replace *commandname* with the actual name of the command.

For example, in the following screen, we examine the on-line documentation for the **passwd** command. The manual entry produced here by entering **man passwd** is that for the Bell System V version of **passwd**. (Some UNIX implementations employ a form of the **man** command that displays a screenful at a time. If your cursor appears to be frozen at the bottom of the screen, press the space bar to get another screenful.)

```
$ man passwd
```

PASSWD(1)   UNIX 5.0   PASSWD(1)

NAME

passwd — change login password

SYNOPSIS

passwd name

DESCRIPTION

This command changes (or installs) a password associated with the login name.
The program prompts for the old password (if any) and then for the new one (twice).
The caller must supply these. New passwords should be at least four characters
long if they use a sufficiently rich alphabet and at least six characters long if monocase. Only the first eight characters of the password are significant.

Only the owner of the name or the superuser may change a password; the owner
must prove he knows the old password. Only the superuser can create a null
password.

The password file is not changed if the new password is the same as the old password or if the password has not "aged" sufficiently; see passwd(4).

FILES

/etc/passwd

SEE ALSO

login(1), crypt(3C), passwd(4).

Page 1   (last mod. 5/19/82)

```
$
```

The entry under the NAME heading lists the name or perhaps names that are
used for the command as well as a brief one-line description of the command's
purpose. The SYNOPSIS section gives the general command line format for
invoking the command. The conventions used to represent this command line
format are the same as those used in this book, even though most CRT terminals
cannot display boldface or italicized characters. The next section, DESCRIP-
TION, explains in some detail the action of the command and documents any
options and arguments taken by the command.

While these first three headings always appear, five subsequent headings may or
may not be present, depending on the nature of the command being documented.

After DESCRIPTION, the EXAMPLES section, if present, will present one or more examples for using the command. Next, the FILES section, if present, lists the file or files that are associated with the command program. In our example, the file **/etc/passwd** is the pathname for the UNIX system password file, which contains, among other things, a list of the passwords for each system account.

The SEE ALSO section, if present, references related commands and other relevant on-line documentation. The number in parentheses is the section number for the other on-line entries. You will see how to use the section numbers shortly. DIAGNOSTICS, if present, discusses some of the more obscure error and warning messages. WARNING, if present, delineates possible problems you may encounter when using the command. And finally BUGS, if present, describes known bugs and deficiencies for the command.

The **man** command displays documentation that is maintained on your system disk. This same documentation is also available in hard-copy form as either *The UNIX User's Manual* for Bell Systems III and V or *The UNIX Programmer's Manual* for other systems. Both the on-line and hard-copy versions are divided into eight sections:

- *Section 1: Commands and Application Programs.* You will use this section of the manual the most. This section contains a description of all the UNIX programs intended to be invoked directly by a system user. The commands in this section are divided further into four subclasses:
  - 1. General-purpose commands
  - 1C. Communication commands
  - 1G. Graphics commands
  - 1M. System Maintenance commands
- *Section 2: System Calls.* This section of the manual documents the low-level kernel routines called from a C language program. Unless you write C programs in the UNIX environment, you won't need to refer to this section.
- *Section 3: Subroutines.* This section documents the higher-level library subroutines called from a C program. Again, you won't need to use this section unless you write C code.
- *Section 4: Special Device Files.* This section describes the characteristics of hardware devices. Typically, disks, tape drives, printers, and terminal interfaces are documented here.
- *Section 5: File Formats.* This section describes the structure of particular files. Generally, these are important system files used by more than one command. For instance, the password file is documented in this section.
- *Section 6: Games.* This section describes the games and educational programs available within the UNIX system.

- *Section 7: Miscellaneous Facilities.* This section includes descriptions of character sets, text formatting macro packages, the file system directory hierarchy, and so on.

- *Section 8: System Maintenance Procedures.* This section describes procedures for maintaining your UNIX system. The information in this section would be of particular interest to your UNIX system administrator.

It's important to know what sections the manual contains because you may wish to display entries from sections other than Section 1, the section that contains the descriptions of the commands and applications programs. To display entries from other sections, use the following command line format:

$$\texttt{\$ man } section \; title$$

Here *section* is the number of the section of the manual you wish to view, while *title* is the name of the section or the name of the command. If you omit the section number, the first manual entry corresponding to *title* will be displayed. Thus, when we used the **man** command to find out about **passwd** a moment ago, we did not specify a section number and we got Section 1. The *title* in our example of using **man** was the name of the command itself.

Finally, if you are using System V and you need to look something up in the hard-copy version of the manual, you should know that the hard-copy manual, which had become too bulky, was divided into two volumes. These volumes are:

- *UNIX System User's Manual.* This volume contains sections that correspond roughly to Sections 1 through 6 of the previous manual. Some sections are rearranged in this release. In particular, the old Sections 4 and 5 are reversed, so that Section 4 now contains a discussion of file formats while Section 5 discusses special device files.

- *UNIX System Administrator's Manual.* This volume contains the system maintenance commands formerly in Section 1M. The descriptions of special device files and of the maintenance procedures are now incorporated into this second volume.

This is the end of your introduction to the fundamentals of using the UNIX system. In order to solidify your grasp of the basics, you should go over any of the concepts or techniques discussed in Chapter 3 that you are unsure about. In Chapter 4, you will learn about some of the sophisticated features of UNIX that allow you to control the execution of your programs as well as the flow of input and output.

4

MASTERING
THE SPECIAL
FEATURES OF THE
UNIX SYSTEM

In this chapter you will learn how to use most of the important features of both the Bourne Shell and the C Shell. You will also learn how to control the execution of programs that you invoke. Here is a session-by-session overview of Chapter 4:

In Session 6, you will learn about several features common to both the Bourne Shell and the C Shell. Among other things, we will explain how to redirect command input and output, how to use pipes and filters, and how to specify related filenames in a convenient shorthand.

In Session 7, you will learn how to control the execution of programs. In particular, we will explain how to execute a program in the background, how to run a program at lower priority, how to continue running a program after you've logged off your system, and how to terminate any program that you initiate. You will also learn how to schedule a program to run at some specific time in the future.

Finally, in Session 8, you will learn about the many useful features particular to the C Shell. For instance, the C Shell allows you to refer to an entire command line with a single word through the *alias feature* and thus to save typing and the chance for errors. In addition, the *history mechanism*, which enables you to refer to and invoke previously executed commands, also provides a shortcut for typing command lines. Session 8 also explains how to use a shorthand notation for your home directory and how to use braces to select groups of files conveniently.

SESSION 6

This first tutorial session introduces you to some of the more useful features common to both the Bourne and C Shells. We will first show you how to specify more than one command on a single command line. Next we will explain how to invoke a subshell to execute a sequence of multiple commands. Invoking a subshell enables you to perform a complex sequence of operations, including changing to any directory in the file system without changing the working directory of your main shell.

A major portion of this session is devoted to explaining how to control the flow of input and output for most UNIX programs. We explain the standard files that are used for data input and output for most UNIX command programs, and show you how to use the shell to redirect the output of a program so that output can be written to a disk file instead of appearing on your terminal screen. And we demonstrate the corresponding process of taking the input data for a program from a disk file instead of the keyboard.

The UNIX shell provides a powerful facility for sending the output from one program directly into the input of a different program to form what is known as a pipeline. Along with pipelines, we will introduce you to filter programs, which can process the data stream in a pipeline to accomplish useful transformations of your data.

While Session 6 focuses on special features common to both the major UNIX shells, Session 8, at the end of this chapter, explains some of the useful features that come only with the C Shell.

The Bourne Shell and the C Shell

Earlier we saw that communication with the UNIX system takes place by way of the shell program. The shell is a command interpreter; that is, it interprets what you type as a command request and then locates and executes the programs that will fulfill your request. Thus you may think of the shell as a program that is used to invoke and execute other programs. It is these other programs that actually fulfill your command request.

The shell operates at the same level as any command program, such as **date** or **who**. When these command programs run, they replace the shell, and when the commands finish, the shell returns once again to replace them.

The shell provides the interface between you as a system user and the kernel program. One shell can be replaced by a different shell quite simply because UNIX shells are not part of the kernel program. In this book we will discuss two of these interchangeable shells: the Bourne Shell developed at Bell Laboratories and the C Shell developed at the University of California at Berkeley. There are other shells available for use on the UNIX system, but the Bourne and C shells are by far the most common.

Multiple Commands on the Shell Command Line

If you wish to give a sequence of commands, you can save some time by specifying them all at once on a single shell command line. To do this, separate each command from the next by a semicolon (;) and end the entire command line with a RETURN. The semicolon tells the shell to execute one command, wait for its completion, and then execute the next command in the sequence. Note that all the commands specified on one line are executed in turn, one after the other.

As an example, enter **date;who** to execute the commands **date** and **who** in sequence. After the current date and time of day, a list of all the users currently logged on to your system is displayed:

```
$ date;who
Thu Nov  1 10:32:09 PST 1984
root           console        Nov 1 09:49
becca          tty32          Nov 1 09:42
$
```

Your particular display will depend, of course, on the actual date and time as well as who is logged on to your system when you enter these commands. You can separate the commands from the semicolon with blanks or tabs if you wish to improve readability. The shell will ignore these whitespace characters.

Invoking a Subshell

You may invoke another shell, known as a *subshell,* to execute a sequence of commands. The advantage of this feature is that it lets you perform a complex sequence of operations without affecting your main shell. In particular, the subshell can change to a different working directory and execute other commands without changing the current directory of your primary shell. Thus when the subshell command has finished executing, you are automatically returned to your primary shell.

To invoke a subshell, place the commands that you wish to be executed by the subshell in parentheses. The subshell will execute all the indicated commands and then return control to your primary shell. To illustrate the command line format, let's employ a subshell to execute the same commands used in the last example:

```
$ (date;who)
Thu Nov  1 10:33:45 PST 1984
root             console        Nov 1 09:49
becca            tty32          Nov 1 09:42
$
```

As you can see, the same results are obtained whether your main shell or a subshell executes the commands.

A more useful feature is to employ a subshell to execute commands in another working directory. After typing the opening parenthesis, you would first specify a **cd** command to change to the desired directory, follow it with one or more commands to be executed in that new directory, and then type a closing parenthesis and press RETURN. After the commands in parentheses have been executed, control will be returned to your primary shell in your original working directory.

To try this now, let's use a subshell and change it to the **Mail/Username/ Jul30.84** subdirectory, and then use **cat** to examine the file **reminder** directly. You will be returned to your **/usr/username** directory without having to issue another **cd** command. We use three **pwd** commands in this example to show the current working directory. The **pwd** commands were included for illustrative purposes only. They are not required.

```
$ pwd
/usr/username
$ (cd Mail/Username/Jul30.84;pwd;cat reminder)
/usr/username/Mail/Username/Jul30.84
```

From username Thu Nov 1 12:32:07 PST 1984

Board meeting this Monday evening.

$ pwd

/usr/username

$

The first **pwd** command shows that the current directory of your main shell is /usr/username. Then a subshell is created to execute the commands shown in parentheses. The subshell changes to the **Mail/Username/Jul30.84** directory first, as verified by the output of the second **pwd** command. There the **cat** command process displays the contents of **reminder**. Notice that only the basename, **reminder**, need be typed as the argument for **cat**, since the current directory of the subshell (and thus of the **cat** process) is the directory containing the file **reminder**. After the **cat** program finishes, the subshell terminates and control is returned to your main shell. The last **pwd** command shows that your main shell remains in your original current directory, **/usr/username**.

The Standard Input and Output Files

When a UNIX program is running, it communicates with you by displaying information on your terminal screen. This information may be either data produced by the program or else error or warning messages alerting you that something is wrong. To communicate with a program, in turn, you type characters on your keyboard. You may type either command requests or data for a program to process.

Communication between you and your UNIX programs by means of the terminal keyboard and screen is so fundamental that these *communication channels* are given special names. The keyboard input channel is known as the *standard input*, while the terminal screen output channel for data (results produced by the program) is the *standard output*. The channel for diagnostic messages produced by a program is called the *standard error* or sometimes the *diagnostic output*.

Furthermore, the UNIX system treats these communication channels as files, so that you will hear the terms *standard input file, standard output file*, and *standard error file*. In this way the useful features of UNIX files, such as access permissions, apply to the standard communication channels as well.

Normally the standard input, output, and error files for a program are "attached" to your terminal; that is, the standard input file refers to your keyboard, and the standard output and standard error files refer to your terminal screen.

Thus when a program writes to its standard output file, it is writing to the terminal screen. Conversely, when a program reads from its standard input file, it is reading information from the terminal keyboard.

The standard input and the standard output are not always synonymous with your keyboard and screen, however. Your shell has the ability to redirect the data flow to and from a program. In other words, instead of having the program output appear on your terminal screen, you may ask the shell to redirect that output to a disk file or to a different terminal screen. And instead of having program input come from your keyboard, you may ask the shell to take the input data from a disk file.

The shell performs these feats of *redirection* by changing the identity of the standard files. For instance, the shell can "detach" the standard output file for a program from the terminal screen and "reattach" it to a disk file, so that the standard output file for that program refers to the disk file. Thus when the program sends data to its standard output file, the data is written to a disk file where it can be accessed later instead of appearing on your terminal. You will practice using redirection in the next few sections of this tutorial.

Redirecting Standard Output to a File

The shell command line format for redirecting output to a file on your system disk is relatively simple:

$$\$ \ command \ >file$$

Here *file* is to receive the data output from *command*. The data information will not be displayed on your terminal but will be stored in *file* instead. If *file* does not already exist, it will be created by the shell. If *file* does exist, the shell will delete its contents in preparation for storing the output of *command*.

When you specify the redirection symbol ($>$), you may use whitespace on either side of the symbol. We recommend, however, that you put the redirection symbol immediately next to the name of the file that will receive the redirected material, but use whitespace in front of the redirection symbol itself. A command line in which redirection occurs is easier to read when it is set up in this way. Options and other file arguments may, of course, be included on the command line. The order of items in a command line that employs redirection is first the command name, then the options, then the other arguments, and finally the redirection expression, as shown here:

$$\$ \ commandname \ [\ option... \ ] \ [\ argument... \ ] \ >file$$

For our first example, let's redirect the output of the **date** program to a disk file named **date.now**. No output appears on your terminal screen because it was written to the disk file instead:

```
$ date >date.now
$
```

Now use **cat** to examine the contents of **date.now** to show that the current date and time were stored successfully:

```
$ cat date.now
Thu Nov  1 10:44:49 PST 1984
$
```

Note that you could have named the output file **date** because the shell would know from the structure of the command line that the first instance of **date** refers to a program named **date** while the second occurrence of **date** indicates the name of the file to receive the redirected data.

As another example, enter **who >who.now** to store the output of the **who** command in **who.now**. Use **cat** to verify that **who.now** contains the output from **who**:

```
$ who >who.now
$ cat who.now
root              console         Nov 1 09:49
becca             tty32           Nov 1 09:42
$
```

Now let's redirect the output from both the **date** and **who** commands to the same disk file. First try entering **date;who >date.who.now**, but note that the contents of the disk file are not quite what you wanted:

```
$ date;who >date.who.now
Thu Nov  1 10:46:04 PST 1984
$ cat date.who.now
root              console         Nov 1 09:49
becca             tty32           Nov 1 09:42
$
```

As you can see, the shell executed **date** as the first command and displayed the result on the terminal. Then **who >date.who.now** was executed as the second command, the result of which was saved in the file **date.who.now**.

The correct way to redirect the output of two or more commands to the same file in one step is to enclose in parentheses the commands whose combined output you wish to redirect. Try this now by entering **(date;who) >date.who.now**, and you will see that the disk file contains the desired result. Note that the previous contents of **date.who.now** were erased and then overwritten with the output from this last command sequence:

```
$ (date;who) >date.who.now
$ cat date.who.now
Thu Nov  1 10:47:44 PST 1984
root            console         Nov 1 09:49
becca           tty32           Nov 1 09:42
$
```

For our next example, let's store what you type at your keyboard directly into a disk file. This useful technique provides an easy way to enter text into a file quickly without the use of an editor.

The **cat** program will take its input from your keyboard if you don't specify a file argument on the command line. As you have already seen, if you do indicate a file argument, **cat** will take its input from that file instead.* On the output side, you would use the shell to redirect the result of the **cat** program, which normally appears on your terminal screen, to a disk file instead.

Try this now. First enter **cat >verse**, and then enter the text of our practice poem, as shown in the following screen simulation. If you make a typing mistake, use your erase or line-kill characters or both to correct the input line *before* you press RETURN. (Recall that these correction codes work here because they operate at the level of the kernel program before the data is input to the **cat** program; that is, the characters are read from the keyboard by the kernel program, which passes them on to **cat**.) Finally, type your end-of-file code (a ^D) to inform **cat** that there is no further input. **cat** will terminate and control will be returned to your shell.

---

* The on-line manual entry for the **cat** command explains that "if no input file is given, or if the argument − is encountered, **cat** reads from the standard input file."

```
$ cat >verse
Roses are Red
Violets are Blue
Sugar is Sweet
And so are You.
[ ^D ]
$ 
```

The text that appears on your screen is echoed by the kernel program. Generally, whenever you type a character, it is displayed immediately after you type it because the kernel program sends a copy of your keyboard input back to your terminal screen. (Another copy is sent to the program reading your keyboard input, which is the **cat** command in the last example.) This echo feature is a kernel phenomenon and is independent of any UNIX command program, including your shell.

Now use the **cat** command to verify that a copy of what you typed at the keyboard was stored in the file **verse**. Because you specify **verse** as a file argument to **cat**, **cat** takes its input from the file **verse**, rather than from the keyboard:

```
$ cat verse
Roses are Red
Violets are Blue
Sugar is Sweet
And so are You.
$ 
```

Previously you saw that if the disk file already exists, any output redirected to the file will overwrite the previous contents of the file. You may, however, ask the shell to add the output of a command process to a file without deleting what is already there. To do this, use the following command form:

$ *command* >>*file*

The double ouput redirection symbol (>>) tells the shell to redirect the standard output to the end of *file*, so that the output of *command* will be appended to the existing file. As before, if *file* does not already exist, the shell simply creates it.

Now enter **date >>date.who.now** and display the contents of **date.who.now** on your screen. Note that the current date and time now appear at the end of the file.

```
$ date >>date.who.now
$ cat date.who.now
Thu Nov  1 10:47:44 PST 1984
root              console        Nov 1 09:49
becca             tty32          Nov 1 09:42
Thu Nov  1 10:54:13 PST 1984
$
```

Before continuing, let's remove the extra files created in this section. Carefully enter **rm *now verse**, making sure that you do not leave any space between the asterisk and **now**.

Reading Standard Input From a File

Just as you can redirect output to a disk file, so you can redirect the input for a command to come from a file on your system disk instead of from your terminal keyboard. The shell command line that allows you to redirect input is relatively simple:

$$\$ command < file$$

Here *file* is the source of the data for *command*. If *file* does not exist, the shell will issue an error message and abort the operation. When you request input redirection in this way, the shell detaches the keyboard from the program's standard input file and attaches the disk file to the standard input file in its place.

Like the output redirection symbol, the input redirection symbol (<) is easiest to interpret when whitespace appears in front but not after it. If you employ options and other file arguments on a command line that also uses input redirection, the command line format is as follows:

$$\$ commandname [option...] [argument...] < file$$

For our first example, let's use the shell to redirect the input for the **cat** command to come from the disk file **poem** instead of from the keyboard. Enter **cat <poem**:

```
$ cat <poem
Roses are Red
Violets are Blue
Sugar is Sweet
And so are You.
$
```

The shell reassigned the standard input file to be **poem** instead of the terminal keyboard. The **cat** program displays its output on the terminal because the standard output file is still attached to the terminal screen. Note that **cat** is designed to take its input from a file if a file argument is specified on the command line. For this program at least, therefore, input redirection is not necessary for taking data from a file. As you will see in the next example, however, a program like **mail** *requires* redirection if it is to take input data from a file.

When you invoke **mail** to send a message, the program takes the text that you enter at your keyboard and places it in a buffer. The contents of the buffer are sent to the desired recipient(s) when you indicate the end-of-file code (a ^D or a period on a line by itself). Thus the standard input file for **mail** is attached to your keyboard. The main drawback with this arrangement is that you cannot change or correct text that you have already entered in the buffer (that is, you can change only the current line before you have pressed RETURN).

To get around this drawback of the **mail** program, you may wish to create and change your message text apart from the **mail** program — for example, with an editor — and then instruct **mail** to send that message. The problem lies in how to get **mail** to take your message into its buffer, without your typing it in directly, since the **mail** program does not recognize any command line option or argument specifying a file containing your message. For instance, if you had entered **mail username reminder**, the **mail** program would have interpreted the **reminder** argument as another account to which you wished to send your message, rather than as the file containing the message itself. Of course, this is not correct. However, you may instruct the shell to detach the standard input file for **mail** from the keyboard and attach it to a disk file containing your message using command line redirection.

To practice this technique, let's use an editor to create a short reminder message and to store the message in a file named **reminder**. Then invoke the **mail** program to send yourself the message by asking the shell to redirect the input for the **mail** program so that it will come from the file **reminder**. Enter the commands as shown here, but replace **username** with your own user name:

```
$ ed reminder
?reminder
P
*a
Board meeting Monday.
.
*w
22
```

```
*q
$ mail username <reminder
you have mail
$ mail
From becca Thu Nov  1 11:01 PST 1984
Board meeting Monday.

? q
$ ▓
```

Some UNIX implementations inform you as soon as new mail arrives. After the current command has completed execution and control is returned to the shell, a message such as "you have mail" or "new mail arrived" will be displayed.

Redirecting Both Standard Input and Standard Output

You may use the shell to redirect both the standard input and standard output for a command at the same time. The command line format that enables you to do this is

$$\$ \; command \; <source \; >destination$$

where *source* becomes the source of input for *command* and the output is directed to *destination*. Notice that by *command* here, we mean a command name and any options or other command line arguments required by the command program, even though these are not shown explicitly.

One use for redirecting both input and output at once is to make the **cat** program behave like the UNIX **cp** program, which duplicates a disk file. For instance, to produce a backup copy of the disk file **poem**, enter **cat <poem >poem.bak**. The shell redirects the standard input for **cat** to come from **poem** and redirects the standard output to go to **poem.bak**. After **cat** is finished, verify that the destination file **poem.bak** has the same contents as the source file **poem**, as shown here:

```
$ cat <poem >poem.bak
$ cat poem.bak
Roses are Red
Violets are Blue
Sugar is Sweet
And so are You.
```

$ cat poem

Roses are Red

Violets are Blue

Sugar is Sweet

And so are You.

$ ▓

It's important to note that once the name of the command and its options and arguments have been specified, the redirected input and output filenames can be placed in any order on the command line. In other words, in the preceding example we could have specified the output file before the input file rather than vice versa:

$ **cat** >poem.bak <poem

Since both output and input redirection operations center around the **cat** command here, the order in which input and output redirectives appear is immaterial.

Do *not* specify the *same* filename for both the source and destination files. If you do, the shell will delete the contents of the source file before its contents are processed by the command and stored in the destination file. For instance, if you were to type

$ **cat** <poem >poem

and then to look at **poem**, you would find it empty.

As a mnemonic device to help you remember which redirection symbol does what, think of the >, >>, and < symbols as arrows pointing to (→) or from (←) the file specified with this symbol. Thus, >*file* sends output to *file*, while <*file* takes input from *file*.

Pipelines and Filter Programs

Often you will need to have data processed by two or more programs in succession. As an example, let's say you wish to produce mailing labels from a mailing list data base file. You might need to sort the mailing list by ZIP code, format the results into a mailing label format, and finally send the data to your printer. The UNIX system can accomplish this task by employing three simple programs in succession: a sorting program, a label-formatting program, and a print spooler program. Each program takes the necessary data as input, processes it, and sends it directly to the next program. This approach would save time and disk space because the intermediate data does not have to be stored in a file. The connected programs that process a stream of data in this way are known as a *pipeline* or simply *pipe*. The pipeline concept is one of the novel and powerful features of the UNIX system.

The command line format for establishing a pipe between two command programs is simply

$$\$ \; command1 \mid command2$$

where the pipeline connection between commands is denoted by a vertical bar (|). The pipe symbol tells the shell (in this case) to connect the standard output of *command1* directly into the standard input of *command2*.

The output from *command1* does not appear on the terminal, nor is it stored in some intermediate temporary file. Instead, the UNIX system "buffers" the output of the first command process for input to the second command process. All the commands in the pipeline are invoked at the same time, and each command process begins working as soon as some input data is available to it. Thus *command2* can begin work even before *command1* has finished executing. This helps speed up the overall processing.

Pipelines may be extended to include additional commands. For instance, three or more commands may be connected together in a pipeline as follows:

$$\$ \; command1 \mid command2 \mid command3$$

Here the standard output of *command1* is fed into the standard input of *command2*, and the standard output of *command2* is in turn fed into the standard input of *command3*. *Command1* is said to be at the "head" of the pipeline, while *command3* is at the "tail." Also note that we can use "pipe" as a verb in describing this command line: the output of *command1* is piped into *command2*, and so on.

In order for a command program to be used in a pipeline, it must meet one of three conditions: it must be designed to take its input from the standard input file, send its output to the standard output file, or both. Some programs don't take their input from the standard input file. An example would be the **who** command, which takes its input directly from a system file containing a list of logged in terminals. Such a program could be used at the head of a pipeline to initiate the pipeline data stream, since it does send its results to the standard output file, but it could not be used at the tail or at an intermediate point. Several other programs do not send their output to the standard output file. An example would be the UNIX electronic mail program, **mail**, which only sends a message to a mailbox file. (However, when you invoke **mail** to read your messages, the text is sent to the standard output file.) Such a program could be used at the tail of a pipeline to terminate the pipeline data stream, since it does take its input from the standard input file, but it could not be used at the head or at an intermediate point in the pipeline.

Programs that both take their input data from the standard input file and send their results to the standard output file may be used anywhere in a pipeline — at the head, tail, or at some intermediate position. These programs are frequently used in a pipeline to transform the data as it passes from the input to the output channel. Such programs are given the special name *filter programs* because they are used to *filter* the data that passes through them. Generally, the filtering process performs some useful transformation of the data, such as sorting lines of text or selecting text lines containing a certain pattern of characters. It's important to note, however, that the most essential characteristic of a filter program is not that it transforms the data on which it operates; that is, the output of a filter program does not necessarily look any different from the input and can in fact be unchanged. The defining feature of a filter program in UNIX is rather its ability to stand anywhere in a pipeline because it is designed to take input and issue output through standard files.

We shall illustrate pipes by several examples. In order to present realistic examples, we need to introduce some new UNIX utility programs in some cases. All the programs introduced to illustrate the operation of pipes are relatively simple and are also described more thoroughly in Chapter 6.

For our first example, we will introduce the UNIX **sort** utility. If no options or file arguments are specified for **sort** on its invocation command line, **sort** will reorder lines of input text from its standard input and send the sorted result to its standard output. Thus, unless **sort** is instructed otherwise, it will order its input according to *ASCII collating sequence*. (The ASCII character set is reproduced in Appendix E.)

Let's construct a pipeline now by connecting the output of the **who** command to the input of the **sort** command. The result, an alphabetical listing of users currently on-line, will appear on your terminal screen. To compare the unsorted output of **who** with the sorted output, first type **who** alone and then enter the command line **who | sort** to demonstrate the effect of sorting the output of the **who** command:

```
$ who
root              console          Nov 1 09:49
becca             tty32            Nov 1 09:42
june              tty43            Nov 1 09:51
$ who | sort
becca             tty32            Nov 1 09:42
june              tty43            Nov 1 09:51
root              console          Nov 1 09:49
$
```

As you can see, the **who** program orders its output by the terminal designation (second column). When piped into **sort**, the output is shown sorted by the account name (first column). Note that the use of whitespace around the pipe symbol (|) is optional. We employ at least one space for clarity.

Our next example utilizes the **wc** command, which counts the number of lines, words, and characters in its standard input. Let's pipe the output of **who** into this counting utility to determine the number of terminals currently logged on the system. The −l option causes **wc** to report only the number of lines in its standard input.

```
$ who | wc −l
     3
$
```

Since **who** generates one line of output per terminal, counting the lines tells you the number of terminals currently logged on your UNIX system. Because one user may log on to more than one terminal, however, the number of terminals may be greater than the number of active system users.

The UNIX **grep** program is useful for locating lines of text that contain a specified text pattern. It reads lines of text from its standard input file and writes out only those lines containing the pattern onto its standard output file. The command line format for invoking **grep** is

$ **grep** *pattern* [*file*]

where all lines in *file* containing *pattern* are sent to the standard output. If *file* is not specified on the command line, the input data for **grep** is taken from its standard input file. Thus **grep** may be employed anywhere in a pipeline if no input file is specified, but only at the "head" if an input file is indicated on the command line.

As an example, let's display the names of the files in your current directory containing the pattern "poem". Enter **ls** | **grep poem**:

```
$ ls | grep poem
poem
poem.bak
$
```

The result shows that only the files **poem** and **poem.bak** in the current directory have the characters "poem" in their filenames. It's also important to note that **ls** can only be used at the head of a pipeline since its input only comes from the file system.

If you were only interested in the number of files containing "poem" in their name, you could extend the pipeline and simply count the instances with **wc**:

```
$ ls | grep poem | wc -l
       2
$
```

Sampling a Pipeline With tee

There may be times when you wish to sample data in a pipeline at an intermediate point. You might, for example, wish to debug a pipeline that isn't producing the results you expected. Or you might wish to use a pipeline to get more than one kind of report. A UNIX program named **tee** makes it possible to send a copy of the data passing through a pipeline to a file on disk or to your terminal screen.

The command line format for using **tee** at an intermediate point in a pipeline is

$$\text{\$ } command1 \text{ | } \textbf{tee } file \text{ | } command2$$

where the standard output of *command1* becomes the standard input for **tee**. The data is passed unchanged from the standard input to the standard output of **tee**, but a copy is stored in *file*. The standard output of **tee** is connected to the standard input of *command2*. Sometimes the use of **tee** is referred to as *pipe fitting* because of the analogy to a "T" connection in a pipeline. Figure 4-1 sketches the operation of the **tee** command. Note that while **tee** is a filter program, it is one of those filters that does not transform data but instead passes it along the pipeline unchanged.

To practice using **tee**, let's divert a copy of the data passing from **grep** to **wc** in

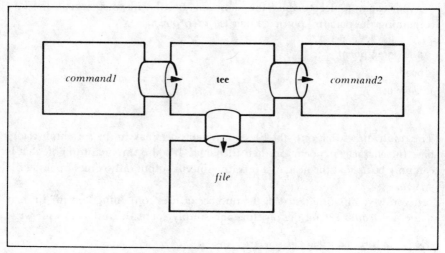

Figure 4-1. *How the tee command works*

the previous example to a disk file named **names** and then display the contents of **names**:

```
$ ls | grep poem |  tee names |  wc −l
       2
$ cat names
poem
poem.bak
$
```

As you can see, **names** consists of a copy of the data that was passed from the **grep** to the **wc** command.

Another way to use **tee** to sample the pipeline is to display the sample directly on your terminal screen. Recall that the UNIX system refers to a physical device, such as your terminal, as a *special file*. The special filename for your terminal is **/dev/tty**. If you read from **/dev/tty**, you are reading from your terminal keyboard, and if you write to **/dev/tty**, you are writing to your terminal screen. The next screen example shows how to use **tee** to divert intermediate data in a pipeline and write it to your terminal screen.

```
$ ls | grep poem | tee /dev/tty | wc -l
```
poem

poem.bak

   2

$ ▓

Because we asked **tee** to divert a sample of the pipeline's contents to the terminal's file (**/dev/tty**), the filenames "poem" and "poem.bak" appear on the screen. These filenames appear first because the **tee** command precedes **wc** −1 in the pipeline.

If you sample the pipeline before **grep**, you will get a different result:

```
$ ls | tee /dev/tty | grep poem | wc -l
```
Mail

letter

names

poem

poem.bak

reminder

   2

$ ▓

As before, the "2" comes from **wc** −1, and the display of the filenames from **tee** /**dev**/**tty**.

Using Redirection With a Pipeline

You can combine redirection with a pipeline on the same command line. For instance, we could store the number of lines in **poem** containing the word "are" by using this pipeline:

```
$ cat <poem | grep are | wc -l >number.are
$ cat number.are
```
   3

$ ▓

Of course, input redirection only makes sense at the head of the pipe and output redirection at the tail; otherwise, the point of using input or output redirection with a pipeline is nullified. If you used output redirection at the beginning of a pipeline, for instance, the pipeline would terminate prematurely.

With a little practice you should be able to combine the various UNIX commands, redirection, and pipes to solve many of your data processing problems.

Now is a good time to remove extraneous files. Enter **rm names number.are poem.bak reminder** to do this.

Selecting Groups of Filenames

Most UNIX commands accept filename arguments. These arguments may serve to specify, for example, the identity of input or output files. The shell provides a shorthand for specifying groups of files and directories with related filenames. Thus, instead of typing out each filename individually when the names differ by only a few characters in the prefix or suffix, you could type a pattern consisting of the characters common to the desired filenames and use special *filename-matching* or *wild card characters* to indicate the characters that differ between the names. The shell creates the complete filename by locating the filenames, usually in the current directory, that match the pattern you specify. The special filename-matching characters are also called *metacharacters* to suggest characters whose meanings can change.

For instance, the asterisk (*) will match any set of adjacent characters. Thus, entering **ls** * is equivalent to entering **ls** followed by *every* filename in your current directory. Entering **ls** *.bak, on the other hand, is the same as entering **ls** followed by *all* filenames with the suffix .bak. Finally, entering **ls poem*** is like typing **ls** followed by all filenames beginning with the prefix **poem**.

It's important to be careful when you use metacharacters. When you enter a command such as **rm** *.bak, for example, you could inadvertently remove every file in the current directory if you leave a space between the asterisk and the .bak. In other words, if you entered **rm** * .bak, the shell would match the "*" to *every* file in the directory instead of just removing all files ending in .bak.

If your related filenames differ by a fixed number of characters, you can use the question mark (?) metacharacter at just those character positions to match all the desired files. For instance, assume that your current directory contains files named **chap1**, **chap2**, and **chap3**. In this case, **chap?** will match all these files but exclude files with names like **chap10** and **chapter**. In contrast, if you use **chap***, you match *all* files beginning with **chap**, so that **chap10** and **chapter** would be included as well. If you use **chap??** as a command argument, you would match **chap10** but not **chap1**, **chap2**, **chap3**, or **chapter**.

To match a subset of related filenames, you may employ square brackets. The left square bracket ([) begins a group of characters and the right bracket (]) ends the group. Thus **chap[ABD]** would match files named **chapA**, **chapB**, and **chapD**, but not **chapC**. You may use a hyphen inside the brackets to indicate a range of characters. Thus **chap[1-3]** would match **chap1**, **chap2**, and **chap3** and exclude all other filenames. And **chap[12B-D]** would match **chap1**, **chap2**, **chapB**, **chapC**, and **chapD**, but exclude **chapA**.

To sum up, here is a list of the characters used for selecting groups of filenames:

- ***** matches any set of adjacent characters, including nothing.
- **?** matches any single character.
- **[** begins a character group.
- **]** ends a character group.
- **-** appears between two characters to indicate a range of characters within a bracketed character group.

In order to practice using some of these metacharacters, let's create a subdirectory named **Test**, change to that directory, and then create five empty files named **chap1**, **chap2**, **chap3**, **ed.man**, and **passwd.man**. The files may be empty because the content of the files is immaterial for this exercise. The steps required to create **Test** and the five files are shown here:

```
$ mkdir Test
$ cd Test
$ pwd
/usr/username/Test
$ >chap1
$ >chap2
$ >chap3
$ >ed.man
$ >passwd.man
$
```

Note that we have used output redirection here to create an empty file. The command line

$$\$ >file$$

creates an empty file named *file* since although the shell creates *file*, there is nothing for the shell to actually write into the file. Note that if you are using the C Shell, you would have to type a different command to create such files. One possibility would be

$$\$ \text{ cp /dev/null } file$$

where **/dev/null** is the empty "null" file.

Now if you type the commands shown in boldface in the next example, you will see that the shell responds to the metacharacters by matching the filenames, which are then passed on to **ls** for display. To save space, we have listed the filenames across the screen instead of down (as the Berkeley **ls** command does by default):

```
$ ls *
chap1 chap2 chap3 ed.man passwd.man
$ ls *.man
ed.man passwd.man
$ ls chap?
chap1 chap2 chap3
$ ls chap??
chap?? not found
$ ls chap[2-3]
chap2 chap3
$ ls ??.man
ed.man
$ ls ????
???? not found
$ ls ?????
chap1 chap2 chap3
$ ls ??????
ed.man
$
```

The command line **ls chap??** caused an error message because there is no filename that begins with **chap** and is followed by exactly two characters. Similarly, the command line **ls ????** caused an error message because there is no filename in the current directory containing exactly four characters.

This is the end of Session 6. Before leaving this tutorial session, remove the extra files we just created. To remove the subdirectory **Test** and the files it contains in one step, enter the following:

```
$ cd
$ rm —r Test
$ ls
Mail
poem
$
```

The —r option causes **rm** to remove all files in the directory **Test** as well as the directory itself.

SESSION 7

While the UNIX kernel program actually schedules programs to run and controls their execution, you can influence the execution of the programs that you invoke. As you will see in this session, it is possible to execute more than one program at a time. These additional programs (or "processes") run as background *tasks so that you may continue to give commands to your shell in the* foreground. *In this session, you will also learn how to leave a program process running even after you've logged off your system, which saves waiting around for time-consuming programs to finish execution. In addition, you will learn how to run a task at a lower priority so that it won't slow down your other work.*

Once you have invoked a program, it's important to know how to terminate it if you wish the program to halt for any reason. In this session, you will learn how to terminate any process that you have started before that process has finished executing on its own, even if that particular process is protected from termination signals.

Finally, this session will teach you two different approaches for starting up a process at some time in the future—perhaps even after you've logged off the system. You might use this technique if, for example, you wanted to start and run tasks in the middle of the night when system loading is light and the computing rates are lowest.

&: Running a Process in the Background

Earlier in this book we explained that the UNIX system is a multitasking operating system, which means that it can schedule the execution of more than one program at the same time. In fact, the system can execute only one program or process at any one instant, but it switches between processes so quickly, usually within one thousandth of a second, that most of the time all the programs seem to be running at the same time. If your system is being used by a large number of users or is heavily loaded for some other reason, however, UNIX may seem sluggish and your programs may take longer than usual to run.

If a program you are running seems to be taking a long time to finish and you'd like to begin work on another task, you may schedule your program to run in what is known as the *background* instead. The main advantage of running programs in the background is that unlike foreground processes, background processes don't have to have finished executing before you can begin another program. After beginning a process in the background, your shell prompt returns immediately to signal the fact that you may invoke another program in the foreground. Then you will have two programs running, since the background process is still executing while the foreground task is running.

Initiating a background process is easy with the UNIX system. Simply type the ampersand character (&) at the end of the command line invoking the process that you wish to execute in the background. The shell will respond by printing an identifying number known as the *process identification number,* or PID, on your terminal and immediately prompt for your next command.

The PID serves to identify your background process uniquely. In a moment you will see how to use this number to inquire about the status of a background process or even to terminate a background process before it finishes of its own accord. It's important to note that all processes, including foreground processes, have PIDs. We mention PIDs here because the & command happens to display the PID of the background process you have invoked.

There are a few other things that you should understand about background processing before you begin working with it. For instance, it's important to note that although you may start more than one background process, the kernel program limits the total number of processes (foreground plus background) to a reasonable value (usually some 20 to 50 per user and 100 to 250 or so system-wide) for your particular UNIX implementation. From a practical point of view, the more processes you start in the background, the slower your system runs overall. Thus you will eventually reach a point of diminishing returns if you start too many background processes. At that point the system response is so slow that you might as well have executed each program one after the other in the foreground.

One inconvenience of background processing is that output that is destined for your terminal from a background process will appear on your terminal screen intermixed with any output from foreground and other background processes. Thus, to avoid a confusing display, you may wish to redirect the output of your background processes to a disk file. Some commands have options that cause their output to be written to a disk file instead of appearing on your terminal. If you are using a command that doesn't have this capability, you can always ask the shell to redirect the program's standard output to a disk file.

Note that you must not initiate a background process that reads input from the keyboard because any foreground process, including your shell, that also reads input from the keyboard would then conflict with the input request of the background process. That is, input destined for the background process might be read by the foreground process, and vice versa. In addition, if the background process reads its input from a disk file, be sure not to modify that file until the background process has finished executing.

Because the shell protects such tasks from terminating in response to an interrupt signal, you cannot terminate a background process with your interrupt character. It is possible to end a background process, however, and later in this session you will learn how to terminate such processes before they finish of their own accord.

To practice running a process in the background, let's select a task that generally requires a minute or so to complete: for example, a task like determining the disk usage for your entire file system. You may use the generally available **du** command to accomplish this. (The **du** program is discussed in detail in Chapter 6.) Furthermore, we'll redirect the output of the **du** command so that the results are placed in a disk file and **du**'s output won't be sent to your terminal screen. Once **du** is placed in the background, you may continue with foreground tasks without the output from the background task disturbing the display on your terminal screen.

To invoke **du** in the background, enter **du / >du.all&** and make a note of the PID number that appears after you press RETURN. The / argument tells **du** to begin examining the file system at the **root** directory. In this way the entire file system will be scanned.

```
$ du / >du.all&
800
$
```

Your process number will probably not be 800. In the examples that follow, use the process number that you get when you initiate your background process, *not* the number shown in the screen examples. Note that the process numbers are unique and are assigned sequentially by the kernel, so that in our example, the very next process that is started in the system would have PID 801, the next 802, and so on.

With **du** in the background, you may go ahead and run a foreground process. To illustrate, let's perform a short directory listing while the background process is still running and note that the file **du.all** has been created, although it is probably still empty:

```
$ ls
Mail
du.all
letter
poem
$
```

Now you should examine **du.all** from time to time, for example with the **cat** command, to check on the progress of the background process you've set up. To do this, enter **cat du.all**. At first the file may be empty — that is, nothing will be displayed and you will get a shell prompt immediately — but as time goes by, the results of the **du** process will be added to the **du.all** file.

ps: Obtaining Process Status Information

If you are running a process in background, you may need to determine if the process is still running or has finished execution. You can monitor the background process with the **ps** (for "process status") command to find out this information. To invoke the process status command, use the following command line format for the Bell Version 7 and Berkeley systems:

$$\text{\$ ps } pid$$

For the Bell System III and V versions, use the following format:

$$\text{\$ ps } -p pid$$

The *pid* is the process identification number that was printed by the shell immediately after you began the background process.

For example, let's start up the **du** command again in background, and this time use **ps** to monitor its progress, as shown here:

```
$ du / >du.all&
805
$ ps -p805
   PID   TTY   TIME   COMMAND
   805    43   0:04   du /
$
```

Most versions of **ps** only display the command name and don't display the entire invocation command line under the "COMMAND" column. (Frequently this column is labeled CMD.) In particular, any redirection directives are not shown (for example, the >**du.all** used in this example). The entry under "TTY" is the terminal number, and the number under "TIME" is the elapsed execution time for the process in minutes and seconds. In addition, your output display for **ps** may be formatted differently than the output we show here since the behavior of the **ps** command is very implementation-dependent.

Now enter **ps** several more times and watch the accumulated execution time in the third column increase as the process continues running in the background.

```
$ ps -p805
    PID  TTY  TIME   COMMAND
    805   43  0:08   du /
$ ps -p805
    PID  TTY  TIME   COMMAND
    805   43  0:30   du /
$ ps -p805
    PID  TTY  TIME   COMMAND
    805   43  1:34   du /
$ ps -p805
    PID  TTY  TIME   COMMAND
$
```

Note that the execution time is the cumulative amount of time that the CPU has spent executing the process and not the elapsed time since the process was started. This is because the process is not actually run continuously, although it seems to be; in fact, the CPU attends to your particular background process only at intervals.

Eventually, the process numbered 805 will no longer exist. The **ps** program will convey that information by the lack of any output, except for the column headings, before the next shell prompt appears, as shown in the last line of the preceding example.

Now let's look at the file **du.all**, where the output from the **du** process was stored. After entering **cat du.all**, we pressed our interrupt character to keep the output for this example short:

```
$ cat du.all
 1600   /bin
  603   /dev
 1698   /etc
  503   /lib
   10   /tmp
  386   /usr/dict
 1158   /usr/bin
[ Interrupt ]
$
```

The numbers to the left of the directory names, which appear in the right-hand column, are the total number of blocks of disk space used by that directory. If you examine the entire **du.all** file, the very last line tells you the total number of occupied blocks in your file system. To determine how many characters your file system is taking up, you could multiply the number of blocks by the size of blocks in your UNIX system. Generally, there are 512 characters per block.

For example, let's say that you have a Winchester hard disk with a 10-megabyte capacity when formatted, and the **du** command reported your file system was occupying 10,000 blocks. In this case, your disk would be about half-full, as shown by this simple calculation: $10,000 \times .5K = 5000K$, or 5MB.

nohup: Protecting a Process From Hangup and Quit Signals

In general, when you log off your UNIX system, any background processes that you have started will terminate. When you log off, the kernel sends a *hangup signal* to all processes that you have started, and they are terminated by this signal.

This feature is a mixed blessing. It is desirable when, for example, as you are working with your system, a program suddenly seems to be suspended and the system no longer responds to anything you type on your keyboard. If you are communicating with your system via modem, you can simply hang up the telephone. With many systems, you will automatically be logged off and a hangup signal will be sent to your suspended or "hung" process, causing it to terminate. You may then log on and start over.

The system's response to the hangup signal is not desirable if your phone hangs up by mistake. In this case, you would be logged off and the programs that you were running would be terminated. Fortunately, the UNIX system provides an easy way to ensure that any program you wish to continue running, either in the foreground or in the background, will do so after you log off the system.

The command that enables you to prevent the hangup signal from terminating your programs is the **nohup** command. The command line format for using **nohup** is

$ **nohup** *commandline*

where *commandline* is the command line that you wish **nohup** to protect. Note that the hangup signal is generated whether you log off from a dial-up connection or from a direct terminal connection; in either case, **nohup** prevents the hangup signal from terminating *commandline*.

The **nohup** command causes any output of *commandline*, including both standard output and standard error output, to be appended to a file in your current working directory named **nohup.out**. If this file cannot be written to in the current directory, the output will be appended to a file with the same name in your home directory.

To practice using **nohup** to ignore the hangup signal, start the disk usage command in the background and immediately log off your system. Log back on in a few minutes and note that **nohup.out** contains a copy of the expected result proving that the command successfully completed execution. If you use **nohup**, you don't have to redirect the output of your background process to a disk file since **nohup** does this anyway.

```
$ nohup du /&
820
Sending output to nohup.out
$ [ ^D ]
(YOUR UNIX SYSTEM BANNER)
login: username
Password:
(YOUR UNIX SYSTEM MESSAGES)
$ cat nohup.out
1600  /bin
603   /dev
1698  /etc
...
9607  /
...
$
```

Your version of **nohup** may or may not display a message such as "Sending output to nohup.out". To keep the example short we have used ellipses (...) to indicate the intermediate results that we don't show. The last line of **nohup.out** is a summary of the disk usage for the entire file system (9607 blocks in this example).

So far you know about two different signals that terminate commands: the interrupt and hangup signals. Another signal, the *quit signal,* is occasionally used to terminate command execution. A process that is immune to termination by the interrupt signal can usually be terminated by the quit signal.

The quit signal is generated from your keyboard by pressing your quit character. The default quit character is a ^ \, which is produced by holding down the

CTRL key and pressing a backslash. Because some terminals may not generate the correct code when you press ^ \, we recommend reassigning the quit character as shown here:

```
$ stty quit '^u'
$
```

Of course, you may choose a different quit character, but we have found ^U to be a convenient choice. Note that the quit signal terminates foreground processes only. Thus when you press ^U, no background processes will be terminated.

While most versions of the **nohup** command will prevent the quit signal from terminating a foreground process, some versions of **nohup** will not. All versions of **nohup**, however, will protect processes from hangup signals.

When a process is terminated by the quit signal, you will find that a new file named **core** was created in your current working directory. This file contains a snapshot of the process at the instant it was terminated. Since this core file is relatively large and takes up a lot of disk space, you should erase it from your file system once you have no more use for it.

To test **nohup**'s ability to prevent the quit signal from terminating a process, let's use the disk usage example again. This time let's just enter **du /** to run this command in the foreground, and then press your quit character. You should get the shell prompt back immediately. Meanwhile, a file named **core** will have been written in your current working directory, and you may be informed of this by a message like "Quit—core dumped", as shown here.

```
$ du /
[ Quit ]
Quit—core dumped
$ ls
Mail
core
letter
poem
$
```

We represent the quit signal as "[Quit]" in this screen display simulation. You will not actually see the quit code on your screen.

Now let's use **nohup** in conjunction with the disk usage request to prevent the quit signal from terminating the command. The results are sent to both **nohup.out** and to the terminal screen in this case.

```
$ nohup du /
Sending output to nohup.out
[ Quit ]
1600    /bin
 603    /dev
1698    /etc
...
9607 /
$
```

If your version of **nohup** doesn't protect processes from the quit signal, however, your shell prompt will return immediately. A message like "Quit—core dumped" would be displayed, **core** would be written to your current directory, and the **nohup.out** file would remain empty.

Before proceeding with this tutorial session, enter **rm core** to delete the large **core** file.

nice: Running a Process at Low Priority

A process runs because it is being executed by the CPU. Processes run in spurts. Each segment of time during which a process is being executed by the CPU is known as a *time slice*. The CPU will execute each process for its slice of time and then run the next process for its time slice. The size of the time slice is affected by the *priority* that the kernel assigns to each process scheduled to run. The higher the priority, the longer the time slice allotted for a process.

Occasionally you may want to run a program at a lower priority than usual so that the program's demand on CPU time is reduced and other programs can get a little more CPU time. By assigning certain programs a lower priority, you can run these programs without being concerned that they will slow down other more important programs as much. Programs that consume a lot of system resources tend, of course, to slow down the system more than others. These programs would be good candidates for assignment to run at a lower priority. A common example of such a program is **nroff**, the UNIX text-formatting program, which we discuss in Chapter 5. Of course, there is a trade-off involved: a program run at a lower priority will take somewhat longer to finish. This is because a low priority program gets a smaller amount of CPU time when it runs and thus takes more time overall to finish.

The **nice** command enables you to reduce the priority of a process. The command line format is similar to that for **nohup**:

$$\text{\$ nice } commandline$$

Here *commandline* is the command line that you wish to place at a lower priority.

How is lower priority processing related to background processing? Usually the kernel runs a background process at the same priority as any foreground task. You may use **nice** to run a background task at a lower priority just as you would a foreground task. However, it makes little sense to run a foreground task at a lower priority, since running a process in the foreground in the first place indicates that you are more interested in quick response from that process.

As an example, let's run the disk usage command at a lower priority in the background so that you may continue with other higher priority tasks in the foreground. In this way the background task won't slow down any of your foreground tasks as much.

```
$ nice du / >du.all&
828
$
```

You might notice that the **du** command takes a little longer to complete than if **nice** were not specified. The priority has been lowered, giving **du** a smaller amount of CPU time each time it runs.

The **nice** command may be used in conjunction with **nohup**. In this case the invocation command line would be set up like the one we show here. You would specify **nohup**, then **nice**, and finally the command name and any arguments.

```
$ nohup nice du / &
829
Sending output to nohup.out
$
```

As before, since the output is stored in **nohup.out** anyway, you do not have to redirect the output explicitly to disk.

nice is not a panacea for reducing the demands a process makes on the system. A better approach is to run a process that places a large demand on the system during a slack period; for example, the middle of the night is usually a good time to run resource-consuming processes on systems employed by many users. Later you will learn how to use either the **at** or **sleep** command to run a command at a specified time in the future, even after you've logged off the system.

kill: Terminating a Process

Occasionally you will need to halt the execution of a background process that you started. For instance, you may decide that you don't need to run the program anyway, or else the background process may not be functioning correctly.

Neither the interrupt nor the quit signal will terminate a process running in background because the shell protects background processes from these signals. But you can terminate a background process by sending a *software termination signal* to the process since the shell doesn't protect processes it places in the background against this signal.

To send a software termination signal to a process, use the **kill** command with the command line format

$$\text{\$ kill } pid$$

Here *pid* is the identification number, of course. This is the number displayed by the shell immediately after it places a process in the background. If you have forgotten that number, you can always reproduce it by entering **ps**. When you enter **ps**, all processes associated with your terminal that are currently scheduled to run will be listed.

For our next example, let's enter the disk usage command in the background and save the result in the file **du.all.2**. In this example, we demonstrate that although an interrupt signal will not terminate the background command, the software termination signal, generated by the **kill** command, will do the job. First, enter **du / >du.all.2&** to place the disk usage command in the background, and note the PID for your particular background process. Then enter the **ps** command without any arguments to display all processes currently running:

```
$ du / >du.all.2&
830
$ ps
    PID  TTY  TIME  COMMAND
    740   43  0:07  sh
    830   43  0:00  du /
    831   43  0:01  ps
$
```

Some versions of **ps** may not display status for the **ps** command itself (denoted here by "ps" in the right-hand column) or for the shell process (denoted by "sh"). This display shows that three processes are running: the shell process, the **du** command that runs in the background, and the **ps** command itself. There is no obvious way to distinguish foreground from background processes by such a **ps** display.

Now press your interrupt character a few times to send an interrupt signal to all processes. To see if the background disk usage process was affected, enter **ps** again:

```
$ [ Interrupt ]
$ [ Interrupt ]
$ ps
   PID   TTY   TIME   COMMAND
   740    43   0:07   sh
   830    43   0:20   du
   832    43   0:01   ps
$
```

As you can see, the background process (PID 830) was not affected when you generated the interrupt code. Of course, the shell is always protected from interrupt signals and from quit signals as well.

To demonstrate that the **kill** command does indeed abort the background process, enter **kill** *pid*. Here *pid* is the actual process number for your background disk usage process.

```
$ kill 830
$ ps
   PID   TTY   TIME   COMMAND
   740    43   0:07   sh
   834    43   0:01   ps
$
```

After you enter the **kill** command, the background process disappears from the **ps** command display. Some systems may also display a message such as "830:Terminated" to indicate that the process with PID 830 was just terminated.

To further verify that the disk usage process was terminated, compare the size of **du.all.2** to **du.all** with a long directory listing:

```
$ ls −l du.all*
−rwxrwxrwx  1  username docum    2338 Nov   1  15:23 du.all
−rwxrwxrwx  1  username docum    1024 Nov   1  15:23 du.all.2
$
```

You should see that the number of characters in **du.all.2** is less than in **du.all** since **du** was terminated before it had a chance to scan the entire file system and write the results to **du.all.2**. Also note that the size of **du.all.2** is some multiple of 512 (or of whatever your system's block size is). This is because the output of **du** is written block by block to the disk file, and since the **du** process didn't finish executing, the remaining blocks of data were not written.

Sometimes programs are designed to be immune to software termination signals. In this case the form of the **kill** command shown in the preceding example would not terminate the process. However, you may request that **kill** send a *kill signal* instead. This signal *always* terminates any process that you own. The command line format is

$$\text{\$ kill } -9 \; pid$$

where *pid* is the process identification number for the process you wish to terminate and the **−9** argument tells **kill** that you'd like to send the "sure kill" signal.

at: Executing a Process at a Specific Time

Generally your interactions with the UNIX system take the form of a dialogue: you type a command and you get a response; you type another command request and get another response, and so on. Occasionally, however, you may want to have the system execute a command at a given time in the future.

Older versions of the Bell UNIX system, such as Version 7, as well as the Berkeley UNIX system provide the **at** command for executing a process at a specific time. This command is not distributed with the newer Bell releases (Systems III and V). One reason for discontinuing this command is that the associated publicly accessible directories constitute a security problem.

The **at** command has the following command line format:

at *time* [*month month day*] [*day of week*] [**week**]

Because this format is rather complicated, we will describe the command line elements one by one. The first element, *time*, consists of one to four digits. An optional A, P, N, or M represents A.M., P.M., noon, or midnight. One- and two-digit numbers represent hours; three- and four-digit numbers represent hours and minutes. If no letters follow the digits, a 24-hour clock time is assumed.

The *month* is the month name (such as jan). The *month day* is the number for the day of the month (in the range of 1 to 31). The square brackets indicate that the *month* and *month day* are optional.

Alternatively, you might specify a day of the week, *day of week*, instead of the *month* and *day of month*. The *day of week* is also optional. Finally, if you specify **week** on the command line, the process will be executed a week later. Thus, if you indicated **wed week**, the process would be executed a week from next Wednesday, instead of next Wednesday.

Names of months and days of the week may be abbreviated, but the abbreviation must be unambiguous. For instance, "ju" could mean either June or July, so you would have to use at least three letters: "jun" for June and "jul" for July.

Examine the following examples of valid specifications of the date and time:

at 8am	Today at 8 o'clock in the morning
at 2130 tue	Next Tuesday at 9:30 P.M.
at 12N fri week	Noon a week from next Friday
at 2pm apr 3	Next April 3rd at 2 P.M.

The **at** command may be used in two different ways. You may supply the command lines to be executed when you invoke **at**, or you may specify the name of a file that contains the commands to be executed. We will discuss the first way of using **at** in this session and the second way in Chapter 6's discussion of **at**.

For our first example, let's say that you wish to leave yourself a reminder to log off the system at 5 P.M. We will ask the **at** command to run the **echo** command with an argument that rings the terminal bell to get your attention (if your terminal has a bell that responds to ^G) and then displays the reminder "Time to log off". The **echo** command, discussed further in Chapter 6, simply sends a copy of its command line arguments to its standard output.

Whenever you employ **at** to run a command that places its output on your terminal, you should specify that the output of the command be redirected to your terminal file. (All devices, including terminals, are represented as files with the UNIX system.) The files for terminals generally have names beginning with **/dev/tty** and followed by the terminal number. Recall from earlier **ps** displays that our terminal number was 43 (under the TTY column). You may also determine your terminal number from the second column of a **who** display or by executing a **tty** command. So for our example, the full terminal name would be **/dev/tty43**.

Continuing with our example, first enter **at 5pm** and the cursor will wait at the beginning of the next line for more input. Next type **echo** and one or more ^G's (terminal bell characters) followed by the reminder **Time to log off**. Finally, press the space bar and type the redirection directive >, then **/dev/tty43**, and press RETURN. Of course, you should substitute the actual name for your terminal for **/dev/tty43**. The cursor will now move to the beginning of the next line and wait for further input. Although you could type additional commands at this time, let's leave the input mode for **at** and return to the shell by typing your end-of-file character, which is usually a ^D.

```
$ at 5pm
echo ^G^GTime to log off >/dev/tty43
[ ^D ]
$
```

Neither the ^G nor the ^D (shown in brackets) will appear on your screen. At 5 P.M. your terminal bell should ring and you will see the reminder message displayed:

```
...
[ Ring Ring ] Time to log off
...
```

The ellipses here are meant to indicate other activity on your terminal screen as the reminder might well appear while you were interacting with another command.

Alternatively, you might wish to have the reminder message sent to you by electronic mail. If so, simply pipe the output of the **echo** command to the **mail** program, as shown here:

```
$ at 5pm
echo ^G^GTime to log off | mail username
[ ^D ]
$
```

At 5 P.M. the message "Time to log off" should appear in your mailbox. Many UNIX systems will announce the arrival of new mail when you return to the shell after executing a command, with the result that you will receive a message like "Mail has arrived" sometime after 5 P.M. This approach is less direct than the previous one, but it does have the advantage that you aren't as likely to miss seeing the message in case you are running a command whose output obscures it. If your system doesn't inform you when new mail arrives, however, you would miss the reminder message completely. In this case, the first approach would of course be the only viable one.

Now let's use **at** to execute the disk usage command at a slack period. You might enter **at 2am** followed by **du / >du.all.3** to initiate the delayed function. The next day you should see the result stored in **du.all.3**:

```
$ at 2am
du / >du.all.3
[ ^D ]
$ ▓
```

You don't need to use **nohup** with the **at** command. Since the **at** command is actually stored in a *memo file* that is only run at the specified time, it will not actually be running when you log off and therefore will not be affected by the hangup signal.

The discussion of **at** in Chapter 6 examines the implications of the memo file in more detail. To use **at** at this point, however, you should understand that the memo file is examined periodically — every 5, 10, 20, or 30 minutes, depending on your system implementation — and any memo files scheduled to run are executed. Thus, if you specify a *time* between the scheduled examination times, the request will not be executed until the next scheduled time. For instance, if the memo file were examined on the hour, 20 minutes past, and 20 minutes before the hour, and you specified that a command be run at half past the hour, the command would not be run for 10 more minutes.

sleep: Delaying a Process for an Interval

If your system doesn't have the **at** command, you may simulate the function to some extent by using the **sleep** command. Some of the restrictions in using **sleep** for this purpose include the following:

- There is a practical limit to the delay time that you can specify: namely, 65,535 seconds or approximately 18 hours in the future without employing chained or nested **sleep** requests.
- The **sleep** process must run continuously.
- If you need to log off the system, you must specify the **nohup** directive so that the hangup signal won't terminate the **sleep** command.

Now let's see how to use the **sleep** command to delay the execution of one or a sequence of command programs. First let's see how the **sleep** command delays return of your shell prompt. Use the command line format

$ **sleep** *time*

where *time* is a decimal integer indicating the number of seconds up to a maximum of 65,535 seconds (over 18 hours).

For instance, looking at your watch, enter **sleep 10** and note that the shell prompt doesn't return for about 10 seconds.

```
$ sleep 10
```

If you specify more than one command on a command line with **sleep** as the first command, the execution of the subsequent command(s) will be delayed by the **sleep** process. For instance, enter **sleep 10;echo Hello**. It will take about 10 seconds before "Hello" is displayed, and you will then be returned to your shell.

```
$ sleep 10;echo Hello
Hello
$
```

You may use the **sleep** command to suspend a background process. Let's say that it's 2 P.M. and you wish to leave yourself a reminder to log off at 5 P.M. You would need to suspend the reminder 10,800 seconds, which we calculate as shown here:

$$(5\text{P.M.} - 2\text{P.M.}) \times 60 \text{ minutes} \times 60 \text{ seconds} = 10,800 \text{ seconds}$$

Now enter the command shown here:

```
$ (sleep 10800;echo ^GTime to log off)&
850
$
```

It's important to remember to use the parentheses to put the entire command line in the background to be executed by a subshell. Otherwise, your main shell would be put to sleep for three hours and you would not even be able to log off unless you interrupted the sleep process.

If you decide to cancel the reminder, simply enter **kill** *pid*, where *pid* is the process identification number for your particular background process.

If you wish to suspend execution of a process and then to log off before the process is to be awakened, you must first specify the **nohup** directive on the command line in order to prevent the hangup signal from terminating the **sleep** process.

For instance, let's say that you are on-line until 5 P.M. and you wish to run the disk usage command at 2 A.M. The delay time would be calculated as

$$(12\text{P.M.} - 5\text{P.M.} + 2\text{A.M.}) \times 60 \times 60 = 32,400 \text{ seconds}$$

Thus you would enter (**nohup sleep 32400;du / >du.all.4)&**. When you next log on, your result should be in **du.all.4**.

$ (nohup sleep 32400;du / >du.all.4)&

851

Sending output to nohup.out

$ [^D]

(YOUR UNIX SYSTEM BANNER)

login: ▓

The reason for redirecting the output of **du** to **du.all.4** is that although the output of the **sleep 32400** command will be written to **nohup.out**, there is no output from the **sleep** command itself, with the result that **nohup.out** will be empty. The **nohup.out** file only accommodates the command that immediately follows it. Thus you have to redirect the output from **du** explicitly to a file, such as **du.all.4**, if **du** is to have anywhere to put its output.

After you log back on, erase all the **du.all** and **nohup**-related files by entering **rm du.all* nohup.out**. Be careful not to type a space between **du.all** and the asterisk.

This is the end of Session 7.

SESSION 8

In this session we focus primarily on the Berkeley C Shell. The first session on the shell, Session 6, discussed features common to both the Bourne and the C shells, such as I/O redirection and pipelines. In this session, we will focus on several additional features of the C Shell.

You should invoke an instance of the C Shell for this tutorial session. After signing on to your UNIX system, you may or may not be using the C Shell. In any case, type the pathname of the C Shell for your system to invoke another instance of this shell.

Generally the pathname of the C Shell will be either /bin/csh or /usr/ucb/csh (on a Berkeley system). If the pathname is /bin/csh, enter /bin/csh to invoke the C Shell. If the pathname is /usr/ucb/csh, enter this pathname. Ask your system administrator for assistance if you cannot locate the C Shell.

As an example, the next screen shows a login sequence in which the Bourne Shell, denoted by the dollar sign prompt ($), is the login program. When the user types the full pathname of the C Shell on his or her system, /bin/csh, the default C Shell prompt, which is a percent sign (%), appears after a few seconds.

(YOUR UNIX SYSTEM BANNER)

login: **username**

Password:

(YOUR UNIX SYSTEM MESSAGES)

$ **/bin/csh**

%

While the C Shell prompt is usually a percent sign, on your system this prompt may have been reassigned to a different set of characters. You will see how to reset the prompt yourself later in this session.

As we explained earlier, both the Bourne and C shells are programs operating at the same level in the UNIX system as any command program. This is why you can invoke one shell from another just as you would any other command program, such as **date** or **who**. From either shell you can enter **/bin/sh** to invoke a Bourne Shell program and **/bin/csh** to invoke a C Shell program. The shells are mutually exclusive: you can interact with one shell or the other but not with two or more at the same time.

Shell Variables

We begin this tutorial session with a discussion of shell variables. The most important function of shell variables is to enable you to customize the operation of your shell. For instance, using variables you can establish a different shell prompt, specify a new home directory, or prevent the shell from recognizing a ^D as a signal that you wish to log off your system. In addition, variables make it possible to use a shorthand for specifying command line elements. For instance, you could use a shell variable to refer to a long pathname prefix by a single letter.

By definition, a *variable* is a quantity that can take on different values. A variable is thus a kind of storage place for a value. For instance, in the simple algebraic expression

$$x = 2$$

x is a variable, which is assigned the numerical value 2.

A shell variable is a variable whose value is known to your shell program. You could define (select) a C Shell variable named x and assign it the value 2 with the **set** command, as shown in the next example. While the whitespace around the equal sign is optional, we use one space on each side for clarity, as in the following.

```
% set x = 2
%
```

The **set** command is built into the C Shell and is used to assign and display the values assigned to shell variables. The Bourne Shell allows you to define shell variables as well. Instead of the **set** command, however, the Bourne Shell defines variables with an equal sign. For instance, if you were using the Bourne Shell, you would assign variable **x** the value 2 in one step, as follows:

$$ \$ \ x=2 $$

Here there should be *no whitespace* on either side of the equal sign.

You may easily determine the value of a C Shell variable in two different ways. If you enter **set**, the C Shell will display the values for all the currently defined shell variables. Do this now. Your display should look similar to the following:

```
% set
argv        ( )
home        /usr/username
path        (. /bin /usr/bin)
prompt      %
shell       /bin/csh
status      0
x           2
%
```

At this point in your knowledge of UNIX, the names **home**, **path**, **prompt**, and **shell** will probably look familiar. We discuss each of these particular variables later in this chapter and in Appendix C, "Interacting With Your UNIX System." The last entry shows the variable named **x** has the value 2. The variables **argv** and **status** apply to programming the shell, a topic that is outside the scope of this book.

If you simply wish to display the value of **x**, use the **echo** command with the argument **$x**, where the dollar sign stands for "the value of." The **echo** command simply displays the value of its command line argument(s) (the value of **$x** in this example) on the standard output (the terminal screen by default). This approach works both for C Shell and Bourne Shell variables:

```
$ echo $x
2
$
```

C and Bourne shell variables fall into two different categories, depending on the types of values the variables can assume. The simplest type of variable has a logical value: that is, either it is defined or it is not defined. The other type of variable has a value that is assigned when the variable is defined. The value may either be numerical, or it may be a *string* value, consisting of one or more characters.

An example of a logical C Shell variable is **ignoreeof**. If this variable is defined, the shell ignores the end-of-file (EOF) code (generally a ^D) for logging off the system. When this variable is in effect, you have to enter **logout** instead of typing ^D to log off your system. This approach has the advantage of preventing accidental log off in case you type one too many ^D's when, for example, you exit from a program like **mail**. To set **ignoreeof**, use **set** as shown here:

```
% set ignoreeof
%
```

Now if you enter **set**, you will see that **ignoreeof** is displayed among the list of currently defined variables.

You can undefine this variable by using the related **unset** command, as shown here:

```
% unset ignoreeof
%
```

Now if you enter **set**, you will see that **ignoreeof** is no longer listed. What is more, you could now log off the system by pressing a ^D instead of having to enter **logout**.

An important example of the second type of C Shell variable (the kind that takes on a value when it is defined) is **prompt**. The shell prompt that your C Shell displays is the string value that has been assigned to **prompt**. When you log on to the system initially, the value of **prompt** is % followed by one space character; thus, the shell prompt that was set is a percent sign followed by a space. To practice using **prompt**, let's reset this variable to a different string, as shown in the following example. Notice that you must enclose a string value in single or double quotation marks if it contains whitespace characters (space or tab characters):

```
% set prompt = "Your wish is my command: "
Your wish is my command:
```

This new C Shell prompt will remain in effect until you reset it or until you log off your system and log back on. When you are ready to reset **prompt** to its original (and default) value, enter the command line **set prompt = '% '**. Here we included one space character after the percent sign so that the prompt would always be separated by one space character from anything you type on the command line:

Your wish is my command: **set prompt = '%'**

%

As another example, let's define a variable and assign it the value of a long pathname prefix. In this way, we may use the variable in lieu of the pathname prefix on the shell command line.

For instance, let's say you wish to refer to files in the **/usr/username/Mail/ Username/Jul30.84** directory without leaving your home directory. One simple way to do this is to define a variable to be this directory string, as shown:

% **set D = /usr/username/Mail/Username/Jul30.84**

%

We chose to call the variable **D** (for directory). You could choose an single word for the name of the variable.

Now when you need to refer to the directory, simply substitute the expression **$D** in its place. For instance, the following screen shows two equivalent ways to display the contents of the ordinary file **reminder**, which resides in the directory **/usr/username/Mail/Username/Jul30.84**:

% **cat /usr/username/Mail/Username/Jul30.84/reminder**

From username Thu Nov 1 12:32:07 PST 1984

Board meeting this Monday evening.

% **cat $D/reminder**

From username Thu Nov 1 12:32:07 PST 1984

Board meeting this Monday evening.

%

Notice that you must type a slash (/) after the **$D** and before **reminder** to specify the complete pathname correctly.

Several shell variables are set initially by the shell. All the variables listed in the second screen, for instance, were predefined by the shell when you logged on. Of course, you may reset these variables to other values using the **set** command. In fact, resetting these variables is part of customizing your shell environment, a topic that we discuss at length in Appendix C, "Interacting With Your

UNIX System."

The predefined variables for the C Shell are generally different than those for the Bourne Shell. However, the principle of resetting the values of shell variables to customize the shell environment applies to the Bourne Shell as well.

In the section called "The Shell Startup Files" at the end of this session, you learn how to automate the process of customizing your shell so that all the appropriate steps are performed right after you sign on to your system and before you even get your first shell prompt.

Command Aliases

The C Shell has a *command alias feature*, which allows you to specify an entire UNIX command line with a single word. You can use this feature to reduce the amount of typing involved in frequently used command lines or to replace the rather cryptic UNIX command names with more descriptive names.

Command aliases are defined by the C Shell **alias** command. The command line format for establishing an alias is

% **alias** *newcmdline oldcmdline*

After the alias is defined, *oldcmdline* will be executed by the C Shell whenever *newcmdline* is typed.

For our first example, let's see how you might give a lengthy command line a simpler alias to help avoid typing errors and fatigue. As we learned in an earlier session, you may read your mail directly by displaying the contents of your mailbox with **cat**. Your mailbox is an ordinary file with the same basename as your account name. Your mailbox file is located in the **/usr/mail** directory on the Bell UNIX system and in the **/usr/spool/mail** directory on most Berkeley systems. Thus, messages for the account **username** would be contained in the ordinary file **/usr/mail/username** or **/usr/spool/mail/username**. To have the C Shell execute the command line **cat /usr/mail/username** whenever you enter **readmail**, give the alias command shown in the next screen. Then type **readmail** to test the new alias.

```
% alias readmail cat /usr/mail/username
% readmail
From username Thu Nov  1 12:32:07 PST 1984
Board meeting this Monday evening.


%
```

Another application for the alias feature would be to rename a terse UNIX command so that it is easier to remember. For instance, if you are used to using a CP/M-based computer, you could assign some of the UNIX commands to have the same names as the equivalent CP/M command names.

Here are three UNIX commands that have CP/M equivalents:

UNIX	CP/M
ls	dir
cat	type
rm	era

To actually give these UNIX commands their CP/M aliases enter the following:

```
% alias dir ls
% alias type cat
% alias era rm
%
```

The order of the arguments for the **alias** command is important. Be careful to remember that the new command name comes before the old name.

Now you may use the aliases. The aliases **dir** and **type** are used in the following example:

```
% dir
Mail
letter
poem
% type poem
Roses are Red
Violets are Blue
Sugar is Sweet
And so are You.
%
```

Because the alias feature creates additional names that are recognized by the shell, you may still use the old command names — ls, **cat**, and **rm** — as well as the new names — **dir**, **type**, and **era**.

You might wish to use the alias feature to replace a command line by a shorter version of the command line or by a single word. For example, you may wish to have the C Shell actually execute the command line **rm −i** whenever you type **rm**. The interactive option (−i) for the **rm** command gives you a "second chance" when deleting files. This way the interactive option for **rm** is automatically specified, for safety's sake, when you delete files.

Enter **alias rm rm −i** to define the new alias. Then enter **rm poem** to verify that the alias is working. The **rm** command will prompt you by displaying a message such as "poem:" (for the Bell version of **rm**) or "rm: remove poem?" (for the Berkeley version of **rm**). If you enter a line beginning with a **y**, **rm** will delete the indicated file; otherwise **rm** will not delete the file. To see this for yourself, enter **n** and the operation will be aborted.

```
% alias rm rm −i
% rm poem
poem: n
%
```

Note that if more files are specified on the command line, **rm** will prompt you for each file in turn until all files have been processed.

Type the command **alias** to display all the aliases currently in effect:

```
% alias
dir           ls
era           rm
readmail            (cat /usr/mail/username)
rm            (rm −i)
type          cat
%
```

Note that if you specified **era**, the C Shell would replace **era** by **rm**. But since **rm** also has an alias (**rm −i**), **rm** would be replaced by **rm −i**. Thus, in effect, **era** actually has the alias **rm −i** as well.

You can remove an alias definition with the **unalias** command. The command line format is simply

% **unalias** *newcmdline*

where *newcmdline* is the alias. For example, let's remove the alias definition for **dir** and then see what happens when we enter **dir**:

```
% unalias dir
% alias
era             rm
readmail                        (cat /usr/mail/username)
rm              (rm −i)
type            cat
% dir
dir: Command not found
%
```

Because the **dir** command no longer stands for **ls** and does not exist as a file for execution, the shell issues an error message.

A Convenient Shorthand for the Home Directory Pathname

The C Shell uses the tilde character (~) as a shorthand to represent your home directory. The shell will replace the tilde in a command line with the full pathname of your home directory. You will find this feature convenient, for instance, if you need to reference files in your home directory when you are working in a different directory.

As an example, let's say you are working in the **Mail/Username/Jul30.84** subdirectory (relative to your home directory) and you wish to display the contents of **poem** in your home directory. In fact, you could be working in any directory on your system and still display **poem** with the same command. You only need to type **cat ~/poem** to accomplish this:

```
% cd Mail/Username/Jul30.84
% pwd
/usr/username/Mail/Username/Jul30.84
% cat ~/poem
Roses are Red
Violets are Blue
Sugar is Sweet
And so are You.
%
```

The C Shell replaced the ~ in the command line with the home directory pathname /usr/username. Thus cat ~/poem was interpreted as cat /usr/username/poem, as desired.

If an account (user) name is suffixed to the tilde, the shell replaces the combination with the full pathname for the home directory of that user's account. In this way, you can specify the home directory for other accounts on your system more easily.

For example, you could list the contents of the home directory for the **friend** account, if you have access permission, as shown:

```
% ls ~friend
Letters
Report
%
```

In addition, the **echo** command provides a convenient way to display the pathname for the home directory of any user account. You may always display the home directory pathname for another account, even if you aren't allowed access to the home directory itself. We illustrate this approach here:

```
% echo ~friend
/usr/friend
%
```

Using Braces To Select Groups of Files And Other Objects

In Session 6 you learned a shorthand notation for specifying filenames on the command line for either the Bourne or the C shell. Filenames in a directory that have basenames with characters in common could be specified by literally typing the characters in the common part of the basename and using wild card characters to indicate the remainder. For instance, if chap1, chap2, and chap3 exist in your working directory, you could specify all three files by typing the common characters, **chap**, followed by either an *, a ?, or in this case [1-3].

The C Shell extends this idea to provide a shorthand for specifying pathnames even when the basename components have no characters in common. In this case the basenames are grouped in braces ({ }), each separated from the next by a comma with optional whitespace, and the grouping may be combined with a common pathname prefix or even other such groupings to yield full or partial pathnames. Note that the resulting pathnames don't have to exist in order to be included on the shell command line. Thus the group expansion could be used for specifying command line arguments that are not necessarily pathnames. These concepts will become clear after you see a few examples.

For our first example, change to the **Mail/Username/Jul30.84** subdirectory, entering **cd Mail/Username/Jul30.84**, and verify with **pwd**. Now let's use the C Shell grouping mechanism to reference the files **letter** and **poem** in your home directory in order to copy them to your new current directory:

```
% cd Mail/Username/Jul30.84
% pwd
/usr/username/Mail/Username/Jul30.84
% cp /usr/username/{letter,poem} .
% ls
letter
poem
reminder
%
```

Since you may also use the tilde (~) to signify your home directory, you could have abbreviated the **cp** command line even further, as shown:

```
% cp ~/{letter,poem} .
%
```

You may use the **echo** command to preview the final form of a shell command line without actually executing it. This technique is especially useful if you are unsure about how to set up a command line. Thus, if you were to use **echo** to preview the last two example command lines, you would see this:

```
% echo cp /usr/username/{letter,poem} .
cp /usr/username/letter /usr/username/poem .
% echo cp ~/{letter,poem} .
cp /usr/username/letter /usr/username/poem .
%
```

Before continuing, you will need to create a few more files in your home directory. First change to your home directory by entering **cd**, and then create the new files **poem.bak**, **poem.tmp**, **letter.bak**, and **letter.tmp**, as shown here:

```
% cd
% cp poem poem.bak
% cp poem poem.tmp
% cp letter letter.bak
% cp letter letter.tmp
% ls
Mail
letter
letter.bak
letter.tmp
poem
poem.bak
poem.tmp
%
```

First let's use groupings to list the files with the **.bak** extensions, then the **.tmp** files, and then both at once:

```
% ls {letter,poem}.bak
letter.bak poem.bak
% ls {letter,poem}.tmp
letter.tmp poem.tmp
% ls {letter,poem}{.bak,.tmp}
letter.bak letter.tmp poem.bak poem.tmp
% ls {letter,poem}{,.bak,.tmp}
letter letter.bak letter.tmp poem poem.bak poem.tmp
%
```

The last two command lines show how two groupings may be combined. All possible combinations of **letter** and **poem** with **.bak** and **.tmp** were obtained. You may combine even more than two groupings together if you wish.

So far we have shown examples where the results refer to basenames or pathnames that exist in the file system. You could even use the braces to group names of objects that aren't filenames. For instance, you could form combinations of prefixes with suffixes, as in the following.

```
% echo {edit,print}{ed,ing}
edited editing printed printing
%
```

You should experiment with various combinations of filename groups and string constants to become proficient in using this C Shell feature.

Before proceeding, erase the backup and temporary files you just created by entering **rm *.bak *.tmp**, and enter **y** in response to each prompted filename. Recall that the **rm** command was changed to **rm** −**i** earlier with the **alias** command.

The History Mechanism

The C Shell has a feature called the *history mechanism,* which enables it to "remember" the command lines that it executes. You may display this list of commands at any time. More importantly, you may select a previous command line or parts of previous commands for reexecution. The history mechanism is a great convenience: it enables you to work more quickly with the shell since command lines that are used often may be specified with a shorthand and the amount of typing you must do is greatly reduced.

The History List and Command Events

The command lines are stored in a buffer known as the *history list.* You may enable the history storage buffer and set the size of the history list with one command line:

$$\% \textbf{ set history} = \textit{listsize}$$

The *listsize* is a decimal number that specifies the maximum number of command lines stored in the buffer. We recommend a size of some 10 to 20 commands for most purposes. A larger list would scroll off the screen when you displayed it, and a smaller list might not contain enough of the previous commands to be useful.

After **history** has been enabled, you may examine the contents of the list at any time by simply entering **history**. Note that after the history list is full, the oldest command lines are deleted as the most recent command lines are added, a kind of first-in, first-out situation.

The following example shows a brief terminal session scenario whose "history" the **history** command is used to recap. First, to simplify matters, start up a new instance of the C Shell and then enable the history mechanism. Use the same pathname that you employed previously for this shell. Now type in the commands shown in boldface, and you should obtain the results shown in regular type:

```
% /bin/csh
% set history=10
% cd
% pwd
/usr/username
% cat reminder
cat: cannot open reminder
% ls
Mail
letter
poem
% history
    1       set history=10
    2       cd
    3       pwd
    4       cat reminder
    5       ls
    6       history
%
```

The command line **cat reminder** generated an error message because the file **reminder** is not located in the current working directory, /**usr**/**username**. The **history** command displayed only six commands even though the list size is ten. This is because only six commands have been typed (including **history** itself) since the new shell program was started. If more than ten commands had been typed into the history buffer, only the most recent ten would be "remembered" for display or subsequent manipulation.

A command line in the history list is known as a *command event* or simply *event*. The number preceding the command event (as shown in the history list display) is known as an *event number*. The event number serves to uniquely identify a command event.

Now examine the output from the **history** command shown in the last example again. The numbers preceding the command lines are the event numbers. They are numbered sequentially, starting with 1. In a moment you will see how each command line may be referenced by its unique event number.

The use of **history** to reference previous command lines as events enables you to run a frequently used command often without having to type out the entire command line. This feature helps prevent typographical errors and typing fatigue.

The following sections show several different ways to construct a command line by retrieving previous command lines or parts of previous command lines from the history list. These command line elements may be reintroduced into the current command line that you are constructing.

Retrieving an Event by Number

The exclamation point (!) is employed as the *event specifier*. The event specifier is prefixed to numbers and characters to indicate a specific event (that is, a command line) in the history list.

Continuing with our **history** practice session, first enter the command line **cd Mail/Username/Jul30.84** to change to the **Mail/Username/Jul30.84** subdirectory, where the file **reminder** is located. Then rerun command event number 3. To do so, enter **!3**:

```
% cd Mail/Username/Jul30.84
% !3
pwd
/usr/username/Mail/Username/Jul30.84
%
```

The C Shell replaced !3 by event 3, which is **pwd**, displayed the name of this command event on the next line, and then executed the **pwd** command. Now command event 8 is also **pwd**.

If you use event numbers frequently, it's a good idea to reset the C Shell prompt so that the current event number is displayed. If you prefer to have the default prompt (the percent sign) as part of the prompt, enter **set prompt='\! % '**. Another approach is shown here:

```
% set prompt='\!) '
10)
```

Because the command line we just entered was event number 9, the next command event will have event number 10. Also note that we have used the backslash (\) in front of the exclamation point (!) to prevent the exclamation point from being interpreted by the shell as indicating a previous event.

You may refer to a previous event by subtracting the number of intervening events from the event specifier (!), which signifies the current event in this case. For instance, let's say you wish to rerun event 8, **pwd**. Since the current event is 10, you would enter !−2 to accomplish this:

```
10) I−2
pwd
/usr/username/Mail/Username/Jul30.84
11)
```

Retrieving an Event by a Command Name Substring

You will recall that a string is a collection of characters. A *substring* refers to one or more characters within a string. In the following discussion, the command name, which always begins the command line, will be the string under consideration.

A command event may be referenced by an event specifier (!) followed immediately by a substring that is composed of one or more characters at the beginning of the command name. Thus, if you forget the number associated with a previous command event, you can execute it by referencing the event in this manner. The C Shell will search backward through the history list for the indicated substring. If a command name is found beginning with that substring, the associated event will be retrieved and executed.

Now let's try to retrieve the **cat reminder** command from the history list without spelling out **cat** completely. First let's use the first letter of **cat** to specify the substring "c" by entering !c:

```
11) !c
cd Mail/Username/Jul30.84
Mail/Username/Jul30.84: No such file or directory
12)
```

We didn't retrieve the desired event. The shell did search backward for the first command event that began with the substring "c" and found **cd Mail/Username/July30.84** instead of **cat reminder**, as desired. The shell's error message

"No such file or directory" indicates that the directory **Mail/Username/Jul30.84** is not a subdirectory of /usr/username/Mail/Username/Jul30.84.

Clearly, if you use this technique to specify an event, you must include enough characters in the substring to identify the command name of the desired event uniquely. Now try the substring **ca** by entering !ca:

```
12) !ca
cat reminder
From username Thu Nov  1 12:32:07 PST 1984
Board meeting this Monday evening.

13)
```

This time the shell found the desired event. The event was executed correctly because **reminder** is located in the current directory (to which you changed in event 7). If **reminder** were not in the current directory, you would have gotten a "file not found" message, just as you would have if you had entered **cat reminder**.

If the shell cannot find a command event, it will also issue an error message. For instance:

```
13) !cb
cb: Event not found.
13)
```

The event number for the next command line remains the same because no command was actually executed. The history buffer is likewise unchanged by such an error.

Rerunning the Previous Event

If you wish to rerun the previous command event, use the shorthand !! to retrieve that event for execution. To try this, type !!:

```
13) !!
cat reminder
From username Thu Nov  1 12:32:07 PST 1984
Board meeting this Monday evening.

14)
```

The previous event (number 12) was retrieved and executed. The intervening command, !cb, was not retrieved because it wasn't entered into the history list.

Obtaining Arguments From the Previous Event

Frequently you can construct a command line by acquiring one or more arguments from the previous command line and placing them in the command line that you are constructing. The C Shell can reference such arguments by special characters analogous to those used in the UNIX line editors for referencing words in a line of text. For instance,

- !^ references the first argument
- !$ references the last argument
- !* references all arguments from the previous event.

For our next example, let's create a backup copy of **reminder** named **reminder.-bak** as shown:

```
14) cp !$ !$.bak
cp reminder reminder.bak
15)
```

You may use the !$ in any argument position in the new command line. Here we used it twice to save typing the string **reminder**.

Now let's use the word count command, **wc**, on all arguments from the previous event to help verify the backup operation:

```
15) wc !*
wc reminder reminder.bak
     3      11      70 reminder
     3      11      70 reminder.bak
     6      22     140 total
16)
```

The first column shows the number of lines, the second the number of words, and the third the number of characters in the indicated files.

Finally, let's remove the original file **reminder** by referencing the first argument of the previous command.

16) **rm !^**

rm reminder

17) ▓

Correcting the Previous Event

If you make a typing mistake and do not catch it before pressing RETURN, you may correct the previous command line after the shell prompt returns. You would change the last command typed by delimiting the incorrect and correct text string with the circumflex (^), as shown here:

$$\% ~^{\wedge}oldstring^{\wedge}newstring^{\wedge}$$

The *newstring* in the new command line will replace *oldstring* from the previous command line. You may omit the trailing circumflex delimiter if a RETURN follows next.

For example, first purposefully enter the incorrect command **mv remindr.bak reminder**, and then correct the mistake by entering **^remindr^reminder**:

17) **mv remindr.bak reminder**

mv: cannot access remindr.bak

18) **^remindr^reminder**

mv reminder.bak reminder

19) ▓

You do not actually have to specify the entire word, but you do have to enter enough characters to make the change unambiguous. For instance, in the preceding example, entering **^d^de** would have produced the same result. Notice, however, that since the shell scans the previous command line from left to right, the construction **^r^er** would have given **mv eremindr.bak reminder**.

The more you use the history substitution features of the C Shell, the more adept you will become at using them. This is a good time to go over the basic information about the history mechanism that you've just read and then to experiment for yourself.

The Shell Startup Files

A shell startup file is an ordinary file containing a list of one or more shell command lines. Thus instead of typing commands one at a time as you interact with the shell, you can place these commands in a file with a special name that tells the shell to execute them sequentially as a *batch*. Generally, commands that are used to customize or change your environment are placed in these files. It's important to note that the start-up files *must* be located in your home directory if they are to be executed "automatically."

The C Shell distinguishes between two startup files. The commands in the file **.login** are executed by the login shell only once, right after you sign on to your UNIX system. The commands in the **.cshrc** file are executed every time another instance of the C Shell (that is, a subshell) is invoked. You would invoke a subshell, for instance, if you ran a UNIX command while still in an editor or in the **mail** program. You can also invoke a subshell explicitly, of course, by enclosing a command sequence in parentheses.

The next screen illustrates some of the commands we introduced in this chapter that are appropriate for including in the C Shell startup files:

```
19) cd
20) cat .login
alias rm 'rm —i'
alias readmail cat /usr/mail/username
set history=10
set prompt='\!) '
stty erase '^h' kill '^u' intr '^c' quit '^x'
date
alias
set
21) cat .cshrc
alias rm 'rm —i'
alias readmail cat /usr/mail/username
set history=10
set prompt='\!)) '
22) ▓
```

Notice that when we constructed these files, we made the prompt for subsequent subshells distinct from the login shell by defining the **prompt** variable slightly differently in **.cshrc** (for the subshells) than in **.login** (for the login shell). The **login** file here includes several commands that you might normally put in a **.login** file but which wouldn't be appropriate for the **.cshrc** startup file. For instance, the **stty** command only needs to be executed once during the terminal session. Also the **date, alias,** and **set** commands at the end of the **.login** file are helpful because they provide information about the environment after you sign on to the account.

Note that immediately after logging on to your system, the commands in **.cshrc** and then those in **.login** will be executed. If this were not the case, your shell prompt would be 1)) and not 1).

This concludes the C Shell tutorial. You should now have most of the basic information you will need for using this powerful command interpreter effectively in interactive terminal sessions with your UNIX system.

CHAPTER 5

TEXT PROCESSING

In Chapter 5, we resume our study of the UNIX line editors, **ed** and **ex**. In Chapter 3 you learned how to use these editors to create a simple text file and save it on disk. In this chapter you will extend your knowledge of **ed** and **ex**. You will learn the most frequently used commands for changing your text file in Session 9. All the important disk file operations that are possible with these line editors will be explained in Session 10.

We will present **vi**, the screen-oriented counterpart of **ex**, in Session 11. **ex** and **vi** are, in fact, two different names for the same program: the program behaves like a line-oriented editor when invoked as **ex**, and like a screen-oriented editor when invoked as **vi**. The editor lets you view your text file through a window on your terminal screen. This window can be moved so that you can view any part of your text. You can move the cursor anywhere within the window to add, change, or delete text precisely at the cursor's position. By contrast, you have manipulated entire lines when you use a line-oriented editor.

The last session in this chapter, Session 12, shows you how to use the **nroff** program, the powerful UNIX text formatter. You can control the appearance of

179

your printed text by selecting the proper formatting commands. You will learn about **nroff** formatting requests in this session.

In combination, the UNIX text editor and formatters enable you to produce high-quality documents suitable for publication. Whether you need to write interoffice memos or long and complex technical reports, these text processing facilities can help you do the job quickly and efficiently.

SESSION 9

*This session focuses on the editing commands for **ed** and **ex** that change the buffer's contents. The next session, Session 10, discusses operations involving exchanges between the edit buffer and the disk files for these line editors.*

Here is an overview of what you will learn in this session:

*After a quick review of **ed** and **ex**, we teach you how to locate lines containing text patterns and then how to substitute a different pattern for the original one. You will also learn a couple of ways to set up editing commands so that they affect the entire buffer rather than just a few lines.*

Session 9 also explains the special meaning several different characters have for the editors and how you combine these special characters to create shorthand notations that facilitate your interactions with the editors when you make search and substitute requests.

*In addition to their extensive search and substitute capabilities, **ed** and **ex** provide a command that allows you to undo your last editing command, in case you make a mistake. In this session, you will practice working with that command, which is aptly called the **undo** command.*

*You will also learn how to cut and paste the text in the edit buffer using delete, move, and text copy operations. The **append**, **insert**, and **change** commands allow you to enter text entry mode in order to add or change existing text.*

Once you have made all the editing changes you want to make, you can write the buffer's contents to a file other than the one you began editing from.

Finally, you will learn how to display the nonprinting characters, such as the control characters, in your edit buffer.

*It's important to note that in many cases you will find that **ex** and the newer versions of **ed** allow a somewhat shorter editing command line. In the text we will indicate the verbose form of an editing command for **ed** and the more succinct form for **ex**, but you may be able to use the shorter form for **ed** as well, if your version of **ed** is one of the newer ones. If the shorthand form doesn't work with your version of **ed**, however, you can always use the more verbose form. Thus, while our examples depict the **ed** editor on the left and **ex** on the right-hand side, the newer versions of **ed** can frequently recognize the shorthand editor command shown on the right for **ex**.*

Also note that only the first letter or letters of UNIX editor commands should be entered when you use a command. To make the commands easier to identify, we have used the whole word in most instances, but you should enter only the boldfaced portion of the word.

A Short Review of ed and ex

First let's quickly review the editing procedures we learned in Session 3: creating a file, entering some text, saving that text, and leaving the editor. At the end of this review, we will present the general format for setting up the new editing commands you will be learning in the remainder of this session.

After logging in, call up the editor program you wish to use to create and edit a file to be named **appeal**. Enter **ed appeal** or **ex appeal** as appropriate. Then enter the commands and text shown in boldface here ("citizen" is purposely misspelled):

$ **ed appeal**	% **ex appeal**
?appeal	"appeal" [New file]
P	:**a**
*****H**	**Now is the time**
cannot open input file	**for all good citizens**
*****a**	**to come to the aid**
Now is the time	**of their country.**
for all good citizens	.
to come to the aid	: ▓
of their country.	
.	
* ▓	

Here is a line-by-line account of your interaction with the computer in this example. First a warning message such as "? appeal" or "[New file]" appears because the file **appeal** does not yet exist on disk in your current directory. The name **appeal** does not refer to a disk file until the buffer's contents are written to disk and given that filename.

Next recall that newer versions of **ed** (System III and later) have a prompt in command mode that may be enabled by entering a capital **P**. These versions also have a help mode. When the help mode is enabled, the editor gives more descriptive error messages. In the preceding example, you entered a capital **H** to enable help mode. In response, **ed** warned you that the file **appeal** could not be found by displaying the message "cannot open input file" — a more descriptive version of "?appeal".

Finally, you entered text entry mode with the append command, and then you entered the text, including any mistakes, of **appeal**. By entering a period on a new line as the first and only character and then immediately pressing RETURN, you returned to the command mode of either editor.

You should verify that you have left text entry mode and have returned to command mode before proceeding. If you see a prompt (an asterisk for **ed**, a colon for **ex**), you are in command mode. If you are using an older version of **ed** that doesn't display a prompt, you will know that you have returned to command mode if you see the current line "of their country" displayed when you type a period and press RETURN. If not, try again. Be sure to press a single period at the beginning of a new line and follow it immediately by pressing RETURN.

Before proceeding, let's make a copy of your edit buffer. It's a good idea to write the contents of the buffer to the disk from time to time. In this way, if your system crashes or you get logged out accidentally, you still will have a recent copy of your work. To copy the edit buffer, simply enter **w**. Either editor will display a character count (this should be 75 characters):

```
*w                          :w
75                          "appeal" [New file] 4 lines, 75 characters
*                           :
```

The edit buffer was saved to disk creating a new file, named **appeal**, in your current directory.

Sometimes you may need to stop an editing command abruptly. For instance, you might decide that an operation is taking too long and you don't wish to wait. Simply press your interrupt character to interrupt whatever the editor is doing. The editors respond to the interrupt signal, stop whatever they are doing, and return to their command mode.

Turning now to the command line format for these editors, notice that **ed** and **ex** use the same general format:

line-number range   command [*parameter*]

All of the editing commands you will be learning in this session use this format. When you specify a single line number (sometimes called a *line address*) in an editor command line, the current line will be changed to the line with that line number, and the operation indicated by *command* will be carried out. When you indicate a range for the line numbers by separating them with commas, the command operation is performed in turn on each line within that range. After the operation is complete, the current line will be the last line affected by the command.

There are many ways to specify line number or address ranges. Some examples are

1	Line number 1.
$	The last line in the buffer.
$−1	The next to the last line.

1,3	Lines 1 through 3.
.	The current line.
none	The current line (. is assumed).
1,.	From the beginning of the buffer (line 1) through the current line.
.,$	From the current line through the end of the buffer ($).
1,$−1	From the beginning to the next to the last line.
$−1,$	The last two lines in the buffer.
1,$	All lines in the buffer.

Let's look at the last element in the command line format statement, the *parameter*. The most commonly employed **ed** parameter is **p** for the print operation. When you suffix **p** to **ed** commands, the last line that was changed will be displayed (this line will become the current line). On the other hand, **ex** normally prints the current line after each buffer change anyway, and thus **p** is rarely necessary when you are using **ex**. Several commands accept a count parameter, which is a decimal number that serves to indicate the number of lines to be involved in the command. For instance, the command **d5** will delete five lines starting with the current line.

You may specify more than one command on an editing command line with the **ex** editor. Separate each command from the next with a vertical bar (|) and end the command line with RETURN. The only exceptions to this are some global commands, which will be discussed later in this session, and the shell escape command, which will be discussed in Session 10. Only a RETURN and not a | can end these requests.

Changing Your Position In the Buffer

Your position in the edit buffer is always the current line. For this reason, we use the terms *position in the edit buffer* and the *current line* to mean the same thing. The current line provides a reference point. If a line address is not specified in a command, the current line is assumed to be the line being addressed.

Frequently, you may not know which line in the text buffer is the current line. One way to determine your position is to display the current line. There are three ways to display the current line without changing your position in the buffer. You can enter the period (.) alone, you can enter a **p** alone, or you can use the complete form of the print command for displaying the current line, **.p**.

*.p	**:.p**
of their country.	of their country.
*p	**:p**
of their country.	of their country.
*.	**:.**
of their country.	of their country.
* ▓	**: ▓**

Notice that the current line here is the last line of **appeal** that we entered into the buffer. When you leave text entry mode and return to command mode, the current line will always be the last line you entered into the edit buffer. If you are in command mode, the current line will be the last line that was affected by an editing command.

You may change the current line to any line in the edit buffer simply by entering the line number of the desired line. Of course, all editing commands including movement commands require that you be in command mode, not text entry mode.

Let's try this now. Type a 1 and press RETURN to change the current line to the first line in the buffer (line number 1). The contents of line 1 will also be displayed since the print command is understood after a movement operation. Thus entering a one (1) is shorthand for entering **1p**.

*1	**:1**
Now is the time	Now is the time
* ▓	**: ▓**

Now practice positioning the current line to line addresses 2, 3, and $. Remember that the $ addresses the last line of the edit buffer.

*2	**:2**
for all good citozens	for all good citozens
*3	**:3**
to come to the aid	to come to the aid
*$	**:$**
of their country.	of their country.
* ▓	**: ▓**

Now return to the first line of the buffer by entering 1. Then press RETURN several times; you will observe the successive display of each line until the end of the buffer. Pressing RETURN is, in fact, a convenient way to move forward through the text a line at a time. Pressing RETURN is equivalent to entering the verbose command .+1p, where the period (.) denotes the current line, plus one (+1) moves you to the next line, and p displays it.

*1	:1
Now is the time	Now is the time
*	:
for all good citozens	for all good citozens
*	:
to come to the aid	to come to the aid
*	:
of their country.	of their country.
*	:
?	At end-of-file
line out of range	:
*	

As you can see, when you reach the last line and you press another RETURN, the editors display a warning message informing you that you have requested a "line out of range" or that you are "at end-of-file".

To display the previous line, type a minus sign (−) and press RETURN. This operation changes the current line to the previous line. The minus sign is actually a shorthand for .−1p: that is, the current line (denoted by .), minus one (−1), and display (p). If you type successive minus signs, you will move backward through the edit buffer. After you reach the first line in the buffer and attempt to continue backward another line, the editor will display a warning, again indicating a line-addressing error.

*−	:−
to come to the aid	to come to the aid
*−	:−
for all good citozens	for all good citozens
*−	:−
Now is the time	Now is the time
*−	:−
?	Nonzero address required on this command
line out of range	:
*	

You may also move forward line by line by typing successive plus signs (+). The plus sign is a shorthand for .+1p, or the current line (.), plus one (+1), and display (p).

*+	:+
for all good citozens	for all good citozens
*+	:+
to come to the aid	to come to the aid
*+	:+
of their country.	of their country.
*+	:+
?	Not that many lines in buffer
line out of range	: ▓
* ▓	

To skip forward or backward by more than a single line, type a decimal number after the plus or minus sign. For example, now position yourself on the first line of the buffer by entering 1, and then enter +2. This will position you two lines down from where you were: that is, at the third line.

*1	:1
Now is the time	Now is the time
*+2	:+2
to come to the aid	to come to the aid
* ▓	: ▓▓

Note that +2 is shorthand for .+2p, that is, the current line (.), plus two (+2), and display (p). You could also have typed ++ instead of +2, since both mean .+2p.

In the preceding operations, the current line was changed to the line with line number 3. If you wish to display the line number of your current line without changing position in the buffer, enter the command .=.

*.=	:.=
3	3
* ▓	: ▓

You may determine the total number of lines in the buffer by entering the command to display the line number of the last line in the edit buffer. This display operation does not change the current line, which remains line number 3 in this case.

```
*$=                    :$=
4                      4
*▓                     :▓
```

You may wish to display one or more lines surrounding the current line. Displaying the context of the current line serves to orient you in the edit buffer. Although this technique is only really useful in a file larger than **appeal**, let's practice it now just to illustrate the principle. Enter the command **−1,+1p** (**−1,+1**) to display the line before and the line after the current line.

```
*−1,+1p                :−1,+1
for all good citozens  for all good citozens
to come to the aid     to come to the aid
of their country.      of their country.
*▓                     :▓
```

This operation does change the current line to the last line displayed (4 in this case). Note that **−1,+1** is actually shorthand for **.−1p,.+1p**.

Here is a summary of the rules involved in determining the buffer position and in movement operations:

- All editing commands, including display movement commands, require that you be in command mode, not text entry mode.

- A line editor handles text in terms of entire lines.

- The lines are referenced by a line number. The first line of text has line number 1. The last line may be referenced by the dollar sign ($).

- The last line operated on is known as the current line. The period (.) (also known as the dot) is the symbol for the current line. Your position in the edit buffer is the current line.

- You may change the current line to another line by entering the line number of the desired line.

- You can move forward in the buffer a line at a time by pressing successive RETURNs. The new current line is then displayed.

- You can move forward one line by entering a plus sign (+). The plus signs are additive. Entering ++, would advance the current line by two lines.

- You can move backward one line by entering a minus sign (−). The minus signs are also additive. Entering − − − moves the current line backward three lines.

- You may skip a specified number of lines by entering a plus sign (to move forward) or a minus sign (to move backward) followed by the number of lines to skip in either direction.

- If you attempt to move backward past the beginning of the buffer or forward past the end of the buffer, the editor will issue a warning message and will not honor your request.

Appending Text to the Buffer

Now let's add some text to **appeal.** First, move to the end of the buffer using one of the methods we have described. Then get into text entry mode with the append command, and enter the sample text shown in the next example. Exit text entry mode by typing a period as the first and only character on a new line and then pressing RETURN.

`*$`	`:$`
of their country.	of their country.
`*a`	`:a`
This is the time	**This is the time**
to get on the UNIX bandwagon.	**to get on the UNIX bandwagon.**
.	.
`*`█	`:`█

It would also have been fine to combine the movement and append command by entering $a.

Now you should be back in command mode. Verify that the append operation was performed correctly by displaying the contents of the edit buffer. Enter **1,$p** for either editor or the shorthand **%** for **ex** only.

`*1,$p`	`:%`
Now is the time	Now is the time
for all good citizens	for all good citizens
to come to the aid	to come to the aid

of their country.

This is the time

to get on the UNIX bandwagon.

* ▓

of their country.

This is the time

to get on the UNIX bandwagon.

: ▓

This would be a good time to save the contents of the edit buffer before proceeding. Simply enter w to do this.

*w

122

* ▓

:w

"appeal" 6 lines, 122 characters

: ▓

Locating a Text Pattern:
The Context Search Operation

You may also locate a line in the edit buffer by specifying some or all of the text in the desired line as a pattern to be found. The search for a pattern of text uses the editor command line format

/pattern/

You may omit the trailing slash with newer versions of **ed** and with the **ex** editor:

/pattern

When you enter such a command line, the editor searches forward for the pattern in the edit buffer, stops at the first occurrence, and displays the line where the match occurred. This line becomes the current line. You must include enough characters in the pattern to find only the desired line and no other; fewer characters may locate additional lines that are not desired. If the specified pattern can't be located, the current line is not changed and the editor displays a warning message.

It's important to note that one or more blanks within a pattern are also considered to be characters and are part of the pattern you are asking the editor to locate. For instance, "the" is distinct from " the", which is distinct from " the ". As an example, position yourself at line 1 of the edit buffer by entering 1:. The line "Now is the time" should appear. Then locate the next line containing the pattern "the time" by entering the command /the time/ or /the time, as appropriate for your editor.

```
*1                              :1
Now is the time                 Now is the time
*/the time/                     :/the time
This is the time                This is the time
*▓                              :▓
```

The match occurred in line 5 ("This is the time"), the first line after line 1 that contained the characters "the time". If you had specified fewer characters in the pattern, such as "the ", the line "to come to the aid" would have become the current line and would have been displayed instead. If you had specified "time" as the pattern, only the desired line would have been displayed. With a little practice, you should be able to construct patterns having the fewest number of characters.

The editor remembers the pattern "the time" until you enter a different search pattern. To find the next occurrence of "the time" in the buffer, simply enter the shorthand command // for **ed** or / for **ex**.

```
*//                             :/
Now is the time                 Now is the time
*▓                              :▓
```

After reaching the end of the buffer (line 6), the editor wrapped around to the beginning of the buffer in order to find the line containing the desired pattern. In Session 10, we will show you how to disable this wraparound feature for **ex**.

You may search backward through the buffer by bracketing the search pattern with question mark (?) characters. This would be useful, for example, if you realized that the line you wanted was farther up the page from the current line. For this example, position yourself at the end of the edit buffer by entering $. Now enter the command ?the time? for **ed** or ?the time for **ex**.

```
*$                              :$
to get on the UNIX bandwagon.   to get on the UNIX bandwagon.
*?the time?                     :?the time
This is the time                This is the time
*▓                              :▓
```

The editor found the line shown in our screen after searching backward through the buffer to line 5.

Since you employed the same pattern as in the forward direction searches, you could have used **??** for **ed** or **?** for **ex**. Let's do this now.

```
*??
Now is the time
*
```

```
:?
Now is the time
:
```

This time the editor wrapped around to the beginning of the buffer to find the line with the pattern you specified.

You will find the special characters that indicate the beginning (^) or end ($) of a line useful in a search request. The editor knows from the context that the dollar sign in a search request doesn't refer to the last line of the buffer. The command formats

/^pattern/   or   /^pattern

will locate the next line that contains *pattern* at the beginning of the line. The command format

/pattern$/   or   /<em>pattern</em>$

will locate the next line with *pattern* at the end of the line.

For instance, if you enter /^**the time**/ for **ed** or /^**the time** for **ex**, no lines will be displayed and you will get a warning message indicating that "the time" doesn't occur at the beginning of any line in the buffer:

```
*/^the time/
?
search string not found
*
```

```
:/^the time
Pattern not found
:
```

But specifying /**the time**$/ for **ed** or /**the time**$ for **ex** gets the desired result:

```
*/the time$/
This is the time
*//
Now is the time
*
```

```
:/the time$
This is the time
:/
Now is the time
:
```

The pattern "the time$", not "the time", is one that the editors will remember until you make another pattern search request.

A useful trick is to specify the search pattern as /^$/ if you wish to find the next blank line in the edit buffer. The expression ^$ is the pattern for a blank line since there are no characters shown between the symbols indicating the beginning (^) and end ($) of the line.

Context search expressions are interchangeable with line numbers. They can be used by themselves to find and print a desired line, or they can be used as line numbers for some other command, like the substitute command, as we will explain later in this session.

For example, /Now/+1, /good/, and /country/− 2 all refer to the same line (line 2). You may use the context search in place of one or more line numbers in a command. For instance, /Now/,/Now/+2p, and /good/−1,/country/−1p, and /Now/,/aid/p are all equivalent to 1,3p. All four display the first three lines of the buffer.

Global Search Operations

So far, the search operations we have learned will only find the next line in which the indicated pattern occurs. Thus you have to type the search request repeatedly to locate all occurrences of the pattern in the buffer. You may, however, specify the global prefix (g) to instruct the editor to search for and display every line in the buffer containing the desired pattern. The current line will become the last line displayed. As before, if the indicated pattern can not be located, the current line remains unchanged. The command format for global searches in older versions of ed is

g/pattern/

Note that a trailing p (for print) is not necessary for the global search request. For newer versions of ed and for ex you may omit the trailing slash:

g/pattern

For instance, enter g/the time/ for ed or g/the time for ex. You display should look like the following:

```
*g/the time/              :g/the time
Now is the time           Now is the time
This is the time          This is the time
*                         :
```

If you need to locate all lines in the buffer that *do not* contain a pattern, use this variation of the global prefix for **ed**:

v/*pattern*/

Or you may use this shorter form for newer versions of **ed** and **ex**:

v/*pattern*

The **ex** editor also recognizes **g!** instead of **v**:

g!/*pattern*

For example, if you enter the command **v** for **ed** (**g!**/ for **ex**), you should see all lines that do not contain "the time". You don't have to specify this pattern again since it was remembered from the last example.

*v//	**:g!/**
for all good citozens	for all good citozens
to come to the aid	to come to the aid
of their country.	of their country.
to get on the UNIX bandwagon.	to get on the UNIX bandwagon.
*	:

If you wish, you may precede the global prefix by line numbers to restrict the lines that the global operation will affect. The command line format

line-address range   **g**/*pattern*/

would only affect lines with line numbers in *line-address range.*

The Substitute Command and Search And Substitute Operations

The substitute command is one of the most useful and versatile editing commands. While it is probably the most complex editing command to use, it has the greatest potential for effective use. It allows you to change the text in a line almost anyway you wish. In combination with the global prefix, the substitute command becomes a flexible and powerful tool for changing text anywhere in the edit buffer, usually with just a single command line.

The general format of the substitute command for **ed** is

s/old pattern/new pattern/

This may be shortened further for **ex** and newer versions of **ed**:

s/old pattern/new pattern

For older versions of **ed** (and newer versions if you type a trailing slash), you must append the **p** (for **print**) command letter to display the result. The **ex** editor and newer versions of **ed** will display the last line on which a substitution occurred anyway. It is a good idea to display the result so that you can verify that the substitution operation was performed correctly.

Recall that earlier you were asked to mistype "citizen" in the second line, entering it as "citozen". We will now correct this misspelling in order to illustrate the substitute command.

Before specifying the substitute command, you need to position yourself at the line where the substitution is to occur. There are several different ways to move to the desired line. One approach is to use a *context search* to locate (and display) the line with a search operation by entering /**citozens**/ for **ed** and /**citozens** for **ex**. Then you may use the substitute command, as shown here:

*/citozens/	**:/citozens**
for all good citozens	for all good citozens
*s/citozens/citizens/p	**:s/citozens/citizens**
for all good citizens	for all good citizens
* ▇	**:** ▇

It's interesting to note that you only have to specify enough characters in the substitute command to make the request unambiguous. Thus, you could have entered **s/to/ti/p** for **ed** or **s/to/ti** for **ex** to obtain the same result as in the last example. Be careful to specify enough characters. For instance, **s/o/i/p** (**s/o/i**) would yield the incorrect result "fir all good citozens". You should also know that since the editors scan the line from left to right to locate the first occurrence of *old pattern* and to replace it with *new pattern,* any further occurrences of *old pattern* are ignored.

The editors allow you to combine the search operation and the substitute command on one command line. Here the search operation serves to locate and effect the change to the desired line, while the substitute command performs the indicated replacement. To try this now, enter /**citizens/s/citizens/citozens/p** for **ed** and

/citizens/s/citozens/citizens for **ex**. The result should be to change "citizens" back to "citozens". Here we show the operation for **ed** only:

```
*/citizens/s/citozens/citozens/p
for all good citozens
*
```

The combined search and substitute operation may be abbreviated even further because the pattern specified in the search request becomes the "remembered" pattern. Thus, you don't have to repeat it in the *old pattern* side of the substitute portion of the command line. Let's find "citozens" and change it back to "citizens":

```
*/citozens/s//citizens/p
for all good citizens
*
```

```
:/citozens/s//citizens
for all good citizens
:
```

Internally, the editors replace the empty double slash with the remembered pattern "citozens", so that **/citozens/s//citizens/p** becomes **/citozens/s/citozens/citizens/p**.

You may employ the special characters ^ and $ to indicate the beginning and end of a line, respectively, in the *old pattern* side of the substitute command. The editor knows from the context that here ($) doesn't refer to the last line of the buffer. Some examples will show what we mean.

Enter the command **1s/^/Right /p** for **ed** and **1s/^/Right** plus a space for **ex**. The 1 tells the editor to change the current line to line 1 of the edit buffer. (This is another way to locate and change to the line on which you wish to make a substitution. Of course, you have to know the line number beforehand. The methods we demonstrated earlier did not require knowledge of the line number since a *context search* was used to locate the desired line.) Then "Right" is substituted for the circumflex (^), which indicates the beginning of the line, and the result is displayed. Don't forget the space after "Right " so that there will be a space between the words "Right" and "Now".

```
*1s/^/Right /p
Right Now is the time
*
```

```
:1s/^/Right
Right Now is the time
:
```

If you omit a trailing slash with the **ex** editor or newer versions of **ed**, you must type exactly one space after "Right" before pressing RETURN.

Now move to line number 5 of the edit buffer and append the phrase ", isn't it," to the end of the line by entering the command **5s/$/, isn't it,/p** for **ed** or **5s/$/, isn't it,** for **ex**. Note that no space is used before the comma in the *new pattern*. This is because we do not wish to separate the comma from the preceding word, "time".

*5s/$/, isn't it,/p

This is the time, isn't it,

*

:5s/$/, isn't it,

This is the time, isn't it,

:

If you surround text in a search pattern or text in a substitution expression with spaces, only that portion of text will be located or substituted. Thus the pattern "the" would match "their" as well, but " the " only matches the single word "the".

At this point, display the entire buffer, entering **1,$p** for either editor or the shorthand **%** for **ex**:

*1,$p

Right Now is the time

for all good citizens

to come to the aid

of their country.

This is the time, isn't it,

to get on the UNIX bandwagon.

*

:%

Right Now is the time

for all good citizens

to come to the aid

of their country.

This is the time, isn't it,

to get on the UNIX bandwagon.

:

Here is another timesaver. If the text of *old pattern* occurs as part of *new pattern*, you don't have to retype *old pattern* on the *new pattern* side of the substitute command. In this case you may indicate the *old pattern* text within *new pattern* by the ampersand character (**&**). Note that this character only has a special meaning within the context of the *new pattern* side of a substitute expression and not elsewhere.

For instance, let's replace "time" in line 1 by "right time" using the ampersand to stand for "time" in *new pattern*, as follows:

*1s/time/right &/p

Right Now is the right time

*

:1s/time/right &

Right Now is the right time

:

Don't forget the space between "right" and the ampersand so that there will be a space between the words "right" and "time".

The ampersand provides a quick way to enclose text in quotes or parentheses. For instance, you could enter s/right/"&"/ for **ed** or s/right/"&" for **ex** to get

*1s/right/"&"/p

Right Now is the "right" time

* ▓

:1s/right/"&"

Right Now is the "right" time

: ▓

You may repeat the ampersand as often as needed on the *new pattern* side; it will be replaced each time by *old pattern*.

You may use the substitute command to delete text on a line. If *new pattern* contains no characters, the text of *old pattern* will be deleted. For example, we may remove the word "right" and the surrounding quotation marks by entering s/"right" //p for **ed** or s/"right", plus a space, for **ex**.

*s/"right" //p

Right Now is the time

* ▓

:s/"right"

Right Now is the time

: ▓

Metacharacters, Escape Characters, And Regular Expressions

In our discussion of search and substitute operations, you have used the circumflex (^) and dollar sign ($) as special characters to signify the beginning and end of a line, respectively. These and other characters that have a special meaning for the editors are known as *metacharacters*. It's important to note that these characters may or may not have a special meaning, depending on the context in which they are used. For instance, it is often but not always the case that a character has a special meaning if it is used in a context search expression or on the *old pattern* side but not on the *new pattern* side of a substitute command expression.

For example, the dollar sign only has a special meaning in a context search expression or on the left side (*old pattern* side) of the substitute command. Thus, the search and substitute expression $s/$/$ is interpreted to mean "move to the last line of the buffer (first $), then replace the end of the line (second $), with a dollar sign (third $)." Only the first and second instances of $ have a special meaning; the third instance is treated literally.

The pattern used to locate text or in a substitution command is also known as a *regular expression*. Regular expressions consist of ordinary characters and perhaps some metacharacters as well. For instance, the regular expression pattern "^The" would match all text lines beginning with the word "The". The regular expression "^The" contains the ^ metacharacter and the ordinary characters "T", "h", and "e".

The period (.) acts as a metacharacter when it occurs in a pattern for the search command or on the left side, or *old pattern* side, of a substitute command expression. This metacharacter stands for *any* single character. For instance, if you enter **g/ i. /p** for **ed** or **g/ i.** plus a space for **ex**, you will display all lines in the buffer containing a two-letter word beginning with "i":

```
*g/ i. /p                              :g/ i.
Right Now is the right time            Right Now is the right time
This is the time, isn't it,            This is the time, isn't it,
*                                      :
```

And if you enter **1s/.ow/now/p** for **ed** or **1s/.ow/now** for **ex**, you will change the first text line as shown here:

```
*1s/.ow/now/p                          :1s/.ow/now
Right now is the time                  Right now is the time
*                                      :
```

Here the ".ow" pattern, which means any character followed by "ow", is matched by "Now".

How would you use the substitute command to change a period already imbedded in the text into a different character? For instance, let's say we wished to change "of their country." into "of their country!". Entering **4s/./!/p** for **ed** or **4s/./!** for **ex** would yield the following:

```
*4s/./!/p                              :4s/./!
If their country.                      If their country.
*                                      :
```

This is not what we intended. Since a period on the left side of the substitution expression **s/./!/** is a metacharacter that stands for any single character, the first character in the line "of their country.", which is an "o", was matched by the period and the exclamation point (!) was put in its place.

The way around this is to use an *escape character* to remove the special meaning given to the period. The backslash (\ ) serves as this escape character for the UNIX line editors and will remove the special meaning given to any metacharacter. If you put the backslash immediately in front of the metacharacter, the editor will interpret the character literally, ignoring the metacharacter's special meaning.

Thus, if you mean to specify a circumflex or a dollar sign literally in a search or substitute command, precede these characters by a backslash. For instance, the search pattern "^D" would locate lines beginning with a capital "D", but "\^D" would locate lines containing a circumflex (^) followed by a capital "D" anywhere on the line.

If you need to search for or use a slash (/) in a substitute command, you can precede it with a backslash (\) to keep the editor from interpreting it as delimiting the expression. Thus you would specify "/ \//" to locate the next line containing a slash, and then "s/ \// \/ \//p" to substitute two slashes in its place.

Command lines that contain metacharacters, slashes, backslashes, and so on may appear very confusing to you at first. You have to read carefully and interpret the line from left to right. After a while you will become adept at reading and writing such expressions.

Note that the backslash also functions as an escape character to remove the special significance given to your erase or line-kill characters, even though these editing characters act at the level of the kernel program. If you do use the backslash in front of these characters, they are ignored by the kernel and can be read by the editor program. In this way, you could, for instance, enter these characters into editing commands or your edit buffer.

Returning now to the problem of changing a period embedded in the text to a different character, let's fix our mistake by entering s/!/o/p or s/!/o, and then use the backslash as shown:

*s/!/o/p	:s/!/o
of their country.	of their country.
*s/ \./!/p	:s/ \./!
of their country!	of their country!
*	:

Notice that this problem doesn't occur if the period is specified on the right-hand side (*new pattern* side) of the substitute command. The period is only interpreted in a special manner if it occurs on the left-hand side of a substitute command expression, as the following example shows:

*s/!/./p	:s/!/.
of their country.	of their country.
*	:

Our next topic in this discussion of notations you can use in search and substitute operations is the square brackets. You can use the square brackets when you need to search for any particular character or set of characters in a larger set of characters.

For instance, let's say you wish to ignore the distinction between upper- and lowercase alphabetical characters. An easy way to specify a search pattern that would select either the upper- or lowercase character in question is to enclose both characters in square brackets and use this expression in your search pattern. Thus, you can indicate a search for either a capital "T" or a lowercase "t" by the regular expression "[Tt]".

To practice using the square brackets, let's display all lines in our edit buffer that begin with either "T" or "t". Enter g/^[Tt]/ for ed or g/^[Tt] for ex to locate and display these lines:

```
*g/^[Tt]/                          :g/^[Tt]
to come to the aid                 to come to the aid
This is the time, isn't it,        This is the time, isn't it,
to get on the UNIX bandwagon.      to get on the UNIX bandwagon.
*                                  :
```

The pattern "^[Tt]" matches all lines that begin (indicated by the circumflex) with a "T" or "t". Compare this result with what you get when you enter either g/^T/ or g/^t/ for ed and g/^T or g/^t for ex:

```
*g/^T/                             :g/^T
This is the time, isn't it,        This is the time, isn't it,
*g/^t/                             :g/^t
to come to the aid                 to come to the aid
to get on the UNIX bandwagon.      to get on the UNIX bandwagon.
*                                  :
```

You can easily reverse the logic of the search by placing a circumflex immediately inside the left square bracket. The editor does not interpret a circumflex just inside the left bracket as "beginning of a line," but rather as "anything except" the characters following. Thus, the pattern "^[^Tt]" matches all lines that don't begin with "T" or "t":

```
*g/^[^Tt]/                         :g/^[^Tt]
Right now is the time              Right now is the time
for all good citizens              for all good citizens
of their country.                  of their country.
*                                  :
```

Another search operation shorthand you should know about is the dash ($-$). When used with the square brackets, the dash allows you to specify characters that fall in a range within the ASCII character set — that is, characters that are adjacent in this character set. (The ASCII character set listed in Appendix E shows which characters are adjacent.)

To use the dash, specify the first character inside a bracket, then the dash, and finally the last character in the range followed by the closing bracket. For instance, the regular expression "[0123456789]", which is used for locating any numerical digit, could be abbreviated as "[0$-$9]".

Likewise, the pattern "[A$-$Za$-$z]$" would be matched by all lines that end with either an uppercase or lowercase alphabetical letter, as shown here:

*g/[A$-$Za$-$z]$/   :g/[A$-Za-$z]$

Right now is the time   Right now is the time

for all good citizens   for all good citizens

to come to the aid   to come to the aid

*   :

And if you used the pattern "[^A$-$Za$-$z]$", you'd select all lines that don't end in an alphabetical character.

*g/[^A$-$Za$-$z]$/   :g/[^A$-Za-$z]$

of their country.   of their country.

This is the time, isn't it,   This is the time, isn't it,

to get on the UNIX bandwagon.   to get on the UNIX bandwagon.

*   :

Remember that the circumflex only has a special meaning within the square brackets if it occurs immediately after the opening bracket ([). Thus, the expression "/^[^^]/" will match any line that doesn't begin with a circumflex.

Finally, if you wish to locate a character that may be repeated an arbitrary number of (zero or more) times, follow the character with the asterisk (*). Table 5-1 shows some examples of the asterisk used with ordinary characters and other metacharacters and an explanation of what each use of the asterisk means.

Now that you know the basic metacharacters and how to combine them into regular expressions, you are in a position to set up very powerful search and substitute operations. In fact, the **ed** and **ex** line editors far surpass the UNIX visual editor, **vi**, in this regard.

Table 5-1. *Use of the Asterisk and Other Metacharacters in Search Operations*

Search Pattern	Locates a Line Containing
/x*	Zero or more "X" characters
/ *	Zero or more space characters
/.*	Zero or more characters of any type
/[0-9]*/	Zero or more digits
/[A-Za-z]*	Zero or more alphabetical characters
/^.$	Exactly one character
/^..$	Exactly two characters
/^.*$	Zero or more characters
/^ *$	Only blanks
/^[0-9]*$	Only digits
/^[^0-9]*$	Characters not containing digits

Substituting Globally Within a Line or the Buffer

In the last section you learned how to use the substitute command to replace the first occurrence of a pattern on a line by another pattern of text. In this section we will demonstrate first how to execute the substitute command with a global suffix so that all occurrences of a pattern on a line are substituted for. Then we will show you how to combine the global prefix with the global suffix in order to make a substitution at every occurrence of a pattern in the entire buffer. The latter technique would be useful, for instance, if you needed to correct a word that was misspelled throughout a text; however, the misspelling would have to be consistent.

The basic substitute command changes only the first occurrence of a pattern on a given line. To illustrate, enter **5s/is/IS/p** for **ed** or **5s/is/IS** for **ex**.

*5s/is/IS/p	:5s/is/IS
ThIS is the time, isn't it,	ThIS is the time, isn't it,
*	:

Only the first instance of "is", the one in "This", is changed. In order to change just the word "is", you would use the command form **5s/ is / IS /p** for **ed** or **5s/ is/ IS** plus a space for **ex**. The " is " pattern matches the word "is" only if it is preceded and followed by at least one space.

Now let's use the **g** (for global) parameter as a suffix to change all occurrences of a pattern on a line. (Note that **g** will be used as a suffix rather than as a prefix as it was earlier in this session.) For instance:

*5s/is/IS/gp	**:5s/is/IS/g**
ThIS IS the time, ISn't it,	ThIS IS the time, ISn't it,
*s/IS/is/gp	**:s/IS/is/g**
This is the time, isn't it,	This is the time, isn't it,
*	:

Notice that the slash before the global parameter suffix is required for both the **ex** and the **ed** editors in order to prevent "is" from becoming "ISg".

You have already learned how to use the global prefix to locate all lines in the buffer containing a specified pattern. Now let's combine the global search request with the substitute command to locate every line in the buffer containing *old pattern* and then to substitute *new pattern* in its place.

For example, let's change the first occurrence of the pattern "the" into "THE" on all lines of the buffer. Enter the command line **g/the/s//THE/p** for either editor. The **p** suffix is required even for **ex** since otherwise only the last line substituted is displayed in a global substitution request.

*g/the/s//THE/p	**:g/the/s//THE/p**
Right now is THE time	Right now is THE time
to come to THE aid	to come to THE aid
of THEir country.	of THEir country.
This is THE time, isn't it,	This is THE time, isn't it,
to get on THE UNIX bandwagon.	to get on THE UNIX bandwagon.
*	:

Notice that the global search request (**g/the/**) *must* precede the substitution request (**s//THE/**). This is the reason why the command **gs/the/THE/p** would not be sufficient.

Alternatively, you may perform a global substitution by specifying the line number range for the entire buffer followed by the substitution request. To illustrate this approach, let's change "THE" back to "the", as shown:

*1,$s/THE/the/p	**:%s/THE/the**
to get on the UNIX bandwagon.	to get on the UNIX bandwagon.
*	:

Only the last line substituted is displayed, although all instances of "THE" were actually replaced by "the", as you can see if you display the buffer's contents:

*1,$p	**:%**
Right now is the time	Right now is the time
for all good citizens	for all good citizens
to come to the aid	to come to the aid
of their country.	of their country.
This is the time, isn't it,	This is the time, isn't it,
to get on the UNIX bandwagon.	to get on the UNIX bandwagon.
*▮	:▮

Finally, you can combine the global prefix with the global suffix to change all occurrences of a pattern within the edit buffer. For example, enter **g/is/s//IS/gp** for either editor since the trailing print directive (**p**) is required by both editors if you wish to display all substituted lines:

*g/is/s//IS/gp	**:g/is/s//IS/gp**
Right now IS the time	Right now IS the time
ThIS IS the time, ISn't it,	ThIS IS the time, ISn't it,
*▮	:▮

Now let's use the substitute command twice in succession to convert all occurrences of "IS" back to "is". First let's convert the first four lines by entering **1,4s/IS/is/gp** and then displaying the entire buffer:

*1,4s/IS/is/gp	**:1,4s/IS/is/gp**
Right now is the time	Right now is the time
*1,$p	**:%**
Right now is the time	Right now is the time
for all good citizens	for all good citizens
to come to the aid	to come to the aid
of their country.	of their country.
ThIS IS the time, ISn't it,	ThIS IS the time, ISn't it,
to get on the UNIX bandwagon.	to get on the UNIX bandwagon.
*▮	:▮

Finally, restore the last two lines of the buffer by entering the command

5,$s/IS/is/gp and then display the entire buffer to verify:

```
*5,$s/IS/is/gp
This is the time, isn't it,
*1,$p
Right now is the time
for all good citizens
to come to the aid
of their country.
This is the time, isn't it,
to get on the UNIX bandwagon.
*
```

```
:5,$s/IS/is/gp
This is the time, isn't it,
:%
Right now is the time
for all good citizens
to come to the aid
of their country.
This is the time, isn't it,
to get on the UNIX bandwagon.
:
```

The undo Command:
Reversing the Last Change Made to Buffer

Sometimes you make a mistake when changing the contents of the edit buffer. The newer versions of **ed** and **ex** recognize a general undo command (**u**) that reverses any changes made in the buffer by the last command that changed the buffer. It's important to realize that only the last change made by the last command may be undone: in other words, you must catch your mistake before entering another command that changes the buffer. Note that intervening commands, such as print, that do not change the buffer, are ignored by the undo command.

If you can't recover from a major error with undo and you wish to undo the entire editing session, exit the editor without saving the edit buffer and reinvoke the editor to begin again. The possibility that you might need to reverse some of the editing you've done in this drastic way is another reason to save your changes periodically. In this way, you only have to recreate the last few minutes of work if it were necessary to discard the entire buffer.

Let's use the undo command now to return the edit buffer to the state it was in prior to the last substitute command. To do this simply enter **u**. The one intervening print command, which was used to display the entire edit buffer, has no effect on undo because the print operation does not change the buffer's contents.

```
*u
*1,$p
Right now is the time
for all good citizens
to come to the aid
```

```
:u
ThIS IS the time, ISn't it,
:%
Right now is the time
for all good citizens
```

of their country.

ThIS IS the time, ISn't it,

to get on the UNIX bandwagon.

*▓

to come to the aid

of their country.

ThIS IS the time, ISn't it,

to get on the UNIX bandwagon.

:▓

Interestingly, the undo command can also undo itself, as shown in the next example. Here the undo command reverses the last undo operation to give the result seen in the screen before last. Enter up for ed or u for ex. The p suffix is required to make ed display the current line after an undo request.

*up

This is the time, isn't it,

*1,$p

Right now is the time

for all good citizens

to come to the aid

of their country.

This is the time, isn't it,

to get on the UNIX bandwagon.

*▓

:u

This is the time, isn't it,

:%

Right now is the time

for all good citizens

to come to the aid

of their country.

This is the time, isn't it,

to get on the UNIX bandwagon.

:▓

As this example suggests, you may apply undo again and again as a toggle operation.

It's important to note that older versions of ed (before System III) have a limited undo command. They could only undo the last substitute command and then only if the current line were the affected line. Newer versions of ed and ex have a general undo command that can undo any kind of change to the buffer, as long as it is the last change.

The delete Command: Removing Lines

The delete command is used to remove one or more lines from the edit buffer. Both line editors automatically renumber all the lines remaining in the buffer. The most general command line format for delete is

line-address range   **d**

The *line-address range* is formed just as it is for other editing commands. White-space between the address range and the **d** command letter is optional. If you append a **p** after the **d** command letter, **ed** will display the current line after the deletion. The **ex** editor will display the current line in any case.

In our first example, we will delete one of the lines in the buffer. You may delete a particular line by prefacing the **d** command letter with the line number of the line to be removed. For instance, enter **4dp** for **ed** or **4d** for **ex** to remove line number 4 and to display the current line, which will be the line after the deleted line. Then display the entire buffer to verify.

*4dp	**:4d**
This is the time, isn't it,	This is the time, isn't it,
*1,$p	**:%**
Right now is the time	Right now is the time
for all good citizens	for all good citizens
to come to the aid	to come to the aid
This is the time, isn't it,	This is the time, isn't it,
to get on the UNIX bandwagon.	to get on the UNIX bandwagon.
*	:

If you are using a newer version of **ed** or **ex**, you can use the **undo** command to restore the line you just removed. Enter **u** and then display the entire buffer by entering **1,$p** for **ed** or **%** for **ex**.

*up	**:u**
of their country.	of their country.
*1,$p	**:%**
Right now is the time	Right now is the time
for all good citizens	for all good citizens
to come to the aid	to come to the aid
of their country.	of their country.
This is the time, isn't it,	This is the time, isn't it,
to get on the UNIX bandwagon.	to get on the UNIX bandwagon.
*	:

The **undo** command worked. All the lines are intact.

If you are using an older version of **ed** that lacks the general **undo** command, you can enter **3** to change to line 3 and then get into text entry mode with the append command. Then enter **of their country** and a period as the first and only character on the next line followed immediately by RETURN. Display the entire buffer to verify:

```
3
to come to the aid
a
of their country.
.
*1,$p
Right now is the time
for all good citizens
to come to the aid
of their country.
This is the time, isn't it,
to get on the UNIX bandwagon.
```

The delete command also allows you to delete more than one line at a time. To do this, specify the beginning line number, a comma, the ending line number, and the **d** command letter.

For example, let's delete the last two lines in the buffer. Since you know that the buffer contains six lines, you could specify **5,6dp** for **ed** or **5,6d** for **ex**. However, if you don't know how many lines are in the buffer, you can still delete the last two lines by using line numbers relative to the last line ($). Let's try this now. Enter **$−1,$dp** for **ed** or **$−1,$d** for **ex**. Recall that **$−1** stands for the next to the last line and $ for the last line. Now verify the deletion by displaying the entire buffer:

```
*$−1,$dp                      :$−1,$d
of their country.             of their country.
*1,$p                         :%
Right now is the time         Right now is the time
for all good citizens         for all good citizens
to come to the aid            to come to the aid
of their country.             of their country.
*                             :
```

The current line becomes "of their country." after the deletion. This time we won't restore the deleted lines since we won't need them anymore.

For our last example, let's delete the entire edit buffer in one step. But first, in order to have a copy of **appeal** as we proceed through this session and also in order to update the disk copy, which currently still has six lines instead of four, let's write out the buffer contents by entering **w**. Now delete the buffer by entering **1,$dp** for **ed** or **1,$d** for **ex**. Verify with **1,$p** for **ed** or **%** for **ex**.

*w	:w
81	"appeal" 4 lines, 81 characters
*1,$dp	:1,$d
?	:%
line out of range	No lines in the buffer
*1,$p	: ▓
* ▓	

The error message from **ed**, "line out of range", indicates that the buffer's contents have been deleted. In effect, although you requested that the current line be displayed (by the **p** suffix appended to **1,$d**), there is no current line after all lines have been removed from the buffer.

The move Command: Moving Lines

You can use the **move** command to rearrange one or more lines in the edit buffer. The line-numbering specification is somewhat more complex than what you've used before because you must specify not only what lines to move but also where they should be moved to. Use the following editor command line format with **move**:

move from line, to line inclusive **m** *to after line*

As before, whitespace between the line addresses and the **m** command letter is optional, but does serve to improve readability.

Since we deleted the buffer's content in the last example, we need to read **appeal** back into the buffer in order to practice the **move** command. To read **appeal** into the buffer, simply enter **e!** and **appeal** will be automatically read in since it is the remembered filename.

Now let's try an example of the **move** command. Move the first two lines to the end of the buffer by entering **1,2m$p** for **ed** or **1,2m$** for **ex**. Then verify the operation by displaying the buffer's contents:

*1,2m$p	:1,2m$
for all good citizens	for all good citizens
*1,$p	:%
to come to the aid	to come to the aid
of their country.	of their country.
Right now is the time	Right now is the time
for all good citizens	for all good citizens
* ▓	: ▓

To move the lines back, enter $-1,$m0p for **ed** or $-1,$m0 for **ex** and verify.

*$-1,$m0p	:$-1,$m0
for all good citizens	for all good citizens
*1,$p	:%
Right now is the time	Right now is the time
for all good citizens	for all good citizens
to come to the aid	to come to the aid
of their country.	of their country.
* ▓	: ▓

The line number range $-1,$ we have used here means "from the line before the last line ($-1) to the last line ($), inclusive." The editor allows the destination address to be line 0 in order to specify a move to the beginning of the buffer. There is actually no text associated with line 0; rather, line 0 is a means of specifying a destination that is in fact the beginning of the edit buffer.

Try moving other lines yourself and then verify the moves by printing the entire buffer before and after each operation. Restore the buffer to its original order before proceeding to the next section.

The append and insert Commands: Adding Lines

Both the append and insert commands are used to enter text entry mode so that text may be entered into the edit buffer. The commands differ only in where they place the new text.

While the insert command adds text before the specified line, the append command adds text after the indicated line. The command line format is the same for both editors:

[*line number*] **a** or [*line number*] **i**

If no line number prefix is specified, the current line is used. When you are finished appending or inserting text, you must formally leave text entry mode and return to command mode. To do this, type a period as the first and only character on the line and immediately press RETURN.

To see the difference between the append and insert commands, consider this simple example. First, use the append command to enter the text "who are patriotic" after the second line of the buffer and then check to see that this line was added:

*2a	**:2a**
who are patriotic	**who are patriotic**
.	**.**
*1,$p	**:%**
Right now is the time	Right now is the time
for all good citizens	for all good citizens
who are patriotic	who are patriotic
to come to the aid	to come to the aid
of their country.	of their country.
* ▓	**:** ▓

Now delete the line you just added by entering the command **3d**. Enter the same text using the insert command, but notice that you must use the argument 3 instead of 2 since insert adds text before the specified line. Finally, once you have left text entry mode, verify the insert operation.

*3dp	**:3d**
to come to the aid	to come to the aid
*3i	**:3i**
who are patriotic	**who are patriotic**
.	**.**
*1,$p	**:%**

Right now is the time   Right now is the time
for all good citizens   for all good citizens
who are patriotic   who are patriotic
to come to the aid   to come to the aid
of their country.   of their country.
* ▓   : ▓

As you can see, inserting before line 3 and appending after line 2 yields the same result. If you do get confused in using insert and append and find that you have entered the text in the wrong place, you can always use the **move** command to rearrange the buffer after you return to command mode.

Notice that while we have only added a single line here, you are not restricted to adding a single line when you use insert and append; in fact, you can enter as much text as you wish once you have entered text entry mode.

After you leave text entry mode, the current line will be the last line entered. This property is useful for entering and correcting text almost simultaneously. For instance, let's say you just entered a few lines and noticed, after you had pressed RETURN, that the last line had an error. In this situation, you could simply exit text entry mode, return to command mode, and then correct the last line, which is now the current line, with, for example, the **substitute** command. Using append, you could then reenter text entry mode and begin adding text right after the line you just corrected.

The transpose or copy Command: Duplicating Lines

To duplicate one or more lines in the buffer without moving the original lines, use the **ed** transpose or **ex** copy command. The command line format is identical to that for the move command except that **ed** uses the **t** command letter and **ex** recognizes either the **t** or the pair of characters **co**:

> *move from line, to line inclusive* **t** *to after line*

Unlike the move command, the transpose command makes a copy of the text after the destination line, leaving the source line or lines intact.

For instance, to make a copy of the last two lines and position them at the beginning of the file, enter the command line $-1,$t0p for **ed**. If you are using **ex**, enter either $-1,$t0 or $-1,$co0. Verify by displaying the entire buffer.

```
*$-1,$t0p                          :$-1,$co0
of their country.                  of their country.
*1,$p                              :%
to come to the aid                 to come to the aid
of their country.                  of their country.
Right now is the time              Right now is the time
for all good citizens              for all good citizens
who are patriotic                  who are patriotic
to come to the aid                 to come to the aid
of their country.                  of their country.
*                                  :
```

This line duplication feature would be useful, for example, if you wished to create several lines, each differing only a little from the other. After duplicating the first line the necessary number of times, you could use the substitute command to make the small changes that were necessary to the other lines.

Before proceeding with this tutorial session, delete the two extra lines by entering **1,2d**.

The change Command: Changing Entire Lines

Previously you learned how to change phrases of text within a line using the substitute command. If you wish to change one or more entire lines, a different approach is necessary.

You can change the contents of text lines in your edit buffer in two different ways. One approach would be to remove the text lines in question with the delete command and then get into text entry mode with the append or insert commands in order to enter the new text. Another approach would be to use either editor's change line command. The command line format for this command is

line-address range   c

The editor deletes the line or lines indicated in *line address range* and then enters text entry mode so that you can add the new text. You do not have to add the same number of lines that were deleted. Text will be added until you terminate the text entry mode by typing a period alone on a line and pressing RETURN.

For practice, let's change the line "who are patriotic" to the two lines "whose skills are needed" and "in the peace effort". Then verify by displaying the buffer's contents.

*3c	:3c
whose skills are needed	**whose skills are needed**
in the peace effort	**in the peace effort**
.	.
*1,$p	:%
Right now is the time	Right now is the time
for all good citizens	for all good citizens
whose skills are needed	whose skills are needed
in the peace effort	in the peace effort
to come to the aid	to come to the aid
of their country.	of their country.
*	:

Joining and Splitting Lines

The join command allows you to connect two or more lines. The end of one line is abutted to the beginning of the next line. The command line format is simply

line-address range   **j**

where all lines addressed by *line-address range* will be joined end to end. If no line addresses are specified, the current line is joined to the following line, if there is a following line.

With the **ed** version of this command, you may need to manually insert a space at the beginning of the second line so that there will be a space inserted between the last word on the first line and the first word on the second line. If you are using **ex**, a space is inserted automatically, if it is needed, when you join the lines. However, you may override this **ex** feature by specifying the join command as **j!** instead of **j**.

As an example, let's join the first two lines in the edit buffer. Follow the steps in the next screen for the **ed** editor. First insert a space at the beginning of the second line using the substitute command. Then join the lines:

```
*2s/^/ /p
   for all good citizens
*1,2jp
Right now is the time for all good citizens
```

```
*1,$p
Right now is the time for all good citizens
whose skills are needed
in the peace effort
to come to the aid
of their country.
* ▓
```

Notice that if you had not provided the extra space, the lines would have been connected by the word "timefor".

If you are using **ex**, the space at the beginning of the second line would be inserted automatically by join. However, if you were to insert a space first, it would be ignored, with the result that after the join operation, there would still be only a single space between the words "time" and "for":

```
:1,2j
Right now is the time for all good citizens
:1,$p
Right now is the time for all good citizens
whose skills are needed
in the peace effort
to come to the aid
of their country.
: ▓
```

You may join more than two lines by extending the *line-address range* to include those lines. For instance, **1,$j** would join all the lines in the buffer to create one long line.

You may split a line apart by inserting a new line character at the desired point in a line to give two shorter lines. You may use the substitute command to insert the new line character, which will separate the lines and which in this instance is generated by pressing RETURN. Normally, when you press RETURN at the end of a command line, the command is considered complete by the editor. You may remove the significance of RETURN to the editor by using the backslash (\ ), the escape character. Having split the lines, you can complete the substitute command on the next line.

An example will help make this method of splitting lines clear. Let's split the line we joined earlier. The technique is the same for either editor. Type **1s/time for/time ** and then press RETURN. The cursor jumps to the next line and nothing else seems to happen. Now complete the substitute command by typing **for/p** if you are using **ed** or **for/** if you are using **ex**. To verify that this operation was performed correctly, display the entire buffer. Finally, end the command line with RETURN.

*1s/time for/time \	:1s/time for/time \
for/p	for/
for all good citizens	for all good citizens
*1,$p	:%
Right now is the time	Right now is the time
for all good citizens	for all good citizens
whose skills are needed	whose skills are needed
in the peace effort	in the peace effort
to come to the aid	to come to the aid
of their country.	of their country.
* ▓	: ▓

Writing the Buffer to a Different File

Earlier we suggested that from time to time you should save a copy of your edit buffer to disk. When you enter **w**, the buffer's contents are written to the file you specified when you invoked the editor. In the context of this session, that file would be **appeal**. Sometimes, however, you might wish to save different versions of the buffer. In this case instead of overwriting the first version of **appeal**, you would want to create a new file in which to store the buffer's altered contents.

The general command line format for writing to another file with *filename* is

w *filename*

Let's practice this now by writing the present contents of the buffer to a new file named **appeal2**. To do so type **w**, a space, then the desired filename, **appeal2**, and press RETURN. After you enter the write command, the editor will display the number of characters written to the disk.

*w appeal2	:w appeal2
125	"appeal2" [New file] 6 lines, 125 characters
* ▓	: ▓

Now exit the editor with the **q**uit command and request a listing of your directory:

```
*q                          :q
$ ls                        % ls
Mail                        Mail
appeal                      appeal
appeal2                     appeal2
poem                        poem
$                           %
```

Remember that if you make any changes to the file and attempt to exit before saving the contents of the edit buffer, the editors will issue a warning message and ignore your request. The write operation may be to any file on the disk; that is, if you write the buffer to **appeal2**, the buffer's contents will be saved just as well as if you write the buffer to **appeal**. If you don't save the buffer and insist on exiting, by typing the **q**uit command again, **ed** will let you exit. If you are using **ex**, however, you will not be able to exit until you either save the buffer to a disk file or enter **q**uit! (or simply **q!**).

To further verify that two different versions of **appeal** now exist, use the **cat** command to examine the contents of the files **appeal** and **appeal2**.

```
$cat appeal
Right now is the time
for all good citizens
to come to the aid
of their country.
$cat appeal2
Right now is the time
for all good citizens
whose skills are needed
in the peace effort
to come to the aid
of their country.
$
```

The **ex** command recognizes another form of the write command that writes the contents of the buffer to the end of the file you specify. The format for this version of the write command is

$$\mathbf{w}>>filename$$

Using this version of write means that even if *filename* exists, it will not be overwritten by the write request.

The list Command: Displaying Control Characters

The list command is a variation of the print command that displays not only text characters, but also nonprinting characters like control characters. Like the print command, the list command can be used as a parameter suffix for many other commands.

One use for list would be to locate and display nonprinting characters that were inserted into your edit buffer inadvertently as you were editing a file. After pinpointing the line or lines containing the control characters, you could remove them in one of two ways: by changing the entire line containing the characters or by deleting the individual control characters with the substitute command. We shall demonstrate the latter technique in a moment.

Before we put list to work, you should note that **ed** and **ex** will display control characters and other nonprinting characters differently. The **ed** editor displays nonprinting characters either with a backslash (\ ) preceding the octal value of the character (the numerical value of the character using the base 8, or octal, number system) or by a special symbol. (You may look up the octal value of any character in the ASCII character chart provided in Appendix E.) The **ex** editor displays control characters as a circumflex (^) followed by the printing character. For instance, a tab character, which is generated by a CTRL-I, is displayed as "^I", and the nonprinting ASCII delete character (octal value 177) is displayed as "^?". When you use list with **ex**, the end of each text line is marked with a dollar sign ($) and lines longer than 72 characters are folded into two or more lines.

Here are some examples of how the different editors display some of the normally invisible characters when you use list:

ASCII Character	Octal Value	Representation	
		ed	ex
Tab	011	→	^I
Backspace	008	←-	^H
Bell	007	\07	^G
Form feed	014	\14	^L

Note that all control characters except tabs are normally displayed by **ex's** print command anyway.

In our first example of list, we will purposely enter some nonprinting control characters into your edit buffer and then display them with list. First invoke your line editor to create a file named **testlistcmd**. If you are using a recent version of **ed**, enable your command mode prompt in the usual fashion.

$ ed testlistcmd	**% ex testlistcmd**
?testlistcmd	"testlistcmd" [New file]
P	:
*	

Then enter text entry mode with the **append** command and type in the text shown in the following example. Enter the control characters by holding down the CTRL key and pressing the appropriate letter key. The control characters themselves are shown in square brackets, indicating that they do not actually appear on the screen at this point. If your UNIX erase character has been reassigned to ^H, you will need to precede the backspace character by a backslash (\ ) in order to turn off its special interpretation by the kernel and enable the editor program to insert it in the edit buffer. Finally, return to command mode by typing a period as the first and only character on a new line followed immediately by RETURN.

*a	**:a**
tab: [^I]	**tab: [^I]**
bell: [^G]	**bell: [^G]**
form feed: [^L]	**form feed: [^L]**
backspace \[^H]	**backspace \[^H]**
.	.
*	:

There may be no colon after the word **backspace** because the backspace character may have erased the colon. This is usually the case with CRT video terminals since a backspace causes the cursor to back up, erasing the character underneath.

Now let's display the edit buffer with the print command. Notice that the "^G" and "^L" are displayed by **ex** anyway, but no control characters are visible with **ed**.

```
*1,$p                              :%
tab:                               tab:
bell:                              bell:^G
form feed:                         form feed:^L
backspace:                         backspace:
*                                  :
```

To get the editors to display the remaining control characters, let's use the list command, typing 1,$l for **ed** or %l for **ex** and RETURN. Note the dollar signs displayed at the end of each line by **ex**:

```
*1,$l                              :%l
tab:>                              tab:^I$
bell: \07                          bell:^G$
form feed: \14                     form feed:^L$
backspace:<                        backspace:^H$
*                                  :
```

Video display terminals will not display the dash portion of the arrows for tab (→) or backspace (←) in **ed** for the following reason. What **ed** actually outputs is a dash followed by a backspace code and then the appropriate arrow. The backspace causes the cursor in most CRT displays to back up and erase the dash; thus only the tip of the arrow remains. If you have a hard-copy terminal, you will see the arrows.

Once you enter the list command, **ex** will continue to display all characters this way until you type a print command explicitly. In other words, if next time you enter %, for example, to display the entire buffer, all characters will be displayed as if %l has been entered. You would have to enter %p to reset the display mode to the default situation.

Now let's see how to use the substitute command to delete an unwanted control character. If you can enter the control character from the keyboard, indicate it on the *old pattern* side and replace it with nothing on the *new pattern* side. For example, enter /^I/l to locate the line containing the tab (^I) character. Then enter the substitution command itself in the third line here:

```
*/[^I]/l                           :/[^I]
tab:>                              tab:^I$
*s///l                             :s///l
tab:                               tab:$
*                                  :
```

The command **s///l** for **ed** (**s//** for **ex**) substitutes nothing for the tab character, which is the pattern remembered from the last search request. Substituting nothing for the tab character deletes the tab character.

Under some circumstances, the control character you type may not reach your editor program. If you cannot enter the control character from your keyboard, you may always use the period (.) metacharacter to stand for the position of the control character in the old pattern side of the substitute command. For instance, to delete the ^G, enter **2s/.$//l** for **ed** or **2s/.$/** for **ex**:

```
*2s/.$//l                    :2s/.$/
bell:                        bell:$
*                            :
```

Finally, exit the editor without saving the buffer's contents in order to erase the material we have entered during our practice with list. Type **q** twice for **ed** or **q!** for **ex**.

This is the end of Session 9. Unless you wish to continue with the next session, in which we extend our study of **ed** and **ex**, log off your UNIX system from your login shell by typing the end-of-file code (the default is ^D) or by entering **logout** from the C Shell if the **ignoreeof** variable is in effect.

SESSION 10

In the last session, we focused on various editing processes: that is, on ways of changing text in the edit buffer. In this session we move outside the buffer to focus on a different kind of editor operation: namely, methods of reading and writing text between the edit buffer and disk storage.

Here is an overview of this session: First you will learn about the file recovery features of the Berkeley ex editor which allow you to recover a file, if the system crashes or you log out by mistake before you saved the buffer's contents to disk. You will also learn to invoke either the ed or the ex editor without specifying a filename, but that you must specify a name in order to save the buffer's contents to disk.

Next, we explain a technique for editing several files successively in one session without leaving the line editor. In addition, the ex editor allows you to specify all the files you wish to edit on the command line when ex is first invoked. You will also learn about the remembered filename and how to use the file command to display or change it.

The next group of topics in this session concern cutting and pasting text between files. With the ex and ed editors, you can write out certain parts of the buffer and then later read them in, perhaps after they've been edited separately, to different places in the buffer.

Finally, you will learn about ex editing options, which may be used to change your editing environment. For instance, you can disable ex's special interpretation *of metacharacters, enable line numbering while the buffer's contents are being displayed, disable wraparound scan during context pattern searches, and much more. These options are actually variables recognized by the **ex** editor. They act like shell variables because they control the overall behavior of the editor program just as shell variables control the behavior of the shell program.*

Recovering From Hangups and Crashes

So far, when you have invoked a UNIX line editor to create and edit a file, you used the following command line format for **ed**:

$$\text{\$ \textbf{ed} } filename$$

And you used the same command line format for **ex**:

$$\text{\% \textbf{ex} } filename$$

If *filename* doesn't already exist, it will be created when the buffer's contents are written to disk. If *filename* exists, its contents will be read into the edit buffer and the current line will be set to the last line of the file.

The **ex** editor can often recover the majority of your buffer's contents even if you get logged out by mistake (that is, your editor program is terminated by a hangup signal) or if your UNIX system crashes (that is, comes down unexpectedly) before you've had a chance to save your edit buffer to disk. If the disk copy of your edit buffer is not as up to date as your edit buffer's contents, **ex** will attempt to preserve your edit buffer. This is possible because the buffer is actually a file on disk (usually in the /tmp directory) instead of a memory image.

When you log in again, you should be able to recover most of the buffer's contents. Some UNIX implementations may inform you by electronic mail that a file you were editing with **ex** is recoverable. You may resume editing the saved file if you invoke **ex** using the recover (−r) option. To do this, first change to the same directory in which you were editing your file and use the command line format

$$\text{\$ \textbf{ex} } -\textbf{r} \, filename$$

replacing *filename* with the name of the file you were editing. This will recover most of the file except perhaps the last few lines you added or changed. You should check the recovered buffer and if it appears to be intact, you should update your permanent disk copy.

Invoking **ex** with the −**r** option will also cause the **ex** editor to list most of the files you may recover. If the editor program was terminated by a hangup signal, however, the file you were editing may not be reported in this way, even though you may still be able to recover it.

Invoking the Line Editors Without Specifying Filenames

You may associate the contents of the edit buffer with whatever filename you choose. The buffer's contents are, in fact, quite separate from any particular disk file until you make the connection through a naming operation: that is, until you specify a filename. In the following sections we will show you some techniques for relating the contents of the buffer to different files.

One consequence of the buffer's independence of any particular disk file is that you don't have to specify a filename when you first call up **ed** or **ex**. You only need to do this before you quit (exit the editor program). In other words, you must specify a filename with the write command before you quit if you didn't specify one when you began the session—unless, of course, you do not wish to save the buffer's contents.

As an example, let's invoke **ed** or **ex** without a filename. If you are using a newer version of **ed** that can display a prompt, enter a capital **P** to turn on the command mode prompt. In addition, newer versions of **ed** have a help mode that you may enable by entering a capital **H**. You should see an asterisk prompt (∗) for **ed** and a colon prompt (:) for **ex**.

Now enter text entry mode with the append command and add the text **This is the time** on the first line and **to get on the UNIX bandwagon.** on the second line. Then exit text entry mode and return to command mode by typing a period as the only character on the next line followed by RETURN. Now attempt to write the buffer contents to disk by entering **w**. The error message you will receive indicates that you haven't associated the buffer's contents with the filename yet.

*a	:a
This is the time	This is the time
to get on the UNIX bandwagon.	to get on the UNIX bandwagon.
.	.
*w	:w
?	No current filename
illegal or missing filename	:▒
* ▒	

Now let's write the buffer's contents to disk with the filename **unixappeal**. Use the form of the editor write command introduced at the end of the last session:

> w *filename*

Replace *filename* by **unixappeal**:

*w unixappeal	:w unixappeal
47	"unixappeal" [New file] 2 lines, 47 characters
* ▒	·:▒

Now the buffer's contents are associated with the filename **unixappeal**. This filename is also known as the *current* or *remembered filename* since the editors remember and will use this filename for all subsequent operations involving reading and writing of files between the edit buffer and disk until a different filename is specified.

The enter or edit Command: Editing Several Files in One Session

If you wish to edit several files in one session, you can use a combination of the enter and write commands to enter (read in) and save (write out) files between the edit buffer and the disk without leaving the editor. Notice that the enter command is also known as the edit command.

Now that we've saved the contents of the edit buffer to disk, let's use the enter command to begin editing a completely new file without leaving the editor. The command line format for using the enter command to read in *filename* is simply

> e *filename*

where *filename* may or may not already exist. You may use enter whether or not the editor was originally invoked with a filename argument. When you enter **e** *filename*, in effect, the buffer is cleared and the remembered or current file becomes *filename*. If *filename* exists, it is read into the buffer; if not, the editors issue the warning messages indicating that the file will be created later. For **ed** the message is "cannot open input file", and for **ex** the message is "*filename* [New file]". Finally, the current line will be set to the last line read into the buffer, although **ex** allows the following alternative format:

$$e +n \; filename$$

Here the current line is set to line number n.

Now enter **e appeal** for either editor and the number of characters read into the buffer (that is, the number of characters in **appeal** will be displayed):

*e appeal	:e appeal
81	"appeal" 4 lines, 81 characters
* ▓	: ▓

Now the current line is set to the last line read into the buffer. The filename **appeal** will be remembered by the editor as a default filename for any subsequent file read, write, or enter commands. The contents of the edit buffer have been overwritten by the contents that were previously in the buffer, **unixappeal**.

If you do not save the contents of the edit buffer after it has been changed and you then specify the enter command, the line editors will issue an error message. To illustrate, let's change the buffer contents slightly and issue another enter command request.

To try this now, let's just delete the last line and then verify by displaying the entire buffer as shown in the following example. Then type **e** and note the warning messages. You do not need to indicate a filename after the **e** command letter since your intention is to read the file with the remembered filename, **appeal**.

*$dp	:$d
to come to the aid	to come to the aid
*1,$p	:%
Right now is the time	Right now is the time
for all good citizens	for all good citizens
to come to the aid	to come to the aid
*e	:e

?   No write since last change (:edit! overrides)
warning: expecting 'w'   : ▓

* ▓

The **ed** editor displays a question mark and prints the message "warning: expecting 'w'" on the next line to signify that it expects a write operation before an enter command because the contents of the buffer were changed and no save operation was performed. If you specify the enter command a second time, however, **ed** will allow the buffer contents to be overwritten.

The second enter command will replace the buffer's contents with the contents of the remembered filename, **appeal**. Under the same circumstances, **ex** will also display an error message. It will display "No write since last change..." and "edit! overrides", but it will refuse to acknowledge your enter command request until you change the form of the enter command to either edit! or simply **e!**, as shown here:

*e   :e!
81   "appeal" 4 lines, 81 characters

* ▓   : ▓

Now exit the editor to prepare for the next few sections. Don't bother saving the buffer. Simply type **q** twice for **ed** or **q!** for **ex**.

The next Command:
Editing More Than One File With ex

The **ex** editor provides an even easier way to edit one file after another without leaving the editor program. This editor allows you to specify more than one filename on its invocation command line. The invocation command line format is simply

$$\% \textbf{ex} \ [\ \mathit{filename...} \ ]$$

where one or more files (denoted by *filename...*) are indicated when you invoke **ex**. The editor places the filenames in a queue for later editing. After you press RETURN, the first file is read into the buffer. Then when you want to edit the next file, you can use the next command to call it into the edit buffer.

As an example, if you have access to **ex**, invoke this editor to edit **appeal** and then **poem**. (If you don't have **ex**, read this discussion anyway to be sure that you understand the principles involved.) First type the letters shown in boldface, and note that although **ex** displays the message "2 files to edit", only the first file, **appeal**, is read into the edit buffer.

```
% ex appeal poem
2 files to edit
"appeal" 4 lines, 81 characters
:
```

The second message, indicating the number of lines and characters in **appeal**, tells us that **appeal** is now in the buffer awaiting any editing changes we might wish to make.

At this point if you decide to exit the editor by typing **quit**, you'd get a warning message, such as

```
:q
1 more file to edit
:
```

In this case you would either enter **n** to edit the next file or **quit!** or **q!** to force **ex** to allow you to exit.

Instead of either exiting the editor or editing a new file at this point, however, let's change the buffer's contents by deleting the last line. Verify with **%**:

```
:$d
to come to the aid
:%
Right now is the time
for all good citizens
to come to the aid
:
```

Now that you have finished editing this first file, let's use the **next** command to read the next file into the buffer. Enter **n** as shown here:

```
:n
No write since last change (next! overrides)
:
```

As you can see, the editor realized that you had changed the buffer without saving it to disk before requesting the next file to be read into the buffer. Since the next file that you call into the buffer will overwrite **appeal**'s contents, you should update the disk copy if you wish to save the most recent version of **appeal**. Otherwise, you must specify the alternate form of the next command, **next!** (or simply **n!**) to force the next file, **poem**, to be read into the buffer. Let's use the latter approach now and purposely overwrite the buffer's current contents with the contents of the disk file **poem**.

```
:n!
"poem" 4 lines, 62 characters
:%
Roses are Red
Violets are Blue
Sugar is Sweet
And so are You.
:
```

We used % here to verify that **poem** did indeed overwrite **appeal** and now constitutes the current contents of the buffer. The current filename — the one remembered by **ex** — is now **poem**.

Now let's enter the next command again to see what happens:

```
:n
No more files to edit
:
```

As might be expected, **ex** complained that there are no further files to edit. Now enter **args** to display the filenames in the editing list:

```
:args
appeal [poem]
:
```

You can use **args** from **ex**'s command mode if you need to find out what files were specified on the **ex** command line. The name of the current file will be enclosed in brackets. In this case, the current or remembered filename is, of course, **poem**.

At this point you have a number of options. You could stay in the editor program and edit another file using the enter command, or you could simply exit. You could begin editing the original list of files over again by entering **rew** (for **rewind**). Or you could type the next command directive again followed by one or more filenames. These filenames will become the new list of files to be edited; the old list will be discarded.

Let's exit **ex** now in order to prepare for the next section.

The file Command: Displaying or Changing the Current File

Earlier in this session we explained that the buffer's contents may or may not be associated with a filename, and furthermore that the associated filename may be easily changed using the enter or next command (next can only be used with **ex**, of course). Because of the fluid relations between edit buffer and files permitted by the UNIX editors, you may sometimes lose track of what the current or remembered filename is. In this situation, you can display the current or remembered filename for either editor by using the file command.

As an example, invoke either editor without a filename, enable the prompt (for **ed**) by entering **P**, and then enter **f** (for file) to display the current filename:

```
$ ed                    % ex
P                       :f
*f                      No file line 0 of 0 --0%--
                        : ▓

*
```

Here **ed** simply displays a blank line to indicate that there is no current filename. The **ex** command is more informative, displaying the message "No file line 0 of 0 --0%--", which tells us that there is no current file. The message "line 0 of 0" means, in effect, "the current line is 0 (the first zero) out of a total number of lines (also zero)." The percentage of the buffer's contents that your current line represents is denoted by the last part of the message: "--0%--" in this case.

In addition to determining the current filename, the file command allows you to change the current or remembered filename. The command line format is simply

f *filename*

Here *filename* will become the new current filename. All subsequent read, write, or enter operations would assume this filename unless you indicate a different one when specifying the operation.

Picking up our example where we left off, let's set the current filename to **appeal** by entering **f appeal**; both editors will display the new current filename when you reset it in this manner. In addition, **ex** tells us that the file is "Not edited" since no request to read the contents of **appeal** into the buffer has yet been made. Now issue an enter command, and note that the contents of **appeal** are read in from the disk without your having to use the longer form **e appeal**. Now enter **f** again to see what the response is:

*f appeal	:f appeal
appeal	"appeal" [Not edited] line 0 of 0 --0%--
*e	:e
81	"appeal" 4 lines, 81 characters
*f	:f
appeal	"appeal" line 4 of 4 --100%--
* ▓	: ▓

The "Not edited" message disappears and the display shows that the current line is 4, the last line in the buffer.

The **ex** editor recognizes the shorthand % for the current filename in operations involving read, write, enter, and some other commands that will be discussed later. (The editor will not confuse % used in this context with its use as shorthand for **1,$p**). One application for this abbreviation might be to create a backup version of the buffer's contents without retyping the current filename. For instance, let's create a backup copy of the buffer and name it **appeal.bak** by simply entering w %.bak (for **ex** only):

:w %.bak
"appeal.bak" [New file] 4 lines, 81 characters
: ▓

Note that the remembered filename is still **appeal** even though we specified a write operation to **appeal.bak**.

Recall that at the end of the last session, you wrote the buffer's contents to a file different from the one you began editing from. This technique is useful for saving different versions of the edit buffer for later inspection or manipulation. The file command can help automate this process by enabling you to change the current filename ahead of time so that you simply have to type **w** whenever you wish to save the buffer's contents to the new file.

To practice this procedure, let's change the buffer's contents by deleting the last line. Now when you enter **f**, the current filename and the modified status of the buffer's contents are reported.

*$dp	**:$d**
to come to the aid	to come to the aid
*f	**:f**
appeal	"appeal" [Modified] line 3 of 3 --100%--
* ▨	: ▨

Now let's change the current filename to **appeal3** by entering **f appeal3**. Note that **ex** considers **appeal3** "Not edited" and the buffer (former contents of **appeal**) "Modified".

*f appeal3	**:f appeal3**
appeal3	"appeal3" [Not edited][Modified] line 3 of 3 --100%--
* ▨	: ▨

Now if you specify an operation involving read, write, or enter commands without indicating another filename, the current filename, **appeal3**, will be assumed. For instance, enter **w** to save the buffer's contents to the disk in the file **appeal3**:

*w	**:w**
63	"appeal3" [New file] 3 lines, 63 characters
* ▨	: ▨

Alternatively, you could have left the current filename as **appeal** and have used **w appeal3** to write the buffer to the disk file **appeal3**. The first approach saves time, however, and also means that you don't have to remember what disk file you'd like to update with the buffer's contents, since you only have to type **w** after resetting the current filename.

Before proceeding to the next section, let's put the line we just deleted back into the buffer. For the editors that have a general **undo** command, simply enter **u**. If you are using an old version of **ed** you need to get into text entry mode with **$a** and enter **of their country**. Leave text entry mode and return to command mode by typing a period as the first and only character on the line followed immediately by RETURN.

Before we move on to the next topic, make sure you have a clear sense of the difference between the enter and file commands. The file command just changes the identity of the current filename, but doesn't alter the buffer's contents. The enter command, on the other hand, causes the buffer's contents to be overwritten — either with the contents from the current file (if it exists on disk and the **e** form of the command is used) or with the contents of the file specified in the enter command line. In the latter case, the current filename is reset to the filename specified.

Executing System Commands From Within the Editors

You may execute UNIX system commands without leaving the editor by typing an exclamation mark (!) and then the shell command line. This feature is sometimes called the *shell escape feature*. The editor command line format is

! command line

where *command line* is the same shell command line you'd type if you were interacting with the shell directly. The editor spawns a subshell to execute the command. Any command output destined for your terminal will be displayed, followed by an exclamation mark on the next line to indicate the end of command output. You are then back in command mode of your editor program.

For instance, to display your current directory, enter !ls:

```
*!ls
Mail
appeal
appeal.bak
appeal2
appeal3
poem
unixappeal
!
:
```

```
:!ls
[No write since last change]
Mail
appeal
appeal.bak
appeal2
appeal3
poem
unixappeal
!
:
```

The message "[No write since last change]" issued by **ex** is warning you that the buffer's contents have been updated more recently than the disk copy of the current file. This may be important to know if you intend to use a shell command to manipulate the current file on disk. In this case, you may wish to update the disk copy before issuing the shell command that uses the disk copy.

As another example, let's use the shell escape feature to examine the contents of the disk copy of the current file without leaving the editor. This might be useful, for instance, to check what is on the disk copy of a file before writing the buffer's

contents to it and thus avoid overwriting something you may wish to save. For the
ed editor, enter **!cat appeal3**. With **ex** you may use the **%** shorthand for the current
file, which is **appeal3**, so that you would enter **!cat %**:

```
*!cat appeal3                        :!cat %
Right now is the time                !cat appeal3
for all good citizens                Right now is the time
to come to the aid                   for all good citizens
!                                    to come to the aid
*                                    !

                                     :
```

Using **cat appeal3** with **ex** will, of course, work as well.

Now examine the buffer's contents and see that they are more up to date. Note
that here the percent sign (%) is an abbreviation for **1,$p**, not the current filename:

```
*1,$p                                :%
Right now is the time                Right now is the time
for all good citizens                for all good citizens
to come to the aid                   to come to the aid
of their country.                    of their country.
*                                    :
```

Now update the disk copy of the current filename and verify the operation by
displaying the contents of the disk copy directly from inside the editor:

```
*w                                   :w
81                                   "appeal3" 4 lines, 81 characters
*!cat appeal3                        :!cat %
Right now is the time                !cat appeal3
for all good citizens                Right now is the time
to come to the aid                   for all good citizens
of their country.                    to come to the aid
*                                    of their country.

                                     :
```

You may execute any UNIX command using the shell escape feature. In fact,
you could invoke another instance of your editor program to create or change a

file. After you exit from the new instance of the editor program, you will be returned to the first editor program. This "nested editing" technique lets you keep your current editing environment (that is, the current filename, the current line, and so on) while you edit a different file.

The **ex** editor program recognizes three other variations of shell escape commands. First, a **shell** command (abbreviated as **sh**) may be used to start up a new shell program. This **shell** escape command would be useful if you needed to interact with a shell for more than a few commands. The subshell you invoke from within the editor with the **sh** command will generally be of the same type as the shell within which you invoked the line editor. For example:

```
:sh
% ls
Mail
appeal
appeal.bak
appeal2
appeal3
poem
% ▓
```

Because we entered **ex** from the C Shell, **sh** caused another instance of the C Shell to be invoked.

To exit from this shell, you would type a ^D (or **logout** if you are using the C Shell and **ignoreeof** is in effect). You will be returned to the editor at the point where you left off before you entered the **shell** command.

```
% [ ^D ] !
: ▓
```

The ^D will not appear on your terminal, of course, but **ex** does print the exclamation point indicating the end of the **sh** shell escape sequence.

Another useful shell escape command uses this command line format:

line-address range **w** !*command line*

Here lines from the buffer in *line address range* are "written" to the standard input of the first command in *command line*. Note that there must be whitespace between the **w** command letter and the exclamation mark.

As an example, enter **%w** **!pr** to send the entire buffer to the **pr** command, which paginates the listing and supplies an identifying header, as shown here:

```
:%w !pr
```

```
Nov 1 14:26 1984  Page 1
```

```
Right now is the time
for all good citizens
to come to the aid
of their country.
```

```
...
:
```

The ellipses (...) stand for the blank lines output by **pr** to make a 66-line page. The buffer contents were not changed by this last shell escape command. We verify this here:

```
:%
Right now is the time
for all good citizens
to come to the aid
of their country.
:
```

There is, however, another variation of shell escape that is used when you wish to replace part or all of the buffer's contents by the output from a shell command line. The following command line format

line-address range! *command*

will send the contents of the buffer indicated by *line address range* to the standard input of the first command in *command line*. The resulting standard output from the last command is read back into the buffer and replaces the lines you sent to *command*. While there should be no whitespace between the line address range and the exclamation point, whitespace may be used elsewhere.

As an example, let's replace the buffer by the output of the same **pr** command we used in the last example.

```
:%! pr
!
62 more lines in file after !
:
```

The report "62 more lines ..." is issued by **ex** to indicate that the buffer has been changed by more than a particular number of lines (5 is the default). Now let's examine the buffer:

```
:%

Nov 1 14:28 1984   Page 1

Right now is the time
for all good citizens
to come to the aid
of their country.
...
:
```

Cut and Paste Buffer/File Operations

You may perform "cut and paste" operations to move blocks of text around the edit buffer. In this part of Session 10 you will learn how to write out part of the edit buffer (a text block) to a disk file. You will also learn how to insert the contents of a disk file containing the text block anywhere in the edit buffer. These operations enable you to move blocks of text around the edit buffer using disk files as intermediate repositories.

Of course, you may use the **move** and **copy** (or transpose) commands introduced in the last tutorial session to move text around the buffer. However, if you create an intermediate disk file, you have more options. By creating such an intermediate file, you could edit or manipulate the file's contents with one or more UNIX utilities programs before reinserting the file in the main body of text, which is waiting in the edit buffer.

Let's begin our study of cut and paste operations with a technique for cutting a block of text from a file, changing it, and then reinserting it in the file. Although the example we will give is very simple in comparison with the day-to-day editing tasks you may have, it does serve to illustrate the technique. Moreover, you could use this technique to move different text blocks between several files, if necessary.

Partial Buffer write Operations

You may use the write command to save only a part of the edit buffer in a disk file. The editor command format is

line address range **w** [*filename*]

where the indicated buffer lines in *line address range* are to be written to *filename* or to the current filename, if *filename* is not specified. Note that although you must use whitespace between the **w** command letter and the *filename*, if a filename is specified, whitespace between the *line address range* and the command letter is optional.

As an example, use the write command to single out the two lines that you inserted into **appeal2** in the last session with the change command, and write them to a file to be named **appeal4**. Enter **e! appeal2** for either editor to read the contents of the source file into the buffer. Then enter **3,4w appeal4** to save lines 3 and 4 in the file **appeal4**. Now display the buffer to verify that it was unchanged by the disk write operation. Finally, examine the contents of **appeal4** without leaving the editor by typing **!cat appeal4**.

*e! appeal2	:e! appeal2
125	"appeal2" 6 lines, 125 characters
*3,4w appeal4	:3,4w appeal4
44	"appeal4" [New file] 2 lines, 44 characters
*1,$p	:%
Right now is the time	Right now is the time
for all good citizens	for all good citizens
whose skills are needed	whose skills are needed
in the peace effort	in the peace effort
to come to the aid	to come to the aid
of their country.	of their country.
*!cat appeal4	:!cat appeal4
whose skills are needed	whose skills are needed
in the peace effort	in the peace effort
!	!
*	:

With **ex** you can't display **appeal4** by using the shorthand **!cat%** because the current file is still **appeal2**, not **appeal4**.

To prepare for the next section, cut out (delete) these same lines with the command 3,4dp for **ed** or 3,4d for **ex** and verify by displaying the entire buffer:

*3,4dp	**:3,4d**
to come to the aid	to come to the aid
*1,$p	**:%**
Right now is the time	Right now is the time
for all good citizens	for all good citizens
to come to the aid	to come to the aid
of their country.	of their country.
* ▓	: ▓

File read Operations

The read command enables you to read in text from a disk file after any line in the buffer without affecting the text alread in the buffer. By contrast, when you use the enter (or edit) command to read in text from a file, the previous contents of the buffer are completely overwritten.

The editor command line format is

$$[\; line \; address \;] \; r \; [\; filename \;]$$

where the contents of *filename* will be placed after the indicated *line address* (or line number). If you do not specify *filename,* the contents of the current (or remembered) file will be read in. If no line number is specified with the read request, **ed** will place the text at the end of the buffer, whereas **ex** will place the text read from *filename* (or the current file) after the current line.

For our next example, let's begin by first changing the contents of the disk file **appeal4** — that is, the two lines which we cut out of **appeal2** in the last section. One way to do this without disturbing the present buffer contents would be to invoke another instance of the editor using a shell escape. To do this now, enter !ed appeal4 or !ex appeal4.

*!ed appeal4	**:!ex appeal4**
44	"appeal4" 2 lines, 44 characters
*1,$p	**:%**
whose skills are needed	whose skills are needed
in the peace effort	in the peace effort

```
*/peace/s//war/p              :/peace/s//war
in the war effort             in the war effort
*1,$p                         :%
whose skills are needed       whose skills are needed
in the war effort             in the war effort
*w                            :w
42                            "appeal4" 2 lines, 42 characters
*q                            :q
!                             !
*                             :
```

Now paste in (read) the contents of **appeal4** into the buffer's current contents (still **appeal2**). Let's put **appeal4** after the line containing "citizens" by entering /**citizens**/**r appeal4** for either editor. Then display the entire buffer:

```
*/citizens/r appeal4          :/citizens/r appeal4
42                            "appeal4" 2 lines, 42 characters
*1,$p                         :%
Right now is the time         Right now is the time
for all good citizens         for all good citizens
whose skills are needed       whose skills are needed
in the war effort             in the war effort
to come to the aid            to come to the aid
of their country.             of their country.
*                             :
```

Here the *line address* for the read command was indicated by a context search pattern, "/citizens/", instead of a line number. You could have specified **2r appeal4** to obtain the same result in this case.

Editing Options for ex

Just as you may customize the operation of your shell by defining variables, you may customize the overall operation of your **ex** editor by setting or unsetting editor options. The options can be set (enabled) and unset (disabled) or, in some cases, assigned a value by the **set** command, which is built into the editor. As with other editor commands, you must invoke the **set** command from command mode.

There are three kinds of editor options:

* *Numeric options*, which take a numerical value.
* *String options*, which take a string value.
* *Toggle options*, which can be enabled and disabled.

You can assign a value to a numeric or string option using the following **set** command syntax:

:**set** *option=value*

There should be no whitespace around the assignment operator, the equal sign (=).

The toggle options can be set (enabled, turned on) or unset (disabled, turned off) by the command forms:

:**set** *option*
:**set** **no***option*

Table 5-2 lists many useful editor options with their full names, abbreviations, if any exist, their default values, and a brief description of how they modify the operation of **ex**. Note that some of the default values we indicate in the table may be different in your editing environment.

Table 5-2.   *Useful Editing Options for the ex Editor*

Name(abbrev)	Default	Effect on ex
autoprint(ap)	ap	Causes the current line to be displayed after each delete, copy, join, move, substitute, or undo command. ex suppresses autoprint in global operations.
beautify(bf)	nobf	All control characters except tab, new line and form feed are prevented from being input into the edit buffer while you are in text entry mode. They are still recognized in command mode.
errorbells(eb)	noeb	Causes error messages to be preceded by ringing of the terminal bell.
ignorecase(ic)	noic	All uppercase characters are treated as if they were lowercase in regular expressions used for matching.

Table 5-2. *Useful Editing Options for the* ex *Editor (continued)*

Name (abbrev)	Default	Effect on ex
list	**nolist**	Show tabs as ^I and mark the end of lines with a $.
magic	**magic**	When **magic** is set, all metacharacters are recognized by the editor. You may remove the special meaning of a metacharacter by preceding it with a backslash. When **nomagic** is set, only the ^ and $ are recognized as being special. However, even if **nomagic** is set, you may reestablish the special meaning of a metacharacter by preceding it with a backslash (\ ).
number(nu)	**nonu**	Prefix the display of each line by its line number.
prompt	**prompt**	The editor uses a prompt in command mode.
report	**5**	Provide feedback for commands which modify more than the specified number of lines (5 lines is default). This helps detect large, undesirable changes while they may still be reversed by **undo**.
terse	**noterse**	Use shorter error messages. Useful for the experienced user.
warn	**warn**	Warn user with the message "No write since last change," if the current file has not been updated more recently than the buffer when a shell command is requested.
wrapscan(ws)	**ws**	Wrap around the end of the buffer when locating text.
writeany(wa)	**nowa**	Allow a write operation to any disk file allowed by permission settings.

You may list all the options that have been changed from their default values by entering **set**. If you wish to determine the value of a particular option, regardless of whether it has been changed from the default value, enter **set** *option*?, replacing *option* with the actual option name. The question mark is only required for toggle options (to prevent the editor from interpreting the request as a request to set or enable the option). You may display the current setting of all possible options by entering **set all**.

We have reproduced a typical display of all possible options in the following screen example. Some of the options listed here are only relevant for the visual editor, **vi**, which we will study in Session 11:

```
:set all
noautoindent          open                        noslowopen
autoprint             nooptimize                  tabstop=8
noautowrite           paragraphs=IPLPPPQPP LIbp   taglength=0
nobeautify            prompt                      ttytype=adm3a
directory=/tmp        noreadonly                  term=adm3a
noerrorbells          noredraw                    noterse
hardtabs=8            report=5                    warn
noignorecase          scroll=8                    window=8
nolisp                sectins=NHSHH HU            wrapscan
nolist                shell=/bin/sh               wrapmargin=0
magic                 shiftwidth=8                nowriteany
nonumber              noshowmatch
:
```

You may place more than one option argument on the same **set** command line. Simply separate each argument from the next by whitespace. You may also abbreviate **set** to **se**, as shown:

:se bf eb report=10 terse nows

In this example the user enables the **beautify** option (**bf**), turns on **errorbells** (**eb**), sets **terse**, and unsets the **wrapscan** option (**nows**). The **report** option is also set to 10 (default 5). Type this command line and then enter **set** without any arguments to display all editor options that have been changed from their default settings.

```
:se bf eb report=10 terse nows
:set
beautify errorbells report=10 slowopen term=du terse nowrapscan
:
```

The options **slowopen** and **term=du** are relevant to the visual editing mode and will be described in the next tutorial session.

Before leaving this session, exit the editor and then remove the extra files you created by entering **rm appeal? appeal.bak unixappeal**, and then use **ls** to verify the fact that these files have been removed.

The ex Editor Startup File: .exrc

Options changed by the **set** command are only in effect while you are in the editing program. If you wish to set certain options whenever you use the editor, you may create a list of **set** directives and place them in a file named **.exrc** in your home directory. Any commands in the **.exrc** file will be executed when the editor, either **ex** or **vi**, is invoked.

Here we show a sample **.exrc** file that will set or unset the same options shown in the last example:

```
$ cd
$ cat .exrc
se bf eb report=10 terse nows
$
```

At this point you have completed your introduction to the UNIX line-oriented editors. Even though we did not have the space to document every aspect of these editors, you should now be able to create and edit text files efficiently. You have a solid foundation for further instruction from your UNIX system documentation.

SESSION 11

Session 11 teaches you how to use the Berkeley vi screen-oriented editor for creating, changing, and storing text documents.

What Is vi

The visual editor or **vi** (pronounced v-eye) displays a window of text. The window shows a certain portion of the edit buffer, and you may position the window to view any part of the buffer.

Changes to the text take place at the cursor position. The editor allows you to move the cursor around in the edit buffer window easily. For instance, the cursor may be moved forward or backward a character, a word, a sentence, or a paragraph at a time or it may be moved vertically, up, or down the page.

The visual editing commands have a uniform and consistent structure that makes the commands easier to learn. Many operations — for example, an operation in which you would change or delete text — may be combined in a natural way with the cursor motion directives to form a combined command. Thus, you may change or delete text in terms of characters, words, sentences, and paragraphs. This regularity in combining operations to form commands helps make them easier to remember and use effectively.

Editor options are available for **vi**. These options enable you to customize your visual editing environment just as you customized **ex**'s line-editing environment. For instance, you may adjust the size of your display window to accommodate different data transfer rates between the terminal and the central computer. Generally the faster the communication speed, the more quickly the window can be updated, with the result that you may use a larger window more efficiently.

The **vi** program needs to know the name of your type of terminal before you can use its full screen-editing capabilities. This name is used by **vi** to access the entry for your terminal in the **/etc/termcap** database file. Thus, your system also needs to have this file on-line before you can use the full capabilities of **vi**.

The **termcap** file is a database describing the capabilities and codes needed to control a large number of display terminals. For instance, the entries in this file tell **vi** what codes to send your terminal in order to address the cursor (that is, move to a particular location on the screen), delete a line, and so forth. If there is no system administrator (whose job it is to set up your editing environment), see the section entitled "Telling UNIX Software Your Terminal Type" in Appendix C, "Interacting With Your UNIX System."

The Editing Modes of ex and vi

The **vi** and **ex** editors are actually the same program. This program may act as either a visual or a line editor depending on the name used to invoke it (**ex** invokes the program as a line editor and **vi** as a screen editor). Furthermore, this editor program can behave in four fundamentally different ways, known as *modes*.

The line-oriented and screen-oriented states of the **ex/vi** program each constitute a mode, and each of these states or modes may be further divided into a command and text entry mode. The result is four basic modes: line-oriented command mode, line-oriented text entry mode, visual-oriented command mode, and visual-oriented text entry mode.

Like **ed** and **ex**, **vi** is in command mode when you first invoke it. Recall that in command mode, whatever you type will be interpreted as an editing command instead of being entered into the edit buffer. The visual editor's commands are sometimes similar but generally different from line-editing commands. If you wish to enter or change text in the edit buffer, you must change to **vi**'s text entry mode by specifying the append, insert, change, open, or substitute command. You may return to command mode from text entry mode at any time by typing either an ASCII escape character, which we represent as ESC, or by typing your interrupt code. The interrupt signal stops whatever the editor is doing and returns **vi** to command mode.

It is relatively easy to change from one of the four **ex/vi** modes to another. For instance, you may enter visual command mode from line editor command mode by entering **vi**; and you may change to line editor command mode from visual command mode by typing a capital **Q** (it is not necessary to press RETURN). You can also have access to the powerful **ex** command set as a temporary escape from the visual command mode, so that you don't have to actually change over to the line-editing state, execute a **ex** command, and then change back to the visual state. All you have to do is type a colon (:) to get into the command mode of **ex** temporarily. Enter your **ex** command, and when the command has been executed, you will be returned to **vi**'s command mode.

Figure 5-1 illustrates the four basic modes and the commands used to change between them schematically.

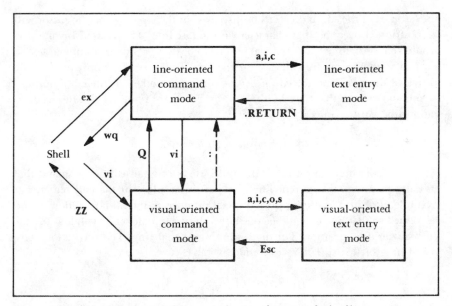

Figure 5-1. *The four basic editing modes for the ex and vi editors*

Invoking vi From the Shell

You may invoke **vi** from the shell level by entering

$ **vi** [*filename...*]

The ellipses indicate that more than one file may be specified. If the file doesn't already exist, it will be created when the edit buffer is written to disk. If the file exists, it will be read into the edit buffer, the terminal screen will be cleared, and the window will be set to display the first part of the file (in other words, the first part of the edit buffer). The cursor will be positioned on the first character of the first line of the window.

As with **ex**, if you specify more than one filename, the first file will be read into the edit buffer for display. After you finish editing the first file and save it, enter **:n** to edit the next file. Of course, the **args** and file commands discussed in Session 10 are easily accessible as line-editing command mode commands.

You may also invoke **vi** with the plus (or forward) option (+) to change the initial position of the display window. If you specify

$ **vi** + [*filename...*]

the last part of the edit buffer will be displayed in the window and the cursor will be positioned over the first character on the last line. This way of invoking **vi** would be useful, for example, if you wished to begin appending additional text to the end of an existing file. But if more than one file is specified, only the first file is treated this way, and the editor begins editing the others at their beginning.

You may request that the editor reposition the cursor immediately after its invocation using this syntax:

$ **vi** +*position* [*filename...*]

The most common reason for doing this is to specify an editor command that initially positions the current line to a particular place in the edit buffer. For example, if *position* were simply a decimal number, n, the initial window would be located so that line n would be positioned in the middle of the window and the cursor would be positioned at the beginning of that line. The invocation command line for this special case would be

$ **vi** +n [*filename...*]

Another common use of this feature would be to specify a search pattern as *position* in order to position the current line to the first line in the buffer containing that pattern. The initial window would be positioned so that the current line would be in the middle of the window and the cursor would be at the beginning of that line. The invocation command line for this special case would appear as follows:

$$\text{\$ vi } +/pattern \text{ [} filename... \text{]}$$

Even if more than one file is specified to be edited, **vi** changes *position* only for the first file.

As with the **ex** editor, you may invoke **vi** for editing one or more recovered files using this syntax:

$$\text{\$ vi } -\text{r } filename...$$

Here you would replace *filename* by the name of the file or files that the system saved when it crashed or when the editor was terminated by a hangup signal. Invoking **vi** in this way will recover most of the file except perhaps the last few lines you added or changed.

If you type **vi** −r from the shell level, the editor will name all the files you may possibly recover after a system crash. Although this command doesn't tell you the names of files recoverable if the editor was terminated by a hangup signal, those files are still recoverable if you can specify their names with the recover (−r) option.

Adjusting Display Window Size

One useful thing to know before using **vi** is how to adjust the size of the display window. The editor always uses the full width of the terminal screen (usually 80 columns) for the display window; thus, this particular window dimension is fixed. Lines of text that contain more than 80 characters will wrap around to the next line. Even though this may seem a little disconcerting, the wrapped text is treated no differently than text on the previous line.

The window length dimension may be adjusted to change the overall display window size. The larger the display window, the longer it takes to update the screen after a change. Thus at a communication rate between your terminal and central computer that is relatively slow, you would want a smaller display window so that it may be updated in a reasonable length of time. Nothing can seem more frustrating than waiting for the screen to update.

The visual editor will set the default (initial) window size according to the communication speed between your terminal and the CPU as follows:

- Slow speeds (600 baud or less): 8 lines of text will be displayed in the window.
- Medium speed (1200 baud): 16 lines will be displayed in the window.

- High speeds (greater than 1200 baud): the full 24 lines will be displayed. Actually only 23 lines of text and 1 line as a status line to show messages and to echo some commands.

You may set the window size to be *n* lines by invoking **vi** like this:

$ **vi** −w*n* [*filename...*]

This is especially useful if you're using a dial-up line.

You may use the **set** command from line editor command mode to change the window size. However, you must be in "permanent" line editor command mode because a temporary escape to this line-editor mode from **vi** is not effective for resetting this parameter.

As an example, let's say you are communicating over a 300-baud phone line and wish the maximum window size to be four lines for even quicker updating of the screen display. From visual command mode enter **Q** in order to enter line editor command mode. Then enter **set window=4**. Finally, return to visual command mode by entering **vi**. Alternatively, you could place this same command in your editor startup file, **.exrc**, if you wish it to be executed automatically when you invoke **ex/vi**.

In the screen examples shown in this book, we use a small window size (eight text lines) to keep the examples short. Thus, our simulation may look slightly different from your display, unless, of course, you use an eight-line window.

Exiting vi

You may exit **vi** and save the contents of your edit buffer to disk in one step by typing **ZZ** (no RETURN necessary) while in visual command mode. The editor will write the contents of the edit buffer to your disk file (if you made any changes to the buffer since the last write) and return you to the shell.

You may also leave the editor by escaping to line-editing mode by entering a colon (:) and **wq** (or simply **:x**). If you wish to abandon any changes you made to the edit buffer, exit via the line-editing mode by entering **:q!**.

vi Editor Command Structure

Almost every character you can type — lower- and uppercase letters, punctuation, and control characters — is a command for **vi**. The distinction between lower- and uppercase letters is important: lower- and uppercase letters generally refer to different commands.

The structure for most **vi** commands is

[*count*] *operator* [*count*] *operand*

The *operator* is the command character specifying the action to be taken, such as **delete** or **change**. The *operand*, in contrast, identifies the object that is to be acted upon. For instance, in the command **r***c*, which replaces the next character by the character *c*, **r** is the replace *operator* and *c* is the *operand* or text object — a character in this case that is to replace the next character after the cursor.

The *count* is a decimal integer that indicates the number of times a command is to be repeated. The *count* may appear before the *operator*, between the *operator* and *operand*, or in both places. If *count* appears both places, the actual repeat count is obtained by multiplying the two individual *count* entries. For instance, you could specify **3dw** to delete the next three words, **d2w** to delete the next two, and **3d2w** to delete the next six words.

Some Special Characters for vi

The ASCII escape character, which we denote as ESC, is used to leave visual text entry mode and return to visual command mode. In addition, you may cancel a partially formed command if you haven't yet pressed RETURN by typing the escape character. If you are unsure of what mode you are in, type the escape character and you should hear the terminal bell ring (if available). Then you will be back in visual command mode. The escape character is generated by pressing the ESC key, which may be called ALT on some keyboards and which is usually located on the upper left-hand side of your terminal's keyboard.

The RETURN key is used to end input for editing commands that take a variable length argument (for example, when you specify the string to be used in a search request).

The interrupt signal may be used to terminate whatever the editor is doing. The editor catches the interrupt and returns to command mode. The interrupt signal is generated by pressing your interrupt character. The default interrupt character is the ASCII delete character, which may be labeled DEL or RUB on your keyboard. Note that your interrupt character may have been reassigned (with **stty**) to some other character, such as ^C.

You may discover your interrupt character using the **stty** command. From your shell, enter **stty**. From visual command mode, use a temporary escape to line-editing command mode and then a shell escape: enter **:!stty**. If you are already in line-editing command mode, simply enter **!stty**. Examine the **stty** command output; if you see an entry such as "intr = ^c", you know that the interrupt character is a ^C. If you don't see an entry for "int" or "intr", the interrupt character is the default, an ASCII delete character.

Moving Around the Screen With *vi*

At this point we are ready to begin actually working with the visual editor. In the next several sections you will learn the basic movement commands for **vi**. First, you will learn how to move the display window around the buffer, and then you will learn how to move the cursor within the display window. Next, you will learn how to move the cursor within a given line of text, and then how to make the cursor jump over words, sentences, and paragraphs of text. Finally, you will learn how to move the cursor vertically within a display window. In combination these basic movement commands enable you to position your cursor anywhere in your edit buffer. Since the editing "action" takes place at the cursor position, you will then be ready to add or modify text anywhere in the edit buffer.

Moving the Display Window

There are a number of commands for moving the window around in the edit buffer. Some of these commands affect the window without changing the cursor position, while others change the cursor position with respect to the window.

The first two commands we will discuss are used to scroll the display window up or down by half a window (or page) length:

- ^D is used for scrolling down half a window. The upper half of the window scrolls up off the screen to be replaced by the original bottom half. Half a window of text lines from farther in the buffer appears in the bottom half of the window.

- ^U is used for scrolling up half a window. The lower half of the window moves off the screen and is replaced by the original top half. Half a window of text from toward the beginning of the buffer comes into view in the upper part of the new window.

These window movements position the cursor so it remains near the beginning of the window.

If you wish to move the window through the edit buffer almost a window length (or page) at a time, use these commands:

- ^F, to move forward
- ^B, to move backward

Figure 5-2 depicts these window movements diagrammatically. The 1 and $ in the figure indicate the first and last line of the edit buffer, respectively.

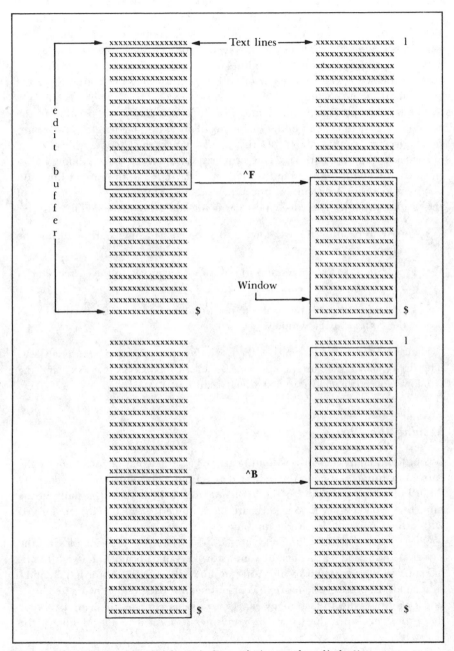

Figure 5-2. *Moving the display window relative to the edit buffer*

You will notice that a couple of lines from the previous window are kept in the new window for continuity. You could use these commands for reading (also known as *paging*) through a file. Thus if you type a ^F, the entire window moves forward (down), so that the last two lines on the old window become the first two lines in the new window. The cursor will be positioned at the beginning of the first line in the new window.

The window movement commands just discussed change the position of the window relative to the edit buffer's contents in absolute page lengths. The z window movement command, on the other hand, changes the window relative to the current line (and the cursor). There are three variations of the z window movement command for positioning the window with respect to the current line: you can use z to position the current line at the top, in the middle, or at the bottom of the display window. The cursor position is unchanged by these commands:

- Enter z to position the window so that the current line is at the *top* of the window.

- Type z. (no RETURN necessary) to position the window so the current line is in the *middle* of the window.

- Type z— (no RETURN necessary) to position the window so the current line is at the *bottom* of the window.

Figure 5-3 depicts the result of these window movements diagrammatically. The figure shows the current line as a boldfaced "xxxxxxxxxxxxxxx" and the window movement relative to a stationary edit buffer.

Moving the Cursor

If your terminal has cursor-positioning arrow keys, they may be used to move the cursor one unit at a time in the indicated direction. These four keys are generally located either on the right- or the left-hand side of the keyboard, usually in the numeric keypad cluster if your keyboard has a numeric keypad. They are labeled with arrows pointing left, right, up, and down.

Older versions of the editor may not support the arrow keys for moving the cursor. Also the codes generated by your arrow keys must be noted for your terminal entry in the /etc/termcap file. You can, however, usually use the h, j, k, and l commands, respectively, to move the cursor one unit backward, down a line, up a line, or to the right. In fact, many experienced vi users prefer the letter keys over the arrow keys since the letters are conveniently located in the middle of the keyboard.

Figure 5-4 illustrates these cursor motion directives. The movements in this

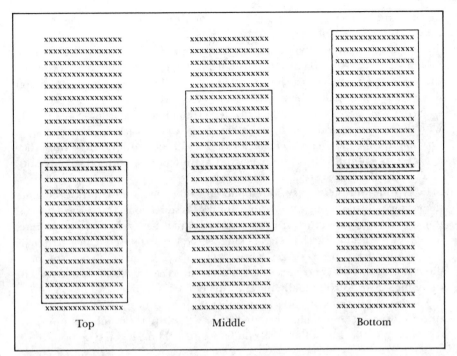

Figure 5-3. *Repositioning display window relative to current line*

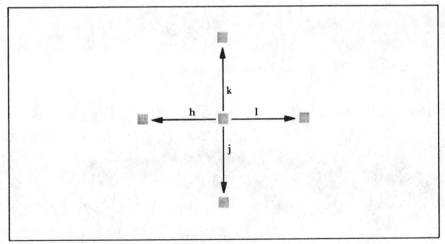

Figure 5-4. *Some cursor movement commands*

diagram are exaggerated for clarity. The cursor actually moves only one character unit each time the letter command key is pressed.

Some older versions of **vi** do not even support the letter commands for cursor motion. Try the letter commands illustrated in Figure 5-4. If they don't work, use the alternative command set shown in Figure 5-5. The commands shown in Figure 5-5 are recognized by newer versions of **vi** as well.

Even if your editor supports the letter keys, you might still prefer to mix the old with the new commands. For instance, the space bar and backspace key (^H) seem very natural for moving the cursor forward and backward on a line since they generally perform this function when you are interacting with other programs, such as the shell.

Every time you press a key corresponding to the cursor movement command, the cursor will move one unit in the appropriate direction. To move additional units, you would repeat the keypress. Some terminals have an auto repeat feature, which will generate the character as long as the key is pressed. Other terminals may require that you press a key labeled REPEAT at the same time that you press the character key to generate a character stream. The stream of characters will cause the cursor to continually move in the desired direction.

Another way to move a specified number of units is to specify a count for the cursor movement command. Then the cursor will move the number of units corresponding to the decimal number you have typed. Thus, if you type 4h (or 4^H),

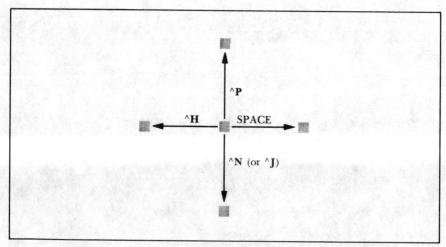

Figure 5-5. *Some alternative cursor movement commands*

the cursor will back up four units; and if you type **8k** (or **8^P**), the cursor will move up eight lines.

You cannot wrap the cursor around the beginning or end of a line of text with these commands. However, you can move the cursor beyond the top or bottom of the display window, and the window will shift to keep the cursor in view.

This would be a good time to invoke the visual editor to read in a file that is several pages in length. Practice with the window- and cursor-positioning commands until they are second nature to you.

Moving the Cursor Within a Text Line   You can move the cursor quickly within a line of text. Some basic commands are listed here:

- The circumflex (^) may be used to move the cursor to the beginning of a line. Actually the cursor moves to the first nonblank character on a line. If you wish to move to the very first character position on a line, use the **0** command instead.

- The dollar sign ($) may be used to move the cursor to the end of the line.

Moving the Cursor Over Words, Sentences, and Paragraphs   You will find it convenient to cause the cursor to jump from word to word. As far as **vi** is concerned, a *word* is a sequence of alphanumeric characters and underscores (_) surrounded by characters that are not alphanumeric or underscores: spaces, tabs, or punctuation characters.

The basic commands for moving the cursor in units of words are as follows:

- The **w** command advances the cursor to the beginning of the next word.

- The **b** command moves the cursor back to the beginning of the current word. If the cursor is already at the beginning of the word, it will be moved back to the beginning of the previous word.

- The **e** command will advance the cursor to the end of the current word. If the cursor is already at the end of a word, a subsequent **e** command advances the cursor to the end of the next word.

You may precede these command letters by a whole number to move that many words in the specified direction. The cursor will stop at each punctuation character when these commands are used. If you wish to move forward or backward a word at a time without stopping at punctuation characters, use the uppercase equivalents: **W**, **B**, and **E**.

Unlike the cursor motion commands discussed in the preceding section, the word cursor-movement commands will wrap around to the previous or next line instead of stopping at the beginning or end of the current line.

In addition to moving the cursor by words, you may move the cursor sentence by sentence. The **vi** editor considers a *sentence* to be a sequence of words that ends with either a period (.), an exclamation point (!), or a question mark (?). These sentence termination characters may be followed by two spaces or occur at the end of a line of text. Note that any number of closing parentheses, closing square brackets, or single or double quotation marks may appear after the sentence termination character and before the spaces or end of the line.

The commands for moving the cursor a sentence at a time are as follows:

- The **)** command moves the cursor to the first character that begins the next sentence.

- The **(** command moves the cursor back to the beginning of the current sentence. If the cursor is already at the beginning of the sentence, it will be moved back to the beginning of the previous sentence.

As with the word movement commands, the sentence movement commands may be preceded by a whole number for skipping multiple sentences.

The **vi** editor defines a *paragraph* as one or more sentences preceded by at least one blank line or as an **nroff** paragraph command. You will learn about such commands in the next session.

The commands for moving the cursor a paragraph at a time are as follows:

- The **}** command moves the cursor to the beginning of the next paragraph.

- The **{** command moves the cursor back to the beginning of the current paragraph. If the cursor is already at the beginning of the paragraph, it will be moved back to the beginning of the previous paragraph.

As with the word and sentence movement commands, you may use a decimal count to skip multiple paragraphs.

Moving the Cursor Vertically Within a Window   You may move the cursor up and down a line at a time either by typing a dash (−) or by pressing RETURN. Using RETURN as a command is a particularly natural way to move the cursor down and is preferred by many users over either the **j** or **^N** commands. Figure 5-6 shows the − and RETURN commands in operation.

You may precede either of these commands with a whole number to move vertically by more than one line at a time. The display window will shift as necessary to follow the cursor.

The cursor may be quickly moved to the beginning, middle, or end of the display window using the capital **H** (for home), **M** (for middle), and **L** (for last) commands. The cursor will be positioned over the first nonblank character of the

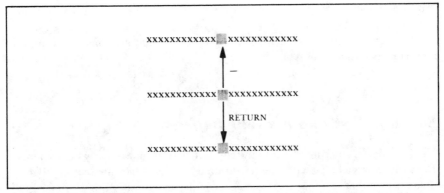

Figure 5-6. *Commands for moving the cursor vertically a line at a time*

new line. Figure 5-7 shows the cursor quickly moving within the window in response to these commands.

You may precede the **H** and **L** commands by a numerical count. Thus, *n***H** would position the cursor *n* lines from the top, and *n***L** would place the cursor *n* lines from the bottom line in the window.

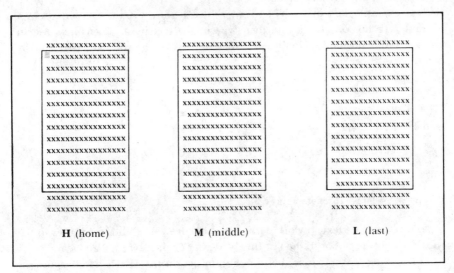

Figure 5-7. *Moving the cursor quickly within the window*

Before moving on to the next section where we will begin text entry, you should be familiar with the cursor and window movement commands introduced so far. Invoke **vi** to read in a document several pages in length and practice using the commands we have discussed.

Entering Text Into the Edit Buffer

The first step in entering text into the edit buffer is to change to text entry mode. Then whatever you type will be entered into the buffer. There are several different **vi** commands that you may use to enter text entry mode. They differ primarily in where the new text will be inserted (that is, before versus after the cursor) and whether or not the new text will overwrite existing text.

The append and insert commands are used most frequently to initiate text entry. After you type a lowercase **a** (for append) or a lowercase **i** (for insert), the editor switches from command to text entry mode. After the append command is issued, the cursor moves one unit to the right and any new text will be entered after the new cursor position. If you use the insert command, the cursor does not move and the new text will be entered before the original cursor position.

Remember that you may leave text entry mode and return to the command mode of **vi** at any time by pressing ESC.

As an example, let's invoke **vi** and enter the text shown in the following screen example. To do so, enter **a** and then type in the text itself. Then press ESC to reenter command mode. Finally, save the contents of the edit buffer to disk by entering **:w appeal**.

```
Now is the time
for all good citizens
to come to the aid
of their country.
~
~
"appeal" 4 lines, 75 characters
```

To give us more text to work with as we practice **vi**, let's add two lines to the file. Position the cursor to the last line by typing **L**; then type a **$** and **a** and press RETURN. Now enter **This is the time** and **to get on the UNIX bandwagon.** on separate lines. Finally, exit text entry mode and return to command mode by pressing ESC. Type **H** to move the cursor to the beginning of the first line.

Now let's insert the word "Right" at the beginning of the first line. Since we wish to enter text in front of the cursor, it is easiest to use the insert command to enter text entry mode. Type **i**, followed by **Right**, press the space bar, and then press ESC to return to command mode. Then the first line should look like this:

Right ▮Now is the time

On some terminals, it may seem that the new text is overwriting the old text; after you press ESC, however, the line will be updated to correct the display. If you had used the **append** command instead, the cursor would have moved to the right (over the "o" in "Now"). Then typing **Right** and pressing the space bar and ESC would have given the following incorrect result:

NRight ▮ow is the time

Continuing with our example, let's move to the end of the fifth line by typing **4j**, which moves the cursor down four lines. Now type **$**, which moves the cursor to the end of the line. Begin text entry with the **append** command and type in the text **, isn't it,**. Return to command mode by pressing ESC. The fifth line should look like this:

This is the time, isn't it ▮

We may summarize the text entry commands discussed so far as follows:

- Use **a** (for append) to place text after (right of) the cursor.
- Use **i** (for insert) to place text before (left of) the cursor.

Here are two variations on the **append** and **insert** commands that might come in handy at times as a shorthand:

- The uppercase **A** command may be used to begin appending text at the end of the current line. This is equivalent to typing **$a**.
- The uppercase **I** command may be used to begin insertion of text at the beginning of the current line. This is equivalent to typing **^i**.

In addition to entering text by changing to visual text entry mode with the **append** or **insert** commands, you may also enter text entry mode with the **open** command. When the editor enters text entry mode with the **open** command, a one-line window is inserted (opened) either below or above the current line and the cursor is placed at the beginning of that blank line. If you enter a lowercase **o**, a blank line will appear below the current line; and if you use an uppercase **O**, the line above will be opened. Then whatever you type will be entered into the edit buffer. If you type more than one line, the one-line window follows the current line (that is, the line on which you are typing). When you have completed text entry, press ESC to return to visual command mode.

The open command makes it possible to use most of the **vi** commands on CRT terminals that cannot support the full-screen visual mode (this is true, for example, of hard-copy and single-line display terminals). You could use the **open** command, for instance, if you can't set your terminal type correctly, or if there isn't an entry for your terminal in the **/etc/termcap** database file, or if your system doesn't have **/etc/termcap** on-line.

As an example, first position the cursor on the second line by typing **3k** to move up three lines. Then type a lowercase **o** to enter text entry mode. A blank line should appear below the current line, and the cursor should be positioned at the beginning of this line:

```
Right Now is the time
for all good citizens
▉
to come to the aid
of their country.
This is the time, isn't it,
to get on the UNIX bandwagon.
~

~

"appeal" 6 lines, 121 characters
```

As an alternative, you could have positioned the cursor on the third line and then typed an uppercase **O** to open the line above the current line.

Now type **who are patriotic** and return to command mode by pressing ESC.

On some dumb terminals the display may not look correct after an insertion. A *dumb terminal* does not have a local screen display memory like an *intelligent terminal*. For this reason, **vi** can't direct it to insert or delete a line locally without the entire screen being redrawn — a time-consuming process, especially at slower baud rates.

If your display doesn't look correct because you have a dumb terminal, type the ASCII form feed character (press ^L). This command directs the editor to clear the screen and redraw the display. Because your editor may not be set up to redraw the screen automatically, ^L is helpful for dumb terminals: it refreshes the screen so that you can see the actual text in the edit buffer.

At this point, your display should look like this:

```
Right Now is the time
for all good citozens
who are patriotic
to come to the aid
of their country.
This is the time, isn't it,
to get on the UNIX bandwagon.
~
~
```

Making Simple Corrections in Text Entry Mode

While you are entering text into the edit buffer, you may wish to correct any typing mistakes as you go. It's important to know that you can always use the UNIX character-erase and line-kill functions from any program to correct text entry before pressing RETURN. This is because these editing functions are effective at the level of the kernel program; that is, they are processed before the characters are even sent to the command program, which is the visual editor in this case.

The character codes assigned to these editing functions are frequently reassigned to characters different from the default values, as we saw in Session 2 of Chapter 3. You may use the **stty** program to determine the current values of these correction codes. Some common values for these correction codes are

- *Character-erase* code: # (default) or ^H (a backspace)
- *Line-kill* code: @ (default), ^X, or ^U

The visual editor supports two other correction codes that are used to back up the cursor and correct an insert. These commands are only effective from **vi** during text entry mode:

- Press ^H to backspace over the last character typed.
- Press ^W to back over the last word typed, leaving the cursor at the beginning of the incorrect word.

Note that in both cases, the new text you type will overwrite the incorrect text that was backed over.

Making Simple Corrections in Command Mode

You may easily make small corrections to existing text while in visual command mode. First position the cursor over the incorrect character. Type an **x** and the character will be deleted from the edit buffer. As a memory aid you may think of this command as "x-ing out" the incorrect character. If you need to enter another character, give the insert command to enter text entry mode, type the correct character (or characters), and return to command mode by pressing ESC.

You may replace an incorrect character with another character easily in a single step using the **r** (for replace) command. As before, position the cursor over the incorrect character, but this time type a lowercase **r** followed immediately by the correct character. Now you are back in command mode.

Alternatively, you may replace an incorrect character with a string of characters using the **s** (for substitute) command. Position the cursor over the incorrect character, type a lowercase **s**, and the editor will print a $ over the character and enter text entry mode. Type in the correct characters, and then return to command mode by pressing ESC.

To get some more practice, let's use one of these methods to correct the second word of the first line. While in command mode type a capital **H** to return the cursor to the home position (the first character of the first line); then type a **w** to place the cursor over the first character of the next word (the incorrect character). Now type **rn** to replace the uppercase **N** with a lowercase **n**.

Finally, press ^L to redraw the screen. If you are using a dumb terminal, the screen may need updating to reflect the corrections you have made.

This would be a good time to save the contents of the edit buffer to your disk file, **appeal**. Do this by typing a colon (:) and note that the cursor jumps to the bottom line of the screen (the status line). Then type **w**, press RETURN, and your screen should look like this:

```
Right now is the time
for all good citizens
who are patriotic
to come to the aid
of their country.
This is the time, isn't it,
to get on the UNIX bandwagon.
~
~
"appeal" 7 lines, 157 characters
```

Locating a Text Pattern:
The Search Pattern Commands

You may locate text in the edit buffer by specifying the text to search for as a pattern for the search function. You can request the editor to search forward or backward to find the pattern. Normally, the search will wrap around the end (or beginning) of the edit buffer so that the entire buffer is scanned for the pattern. You may disable the **wrapscan** option if you wish.

The **vi** search command is analogous to the **ex** search function discussed previously. Type a slash (/) to initiate the search. The editor will echo the slash on the status line (the last line on your terminal screen), place the cursor immediately after the slash, and wait for further input. At this point, you should carefully type in the text pattern to search for. If you make a typing mistake, correct the entry with the UNIX erase and line-kill characters. Terminate entry of the pattern string by pressing a RETURN or ESC.

The editor will then search forward to locate the next occurrence of the *pattern*. If the pattern is found, the cursor will be positioned at the beginning of the pattern. If pattern cannot be located, the editor displays an error message, such as "Pattern not found", and the cursor will be returned to its position before the search began. Note that this search request can only locate one instance of a *pattern* at a time.

To try this now, first enter $ to move to the end of the line, thus bypassing the pattern "the time." Then type /**the time** and press RETURN: the cursor moves forward from the first line to the next appearance of "the time", which is on the sixth line, as shown in the following example. In this split screen, the left-hand side depicts the display just before RETURN is pressed to enter the search request. The right-hand side shows the result of the search. We will use such a double screen simulation to illustrate "before" and "after" displays for some of the examples that follow.

Before Pressing RETURN	**After Pressing** RETURN
Right now is the time	Right now is the time
for all good citizens	for all good citizens
who are patriotic	who are patriotic
to come to the aid	to come to the aid
of their country.	of their country.
This is the time, isn't it,	This is the time, isn't it,
to get on the UNIX bandwagon.	to get on the UNIX bandwagon.
~	~
~	~
/the time▮	/the time

You may find the next occurrence of the same pattern by typing either / and pressing RETURN or by simply typing n (for next). In our example, if you elect to search for the next occurrence of "the time", the search will wrap around the end of the buffer to find the pattern on the first line, as shown here:

Before Pressing RETURN	After Pressing RETURN
Right now is the time	Right now is the time
for all good citizens	for all good citizens
who are patriotic	who are patriotic
to come to the aid	to come to the aid
of their country.	of their country.
This is the time, isn't it,	This is the time, isn't it,
to get on the UNIX bandwagon.	to get on the UNIX bandwagon.
~	~
~	~
/	/

If you wish to return the cursor to its position in the edit buffer before the last search request, type two backquotes (``). This "undo" function might be useful, for example, if you accidentally typed any command that moved the cursor and you wished to return to the position at which you had been working.

You may search backward in the buffer for a string pattern by entering ?*pattern* from command mode. If you wish to search backward for the same pattern again, simply enter ?. Alternatively, you may type n to search again in the same direction or a capital N to search for the same pattern in the opposite direction.

Continuing with our example, let's enter ? to search backward for "the time". This time the search wraps around the beginning of the buffer and the pattern is found on the sixth line. The left-hand side of the following example depicts the terminal display immediately before RETURN is pressed (to enter the search request) and the right-hand side of the example shows the result of the search:

Before Pressing RETURN	After Pressing RETURN
Right now is the time	Right now is the time
for all good citizens	for all good citizens
who are patriotic	who are patriotic
to come to the aid	to come to the aid
of their country.	of their country.

Before Pressing RETURN	After Pressing RETURN (*cont.*)
This is the time, isn't it,	This is the time, isn't it,
to get on the UNIX bandwagon.	to get on the UNIX bandwagon.
~	~
~	~
?	?

You may use the circumflex (^) and dollar sign ($), respectively, to indicate a search pattern at the beginning or end of a line. For instance, if you specify the pattern "time$", the editor would locate the string "time" at the end of line 1 and not on line 6, where the pattern "time" would locate the same four characters in mid-line. Similarly, if you specify the pattern "^to", the editor will locate the letters "to" either at the beginning of line 4 or line 7, but not the occurrence in the middle of line 4.

The **vi** search commands we have introduced are summarized in Table 5-3.

Remember to include spaces in your search pattern to match whole words. For instance, the pattern "the" would be matched by "their" on line 5; however, the pattern " the " would not.

Table 5-3. *Some vi Pattern Search Commands*

Command	Action
/*pattern*	Search forward for *pattern*.
?*pattern*	Search backward for *pattern*.
/^*pattern*	Search forward for *pattern* at the beginning of the line.
/*pattern*$	Search forward for *pattern* at the end of the line.
?^*pattern*	Search backward for *pattern* at the beginning of the line.
?*pattern*$	Search backward for *pattern* at the end of the line.
/	Repeat forward search for last *pattern* specified.
?	Repeat backward search for last *pattern* specified.
n	Search for *pattern* again in the same direction.
N	Search for *pattern* again in the opposite direction.
··	Undo the last search request and return cursor to original position.

You may use the **set** command to disable the wraparound feature. You might wish to prevent the search request from wrapping around the end (or beginning) of the buffer, for instance, when you are systematically searching the buffer from beginning to end (or vice versa) for all occurrences of *pattern*. This way when the message "Pattern not found" is displayed, you know that you've already located all occurrences of the pattern in question.

The **wrapscan** option is enabled by default when the editor is invoked. Enter **:set nowrapscan** from visual command mode to disable wraparound. You may reenable **wrapscan** by entering **:set wrapscan**. We will describe other **vi** editor options at the end of this chapter.

Executing Line-Editing Commands From *vi*

As we mentioned earlier, you may temporarily escape to line-editing mode to give an **ex** command by typing a colon (:) from visual command mode. When you do this, the cursor will move down to the status line. Then type in the line-editing command (**ex**), ending the input with RETURN. After the request has been serviced, you will be returned to visual command mode.

The main reason why you would want to escape to line-editing mode would be to perform operations not duplicated in the visual mode. Some examples of such operations are disk file operations, such as writing part of the edit buffer to a disk file, or invoking a subshell to execute a UNIX command, such as listing the contents of your current directory. In addition, global searches and substitutions are only possible in line-editing mode.

As an example, let's use the **ex** pattern search function. Enter **:/the time**. Your display should look like this:

Before Pressing RETURN	After Pressing RETURN
Right now is the time	Right now is the time
for all good citizens	for all good citizens
who are patriotic	who are patriotic
to come to the aid	to come to the aid
of their country.	of their country.
This is the time, isn't it,	This is the time, isn't it,
to get on the UNIX bandwagon.	to get on the UNIX bandwagon.
~	~
~	~
:/the time	**:/the time**

Note that a line-editing mode search request places the cursor at the beginning of the line where the pattern is located instead of immediately before the pattern, as is the case with a **vi** search request.

If you wish to execute several **ex** commands, it would be more efficient to switch permanently to line-editing mode. From **vi**, type **Q** to get the **ex** colon prompt, indicating that you are in the command mode of **ex**. You may return to visual mode by typing **vi** and pressing RETURN.

While in visual mode, the editor may occasionally switch to line-editing mode in response to an internal error (as opposed to user-initiated error). In this case, go ahead and save the contents of the buffer to disk, just to be safe, before reentering visual mode.

Operators and Text Objects

Many visual mode commands are formed in a regular way by combining numerical counts, operators, and operands. The three operators used most frequently in this way include

- **d** for delete
- **c** for change
- **y** for yank.

We shall be explaining how to use these operators along with other commands in the next few pages.

The operands may refer to units of text called *text objects*. The text objects of interest include:

- **w** for current word
- **b** for previous word
- **)** for current sentence
- **(** for previous sentence
- **}** for current paragraph
- **{** for previous paragraph.

Whole lines of text are usually indicated by doubling the operator. For example, you would use **dd** to delete an entire line.

The operands and the operators from the previous lists may be combined to form commands. Some examples would be **3dw**, which would delete the next three words; **yy**, which would yank the current line (through a copy operation) into a buffer area; **2c**), which would change the two following sentences, and **d(**, which would delete the previous sentence.

Deleting Text

Earlier we introduced the visual editor's **x** command for deleting characters. Using **x** to delete larger amounts of text, such as lines and sentences, would be tedious, to say the least. Instead, you may use the **d** (for **d**elete) operator to delete text in terms of lines, words, sentences, and paragraphs.

A complete delete command consists of the delete operator, the text object operand, and perhaps a count, all of which are combined as we explained earlier in this session. You must place the cursor at the beginning of the word, sentence, or paragraph you wish the delete command to refer to. If the cursor is placed in the middle of a text object, only the text before or after the text object will be deleted.

For instance, the command **d)** deletes after the cursor to the end of the current sentence, while a **d(** deletes from the beginning of the sentence to the cursor. You would place the cursor in the middle of the text object and give the delete command only if you intended to delete part of a text object.

Type **dd** to delete an entire line of text on the screen. The cursor may be placed anywhere on a line when deleting an entire line.

If you are using a dumb terminal, which can't delete a line locally in response to being sent a character sequence, the remaining text may need rearranging for proper appearance. For instance, if the **redraw** option is not in effect when a line of text is deleted, the editor will leave an **@** symbol in the first column of an otherwise blank line instead of redrawing the rest of the screen. The delay involved in redrawing the screen on a terminal may be intolerable. If too many of these blank lines accumulate, you may direct the editor to redraw the screen to close up the gaps so that there is more text in the display window. The redraw command is a **^R**. Alternatively, you could enable the **redraw** editing option to simulate an intelligent terminal so that the text after a deletion will automatically be rearranged correctly. However, the **redraw** option requires a large amount of output to simulate an intelligent terminal. This may slow down the editor too much to be practical, unless you are using a high communication speed for your terminal on a lightly loaded UNIX system.

You may delete a part of a line by positioning the cursor to the place at which you wish to begin and typing **d$**, which will delete all characters from the cursor position to the end of the line. Alternatively, you may use the less regularly formed command, **D**, to accomplish the same thing. Similarly, you would type **d^** to delete all characters from the beginning of the line to the cursor's position.

Now you should practice using the delete command, but first save the contents of your edit buffer to disk by entering :w to update the disk copy of **appeal**. This way you may easily restore the edit buffer to its original state after you have completed the practice session. Now try deleting characters, lines, words, sentences, and parts of lines, words, and sentences both in the forward and reverse direction until you feel proficient with the visual mode delete command. Finally, restore the edit buffer to its original state by reading in the copy of **appeal** you saved previously. To do this, enter the (force) reedit command, :e!. Recall that the e! form of the enter (or edit) command will force the current file to be read into the buffer, even if the buffer contents have been changed since the last disk update operation.

Undoing a Change

The visual mode has two undo commands. The lowercase u command returns the edit buffer to the state it was in before the last change to the buffer was made. The cursor or the display window or both will be returned to their position before the last change. This command undoes even extensive changes to the edit buffer. A second u command will undo the first u command as a toggle, so that the last change will again apply to the edit buffer.

The uppercase U command will undo all changes that have been made to the current line. However, if the cursor is moved from the current line and back again, the U command will no longer be able to undo the changes made before moving the cursor. This form of the undo command would be useful, for instance, if you have made extensive changes to a single line and wish to restore it completely to its original state. The U command will not undo itself; thus typing a second U on the same line has no effect. In addition, the u and U commands will not undo each other.

Repeating a Change

The repeat command, specified by typing a period (.), is used to repeat the last command that changed the edit buffer. This command would be useful, for instance, to apply the same change in different parts of the text. Because moving the cursor or window or both does not change the buffer, the repeat command can be used to reproduce the last change in a new location.

As a simple example, let's say you wish to delete several words in a sentence. Instead of bothering to count each word so that you can use the delete word command with a count, you could simply position the cursor to the beginning of the first word, type **dw**, and then type enough periods to erase all the desired words. Be careful not to delete too much. Remember that the u command only will undo the last change—in this case, the last word deleted. You could, however, use the **U** command to repair an entire line and start over.

Rearranging Text

You've already learned how to rearrange text in the edit buffer by using the move command while in line-editing mode. You may also rearrange text while in visual command mode. Furthermore, in visual mode you may rearrange text in terms of words, sentences, and paragraphs rather than just in terms of whole lines as is the case of **ex**.

The text that you deleted with the last command is saved in what is known as the *unnamed buffer*. You can still access this text by using the put command if no other changes to the edit buffer have been made in the meantime. Thus you could use a delete command, then a cursor movement command, and finally a put command to rearrange text conveniently in the edit buffer.

There are two put commands that only differ in where they place the text retrieved from the unnamed buffer. The lowercase **p** command places the contents of the unnamed buffer after the cursor and the uppercase **P** command places the text before the cursor. However, if text was deleted in terms of one or more entire lines, the lowercase **p** command places the retrieved lines or lines *after* the current line while uppercase **P** places the retrieved lines *before* the current line.

As an example, let's use delete and put to move the last two lines to the beginning of the buffer while in visual mode. First, position the cursor anywhere on the next to the last line and type **2dd** to delete the current line and the next line. Move the cursor to the home position by typing **H**. Then type an uppercase **P** to place the contents of the unnamed buffer, which contains the last two lines, before the current line. The next few screen examples illustrate the procedure.

The following screen example shows the display immediately after the two lines have been deleted. The **@**'s appear because the **redraw** option was disabled, so that the screen is not redrawn after the decision:

```
Right now is the time
for all good citizens
who are patriotic
to come to the aid
of their country.
@
@
~
~
```

The next screen simulates the display after the **put** command:

This is the time, isn't it,
to get on the UNIX bandwagon.
Right now is the time
for all good citizens
who are patriotic
to come to the aid
of their country.
@
@
~
~

Now let's move the lines back. If the cursor is not already home, move it to the new home position by typing **H**. Then type **dd** to delete the current line. Now delete the other line by typing **dd** again.

@
@
Right now is the time
for all good citizens
who are patriotic
to come to the aid
of their country.
@
@
~
~

Now move the cursor to the last line by typing **L**. Then use the lowercase **p** command to place the contents of the unnamed buffer after the current line, which is also the last. Note that only the last line deleted was retrieved.

Right now is the time
for all good citizens
who are patriotic
to come to the aid
of their country.

to get on the UNIX bandwagon.
@
~
~

This example has shown that you must delete *all* the text you wish to move with a single command. Otherwise, the contents of the unnamed buffer from one deletion will be overwritten by the text from the next deletion.

Even though these examples have demonstrated text movements in terms of whole lines, you can use the same approach to move words, sentences, paragraphs, parts of words and sentences, and so on.

A very common typing mistake is to transpose two adjacent characters. You may use the character delete and the put command to quickly correct such an error. Position the cursor over the first character of the transposed pair and then type **xp**. The **x** command will delete the character, placing it in the unnamed buffer, and the cursor will move over to the second character. The **p** command retrieves the character just deleted and places that character back in the word in the correct place after the cursor.

This would be a good time to practice moving text around the edit buffer. You might want to rearrange characters, words, lines, and sentences. When you feel proficient using delete and put, you should restore the edit buffer to the state it was in before you began your practice. To do this, enter **:e!**.

Duplicating Text

You've already learned how to duplicate text in the edit buffer using **ex**'s transpose or **co**py command. You may also duplicate text while you are in visual command mode. In visual mode, as you know, you may duplicate text in terms of words, sentences, and paragraphs. You are not limited to working with whole lines, as is the case with line-editing mode.

Text may be copied into the unnamed buffer with the **y** (for yank) command. In this way the original text (the source text) is not affected. You may then move the cursor to another position in the edit buffer and place a copy of the original text in a new position. This technique allows you to duplicate text without altering the original.

As an example, this time let's duplicate the same two lines from the end at the beginning of the buffer using yank and put. Place the cursor on the next to the last line. Type **2yy** to yank a copy of the current line and the following line into the unnamed buffer. As the following screen example shows, the source lines remain in the buffer.

Right now is the time
for all good citizens
who are patriotic
to come to the aid
of their country.
This is the time, isn't it,
to get on the UNIX bandwagon.
~
~

Now move the cursor to the home position. Type an uppercase **P** to place the yanked text before the current line — that is, at the beginning of the edit buffer. As before, be sure to yank all the text you wish to duplicate in one operation because a second yank will overwrite any text from the first yank. The next screen shows the display after the put operation:

This is the time, isn't it,
to get on the UNIX bandwagon.
Right now is the time
for all good citizens
who are patriotic
to come to the aid
of their country.
This is the time, isn't it,
to get on the UNIX bandwagon.
~
~

You should practice duplicating text using yank and put. You can duplicate text in terms of words, sentences, and parts of words and sentences. Just combine the yank operator with the appropriate text object operand and add a count if necessary. Finally, to restore the edit buffer, enter :e!.

Changing Text

You may modify the text in the edit buffer by deleting the old text and inserting the new text. Alternatively, you may use the change command to perform the alteration in a single step. Use the c (for change) operator to form combined change commands with the same syntax you used with the delete and yank operators just discussed.

As an example, let's change the word "good" on the second line to "able-bodied". First position the cursor at the beginning of the word to be changed. Then type **cw** (for change word) and the editor will replace the character at the end of the word with a dollar sign ($) to indicate the end of the change operation, as shown here:

```
Right now is the time
for all goo$ citizens
who are patriotic
to come to the aid
of their country.
This is the time, isn't it,
to get on the UNIX bandwagon.
~
~
```

Now type in **able-bodied** and then press ESC immediately to end text entry and return to visual command mode. Your display should look like this:

```
Right now is the time
for all able-bodied citizens
who are patriotic
to come to the aid
of their country.
This is the time, isn't it,
to get on the UNIX bandwagon.
~
~
```

The editor adjusted the text so that the longer word "able-bodied" fit where "good" did originally.

Joining and Splitting Lines

Occasionally you may need to join two or more lines. There is no way to use a delete command to erase the ASCII new line character, which separates the lines, in order to join them together. Instead, you can use the uppercase **J** command. (The lowercase **j** is reserved for cursor movement.)

As an example, let's join the last line in the buffer to the end of the preceding line. Place the cursor anywhere on the next to the last line and type **J**. The result should look like this:

```
Right now is the time
for all able-bodied citizens
who are patriotic
to come to the aid
of their country.
This is the time, isn't it, ▓ to get on the UNIX bandwagon.
~

~
```

The **vi** editor automatically puts a space between the last word of the previous line and the first word of the next line. If the previous line ends in a sentence termination character (a period, a question mark, or an exclamation point), two spaces will be inserted. If you wish to delete the spaces, the cursor is positioned so that you may easily do so.

You may join together more than two lines in one step by specifying a count. Place the cursor on the first line to be joined to the remaining lines. Then perform the appropriate combined join operation. For instance, you could have joined the five lines making up the first sentence by typing **5J** after placing the cursor anywhere on the first line.

Splitting lines is very easy with **vi**. Simply place the cursor at the position at which you'd like to divide the lines. Then enter text entry mode with the append command and press RETURN. Press ESC to return to visual command mode.

Continuing with our screen example, leave the cursor where it is and type **a** to enter text entry mode. Press RETURN and then ESC to return to command mode, and notice that the line is divided in the same place again:

```
Right now is the time
for all able-bodied citizens
who are patriotic
to come to the aid
of their country.
This is the time, isn't it,
▓to get on the UNIX bandwagon.
~

~
```

Automatic Word Wrap

You may input text continuously into the edit buffer without having to press RETURN to end each line if you enable the **wrapmargin** option. When you reach a certain distance from the right margin, the next word you would type will be moved (or wrapped) automatically around to the beginning of the next line.

To enable this feature and set the right margin in one step, set the **wrapmargin** option to a positive value. Then whenever you type a space less than the value of **wrapmargin** spaces from the right side of the screen, the space is converted into a new line and the text input will continue on the next line. For instance, if you type from visual command mode **:set wm=10** and press RETURN, whenever whitespace is typed after column 70 (80 − 10 = 70), any subsequent text will appear on the next line in the edit buffer. Thus you have to press RETURN explicitly only when you actually wish to end a paragraph or insert a blank line.

Let's practice setting and using the **wrapmargin** option now. First erase the edit buffer by typing, from visual mode, **:%d** and then pressing RETURN. Now set the **wrapmargin** value to 8 by entering **:set wm=8**. Then enter text entry mode with the **append** command and type the sentence "Right now is the time for all good citizens who are patriotic to come to the aid of their country." and press RETURN. Now press ESC to return to command mode. Change the margin setting to 10 by entering **:set wm=10**, and enter the same sentence. Where the editor breaks, the line has changed:

```
Right now is the time for all good citizens who are patriotic to come to
the aid of their country.
Right now is the time for all good citizens who are patriotic to come
to the aid of their country.
```

```
~
~
```

The right margin for the first sentence is at column 72. It is at column 70 for the second.

Now type **:q!** to exit the editor, to abandon the contents of the edit buffer, and return to the shell.

Executing UNIX
System Commands From Within *vi*

If you wish to execute a UNIX command while still in visual command mode, type a colon (:) to escape to line-editing mode temporarily. After the cursor moves to the status line, enter an exclamation point (!) followed by the desired shell command line. Terminate the entry by pressing RETURN. After the command has finished, the editor will prompt you with the message "Hit return to continue", refresh the screen, and return you to command mode. Of course, if you are in line-editing command mode already, you simply need to type !, the command line, and then press RETURN, as we saw in the **ex** tutorial.

As a convenient shorthand, you may repeat the last shell command request by simply typing :!! from visual command mode, followed by RETURN.

vi Editor Options

In Session 10, we learned that the **ex/vi** program has a set of options that are used to change the overall behavior of line editor. These and other options may be used to influence the behavior of the visual editor as well. The options are enabled and disabled using the **set** command, but you must be in line-editing command mode in order to run **set**. Thus you can set the options for the visual editor in two ways. You may switch to line-editing command mode, run the **set** command, and then return to visual mode. The more convenient method is to perform a temporary escape from visual mode to line-editing command mode just to use **set**. But note that you must be in "permanent" line-editing mode to reset the **window** and **term** options.

Table 5-4 lists many useful editing options for visual mode with the full name of each option, the abbreviation of the name (if there is one), the default values, and a brief description of the option's effect on **vi**. Note that this table does not duplicate any options discussed in Table 5-2 in Session 10, although the options listed in Table 5-2 apply to **vi** as well. Note that some of the default values listed in Table 5-4 may be different for your editing environment.

Now you should have all the basic information for using the visual editor to create and change text. We do not have the space to document all the features and nuances of the editor; however, the basic operations have been presented. For more information on **vi**, read *An Introduction to Display Editing with vi* by William Joy (see Appendix G for complete bibliographical information).

Table 5-4.   *Useful Editing Options for the vi Editor*

Name(abbrev)	Default	Description
autowrite(aw)	noaw	Edit buffer will be automatically written to disk file (if buffer was modified) before certain visual mode commands are executed.
mesg	mesg	Disable write permission for the terminal you are using so other system users can't communicate with you via the UNIX write command.
open	open	If **noopen** is set, you cannot change from line editing to visual (or open) mode.
optimize(opt)	opt	Speed up editing with terminals that do not have addressable cursors since automatic RETURNs are not enabled when more than one logical line of output is being printed.
redraw(re)	(none)	Simulate an intelligent terminal on a dumb terminal. Useful only at high data communication (baud) rates.
scroll	(1/2 window)	The number of lines scrolled in response to either a ^D or ^U command; also half the number of lines displayed by a z command.
slowopen(slow)	slow	Postpone display updates during text insertion. Useful for dumb terminals at slow communciation rates between terminal and CPU.
term	(from **TERM** environmental variable)	Your terminal type name. Must be set appropriately for your terminal so you can use full screen editing mode.
window	(baud rate)	The number of lines displayed in visual mode. The actual default value depends on the data communication speed between terminal and CPU.
wrapmargin(wm)	=0	Define a margin for automatic word wrap during continuous text entry. Normally disabled (**wm**=0).

SESSION 12

The UNIX system is renowned for its extensive and powerful text processing facilities. Because the UNIX text processing system was developed in the days of hard-copy terminals, however, it differs substantially from modern word processing facilities, which are based on the CRT display terminal.

Word processing systems generally combine editing and document printing functions into one program. The primary advantage of using a single program for both functions is that the program may be designed so that you can see on the CRT display exactly how your document will look when it is printed.

By contrast with such word processing, text processing systems generally use two or more separate programs: at a minimum, an editor program for creating and editing the document and a separate formatting program for printing the document. In this situation you do not know how the printed document will look until after it has been formatted (that is, printed). This is considered to be a disadvantage, although it is possible to preview **nroff**'s *output on your terminal screen.*

Using two separate programs does have its advantages, though, especially for larger documents. One advantage is that it is easier to make global changes that affect the printed output. For instance, if you wished to convert a single-spaced document to double-spaced, you'd only have to add a simple directive for the formatter program at the beginning of the document file, no matter what the length of the file. With some word processing systems, however, you'd have to format the entire document manually to make it double-spaced. This would be a very time-consuming procedure with a large document.

Thus we have found that word processing programs are most useful for smaller documents, such as business letters, interoffice memos, and short reports. Larger documents like books, manuals, treatises, and complex reports are more efficiently handled using a system like the UNIX text processing system.

Text processing systems can be very effective for producing short documents as well. After you have created the appropriate short document containing all the necessary directives for the formatting program, you could use this document as a guide or template for producing other documents of the same type. (The guide or template is also known as a boilerplate.) *It is often possible to produce a new document just by changing the text contents and letting the formatting directives stand.*

With the UNIX text processing system, you first create a text file with an editor program. Then in a separate step the resulting text file is printed by a formatting program to produce the finished document. Formatting directives, also called commands or requests, are imbedded in the text file at the editing stage. The imbedded formatting requests tell the formatting program how the final document should look when printed.

The most widely used and generally available formatting program for the UNIX system is the **nroff** *program. The name is derived from "new run off," indicating a newer version of the original UNIX "run off" (or* **roff**) *program that was used to "run off" a hard copy.*

In this tutorial session, you will gain experience using the **nroff** *text formatting program. In the process, you will learn how to use two fundamentally different types of formatting requests. First you learn the universally available low-level* *formatting requests, which happen to be perfectly adequate for producing small documents. Then you will be introduced to macro requests and macro packages, which are important aids for creating documents that extend for many pages.*

Macro formatting requests consist of frequently used low-level formatting requests combined in a group so that nroff can execute them all at once. This session will teach you how to define some simple macro requests for your own use. You will also learn about powerful predefined sets of macros called macro packages, which are available with most UNIX systems.

Running nroff

Before going into particulars about using the low-level formatting requests, let's learn how to invoke and use the **nroff** program itself. The basic command line for invoking **nroff** to format one or more files is

$ **nroff** [*filename...*]

As usual, the ellipses indicate that you may specify more than one filename on the **nroff** command line. The contents of all the file arguments specified on the command line will be concatenated and the combined contents will then be formatted.

If no *filename* is specified, **nroff** takes its input from the standard input file, which means that you can pipe the input text into the **nroff** program.

The output of **nroff** is directed to the standard output (your terminal screen). This is convenient for previewing the result before you request a hard copy. This way you can see on your screen what you'll get when you do print out the document. When you are satisfied that the output is what you desire, you may easily obtain a hard copy by piping the standard output of **nroff** into the line printer spooler program, **lpr** (discussed in Chapter 6), as shown here:

$ **nroff** [*filename...*] | **lpr**

See the section "Redirecting **nroff**'s Input and Output" later in this session for other ways to manipulate the input and output of the **nroff** program. Note that in this session on **nroff**, we will generally show the output as it is directed to your terminal screen for your perusal before printing.

Even in the absence of any formatting requests in the input text file, **nroff** produces output with a pleasing appearance. The lines are filled with text to make them uniform in length, if possible. The whitespace between words is adjusted to produce justified (straight) left and right margins, while indented paragraphs and blank lines in the input file are passed to the output unchanged.

The first two screens show an example of running **nroff** on a text file without embedded formatting requests. The choppy looking input text is an edited version of the on-line manual entry for the System V password command that we stored in the file **passwd.txt**. The first screen shows the input text for **nroff**:

```
$ cat passwd.txt
    This command changes (or installs) a password associated
with the login name.
    The program prompts for the old password (if any) and then
for the new one (twice). The caller must supply these. New
passwords should be at least four characters long if they use
a sufficiently rich alphabet and at least six characters long if
monocase. Only the first eight characters of the password are
significant.
    Only the owner of the name or the super-user may change a
password; the owner must prove he knows the old password.
    Only the super-user can create a null password.
    The password file is not changed if the new password is the
same as the old password, or if the password has not "aged"
sufficiently.
See also passwd(4).
    $ ▓
```

If you use this same text as input for **nroff**, its standard output consists of text that has been formatted to produce a 66-line page, with uniform lines 65 characters long, that have both left- and right-justified margins. This is the default output from the **nroff** program when no formatting directives are used:

```
$ nroff passwd.txt
    This command changes (or installs) a password associated
with the login name.
    The program prompts for the old password (if any) and then
for the new one (twice). The caller must supply these. New
passwords should be at least four characters long if they use
a sufficiently rich alphabet and at least six characters long if
monocase. Only the first eight characters of the password are
significant.
    Only the owner of the name or the super-user may change a
password; the owner must prove he knows the old password.
    Only the super-user can create a null password.
```

The password file is not changed if the new password is the
same as the old password, or if the password has not ¢¢aged"
sufficiently.

See also passwd(4).

...

$ ▓

Note that the ellipses (...) indicate the blank lines that were output to make up a
total line count of 66 lines for the page.

Any input text that is indented from the left margin is assumed to start a paragraph; **nroff** therefore leaves it indented the same amount on output. In addition,
if the input text contains any blank lines, they are passed to the output
unchanged. Otherwise words from one line are shifted to fill up shorter lines, and
then space between words is added so that the lines are uniform in length.

The preceding example demonstrates the usefulness of **nroff** even if formatting
requests are not embedded in the input text. Of course, in the absence of such
requests the result will always be the default situation: 66-line pages with each
line 65 characters long. Frequently, you will find the default format is perfectly
adequate for short memos or reports. Simply type your document paying no attention to the right margin; then run it through **nroff** to get nicely justified margins.

In the next section we will introduce you to formatting requests that enable you
to control the appearance of the formatted output text exactly.

Formatting Requests

The input for the formatting program generally consists of text lines that are to
be printed and control lines that contain requests which control the appearance of
the text on the printed page.

A control line begins with a formatting control character (not to be confused
with an ASCII control character), usually a dot (.) or sometimes a single quotation mark ('), followed by one or more characters that name the request. The
request may take an argument, and any argument must be separated from the
request name by whitespace (one space character is sufficient). Because any
remaining text on the control line is ignored, the request must be on a line by
itself.

Some formatting requests must be embedded within a line of text so that they
affect only selected words instead of the entire line. These requests are preceded by
a formatting escape character, the backslash (\ ), and are called *escape sequences*.

In this tutorial you will learn about the low-level **nroff** requests that

• Set line and page length

- Set the left margin and adjust text to produce justified or ragged margins
- Enable or disable line filling
- Control hyphenation and vertical spacing
- Force the start of a new page or keep a group of lines together
- Center text on a line
- Underline text
- Provide flexible indentation
- Produce titles for documents
- Define macros.

Most of the requests that we discuss occur on a control line and begin with a dot. We will refer to such requests as *dot requests*. A dot request may take a numerical or string argument. An unsigned numerical argument specifies a particular value, whereas a signed number specifies a change to an existing value. For example, the following request specifies an absolute line length of 55 characters:

.ll 55

The following requests specify an increase and decrease in the length by the amount shown:

.ll +10
.ll −5

Generally, omitting a numerical argument indicates that the default value should be used. Thus, the request

.ll

would specify that the line length be returned to 65 characters (the default value).

Controlling Page Layout

In the absence of any formatting requests, the **nroff** program produces output that fits on a standard 8 1/2 × 11-inch page. A vertical spacing of 6 lines per inch is assumed; thus 66 lines fit on the 11-inch-long printed page. The default line length is 65 character columns across, so that if you specify the customary one-inch left margin, the right margin will be about the same width. However, in the absence of any formatting requests, **nroff** *does not* provide a left margin. You therefore have to specify a left margin explicitly.

The dot requests that control layout of the text on the printed page include the following.

- *Page length*, **.pl**, specifies the number of lines on a page. The initial (default) value is 66 lines. The value specified for the page length must agree with the physical length of the paper.

- *Line length*, **.ll**, specifies the number of characters on a line of text. The initial (default) value is 65.

- *Page offset*, **.po**, specifies the number of spaces in the left margin. The initial (default) value is 0, giving no left margin. Generally a value of 8 to 10 is employed with 65-character lines to give roughly equal left and right margins.

Figure 5-8 shows how the values for page length, line length, and page offset control the appearance of the printed page.

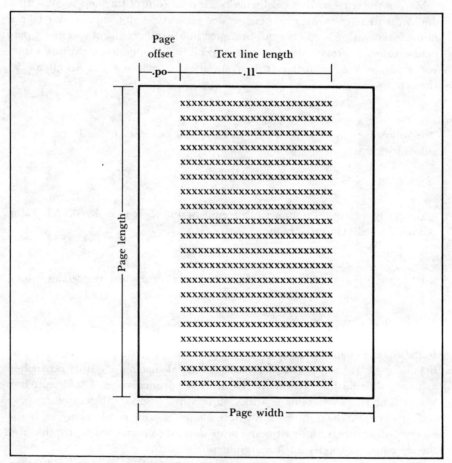

Figure 5-8. *Elements controlling printed page layout*

To see how changing the page offset and line length affect the page layout and in particular the margin settings, let's first format a paragraph using a page offset of 8 columns with a line length of 65. Note that the input text has no left margin since there is no space between the text and the left side of the screen (or of the paper when the output is printed):

```
$ cat input.txt
.ll 65
.po 8
    The program prompts for the old password (if any) and then for the
new one (twice). The caller must supply these. New passwords should be
at least four characters long if they use a sufficiently rich alphabet and
at least six characters long if monocase. Only the first eight characters of
the password are significant.
$
```

And after formatting, here is the result:

```
$ nroff input.txt
        The program prompts for the old password (if any) and then for
    the new one (twice). The caller must supply these. New passwords
    should be at least four characters long if they use a sufficiently rich
    alphabet and at least six characters long if monocase. Only the first
    eight characters of the password are significant.
...
$
```

As you can see, the combination of a 65-character line length and an 8-character left margin gives approximately equal left and right one-inch margins.

Now let's change the formatting directives to decrease the line length by 10 (to 55 characters) and compensate by increasing the page offset by 5 to keep the left and right margins the same width. Here is the input text:

```
$ cat input.txt
.ll 55
.po 13
    The program prompts for the old password (if any) and then for the
new one (twice). The caller must supply these. New passwords should be
at least four characters long if they use a sufficiently rich alphabet and
```

at least six characters long if monocase. Only the first eight characters of
the password are significant.

$ ▉

And the next screen shows the formatted result:

$ nroff input.txt

> The program prompts for the old password (if any) and
> then for the new one (twice). The caller must supply
> these. New passwords should be at least four characters
> long if they use a sufficiently rich alphabet and at least
> six characters long if monocase. Only the first eight
> characters of the password are significant.

$ ▉

Filling and Adjusting Text

Earlier we saw that without any formatting requests, **nroff** fills and adjusts lines
to produce text that looks like a block. The text is *filled* by first rearranging the
words on the lines so that the lines are as uniform in length as possible. Words at
the end of the line are hyphenated, if necessary, during the filling process. The
text is *adjusted* by inserting additional space between words to create a *justified*
(that is, straight) right margin.

The dot requests that control adjusting include the following:

- *No adjust,* **.na**, turns off adjusting. The right margin will not be justified and
  will thus be *ragged*. However, the left margin will be straight.
- *Adjust left,* **.ad l**, gives a flush left and ragged right margin (the same result
  as using **.na**).
- *Adjust right,* **.ad r**, gives flush right and ragged left margins.
- *Adjust center,* **.ad c**, centers text on a line and thus both margins will be
  ragged.
- *Adjust both,* **.ad b**, or *adjust normal,* **.ad n**, produces justified right and left
  margins.
- *Adjust last,* **.ad**, reenables adjusting. The adjusting style will be the same as
  the last style used.

Here are some examples of how these adjusting styles work. No **nroff** request or the request **.ad b** or **.ad n** would produce

```
| This paragraph has been filled and adjusted. The
| formatter will fill and adjust text in the absence of
| any requests. You have to disable filling or adjust-
| ing or change adjusting style by request.
```

The **nroff** request **.na** or **.ad l** would produce

```
|This paragraph has been filled but not adjusted.
|The left margin is flush but the right margin is
|ragged. This style is generally used for corre-
|spondence.
```

The **nroff** request **.ad r** would produce

```
|     This paragraph has been right adjusted. The
| right margin is flush but the left margin is ragged.
|     This format is sometimes called "Swiss style".
```

The **nroff** request **.ad c** would produce

```
| This paragraph has been adjusted so each line of
| text is centered on the page. Note, that both margins
| are ragged. This style might be used for centering
|             headings and titles.
```

You may use the *no fill* request, **.nf**, to disable filling of the output text. Each output line will appear exactly like the corresponding input line because adjusting as well as filling is disabled. You may reenable filling with the *fill* request, **.fi**. If adjusting has not been disabled, it will be reinstituted using the previous adjusting style.

Controlling Hyphenation

During the text filling process, **nroff** attempts to include as many words as possible on an output line. If the last word on a line is too long — that is, if it would cause the line length specification to be exceeded — **nroff** may divide the word with a hyphen (-) and place the "overhang" on the next line. Generally, **nroff** divides the word correctly between syllables, but occasionally it may hyphenate the word incorrectly or hyphenate a word that should not be hyphenated, such as a proper name.

Without any requests, **nroff** provides hyphenation as a default case. You may control hyphenation in several ways. You may turn hyphenation off for an individual word or for all words on one or more lines. Alternatively, you can allow a restricted form of hyphenation. In addition, you may specify how you wish to hyphenate particular words.

To prevent a word from being divided during the filling process, put the escape sequence \% immediately before a particular word (with no intervening whitespace). The following examples illustrate how to protect a proper name from being hyphenated. First, without any requests, the proper name "California" is hyphenated:

```
$ cat input.txt
.ll 55
    The examples were checked at the University of
California at Berkeley.
$ nroff input.txt
    The examples were checked at the University of Cal-
ifornia at Berkeley.
$
```

But when the \% escape sequence precedes the proper names, hyphenation is prevented:

```
$ cat input.txt
.ll 55
    The examples were checked at the \%University of
\%California at \%Berkeley.
$ nroff input.txt
    The examples were  checked  at  the  University of
California at Berkeley.
$
```

You may disable hyphenation completely by specifying the *no hyphenation* request, **.nh**. If you wish to reenable hyphenation, you may specify the *hyphenation* request, **.hy**. Note that words that already contain hyphens may still be divided at the existing hyphen whether or not hyphenation is enabled.

You may use a numerical argument with the hyphenation request to restrict the *hyphenation level,* as follows:

- **.hy 2** prevents hyphenation of the last word on a page.
- **.hy 4** prevents dividing the last two letters from a word, as in "request-ed."
- **.hy 8** prevents dividing the first two letters from a word, as in "re-quested."
- **.hy 14** combines all of these restrictions.

Notice that these restrictions are additive, so that **.hy 12**, which combines **.hy 4** and **.hy 8**, prevents the first or the last two letters from being split from a word, although the last word on a page could still be hyphenated.

You may specify where you wish hyphenation to occur by following the *hyphenate words* request, **.hw**, with a list of words. Indicate the desired hyphenation position by explicitly placing a hyphen (-) where you wish the word to be hyphenated. Use the request syntax

.hw *word...*

These *words* will be hyphenated only at the indicated place. Also the size of the hyphenated word list is limited, usually to 128 characters in all.

Controlling Vertical Spacing

As you have seen, a blank line in the input text is passed by **nroff** unchanged to its standard output. Thus you may specify one or more blank lines in the output by actually inserting them in the input text. If you wished to change the number of lines later, however, you'd have to use an editor to add or remove blank lines from the input. To specify a blank line, we recommend using the *spacing* request, **.sp**, instead. To indicate more than one blank line, you may specify an argument to this request. For instance,

.sp 2

would leave the next two text lines after this request blank in the output. If the argument for **.sp** is negative, the blank lines will be inserted before the formatting request.

The formatted output is single-spaced by default. You may change the spacing between lines from this default to some other value by using the *line spacing* request, **.ls**, with a numerical argument. The number of blank lines inserted between each text line will be the value of this argument minus one. For instance,

.ls 3

specifies triple spacing, or that two (3 − 1 = 2) blank lines be inserted after each line of text.

As an example, the following input text has spacing requests to specify a blank line and a line spacing request to cause double spacing of the output text:

```
$ cat input.txt
.ls 2
Only the owner of the name or the super-user may change a
password; the owner must prove he knows the old password.
.sp 1
Only the super-user can create a null password.
.sp
The password file is not changed if the new password is the
same as the old password, or if the password has not
"aged" sufficiently.
.sp 1
See also passwd(4).
$
```

When formatted, the **.ls 2** request causes a blank line to be inserted after *every* text line. Note that **.sp** gives the same result as **.sp 1**.

```
$ nroff input.txt
    Only the owner of the name or the super-user may change a password; the owner

must prove he knows the old password.

    Only the super-user can create a null password.

    The password file is not changed if the new password is the same as the old pass-

word, or if the password has not "aged" sufficiently.

See also passwd(4).
$
```

There are two blank lines between paragraphs. One blank line results from the **.sp** request and the other from the **.ls 2** request.

Controlling Pagination

You may force a new page by inserting the *break page* request, **.bp**, in the text where you wish the new page to begin. When **nroff** encounters this request, it ends the current page and immediately begins a new page. (If you want a one-inch margin at the top of the new page, follow the break request with the space request, **.sp 6**. You have to use a macro package to get top and bottom page margins automatically.)

Occasionally you will need to keep a group of lines together on a page. For instance, you wouldn't want to start tabulated information on the bottom of one page and have it divided and continued on the next page. You could use the *need line* request, **.ne**, to keep all the lines in the table together. This request takes a numerical argument that specifies the number of lines that should remain together. For instance,

.ne 10

specifies that the ten lines containing text (control lines don't count) after this request should remain together. If less than that number of lines would remain on the current page, a page break would occur to place all the lines together on the following page.

Centering Text

Earlier in this session we mentioned using the *center adjust* request, **.ad c**, for centering lines of text. The results of this request may not be what you expect, because filling may cause words to be shifted between lines. For this reason it is preferable to use the *center* request, **.ce**, instead. A numerical argument indicates the number of subsequent text lines that are to be centered. The center request without an argument only centers the next text line.

As an example, let's center the heading for a document. The input text and the resulting formatted output are shown in this screen simulation:

```
$ cat input.txt
.ll 55
.ce 4
Chapter 5
Tutorials
```

```
.sp
Session 12
.sp
The UNIX text formatter—nroff
.sp 2
    The UNIX system is noted for its powerful and
extensive text processing facilities. UNIX text
processing involves two separate steps.
$ nroff input.txt
                    Chapter 5
                    Tutorials
                    Session 12
        The UNIX text formatter—nroff
    The UNIX system is noted for its powerful and ex-
tensive text processing facilities. UNIX text process-
ing involves two separate steps.
    $ ▇
```

Since only lines of text are counted for centering, the blank lines specified by the *space* requests, **.sp**, have no effect.

A way to avoid counting the lines to be centered is to specify an arbitrarily large number of lines to center—for example, 50—and then disable centering immediately after the last line you wish centered by using the request **.ce 0**. An additional advantage of this approach is that it keeps you from having to change the argument to **.ce** if lines to be centered are added or deleted. For practice, try this now with the last example.

Underlining Text

There are two different dot requests for underlining text:

- *Underline*, **.ul**, underlines *only* alphanumeric characters.
- *Continuous underline*, **.cu**, underlines *all* characters, including whitespace.

Either dot request may take a numerical argument to indicate the number of text lines to underline. As with the centering request, you may specify a zero argument to either **.ul** or **.cu** to stop the underlining process.

The distinction between the two styles of underlining is shown by the next example:

```
$ cat input.txt
.ul
5.12.2 Formatting Requests
.sp
.cu
5.12.2.1 Controlling Page Layout
$ nroff input.txt
5.12.2 Formatting Requests
5.12.2.1 Controlling Page Layout
$
```

In the first instance, only the alphanumeric text is underlined. In the second case, both the text and any intervening whitespace and punctuation are underscored to create a continuous underline.

If you wish, for example, to underline one or more words in the middle of a sentence for emphasis, place the words on their own line in the input file. Here is an example:

```
$ cat input.txt
.ll 55
    Any remaining text on the control line is ignored so the request must be
.ul
on a line by itself.
Some requests may appear on text lines.
$ nroff input.txt
    Any remaining text on the control line is ignored
so the request must be on a line by itself. Some re-
ests may appear on text lines.
$
```

Notice how the filling process placed the underlined text properly within the paragraph, even though it appeared on a separate line in the input.

Controlling Indentation

If any blanks occur at the beginning of a line, **nroff** treats this as a *break* and stops the filling process. So far we have used paragraphs that were indented manually through the insertion of several space characters (or a tab) on the first line. These spaces cause a break in the filling so that the previous paragraph isn't merged into the current paragraph. If you wish to use block style paragraphs instead of indented paragraphs, simply insert one or more blank lines between paragraphs to provide a break to interrupt the filling process.

The spaces at the beginning of a manually indented paragraph provide a break in the filling process, as shown here:

```
$ cat input.txt
.ll 55
    Only the owner of the name or the super-user may change a
password; the owner must prove he knows the old password.
    Only the super-user can create a null password.
    The password file is not changed if the new password is the
same as the old password, or if the password has not
"aged" sufficiently; see passwd(4).

$ nroff input.txt
    Only the owner of the name or the super-user may
change a password; the owner must prove he knows
the old password.
    Only the super-user can create a null password.
    The password file is not changed if the new pass-
word is the same as the old password, or if the pass-
word has not "aged" sufficiently; see passwd(4).
$
```

Because the block paragraph style doesn't use indentation, a blank line is used to provide a break in the filling process:

```
$ cat input.txt
.ll 55
Only the owner of the name or the super-user may change a
password; the owner must prove he knows the old password.

Only the super-user can create a null password.
```

The password file is not changed if the new password is the
same as the old password, or if the password has not
"aged" sufficiently; see passwd(4).

$ nroff input.txt

Only the owner of the name or the super-user may change
a password; the owner must prove he knows the old password.

Only the super-user can create a null password.

The password file is not changed if the new password is
the same as the old password, or if the password has not
"aged" sufficiently; see passwd(4).

$ ▓

You may wish to emphasize a block of text by indentation. Use the *permanent
indent* request, **.in**, to indent all text lines that follow by the amount specified as a
numerical argument. This level of indentation remains in effect until changed by
another permanent indentation request. For example:

$ cat input.txt

.ll 55

This command changes (or installs) a password associated
with the login name.

.sp

.in 5

The program prompts for the old password (if any) and then
for the new one (twice). The caller must supply these. New
passwords should be at least four characters long if they
use a sufficiently rich alphabet and at least six characters
long if monocase. Only the first eight characters of the
password are significant.

.sp

.in −5

Only the owner of the name or the super-user may change a
password; the owner must prove he knows the old password.

$ nroff input.txt

This command changes (or installs) a password associated with the login name.

> The program prompts for the old password (if any) and then for the new one (twice). The caller must supply these. New passwords should be at least four characters long if they use a sufficiently rich alphabet and at least six characters long if mono-case. Only the first eight characters of the password are significant.

Only the owner of the name or the super-user may change a password; the owner must prove he knows the old password.

$ ▆

Since we specified no page offset (left margin) here, the **.in 5** request causes the second paragraph to be indented 5 spaces from the left-hand edge of the paper. We used the **.in −5** request to reset the permanent indentation, however in this instance either **.in 0** or even **.in** would have worked as well.

The **nroff** program also recognizes a *temporary indent* request, **ti**. This request causes indentation of only the *next* text line by an amount specified by its argument. The indentation for the remaining text lines returns to the current permanent indentation level.

Here is an example in which permanent and temporary indentation are combined:

```
$ cat input.txt
.ll 55
.po 5
.ti +5
This command changes (or installs) a password associated
with the login name.
.sp
.in 5
.ti +5
The program prompts for the old password (if any) and then
for the new one (twice). The caller must supply these. New
passwords should be at least four characters long if they
use a sufficiently rich alphabet and at least six characters
```

long if monocase. Only the first eight characters of the
password are significant.

.sp

.in −5

.ti 5

Only the owner of the name or the super-user may change a
password; the owner must prove he knows the old password.

$ nroff input.txt

This command changes (or installs) a password associated with the login name.

The program prompts for the old password (if
any) and then for the new one (twice). The caller
must supply these. New passwords should be at
least four characters long if they use a sufficiently rich alphabet and at least six characters
long if monocase. Only the first eight characters
of the password are significant.

Only the owner of the name or the super-user may
change a password; the owner must prove he knows
the old password.

$ ▮

In this case, both **.ti +5** and **.ti 5** work the same way.

In the previous example, since we have specified a page offset, the overall
indentation is the sum of the page offset, the permanent indentation, and any
temporary indentation. Figure 5-9 shows how these indentation elements control
page layout.

As another example, let's use a negative argument with the temporary indent
request to produce an indented list of paragraphs, where each paragraph is
marked with a bullet:

$ cat input.txt

.ll 55

There are several things to consider
when choosing a password:

.sp

.in 10

.ti −5

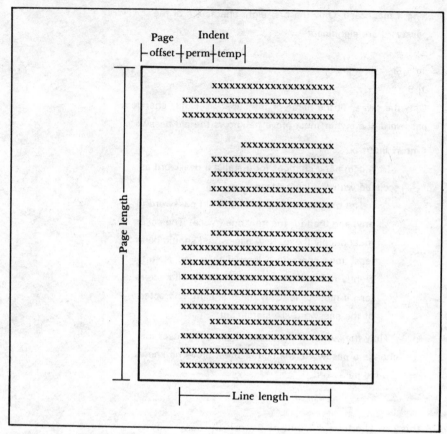

Figure 5-9. *Indentation elements control page layout*

· The password must be at
least four characters long if you
use only lower- and uppercase
letters and numerals.
.sp
.ti −5
· Your password should be
at least six characters long
if you use only lower- or
uppercase letters.

```
.sp
.ti -5
```
· Only the first eight characters
of a password are significant.
Extra characters are simply ignored.

$ nroff input.txt
There are several things to consider when choosing a
password:

- The password must be at least four characters
  long if you use only lower- and uppercase
  letters and numerals.

- Your password should be at least six characters long if you use only lower- or uppercase
  letters.

- Only the first eight characters of a password
  are significant. Extra characters are simply
  ignored.

$

Providing Titles

The **nroff** formatter provides title lines that may contain up to three parts: a left, right, and center field. The *title line* request, **.tl**, is used to define a title. Use the following request syntax:

$$.tl \ ' \ lstr \ ' \ cstr \ ' \ rstr \ '$$

Here you would replace *lstr, cstr,* and *rstr* by the appropriate text or by nothing if you wished the field left blank. The formatter will place the left string against the left margin, and the right string will end at the right margin of the title line. The center string will be located midway between the title line margins.

You may set the length of the title line separately from the line length. Use the *length of title line* request, **.lt**, where the numeric argument determines the title line length. The initial default length of the title line is 65 characters (the same as the default line length). Note that the title line may be offset by a preceding page offset request (**.po**), but it is unaffected by a permanent indent request (**.in**).

Here is an example of setting up a title line. The input text is

```
$ cat input.txt
.bp
.sp 2
.tl 'A  User Guide to the Unix System' 'Second Edition'
.sp 3
$
```

The following shows how the top of the titled page would look when formatted and printed. After the page break (produced by **.bp**), there are two blank lines (produced by the **.sp 2** request) between the top of page and the title line. Then three blank lines (produced by **.sp 3**) follow before any text begins.

————————————————— (top of page) —————————————————

A User Guide to the Unix System   Second Edition

(beginning of text)

You may easily provide for page numbering in a title line. Whenever a percent sign (%) occurs in the title line request, it will be replaced by the current page number. Here we show the input text in our screen simulation:

```
$ cat input.txt
.bp
.sp 2
.tl 'A User Guide to the Unix System'Page %'Second Edition'
.sp 3
$
```

When formatted, however, a title is produced in which the left field overlaps the middle field.

————————————————— (top of page) —————————————————

A User Guide to the Unix SystePage 2   Second Edition

(beginning of text)

When the fields overlap, you need to compensate by increasing the length of the title line, such as shown here:

```
$ cat input.txt
.lt 70
.bp
.sp 2
.tl 'A User Guide to the Unix System'      Page %'Second Edition'
.sp 3
$
```

Now when the title is formatted, there is sufficient room for all three elements of the title line:

———————————————— (top of page) ————————————————

A User Guide to the Unix System   Page 2   Second Edition

(beginning of text)

We added some space before the "Page %" string in the middle field for a more balanced appearance.

These last few examples really demonstrate the virtue of previewing the result on your terminal screen before requesting a hard-copy printout.

Some Useful Escape Sequences

Previously we introduced the escape sequence \%, which prevents hyphenation of the attached word. Generally escape sequences are used to specify formatting directives that affect only a portion of a line instead of the entire line. Other escape sequences are used when adjacent text or control lines must be connected logically.

Here are several escape sequences that you may find useful:

- \<SPACE>, the *unpaddable space,* is used to keep text together on a line. If an unpaddable space is used instead of an ordinary space between words, the words on either side of the space are kept on the same line.

- \&, the *unpaddable zero width character,* may be used to remove the significance of the dot (.) or acute accent (') located at the beginning of a line as beginning an **nroff** request.

- \'' is used to begin a comment on a line. The remaining characters on the input line are ignored.

- \c, the *continuation indicator,* is used to indicate that a given input line is a continuation of the previous input line so that no spaces are inserted between the two lines during filling.

- **\u**, the *upward half-line motion*, is used to produce superscripted text. Follow the text to be superscripted by the **\d** sequence to bring the printer down to the baseline again.

- **\d**, the *downward half-line motion*, is used to produce subscripted text. Follow the text to be subscripted by the **\u** sequence to bring the printer up to the baseline again.

- **\<NEWLINE>**, the *concealed* (or *ignored*) *new line* (generated by pressing RETURN immediately after typing backslash) is used to continue a long **nroff** request on the next line.

Macro Requests

So far you have learned about the lowest level or *primitive* **nroff** requests that control the appearance of the printed document. Each primitive performs what might be called an *atomic operation*, in that they each specify only one low-level format directive. You will find these low-level requests adequate for most single-page documents.

In some of our earlier examples you might have noticed that a number of primitive requests were specified sequentially one after the other in order to perform a practical task. As an example, the following operations are commonly specified to start a new paragraph:

- Leave one or more blank lines between the new and the previous paragraph. A blank line request would stop the filling process so that the previous paragraph won't merge with the next one.

- Make sure that there are enough lines left on the current page to start the new paragraph. If not, force a page break and begin the paragraph on next page.

- Cancel any permanent indentation that may be in effect so that the left margin is determined solely by the current page offset.

- Provide temporary indentation for the first line of the new paragraph.

These operations could be performed by specifying the following sequence of low-level directives:

    .sp 1   Insert one blank line before the next paragraph.
    .ne 3   Keep at least the first three lines of the next paragraph together on the same page.
    .in 0   Reset permanent indentation level to zero.
    .ti 5   Temporarily indent the first line of the next paragraph.

Now you might ask yourself, "Do I have to type these same four requests each time I wish to begin a new paragraph?" The answer is no: you can use a *macro* request, often called simply a *macro*, to stand for these same four requests. Whenever **nroff** encounters the higher-level macro request in the input text file, all the low-level requests that constitute it are actually executed. In fact, the macro request looks very much like a low-level request and is used the same way.

In the next section you learn how to define and use several macros, including the paragraph macro we have been discussing.

Defining and Using Some Simple Macros

Let's name our paragraph macro **PG**. The convention in naming macro requests is to use capital letters although **nroff** will accept lowercase macro names too. Using capital letters is helpful in that it allows you to distinguish the macro requests from low-level requests, which have lowercase names, when you are reading an input text file.

The macro definition begins with the *define* request, **.de**, followed by the name you wish to give the macro. You can provide comments on the control lines in the macro definition by preceding the comment text with the \" escape sequence. We recommend using comments generously so that other users can immediately understand your macro definition and its purpose. (Comments also serve as useful reminders if you return to the macro after time away.) Finally, you should end the macro definition with a control line containing two dots (..). In general, macros are defined in terms of low-level **nroff** requests and other previously defined macros. Thus our paragraph macro would be defined as follows:

```
.de PG   \" Paragraph macro definition.
.sp      \" One blank line between paragraphs.
.ne 3    \" Need to keep 3 lines together.
.in 0    \" Reset permanent indentation level.
.ti 5    \" Temporarily indent first line.
..       \" End definition.
```

Now whenever you wish to start a new paragraph, you can simply specify

.PG

in the first column of your input text file, and whenever **nroff** encounters a **.PG** in the text, it will actually execute the four low-level requests that constitute it.

You must place your macro definition before your first usage of that macro. The following input text illustrates the placement of the paragraph macro definition and its use for formatting two short paragraphs.

```
$ cat input.txt
.de PG  \" Paragraph macro definition
.sp     \" One blank line between paragraphs
.ne 3   \" Need to keep 3 lines together
.in 0   \" Reset indentation level
.ti 5   \" Temporarily indent first line
..  \" End definition
.ll 50
.PG
The password must be at
least four characters long if you
use only lower- and uppercase
letters and numerals.
.PG
Your password should be
at least six characters long
if you use only lower- or
uppercase letters.
$ ▓
```

When this input text is formatted with **nroff**, the output will look like this:

```
$ nroff input.txt
    The password must be at least four characters long if you use only lower- and
uppercase letters and numerals.
    Your password should be at least six characters long if you use only lower- or
uppercase letters.
$ ▓
```

You may wish to place your macro definitions in a separate file and use the source request, **.so**, to include the contents of the macro definition file at formatting time. In this way, you can keep your main text document shorter and easier to manage. In fact, you may use the source request to combine several smaller input text files into a single larger input file at formatting time. The syntax for using this request to include a file named *filename* is simply

.so *filename*

When **nroff** encounters the source request, the contents of *filename* replace the request control line.

To implement our last example in this tutorial session, we need to define two more simple macros. One is used to center a title at the top of the page and the other is used to create a list that employs bullets.

The title macro is simply

```
.de TL   \" Title for document.
.bp      \" Begin a new page.
.sp 2    \" Two blank lines before title.
\\$1     \" The title argument.
.sp 3    \" Three more blank lines before the text.
..       \" End definition.
```

The \\$1 will be replaced by the argument for the macro. The argument is separated from the macro call (.**TL**) by whitespace on the same line, and the argument must be enclosed in quotation marks if it contains whitespace. For instance, after defining the title macro, you'd specify the macro request as

.TL "Title Line"

to produce a centered title containing the text "Title Line".

One possible definition for the **BL** bullet macro would be

```
.de BL   \" Bullet list macro definition.
.sp      \" One blank line between bullet paragraphs.
.ne 3  . \" Need to keep 3 lines together.
.in 10   \" Add permanent indentation.
.ti −5   \" Create hanging indent on first line.
..       \" End of definition.
```

Now let's add the definitions for **TL**, **PG**, and **BL** to a file named **mymacros**. The contents of this are as follows:

```
$ cat mymacros
.de TL   \" Document title macro definition.
.bp      \" Begin a new page.
.sp 2    \" Two blank lines before title.
\\$1     \" The title argument.
.sp 3    \" Three more blank lines before the text.
..       \" End definition.
.de PG   \" Paragraph macro definition.
.sp      \" One blank line between paragraphs.
.ne 3    \" Need to keep 3 lines together.
```

```
.in 0      \" Reset permanent indentation level.
.ti 5      \" Temporarily indent first line.
..         \" End definition.
.de BL     \" Bullet list macro definition.
.sp        \" One blank line between bullet paragraphs.
.ne 3      \" Need to keep 3 lines together.
.in 10     \" Add permanent indentation.
.ti −5     \" Create hanging indent on first line.
..         \" End of definition.
$ ▓
```

At this point, we're ready to employ these macros to format the short document entitled "Style Recommendations for Input Text," the input text for which follows:

```
$ cat style.guide
.so mymacros
.hw un-avoidable
.TL "Style Recommendations for Input Text"
.PG
We recommend the following guidelines for
preparing your input file for the
.ul
nroff
program:
.BL
• Text lines should
.ul
never
begin with a control character, that is,
a dot (.) or acute accent ('). If this is
unavoidable then precede the control
character by the escape sequence, \ \&.
.BL
• Use
.ul
every
```

line in the input file for either a

formatting directive or text.

.BL

• Don't provide breaks manually. That is,

don't begin a line with a space or

leave blank lines in the input file.

Use formatting directives for indenting

text and inserting blank lines in output.

.BL

• Keep input lines short, say, half-way

across the page for easier editing and reading.

.BL

• Keep input files short, say 500 lines or less,

so they are manageable. Divide long documents

into shorter files which can be combined

when formatting commences.

Note that we used the hyphenate word request, **.hw**, to specify how to hyphenate "unavoidable" because **nroff** would have divided it incorrectly as "una-voidable". When formatted, the result is this:

$ nroff style.guide

Style Guidelines for Input Text

We recommend the following guidelines for preparing your input file for the <u>nroff</u> program:

• Text lines should <u>never</u> begin with a control character, that is, a dot (.) or acute accent ('). If this is unavoidable then precede the control character by the escape sequence, \&.

• Use <u>every</u> line in the input file for either a formatting directive or text.

• Don't provide breaks manually. That is, don't begin a line with a space or leave blank lines in the input file. Use formatting directives for indenting text and inserting blank lines in output.

- Keep input lines short, say, half-way across the page for easier editing and reading.

- Keep input files short, say 500 lines or less, so they are manageable. Divide long documents into shorter files which can be combined when formatting commences.

$

Macro Packages

Frequently used macros may be collected together and placed in a *macro package*. There are several macro packages available for use with **nroff** on the UNIX system.

The **ms** (for manuscript) macro package is the most widely available and frequently used macro package. It was originally developed at Bell Labs for formatting long manuscripts like internal technical papers. It is available on most Version 7 UNIX systems.

The **mm** (for memorandum) macro package was also developed at Bell Labs. It was originally only available with the Programmer's Workbench UNIX system, but is now available with Systems III and V UNIX releases. Bell Labs has replaced the older **ms** package with the more powerful **mm** macro package.

The **me** macro package was developed at U.C. Berkeley and is available with the Berkeley UNIX software distribution. This package is somewhat easier to learn and use than the Bell Labs packages. However, the macro names use lowercase letters, which makes them difficult to distinguish from the low-level **nroff** requests.

The **man** macro package was developed at Bell Labs and is used to prepare the *UNIX User's Manual*. In addition, the **man** program uses this package for reproducing the manual on-line.

Redirecting nroff's Input and Output

The general command line for invoking **nroff** to format one or more files is

$ **nroff** [−*option*...] [−] [*file*...]

where one or more *options* may appear in any order, although they must appear before the names of the input files. See the last section in this session, "Some **nroff**

Invocation Options," for a discussion of some commonly used options. The formatter treats a minus ($-$) argument as being an input that corresponds to its standard input file. Output from the **nroff** program is directed to its standard output file (your terminal screen, by default).

At the beginning of this session, you learned about the basic command lines for viewing **nroff**'s output on your terminal and piping the output to the line printer spooler, **lpr**, for producing a hard copy. Here are some other command lines that are useful with the text formatter. The following command line allows you to redirect the output to a disk file, *output file*, for storage or subsequent manipulation with an editor:

$$\text{\$ nroff } \textit{input file} > \textit{output file}$$

To pipe the output to another UNIX utility for further processing, such as the program used to check for spelling mistakes, use this command line:

$$\text{\$ nroff } \textit{input file} \mid \textbf{spell}$$

Finally, with the command line, the output of another UNIX utility, such as **sort**, may provide the input data for **nroff**.

$$\text{\$ sort } \textit{file} \mid \textbf{nroff}$$

If more than one input file is specified on the shell command line when you invoke **nroff**, the contents of each file are first joined in the order specified and the combined result is formatted. For instance, in the next sample command line, we show a mailing list being sorted by the UNIX **sort** program, the result piped into **nroff** to be appended to a heading (contents of *header file*), to which is appended a footing (contents of *footer file*). The concatenated text is formatted and the output passed on to **lpr** for printing on the system line printer:

$$\text{\$ sort } \textit{mail list} \mid \textbf{nroff } \textit{header file} - \textit{footer file} \mid \textbf{lpr}$$

Problems may arise if each input file was actually designed to be formatted separately. The files may format differently when concatenated if the formatting requests from one file influence the formatting of the next file. For instance, let's say that a formatting request in one file specifies a change from a default value and that the next file uses the same value as if it were the default. The product of such a chain of influence would be unpredictable and quite different from what you wanted. Thus if you plan to concatenate input files, be sure to return values to their default at the end of each input file.

Some nroff Invocation Options

Although the **nroff** program has many invocation options, here we will mention only some of the options that you are most likely to need. If you are interested in using some of the more esoteric options for **nroff**, consult the Bell Labs documentation.

The following options control the printing of specific pages. The

$$-opagelist$$

option specifies printing of pages in *pagelist*. The *pagelist* consists of individual page numbers separated by commas or ranges of page numbers separated by a dash. For instance, $N-M$ indicates pages N through M, inclusive; $-N$ indicates all pages from page 1 through page N; $N-$ indicates page N through the end of the document.

You would use this option when you need to print only part of a document. For instance, if you specify

$$\text{\$ nroff } -o2-4 \text{ } input \text{ } file$$

you would print pages 2, 3, and 4 of *input file*.

The option

$$-nN$$

resets the page number to N for the first page that is printed. This option enables files that make up a large document to be formatted separately but still to be numbered correctly with reference to the combined document. For instance, if you specify

$$\text{\$ nroff } -n20 \text{ } input \text{ } file$$

the first page formatted of *input file* will have the page number 20.

The option

$$-sN$$

allows the printing to be suspended every N pages. This option would be useful to allow paper changing or loading during printing. Formatting continues after you press RETURN. For instance, specify

$$\text{\$ nroff } -s1 \text{ } input \text{ } file$$

to suspend printing of *input file* at the end of every page.

The next option enables you to specify that a particular macro package be employed:

$$-\mathbf{m}name$$

This option specifies that the macro definitions contained in the file with pathname **/usr/lib/tmac/tmac.***name* be prepended to your document before formatting commences. Note that the name of the macro package file must conform to this pathname when you use this option. If you have your own custom macro package named, for example, **mymacros**, then that file will have to be specified explicitly on the command line before the names of any files to be formatted. For example, if **mymacros** is in your current directory, specify

$$\$ \text{ nroff mymacros } input \ file$$

Here is an example of using this option. The definitions for standard macro package **ms**, are contained in the file **/usr/lib/tmac/tmac.s** and thus may be referenced by specifying −**ms** on the invocation command line, as follows:

$$\$ \text{ nroff } -\mathbf{ms} \ input \ file$$

If you wished to employ both the **ms** macro package and your custom macro package, **mymacros**, you would use the command line

$$\$ \text{ nroff } -\mathbf{ms} \ \mathbf{mymacros} \ input \ file$$

You may indicate the output device for which **nroff** should prepare output for using the next option in this way:

$$-\mathbf{T}name$$

This option specifies the device *name* for which **nroff** is to prepare its output. All devices designated by *name* require driving tables installed in the **/usr/lib/term** directory. Thus, if there is no driving table file in **/usr/lib/term** corresponding to your output device, such as a printer, **nroff** cannot prepare output for your printing device. In this case, specify −**Tlp** or −**Tcrt** so that you can at least obtain a hard copy, even if not all of the printing features would then be available.

If no −**T** option is used, **nroff** prepares output for a default case, the Teletype Model 37 hard-copy terminal, which is capable of backspacing. If you are using a line printer that is not capable of backspacing, specify **lp** for *name*. Consult your system administrator for assistance with specifying an output device for **nroff** if the output produced by your printer doesn't look correct.

PART THREE

CHAPTER 6

COMMONLY USED UNIX SYSTEM COMMANDS

6
COMMONLY
USED UNIX
SYSTEM
COMMANDS

In this chapter we present 44 commonly used UNIX system commands. You may read the chapter from beginning to end, trying all the examples on-line for an in-depth understanding of these commands and additional UNIX concepts. While the chapter lends itself to tutorial practice with each of the commands presented, either in sequence or individually, it is also structured to serve as a handy reference tool.

To facilitate the reference process, the command line and the options for each command are summarized in a box located at the head of the text describing each command. One of the major differences between versions of UNIX is the different constellation of options available for each command. The options box gives you a quick way to determine which invocation options for a command apply to your version of UNIX. Some commands, of course, have no options, while others have several. Some commands are very "implementation-dependent," which means that there is considerable variation in the options that the customized version of UNIX—for instance, a tailored version of System III—recognizes. Whenever a command is highly implementation-dependent, the overview of the command informs you of this characteristic.

The overview, which is located immediately after the options box, describes the purpose and overall operation of the command. From this general introduction you will learn how to set up the command line both in its most general form and in any other particularly useful ways. The most important options for the command are presented, and any idiosyncracies in the command's operation or results are outlined as well.

The overview for each command is followed by examples that you may enter directly into your computer. The examples illustrate most of the facets of the command described in the overview. By working closely with the examples, you should become thoroughly familiar with how the command and some of its most useful options behave. Once you practice with the examples, you will be able to adapt the command to your own needs. You should also feel free to experiment with any options that appear in the options box or in the overview that are not put to use in the examples.

The final section for each command consists of explanations of commonly occurring error and informational messages. Once again the messages are divided by UNIX versions for easier access, and any messages that vary greatly in particular UNIX implementations are noted. Because the *UNIX User's Manual* does not treat these error messages, you should find the explanations provided here especially helpful whenever you obtain unexpected results.

To understand the description of each command in this chapter, you should have read Chapters 3, 4, and 5 and have a working knowledge of the material explained there. In this chapter, we use the same conventions in screen displays and in referring to aspects of UNIX in the text as were used in Chapters 3, 4, and 5. Thus to "enter" a command line or a reply to a query, for example, means to type the command or response and to press RETURN. See the introduction to Chapter 3 for a full description of these conventions.

In addition, the examples in this chapter assume that you are using essentially the same sample file system that was used in Chapters 3 through 5 and that is shown here in Figure 6-1. Note that the directories **username** and **Username** are distinct and unrelated. These names should be replaced by your actual account name, as long as you do so consistently. Similarly, while the parent directory to your home directory doesn't have to be /usr, you must consistently replace **usr** with the actual name of your parent directory.

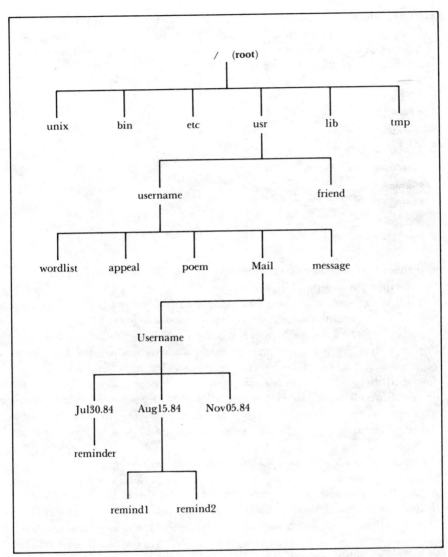

Figure 6-1.   *The sample file system*

Follow the steps outlined here to prepare for all the examples in this chapter. First change to your home directory by typing **cd** and pressing RETURN, and verify by entering **pwd**. Your result should be the same as if you had entered **echo**

$HOME, which also reveals the full pathname of your home directory. If this is not the case, see your system administrator for assistance.

Now set your user file creation mask (**umask**) value to zero by entering **umask 0** and verify the result by entering **umask**.

```
$ cd
$ pwd
/usr/username
$ echo $HOME
/usr/username
$ umask 0
$ umask
0000
$
```

You should set your umask value to zero in order to obtain the same results as shown when you enter and execute the suggested examples.

If you want to restrict the permissions automatically for newly created files, ask your system administrator for a recommended **umask** value.

The examples for some commands require a list of words, one word per line. If your system has a copy of the spelling dictionary on-line, use this file as your word list when necessary. The pathname for this dictionary is either **/usr/spell/dict** for Bell Version 7 and the Berkeley version and **/usr/lib/spell/list** or **/usr/lib/spell/words** for Bell System III and V. If you are using the on-line spelling dictionary, you should create a link to it by entering **ln** *dictionary* **wordlist**. Replace *dictionary* with the actual pathname of your system's spelling dictionary.

If your system doesn't have a readable form of the on-line spelling dictionary or some other convenient list of words, you can create such a list simply by typing **ls /bin >wordlist** and pressing RETURN. Of course, if your dictionary has been modified or if you are using a different word list, your results would be different in content than the results we depict in the examples. The principles of command operation, however, will be the same. In all cases, remove the link to **wordlist** when you are finished with it by entering **rm wordlist**.

The interrelated nature of the UNIX system becomes apparent in this chapter. Many of our examples use several commands to perform a realistic task. We suggest that you focus on the command being addressed and keep in mind that additional information on related commands will be addressed in other sections.

The screen displays reflect the UNIX system as distributed by Bell or Berkeley and may be somewhat different from other system implementations. Even if the details differ, however, the content and operation of each command should be essentially the same as we describe here.

Access Control

This section discusses the **login** and **passwd** commands. These commands are necessary for getting and controlling access to your UNIX system.

login — Sign On to Another Account

Bell Version 7 and Berkeley Versions:
$ **login** [*Username*]

Bell Systems III and V Versions:
$ **exec login** [*username*]

No Options

The sign-on procedure, which is called automatically by your UNIX system, makes it possible for you to log on initially. Before you do log on, your terminal is in an idle state, and the only procedure your system will perform is the sign-on procedure. After you have logged on to your account, you may invoke **login** as a command to sign on to another account. You might wish to log on to another account if, for instance, you are working on a small system and you would like to use different accounts for different purposes.

The UNIX sign-on procedure performs several functions, including

- Restricting system access to authorized users.

- Initiating accounting functions to bill users for their usage of the UNIX system.

- Displaying important system messages and informing you if mail is in your mailfile.

- Setting up a working *environment* for each user.

See the section "Customizing Your Working Environment" in Appendix C for information on how to customize your UNIX system environment.

The "login:" prompt will appear automatically on your terminal screen once you have turned the system on or dialed up properly. You simply need to type your login or user name, and perhaps a password, to begin interacting with the shell.

If you then wish to change the account you are logged on to, use the following command line format to invoke the **login** command:

$$\$ \text{ login } username$$

The *username* here refers to the user name that identifies the other account you wish to log on to. If you do not specify a user name, the **login** program will request one and perhaps a password as well.

If you are using either the Bell System III or V Bourne Shell, however, use the following command line format to change from one account to another:

$$\$ \text{ exec login } username$$

It is important to note that you can invoke other shells from the shell you initially interact with once you have logged on to the system. These secondary shells are known as *subshells*. When logging on to a new account, you should always invoke **login** from your login shell rather than from a subshell. Otherwise, you really haven't logged off the old account, and when you attempt to log off the new account, you will be returned to the old account. On some systems, you may get an error message if you try to log on to another account from a subshell.

Examples   Prepare for these examples as directed in the introduction to this chapter, but do not link **wordlist.**

For purposes of illustration, we assume that you are logged in as **username** and u wish to change to the account with the user name **friend.** Of course, you should replace **username** with your actual user name and **friend** with an actual account name on your UNIX system. If you are using a Version 7 Bourne or the Berkeley C Shell, simply type **login**, press RETURN, and answer the queries as you would for initial system access:

```
$ login
login: friend
Password:
(YOUR UNIX SYSTEM MESSAGES)
$ 
```

The actual text of YOUR UNIX SYSTEM MESSAGES depends on the version you are using and on the date and time of system access. Note that on some implementations, the system messages may not be displayed when you log in.

If you are working with a System III or V Bourne Shell, the procedure you would use is similar:

```
$ exec login friend
Password:
YOUR UNIX SYSTEM MESSAGES
$ ▓
```

If the **friend** argument is omitted, the **login** program will prompt you with the "login:" prompt for the name of the account you wish to change to, as shown in the first example.

Messages The following messages apply to all versions of **login**. If you receive any of these messages, see your system administrator for assistance.

No directory
Your system can't locate your home directory.

Cannot open password file
The password file cannot be read.

No shell
The program normally invoked immediately after system sign-on, which is usually a general-purpose shell, cannot be executed.

No utmp entry
Either you attempted to invoke the **login** program from a subshell or you need to enter **exec login** instead of just **login**.

Invalid ID
You do not have permission to execute **login**.

Not on system console
The **login** program may only be executed from the system console.

The following message might be obtained on a UNIX system with the **chroot** (for "change root") function, such as Bell System III or V:

Subsystem root: *pathname*
Prompt for repeating login sequence at the new level in the file system

No login in /etc or /bin on root
The **login** program is not present in either /etc or /bin in the new root directory.

Your pasword has expired. Choose a new one
You must select a new password before the file system will let you log in.

passwd — Change Login Password

$ passwd [*username*]

No Options

The **passwd** command changes or installs the password associated with your account. On some systems your account may be created without any password at all, while on other systems your account may be established with a password assigned by the system administrator. In either case, you can use this utility in your first session to change the password you have been using or to install a password and thus help prevent unauthorized use of your account.

Passwords may consist of as many as eight ASCII characters. Any ASCII character may be used except those which your UNIX system interprets in a special way. Until you become acquainted with these special characters, you should employ only alphabetic characters (both lowercase and uppercase) and numerals in your password.

Your password becomes more difficult to discover as (1) the number of characters in the password is increased, and to a lesser extent, as (2) the size of the character set from which the characters are selected is increased. We recommend that you employ eight characters from the set of all alphanumeric characters. This provides $(2 \times 26 + 10)^8$ or over 200 trillion permutations for your password. If security is of great concern, do not select a password that might be easily guessed — for example, a password derived from your name, license plate, or telephone or Social Security number. You should, however, select a password that you can type easily, since the UNIX system will not display your password as you are entering it.

Only the owner of an account, or the superuser, may change the password for an account. The account user must prove that he or she knows the old password.

Remember your password. You cannot log on to the system without it. If you do forget it, you will have to ask the person in charge of system accounts to delete your account password so that you may log on and install a new password.

The password is stored in encrypted form in the system password file that is called **/etc/passwd**. See Appendix D, "The Password and Group Files," for more information.

Examples　In this tutorial session we first demonstrate installation of a new password and then the changing of an existing password. The procedure is similar in both cases. Your version of the **passwd** command should act as described here, but some details, such as the exact text of prompt or error messages, may differ slightly.

If you are installing a password for the first time, type **passwd** and press RETURN. A message like "Changing password for *username*" may appear with some versions of **passwd**. In any case, you will be prompted for your new password:

```
$ passwd
Changing password for username
New password: ▓
```

Type in your new password carefully since what you type will not be echoed back to your terminal. Be sure to end your response with RETURN. The **passwd** command prompts you to retype the new password to verify that you did type in your desired password correctly.

```
$ passwd
Changing password for username
New password:
Re-enter new password: ▓
```

If both password entries match, **passwd** exits and you get a shell prompt. If they don't match, **passwd** issues an error message and may give you another chance.

If you are changing an existing password, enter **passwd** as before, but this time you will be prompted for your previous password. This is a security measure to help prevent an unauthorized user from changing your password.

```
$ passwd
Old password: ▓
```

As before, the system will not echo your response back to you. If you didn't type the correct password, the **passwd** program will complain "Sorry" and exit. If you typed in your password correctly, **passwd** will prompt you to type in the new password.

```
$ passwd
Old password:
New password: ▓
```

Finally, since you cannot see what you typed, the system will verify that your entry is the password you wanted by prompting you to type it again.

$ passwd

Old password:

New password:

Re-enter new password: ▮

If both responses are the same, the system password file will be updated to reflect your new password. If not, **passwd** may give you another chance before exiting.

Messages   The following messages apply to all versions of **passwd**:

Usage: passwd user
   In this case, you must specify your user name as an argument to **passwd**.

Permission denied
   Unless you are the superuser (**root**), you can only change the password for the account you are logged on to.

Sorry
   You didn't type your "Old password" correctly.

Too short. Password unchanged
   Your new password doesn't contain enough characters. Choose a longer password.

Please use at least one nonnumeric character
   You cannot choose a password containing only numerals.

Please use a longer password
   The **passwd** program recommends that you choose a longer password or use a more extensive character set. However, if you insist on using the password you specified, the system will accept it after the third try.

They don't match; try again
   Both new password entries must match. Here the **passwd** program is giving you another chance.

Too many tries; try again later
   You still didn't match both new passwords after two tries, so **passwd** terminates.

Temporary file busy; try again later
   Another system user is already changing his or her password. Since only one user is allowed to do so at a time, you must try again later.

The following messages apply only to System V versions of **passwd**:

Sorry: < *num* weeks since the last change
   The minimum number of weeks, *num*, that must elapse before your password may be changed has not been reached.

You may not change the password
   In this case only the superuser is allowed to change your password.

On-Line Documentation

A copy of the UNIX reference manuals for your system may be kept on-line for your immediate access and perusal. However, some smaller systems may not have sufficient disk space to maintain the on-line version of the *UNIX User's Manual*.

man — Display On-Line UNIX User's Manual

$ man [*options*] [*section*] *entry...*

Bell Version 7 Options:

—t	Phototypeset the section using **troff**.
—n	Print on the standard output (terminal screen) using **nroff**.
—k	Display the output on a Tektronix 4014 terminal using **troff** and **tc**, which processes **troff** output for phototypesetter simulation on the 4014 graphics terminal.
—e	Concatenated with —t or —n to invoke **neqn** or **eqn**, which are preprocessors for typesetting mathematical equations; —e alone means —te.
—w	Display only the pathname of the manual *entry*.

Bell Systems III and V Options:

—t	Typeset *entry* in normal 8.5×11 format.
—s	Typeset *entry* in small 6×9 format (usable with the next four options).
—T4014	Display typeset output on a Tektronix 4014.
—Ttek	Display typeset output on a Tektronix 4014.
—Tvp	Display typeset output on the Versatec printer.
—12	12-pitch (effective only with DASI terminals).
—c	Filter **nroff** output through **col**, which processes multicolumn output.
—d	Find *entry* in the current directory rather than in the standard directory, **/usr/man**; you must use a complete filename, such as **acct.lm**, with this option.
—w	Show only the pathnames of *entry* (relative to **/usr/man** or the current directory if —d is also specified).
—y	Use the uncompacted version of **man** macros. Generally compacted versions are used to save disk space.
other	Other options are passed to **nroff** or **troff**, which actually format the entries.

Berkeley Options:

none   Display a preformatted manual entry; if not available, format the manual page using **nroff**.

—   Simulate underlining even if output is not directed to a terminal.

—t   Arrange to use **vroff** for the Versatec printer.

—k *keyword*...
    Display manual entry headings containing *keyword*.

—f *commandname*...
    Display a one-line description for *commandname*.

This command displays entries from the on-line *UNIX User's Manual,* formerly called the *UNIX Programmer's Manual.* The exact behavior of the **man** program will depend on your UNIX implementation. We discuss the widely used Bell and Berkeley versions.

The Bell UNIX **man** command is distinctly different from the Berkeley UNIX variation. The Bell command is a shell script, and the Berkeley command is a compiled C program. However, both commands act similarly if you do not use any options.

The on-line manual is arranged like the hard-copy version of the *UNIX User's Manual.* See Chapter 3, Session 5 for an explanation of how the Bell or Berkeley hard-copy version of the *UNIX User's Manual* is organized.

To display the on-line description of a UNIX system command, use the following command line format:

$ **man** *command*

If you wish to keep a copy of the manual section on your disk for subsequent editing, redirect the output as shown here:

$ **man** *command* >*filename*

We recommend that you make *filename* something like *command*.**man** so you can remember the origin of the file.

The general invocation command line for the **man** command is

$ **man** [*options*] [*section*] *entry*...

The *entry* is entered in lowercase. The *section* number does not need a letter suffix. If no *section* is specified, the whole manual is searched for *entry* and the first occurrence is displayed on your terminal.

Some entries occur in more than one section of the manual. However, only the entries in the first section refer to the command itself. Other sections may describe system files related to the command. For instance, the **passwd** command is described in Section 1, and the related password file is described in either Section 4 (Bell System V) or Section 5 (other UNIX versions).

During display of the manual entry, your terminal may be write-protected so that other users cannot send messages using **write**. In this way, the formatting of the manual entry will not be disturbed.

When no options are specified, the Bell versions format the *entry* with **nroff** on your terminal, using the **TERM** environment variable (or **450** if **TERM** is undefined) to identify your terminal type. (The −**T** options of the **mm** command—for example, −**Tlp**—are also recognized and override the value of **TERM**.) For a discussion on how to set shell variables, such as **TERM**, see Session 8 in Chapter 4 and the section entitled "Customizing Your Working Environment" in Appendix C.

The Berkeley version also stores preformatted entries that can be displayed more quickly since the relatively slow **nroff** program doesn't have to be invoked.

With the Berkeley version, if the standard output is your terminal or if you specify a dash (−) on the command line, the formatted output is first piped through **cat** −**s**, which removes extra blank lines, then through **ul**, which underlines or uses enhanced video, and finally through **more**, which causes output to be suspended after each screen is displayed.

The Berkeley version has two different keyword lookup features. When either is specified, the remaining arguments are used as patterns for a **grep**-like search in the **/usr/lib/whatis** database file. This file consists of the title (or header) lines from the on-line manual entries.

One keyword lookup feature may be used to find the name of a command to perform a particular task. The command line format for this Berkeley keyword lookup feature is

$ **man** −**k** *keyword*...

This variation of the Berkeley **man** command displays all headings (under the NAME section of manual for each entry) that contain *keyword* anywhere in the heading. The case (upper- or lower-) is ignored. Note that the Berkeley **apropos** command is the same as the **man** command with the −**k** option.

The other keyword lookup feature gives a one-line description for the manual entry for the command name you supply. In this case only manual entries that contain *commandname* on the left-hand side of the header line are displayed. The command line format is

$ **man** −**f** *commandname*...

Note that the Berkeley **whatis** command is a synonym for the **man** command with the −f option.

Some systems do not display certain sections of the *UNIX User's Manual* because these sections are not operational in that system implementation or because they operate in a substantially different way. Check the documentation for your particular UNIX system installation for pertinent details.

Examples   Prepare to enter these examples as discussed in the introduction to this chapter. The **wordlist** is not necessary for this command.

As an example of using **man**, display the on-line manual entry for the **passwd** command. Enter **man passwd**, and if you are using the Bell System V, you will observe a display like the following:

```
$ man passwd
```

PASSWD(1)   UNIX 5.0   PASSWD(1)

NAME

 passwd - change login password

SYNOPSIS

 passwd name

DESCRIPTION

 This command changes (or installs) a password associated with the login name.

 The program prompts for the old password (if any) and then for the new one (twice). The caller must supply these. New passwords should be at least four characters long if they use a sufficiently rich alphabet and at least six characters long if mono-case. Only the first eight characters of the password are significant.

 Only the owner of the name or the superuser may change a password; the owner must prove he knows the old password. Only the superuser can create a null password.

 The password file is not changed if the new password is the same as the old password, or if the password has not "aged" sufficiently; see passwd(4).

FILES

 /etc/passwd

SEE ALSO

 login(1), crypt(3C), passwd(4).

$

If you were using a Berkeley version of **man**, the display would be similar but it would be suspended after one screenful, and a prompt, such as "—**More**—", would appear. At this point press either RETURN to display the next line or the space bar to display the next screenful.

Occasionally, you will need to display an entry from another section of the on-line manual. In this case you need to specify the section number in addition to the entry name. For example, you must specify Section 4 (Bell System V) or Section 5 (with other UNIX versions) to obtain the manual entry related to **passwd** that describes the password file itself. Type **man 4 passwd** and press RETURN. Substitute 5 for 4 in this example if you are not using Bell System V. Here we interrupted the display to keep the example short:

```
$ man 4 passwd

PASSWD(4)                    UNIX 5.0                    PASSWD(4)

[ Interrupt ]

$
```

With any of the Bell versions, you may display the partial pathname of the manual entry (relative to the /**usr**/**man** directory) instead of the contents of the entry by using the —**w** option. For instance, if you enter **man** —**w passwd**, you would see a display like the following with the Bell System V version:

```
$ man —w passwd
man1/passwd.1   man4/passwd.4

$
```

These results tell us that the actual manual entries for sections 1 and 4 of the manual's discussion of **passwd** have the full pathnames /**usr**/**man**/**man1**/**passwd.1** and /**usr**/**man**/**man4**/**passwd.4** respectively.

To try some other examples, enter **man 7 ascii**, and a chart of the ASCII characters and their octal equivalents will be displayed. Another informative manual section is a description of the file system hierarchy, obtained by entering **man 7 hier**. These entries may not be available on some systems.

If you have access to the Berkeley version, try the keyword lookup features. The —**k** option causes **man** to search the /**usr**/**lib**/**whatis** database for any entries containing the word you specified as an argument to the **man**—**k** command. The word can occur anywhere in the database entry line. One use for this feature would be to locate related commands. For example, let's see what manual entries are related to **nroff**.

```
$ man −k nroff
```

checknr (1)	check syntax of nroff/troff files
colcrt (1)	filter nroff output for CRT previewing
deroff (1)	remove nroff, troff, tbl, and eqn constructs
soelim (1)	eliminate \&.so's from nroff input
tbl (1)	format tables for nroff or troff
troff, nroff (1)	text formatting and typesetting

```
$ ▮
```

Note that you may obtain the same result by entering **apropos nroff** since **apropos** is a synonym for **man −k**.

Now use the other Berkeley keyword feature to find the description for a given command. For instance, if a brief description for the **nroff** command was desired, you would type the command line **man −f nroff**. Only the entry containing **nroff** on the left-hand side of the title line is displayed with this option.

```
$ man −f nroff
```

troff, nroff (1)	text formatting and typesetting

```
$ ▮
```

Note that you may obtain the same result by entering **whatis nroff** since **whatis** is a synonym for **man −f**.

For our last example, let's say that you wish to balance your checkbook and that you left your calculator at home. Maybe there is a command to help you:

```
$ man −k calculator
```

dc(1)	desk calculator

```
$ man dc
```

```
   DC(1) ...
...
```

Yes, so there is. Now you can invoke **man** without any option, as we did in this example, to display the manual entry for the **dc** program and thus learn how to use the program to balance your checkbook.

Messages   The following messages apply to Bell System III and V versions of **man**:

Usage: "man [options] [section] entries" where "options" are:

−t	typeset "entries" in normal (8.5×11) format
−s	typeset "entries" in small (6×9) format (usable with next 4 options)
−Tst	display typeset output on the MHCC STARE facility
−T4014	display typeset output on a Tektronix 4014
−Ttek	display typeset output on a Tektronix 4014
−Tvp	display typeset output on the Versatec printer
−12	12-pitch (effective only with DASI terminals)
−c	filter nroff output through col
−d	find "entry" in current directory rather than in /usr/man (must use complete file name, e.g., acct.1m)
−w	show only path names of "entries" (relative to /usr/man or current directory for ^{E}d)
−y	use uncompacted macros

Other "options" are passed to nroff or troff.

Default is to format "entries" with nroff on your terminal, using the $TERM environment variable (or 450 if it is undefined).
The "−T" options of the "mm" command (e.g., "−Tlp") are also recognized and override the value of $TERM.
"Section" is 1 to 8; it may be changed before each "entry".
  You typed an unrecognized option.

man: *entry* **not found**
  The specified manual *entry* could not be located after the appropriate subdirectories were searched.

man: /usr/man: bad directory
  You don't have search permission for this directory. Check with your system administrator.

The following messages apply to the Berkeley version of **man**:

Usage: man [section] name ...
man −k keyword ...
man −f file ...
  You must specify at least one argument to **man**.

Can't chdir to /usr/man
  You don't have search permission for this directory. Check with your system administrator.

But what do you want from section *section*?
  You must specify an *entry* in addition to a *section* number.

No manual entry for *entry*
The specified *entry* could not be located anywhere.

No manual entry for *entry* **in** *section*
The specified manual *entry* in *section* could not be located after the appropriate subdirectories were searched.

Reformatting page. Wait...
The preformatted version of the *entry* could not be found so **man** has to format the *entry*. The message "Done" will be appended when the formatting is complete. If unsuccessful, **man** will append "Aborted (sorry)" instead.

man: −**k what?**
You must specify a *keyword* with the −**k** option.

keyword: **nothing appropriate**
The *keyword* could not be located in the database **/usr/lib/whatis**.

man: −**f what?**
You must specify a *commandname* with the −**f** option.

commandname: **not found**
The *commandname* could not be found in the database **/usr/lib/whatis**.

If you type an invalid option, it will be ignored and **man** will attempt to display the manual entry for any argument that you indicated. Most other error messages would originate from **nroff**, **troff**, **col**, **tbl**, **eqn**, or **neqn**, which are called by the **man** program when necessary.

Working With Directories

Directories, which are files containing information about other files and directories, form the basis of the UNIX file system. The commands described in this section allow you to create new directories or to inspect and manipulate existing directories so that you can organize your UNIX file system.

ls — List Files in a Directory

$ **ls** [*option...*] [*file...*]

Bell Version 7 Options:

−**l**   List in long format. The files are sorted by name, and the permission modes, number of links, file owner, modification date and time, and filename are listed.

−**t**   List in order of last modification time (most recent first).

−a List all entries, including files whose names begin with dot (.).

−s Report number of disk blocks occupied by file.

−d List directory file instead of its contents.

−r Reverse order of sort for listing.

−u List in order of last access time.

−c List in order of last modification time of the inode instead of the file.
   For instance, resetting permissions modifies the inode and not the file
   contents.

−i Display inode number in first column.

−f Force each argument to be interpreted as a directory. This option turns
   off recognition of the −l, −t, −s, and −r options, but turns on −a. (The
   contents of ordinary files are displayed incorrectly.)

−g Give group ID instead of user ID in long listing.

Additional Bell System III Options:

−o List in long format suppressing group name. Normally both user and
   group names are listed.

−g List in long format suppressing file owner name.

Additional Bell System V Option:

−p Append slash (/) to name of each directory file.

Additional Berkeley Options:

−m Force stream output format; list files across the page, each separated
   from the next by a comma.

−l Force one-entry-per-line format.

−C Force multicolumn output format.

−q Display nonprinting characters in filenames as ?.

−x Sort multicolumn output across the page instead of down (the default).

−F Display directories with a trailing slash (/) and executable files with a
   trailing asterisk (*).

−R Recursively list all subdirectories.

Use this command to list the files in your directory files. Not only can you determine the filenames in various directories, but you can also display all the information about a given file, except for the contents of the file itself. Use one of the
file examination commands discussed later to display the contents of a file.

When no arguments to **ls** are specified on the command line, the files in the current directory are listed. If you specify an argument that is a directory, the files in that directory are listed. The output is sorted alphabetically by filename.

If you wish to verify that a particular file is indeed located in a directory, you may specify the name of the file as an argument. In this case, if the file exists in your directory, the filename will be listed. This approach is useful when you need to determine the presence of a file in a directory that contains many files.

Most versions of **ls** recognize a number of options that either request additional information about the file or files or that control the listing format. It is possible to access most of the information contained in the UNIX system for any file or directory by using **ls** with the appropriate choice of options.

The general command line format is

$$\$ \text{ ls } [\text{ option... }] [\text{ file... }]$$

to list one or more ordinary files or the contents of one or more directory files. Most options may be run together: for example, **−ltasdr**.

The primary difference between different versions of **ls** is the number and type of invocation options. The output format for different implementations of this command may also differ. There is an almost unbelievable number of options for this command. In fact, this command is one of the favorites for modification by system implementers who like to add custom options.

The Bell versions list files vertically down a single column by default. If you attempt to list a directory containing a large number of files, the listing will begin scrolling off the screen. If you would like to have **ls** list the contents of a directory in one screen, use an option to give multiple columns, or else pipe the output of **ls** into a **pr** (pagination) process that is invoked to display its standard input in several columns. (The **pr** command is discussed later in this chapter.)

In contrast to the Bell versions, the popular Berkeley version of **ls** lists the files in a multicolumn format with the filenames sorted alphabetically down the column, if the output is directed to a terminal. However, if the output is redirected to a file or to another process (via a pipe), the files are listed one per line in a single column. You may override these default formats with the appropriate options.

Examples   Prepare for these examples as discussed in the introduction to this chapter. Create the link to **wordlist** before you begin your practice with **ls**.

The display format of your **ls** command may differ from that depicted in this tutorial. For instance, if you are using the Berkeley version, the filenames will be listed across the screen by default if the output is to a terminal:

$ ls

Mail appeal poem wordlist

$ ▓

Any or all of these names in the directory could refer to a file or to another directory. A file entry can be distinguished from a directory entry by the use, for example, of the long listing option, −l, which is one of the most commonly used ls options. From your home directory, enter ls −l:

$ ls −l

total 391

drwxrwxrwx	3 username	docum	80	Oct	10	09:34	Mail
−rw−rw−rw−	1 username	docum	78	Oct	9	11:55	appeal
−rw−rw−rw−	1 username	docum	62	Oct	9	12:02	poem
−rw−r−−r−−	2 bin	bin	196513	Jul	30	09:33	wordlist

$ ▓

The "total 391" refers to the total number of disk blocks occupied by the files listed. The first column lists the permission modes. The second column indicates the number of links to the file (see also the ln command), and the third column displays the name of the file owner. The fourth column shows the group owner name. The fifth column indicates the number of characters in the file. Finally, the next to the last column informs you of the date on which the file was last modified (written to), and the last column shows the filename itself. The entries are sorted in ASCII collating sequence by the filename; thus, an uppercase directory name will appear before the lowercase ordinary filenames. (We follow the convention in this book that directory files we create are capitalized and ordinary files are not.)

You may request information about a particular file, directory, or group of files or directories by specifying their names on the ls command line. This is especially powerful when a filename generation wild card, such as *, is used to list a group of filenames.

For instance, let's say that you would like a listing of all the reminders in the **Mail/Username/Aug15.84** directory. To simplify matters, create a subshell using parentheses to move to that directory and then execute the command, as shown. Recall that we labeled our reminder messages **remind1** and **remind2**. The shell matches the **remind*** wild card abbreviation to all filenames beginning with **remind**. Note that the parentheses cause a subshell to be invoked to execute the commands enclosed in the parentheses. In this way your present working directory remains your login or home directory.

```
$ (cd Mail/Username/Aug15.84; ls remind*)
remind1
remind2
$
```

You may also display information about a file or directory that is not in the current directory by entering the absolute or relative pathname to that file or directory. Try this now by entering the following from your home directory:

```
$ ls Mail/Username/Aug15.84
remind1
remind2
$
```

The contents of the directory **Mail/Username/Aug15.84** are listed. The same information appears, but in a slightly different form, if you append the * wild card to **remind**, as shown:

```
$ ls Mail/Username/Aug15.84/remind*
Mail/Username/Aug15.84/remind1
Mail/Username/Aug15.84/remind2
$
```

If you wish information about a directory instead of the files contained within that directory, specify the −**d** option. For instance, to obtain a long listing for your home directory (now the current directory) itself, enter **ls** −**ld**:

```
$ ls −ld
drwxrwxrwx    4 username docum    640 Oct 10 09:34
$
```

The **ls** option −**s** gives the size in disk blocks for each entry and the total for all entries if a directory is being listed. Try this now:

```
$ ls −s
total 391
1 Mail
1 appeal
1 poem
388 wordlist
$
```

In this case, the system displays the directory's size in blocks and indicates that the three entries occupy one block each, while the last occupies 388 blocks. Recall that a file must occupy one block even if it contains less than one block's worth of characters (512 or a multiple).

The −r option is usually concatenated with some other options to reverse the order of the sort. For instance, enter **ls −rt** to reverse the temporal order and list the oldest file first:

```
$ ls −rt
wordlist
appeal
poem
Mail
$ 
```

The files are still listed in the order in which they were last modified (specified by the −t option), but the oldest is listed first (because of the −r option). When used alone, −r simply lists the files in reverse alphabetical order.

Messages   The following messages apply to the Bell versions of **ls**. Note that the **ls** command must read the password or group files in order to find user or group names that correspond to a given user or group ID number.

ls: illegal option −*x*
  The specified option, *x*, is not recognized by **ls**.

/etc/passwd file cannot be opened for reading
  The password file cannot be read. See your system administrator.

/etc/group file cannot be opened for reading
  The group file cannot be read. See your system administrator.

The following messages apply to both the Bell and Berkeley versions of **ls**:

directory **unreadable**
  The directory file named *directory* cannot be opened for reading.

ls: too many files
  There are too many files for **ls** to process.

ls: out of memory
  There is not enough memory for **ls** to function under the requested conditions.

filename **not found**
  The specified file argument named *filename* cannot be located.

pwd — Print Working Directory

$ pwd

No Options

Use the **pwd** command to display the full pathname for the current (or working) directory of your shell. The working directory of your shell informs you of your location in the hierarchical file system. You will find this utility quite handy if you forget where you are in your UNIX file system.

The **pwd** process does its work by successively changing directories — that is, by traversing the directory tree in reverse toward the root directory and noting the name of each parent directory. When it reaches the root directory, it displays the full pathname back to the directory it started from. When a directory between the current directory and the root directory is inaccessible, **pwd** generates an error message.

Each UNIX process has a working directory associated with it. The current directory feature gives you a shorthand when you reference files. Thus you may reference a file easily from your current directory using a relative (or partial) pathname, but a file may always be referenced by its absolute (or full) pathname as well.

You may think of your working directory as the directory in which you are currently working. Actually, your working directory is the current directory for your shell process. You may easily change your working directory by using the built-in **cd** (change directory) shell command.

Examples   Prepare for these examples by following the instructions in the introduction to this chapter. The **wordlist** is not necessary for this command.

Return to your home directory by typing **cd** and pressing RETURN. Then enter the **pwd** command. Your own particular home directory, of course, will not be /usr/**username**, as it is in the following example, but will instead contain your actual login name.

$ cd
$ pwd
/usr/username
$

Here the shell has the current directory /usr/**username**, which is a subdirectory of /usr. The **usr** directory, in turn, is a subdirectory of the root directory, /.

Now change to your **Mail** subdirectory and execute **pwd** again:

```
$ cd Mail
$ pwd
/usr/username/Mail
$
```

Then descend to **Username** and finally **Jul30.84**, executing **pwd** at each stage:

```
$ cd Username
$ pwd
/usr/username/Mail/Username
$ cd Jul30.84
$ pwd
/usr/username/Mail/Username/Jul30.84
$
```

Now return to the root directory one directory at a time and verify each change by using **pwd**. Recall that the dot dot (**..**) entry is the parent directory.

```
$ cd ..
$ pwd
/usr/username/Mail/Username
$ cd ..
$ pwd
/usr/username/Mail
$ cd ..
$ pwd
/usr/username
$ cd ..
$ pwd
/usr
$ cd ..
$ pwd
/
$
```

Now if you attempt to change to the parent directory of the root directory, nothing appears to happen. Actually, the **pwd** command shows you are still in the parent directory, which is the root directory. This is because the parent directory of the root directory is the root directory. The root directory has the same current and parent directory: itself.

Finally, change back to your home directory by typing **cd** and pressing RETURN, and verify with **pwd**.

Messages   Because the **pwd** program ignores the remainder of the invocation command line, there are no correct usage messages. The following messages apply to Bell versions of **pwd**:

> **pwd: cannot stat .!**
> You don't have permission to obtain file status information for your current directory. If you own the directory, use **chmod** to enable search (execute) permission for your current directory.
>
> **pwd: cannot open ..**
> You don't have permission to open your parent directory for reading. If you own this directory, use **chmod** to enable read permission for your parent directory.
>
> **pwd: cannot chdir to ..**
> You don't have search permission for your parent directory. If you own this directory, use **chmod** to enable search (execute) permission for your parent directory.
>
> **pwd: read error in ..**
> There was an error in reading an entry in the parent directory. Try again, and then see your system administrator, if necessary.

The following messages apply to the Berkeley version of **pwd**:

> **pwd: cannot open ..**
> You don't have permission to open your parent directory for reading. If you own this directory, use **chmod** to enable read permission for your parent directory.
>
> **pwd: read error in ..**
> There was an error in reading an entry in the parent directory. Try again, and then see your system administrator, if necessary.

cd — Change Working Directory

```
$ cd
$ cd pathname
No Options
```

Use the **cd** command to change the current directory associated with your shell. If no argument is indicated, you will be returned to your home directory. You may change to any other directory for which you have execute permission by specifying either the absolute or relative pathname to that directory.

You can access files in another directory without using the **cd** command by specifying a file pathname each time. Typing pathnames of files rather than moving to a different directory, however, creates more opportunities to make typographical errors. To minimize errors, just move from your current directory to the directory that contains the desired files.

Examples Prepare for these examples as discussed in the introduction to this chapter.

Suppose you wish to access a file contained in the practice subdirectory **Mail/ Username/Jul30.84**. To avoid specifying long pathnames for every file, move to this subdirectory by entering **cd Mail/Username/Jul30.84**. To verify that you are in the correct directory, enter **pwd**. The full pathname for this directory will be displayed.

```
$ cd Mail/Username/Jul30.84
$ pwd
/usr/username/Mail/Username/Jul30.84
$
```

You may occasionally need to move from one subdirectory to another where both have the same parent directory. For instance, you may change from the **Jul30.84** to the **Aug15.84** directory by jumping "up" to their common parent directory (**..**) and then jumping "down" to the desired directory. To do this, enter the command line **cd ../Aug15.84**. Verify the change with the **pwd** command:

```
$ cd ../Aug15.84
$ pwd
/usr/username/Mail/Username/Aug15.84
$
```

It is easy for a novice to get lost in the complex hierarchical file system. If this happens, you can return to your home directory at any time from any directory simply by typing **cd** and pressing RETURN. Try this now and then give the command **pwd** to verify that you have indeed gotten "home."

```
$ cd
$ pwd
/usr/username
$ ▓
```

Messages   The following message applies to all versions of **cd**:

> **pathname: bad directory**
> Either the argument *pathname* doesn't exist or it exists but is not a direc-
> tory, or else you don't have search (execute) permission for the directory.

mkdir — Make a Directory

> **$ mkdir** *pathname* . . .
>
> No Options

Use the **mkdir** command to create a directory. This new directory will be empty
except for the dot and dot dot entries, which are used by the UNIX system. These
entries are normally invisible; that is, they do not appear in a directory listing
unless the all option (−a) is employed with **ls**.

When you create a directory with **mkdir**, a link is established from the new
directory to the parent directory. In order to create a directory, you must have
execute permission (also known as search permission) for all the levels of directories that are involved in creating that new directory. You must also have write
permission in the parent directory of the new directory. If you did not have write
permission, you would not, of course, be able to create a new directory within the
parent directory since you would not be able to alter the parent directory in any
way, either by adding file entries or deleting them.

The permission modes for the new directory will depend on the current setting
of the **umask** value. If the most permissive value (zero) for **umask** is in effect, the
newly created directory will have all permissions enabled for all user categories.

Only the superuser may create an empty directory; thus during its execution,
mkdir is set up to give you temporary superuser privileges for this purpose. Then
mkdir automatically links the dot entry (.) to the current directory (the new directory itself) and the dot dot entry (..) to the new directory's parent directory.

Each directory entry requires 16 bytes (or characters) for most UNIX implementations. Thus the size of a directory should always be a multiple of 16 bytes. A

directory just created by **mkdir** has a size of 32: 16 bytes each for the dot and dot dot entries.

Examples Prepare for these examples as discussed in the introduction to this chapter. The **wordlist** is not necessary for this command.

First let's create a new empty subdirectory named **Test** in the current directory by typing **mkdir Test** and pressing RETURN. Verify the new entry by a long directory listing. Type **ls −ld Test** to do this (you need to use the directory option, −**d**, with **ls** to examine the name and status of the directory **Test** itself instead of its contents).

```
$ mkdir Test
$ ls −ld Test
drwxrwxrwx  1 username docum    32 Oct 11 10:23 Test
$
```

All permissions were enabled because the value of our file creation mask, **umask**, was zero.

Now move to this new directory by entering **cd Test**. List all files in the new directory by entering **ls −al**. The all option (−**a**) causes **ls** to list the files whose names begin with a dot (.), which are usually invisible (that is, not listed).

```
$ cd Test
$ ls −al
drwxrwxrwx  2 username docum    32 Oct 11 10:23 .
drwxrwxrwx  5 username docum   656 Oct 9 10:23 ..
$
```

The dot entry (shown in the last column as .) refers to new directory **Test**, and dot dot (..) refers to its parent, **/usr/username**. The size of dot (**Test**) is 32 bytes (listed in column 5) because it contains only two entries: . (dot) and . . (dot dot). The size of your parent directory will most likely not be 656, but it should be a multiple of 16. We show two links (indicated in column 2) to dot and five to dot dot. The dot entry is linked to itself and its parent. The dot dot entry is linked to itself, to its parent, and to **Mail**, **appeal**, and **poem**, for a total of five links.

You may create more than one directory at a time with the **mkdir** command. From your current directory, **Test**, enter **mkdir Subtest2 Subtest3**, and then list the directory again.

```
$ mkdir Subtest2 Subtest3
$ ls −l
total 2
drwxrwxrwx    2 username docum        32 Oct 11 10:24 Subtest2
drwxrwxrwx    2 username docum        32 Oct 11 10:24 Subtest3
$
```

Now the directory **Test** has two subdirectories, **Subtest2** and **Subtest3**.

You may not, however, create a subdirectory and a sub-subdirectory in one step unless the first subdirectory already exists. To illustrate, return to your home directory by typing **cd** and pressing RETURN; then attempt to create **Test2/Subtest** in one step:

```
$ cd
$ mkdir Test2/Subtest
mkdir: cannot access Test2/.
$
```

The message "cannot access Test2/." tells us, in effect, that the sub-subdirectory **Subtest** cannot be created because **Test2** has not been created yet. However, you may create both **Test2** and **Subtest** in two steps with one command line, as follows:

```
$ mkdir Test2 Test2/Subtest
$
```

Because we created **Test2** first, we can proceed to create the sub-subdirectory **Subtest**.

Before leaving this tutorial, remove the directories you created by entering the one-line command **rm −r Test Test2**, which removes both **Test** and **Test2** along with the sub-subdirectories that **Test** and **Test2** contain.

Messages   The following messages apply to all versions of **mkdir**:

> **mkdir: arg count**
> You must specify at least one argument.
>
> **mkdir: cannot access *parentdir***
> You don't have permission to write in the directory *parentdir*, which would have become the parent directory of *dirname*.

mkdir: cannot make directory *dirname*
The **mkdir** program is not set up to give you the superuser privileges you need to create an empty directory. See your system administrator.
mkdir: cannot link *dirname/*.
mkdir cannot create the dot directory entry. See your system administrator.
mkdir: cannot link *dirname/*..
mkdir cannot create the dot dot directory entry. See your system administrator.

rmdir — Remove a Directory

Options for All Versions

$ **rmdir** *pathname*...

No Options

The **rmdir** command removes the directories you name as arguments on the command line. This command requires permission to write in the directory that is the parent for the directory you wish to remove. In addition, you must be able to search all directories leading to the specified directory.

A second prerequisite for using **rmdir** is that the indicated directory must be "empty" before **rmdir** can remove it; that is, the directory must contain no entries except for the dot and dot dot entries, which are used by the system. (You may remove a directory that contains additional entries in one step by using the **rm** command with the recursive option, **−r**.)

In contrast to ordinary files that are removed with **rm**, directory files cannot be write-protected against removal with **rmdir**.

Examples Prepare for these examples as discussed in the introduction to this chapter. Create the link to **wordlist** before you begin your practice with **rmdir**.

You will need to create a few extra directories for this tutorial session. Type **mkdir Test Test/Subtest** and press RETURN. Then verify by typing **ls** and pressing RETURN to list the directories, as shown here:

```
$ mkdir Test Test/Subtest
$ ls
Mail
Test
appeal
```

```
poem
wordlist
$ ls Test
Subtest
$ ▒
```

Remember that the names of directory files are capitalized (by our conventions). Now try to erase **Test** by entering **rmdir Test**:

```
$ rmdir Test
rmdir: Test not empty
$ ▒
```

Since directories containing files cannot be erased, let's change to the **Test** directory by entering **cd Test** and then list that directory's contents:

```
$ cd Test
$ ls
Subtest
$ ▒
```

The directory **Test** was not empty: it contained **Subtest**. Now use **rmdir** to delete **Subtest** and verify:

```
$ rmdir Subtest
$ ls
$ ▒
```

Finally, change back to your home directory, delete **Test**, and verify:

```
$ cd
$ rmdir Test
$ ls
Mail
appeal
poem
wordlist
$ ▒
```

Messages The following messages apply to all Bell versions of the **rmdir**

command:

> **rmdir: usage: rmdir dirname ...**
> You must specify at least one argument.
>
> **rmdir:** *dirname* **non-existent**
> The specified directory *dirname* does not exist.
>
> **rmdir: cannot stat ".".**
> **rmdir** cannot obtain file status information for your current directory.
> Type **chmod u+x** *currentdir*, where *currentdir* is the full pathname of
> your current directory. If this doesn't help, see your system administrator
> for assistance.
>
> **rmdir:** *dirname* **not a directory**
> **rmdir** only removes directory files. Use **rm** to remove ordinary files.
>
> **rmdir: cannot remove current directory**
> You are not allowed to remove your current directory.
>
> **rmdir:** *dirname* **unreadable**
> The directory *dirname* cannot be opened for reading. Enable read permis-
> sion and try again.
>
> **rmdir:** *dirname* **not empty**
> **rmdir** will not remove a directory until it is "empty" — that is, until it
> only contains dot and dot dot entries. Remove contents of *dirname* and
> try again.
>
> **rmdir:** *dirname* **no permission**
> You don't have write permission for parent of *dirname* so you can't unlink
> *dirname*. Enable write permission for parent directory and try again.
>
> **rmdir:** *dirname* **not removed**
> You aren't allowed to unlink *dirname* from its parent directory. See your
> system administrator.

Most of the messages for the Berkeley version of **rmdir** are the same as those for
Bell versions, with the exception of these two:

> **rmdir: arg count**
> You must specify at least one argument.
>
> **rmdir: cannot remove . or ..**
> You are not allowed to remove your current (**.**) or your parent (**..**)
> directory.

Examining Ordinary Files

This section describes command programs that are used to examine the contents
of ordinary files. Text files that consist of printable ASCII characters may be

examined directly by these UNIX utilities. Some of these commands have options that enable you to examine files containing nonprinting characters, such as control characters, as well.

cat — Concatenate and Print

$ **cat** [*option...*] [*file...*]

Bell Version 7 Options:

— Take input from the standard input file.

—u Don't buffer the output of the **cat** program. This option enables line-by-line transfer from standard input to standard output.

Additional Bell Versions III and V Option:

—s Be silent about input files that cannot be accessed for reading.

Additional Berkeley Options:

—n Number all the output lines.

—b When used with —n, do not number blank lines.

—s Squeeze multiple adjacent blank lines into a single line.

—v Enable display of nonprinting characters. A CTRL-X is indicated as ^X, and if the next character has its parity bit set, the character is preceded by an M—.

—e When used with —v, mark the end of each line with $.

—t When used with —v, show tabs as ^I.

Note that the —s option is different for Bell and Berkeley versions.

You may use a text editor or word processing program to display or print a file, but if you just want to take a quick look at your program or data, the **cat** program is a timesaver.

Use the simple command format

$ **cat** *filename*

to display the contents of *filename* on your terminal.

The more general command line format for using **cat** is

$ **cat** [*option...*] [*file...*]

which sends the contents of one or more files to the standard output. If *file* is omitted, the input for **cat** is taken from the standard input so that data may be sent to **cat** by means, for example, of a pipeline. There are several options available that change the output display.

Generally, the file you wish to display should contain only printable characters. If you try to display files containing nonprinting characters like control characters, garbage will appear on the screen. You may successfully use the Berkeley **cat** command to list files that contain nonprinting characters if you use the −v (for "visible") option.

You may use **cat** to combine two or more files into another single file by instructing the shell to redirect the command output. Files are combined in the sequence you specify on the command line. Thus, to combine the contents of *file1* and *file2* into *file3*, use the command format

$ **cat** *file1 file2* >*file3*

If *file3* already exists, the shell will delete its contents first. If you wish to append to an existing *file3*, use the alternate command line

$ **cat** *file1 file2* >>*file3*

Make sure that the output file does not have the same pathname as one of the input files; otherwise, the shell will erase the contents of that input file before the **cat** command has a chance to read it. For example, if you specify

$ **cat** *file1 file2* >*file2*

the input file *file2* will be erased first, with the result that once the **cat** command has been executed, *file2* will only contain the contents of *file1*.

Normally the output of the **cat** command is buffered in units of the disk block size. The block size for Bell Version 7 and System III is 512 bytes (characters) and is 1024 bytes or greater for Berkeley and Bell System V. When the output is buffered, the input is written in block-size units to the output. If the **cat** program were terminated, for example by an interrupt, before a block was written, the contents of that block would be lost. To prevent such losses, you can use the unbuffered option (−u), which transfers a line at a time from input to output.

Examples Prepare for these examples as discussed in the introduction to this chapter. The **wordlist** is not necessary for this command.

The first few examples may be tried with either the Bell or Berkeley versions of the **cat** command. Type the command line **cat poem** and press RETURN to display the contents of **poem**:

```
$ cat poem
Roses are Red
Violets are Blue
Sugar is Sweet
And so are You.
$
```

Since **poem** is an ASCII text file, you are able to read its contents. If you tried to display the contents of a non-ASCII file or a directory, cryptic characters would be displayed on the screen. If **poem** were empty, nothing would be displayed.

The **cat** program responds to signals such as hangup, interrupt, or quit. If the **cat** process receives one of these signals, it terminates immediately. You may use this property to display the first few lines of a file to determine its contents. In this case, after you have seen enough, give an interrupt signal by pressing your interrupt code (the delete character, by default) to abort further output. Your shell prompt will reappear. Sometimes you may have to press RETURN to move the cursor to the beginning of the next line.

For our next example, let's use **cat** to display one file after another on the screen.

```
$ cat appeal poem
Now is the time
for all good citizens
to come to the aid
of their country.
Roses are Red
Violets are Blue
Sugar is Sweet
And so are You.
$
```

Now let's combine the contents of **appeal** and **poem** and redirect the result to the disk file named **text**. If you display the contents of **text**, for example by typing **cat text** and pressing RETURN, you should see the same result as shown in the preceding screen example.

```
$ cat appeal poem >text
$ cat text
Now is the time
for all good citizens
to come to the aid
of their country.
Roses are Red
Violets are Blue
Sugar is Sweet
And so are You.
$ ▮
```

In our tutorial file system, **Mail** is a directory. If you typed **cat Mail** and pressed RETURN, the system would display garbage characters intermixed with filenames, proving that you cannot effectively display the contents of a directory with **cat**. Use the **ls** command to list the contents of a directory file. Again, you may have to press RETURN to move the cursor to the beginning of the next line.

```
$ cat Mail
3.0..8Username$ ▮
```

If no filename argument is specified on the command line, **cat** reads its input from the standard input file (the keyboard, by default). If you also redirect the output of the **cat** command to a disk file, you may rapidly enter data into a file without using an editor. To exit the **cat** program, type your end-of-file code.

To illustrate, type **cat >poem2**, press RETURN, and then type the text shown in the following example. If you make a mistake, you may correct it before pressing RETURN by using the usual character-erase or line-kill correction codes. Finally, press ^D to exit **cat** and return to the shell.

```
$ cat >poem2
Roses are Red
Violets are Blue
[ ^D ]
$ ls
Mail
appeal
poem
```

```
poem2
$ cat poem2
Roses are Red
Violets are Blue
$ ▓
```

Checking the directory with **ls**, we see that it indeed contains the file **poem2**. Checking **poem2** with **cat**, in turn, shows that the file does contain the text that the initial **cat** command read from the keyboard.

Note that if you were to exit the **cat** program by an interrupt, no text would be saved in the file **poem2**. Since **cat** terminates immediately upon receiving an interrupt signal, an interrupt causes any text that is buffered internally to be lost. For example:

```
$ cat >poem2
Roses are Red
Violets are Blue
[ Interrupt ]
$ cat poem2
$ ▓
```

Although a file is created by the shell, it is empty since **cat** did not write any characters in it. If you employed the unbuffered option, however, the text would be saved to disk because each line written after it is input:

```
$ cat −u >poem2
Roses are Red
Violets are Blue
Sugar is [ Interrupt ]
$ cat poem2
Roses are Red
Violets are Blue
$ ▓
```

As you can see, any text typed on a line before RETURN is pressed will be lost if you give the interrupt signal. Thus, **Sugar is** was not stored in **poem2**.

You may indicate that **cat** should take its input both from the standard input file and from a disk file by specifying the standard input file as a dash argument

(−). This is sometimes necessary when **cat** is used in a pipeline. For example, pipe the output of **date** into **cat** and also display the contents of **appeal**, as shown here:

```
$ date | cat − appeal
Mon Dec 10 16:45:22 PST 1984
Now is the time
for all good citizens
to come to the aid
of their country.
$
```

Without the dash argument, **cat** would display only the contents of **appeal**. If you reverse the order of the arguments for **cat** in this last example, **appeal** would be displayed followed by the current date and time.

You will need access to the Berkeley version of the **cat** command to enter the remaining examples.

Use the −**n** (number) option if you wish to number the output lines. For instance, the file **poem3** was created from **poem** by inserting blank lines. You can number lines of text as well as blank lines by using −**n** alone:

```
$ cat poem3
Roses are Red

Violets are Blue

Sugar is Sweet

And so are You.
$ cat −n poem3
   1 Roses are Red
   2
   3 Violets are Blue
   4
   5 Sugar is Sweet
   6
   7 And so are You.
   8
$
```

Note that if you do not wish to number the blank lines, you can use the −b option as well. These options must be indicated separately as −n −b, not −nb.

You may use the −v (visible) option to display nonprinting characters. Sometimes a control character may be inadvertently entered into a text file. You can use this option to locate such characters so that you may eliminate them either with an editor or with the **tr** program (the **tr** command is discussed later in this chapter).

The visible option doesn't display tabs directly. If you want to see the tabs, however, specify the −t option with −v (−v −t). Sometimes you might wish to see the ends of the input lines. To accomplish this, use the −e option with the −v option. As an example, use these options to display a text file that contains some tab characters.

The −s (squeeze) option is useful for removing extraneous blank lines in the input: any two or more adjacent blank lines in the input will be "squeezed" into one blank line in the output. This option would also be useful, for instance, to eliminate extra lines produced by commands like **nroff**, **man**, and **pr**. As an example, pipe the output from each of these commands into **cat** with and without specifying the squeeze option.

Before leaving this tutorial, erase the example files **poem2** and **poem3**.

Messages   The following messages apply to all versions of the **cat** command:

cat: cannot stat stdout
The standard output file is closed. See your system administrator.

cat: cannot open *file*
The specified *file* cannot be opened for reading. Either the file doesn't exist or you don't have access permission to read it. If the silent option is in effect, this message will not be displayed.

cat: cannot open −*option*
The **cat** command treats unrecognized options as file arguments. There is no correct usage error message.

cat: cannot stat *file*
The file status for *file* cannot be obtained. See your system administrator. This message is not displayed if the silent option is in effect.

cat: input *file* **is output**
cat: input − **is output**
The output *file* is the same as the input *file*. The output *file* must be different from the input *file* unless it is a special device file like a terminal device file.

head — Display Beginning of a Text File

$ head [*option*] [*file...*]

Option
   −count Display the first *count* lines of *file*.

The **head** command was written at U.C. Berkeley and is distributed with the Berkeley UNIX system, but some other non-Berkeley UNIX implementations also provide this utility. The **head** command is used to display the initial part of a text file. You might think of this command as the complement of the **tail** command, which is discussed in the next section. In contrast to **tail**, however, with **head** you may specify more than one file for display.

Use the following command line format to display the first ten lines (the default) of one or more text files:

$ head [*filename...*]

If no *filename* is indicated, this command takes its input from the standard input file. Thus the command may be used in a pipeline to display the initial portion of a data stream. For instance,

$ ls /bin *filename* **| head**

will display only the first ten commands in **/bin** because **head** filters out all but the first ten lines of its input, which in this case consists of a list of commands with one command per line. The **/bin** directory contains most of the UNIX command programs.

You may display the first *count* lines of one or more files by invoking **head** with an option:

$ head [*−count*] [*filename...*]

The entire file will be displayed if the value of *count* is greater than the number of lines in the file.

Examples Prepare for these examples as discussed in the introduction to this chapter. Create the link to **wordlist** before you begin your practice with **head**.

As a first example, enter **head wordlist** to display the first ten words in your **wordlist** file. Our simulation displays the first ten lines from the on-line spelling dictionary.

```
$ head wordlist
10th
1st
2nd
3rd
4th
5th
6th
7th
8th
9th
$
```

You may examine more than one file in succession:

```
$ head poem wordlist
→ poem ←
Roses are Red
Violets are Blue
Sugar is Sweet
And so are You.

→ wordlist ←
10th
1st
2nd
3rd
4th
5th
6th
7th
8th
9th
$
```

Here **head** displays the entire file **poem**, which contains only four lines, and goes on to display the first ten lines of **wordlist**. The "→ *filename* ←" header precedes the display of the contents of each file if more than one file is given as an argument to **head**.

You may give a *count* argument to change the number of lines that are displayed. Here we display the first six lines from **wordlist**:

```
$ head −6 wordlist
10th
1st
2nd
3rd
4th
5th
$
```

The **head** command is a filter program. Thus it may be used at the end, in the middle, or at the beginning of a pipeline. For example, here we employ **head** at the end of a pipeline to filter out all but the first ten lines from the data stream:

```
$ cat wordlist | head
10th
1st
2nd
3rd
4th
5th
6th
7th
8th
9th
$
```

In the next example, **head** is used in the middle of a pipeline. It filters out all but the first ten lines from its input and passes them on to **wc**, the word count program, which reports the number of lines, words, and characters.

```
$ cat wordlist | head | wc
     10    10    41
$
```

Finally, the **head** command may be used at the beginning of a pipeline. In this case the output of **head** consists of the first ten lines in **wordlist**, which are passed on to **wc**. Note that the **wc** program should report the same statistics for both this and the preceding example.

```
$ head wordlist | wc
     10     10     41
$
```

Messages   The following messages apply to the Berkeley version of **head**, which is the only version of this command.

> *file:* **No such file or directory**
> The *file* doesn't exist.

> *file:* **Permission denied**
> You do not have access or read permission for *file*.

> → *filename* ←
> When more than one file argument is specified, this message precedes the display for each file.

> **Badly formed number**
> The *count* argument must be a whole decimal number. The command terminates after displaying this message.

tail—Deliver the Last Part of a File

> **$ tail** [± *number*[*unit*]] [*option...*] *file*
>
> Options for All Versions:
>   −[*number*]l   *Number* is counted in units of lines (default).
>   −[*number*]b   *Number* is counted in units of the disk block size.
>   −[*number*]c   *Number* is counted in units of characters.
>
> Additional Bell Systems III and V and Berkeley Option:
>   −f   Enable **tail** to follow the growth of *file*.
>
> Additional Berkeley Option:
>   −r   Display lines in reverse order.

When you wish to display the last part of a text file, **tail** copies the "tail end" of the file to the standard output. This utility allows you to access the end of a file without paging through the entire file from the beginning.

There are several applications in which accessing the end of the file is useful. You may wish to place a marker at the end of a file for some purpose; the **tail** program lets you access that marker easily. You may have appended one file to another file and wish to access the end of the appended file first. Since a number of UNIX programs append data at the end of files, you might use **tail** to display the most recently added data. Finally, the **tail** program allows you to check the end of a data stream in a pipeline to verify that the pipeline is operating correctly.

To use **tail**, specify the command line

$$\text{\$ tail } [\textit{ file }]$$

to copy the last ten lines of *file* to the standard output (your terminal screen, by default). Only one file argument is recognized and any others will be ignored. If no *file* is specified, **tail** takes its input from the standard input. Thus you may use **tail** in a pipeline to display the last few lines of a data stream. For instance,

$$\text{\$ cat } \textit{filename} \mid \text{tail}$$

will display the last ten lines of *filename*.

You may display lines of *file* beginning with an offset of $+number$ from the beginning or $-number$ lines from the end by specifying the command line

$$\text{\$ tail } [\pm \textit{ number }] \textit{file}$$

You may also begin the display by counting either the number of lines (the default case), of blocks, or of characters from either the beginning or end of the file by using the command line

$$\text{\$ tail } [\pm \textit{ number}[\textit{unit}]] \textit{file}$$

This command line directs **tail** to copy *file* to the standard output beginning at a distance of *number units* from the beginning or end of the file. The *unit* options may either be lines (indicated by l, or the l may be omitted), disk blocks (indicated by b), or characters (indicated by c).

Lines relative to the end of the file are stored in a buffer that can accommodate only 4096 characters. Thus only the last 4096 characters are displayed if your request is made relative to the end of the file. For instance, Figure 6-2 diagrams a file containing 1000 lines with each line containing 10 characters for a total of 10,000 characters. If you request the last 900 lines to be displayed by entering **tail −900 file**, **tail** begins the display at line 590, since only the last 4096 characters (corresponding to some 410 lines) can be stored and since 1000 − 410 = 590. To resolve this problem, make the request relative to the beginning. For example, enter **tail +100 file** to skip the first 100 lines if you wish the last 900 lines to be printed.

The Bell System III and V and Berkeley versions of **tail** have an option (−f) that allows you to see if any characters are appended to a file. This option may be used to monitor the growth of a file, since any character added to the file will be printed on your terminal screen (unless redirected to a disk file). You might place this "monitoring" process in the background so that you can continue with your interactive session in the foreground.

In addition, the Berkeley version recognizes a reverse option (−r) so that you can display the lines in a file in reverse order. When used without ± *number unit*, the entire file will be printed in reverse.

Examples   Prepare for these examples as discussed in the introduction to this chapter. Create the link to **wordlist** before you begin your practice with **tail**.

Type the command to display the "tail" of your **wordlist** file. Of course, your actual display depends on the entries in your word list.

```
$ tail wordlist
zombie
zone
zoo
zoology
zoom
Zoroaster
Zoroastrian
zounds
zucchini
Zurich
$
```

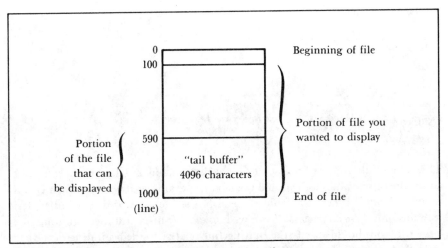

Figure 6-2. *Using* **tail** *to display the end of a file*

The last ten lines were displayed because no offset was indicated. If no ± *number* is named, **tail** assumes the default case, and the display begins with the tenth line from the end of the file.

You can specify an offset from the beginning of the file using **+** *number* or from the end of the file using **−** *number*. For example, type **tail+23996 wordlist** and press RETURN. The result will be similar to the following example:

```
$ tail +23996 wordlist
zoom
Zoroaster
Zoroastrian
zounds
zucchini
Zurich
$
```

Here the display began 23,996 lines from the beginning of the file. Compare this with the result obtained by entering the command **tail −6 wordlist**.

```
$ tail −6 wordlist
zoom
Zoroaster
Zoroastrian
zounds
zucchini
Zurich
$ ▮
```

The same result appears because our word list contains 24,001 entries. You must adjust the offset values for this and the next few examples if your word list is of a different length. Lines relative to the end of the file are stored in a buffer that contains only 4096 characters. If you wish to display lines near the beginning of a large file, you should specify the starting line relative to the beginning of the file instead of to the end of the file.

As an example, enter the command **tail +10 wordlist** followed by the interrupt signal to terminate the listing.

```
$ tail +10 wordlist
9th
a
A&M
[ Interrupt ]
$ ▮
```

However, if you give the apparently equivalent command line **tail −23992 wordlist**, you will observe a different display:

```
$ tail −23992 wordlist
whatever
Whatley
whatnot
[ Interrupt ]
$ ▮
```

In this case, the buffer could only accommodate the last 4096 characters (correspondingly roughly to the last 500 or more words), so the display began approximately 500 words from the end of the file.

So far the offset counts have been in terms of lines. You may specify the offset in terms of characters by concatenating the letter **c** to the offset count value. For example, enter the command line **tail −18c appeal** to begin the display at the eighteenth character from the end of the file.

```
$ tail −18c appeal
of their country.
$
```

As an exercise, try to get this same display by specifying a character offset from the beginning of the file. Don't forget to count each line terminator (new line) character.

You may specify an offset in terms of the disk block size. The block offset is only useful for files that are larger than a block in size. To illustrate, enter **tail −1b wordlist**. The display begins 512 (or a multiple of 512) characters from the end of the file. In this example the word "youngish" was not printed in its entirety because it fell across the disk block boundary.

```
$ tail −1b wordlist
ngish
youngster
Youngstown
[ Interrupt ]
$
```

Your result will differ if your disk block size is not 512 characters (the disk block size on newer versions of UNIX tends to be larger). In any case, verify that an entire block was displayed by piping the output from **tail** into **wc**: enter **tail −1b wordlist | wc −c**. The **wc −c** command counts and displays the number of input characters.

```
$ tail −1b wordlist | wc −c
    512
$
```

If the file is less than one block long, an offset of **+1b** would display nothing because the one-block offset would "reach" past the end of the file. However, the entire file would be displayed if you indicated **−1b**.

If your **tail** command recognizes the follow option (**−f**), try this next example.

Many UNIX utilities append words you misspell to a "history" file associated with the **spell** command. Let's use **tail** to monitor the growth of the spelling history file, which usually has the pathname **/usr/dict/spellhist** (Bell Version 7 and Berkeley), or **/usr/lib/spell/spellhist** (Bell Systems III or V).

Enter **tail −lf** *history file&*, replacing *history file* with the full pathname of your spelling history file. The & in this command line sets up the monitoring process in the background, and the l displays the last line of the history file before the spelling check. Then run the spelling check on **appeal2**, which was created from **appeal** by changing "citizens" to "citozens" and "country" to "coumtry" using an editor. We redirected the output of **spell** to **appeal2.errs** so that the display wouldn't be confused with the output of the **spell** command.

```
$ tail −1f /usr/dict/spellhist&
12475
username tty01    Oct  3 10:14
$ spell appeal2 >appeal2.errs
citozens
coumtry
username tty01    Oct  5 19:57
$ cat appeal2.errs
citozens
coumtry
$
```

The first output (immediately after the **spell** command was given) was generated by the background **tail** process. The output of the **spell** command was redirected to **appeal2.errs** and is displayed next by means of **cat**.

The *pid* of the background monitoring process is shown to be 12475. To terminate your background process, you would enter **kill** *pid*, replacing *pid* with the actual process ID number of your background process.

You should erase any extra files created in this tutorial.

Messages   The following messages apply to the Bell versions of **tail**:

> **usage: tail[±[n] [lbc] [f] [file]**
> You did not set up the invocation command line correctly. (The Bell Version 7 message omits the [f].)

> **tail: cannot open input**
> The specified input file cannot be accessed for reading. An option without a preceding sign would be treated as an input file.

The following messages apply to the Berkeley version of **tail**:

usage: tail [±[n] [lbc] [rf] [file]
You did not set up the invocation command line correctly.

file: **No such file or directory**
The specified input *file* cannot be opened for reading. The exact text of this message may be different for your system.

more — Display a File in Increments

$ more [*option...*] [*filename...*]

$ page [*option...*] [*filename...*]

Options for All Versions:

—windowsize	Set display window to *windowsize* lines, where *windowsize* must be a decimal integer less than the physical screen size.
—c	Clear each screen and begin text display at the top of the screen. Each screen is erased before displaying the next screen.
—d	Display "[Hit space to continue, Rubout to abort]" in addition to the default prompt " — More — ". The verbose form may be useful for inexperienced users.
—f	Display lines using a logical count. This option is useful for displaying lines that contain nonprinting escape sequences. Otherwise, **more** may consider such lines to be longer than they actually appear and fold them in the wrong place.
—l	Don't pause after a line containing a form feed code (^L).
—s	Squeeze multiple adjacent blank lines in the input into one blank line on output display.
—u	Suppress the generation of escape sequences that perform or simulate underlining on a CRT terminal.
+*linenumber*	Start the display at *linenumber.*
+*/pattern*	Start display two lines before *pattern.*

Note that your implementation of **more** may not support all of these invocation options. Any unrecognized options are ignored.

The **more** command allows the display of text in controlled increments on a CRT terminal. You may control the amount of text so that anything from a line to a screenful may be displayed at a time. This command is commonly used to make it possible to read the contents of a long text file or the data stream in a pipeline a screenful at a time. The Berkeley **man** command uses **more** to make the display of the manual page entry stop after each screenful so that you can catch up reading.

The **more** program was developed at U.C. Berkeley and is distributed with the Berkeley UNIX system. However, it is becoming increasingly available on other UNIX systems as well. There are several implementations of **more** that differ primarily by the number of options and commands that control the display. If an option for **more** or the **more** command itself is not recognized by your system, it will be ignored.

If no source file is specified on the **more** command line, input is taken from the standard input file, which should connect to a pipe. If the standard output is not a CRT terminal, **more** acts like the **cat** command, except that a file-identifying header precedes the display of each file if more than one file is being viewed. The command line format for invoking **more** to examine one or more disk files is

$ **more** [*filename...*]

The prompt "—More—" is output whenever the screen display is suspended and the **more** program expects further instructions from the operator. If the input text comes from a file (not a pipe), the message "(*xx*%)" is displayed after the prompt. The value reported—that is, (*xx*)—is the percentage of characters (not lines) in the file from its beginning to the current line.

The **more** program has a number of command line *options* for controlling the display. The general invocation command line for **more** to use one or more *options* is

$ **more** [*option...*] [*filename...*]

The **more** program may also be invoked with the name **page**. When invoked this way, the display will behave as if **more** were invoked with the −c option. Unless instructed otherwise the display window size will be one line larger with **page** than with **more**. The remaining **more** command line options are recognized by **page**.

There are a number of commands you may use for controlling **more** after the display is suspended (that is, after the "—More—" prompt has appeared).

We list each interactive command in Table 6-1. Note that *n* indicates an optional decimal integer. If *n* is omitted, the command acts as if *n* were 1, unless we indicate otherwise. Your version of **more** may not support all the commands listed.

Table 6-1. *Interactive Commands to Control Display With* **more**

Command	Description
n space bar	Display *n* more lines or an entire screen if *n* is absent.
d or **^D**	Display the next scroll size number of lines. Initially the scroll size is 11 lines.
*n***d** or *n***^D**	Reset the scroll size to *n* and display that many lines. If *n* is absent, display the number of lines that is the current scroll size.
*n***z**	Reset the display window size to *n*. If *n* is omitted, another screen is displayed using the current setting for the window size.
*n***s**	Skip *n* lines and display another screenful.
*n***f**	Skip *n* screenfuls and display another screenful.
q or **Q**	Exit from **more** and return to the shell.
=	Display the current line number.
v	Start up the **vi** editor at the current line. When you exit **vi**, you will be returned to **more** command mode.
h	Display a list of all the **more** commands. The file **/usr/lib/more.help** contains the help text.
*n***/***pattern*	Search forward for the *n*th occurrence of *pattern*. If there are fewer than *n* occurrences remaining and the input is from a file, the current line remains unchanged. If found, a screenful is displayed starting two lines before the line containing *pattern*. Use the character-erase and line-kill codes to edit *pattern* before pressing RETURN.
*n***n**	Search for the *n*th occurrence of the last *pattern* that was searched for.
'	Type a single quote to return to the line before the last search operation. If no search has been performed yet, this command will return you to the beginning of the file.
!*commandline*	Invoke a subshell to execute the command line *commandline*. If the characters **%** or **!** are used in *commandline*, they will be replaced by the current filename and previous shell command, respectively. Type a backslash (****) before these characters if you wish to have them interpreted literally in *commandline*.
*n***:n**	Start displaying the *n*th *next* file that was specified as an argument on the command line or the last file if *n* is too large.

Table 6-1.   *Interactive Commands to Control Display With* **more** *(continued)*

Command	Description
n:p	Start displaying the *n*th *previous* file that was specified as a command line argument. If *n* is too large, display the first file. If **more** is not reading input from a file, the terminal bell rings but nothing else happens.
:f	Display the name of the current file and the value of the current line number.
	Type a dot to repeat the previous command.

Note that some of the interactive commands take effect after they are typed. Others require that you press RETURN before they will be recognized. You may cancel any partially formed command by pressing your line-kill character.

The **more** command is terminated by an interrupt signal, and you are returned to the shell. A quit signal, in contrast, does not cause termination, but does cause the display to halt. The prompt " — More — " will be displayed, indicating that **more** has returned to command mode. Some displayed characters may be lost if you halt the display with the quit signal.

The **more** program is designed for perusing a file in the forward direction, but you may employ a few commands to move backward in a given file. However, these commands are related to pattern searching and allow backward movement only in jumps rather than in controlled, progressive increments.

The **more** program must know the characteristics of your CRT display terminal. You must inform **more** of your terminal type so it may find the necessary characteristics for your terminal in the terminal capability database /etc/termcap. You may use the same approach outlined in Appendix C (see the section "Telling UNIX Software Your Terminal Type").

You may predefine any **more** invocation options by assigning them to the shell environment variable **MORE**. In this way you may invoke **more** without specifying those invocation options explicitly. Setting of shell variables is discussed in Chapter 4 and in Appendix C.

Examples   Prepare for these examples as discussed in the introduction to this chapter. Create the link to **wordlist** before you begin your practice with **more**.

Your version of **more** may not support all of the commands illustrated in this tutorial. Type **man more** and press RETURN to see the local documentation for your version of **more**.

For our first example, enter **more wordlist** to display the first 22 lines of the word list. The first several screens indicate that 0% of the file has been displayed, since the word list we are using is so large that over 1950 characters must precede the current line before even 1% of the file has been displayed.

```
$ more wordlist
10th
1st
...
aback
abalone
—More—(0%)
```

Note that in this and many of the remaining screen examples, we use ellipses (...) to indicate lines that we have omitted in our screen simulation in order to save space.

To display the next screenful, press the space bar:

```
abalone
abandon
...
Aberdeen
—More—(0%)
```

To display the next line, press RETURN:

```
abandon
...
Aberdeen
Abernathy
—More—(0%)
```

You may scroll half a screenful by typing either a lowercase d or a ^D:

```
abc
...
Abigail
—More—(0%)
```

You may display both the current line number value and current filename **by** typing **:f**.

...

Abigail

"wordlist" line 56 ▓

Now let's look for the pattern "comput". Enter **/comput** and the display should stop two lines before a line containing the string "comput":

/comput

...skipping

compulsive

compulsory

computation

compute

comrade

...

concert

—More—(19%)▓

Sometimes you'll need to execute a shell command without leaving **more**. To accomplish this, simply type **!** followed by the desired shell command line and end the entry with RETURN. In addition, you may use a shorthand to specify the current filename on the shell command line. To specify the current filename, use the percent sign (**%**).

Try this now. Type an exclamation point (**!**). Then type **ls −l %** and press RETURN; **more** will replace **%** by the name of the current file (that is, by the name of the file that it is currently displaying), **wordlist**. The **more** program draws a dashed line to indicate the end of the shell command output:

—rw—r——r——   1 bin   bin   196513 Oct 10 09:38 wordlist

————————

—More—(19%)▓

If you wish to make changes to a file that you are viewing through the **more** command, you can enter the **vi** editor directly from **more**. When you invoke a **vi** from within **more**, you do not actually exit from **more** and return to the shell, but instead, in effect, you only suspend **more** temporarily.

It is possible to enter the visual editor **vi** from **more** in two ways. First, you can start up a new shell as we just did by typing the **!** and then invoke **vi** to edit any file you choose. If you enter **vi** from **more** in this way, you will be placed at the top of the file. A second way to enter **vi** from **more** is simply to type **v**, in which case you will be placed at the same position in the same file that you were accessing with **more**. In this way, you can begin editing the piece of the file that was on your screen when you decided to invoke **vi** without having to search through the file to relocate your position. Any editorial changes that you make will be reflected in the file when you return to the command mode of **more**. When you return to **more**, you will always be placed at the same location in the file at which you temporarily left **more**.

Messages   There are two kinds of messages associated with the **more** command: error messages and informational messages. The following error messages apply to the Berkeley version of **more**, which is the only version of this command.

> **Usage:** *pathname...*
> The command displays a "usage" message if it was invoked without any file arguments and the input does not come from a pipe. It prints the pathname of the **more** program itself.
>
> ******* *filename*: **directory *****
> You must specify an ordinary file for **more** to display.
>
> ************ *filename*: **Not a text file *********
> You must specify a text file for **more**.
>
> **Can't open help file**
> The file containing the list of the **more** commands, **/usr/lib/more.help**, cannot be opened for reading.
>
> **Pattern not found**
> The specified pattern could not be located by searching forward in the current file.
>
> **Line too long**
> The input line is too long. Generally the maximum length for an input command line is 256 characters.
>
> **No previous command to substitute for**
> You typed two exclamation points to repeat the previous shell command, but there was no previous shell command to replace the second **!** character.
>
> **Regular expression botch**
> This message is displayed when *pattern* is not specified correctly. There are other error messages related to incorrectly formed regular expressions for *pattern*.

The following messages give you information while you're using the **more** command:

—More—
The short form of the **more** program prompt.

[Hit space to continue, Rubout to abort] —More—
The long form of the **more** program prompt.

(xx%)
The percentage of characters in the file from the beginning to the current line.

::::::::::::::
filename
::::::::::::::
The header that precedes the display of each file if more than one file argument was specified on the invocation command line.

[Use q or Q to quit]
Displayed whenever you type the quit signal to remind you that you must use **q** or **Q**, *not* the quit signal, to exit **more**.

"*filename*" line *number*
Display of current *filename* and line *number* in response to **:f** command.

...skipping
Message displayed when lines are being skipped.

...skipping *number* line
Message displayed when skipping *number* lines in current file.

Skipping to file *filename*
Message displayed when skipping forward to another file named *filename* in response to *n*:**n** command.

Skipping back to file *filename*
Message displayed when skipping backward to another file named *filename* in response to *n*:**p** command.

pr — Print File With Pagination

$ **pr** [*option...*] *file...*

Bell Version 7 Options:

−*n*   Produce *n*-column output. The column width is automatically decreased as *n* is increased and thus may truncate the columns unless the page width is increased as well.

+*n*	Start printing at page *n* skipping the first *n*−1 pages.
−**h** *string*	The *string* argument replaces the filename in the header line of the output. Enclose *string* in single or double quotation marks if it contains ASCII space or tab characters.
−**w***n*	Set page width for multicolumn output to *n* columns (the default is 72).
−**l***n*	Set page length to *n* lines (the default is 66 lines).
−**t**	Skip printing five-line header and trailer.
−**s***c*	Separate columns by character *c* or by a tab if *c* is not indicated (space characters are separate by default).
−**m**	Merge and print all the files simultaneously, each in its own column.

Additional Berkeley Option:

−**f**	Output a form feed instead of blank lines to begin a new page. The effective page length remains the same. Generally a form feed does not affect a CRT display terminal; however, it will cause a new page to be ejected with most hard-copy terminals.

Additional Bell Systems III and V Options:

−**a**	Display the multicolumn output across instead of down the page (the default).
−**d**	Double-space the output.
−**e**[*c*][*k*]	Replace tabs (or the character *c*) in the input to *k* space characters on output (the default *k* is 8).
−**i**[*c*][*k*]	Replace *k* successive space characters in input by a tab (or character *c*) on output (the default *k* is 8).
−**n**[*c*][*k*]	Number lines (integer digits for *k*, with the default *k* at 5), and then append a tab (or character *c*).
−**o**[*k*]	Start printing at column *k* (the default *k* is 0).
−**p**	Suspend the CRT display at the beginning of each page and ring the terminal bell if directed to a terminal. Resume display by pressing RETURN.
−**r**	Suppress error messages about inaccessible input files.

If you use the **pr** command to display the contents of a text file, you will get a paginated and nicely formatted listing. You can control the appearance of the output by several different command line options.

Each page of the output begins with a five-line header containing a line with the last date and time of file modification, the filename, and the page number. A trailer consisting of five blank lines at the end of the page is also supplied. The output is formatted to fit on a standard 8 1/2- × 11-inch page, which has 66 lines and 72 columns. If no file argument is specified, **pr** takes its input from the standard input file (the keyboard, by default) and thus may be used in a pipeline to paginate the data stream.

The general invocation command line for printing one or more files under direction of one or more options is

$ **pr** [*option...*] *file...*

You will find **pr** useful for preparing nicely formatted hard-copy output. Pipe the output of **pr** into the input of **lpr**, which places its input data in a queue for subsequent printing on the system line printer. For instance,

$ **pr poem | lpr**

sends the output of **pr** to **lpr** to produce a hard copy of **poem** with an identifying header and trailer on each page. (The **lpr** utility is the next command to be discussed in this chapter.)

Like the **cat** command, **pr** buffers its output in units of the disk block size, which is 512 bytes (characters) for Bell Version 7 and System III, and 1024 bytes or greater for the Berkeley UNIX system and some implementations of Bell System V.

Interterminal messages (that is, messages sent between two users who are using the **write** command) are suppressed during the operation of the **pr** command. This ensures that the formatted listing is not disturbed.

Examples   Prepare for these examples as discussed in the introduction to this chapter. Create the link to **wordlist** before you begin your practice with **pr**.

As a first example of using **pr**, type **pr poem** and press RETURN. The ellipses (...) in our example represent the remaining 57 blank lines on the page. The date and time reflect the last modification time of the file being displayed, **poem**.

```
$ pr poem

Oct 7 18:19 1984 poem   Page 1

Roses are Red
Violets are Blue
Sugar is Sweet
And so are You.

   ...

$ 
```

You will see a five-line header consisting of two blank lines, a line containing an identifying header ("Oct 7 18:19 1984 poem   Page 1"), and two more blank lines. Then **pr** displays the contents of the file. Finally, enough blank lines are output to make a 66-line page, including a five-line trailer consisting of blank lines. If **poem** contained enough text to require a second page, another header similar to the first but indicating "Page 2" would be displayed.

On terminals with high-speed display rates, you will need to pipe the output of **pr** into a utility (such as the Berkeley **more** command) that lets you view one screenful at a time. Check your system documentation for such a utility. Later we show you how to simulate this function if you have Bell Systems III or V **pr** with the pause option (−**p**).

There are a number of options that you can use to customize the appearance of the formatted output. You must specify the options before the file arguments.

For example, if you don't want **pr** to print the five-line header and the five-line trailer normally supplied for each page, use the −**t** option. If you are using the Bell Version 7 or the Berkeley version of **pr**, the display will continue for 66 lines. The Bell Systems III and V versions, however, stop the display after the last line of the file. This display will then be the same as that produced by the **cat** utility, as shown here:

```
$ pr −t poem
Roses are Red
Violets are Blue
Sugar is Sweet
And so are You.
$ 
```

You may use the −l option to change the output page length. If the output is destined for a hard-copy device, the page length specification should agree with the physical page length. For instance, to change the length of the printed page to fit 8 1/2- × 14-inch legal paper, multiply 14 inches per page by 6 lines per inch to get 84 lines per page and specify −l84 as an option.

pr produces multicolumn output if you specify a decimal digit *n* after the dash, where *n* is the number of columns desired. As an example, let's display your word list in five columns. Type **pr −5 wordlist** and press RETURN to produce a display with five columns.

```
$ pr −5 wordlist

Oct 9 14:57 1984   wordlist Page 1

10th     abject      abstinent     accountant   across
1st      ablate      abstract      accouter     acrylate
2nd      ablaze      abstractor    Accra        acrylic
[ Interrupt ]
$
```

The "[Interrupt]" here indicates that we terminated **pr** with an interrupt signal to save space.

The **pr** command will take the words that will fit on one page and display them from top to bottom down each column, beginning with the left-hand column and ending with the column on the extreme right. An alternative is to list all the words in succession from left to right across the page by suppressing the page header with the −t option and specifying a page length of one line:

```
$ pr −t −5 −l1 wordlist
10th     1st       2nd       3rd       4th
5th      6th       7th       8th       9th
a        A&M       A&P       a's       AAA
[ Interrupt ]
$
```

If you are using the Bell Systems III or V version, on the other hand, specify the −a (across) option with the column count option. Thus, you would enter **pr −a −5 wordlist** with this version to achieve the same effect as that shown in the preceding screen.

Use the −w*n* option to change the width of the page for multicolumn output. The default value is 72 columns for the page width. As an example, to utilize the

entire 80 columns that are available on most modern terminals, you would enter
the command line **pr −5 −w80 wordlist**.

The option **+n** means "begin printing on page *n*." If you were printing a long
document and stopped in the middle, you could use this option to resume printing from the point of interruption rather than from the beginning. To illustrate,
print a few pages of the your word list and abort the listing with an interrupt
signal. Note the page number you were on when you aborted. Now resume printing on that page using the **+n** option.

To design your own customized page header, use the **−h** option. Be sure to
insert at least one space between the option letter and the text for the header.
Surround the text with single or double quotation marks if it consists of more
than one word.

```
$ pr −5 −h "SPELLING DICTIONARY" wordlist

Oct 9 14:57 1984   SPELLING DICTIONARY Page 1

10th     abject      abstinent    accountant   across
1st      ablate      abstract     accouter     acrylate
[ Interrupt ]
$
```

If you want to separate the columns by a particular character rather than by
spaces, use the **−s**c option, where *c* is the separation character. The separator is
taken to be a tab if you do not explicitly designate a character after **−s**. If the
separation character normally has a special interpretation by the shell, you must
enclose it in single quotation marks. As an example, display your word list in five
columns, each separated by a vertical bar. Enter the command line **pr −5 −s'|'**
wordlist. (The vertical bar must be enclosed in single quotation marks because the
shell normally interprets it to mean "to pipe.")

```
pr −5 −s'|' wordlist

Oct 9 14:57 1984 wordlist Page 1

10th|abject|abstinent|accountant|across
1st|ablate|abstract|accouter|acrylate
2nd|ablaze|abstractor|Accra|acrylic
[ Interrupt ]
$
```

Multicolumn output consists of columns of the same width that are separated
by at least one space. If some words do not fit in the column width, they are

truncated. When you use the −s option, the words are separated by the designated character and are not truncated. For example, displaying eight columns of the word list causes some words to be truncated. If you use −s' ' to separate the columns by a space, however, they are not truncated, as we see here:

```
$ pr −8 wordlist

Oct 9 14:57 1984   wordlist Page 1

10th  abject   abstinen   accounta   across    adenoma   Adrian    affair
1st   ablate   abstract   accouter   acrylate  adept     Adriatic  affect
[ Interrupt ]
$ pr −8 −s' ' wordlist

Oct 9 14:57 1984   wordlist Page 1

10th abject abstinent accountant across adenoma Adrian affair
1st ablate abstract accouter acrylate adept Adriatic affect
[ Interrupt ]
$
```

The remaining examples pertain only to the Bell System III or V **pr** command. You may easily double-space the output with the −d option:

```
$ pr −d poem

Oct 7 18:19 1984   poem Page 1

Roses are Red

Violets are Blue

Sugar is Sweet

And so are you.
...
$
```

The **pr** command has a pause (−p) option that will ring the terminal bell and cause the output to be suspended at the beginning of each page until you press RETURN. You could use this feature to display a screenful of text at a time if, for instance, you were using a terminal with a rapid display rate that made the output scroll rapidly off the screen.

For our example, let's pipe the output of the **ls** command into **pr**, which we are invoking simply in order to display a screenful at a time. The terminal bell will beep before the display begins. Each time you press RETURN, a screenful (23 lines) will be displayed and the terminal bell will sound again. When you have finished reading the list, press RETURN again and the next screenful will be displayed, and so on.

```
$ ls /bin I pr −p −t −l23
ar
as
...
echo
```

You may use the −**n** option to number the output lines. For example, enter **pr −n wordlist** to precede each text line by a whole number:

```
$ pr −n wordlist
Oct 9 14:57 1984   wordlist Page 1

    1  10th
    2  1st
    3  2nd
[ Interrupt ]
$
```

Finally, you may use the −**e** option to convert tabs in the input file to a specified number of spaces. This would be useful, for example, if you had a document like a C program with indentation provided by tabs and the text on the right-hand side running off the edge of the printed page. In this case, you could convert each tab that causes an indentation of eight column positions to four spaces so the right margin would fit on the page by entering the command **pr −e4** *program*, where *program* is the file containing the indented program listing.

Messages   The following messages apply to the Bell Version 7 and Berkeley version of the **pr** command:

> **pr: can't open** *file*
> The *file* cannot be accessed for reading. This message is only displayed on your terminal if the standard output has been redirected away from the terminal screen—for example, into a file or pipeline. If the report option (−**r**) is available, this message will not be displayed at all.

pr: Too many args
There are too many input files specified for using the merge (−m) option. Generally, no more than nine file arguments can be merged at a time.

pr: No room for columns
You must specify a number of columns less than the effective width of the output page.

The following messages apply to the Bell Systems III and V versions of **pr**:

pr: can't open *file*
The *file* cannot be accessed for reading

pr: too many files
There are too many input files specified for using the merge (−m) option.

pr: bad option
You specified an unrecognized option.

pr: width too small
You have specified too many columns for the effective page width setting.

pr: page-buffer overflow
You have specified too large an effective page size for the internal page buffer.

pr: file—empty file
The specified *file* argument is empty.

pr: out of space
There is insufficient memory to run **pr** under the specified conditions.

Note that if the standard output of **pr** is directed to a terminal, any error messages are withheld until the command has finished printing all the files that it is able to print.

lpr— Print Files

$ lpr [*option...*] *file...*

Bell Version 7 and System III Options:

−c	Copy *file* to be printed instead of linking.
−r	Remove the *file* after placing on queue.
−m	Have **mail** inform you when printing is done.
−n	Do not inform when printing is complete.

Additional Bell System V Option:

−f*name*	Use (fictitious) file *name* for reporting completion by **mail**.

Use the **lpr** command to print one or more files on your system line printer. This command places one or more files in a printer queue to be printed in the background.

The **lpr** command works like this: first, **lpr** writes a *directive file* and either links or copies the data file(s) specified on the **lpr** invocation command line to a printing "spool" directory, generally **/usr/lib/lpd**. (Spool is an acronym for "simultaneous peripheral output on-line.") Then another program, **lpd**, known as the "line printer daemon," examines this spool directory and prints the files as instructed by the directive file. However, the **lpd** process will not print any files if a file named **lock** is also present in this directory. This *lock file* helps prevent conflicts when more than one printing request is made at the same time.

You may wish to paginate the file with the **pr** command before sending it to the line printer. (The **pr** command and its formatting options are discussed in the preceding section.) In this case, pipe the output of **pr** directly into **lpr**, as shown:

$$\$ \textbf{ pr } [\textit{ option... }] \textit{ file } | \textbf{ lpr}$$

The printing may not occur immediately after the request. This depends on many factors, including how heavily loaded your system is, whether the printer is set up and ready, and so on. If you request that you be informed when printing is complete, **lpr** will invoke **mail** to send you a completion message.

Normally the files you specify to be printed are linked to the spool directory. This approach saves valuable disk space as another copy is not made. If you were to change the original file before it was actually printed, however, the printout would reflect your changes, so that you would not get a printout of the file in the original form. Furthermore, if you deleted the original file after you invoked **lpr**, no output would be produced. Thus, if you intend to change or delete the original file, you should specify the copy (−c) option when you invoke **lpr**. Specifying −c causes a copy of the original file to be made in the spool directory. Then you may change or delete your original file without affecting the printing of the queued copy.

You may wish to specify the remove option (−r) when printing a file you no longer have use for. The **lpr** command will then delete this file after it has been copied to the spool directory. In this way you don't have to remember to delete your original file.

The **lpr** command may not exist in your version of UNIX since this command is being replaced in newer versions. If your system does not have **lpr**, refer to your local documentation for the related **lp** command.

Examples   Prepare for these examples as discussed in the introduction to this chapter, but before you begin, read your system documentation concerning use of the **lpr** command and its options, since this command tends to be more implementation-dependent than most. Our examples illustrate the Bell versions of this command. The Berkeley version is similar in principle but differs in detail.

First, to illustrate why some sort of header is helpful in identifying what you print, type **lpr poem** and then press RETURN; then compare the results with those of **pr poem | lpr**.

Next, if the −m option is available on your system, enter the command **lpr −m poem**. There should be a completion notification message in your *mailfile* when your printing run is complete.

When you modify a file in any way after requesting that it be printed, several factors determine whether you will get a printout of the file in its original form as you requested it. Because the **lpr** command places a file to be printed in a printer queue and because this queue may at times be very short (that is, there are not many requests to use the printer ahead of yours), the original, unmodified file may be the file that is printed; in effect, the **lpr** command is executed at once, before you even have a chance to type in the changes to the file. More often, however, there will be many requests to use the line printer and the spooling system will be backed up. In this case, any changes you make will be reflected in the file that is printed since these changes will be made in the file as it waits in the queue. Thus, if you make changes to a file after the **lpr** request, the only way to ensure that you will get a hard copy of the file in its original form is to use the −c (copy) option.

To illustrate this, first make a backup copy of **poem**: enter **cp poem poem.bak**. Now enter **lpr poem;rm poem**, and if your line printer spooling system is slow enough, the text of **poem** will *not* be printed.

Now restore your original file, entering the command line **cp poem.bak poem**, and then enter **lpr −c poem;rm poem**. This time the text of **poem** *is* printed. The copy option causes **lpr** to make a copy of the file argument in the spool directory instead of simply linking the original file to the directory. In this way, you can change the original file, or remove it as we just did, without affecting the copy to be printed. Restore **poem** because we erased it in the last operation. Enter

cp poem.bak poem.

Next, enter the command **lpr −r poem.bak**, if the −r option is available on your system, and then after the file is printed, examine your directory with **ls** and see that **poem.bak** was removed.

```
$ lpr −r poem.bak
$ ls
Mail
appeal
poem
$
```

You may specify the mail option (−m) if you wish **mail** to inform you when the printing request has been completed. Some implementations may notify you with **mail** by default.

If you are making several requests for printing the same file and are using the System V version of **lpr**, you might specify the −f option so that **mail** can inform you with a dummy filename for each request. For instance, if you need to print **poem** several times, you might use dummy names with the −f option, such as **poem.run1**, **poem.run2**, and so on, to distinguish the different printing run requests for the same file, **poem**.

Let's try this now. Print **poem** twice in succession specifying the runs as **poem.run1** and **poem.run2**, as shown:

```
$ lpr −fpoem.run1 poem
$ lpr −fpoem.run2 poem
$
```

You determine how many files are waiting in the queue to be printed by counting the number of files in **/usr/spool/lpd** whose names begin with **cf** (copied file) and **lf** (linked file). Additional characters are added to give the file a unique name. The numbers are the process identification numbers (the PID numbers) of the **lpr** command process that queued up the file for printing. Letters like **A** and **B** are added to give a unique filename in case the same **lpr** process queues up more than one file.

The following example shows that four data files are queued up to be printed. The two copied files were named **cfA00190** and **cfB00190** since the same **lpr** process (with PID 190) prepared these files for printing. The two linked files, named **lfA00171** and **lfA00188**, were queued by different **lpr** requests. Files whose names begin with **df** contain directives for the program **lpd**, which directs the files to be printed.

```
$ ls /usr/spool/lpd
cfA00190
cfB00190
dfA00171
dfA00188
dfA00190
lfA00171
lfA00188
$
```

Note that your version of **lpr** may name the files differently.

Messages   The following messages apply to Bell versions of **lpr**:

lpr: Unrecognized option: −x
You specified an option that was not recognized by **lpr**.

lpr: Cannot open *file*
The *file* cannot be opened for reading.

lpr: File *file* **is empty**
The *file* exists but is empty.

lpr: File pipe.end is empty
lpr received no input from pipe before end-of-file.

lpr: Too many copy files; *file* **not copied**
You specified too many *files* for the copy (−c) option. The limit is around 50 to 60 files; *file* was not copied for printing.

lpr: Can't create /usr/spool/lpd/tfA*XXXXX*
You don't have permission to write in the spool directory /**usr/spool/lpd**. For assistance, ask your system administrator.

wc — Count Units in a File

$ **wc** [*option...*] *filename...*

Bell Version 7, Systems III and V Options:

none	Display the number of lines, words, and characters.
−l	Display the number of lines.
−w	Display the number of words.
−c	Display the number of characters.

Additional Berkeley Options:

−p	Count the number of pages. The default page length is 66 lines but may be reset with the size (−s) option.
−t	Display the time to transmit the file. The default transmission speed is 300 baud (30 characters per second) but may be reset with the baud (−b) option.
−b*baud*	Calculate the transmission speed using *baud* baud rate instead of the default (300 baud).
−s*pagesize*	Calculate the number of pages based on a page size of *pagesize* instead of the default (66 lines).
−v	Specify "verbose" output format, which prints a header and includes page count and transmission time.

The **wc** command counts the lines, words, and characters in one or more files that you specify on the command line. If no file is named, **wc** counts what is input in the standard input (keyboard, by default); thus **wc** may be used in a pipe to report these same statistics for the pipeline data stream.

It's important to note that the **wc** program includes whitespace characters in its character count. A whitespace character is a space, a tab, or a new line character. A new line character, which is the same as an ASCII line feed character, separates one line of text from the next in the UNIX system.

The **wc** program defines a *word* to be a string of characters that does not contain any whitespace characters.

Both the Bell and Berkeley versions of **wc** recognize three options to limit **wc**'s report to either lines, words, or characters, or to any combination. If you do not indicate a command line option, the line, word, and character count will all be reported.

The Berkeley version of **wc** has an option (−p) for counting the pages using a 66-line default page size. In addition, you may specify a different page size for this calculation by using the −s option right next to the size. The size of the page must be a whole number.

The Berkeley version of **wc** also displays the transmission time for the file argument using a default 300 baud data transmission speed. You may indicate a different transmission speed by specifying the −b option along with a whole number for the new baud rate.

The −v option (for "verbose") displays all possible statistics for the Berkeley version of **wc**. The −v option includes the −p and −t calculations, and as with the −p and −t options, the page size or transmission speed used with −v may be reset with the −s and −b options respectively.

Examples   Prepare for these examples as discussed in the introduction to this chapter. Create the link to **wordlist** before you begin your practice with **wc**. For our first tutorial example, enter **wc poem.**

```
$ wc poem
    4      13        62 poem
$
```

The result shows 4 lines, 13 words, and 62 characters in the file **poem.**

To see how long the other text files in your personal file system are, use this basic command form. If you want statistics on more than one file, simply add the desired files to the command line. Wild card abbreviations for the filenames will also work. For example, enter the command line **wc [a−z]*** to obtain statistics for all ordinary files in your home directory. The directory names are capitalized and will therefore not be included.

```
$ wc [a−z]*
      4      16        75 appeal
      4      13        62 poem
  24001   24001    196513 wordlist
  24009   24030    196651 total
$
```

You may count only lines, words, or characters, or some combination, by specifying the appropriate option letter or letters before the file arguments. Thus, you can enter **wc −lw appeal** to display the number of lines and words in **appeal**, as shown:

```
$ wc −lw appeal
      4      16 appeal
$
```

If no file argument is specified, the input for **wc** is taken from the standard input, which is the keyboard, by default. Thus you may also pipe the output of another program into the standard input of **wc** in order to obtain statistics on the data stream.

For example, enter **who | wc −1**, and the standard output of the **who** program will be piped into the standard input of **wc**. Since **who** produces one line of output for each terminal that is currently logged on to your system, a count of these lines will reveal the number of terminals currently on-line.

```
$ who | wc −l
   7
$
```

This result indicates that seven terminals are currently logged on. Actually, there may be fewer users as a given user may log on to more than one terminal.

If you have access to the Berkeley version of **wc**, try these next few examples. Type **wc −v wordlist** to obtain all statistics for your word list:

```
$ wc −v wordlist
lines   words   chars    pages    time@300
24001   24001   196513   364      1.8 hr wordlist
$
```

Now let's reset the page size to be 55 lines and the baud rate to be 1200 and see how the report differs:

```
$ wc −v −s55 −b1200 wordlist
lines   words   chars    pages    time@1200
24001   24001   196513   437      27.3 mi wordlist
$
```

As you can see, the transmission time is approximately one-fourth the value shown the first time we measured the word list because the baud rate was increased four times. The number of pages increased because the page size specification was reduced.

Messages   The following messages apply to Bell versions of the **wc** command:

> **usage: wc [−clw] [name ...]**
> You specified an unrecognized option.
> **wc: cannot open** *file*
> The *file* argument cannot be accessed for reading.

The following messages apply to the Berkeley version of the **wc** command:

Usage: wc [−lwcpt] [−v] [−u] [−s*pagesize*] [−b*baud*]
You either specified an invalid option letter or didn't specify a positive whole number argument to the −s or −b option. Note that the number *must* be joined to the option letter (that is, no space should separate the two) or else it will be considered to be a file argument.

wc: can't open *file*
The *file* argument cannot be accessed for reading.

Managing Your Files

The commands presented in this section enable you to manage your UNIX filing system. With these commands you can duplicate, rename, or delete your files, as well as place copies of files in different directories. This section also explains the **chmod** command, which allows you to control who has access to your files and what kind of access they have.

While the Bell Version 7 and Berkeley system have three distinct programs corresponding to the **cp**, **ln**, and **mv** commands described in this section, both Bell Systems III and V have combined these three functions into a single program. For this reason, you will find these commands documented under one entry in the *UNIX User's Manual* if you have either System III or System V.

cp — Copy File

$ cp [*option*] *file*... *target*

Berkeley Option:
−i Prevent accidental erasure by invoking an interactive mode in which you are prompted with messages before copying proceeds.

Use the **cp** command to create duplicate copies of ordinary files. The general command line format for making a copy of the ordinary file *file* onto *target*, which may be either an ordinary or directory file, is

$ cp *file target*

If *target* is an ordinary file that already exists, the contents of *target* are erased and the contents of *file* are written onto *target*. If *target* is a directory, a new file with the name *target/file* will be created. The contents of *file* are then copied. If the file *target/file* already exists, it will be overwritten by the contents of *file*. In all cases the original source file *file* remains intact.

You must have permission to read the source file. The **cp** command will not let you overwrite an existing ordinary target file if it is write-protected. If you own *target*, you may use **chmod** to enable write permission and then perform the desired copy operation.

To copy one or more files into a specified *target* directory with their original filenames, use the following command line form:

$$\text{\$ cp } file1 \; file2... \; target$$

This command form may be used for duplicating an entire group of files with a single command line.

You may change the name of the file as you copy it to a directory by specifying an ordinary filename as the target. Thus to duplicate *oldname* as *newname* in directory *target*, use the command line format

$$\text{\$ cp } oldname \; target/newname$$

The Berkeley version has an interactive option ($-i$) that warns you if you are about to overwrite an existing target file, whether or not that file is write-protected. You should employ this interactive option to prevent accidental erasure of *target*.

Use the following command line format to initiate the interactive mode:

$$\text{\$ cp } -i \; file... \; target$$

Whenever the file *target* exists, the Berkeley version of **cp** will prompt you with a message such as "Overwrite *target*?". Answer with a y and press RETURN to proceed with the copy to *target*; otherwise, that particular copy operation will be aborted. (You can answer with the whole word **yes**; the first letter, y, is all that counts.) The **cp** program doesn't terminate until you have been queried for each *file* specified on the invocation command line.

If an existing ordinary file *target* is overwritten, its old permission modes will be preserved. Otherwise, the permission modes of the source file become the permission modes of the new (copied) file.

You may use the **cp** command to create backup copies of files. With backups you can manipulate the original file without worrying that all will be lost if you damage the file. Thus you might enter **cp poem poem.bak** to back up **poem** as

poem.bak. If you damage **poem**, you can reproduce the original file by entering **cp poem.bak poem** and trying again.

Examples   Prepare for these examples as discussed in the introduction to this chapter. The **wordlist** is not necessary for this command.

As a first example, remove read and write permissions for the group and other user categories for **poem** by entering the command line **chmod og−rw poem**. (The **chmod** command is discussed in a later section.) Now verify with a long directory listing by entering **ls −l poem**. Then make a copy of **poem** with the name **poem.bak** by entering **cp poem poem.bak**. Finally, list all the "poem" files by entering **ls −l poem∗**.

```
$ chmod og−rw poem
$ ls −l poem
—rw————————   1 username docum    62 Oct 9    12:02 poem
$ cp poem poem.bak
$ ls −l poem∗
—rw————————   1 username docum    62 Oct 9    12:02 poem
—rw————————   1 username docum    62 Oct 10  09:33 poem.bak
$ ▓
```

The last long directory listing shows that the new duplicate **poem.bak** was created with the same permission modes as the source file **poem**. However, if you created a new duplicate copy using an editor, it would have a different set of permission modes, as shown here:

```
$ ed poem
62
w poem2
62
q
$ ls −l poem∗
—rw————————   1 username docum    62 Oct 9    12:02 poem
—rw————————   1 username docum    62 Oct 10  09:33 poem.bak
—rw—rw—rw—   1 username docum    62 Oct 10  09:35 poem2
$ ▓
```

If the **cp** program overwrites an existing file, this destination file retains its previous set of access permissions, as the following illustrates:

```
$ cp poem poem2
$ ls —l poem*
—rw————————   1 username docum   62 Oct 9    12:02 poem
—rw————————   1 username docum   62 Oct 10 09:33 poem.bak
—rw—rw—rw—     1 username docum   62 Oct 10 09:36 poem2
$
```

Note that if **poem2** didn't exist before the copy operation, it would have been given the same permission modes as **poem**.

If the target file is a directory, you can copy several source files into that directory in one operation and the copied files will retain their original names and access permissions. For example, copy all the "poem" files into the **Mail** directory by entering **cp poem* Mail**. Then verify that the copies retained their original names and access permissions by a long directory listing:

```
$ cp poem* Mail
$ ls —l Mail
total 4
drwxrwxrwx          4 username docum   80 Oct 5    13:04 Username
—rw————————   1 username docum   62 Oct 9    12:02 poem
—rw————————   1 username docum   62 Oct 10 09:33 poem.bak
—rw—rw—rw—     1 username docum   62 Oct 10 09:36 poem2
$
```

You may change the name of a file as you copy it to a directory by specifying the new filename in the destination directory. For instance, entering the command line **cp poem Mail/verse** will create a duplicate of **poem** named **verse** in the **Mail** directory:

```
$ cp poem Mail/verse
$ ls Mail
Username
poem
poem.bak
poem2
verse
$
```

For our last example, let's make a copy of **verse** in the home directory and verify the operation by a directory listing. Here we must specify a pathname to the source file **verse**. The dot (.) stands for the current (and in this case, the home) directory.

```
$ cp Mail/verse .
$ ls
Mail
appeal
poem
poem.bak
poem2
verse
$ ▇
```

Before leaving this tutorial session, restore your home directory to its original state by erasing the files created to exemplify **cp**. Type **rm poem.bak poem2 verse Mail/[a−z]*** and press RETURN.

Messages   The following messages apply to the Berkeley version of **cp**:

Usage: cp: f1 f2; or cp f1 ... fn d2

The command line was not set up correctly. Either you (1) gave an invalid option, (2) specified no *target*, or (3) specified more than one *source* along with a *target* that is not a directory.

cp: cannot open *source*

You don't have permission to read the *source* file.

cp: cannot copy file to itself

The *target* cannot be the same as the *source* file.

overwrite *target*?

You get this query when using the interactive option and the file *target* exists. Enter **y** to overwrite *target*. Other responses will prevent the copy operation.

cp: cannot create *target*

You are not allowed to create the file *target*.

cp: read: *message*

There was a system error indicated by *message* when **cp** tried to read the contents of *source* file.

cp: write: *message*

There was a system error indicated by *message* when **cp** attempted to write to file *target*.

The following messages apply to Bell System III and V versions of **cp**:

Usage: {mv|cp|ln} f1 f2
{mv|cp|ln} f1 ... fn d1
mv d1 d2
The command line was not set up correctly. Either you specified (1) only *source* or (2) more than one *source* file and a file *target* that is not a directory.

cp: *target* **not found**
The specified *target* directory does not exist.

cp: **cannot access** *source*
Either you specified (1) a file *source* that doesn't exist or (2) an option. (The Bell version has no options.) This version of **cp** treats all invocation options as source files.

cp: <*source*> **directory**
The specified file *source* is a directory.

cp: *source* **and** *target* **are identical**
The *target* cannot be the same as the *source* file.

cp: **cannot open** *source*
You don't have permission to read the file *source*.

cp: **cannot create** *target*
You don't have permission to create *target*.

cp: **bad copy to** *target*
There was a system error that either prevented reading of *source* or writing to *target*.

ln — Make Link

Bell Version 7, Systems III and V:
$ ln *firstname secondname*

Berkeley Version:
$ ln *firstname* [*secondname*]
No Options.

Use the **ln** command to establish an additional filename for the same ordinary file. Whereas the **cp** command creates a duplicate copy of a file, the **ln** command creates another name for the same file.

A UNIX directory file associates one or more filenames with a disk file. Each entry in a directory consists of two parts: a filename and a pointer to the file in the disk storage system. This pointer is also known as a *link,* since it links a filename to a physical file on the disk. Hence the names of one file in the same directory must be different, but these same files may have the same name if they are linked to different directories. Nothing prevents two or more links (filenames) to the *same* physical file.

While you can use **ln** to create an alias for the same ordinary file, you cannot create an alias for a directory. The **ln** command has two general command line formats, the first of which is

$$\$ \text{ ln } \textit{firstname secondname}$$

Here *firstname* is the name of the ordinary file for which you wish to establish an additional name or link. The *secondname* is the additional name of the file specified by *firstname.* If *firstname* is pathname, the ordinary file to be linked is in a different directory from the current directory; otherwise, there would be no need, of course, to specify a pathname.

With the Berkeley version you can also use **ln** by designating *firstname* to be the pathname of the file for which you wish to create an alias. The command line format in this case is

$$\$ \text{ ln } \textit{firstname} \text{ [\textit{secondname}]}$$

You can use a shorthand by omitting *secondname.* The name of the resulting link will be the basename of *firstname.* The Berkeley version of **ln** will simply use the last element of *firstname,* which is the basename if you don't supply *secondname.*

In either case, if *secondname* doesn't already exist, the new link is established between the disk file named *firstname* and the current directory. In other words, a new current directory entry is created that also points to the file named *firstname,* but that has the name *secondname,* with the result that *secondname* refers to the same disk file as *firstname.*

Before we move on to the examples, it's important to note that the **rm** command, which is closely allied to **ln**, "removes" files by breaking the link between the filename and the physical file. When the number of links to any physical file becomes zero, the file is no longer accessible. Then the UNIX system reuses the disk space for another file.

Examples   Prepare for these examples as discussed in the introduction to this chapter. Create the link to **wordlist** before you begin your practice with **ln**.

Each physical disk file is identified by a unique number. You may display this identification number by using the −**i** option when you invoke the **ls** utility. We will use this identification number to see if two filenames refer to the same disk file or not. For instance, enter **ls —il** and observe the identification numbers in the leftmost column of the long directory listing. Since each filename (listed in the rightmost column) has a different identification number, these names all refer to different files on the disk. Of course, your identification numbers in all likelihood will not be the same as shown here:

```
$ ls —il
total 391
713 drwxrwxrwx      3 username docum      80    Oct 5 09:36 Mail
665 —rw—rw—rw—       1 username docum      78    Oct 9 12:02 appeal
666 —rw—rw—rw—       1 username docum      62    Oct 9 09:35 poem
521 —rw—r——r——       2 bin      bin    196513   Oct 2 16:28 wordlist
$
```

Now establish another link, called **verse**, to the file **poem** in the same directory by typing **ln poem verse**. Then list the directory again:

```
$ ln poem verse
$ ls —il
total 392
713 drwxrwxrwx      3 username docum      80    Oct 5 09:36 Mail
665 —rw—rw—rw—       1 username docum      78    Oct 9 12:02 appeal
666 —rw—rw—rw—       2 username docum      62    Oct 9 09:35 poem
521 —rw—r——r——       2 bin      bin    196513   Oct 2 16:28 wordlist
666 —rw—rw—rw—       2 username docum      62    Oct 9 09:35 verse
$
```

The **verse** link now refers to the same file (with ID number 666) as the original link, **poem**, does. Note that the number of links to this file, tabulated in the third column from the left, increased from 1 in the previous screen to 2 in this screen.

If you change the contents of **verse**, you change the contents of **poem** since the two names refer to the same file. For instance, if you used an editor and changed either **poem** or **verse** in some way, you would discover that the other file was changed in the same way as the file you edited after saving the edit buffer to disk.

Now use **rm** to erase **poem** by typing **rm poem**. Then list the directory again. Even though one of the links to the file was broken, you may still access the physical file because the one link named **verse** remains. To prove this, type **cat verse** and note that the text of **poem** is displayed.

```
$ rm poem
$ ls -il
total 391
435 drwxrwxrwx        3 username docum          80   Oct 5 09:36 Mail
665 -rw-rw-rw-        1 username docum          78   Oct 9 12:02 appeal
521 -rw-r--r--        2 bin        bin     196513   Oct 2 16:28 wordlist
666 -rw-rw-rw-        1 username docum          62   Oct 9 09:35 verse
$ cat verse
Roses are Red
Violets are Blue
Sugar is Sweet
And so are You.
$
```

You may create a link between an ordinary file in another directory and the current directory. For instance, let's establish a link to **Mail/Username/Jul30.84/ reminder** named **message**. A new entry named **message** appears in the current directory as shown:

```
$ ln Mail/Username/Jul30.84/reminder   message
$ ls
Mail
appeal
message
wordlist
verse
$
```

The file **Mail/Username/Jul30.84/reminder** may now be accessed from the current directory as **message**. By using **ln**, we can create a link to a file that is "buried" deep in a directory hierarchy and thus access that file much more easily.

If you are using the Berkeley **ln** command, you could shorten the link request even more. If you don't specify a new name for the link, it will be named **reminder** because the last component of the pathname (in other words, the basename **reminder**) is used in naming the link:

$ ln Mail/Username/Jul30.84/reminder

$ ls

Mail

appeal

message

reminder

wordlist

verse

$ ▓

Of course, you may specify a different name for the new link if desired by indicating that name as the second argument on the **ln** command line. Here we named the new link **memo**:

$ ln Mail/Username/Jul30.84/reminder   memo

$ ls

Mail

appeal

memo

message

reminder

wordlist

verse

$ ▓

Now if you wish to change **Mail/Username/Jul30.84/reminder**, you may access the contents of this file from the current directory by using any of the names for this file: **message, memo,** or **reminder.**

Before proceeding, let's remove these redundant links by entering **rm message memo reminder**. Of course, the original file is still accessible as **Mail/Username/ Jul30.84/reminder.**

To see how linking differs from the file copy process, use **cp** to make a copy of **verse,** naming it **poem,** and list the files again.

```
$ cp verse poem
$ ls -il
total 392
731 drwxrwxrwx      3 username docum       80   Oct 5  09:36 Mail
665 -rw-rw-rw-      1 username docum       78   Oct 9  12:02 appeal
750 -rw-rw-rw-      2 username docum       62   Oct 11 09:45 poem
521 -rw-r--r--      2 bin      bin     196513   Oct 2  16:28 wordlist
666 -rw-rw-rw-      2 username docum       62   Oct 9  09:35 verse
$
```

Notice that **poem** and **verse** are two physically distinct files since they have different identification numbers. The different dates of last modification reflect the fact that **poem** was created by reading and then writing a copy of **verse** to disk. If **poem** were established as another link to **verse**, they would both share the same modification time (Oct 9 09:35 in this case). Compare this result with that in the second example in this series of examples of the **ln** command.

Alternate file links provide a convenient means of manipulating files. Let's say you have a group of files representing a manuscript, such as the first edition of this book. To facilitate your daily work with these files, you give them descriptive names such as **intro, basic.concepts, tutorials,** and so on. When you are ready to proofread the entire book, however, you might wish to streamline the printing process. You could do this by establishing a set of links with names like **chapter1, chapter2,** and so forth that make for easy wild card manipulation, as shown here:

```
$ ln history chapter1
$ ln basic.concepts chapter2
$ ln tutorials chapter3
$ ln commands chapter4
$ ln office.applic chapter5
$ ln evaluating chapter6
$ ln resources chapter7
$
```

Now you can send all the chapters to the line printer with a one-line command because the shell interprets the wild card abbreviation **chapter?** to include **chapter1, chapter2,** and so on. The command **pr** will paginate the contents of each chapter and **lpr** will place the files in the line printer queue:

```
$ pr chapter? | lpr
$
```

The property that all links to a physical file have to be severed before that file's contents are erased provides another application for linking. You might create a set of "backup" files in another subdirectory that were actually links to the files in your current directory. Then even if you accidentally erased all files in one directory, say by entering **rm ***, you could still access the same file contents from the other directory. Of course, if you change the contents of a file, the contents of the backup copy would be altered in the same way.

Before leaving this tutorial, enter **rm wordlist verse** to restore your home directory to its original condition.

Messages The following messages apply to the Berkeley version of **ln**. Note that if you are using Bell Labs documentation, *firstname* will be called *source* and *secondname* will be called *target*.

Usage: ln f1
or: ln f1 f2
ln f1 .. fn d2
The command line was not set up correctly. Either you specified (1) no command line arguments, or (2) three or more arguments, and either the file *secondname* doesn't exist or else it exists and is not a directory.

firstname **is a directory**
You can't link to *firstname* since it's a directory.

In the following group of messages, because the text of the messages following "*firstname:*" comes from the UNIX system (rather than from **ln**), their content may vary from system to system:

firstname: **file exists**
The link between *firstname* and *secondname* already exists.

firstname: **no such file or directory**
The source file **firstname** doesn't exist.

firstname: **permission denied**
Either (1) the link operation requires writing in a directory for which you don't have write permission or (2) you don't have search permission for a directory in the pathname prefix for *firstname* or *secondname*.

firstname: **not a directory**
A component of the pathname prefix for either *firstname* or *secondname* is not a directory.

firstname: **cross-device link**
You can't link across logical devices (file systems).

The following messages apply to the Bell System III and V versions of **ln**.

Usage: {mv|cp|ln} f1 f2
{mv|cp|ln} f1 ... fn d1
ln d1 d2

The command line was not set up correctly. Either you specified (1) only the *firstname* file, (2) a *firstname* file that is a directory, or (3) more than one *firstname* file and a *secondname* file that is not a directory.

ln: *secondname* **not found**
The specified *secondname* directory doesn't exist.

ln: cannot access *firstname*
Either (1) you specified a *firstname* file that doesn't exist or (2) you specified an option. This version of **ln** treats all invocation options as *firstname* files.

ln: <*firstname*> **directory**
The specified *firstname* file is a directory.

ln: *firstname* **and** *secondname* **are identical**
The *secondname* cannot be the same as the *firstname* file.

ln: *secondname: mode* **mode**
The specified *secondname* exists and is write-protected. The program will wait for a response from the keyboard. If you enter a line starting with a **y**, the link to the existing *secondname* will be severed and the new link will be attempted; otherwise, the linkage operation will be aborted.

ln: cannot unlink *secondname*
The specified *secondname* exists and the existing link cannot be severed to establish the new link.

ln: different file system
You cannot link to a *secondname* on a different file system.

ln: no permission for *secondname*
You don't have the necessary access permission to form a link to *secondname*.

mv — Move or Rename Files or Directories

$ mv [*option...*] *file... target*

Berkeley Options:

 −i Use interactive mode. Whenever the *target* exists, **mv** prompts you with the name of that *target* followed by a question mark. Enter y to initiate that rename operation; otherwise, it is aborted.

 −f The force option will override (1) write-protection for *target* and (2) the interactive mode.

— Interpret all remaining arguments as filenames. This allows filenames that begin with —.

Use the **mv** command to rename ordinary and directory files. You will need both search (execute) and write permission for all directories leading to the file to be renamed and for the directory that is to contain the renamed file.

The **mv** command differs functionally from the **cp** command in that **mv** "moves" a file by establishing a link between the new filename and the physical file and then severs the link between the old filename and the physical file. The **cp** command, on the other hand, actually copies the file, leaving the link to the old filename intact.

To rename a file or directory from *oldname* to *newname*, use the command line format

$$\$ \ \textbf{mv} \ oldname \ newname$$

To "move" one or more files into a specified directory *dirname* with their original basenames, use the following command line format:

$$\$ \ \textbf{mv} \ file... \ dirname$$

After the move, each *file* will have the pathname *dirname/file* relative to the directory containing *file* before the move operation. This command format is useful for moving any number of ordinary files to another directory.

The Bell version of **mv** silently deletes a preexisting target file unless it has a permission mode that forbids writing, in which case **mv** prints the mode (which serves as a warning message) and reads the standard input (terminal keyboard) to obtain your response. If you answer with a **y** and press RETURN, or with a line beginning with **y**, that move takes place and the preexisting target file is overwritten; if not, the move operation is aborted. If more than one file is being moved to a directory, however, **mv** does not terminate until all the files you specified on the invocation command line have been processed.

The Berkeley version's interactive mode, initiated using the —i option, queries you with "remove *newname?*" each time an existing file *newname* is encountered, whether or not it is write-protected. If you answer with a **y** and press RETURN, this file will be overwritten; otherwise, the move operation is aborted. If other files were specified on the invocation command line, the **mv** program will not terminate until all the files have been processed. If the *newname* was retained and is write-protected, you will be queried again, this time with the message "override protection *mode* for *newname?*" (*mode* will be an octal number indicating the file access permissions for the file). If you answer **y** and press RETURN, the existing file will be overwritten; otherwise, the move operation will not occur.

The Berkeley version also recognizes a force option (−**f**) that enables **mv** to erase *any* preexisting target file that you own without asking for permission to override write-protection. If the interactive option is specified with the force option, the interactive option will be ignored.

Examples   Prepare for these examples as discussed in the introduction to this chapter. Create the link to **wordlist** before you begin your practice with **mv**.

Enter **mv wordlist dictionary**, and your home directory should contain the file named **dictionary** in place of **wordlist**. This change may be shown by a directory listing before and after the rename operation:

```
$ ls
Mail
appeal
poem
wordlist
$ mv wordlist dictionary
$ ls
Mail
appeal
dictionary
poem
$
```

To move **dictionary** to your **Mail** directory, enter the following command line: **mv dictionary Mail**. This "move" actually renames **dictionary**, whose full pathname is **/usr/username/dictionary** in our sample file system, to **/usr/username/Mail/dictionary**.

```
$ mv dictionary Mail
$ ls
Mail
appeal
poem
```

```
$ Mail
Username
dictionary
$ ▓
```

You may rename a file as you move it between directories by specifying a different destination filename. For instance, enter **mv Mail/dictionary wordlist** to move **dictionary** back to the current (and home) directory and to name it **wordlist** once again. If you had simply entered **mv Mail/dictionary .** instead, the move from **Mail** to the current directory (.) would have taken place, but the result would still be named **dictionary**.

```
$ mv Mail/dictionary wordlist
$ ls
Mail
appeal
poem
wordlist
$ ls Mail
Username
$ ▓
```

Now let's try moving more than one file into another directory with the **mv** command. Enter **mv appeal poem Mail**.

```
$ mv appeal poem Mail
$ ls
Mail
wordlist
$ ls Mail
Username
appeal
poem
$ ▓
```

Having been moved to the **Mail** directory, both ordinary files have, of course, actually been renamed. The new pathnames are **/usr/username/Mail/appeal** and **/usr/username/Mail/poem**.

You may rename directories with **mv**. For example, enter **mv Mail Messages**:

```
$ mv Mail Messages
$ ls
Messages
wordlist
$ ls Messages
Username
appeal
poem
$
```

Now use **cp** to create a duplicate of both **appeal** and **poem** in current directory (.). Type **cp Messages/[a−z]* .** and press RETURN. You must specify **[a−z]*** instead of simply ***** so that **cp** won't match **Username** as a source argument and abort with a bad usage message (**cp** cannot be used to copy directories).

```
$ cp Messages/[a−z]* .
$ ls
Messages
appeal
poem
wordlist
$ ls Messages
Username
appeal
poem
$
```

If you have access to the Berkeley **mv** command, you may try this next example. Use the interactive option (−i) to selectively move files when their corresponding targets exist. Since files with names **appeal** and **poem** are now in both the **Messages** directory and your home directory, we can demonstrate this feature. Enter the command line **mv −i appeal poem Messages** and move **poem**, but not **appeal**, as shown:

$ mv −i appeal poem Messages
remove Messages/appeal? **n**
remove Messages/poem? **y**
$ ls
Messages
appeal
wordlist
$ ls Messages
Username
appeal
poem
$ ▉

Finally, restore your home directory by entering **rm Messages/appeal**, then **mv Messages/poem .**, and **mv Messages Mail**. Then list the directories to check.

Messages The four messages listed here may occur when you rename either ordinary or directory files. The first two apply to the Berkeley version of the **mv** command:

> Usage: mv [−if] f1 f2; or mv [−if] d1 d2; or mv [−if] f1 ... f2 d1
> The command line was not set up correctly. Either you specified (1) an invalid option, (2) less than two file arguments, (3) more than two file arguments where the first file argument is a directory, or (4) three or more file arguments, and either *secondname* doesn't exist or it is not a directory.
>
> mv: cannot access *firstname*
> You specified a *firstname* file that doesn't exist.

The following messages apply to Bell System III and V versions of **mv**:

> Usage: {mv|cp|ln} f1 f2
>   {mv|cp|ln} f1 ... fn d1
>   mv d1 d2
> The command line was not set up correctly. Either you specified (1) only the *firstname* file, (2) a *firstname* directory and more than one *secondname* file, or (3) more than one *firstname* file and a *secondname* file that is not a directory.

mv: *secondname* **not found**
The specified *secondname* directory doesn't exist.

The following messages occur only when you rename ordinary files:

mv: cannot access *firstname* (Bell)
Either (1) you specified a *firstname* file that doesn't exist or (2) you specified an option. This version of **mv** treats any invocation options as *firstname* files.

mv : <*firstname*> **directory** (Bell)
The specified *firstname* file is a directory and you cannot move (relocate) a directory, only rename it.

mv: directory rename only (Berkeley)
mv: *secondname* **is a directory** (Berkeley)
The *secondname/firstname* exists and is a directory so you cannot rename an ordinary *firstname* file to be this directory.

remove *secondname*? (Berkeley)
You get this query when using the interactive option and not the force option and the *secondname* file exists. Enter a line beginning with **y** to remove the existing *secondname*. Other responses will prevent the rename operation.

mv: *firstname* **and** *secondname* **are identical** (Bell or Berkeley)
The *secondname* cannot be the same as the *firstname* file.

mv: *secondname: mode* **mode** (Bell)
override protection *mode* **for** *secondname*? (Berkeley)
The specified *secondname* exists and is write-protected. The program will wait for a response from the keyboard. If you answer with a line beginning with a **y**, the existing *secondname* will be erased and the rename will be attempted; otherwise the operation will be aborted.

mv: cannot unlink *secondname* (Bell or Berkeley)
The specified *secondname* exists and it cannot be erased.

mv: cannot unlink *firstname* (Bell or Berkeley)
The directory containing *firstname* cannot be written on, so you could not unlink *firstname* after linking to *secondname*.

These error messages may arise when *firstname* and *secondname* are on different file systems so **mv** must invoke **cp** to copy *firstname* to *secondname* and then delete *firstname*. The next three messages apply to Berkeley versions of **mv** only:

mv: try again
The **mv** process cannot run **cp**.

mv: cannot exec cp
The **cp** command cannot be found.

mv: cannot unlink *firstname*
The *firstname* file cannot be erased after the copy.

These messages apply to Bell Systems III and V only:

mv: cannot open *firstname*
You don't have permission to read *firstname* file.

mv: cannot create *secondname*
You don't have permission to create *secondname* file.

mv: bad copy to *secondname*
There was a system error that either prevented reading of *firstname* or writing to *secondname*.

The remaining error messages may occur only when you rename directories. The following error messages occur when the *secondname* exists:

mv: *secondname* **exists** (Bell and Berkeley)
The *secondname* exists and is not a directory.

mv: target name too long (Berkeley)
The pathname for *secondname* is too long.

mv: *secondname* **exists** (Berkeley)
The desired ordinary file *secondname/firstname* already exists.

These six error messages occur when the *secondname* doesn't already exist:

mv: cannot rename . (Bell and Berkeley)
You cannot specify *firstname* to be dot .

mv: cannot rename .. (Bell and Berkeley)
You cannot specify *firstname* to be dot dot ..

mv: cannot rename / (Bell and Berkeley)
You cannot rename the **root** directory /.

mv: cannot rename *firstname/* (Bell and Berkeley)
You cannot specify *firstname* to end in /.

mv: cannot locate parent (Bell and Berkeley)
The parent directory for either *firstname* or *secondname* cannot be located.

mv: no write access to *pathname* (Bell and Berkeley)
You don't have permission to write into the parent directory of *firstname* in order to erase it.

The following messages apply only to the Berkeley version of **mv**:

mv: cannot move directories across devices
You cannot move directories between file systems.

mv: sorry, path names including .. aren't allowed
The pathname for either *firstname* or *secondname* cannot contain ...

mv: cannot access *pathname*
You cannot access the parent directory of *secondname*.

mv: cannot move a directory into itself
Both *firstname* and *secondname* would have the same pathname.

mv: name too long
The pathname of *secondname* is too long.

The following messages are worded slightly differently in the Bell and Berkeley versions:

mv: cannot link *firstname* to *secondname* (Bell)
mv: cannot link *secondname* to *firstname* (Berkeley)
The link between *firstname* and *secondname* cannot be created.

mv: ?? cannot unlink *firstname* (Bell)
mv: cannot unlink *firstname* (Berkeley)
The link to the *firstname* directory cannot be severed.

The following message is generated only by Bell Systems III and V versions of **mv**:

mv: directory rename only
Directories may only be renamed if they have the same parent directory.

rm — Remove Files or Directories

$ rm [*option...*] *file...*

Bell and Berkeley Options:

−i   Interactively ask to delete each file. When you combine −i with the −r option, **rm** asks whether to examine each directory.

−f   Force the removal of files that do not have write permission.

−r   Recursively delete the entire contents of the directory as well as the directory file itself.

Additional Berkeley Option:

−   Treat all arguments following as filenames. This allows removal of files whose names begin with −.

Use the **rm** command to remove one or more files from a directory. This command may be used to delete all files and then the directory itself. If a directory entry was the last link to the physical file, the file is irretrievably lost.

To remove (or unlink) a file, you must have permission to search and write in the directory containing the filename entry. If you own the file to be removed and the file has no write permission for the owner, **rm** lets you override the write-protection. However, if you don't own the file and it is write-protected, **rm** will refuse to remove it.

If you try to remove a file that you own which has no write permission, **rm** will ask you in an implicit way, which we will describe in a moment, if you'd like to delete the file. If you answer the implied query to remove the file with a y (or with a word beginning with y) and press RETURN, **rm** will delete the file. There is no such query if you invoke the **rm** command with the −**f** (force) option.

The interactive option allows you a "second chance" when removing files. If you answer the query affirmatively, the link to the file will be severed; otherwise, that particular file will remain linked—that is, it will not be removed. The −**i** option provides a convenient way to remove a subset of files from a directory. In other words, you may request to delete all files interactively and then answer y and press RETURN for only those files you actually wish to erase.

The recursive option (−**r**) provides a convenient way to erase a directory even if it contains files. This use of **rm** contrasts with the **rmdir** program, which can only remove a directory that is empty. The **rmdir** program is called automatically by **rm** to remove a directory after all its ordinary and directory file entries have been removed.

Be especially careful when you specify filenames for **rm** using wild cards. For example, if you entered **rm poem**∗, **rm** would remove all files from the current directory whose name begins with the letters "poem". However, if you were to type **rm poem** ∗ instead, **rm** would remove not only **poem** but every file in your directory, since the shell expands the lone ∗ to match every file in your current directory. It is important, therefore, to be sure that you don't leave a space here. To play it safe, specify the −**i** option *each* time you use a wild card with **rm**; in this way, you will have an opportunity to catch such a typo before disaster occurs. The extra time involved in answering the queries is nothing compared to what might be involved in recovering the lost files.

Examples Prepare for these examples as discussed in the introduction to this chapter. The **wordlist** is not necessary for this command.

You will need to create a few extra files with which to practice the deleting process. First, create a few ordinary files by entering **cp poem poem2** and **cp appeal appeal2**. Create two additional directories by entering the command line **mkdir Test Test/Subtest Test2**. Now list the contents of the directories to see which files are ordinary and which are directories.

```
$ cp poem poem2
$ cp appeal appeal2
$ mkdir Test Test/Subtest Test2
$ ls —l
total 7
drwxrwxrwx          3 username docum     80      Oct 5    09:36 Mail
drwxrwxrwx          3 username docum     48      Oct 11   09:36 Test
drwxrwxrwx          3 username docum     32      Oct 11   09:36 Test2
—rw—rw—rw—          1 username docum     75      Oct 9    12:02 appeal
—rw—rw—rw—          1 username docum     75      Oct 11   09:36 appeal2
—rw—rw—rw—          1 username docum     62      Oct 9    09:35 poem
—rw—rw—rw—          1 username docum     62      Oct 11   09:36 poem2
$ ls —l Test
total 1
drwxrwxrwx          2 username docum     32      Oct 11   09:36 Subtest
$
```

To remove an ordinary file, simply type **rm**, a space, and the filename, and press RETURN. Try to list the file before and after this operation, as shown here:

```
$ ls appeal2
appeal2
$ rm appeal2
$ ls appeal2
appeal2 not found
$
```

Now let's write-protect the other ordinary file, **poem2**, and attempt to remove it the same way. The **chmod** command removes user write permission, and the long directory listing verifies the change. The octal mode value of "466" displayed by **rm** corresponds to the symbolic mode "r — — rw —rw —" displayed by **ls** —l.

```
$ chmod u−w poem2
$ ls −l poem2
−r——rw—rw—          1 username docum          62  Oct 11  09:36  poem2
$ rm poem2
poem2: 466 mode ▓
```

The cursor next to "466 mode" indicates that the **rm** program is waiting for you to answer the implied query, "Do you want to remove this file anyway?" If you answer affirmatively, the file will be removed. Enter a line beginning with a letter other than **y**, such as **n**, and the file will be retained. For this example, enter **n** and note that the file remains:

```
poem2: 466 mode n
$ ls poem2
poem2
$ ▓
```

Note that if you are using the Berkeley version, the query is more informative: "rm: override protection 466 for poem?".

Specify the force option (−**f**) when you wish to erase write-protected files without query:

```
$ rm −f poem2
$ ls poem2
poem2 not found
$ ▓
```

Now let's try to delete a directory. Type **rm Test2** and note the result. You must use the directory option (−**d**) with **ls** if you wish to list the directory **Test2** instead of its contents.

```
$ rm Test2
rm: Test2 directory
$ ls −d Test2
Test2
$ ▓
```

The **rm** program refuses to delete a directory, even if it is empty, unless you specify the recursive option (−**r**):

```
$ rm Test2
rm: Test2 directory
$ rm −r Test2
$ ls Test2
Test2 not found
$
```

The interactive option (−i) is useful when you wish to be queried for removal of *every* file or directory designated as a command line argument. Let's use this option so we can choose to remove **appeal2** out of all the files remaining in the home directory. (Remember that the shell expands the * wild card to match *all* files in the current directory.) First we need to create another instance of **appeal2** by entering **cp appeal appeal 2**. Then enter **rm−i***

```
$ rm −i *
rm: Mail directory
rm: Test directory
appeal:
```

Notice that since the recursive option (−r) was not specified, **rm** first gives us a warning message that **Mail** and **Test** are directories. Then the cursor pauses after the implied query "appeal:". Answer no by entering **n**, and you will be queried about the next file.

```
appeal: n
appeal2: y
poem: n
$
```

Here we answered **y** to delete **appeal2** and entered **n** to avoid deleting **poem**. If you do not use the −i option, you must be careful when using the * wild card. Always inspect your **rm** invocation command line before pressing RETURN if you use wild cards without the −i option.

As a last example, let's recursively delete the **Test** directory, employing the −i option in the process. First copy the ordinary files **appeal** and **poem** to **Test**, and then attempt the recursive deletion as shown:

```
$ cp appeal poem Test
$ rm —ri Test
directory Test: y
directory Test/Subtest: y
Test/Subtest: y
Test/appeal: y
Test/poem: y
Test: y
$ ls
Mail
appeal
poem
$
```

Two kinds of implied queries have emerged in this process of recursively delet-ing a directory and the files it contains. A query in the form "directory *file:*" asks you if you wish to search the directory *file,* and the query *"file:"* asks if you wish to delete the directory or ordinary file named *file.* (The search-directory query allows you *not* to search a particular subdirectory.) Thus, in our example, "direc-tory Test:" and "directory Test/Subtest:" are asking your permission to search the **Test** and **Test/Subtest** directories respectively. If you answer either of these queries in the affirmative, you will then be queried about whether you wish to remove each empty directory and each ordinary file contained in these directories. (Remember, a directory must be empty before it can be removed.) In the preceding example, you are queried first about removing the subdirectory ("Test/Subtest:"), and then about removing each of the ordinary files that **Test** also contains ("Test appeal:" and "Test/poem:"). Finally, since **Test** is now empty, you are asked whether you wish to remove it ("Test:"). You may do so by entering **y.**

Messages   The form of the following messages for **rm** is slightly different for Bell and Berkeley versions of the command:

> **rm: usage: rm [—fir] file ...** (Bell)
> **rm: unknown option** (Berkeley)
>   You specified an option that **rm** didn't recognize.
> **rm: cannot remove ..** (Bell)
> **rm: cannot remove '..'** (Berkeley)
>   You are not allowed to remove your parent directory (..).

file: (Bell)
rm: remove *file?* (Berkeley)

You get this query when the interactive option is in effect. Enter a **y** to remove the file, and any other letter not to.

file: mode **mode** (Bell)
rm: override protection *mode* **for** *file?* (Berkeley)

You get this query when the *file* is write-protected and the force option (−**f**) is not in effect. If you enter **y**, the file will be removed; otherwise, it will not be. The *mode* is the octal equivalent of the access permission pattern.

The following messages apply to both Bell and Berkeley versions of the **rm** command:

rm: *file* **non-existent**

The file argument *file* cannot be found. This message is not given if the force option (−**f**) is in effect.

rm: *file* **directory**

You cannot remove a directory *file* without specifying the recursive option (−**r**).

rm: *file* **not removed**

This message indicates that *file* cannot be removed. The message appears only if the force option (−**f**) is not in effect (but it does appear if the interactive option (−**i**) is combined with the force option).

The following messages occur if argument *file* is a directory and the recursive option (−**r**) is in effect. Once again, the form of the message in Bell and Berkeley versions is slightly different:

directory *file:* (Bell)
remove directory *file?* (Berkeley)

You receive this query if the interactive option (−**i**) is in effect and the directory contains other directory entries. Answer with a **y** if you wish to search the contents of the directory file recursively.

rm: cannot read *file* (Bell and Berkeley)

The directory *file* cannot be opened for reading.

file **not changed** (Berkeley)

The directory *file* is write-protected and the force option (−**f**) is not in effect.

dirfile/file: (Bell)
rm: remove *dirfile/file?* (Berkeley)

You receive this query if the interactive option (−**i**) is in effect. Answer with a **y** if you wish to remove the indicated ordinary *file*.

No rmdir (Bell)

The command **/bin/rmdir** cannot be located to remove the directory.

rm: can't find rmdir (Berkeley)
The **rmdir** command cannot be located in either the **/bin** or **/usr/bin** directories.

chmod — Change Permission Mode

> All Versions
> $ **chmod** *mode file...*
>
> $ **chmod** [*who*] *op-code mode file...*
>
> No Options

The **chmod** command is the key to UNIX permission modes, which provide a simple yet effective method for controlling access to files. Refer to Session 4 in Chapter 3 for a full discussion of permission modes.

In order to use the **chmod** command to change the access permission for a file, you must own that file. You may specify the desired access modes either in a *symbolic format* or *absolute format*. We will discuss symbolic format first.

The symbolic format consists of up to three letters, which represent information that we'll call *who, op-code,* and *mode.* Table 6-2 lists these symbolic format codes. The *who* letter identifies which kind of user can access a file. The *who* letter may be either **u** (for "owner" — literally, the "file user"), **g** (for "group" user), **o** (for "other" users), or **a** (for "all" users). You may concatenate these categories: for example, **go** stands for "group" and "others."

The *op-code* symbol indicates whether to add (+), take away (−), or assign (=) the *mode.* Thus the *op-code* symbol expresses the kind of operation that will take place.

Finally, the *mode* letters are **r** (for "read"), **w** (for "write"), or **x** (for "execute"). As with the user category letters, you may concatenate these mode letters: for example, **rw** means both read and write permissions are specified.

Use the command line format

$ **chmod** [*who*] *op-code mode file...*

to change the access modes for one or more ordinary or directory files using the *symbolic mode* format. You cannot omit the *op-code* and *mode* fields from the *symbolic mode* expression. However, you may omit the *who* letter if you wish to refer to all user categories. In addition, you may enter more than one set of [*who*] *op-code mode* expressions as long as each set is separated from the next by a comma and there is *no* intervening whitespace. Thus, **u+x, go−rw** would add (+) execute permission (**x**) for the file owner (**u**) and remove (−) read and write access (**rw**) for the group and other user categories (**go**).

Table 6-2.   *Symbolic Format Codes for* **chmod**

---

who

u	File owner (user)
g	Group
o	All others
a	All (default): user, group, and all others

op-codes

+	Add permission
−	Remove permission
=	Assign absolute permission for file

mode

r	Read
w	Write
x	Execute

The second method for changing the permission of a file using **chmod** is called absolute format and is a little more difficult to construct than the symbolic method. The absolute format is based on octal numbers representing the three kinds of access permission. (Octal numbers include the digits 0 through 7, inclusive.) The octal values for read, write, and execute modes are

read	**write**	**execute**
4	2	1

In order to express the ways in which you want a particular file to be accessed, simply add the octal values that correspond to the individual types of permissions (that is, read, write, and execute). For example:

No access = 0

Read access only = 4

Read and execute access = 4 + 1 = 5

Read and write access = 4 + 2 = 6

Read, write, and execute access = 4 + 2 + 1 = 7

Finally, the added octal values are expressed in groups of three octal numbers, which, in turn, indicate the desired access modes for the file owner, group owner, and other user categories, respectively. Several examples of how this works are illustrated here:

user	group	others
r w x	r w x	r w x
(4 + 2 + 1)	(4 + 2 + 1)	(4 + 2 + 1)
7	7	7 octal value = 777

r w x	r — x	— — x
(4 + 2 + 1)	(4 + 0 + 1)	(0 + 0 + 1)
7	5	1 octal value = 751

r w —	— — —	— — —
(4 + 2 + 0)	(0 + 0 + 0)	(0 + 0 + 0)
6	0	0 octal value = 600

In the first example, 777 shows that all access modes for all system users are enabled. In the second example, the 751 mode enables all types of access permission for the file owner, read and execute permission for the group owner, and execute permission for other users. Finally, the 600 mode enables read and write permission for the file owner and no access permission at all for the group or other user categories.

If you use the absolute format to express file access permission, use the following command line format:

$$\text{\$ \textbf{chmod} } mode\ file...$$

Using this command line, you can change the access permission for one or more ordinary or directory files. Note that *mode* must always be expressed before *file*.

Although the absolute format is more difficult to construct than the symbolic format, once constructed, this method of expressing file access permission requires less typing and thus reduces the chance of typographical errors when entering the **chmod** command line.

In all UNIX systems, files and directories are assigned permission modes by default. (For a discussion of default permission modes and how to alter them, see the discussion of **umask** in Appendix C, "Setting the User File Creation Mask."

The **chmod** command, of course, allows you to change the default permission mode for particular files. One common reason to change the permission mode for a particular file is to write-protect files containing important information so that you cannot accidentally overwrite the file and thus lose the original content. A second common use is to keep the contents of a file private by denying access of any kind to other system users.

Examples   Prepare for these examples as discussed in the introduction to this chapter. The **wordlist** is not necessary for this command.

For the examples that follow, it is helpful to examine permissions for the files and directories using the **ls** command with the long listing option (−l) before and after each **chmod** command. The permissions are listed symbolically in the first field.

You will see how to change the access permissions using both the symbolic and absolute mode format. For our first example, let's deny all access to the file **poem** for the group and other user categories. Denying access to other system users is a convenient way to keep the contents of a file private. The desired permission pattern is **rw———————**. Since we are beginning with the pattern rw—rw—rw—, we may change the access permission symbolically by removing read and write access modes for the group and other user categories, as shown:

```
$ ls —l poem
-rw—rw—rw—          1 username docum     62 Oct 9 09:35 poem
$ chmod go—rw poem
$ ls —l poem
—rw————————          1 username docum     62 Oct 9 09:35 poem
$
```

Note that the modification time is not changed. This is because changing the access permissions doesn't modify the contents of the file. The modification time is changed only if the file's contents are modified by a write operation.

Alternatively, you may specify the appropriate absolute mode argument with **chmod**. This mode number is easy to construct. Write out the desired mode pattern, indicating the octal value for each mode. Finally combine the octal values for each user category:

$$
\underbrace{\begin{array}{ccc} r & w & - \\ (4 & + \ 2 \ + & 0) \end{array}}_{6} \quad \underbrace{\begin{array}{ccc} - & - & - \\ (0 & + \ 0 \ + & 0) \end{array}}_{0} \quad \underbrace{\begin{array}{ccc} - & - & - \\ (0 & + \ 0 \ + & 0) \end{array}}_{0} \quad \text{octal value} = 600
$$

Now let's use this octal number to change the permissions for **appeal** so that they are the same as those for **poem**:

```
$ ls —l appeal
—rw—rw—rw—        1 username docum     75 Oct 9 12:02 appeal
$ chmod 600 appeal
$ ls —l appeal
—rw———————        1 username docum     75 Oct 9 12:02 appeal
$
```

You may write-protect a file by removing the write access mode. (Write-protection means that you cannot accidentally erase or overwrite the file contents.) For instance, let's write-protect **poem**. Since we simply wish to remove write access, the symbolic format is easy to construct:

```
$ chmod u—w poem
$ ls —l poem
—r————————        1 username docum     62 Oct 9 09:35 poem
$
```

You could write-protect **appeal** using the absolute mode, as shown here:

```
$ chmod 400 appeal
$ ls —l appeal
—r————————        1 username docum     75 Oct 9 12:02 appeal
$
```

If you then attempt to erase this write-protected file, **rm** may inform you that **appeal** is "mode 400"—that is, write-protected. In the following example, we enter **n** after the prompt "appeal: 400 mode" so that the file will in fact not be erased. If you give any response other than a line beginning with a y, **rm** will not remove the file. For example:

```
$ rm appeal
appeal: 400 mode n
$
```

If you remove read access, you cannot examine the contents of a file. For instance, let's read-protect **poem** and then attempt to read its contents with **cat**.

```
$ chmod u−r poem
$ ls −l
−−−−−−−−−−    1 username docum    62 Oct 9 09:35 poem
$ cat poem
cat: cannot open poem
$
```

Before leaving these examples of using **chmod**, let's restore the original access modes for **appeal** and **poem**. Since we wish to enable the same access modes for all user categories, the "all" who code letter (**a**) may be employed with the *op-code*. First let's restore access to **appeal**:

```
$ chmod a=rw appeal
$ ls −l appeal
−rw−rw−rw−    1 username docum    75 Oct 9 12:02 appeal
$
```

Now, for **poem**, let's use the absolute format, which may be constructed as shown:

$$
\underbrace{\begin{matrix} r & w & - \\ (4 & + \; 2 & + \; 0) \end{matrix}}_{6} \quad \underbrace{\begin{matrix} r & w & - \\ (4 & + \; 2 & + \; 0) \end{matrix}}_{6} \quad \underbrace{\begin{matrix} r & w & - \\ (4 & + \; 2 & + \; 0) \end{matrix}}_{6} \quad \text{octal value} = 666
$$

Let's plug in this octal value:

```
$ chmod 666 appeal poem
$ ls −l
total 3
drwxrwxrwx    3 username docum    80 Oct 5 09:36 Mail
−rw−rw−rw−    1 username docum    75 Oct 9 12:02 appeal
−rw−rw−rw−    1 username docum    62 Oct 9 09:35 poem
$
```

As you can see, read and write access have been restored for the group and other user categories.

Messages Some of the more common error messages for all versions of **chmod** include the following:

Usage: chmod [ugoa] [+ − =] [rwxstugo] file ...
   You didn't specify at least two command line arguments.

chmod: can't access *filename*
   The file argument *filename* cannot be found.

chmod: invalid mode
   Either the symbolic or absolute permissions mode format was not specified correctly.

chmod: can't change *filename*
   You are not the owner of the file you have tried to change.

Getting Status Information

The commands in this section enable you to retrieve vital statistics about your filing system, currently operating processes, or terminal. One of the commands described here — the **stty** command — not only reports the current settings for your terminal line but also allows you to customize the connection between your UNIX system and your terminal. Finally, some of the commands explained here enable you to find out who else is on the system, to inspect a perpetual calendar, or simply to have UNIX report the current date and time.

Do not be concerned if you are not familiar with some of the kinds of information reported or used by the commands in this section. Although we have included some advanced information here for the sake of completeness, you do not need to know everything involved in these commands in order to use them effectively.

ps — Get Process Status

$ ps [*option...*]

Bell Version 7 Options:

none	Display process status information for processes associated with your control terminal.
−a	Display all processes associated with a terminal.
−l	Display in long listing format.
−x	Display information for all system processes.

Bell Systems III and V Options:

—e	Display information about every process.
—d	Display information about all processes except process group leaders.
—a	Display information for all processes except process group leaders and processes not associated with a terminal.
—t*tlist*	Display information for processes associated with the terminals in the terminal list, *tlist*.
—p*plist*	Display information for all processes in the process list, *plist*.
—u*ulist*	Display information for all processes whose user ID or user names are specified in the user list, *ulist*.
—g*glist*	Display information for all process group leaders specified in *glist*.
—l	List the information using the long format.
—f	List the information using full format.

Berkeley Options:

—a	Display information about all processes associated with a terminal except process group leaders.
—g	Display information about all processes associated with a terminal including process group leaders.
—t*x*	Restrict display to processes associated with terminal name **tty***x*.
—x	Display information for processes not associated with a terminal.
pid...	Restrict display to one or more processes with the specified *pid* numbers.
—l	List the information using long format.
—u	List the information with a user-oriented output.
—w	Display the output in 132 columns instead of 80.
—ww	Display the output in arbitrarily wide format.
—c	Print just the command name instead of the command and its arguments.

An executing program is known as a process and is identified by a unique number known as a PID (for process identification number). Processes that have the PID number 0 or 1 are reserved for special system processes. Process identification numbers for other processes can range from 2 to 30,000 on most systems.

The **ps** command is used to display not only the PIDs but also other information about processes running on your system. For instance, you might need a status report on commands that you started running in the background. You might need to determine the PIDs for these processes in order to use the **kill** command to terminate such background processes. You can also find out what processes (or commands) other users are running.

If no options are indicated, most versions of **ps** display information about processes associated with your control terminal (your control terminal is the terminal you signed on to the system from). Four fields of information are generally displayed that include the PID, the control terminal name, the elapsed execution time, and the command name. Generally, the entire command line used to invoke the process is not displayed, although some versions of **ps** might have this capability.

Use this command line format for invoking **ps**:

$ **ps** [*option...*]

The options either select certain classes of processes or determine the format in which **ps**'s report is displayed. In addition, most versions of **ps** allow you to display information about processes associated with other terminals or processes not associated with a terminal at all. Processes that perform tasks in the background (not usually associated with a terminal) are sometimes referred to as *daemon processes* or *daemons*.

The **ps** command is very implementation-dependent, and your version may differ from the description given here. Check your local documentation or ask your system administrator for details.

Examples Prepare for these examples as discussed in the introduction to this chapter; however, linking **wordlist** is not necessary. Enter **ps** to view all the active processes associated with your control terminal. You should see a display similar to the following:

```
$ ps
   PID  TTY   TIME   COMMAND
    25  01    0:09        sh
   156  01    0:01        ps
$
```

Since the **ps** command is so implementation-dependent, your display format may differ. For instance, some versions may not show an entry for the **ps** command itself or your login shell. The login shell is indicated by "sh" in the preceding example.

If you need status information about a particular process, you may specify one or more process numbers. The Bell version requires that you list the PIDs following the −**p** option, whereas the Berkeley version recognizes the process ID numbers without −**p** if they are specified last on the command line.

For instance, given the information in the previous example, to just list your login shell process, enter **ps** −**p 25** if you have a Bell version of **ps**, or **ps 25** if you have a Berkeley version:

```
$ ps −p 25
   PID  TTY   TIME   COMMAND
    25   01   0:09   sh
$
```

Note that the whitespace between the option letter and its argument is not required. (Of course, you should substitute the actual PID of your login shell for this example.)

Let's begin a process in the background and then look at all your current processes. An example of a process that takes a few moments to complete would be a process that determines the disk utilization of your file system. To initiate such a command, enter **du / >/dev/null&** and note the process number for *your* background process. (When you initiate a background process, you are automatically informed of that process's PID; 158 is the PID for our process, as shown in the following example.) Furthermore, we discarded the output from **du** by redirecting it to the *null file,* **/dev/null**.

```
$ du / >/dev/null&
157
$
```

Now type **ps** and press RETURN, and you should observe an additional entry for the background process. Note that the listing does not indicate whether or not a process is executing in the background or foreground.

```
$ ps
   PID  TTY   TIME   COMMAND
    25   01   0:09   sh
   157   01   0:03   du
   158   01   0:01   ps
$
```

You may see the accumulated execution time increase for **du** (third field, under the "TIME" heading) if you wait a few seconds and run **ps** again. But don't wait too long or the **du** command will have finished and will disappear from the screen.

$ ps

PID	TTY	TIME	COMMAND
25	01	0:09	sh
157	01	0:24	du
159	01	0:01	ps

$ ▓

So far we have requested the short form listing, which tells you the process ID number, associated terminal number, cumulative execution time, and an approximation to the command line that began the process. You can use the long listing (−1) option to obtain an extended listing. Try this now by entering **ps** −1. The actual values in the various fields will be different for your display, but the format should be similar to this example:

$ ps −l

F	S	UID	PID	PPID	C	PRI	NI	ADDR	SZ	WCHAN	TTY	TIME	COMD
1	S	70	25	1	0	30	20	39	32	child	01	0:10	sh
1	R	70	160	25	13	56	20	4f	64		01	0:01	ps

$ ▓

Of course, the particular numbers and perhaps some of the fields will be different for your display.

Here is a brief description of what these various fields mean and of the information they contain:

F   Flags associated with the process (additive octal):
               01:   in core
               02:   system process (scheduler)
               04:   locked in core (physical I/O)
               10:   being swapped
               20:   being traced by another process

S   State of the process:
               S: sleeping
               W: waiting
               R: running
               I: intermediate
               Z: terminated
               T: stopped

UID   The user ID of the process owner.

PID	The process ID Number.
PPID	The ID number for the parent process.
CPU	CPU usage for scheduling.
PRI	Priority of the process (high numbers mean low priority).
NICE	Number used in priority computation.
ADDR	If the process is in memory, the address will be an address in memory. Otherwise, the address will be a disk address.
SZ	Size of the process in memory.
WCHAN	When a process requests a system resource that is not available, the process must wait until that resource is available. The event for which it is waiting is listed as an address in this field. If the field is blank, the process is running.
TTY	The terminal controlling the process.
TIME	The cumulative execution time for the process.

Note that your version may list different fields and the field headings may be different, such as **NI** instead of **NICE**.

With the **ps** command, you can examine every process running on your system if you specify the appropriate option. For the Bell Version 7 and Berkeley version, enter **ps —alx**; for Bell Systems III and V, enter **ps —el**. The processes with the names **swapper**, **init**, **getty**, and **cron** are used by the UNIX system.

```
$ ps —el
```

F	S	UID	PID	PPID	C	PRI	NI	ADDR	SZ	WCHAN	TTY	TIME	COMD
3	S	0	0	0	45	0	20	1d	8	runout	?	570:08	swapper
1	S	0	1	0	0	30	20	29	40	child	?	0:01	init
1	S	0	26	1	0	28	20	3d	32	tty[0]	co	0:05	getty
1	S	70	25	1	0	30	20	39	32	child	01	0:10	sh
1	R	70	161	25	13	56	20	4f	64		01	0:01	ps
1	S	0	21	1	0	40	20	4a	40	sleep	co	1:12	cron

```
$
```

The different versions of **ps** have various options for restricting the display to a selected subset of system processes. (Processes can be classified as either *group leaders* or *group followers*. This division is based on systems programming concepts and is beyond the scope of this book.) For instance, if you have Bell Systems III or V and you do not wish to examine processes that are group leaders (such as **init**, **getty**, **login**, or login shells) and processes not associated with a terminal (like **swapper**), enter the command **ps —al**:

```
$ ps  -al
```

F	S	UID	PID	PPID	C	PRI	NI	ADDR	SZ	WCHAN	TTY	TIME	COMD
1	R	70	162	25	13	56	20	4f	64		01	0:01	ps
1	S	0	21	1	0	40	20	4a	40	sleep	co	1:12	cron

```
$
```

Messages The actual error messages depend on your system's implementation for this command. Most versions display a correct usage message if you specify an option or an argument for that option that **ps** does not recognize. The majority of other error messages are due to system-related problems like unreadable system directories. If you get a system-related error message, see your system administrator for assistance.

who — Determine Who Is On the System

$ who [*option...*] [*who-file*]

Option for All Versions:
    am I   Display the name under which you are logged in.

Bell System V Options:
    —u   Restrict listing to users currently logged in.
    —T   Display the *state* for all logged-in users as well (that is, whether someone can write to the terminal).
    —l   Display only the terminal lines that are not being used.
    —b   Display the date and time the system was brought up.
    —t   Display the last change to the system clock.
    —a   Turn on all the above options.
    —s   Display the short form listing, which consists of the *username, line,* and *time* fields.

In a multiuser environment, the more users using the system, the slower the system's response to your commands. You can use the **who** command to get an idea of how heavily the system is loaded. It's also a good idea to use this command before employing the **write** program in order to verify that the persons you intend to write to are currently logged in to the system. (You may also need to know their terminal names if they are logged in on more than one terminal.)

The general command line format for invoking **who** is

$$\text{\$ } \textbf{who } [\textit{ option... }] [\textit{ whofile }]$$

If you do not specify a *whofile*, the file named **/etc/utmp** will be displayed by default. This file lists all the users who are currently logged on, the time they logged on, and the terminal or terminals they are using. You can also call up a history file that contains a history of all accounting information: that is, not only every system login, but every time the system has been booted or the system clock has been reset. In UNIX versions other than System V, this history *whofile* is **/usr/adm/wtmp**. In System V, it is called **/etc/wtmp**. You can use this history file to find out when you last logged on or to see whether anyone else has been using your account.

Most versions recognize an "option" consisting of any two separate arguments after the **who** command name, as in **who am I** or **who are you**. The system responds to these queries with login accounting information for you. This is useful if you need to see what login name you used. In addition, this form of the **who** command gives your control terminal name, just as the **tty** command does.

A major change in the information contained in the login accounting files was made in Bell System V. Several more fields of information were added which may be displayed with the appropriate option for this version of **who**. The most general output format for this version of **who** is

$$\text{\$ } \textit{username } [\textit{state}] \textit{ line time activity pid } [\textit{comment}] [\textit{exit}]$$

The *username* is the user's login name. The *state* field indicates if someone can write to the terminal. The *line* is the name of the terminal line. The *time* is the time the user logged in. The *activity* is the number of hours and minutes since the line was used. The *pid* is the process ID of the user's shell. The *comment* is the content of the comment field (if any) present in the system initialization file **/etc/inittab**. The *exit* field contains the exit status for terminated processes, telling you whether a process terminated under an error condition.

Examples Prepare for these examples as discussed in the introduction to this chapter. The **wordlist** is not necessary for this command.

Enter the command **who** to see a list of all users currently logged on to your UNIX system. The list will be sorted in alphabetical order by terminal designation. Your login name should appear on this list as well. In our simulation, only the superuser ("root") and you ("username") are currently on-line. The first field lists the login name; the second field lists the control terminal name for that user; and the date and time of system sign-on is indicated in the last field:

```
$ who
root          console    Nov  7    08:34
username      tty01      Nov  7    13:57
$ ▊
```

Now enter **who am i.** The system will respond with your user name, terminal name, and time of login. Note that you can type any two words (arguments) after **who** since **who** looks only for an argument count of two (except for System V, where you must enter **who am i** or **who am I**).

```
$ who am i
username      tty01      Nov  7    13:57
$ ▊
```

When the system response to your requests becomes very sluggish, you might enter **who | wc −l** to see how many terminals are on-line. Recall that the output of the **who** command consists of one line per terminal, so that piping **who**'s output to the word count (**wc**) program to display the number of lines will tell us the number of terminals that are logged on. The actual number of users may be less because a user may log in to more than one terminal. Some users like to place this command in their shell start-up file so that they can tell how heavily the system is loaded before they begin working.

You may display all the login accounting information that has been collected since the login history file, or *whofile*, was last created by entering **who** *whofile*. Here *whofile* is either **/usr/adm/utmp** for the Bell Version 7, System III, and Berkeley version, or **/etc/wtmp** for Bell System V. This file contains a record of all the logins since the file was created. Also note that entries after a vertical bar (|) and left brace ({) indicate when the system clock was last reset. We interrupted our simulation after a few lines to keep the example output short.

```
$ who /usr/adm/wtmp
            console    Oct 15    12:06
       |               Oct 15    12:06
       {               Oct 16    10:34
            tty01      Oct 16    10:35
```

```
              console    Oct 16    10:35
root          console    Oct 16    10:40
username      tty01      Oct 16    12:35
[ Interrupt ]
$ ▓
```

Here is an account of the information that this screen gives us. First, the system was brought up (booted) from the console, and then the system clock was reset from the value it had when the system was last brought down (on Oct 15 12:06) to the value when the system was just brought up (on Oct 16 10:34). Next we see that at 10:35 the terminals **tty01** and **console** were made available for system login, so that the system could be used by several users from that point on. Finally, we see that at 10:40 **root** logged on to **console** and that at 12:35 **username** logged on to **tty01**.

If you are using the Bell System V version of **who**, try out the various options to display additional fields of information.

Messages Some common messages from all versions of **who** include the following:

> **who: cannot open utmp**
> The login file, **/etc/utmp**, cannot be opened for reading. See your system administrator.

> **who: cannot open** *whofile*
> The specified *whofile* cannot be opened for reading.

date — Display the Current Date and Time

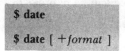

```
$ date
$ date [ +format ]
```

Use the **date** utility to display the current date and time of day. When you press RETURN after typing **date**, your UNIX system's idea of the time and date will be displayed on your terminal. You may discover that your UNIX system clock will gradually lose time because clock ticks will get lost now and then. This time loss will be slight, however. (If you notice an inaccuracy in the system clock, you can write to your system administrator. If you are the system administrator, refer to Appendix D, "Setting the System Clock.")

The Bell System III and V versions allow you to format the date and time display. If you specify an argument that begins with a plus sign (+), the output may be controlled by one or more format directives. These directives may be intermixed with text, which is simply passed to the standard output unchanged. When **date** is executed, the formatting directive will be replaced by its corresponding value. If there is embedded whitespace, you must enclose the entire argument for **date** in single or double quotation marks.

The formatting directives for the date include

%D   The date as MM/DD/YY

%a   Abbreviated weekday (Sun to Sat)

%h   Abbreviated month (Jan to Dec)

%j   Day of the year (001 to 365, or 366 on leap years)

%w   The day of the week (Sunday=0, Monday=1, and so on)

%m   The month of the year (01 to 12)

%d   The day of the month (01 to 31)

%y   Last two digits of the year (00 to 99)

The formatting directives for the time include

%T   The time as HH:MM:SS

%r   The time as HH:MM:SS (A.M./P.M.)

%H   The hour (00 to 23)

%M   The minute (00 to 59)

%S   The second (00 to 59)

You may also embed new lines and tabs in your *format* string using these directives:

%n   Insert a new line character (causes a new line to begin)

%t   Insert a tab character

If you are the person who is responsible for maintaining your UNIX system, your first task after system start-up should be to set the system clock. See Appendix D, "Setting the System Clock," for more information.

Examples   Type **date** and press RETURN to see the current date and time:

$ date
Thu Nov 1 12:45:04 PST 1984
$ ▓

You may also use this utility to record the date and time of a particular event. Perhaps you would like to record the times that you log in to the system. Use an editor and append the command line **echo Your login time is `date | tee —a .login_times`.** to your shell start-up file (**.profile** for Bourne Shell or **.login** for C Shell). If you executed this command line interactively, you would see something like this:

```
$ echo Your login time is `date | tee —a .login_times`.
Your login time is Thu Nov 1 12:46:01 PST 1984.
$
```

You may print all your previous login times at any time by entering **cat .login_times**, as follows:

```
$ cat .login_times
Thu Nov 1 12:46:01 PST 1984
$
```

The Bell Systems III and V versions also allow you to format the output display using various formatting directives. Place the entire argument in quotation marks if you are including blanks. An example is given here:

```
$ date "+ The time is %H:%M:%S%nThe date is %m/%d/%y"
The time is 12:46:50
The date is 11/01/84
$
```

Messages   The following messages apply to all versions of the **date** command:

date: no permission
 You must be the superuser to reset the system clock.

date: bad conversion
 You didn't specify the argument for setting the system clock correctly.

This message applies to the Bell Systems III and V versions of **date**:

date: bad format character - *c*
 The format directive, %*c*, is not recognized by **date**.

date: bad format character - *c*
The format directive, %*c*, is not recognized by **date**.

cal — Print Calendar

$ cal [*month-number*] *year*

No Options

Use this command to print a calendar for a specified year or month of a year. The **cal** command prints a nicely formatted calendar for any year from 1 to 9999, inclusive. If you precede the year with a numeral from 1 to 12, corresponding to a month of the year, the calendar for that month of the specified year is printed.

Examples Display the calendar for 1984 by entering **cal 1984**:

$ cal 1984

1984

	Jan								Feb								Mar				
S	M	Tu	W	Th	F	S		S	M	Tu	W	Th	FS		S	M	Tu	W	Th	FS
1	2	3	4	5	6	7					1	2	34						1	23
8	9	10	11	12	13	14		5	6	7	8	9	1011		4	5	6	7	8	910
15	16	17	18	19	20	21		12	13	14	15	16	1718		11	12	13	14	15	1617
22	23	24	25	26	27	28		19	20	21	22	23	2425		18	19	20	21	22	2324
29	30	31						26	27	2829					25	26	27	28	29	3031

	Apr								May								Jun				
S	M	Tu	W	Th	F	S		S	M	Tu	W	Th	FS		S	M	Tu	W	Th	FS
1	2	3	4	5	6	7				1	2	3	45							12
8	9	10	11	12	13	14		6	7	8	9	10	1112		3	4	5	6	7	89
15	16	17	18	19	20	21		13	14	15	16	17	1819		10	11	12	13	14	1516
22	23	24	25	26	27	28		20	21	22	23	24	2526		17	18	19	20	21	2223
29	30							27	28	29	3031				24	25	26	27	28	2930

```
            Jul                      Aug                      Sep
 S  M Tu  W Th  F  S      S  M Tu  W Th  F  S      S  M Tu  W Th  F  S
 1  2  3  4  5  6  7               1  2  3  4                           1
 8  9 10 11 12 13 14      5  6  7  8  9 10 11      2  3  4  5  6  7  8
15 16 17 18 19 20 21     12 13 14 15 16 17 18      9 10 11 12 13 14 15
22 23 24 25 26 27 28     19 20 21 22 23 24 25     16 17 18 19 20 21 22
29 30 31                 26 27 28 29 30 31        23 24 25 26 27 28 29
                                                  30

            Oct                      Nov                      Dec
 S  M Tu  W Th  F  S      S  M Tu  W Th  F  S      S  M Tu  W Th  F  S
       1  2  3  4  5  6            1  2  3                           1
 7  8  9 10 11 12 13      4  5  6  7  8  9 10      2  3  4  5  6  7  8
14 15 16 17 18 19 20     11 12 13 14 15 16 17      9 10 11 12 13 14 15
21 22 23 24 25 26 27     18 19 20 21 22 23 24     16 17 18 19 20 21 22
28 29 30 31             25 26 27 28 29 30         23 24 25 26 27 28 29
                                                  30 31
```

$ ▓

Now try displaying the calendar for a single month by indicating the number of the month before the year. For example, to display the calendar for January 1985, enter **cal 1 1985**:

```
$ cal 1 1985
     January 1985
 S  M Tu  W Th  F  S
        1  2  3  4  5
 6  7  8  9 10 11 12
13 14 15 16 17 18 19
20 21 22 23 24 25 26
27 28 29 30 31
```

$ ▓

Print the calendar for the year of your birth and display it on your local line printer by entering **cal** *birthyear* **| lpr**.

Display the calendar for your birth month. Did you get the correct year?

Messages The following messages apply to all versions of **cal**:

usage: cal [month] year
You must specify at least one argument. (System V version will display the current month if no arguments are specified.)

Bad argument
Either your specified *month-number* was not between 1 and 12, inclusive, or the *year* was not between 1 and 9999, inclusive.

du — Determine Disk Usage

$ du [*option...*] [*dirname*]

Bell and Berkeley Options:
−s Report only the total number of blocks.
−a Report the size of each ordinary file as well.
Note that these options are mutually exclusive.

Additional Bell Systems III and V Option:
−r Report certain error conditions.

The **du** utility is used to obtain cumulative information about your usage of disk space. By determining how much disk space you are using, you can make an informed decision whether to delete certain unwanted files and directories. The **du** command is an essential part of the housekeeping process in UNIX.

If a directory is named in the **du** command line, information about the disk blocks used for that and all subdirectories is reported. With the appropriate option, furthermore, an entry for all files as well as directories will be generated.

Directories beginning with the specified directory are searched recursively. In other words, after the specified directory, all subdirectories of that directory (and all sub-subdirectories) are searched, and the results are presented as indicated by the options, if any options are used.

If you want only the total number of blocks occupied, specify the summary (−s) option. The all option (−a), which is mutually exclusive with −s, will enable the reporting of all files and their block sizes. Without any option, the sizes of files in each directory are added and given in a simple figure for each directory, but the size of each individual file is not reported. The report option (−r), if available, is useful for enabling error messages regarding directories that cannot be read, files that cannot be opened, and so on.

You may use this command to summarize the disk usage for other files on your UNIX system. Since you may not be allowed to open certain files, the result you get with **du** will probably be less than the actual disk usage.

Examples   Prepare for these examples as described in the introduction to this chapter. The **wordlist** is not necessary for this command.

You will see how to summarize the disk usage in your various subdirectories in several of the examples that follow. Enter **du**, and you should see a display similar to the following:

```
$ du
2          ./Mail/Username/Jul30.84
3          ./Mail/Username/Aug15.84
6          ./Mail/Username
7          ./Mail
11         .
$
```

Since we did not use an argument on the **du** command line, **du** reports the disk space used by the current directory (the home directory in this case). These disk usage results are represented schematically in Figure 6-3. The numbers in parentheses represent the number of disk blocks each directory uses, so that the figure gives you a sense of all the disk space used by directories in your tree.

If you wish to see the usage for every file in the **username** account as well, enter **du** −**a**.

```
$ du −a
1          ./appeal
1          ./poem
1          ./Mail/Username/Jul30.84/reminder
2          ./Mail/Username/Jul30.84
1          ./Mail/Username/Aug15.84/remind1
1          ./Mail/Username/Aug15.84/remind2
3          ./Mail/Username/Aug15.84
6          ./Mail/Username
7          ./Mail
1          ././.profile
11         .
$
```

The total disk usage beginning at the home directory is 11 blocks. The disk

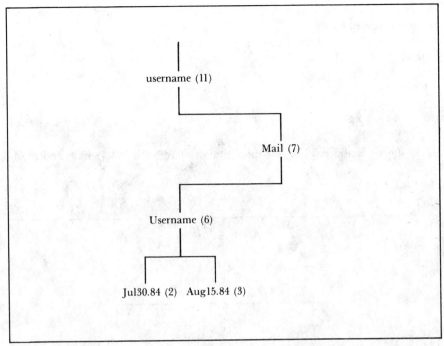

Figure 6-3. Schematic representation of directory disk block usage

usage numbers for the subdirectories and other files don't simply add up to 11 for two reasons. First, the disk usage for a directory includes one block for the directory file itself in addition to the blocks used by the files in that directory. Second, when used with the −**a** option, **du** lists all the parts of the tree along with the sums of those parts, since the sums are associated with the directories. You should not, in other words, try to add up the numbers in the preceding screen to get your total disk block usage.

The numbers do add up, however, when you look at Figure 6-4. Looking, for example, at the lower right-hand portion of the tree, we see that the disk block usage next to the directory **Aug15.84** is 3: one block for **remind1**, one block for **remind2**, and one block for the directory **Aug15.84**. As we move farther up the tree, we see that the number of disk blocks used by **Mail** is 7 because **Mail** is comprised of six files (that is, ordinary files and subdirectories) and takes up one block itself. Disregarding the totals listed in parentheses next to the directories and counting only each item in the tree, we see that the total disk block usage of 11 for **username** is correct.

If you simply wish a total disk usage figure, indicate the summary option, as follows:

```
$ du -s
11
$
```

The **du** command gives information in terms of 512-byte blocks independent of

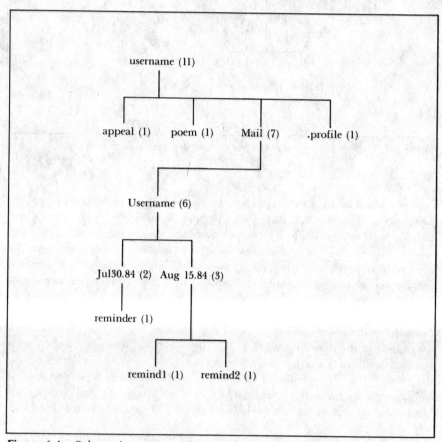

Figure 6-4. *Schematic representation of ordinary file disk block usage*

The **du** command gives information in terms of 512-byte blocks independent of the actual disk block size. For some UNIX file system implementations, the block size may be a multiple of 512 bytes.

Usually only the system administrator is concerned with the amount of disk space occupied by various files besides your own, but you might find it interesting to explore your UNIX system using the **du** command. To do this, specify **du** arguments corresponding to files at the top of the file system tree—that is, to directories like the **root** directory (/), the **/usr** directory, the command directories (**/bin** and **/usr/bin**), or the **/etc** and **/dev** directories.

Messages The following messages apply to Bell Systems III and V versions of **du**:

> **usage: du [—ars] [name ...]**
> You specified an option that **du** did not recognize.

> **Huge directory** < *dirname* >—**call administrator**
> The directory *dirname* is over 32,000 bytes (2000 entries) long. Report this fact to your system administrator.

These error reports occur only if the report option (—r) is specified:

> **du: bad status** < *dirname* >
> Either *dirname* doesn't exist or you don't have permission to obtain status information.

> **du: cannot open** < *dirname* >
> The directory *dirname* cannot be opened for reading.

> **du: cannot read** < *dirname* >
> You don't have permission to read *dirname*.

The following messages apply only to the Berkeley version of **du**:

> **cannot chdir( )**
> The **du** process cannot change to the directory where the disk usage count is to begin.

> **—bad status** < *dirname* >
> Either *dirname* doesn't exist or you don't have permission to obtain status information.

> **—cannot open** < *dirname* >
> The directory *dirname* cannot be opened for reading.

> **—cannot read** < *dirname* >
> You don't have permission to read *dirname*.

> **Bad directory**
> The **du** process cannot change back to the parent directory.

file — Determine File Type

> **$ file [option...]...**
>
> Bell System III Option:
> **—f** *filelist*   Classify the list of files contained in *filelist*.
>
> Additional Bell System V Options:
> **—m** *magicfile*   Use the file *magicfile* instead of **/etc/magic**.
> **—c**   Check format of the *magicfile* (or **/etc/magic**).

The **file** program performs a series of tests on the specified file arguments in an attempt to classify these files. This utility is especially useful if you need a quick idea of the file type or of the nature of the file's contents. If, for example, you have a large filing system and you can't remember the contents of a file, you can use **file** to obtain information in one step, instead of using **cat**, **ls**, and perhaps several other utilities to see a file's contents. As we will see, **file** operates like a kind of detective, making deductions about the file it is investigating through a process of elimination.

Sometimes the file type reported by **file** will be unfamiliar to you. There are several file types that only programmers or system administrators would be concerned with. We will mention the names and types of such files for completeness and in case the **file** command indicates such a file. Further discussion of these files, however, is beyond the scope of this book.

The Bell Systems III and V versions of **file** allow you to indicate a list of files one filename per line, to be classified by **file**. This list would be contained in a text file that you would create. Specify the —**f** option immediately followed by the filename of the list, *filelist*, to use this feature:

$ **file** —f*filelist*

The **file** program goes through a process of elimination in its effort to ascertain a file's type and the nature of its contents. **file** first determines if a file is a directory, a special device file, a fifo (a pipe with a name, Bell Systems III and V), multiplexor (obsolete, Berkeley only), or an ordinary file. The informational messages that indicate these file types are listed in the "Messages" section.

Next, if **file** determines that the file in question is an ordinary file, **file** checks to see if the file is empty. It does this by reading in the first block (512 characters or a multiple). From **file**'s point of view, the file is empty if it can be opened for reading but no characters can be read, in which case **file** displays the message "empty."

If **file** finds that the file is not empty, it checks to see if the file begins with a *magic number* — a numeric or string constant used to indicate the type of file if a file is not of a humanly readable type. Generally, ordinary files that are not ASCII text files, such as executable programs and certain archive library files, begin with an identifying magic number. Some of the informational messages which indicate these file types are listed in the "Messages" section.

System V has a new data file, **/etc/magic**, that contains a list of file types and their corresponding magic numbers. The System V **file** program can reference this data file, or a user-specified file containing a similar list, when attempting to classify a file by its magic number. The existence of this list makes the **file** program more flexible because the list may be easily updated by the user. In the past this list was "hard-coded" in the **file** program itself and could not be changed unless you were a programmer and had access to the source code for **file**.

You may use your own list of magic numbers contained within a *magicfile* list by specifying the following command line format with the Bell System V version:

$$\text{\$ file } -\text{m}magicfile$$

Or you may check such a file for correct format by using the −c option. If a magic file is not indicated on the command line, then **/etc/magic** will be checked by default. No file typing is performed when using the check option.

The next step in **file**'s investigation is taken when the file doesn't have a recognizable magic number: the **file** program examines the first block of the file (512 characters or a multiple) and tries to guess its "language." The language could be English text, a programming language, or some other special data file, such as text containing embedded text-formatting directives. The **file** program sometimes makes mistakes when guessing the language. For instance, it might guess that a file is a C program when it is actually a file of shell commands, or shell script.

A list of the classifications which the **file** program may use to report on the nature of a text file includes

c program text
  C program source code.
fortran program text
  FORTRAN program source code.
assembler program text
  Assembler program source code.

[nt]roff, tbl, or eqn input text (Bell)
roff, nroff, or eqn input text (Berkeley)
  Input text that apparently contains text formatting directives.

troff intermediate output text
  Text that contains Berkeley **troff** intermediate language keywords.

troff output (Bell)
troff (CAT) output (Berkeley)
  Output from the **troff** program.

commands text
  A text file that is executable.

English text
  This text file contains proper punctuation (more than 20% is followed by
  a space or new line), a large proportion of vowels, and a high proportion
  of commonly occurring letters (as compared to letters which rarely occur
  in English text).

ascii text
  A text file that doesn't meet the criteria for English text.

If the file isn't a text file, **file** reports that it is "data," which is **file**'s classification for anything that is an ordinary file, and that it has not been able to classify by this time.

Examples Prepare for these examples as discussed in the introduction to this chapter. The **wordlist** is not necessary for this command.

For your first tutorial example, use the **file** program to guess the types of the files in your home directory. Enter **file**, and if your directory is set up according to our conventions, you should see something like the following display:

```
$ file *
Mail:    directory
appeal:  English text
poem:    English text
$
```

Now add execute permission to the file **poem** by entering **chmod u+x poem** and remove read permission for **appeal** by entering **chmod u−r appeal** and run **file** again. A text file like **appeal** must be readable in order for **file** to be able to read the first block and thus to guess its type:

```
$ chmod u+x poem
$ chmod u-r appeal
$ file *
```
Mail: directory

appeal: cannot open for reading

poem: commands text

$ ▓

After we added execute permission to **poem, file** considered it to be "commands text" — that is, like a shell script.

Now remove search permission for the **Mail** directory by entering **chmod u−x Mail** and try to access the contents of **Mail**. We used the Bell version of the **file** command here. The Berkeley version would say "cannot stat" for the same error condition:

```
$ chmod u-x Mail
$ file Mail/*
```
Mail/Username: cannot open

$ ▓

To get a fuller sense of **file**, use this command to explore the types of files in your UNIX installation. Change to the **root** directory by typing **cd /**, and then have **file** classify the directory's contents by entering the command **file *.** The resulting display should list all the files and their attributes. Choose a subdirectory of the **root** (**/usr**, for example), and investigate that directory. First move to /usr by entering **cd /usr**, and then give the form of the **file** command given in the first and second screen examples. After investigating this directory, change to another of **root**'s subdirectories (**/etc**, for example) with the **ed /etc** command. Some other interesting directories are **/lib, /bin, /dev,** and **/tmp**.

By this time you should have a good idea of the types of files on your system. Display the contents of the files which appear to be worth further investigation, and see if **file** identified them correctly.

Messages   The following messages tell you the file type that **file** is investigating. These three messages apply to all versions of **file**:

    character special (m/n)
        A character device file, such as a terminal. Here m and n are numbers used to identify the device.

block special (m/n)
A block device file, such as a disk or tape drive. Here *m* and *n* are numbers used to identify the device.
directory
A directory file.

These two messages apply to the Berkeley version only:

char multiplexor
A character multiplexed I/O file.
block multiplexor
A block multiplexed I/O file.

And this message may be generated by System III and V versions of the command:

fifo
A FIFO (first-in-first-out) named pipe file.

The following error messages apply to either the Bell or the Berkeley versions of the command or to both:

usage: file [−c] [−f ffile f] [−m mfile] file___(Bell System V)
You didn't set up the invocation command line correctly.
Can't open *filelist* (Bell Systems III and V)
The file argument for the −f option, *filelist*, cannot be opened for reading.
file: **cannot open** (Bell)
file: **cannot stat** (Berkeley)
You cannot obtain status information for the file argument *file*. Either the file doesn't exist or you don't have permission to access it.
file: **cannot open for reading** (Bell)
file: **cannot open** (Berkeley)
The file argument *file* cannot be opened to read in the first block for typing.

The following are additional informational messages that apply to Bell, Berkeley, or both as indicated:

old archive (Bell)
very old archive (Berkeley)
An object library archive file in old format. (Magic number 0177555.)
archive (Bell)
old archive (Berkeley)
An object library archive file. (Magic number 0177545.)

archive (Bell)
archive random library (Berkeley)
An archive library in current Berkeley style format.
cpio archive (Bell)
An archive file in cpio format, which is a format used by the **cpio** program. (Magic number 070707.)
ldp executable (Bell)
Locked process (UNIX/RT system). (Magic number 0401.)
overlay executable (Bell)
Overlay process. (Magic number 0405.)
executable (Bell and Berkeley)
Normal load module. (Magic number 0407.)
pure executable (Bell and Berkeley)
Read-only code segment. (Magic number 0410.)
separate executable (Bell)
jfr or pdp-11 unix 411 executable (Berkeley)
Separate I&D load module. (Magic number 0411.)
demand paged pure executable (Berkeley)
Demand paged load format. (Magic number 0413).

stty — Set Terminal Options

$ stty [*mode* ...]
No options

$ stty [*option*]
Bell Systems III and V Options:

—a	Display all of the current mode settings.
—g	Display the current mode settings in a format suitable for use as an argument to another **stty** command.

Berkeley Options:

none	Report the speed of the communication line and the modes that are different from their defaults.
all	Display all commonly used mode settings.
everything	Display every mode setting.

The **stty** command enables you to tailor the connection between your UNIX system and your terminal device. The connection might be called "the terminal line," "the terminal interface," "the terminal driver," or "the line discipline." All these terms are synonymous and equivalent for our purposes.

In addition to setting your terminal device through **stty**, you can also use the **stty** command to display the current mode settings for your terminal line. The terminal device can be any serial character I/O (input/output) device that can be driven by your UNIX system. This includes CRT display terminals, modems, and hard-copy draft and letter-quality printers. In a sense, the **stty** command makes UNIX more universal and flexible. Because **stty** helps to mediate the communication between UNIX and devices like modems or CRT terminal monitors, a wide variety of hardware devices can communicate with UNIX.

The terminal line and hence the operation of **stty** have changed greatly from Bell Version 7, to Berkeley and to Bell Systems III and V. In addition, an implementation for one of these versions may be somewhat different from another implementation.

Even though the options and modes used by the various implementations are very different, the general command line formats for using the **stty** command are the same. To display the current settings for your terminal line for any version, simply type

$ stty

Generally some basic mode settings and perhaps those which have been changed from a default value will be depicted.

With the Bell Systems III and V and Berkeley versions, you may control the amount of information displayed by using one of several options. The command line format for doing this is simply

$ stty option

The Bell versions recognize an all ($-$a) option to display *all* the current terminal mode settings. The $-$g option will display the mode settings in a compact format that may be used as an argument for another **stty** command. This feature enables you to store all your favorite mode settings in a disk file for later use.

The Berkeley version options also control the amount of information reported. If no option is specified, the speed of the communication line and the modes that are different from their defaults are reported. The **all** option will display most of the commonly used modes, and every mode setting may be displayed by specifying the **everything** option.

When you log on to your UNIX system, you are communicating with the system through a terminal. This terminal device is known as your *control terminal*. It is important to distinguish your control terminal from other terminals because you may use other terminal devices during sessions with UNIX.

The command format for setting the terminal driver for your control terminal, whatever hardware device that may be, to one or more modes for all versions is

$ stty *mode...*

The modes for the Bell and Berkeley terminal drivers are listed in "Terminal Mode Settings" in Appendix C.

You may display the modes for a terminal device other than your control terminal by redirecting the input for **stty** to come from that terminal device file. For instance, if the device is named **/dev/tty***xx*, use the command line format

$ stty </dev/tty*xx*

Notice that the file to which we are redirecting the standard input is a device file, as is indicated by **dev**. The standard input for **stty** must come from a terminal device file. For further background in understanding and using **stty**, refer to the section entitled "The General Terminal Interface" in Appendix C.

You may set the modes for another terminal device in a similar fashion:

$ stty *mode*...</dev/tty*xx*

Note that the *standard input* (not the standard output) must be redirected to come from the terminal device file for both displaying and setting the terminal modes.

One common situation in which you might use the preceding line is to adjust the baud rate for a printer. Suppose, for example, that you have set up your line printer to communicate directly with UNIX. You may need to change the baud rate to accommodate your printer if it cannot receive information as quickly as UNIX can send it. To do this, you would use **stty** to set the baud rate for the printer from your control terminal and then redirect these settings from the printer as a device file.

Another situation in which you might need to use **stty** arises when your terminal settings are inadvertently changed during the execution of a command program. Sometimes a program error, for example, will occur and you will be returned to the shell, but your terminal settings will have changed. In this case, you will need to use **stty** to reinstate the original values.

It might be a good idea to change the mode settings one at a time and note what effect the new settings have on the behavior of your control terminal. Then when some unexpected behavior arises, you should have an idea of its cause and know how to correct it.

Examples Prepare for these examples as discussed in the introduction to this chapter. The **wordlist** is not necessary for this command.

The first several examples in this tutorial illustrate how to display your current terminal mode settings for the various versions of **stty**.

Enter **stty** to display the current mode settings for your control terminal. You should compare the mode settings you see with those available for your version of stty. Our results were obtained using a Bell System III UNIX system unless otherwise indicated.

```
$ stty
speed 1200 baud; -parity
brkint -inpck icrnl onlcr
echo -echoe echok
$
```

Of course, your actual display will depend on your particular version of **stty** and current settings of your terminal driver. With most versions, the line speed, a few basic modes, and modes that have been changed from their default values will be displayed.

If you are using the Berkeley or Bell Systems III or V versions, there are options that allow you to display all mode settings. A sample display for the Bell version is

```
$ stty -a
speed 1200 baud; line = 0; intr = DEL; quit = ^ \;erase = #; kill = @; eof = ^d; eol
    = ^ `
-parenb -parodd cs8 -cstopb -hupcl cread -clocal
-ignbrk brkint ignpar -parmrk -inpck istrip -inlcr -igncr icrnl -iuclc
ixon ixany -ixoff
isig icanon -xcase echo -echoe echok -echonl -noflsh
opost -olcuc onlcr -ocrnl -onocr -onlret -ofill -ofdel
$
```

And for the Berkeley version:

```
$ stty everything
new tty, speed 1200 baud
even odd -raw -nl echo -lcase -tandem tabs -cbreak
-crtbs -crterase -crtkill -ctlecho -prterase -tostop -intrup
-tilde -flusho -mdmbuf -litout -nohang
-etxack -pendin -decctlq -noflsh
erase   kill   werase   rprnt   flush   lnext   susp    intr   quit   stop    eof
#       @      ^W       ^R      ^O      ^V      ^Z/^Y   ^?     ^ \    ^S/^Q   ^D
$
```

Compare the settings listed here with the possible modes tabulated in Appendix C, "Terminal Modes Settings." The settings for Bell and Berkeley represent the basic settings for these respective systems and are therefore a good starting place for learning how to customize your terminal line to your particular needs.

If you are using the Bell Systems III or V versions, you may display all the current mode settings in a format suitable for use as an argument to another **stty** command. This feature makes it possible, for instance, to reproduce these same mode settings easily at any time in the future. All values shown are hexadecimal numbers, which consist of these sixteen characters: 0, 1, 2, 3, 4, 5, 6, 7, 8, 9, A, B, C, D, E, and F.

```
$ stty −g
d26:1805:bd:3b:7f:1c:23:40:4:0:0:0
$
```

The output consists of fields separated by colons. The first four fields are composite numerical equivalents of the input modes, output modes, control modes, and local modes, respectively. The remaining fields are the hexadecimal values for the interrupt, quit, erase, kill, EOF (end-of-file), and EOL (end-of-line) characters. The last two fields are reserved for future expansion.

One application for this feature is to save the mode settings in a file once you have determined the best settings for your control terminal. To try this, first store the modes in a file, for example, **modes.best**, and whenever you wish to reset your terminal, simply enter **stty `cat modes.best`**, as shown:

```
$ stty −g >modes.best
$ stty `cat modes.best`
$
```

You can't simply redirect the standard input of **stty** to come from **modes.best** because the standard input must be a terminal device file, not a disk file. The remaining examples in this tutorial show you how to change some commonly used mode settings for the various terminal drivers.

You may wish to reset some of the control assignments for your terminal. All terminal drivers allow you to reset the erase and kill characters, but only Berkeley allows you to reset stop and start. Other versions generally allow you to reset interrupt, quit, and EOF characters.

As an example, many users of CRTs prefer to use a ^H (backspace) as the erase and ^X (or perhaps ^U) as the kill character. The default erase and kill characters (# and @, respectively) may then be used as printing characters. You may reset both for your control terminal with one command line, as shown here:

```
$ stty erase '^h' kill '^u'
$
```

You may conveniently set both the erase and kill characters back to their default values with almost any version of stty by entering stty ek. Some terminal drivers enable you to reset all control assignments to their original default values by entering stty sane.

If you are using a modem connection, you may need to reset your interrupt character, since the default, an ASCII delete, is frequently generated over noisy dial-up lines. We recommend reassigning the interrupt character to a ^C. For the sake of consistency, go ahead and reset quit to ^U at the same time.

The function of the nl option can be seen by specifying the mode change stty nl. Now the RETURN key will no longer terminate the line; instead you must use the NEW LINE (or LINE FEED) key for this purpose. Now enter date and note that the current date and time are not displayed. You must type date and press NEW LINE instead to execute date. If your keyboard doesn't have a NEW LINE or LINE FEED key, type the equivalent ^J instead. Now switch back to RETURN mode by entering stty −nl and pressing NEW LINE one last time.

Momentarily turn off the echo of your input characters by entering stty −echo. Carefully enter date. You will not see the letters d a t e as you type them, but after you press RETURN, you will see the output from the date program. Now turn on the echo again by entering stty echo. Recall that the input echo is turned off when a password is being requested by your UNIX system.

You can speed up your terminal display if you preserve tabs. To do this, your terminal must respond to a tab character (^I) by moving the cursor to the next tab stop. Enter stty tabs, and then press the TAB key several times. The cursor seems to jump from tab stop to tab stop. Now enter the command stty −tabs, and then press the TAB key several more times. This time the cursor moves between tab stops in a series of one-column increments corresponding to each space character, which is now output to simulate the tab.

You may use stty to configure other terminal devices as long as they use the same type of terminal interface as does your control terminal. As an example, let's say your system has a serial printer with device file name /dev/tty03. Generally, you would communicate with such a device at 1200 baud. However, if your control terminal was set up for 9600 baud, /dev/tty03 might be as well. You may use stty to lower the rate at which data is transferred to the serial printer, as shown:

```
$ stty 1200 </dev/tty03
$
```

After changing the mode, verify by displaying the current mode settings. For this example, you would enter **stty** **</dev/tty03** to observe the new baud rate setting.

You may find, especially with hard-copy mechanical terminals, that characters are "lost" at high transmission speeds. Most terminal drivers can provide delays after sending a carriage return, new line, tab, form feed, or backspace character. These delays in resuming character transmission allow the mechanical components time to position themselves so that they can continue printing the characters correctly. For instance, characters can be lost while the print head returns to the left margin after a carriage return, because it takes time to travel the width of the page. A delay after the carriage return will ensure that you do not lose any characters at the beginning of the next line.

As an example, let's add some delay after the carriage return for our serial printer:

```
$ stty cr1 </dev/tty03
$
```

Experiment using different amounts of carriage return delay for your control terminal and other devices. Also introduce delays after the other characters to see the effects.

Combinations of the various I/O modes for some commonly used terminals have been preset. For example, if you are installing a Texas Instruments Silent 700 thermal printing terminal, you simply need to enter **stty ti700** and all the appropriate modes will be set for you.

Messages The following messages apply to all versions of the **stty** command:

unknown mode: *mode*
  Most versions of **stty** display such a message if the *mode* argument to the **stty** command is not recognized.

stty: : not a typewriter
  The standard input for **stty** is not a terminal device.

***terminal device:* cannot open**
  The standard input is a *terminal device* that cannot be opened for reading.

This message applies only to Bell Systems III and V versions of **stty**:

usage: stty [−ag] [modes]
  You did not set up the command line correctly.

tty — Get Terminal Name

$ tty

No Options

When you log in to the UNIX system, you are assigned a particular terminal from which you control all your processes. This terminal is called your *control terminal*. The UNIX system knows each device by a unique filename; using this filename, you can refer to your control terminal, someone else's control terminal, or another terminal device. When you need to refer to your terminal, you may use the **tty** command to find out the filename for your control terminal.

Sometimes you may use the name **/dev/tty** as a synonym for your control terminal. If this is allowed, you do not have to know the actual filename for your control terminal.

Examples   Prepare for these examples as described in the introduction to this chapter. The **wordlist** is not necessary for this command.

Type **tty** to display the filename of your control terminal.

$ tty
/dev/tty01
$

You can display more information about your terminal now that you know its name. For instance, type **ls —l** *ttyname*, where *ttyname* is the pathname for your terminal reported by **tty**.

$ ls —l /dev/tty01

```
crw——w——w—        1 username docum        2,  1 Nov  7 10:46 /dev/tty01
$
```

The character "c" to the left of the permission modes indicates that your terminal is a special character file. Also observe that while you have read and write permission for your terminal, other users have write but not read permission. This is so that other users can use the **write** command for direct interterminal communication, yet cannot peek at what you are doing.

The numbers 2 and 1 are the major and minor device numbers, respectively. The actual values for these numbers depend on your system implementation. Generally, types of devices, such as terminals, are assigned a particular major device number, and the individual devices of that type are given sequentially increasing minor device numbers.

Messages   The following message applies to all versions of **tty**:

not a tty
    The standard input file is not a terminal device.

Controlling Your Running Programs

The four commands explained in this section enhance the operation of other commands by giving you greater control. Using these commands, you can terminate an executing process or specify a later time at which you want that process to execute. You can also test input information on command lines if you need to diagnose a problem or order the output of a process to be distributed in several places.

kill — Terminate a Process

Bell Versions:
$ kill *pid*...
No Options

Bell and Berkeley Versions:
$ kill — *signo pid*...
No Options

Berkeley Version:
$ kill — *signame pid*...
No Options

An executing program is known as a *process*. Processes are uniquely identified by a number. Generally you reference a given process by specifying this identification number known as a PID (process identification number). Processes with numbers 0 and 1 identify special system processes.

Generally you will use the **kill** command to terminate a process that you began executing in the background. You cannot terminate such a process by issuing an interrupt signal because the shell has instructed the process to ignore the interrupt signal. (The interrupt signal is usually generated from the keyboard by pressing your interrupt character, which is the DEL or RUBOUT key by default.) Instead, you must direct the **kill** command to terminate the process. To do this, you would use the following command format:

$$\$ \text{ kill } pid$$

This sends a *software termination signal* to the process with process identification number *pid*. If the process cannot be terminated with this default signal, use the slightly different command format

$$\$ \text{ kill } -9 \; pid$$

to send the *kill signal* (often called the "sure kill signal") to the process with the number *pid*. The kill signal will always terminate a process. Note that to terminate a process, you must either have superuser privileges or else have initiated that process.

Recall that you initiate a background process by specifying the **&** directive at the end of the command line. After you press RETURN, the shell will reply with a number. This is the PID for the background process you just initiated, and it is this number that you must use when you want to terminate a process with **kill**. If you forgot to jot down this number when you initiated the background process, you may use the **ps** command to determine the identification number for the process. (The **ps** command is discussed in the section "Getting Status Information" earlier in this chapter.)

You may wish to terminate a background process if it seems to overload system resources or if you no longer need the process that you began executing in background. Sometimes a process will cause a terminal not to respond to keyboard input. In this case you could log on to another terminal and use **kill** to terminate the process that was hanging up the other terminal.

Examples   Prepare for these examples as discussed in the introduction to this chapter. The **wordlist** is not necessary for this command.

First start a process executing in the background. For example, enter **sleep 1000&** and note the process number displayed.

```
$ sleep 1000&
300
$
```

The number on your display will most likely be different. Make a note of *your* background process identification number. (For a discussion of the **sleep** command, see Chapter 4, Session 7.)

After you initiate a background process, you may decide to terminate before it finishes on its own accord. Two common reasons for this are that you started a process you later decided not to run or that the process you started seems to be taking "forever," indicating that the system is already heavily loaded. In this case, you might decide to run the process at a later time.

Next press your interrupt character a few times. Then enter **ps** to display the processes associated with your terminal. Note that the keyboard-generated interrupt signal indicated by "[Interrupt]" did not terminate the background **sleep** process.

```
$ [ Interrupt ]
$ [ Interrupt ]
$ ps
   PID   TTY    TIME    COMMAND
   195   01     0:09    sh
   300   01     0:01    sleep
   301   01     0:01    ps
$
```

Now enter **kill** *pid*, where *pid* is the process number for the sleep routine you started in background. Then enter **ps** again. The message with which your UNIX system responds may be somewhat different than "300: Terminated". Some systems don't issue such a message at all.

```
$ kill 300
300: Terminated
$ ps
   PID   TTY    TIME    COMMAND
   195   01     0:09    sh
   305   01     0:01    ps
$
```

Occasionally you may come across a process that can't be terminated by the default software termination signal. In this case you may use the "sure kill" signal, which cannot be ignored by a process.

If you are using the Berkeley version of **kill**, you may specify a signal name in lieu of the signal number. For instance, you would send the kill signal (**KILL**) to a process, as shown here:

$ kill —KILL 666

$ ▓

Note that the Berkeley version allows you to specify the signal by number (9 in this case) as well.

Sometimes you may be executing a program which "hangs"; that is, there was an internal error such that keyboard input has no effect. In this case, log on to another terminal and enter the command line to list every process: **ps —a** (for Bell Version 7 and the Berkeley version of **ps**) or **ps —e** (for Bell Systems III and V versions of **ps**). Then note the number of the offending process that is "hanging" on your original terminal. Finally, use the **kill** command from the second terminal to terminate the process.

Messages   The following messages apply to Bell versions of **kill**:

usage: kill [-signo] pid ...
> Either you didn't specify an argument or specified the *pid* argument incorrectly.

kill: *pid:* permission denied
> You either must own the process or be *superuser* to signal a process.

kill: *pid:* invalid signal
> The signal number you specified is not recognized by **kill**.

kill: *pid:* no such process
> The process you specified does not exist.

kill: *pid:* not a killable process group
> The process group (a group of processes) cannot be killed.

The following messages apply to the Berkeley version of **kill**:

usage: kill [—sig] pid ...
for a list of signals: kill —l
> Either you didn't specify an argument or specified the *pid* argument incorrectly.

kill: *signo:* number out of range
> You specified an invalid signal number, *signo*.

kill: *signame:* unknown signal; kill —l lists signals.
> The signal name was not recognized by **kill**. Type **kill —l** for a list of valid signal names.

kill: *pid:* Not owner
> You either must own the process or be *superuser* to signal a process.

kill: *pid:* **No such process**
The process you specified does not exist.

at — *Execute Commands at a Later Time*

> **$ at** *time* [*month monthday*] [*day of week*] [**week**] [*file*]
>
> No Options

The **at** command is used for scheduling one or more commands to be run at a specified time and date. This command is not supplied with some UNIX systems because of security problems.

You may use **at** to schedule execution of one or more UNIX commands anytime from the next minute to the next year. You may either type the desired commands as you invoke **at**, or specify a file that contains the commands. The **at** utility places your commands together with information necessary for establishing the appropriate environment in a *memo file* in the /usr/spool/at directory. Periodically another program, **atrun**, is invoked by your UNIX system to examine /usr/spool/at; **atrun** will execute any memo file that is scheduled to run. Generally the memo files are examined several times each hour: for example, at ten-, fifteen-, twenty-, or thirty-minute intervals. If you schedule a file to be executed at some intermediate time, the system waits until the regularly scheduled execution of the **atrun** program before executing your commands. You may determine how often your system invokes **atrun** to execute memo files by examining the system file /usr/lib/crontab. The comma-separated numbers at the beginning of the line containing "atrun" tell the system when to execute **atrun**.

If you only need to execute a few commands, enter them immediately after you invoke **at**. After typing the line initiating **at**, press RETURN and enter one or more lines containing shell command lines. Terminate entry by typing your end-of-file code (usually a ^D) on a line by itself. You may schedule commands to run at a particular time of day simply by using the following invocation command line format when invoking **at**:

$ **at** *time*

The *time* argument here can consist of from one to four digits. Add an **A**, **P**, **N**, or **M** to stand for A.M., P.M., noon, or midnight, respectively. One- and two-digit numbers will be interpreted to be an hour, and three- and four-digit numbers represent hours and minutes. If no letters follow the digits, a 24-hour clock time will be assumed. Note that you should not separate the hours and minutes with a colon. To specify half past 12 in the afternoon, for instance, you would type 1230 instead of 12:30 P.

You can schedule commands to be executed on a specified day of the month by using the following command line format:

$$\text{\$ at } time \; [\; month \; monthday \;]$$

This causes the commands you enter on the next line(s) to be executed on *month monthday* at *time:* for instance, **apr 3** for next April 3rd.

You may specify commands to be executed on a particular weekday by using the command line format:

$$\text{\$ at } time \; [\; dayofweek \;] \; [\; \textbf{week} \;]$$

This command line schedules commands supplied on the standard input to be executed on *dayofweek* at *time:* for instance, **thu** for Thursday. If **week** is also specified, the command will be executed a week later on *dayofweek* at *time.* Thus, you would enter **thu week** for a week from next Thursday.

You can use abbreviations for the month or day of the week as long as you use enough letters for **at** to recognize the month or day unambiguously. For instance, because **ju** could stand for either June or July, **at** would issue an error message, but neither **jun** nor **jul** would be ambiguous.

The general command line format for executing commands contained in a disk file is

$$\text{\$ at } time \; [\; month \; monthday \;] \; [\; dayofweek \;] \; [\; \textbf{week} \;] \; file$$

This causes the execution of the shell commands contained in *file* at *time* either on *month monthday*, or on *dayofweek*, or one week later if **week** is indicated.

You would use an editor or some other utility to create the file of commands. Because of its relation to the **at** program, this file is commonly called an "at-file." Note that you *must* redirect the output from the commands to be executed later either to a disk file or to a terminal device file. Otherwise, the output would be lost since a shell different from the one used when invoking **at** is used to execute the commands at a later time.

If you wish to delete the **at** request, simply remove the appropriate memo file in the **/usr/spool/at** directory with **rm**. Since you own the memo file, you can delete it if you have write and execute permission for **/usr/spool/at**; if not, enter **cp/dev/null** *memofile* to destroy its contents. The memo file has the basename *yy.ddd.hhhh.uu*, where *yy* is the year, *ddd* the day of the year (1-365, or on leap years, 1-366), *hhhh* is the time of day (24-hour format), and *uu* is a unique identifying number. The unique number enables a given user to schedule more than one memo file to be executed at the same time.

Examples Prepare for these examples as discussed in the introduction to this chapter. The **wordlist** is not necessary for this command.

For our first example, schedule the two commands shown in the following example by typing **at** followed by a time/date specification, such as 2100 for 9 P.M. Then press RETURN and type the commands shown. (Note that the output of the **echo** commands is redirected to your terminal file to ensure that the output does in fact appear on the terminal from which you invoked **at**.) To complete the entry, press RETURN and then your end-of-file code (a ^D by default). Neither the end-of-file code nor the line you typed it on will appear on your screen. Replace "/dev/tty01" by the device designation of your particular control terminal. You may determine this by entering **tty** and noting the device name.

```
$ tty
/dev/tty01
$ at 2100
echo Time to log off >/dev/tty01
echo It is now 'date'. >/dev/tty01
[ ^D ]
$
```

Now at 9 P.M. you should see the output:

```
Time to log off
It is now Apr 1 21:00:00 PDT 1984.
```

Notice that the shell replaced the string 'date' by the output of the **date** command. Of course, your current date and time would be displayed.

Alternatively, you may place the desired commands in a file. Invoke your favorite editor and place the commands used in the previous example in a file named, for example, **reminder**. Then invoke **at** to execute the file at 9 P.M.

```
$ cat reminder
echo Time to log off >/dev/tty01
echo It is now `date`. >/dev/tty01
$ at 9pm reminder
$
```

The file **reminder** does not require execute permission because instead of being executed, its contents are copied to the memo file for execution.

You may schedule a command to run on a particular date as shown in the next example. Here the **echo** command is scheduled to be executed at 2 P.M. on April 3 within the next year.

```
$ at 2pm apr 3
echo Happy Birthday >/dev/tty01
[ ^D ]
$
```

You may schedule a command to run within the next two weeks by indicating the day of the week when you invoke **at**. In this next example, we also specified **week** so that the **echo** command would be scheduled to run at midnight (**M**) a week from the next Wednesday:

```
$ at M wed week
echo Time to log off >/dev/tty01
[ ^D ]
$
```

Now examine the **/usr/spool/at** directory and you should see a display like the following:

```
$ ls /usr/spool/at
84.92.2100.34
85.94.1400.25
84.103.0000.89
lasttimedone
past
$
```

In this example, the memo file, named **84.92.2100.34**, is scheduled to be executed on or after 2100 hours (9 P.M.) on the 92nd day (April 1) of 1984. The last time that **atrun** examined **/usr/spool/at** is written in **lasttimedone**. The file **past** is the directory to which **atrun** moves the memo file that is scheduled to run. The memo file is actually executed from **past**.

Let's say you wished to remove the last request you made. This request created the memo file with basename **84.103.0000.89**. Thus, simply use **rm** to delete this file:

```
$ rm /usr/spool/at/84.103.0000.89
$ ls /usr/spool/at
84.92.2100.34
85.94.1400.25
lasttimedone
past
$
```

The memo files are executed only at certain periodic intervals depending on how often **/usr/lib/atrun** is executed by the **cron** process. This may occur every ten minutes, every twenty minutes, or even every half hour, depending on your particular system.

You may set up a file of commands to be executed automatically once every 24 hours. For example, use an editor and append the line **at 2100 reminder** to the file **reminder**. Then invoke **at** to execute **reminder** today at 9 P.M. by entering **at 2100 reminder**. At 9 P.M. **atrun** will execute the memo file containing a copy of the commands in **reminder** including the **at** command that specifies when next to execute the file. Once the **at** command from the **reminder** file has been copied to the memo file, this last command "at 2100 reminder" can invoke **at** to execute **reminder** at 2100 hours the next day. This will occur indefinitely until you either remove **reminder** or erase the memo file.

```
$ cat reminder
echo Time to log off >/dev/tty01
at 2100 reminder
$ at 9pm reminder
$
```

You could use such a feature to execute a task (such as a file backup operation or other maintenance duty) once every day, after the initial startup, without your intervention.

Messages The following messages apply to all versions of **at:**

at: arg count
You must specify at least two arguments.

at: bad time format
You didn't specify the *time* argument correctly.

at: time out of range
The specified *time* is not in a 24-hour period range.

at: illegal minute field
The minute field for *time* must be less than 60.

at: ambiguous month
You need to indicate more letters in your abbreviation of *month* for an unambiguous interpretation.

at: illegal day
You didn't specify the *monthday* correctly. If you do specify *monthday* to be greater than the number of days in *month*, the excess will go toward the next month.

at: ambiguous day of week
You need to indicate more letters in your abbreviation of *dayofweek* for an unambiguous interpretation.

at: cannot open input: *file*
Either you specified (1) a *file* that cannot be opened for reading or (2) an argument that was not valid for setting the time or date of execution, so that **at** interpreted it as a command file argument.

at: cannot open memo file
You can't add your command to *yy.ddd.hhhh.uu* in **/usr/spool/at**. See your system administrator for assistance.

at: can't execute pwd
The command **pwd** cannot be executed. See your system administrator.

The following messages are displayed by the **atrun** program. If you get such a message, see your system administrator for assistance.

Cannot read at directory
The **atrun** program cannot read the **/usr/spool/at** directory.

Can't execl shell
The **atrun** program cannot execute a shell to run the command.

can't write lastfile
The **atrun** program cannot update the log file **/usr/spool/at/lasttimedone**.

echo — Echo Arguments

$ echo [*option*] [*arg...*]
Bell Version 7 and Berkeley Option:
—n   Do not terminate output with a new line character.

The **echo** program simply echoes, or plays back on your terminal screen, each of the arguments on the command line used to invoke it. For instance, let's say the **echo** command line is

$ echo Hello there

The output will consist of the first argument, "Hello", a space character, then the next argument, "there", and finally a new line character that moves the cursor to the beginning of the next line. If you are using the Bell Version 7 or Berkeley **echo** command, you can use the **—n** option if you *do not* wish the output to end in a new line character.

The **echo** program is especially useful when it is used in conjunction with metacharacters. Recall that the UNIX shell treats any metacharacters entered on a command line in a special manner. The shell will scan each command argument for the filename generation metacharacters, such as *, ?, and the square brackets [and]. If these constructions appear, the argument is regarded as a pattern to be replaced with alphabetically sorted filenames that match the pattern.

Thus, when the **echo** program writes out its arguments, all metacharacter abbreviations and other special characters and constructions will have been completely interpreted or "expanded" by the shell. This lets you preview the final form of a command line without the shell actually executing it. For instance, let's say you type a command using a metacharacter that doesn't work as you had expected. Now if you type **echo** followed by the same command line, as follows

$ echo *command line*

the shell will interpret the *command line*, which will in turn be passed to **echo** for display instead of being executed by the shell. By inspecting this expanded command line, you should be able to discover why the original command line didn't work as you had expected.

Here are the metacharacters and what they mean:

*   Match any string of characters.

?   Match any single character.

[ ]   Match any character enclosed in the brackets. A pair of characters may be separated by a dash (—) to indicate an inclusive range of characters.

You can also use the **echo** command to display the value of a shell variable (see the discussion of shell variables in Chapter 4, Session 8). To do this, prefix the name of the variable with a dollar sign ($). For instance, the shell variable **HOME** refers to the pathname for your home directory. Thus, you would enter

$$\text{\$ echo \$HOME}$$

to display the value of **HOME**.

The **echo** program can also be used to provide "print" statements in a shell script. A *shell script* is an executable file containing shell-level commands. Any text on the line following the **echo** command name will be displayed on the terminal when the shell script is run.

Finally, the **echo** program enables you to test the operation of a pipeline. More specifically, **echo** allows you to create the data to be input into a pipeline so that you can see how the pipeline will operate on that input. When you make that input data a command line argument for **echo**, **echo** sends that input data into the pipeline.

The Berkeley C Shell has the **echo** function built in; that is, it is not a separate disk file, but a command integral to the shell. If you are using the C Shell, your system may also have a separate disk-based **echo** program, which means that you would have to type **echo's** complete pathname (for example, **/bin/echo**) to invoke the disk-based version. Otherwise, if you simply type **echo**, the C Shell will execute its internal **echo** function.

The Bell Systems III and V versions of **echo** recognize escape sequences in their arguments and replace them with the corresponding ASCII character. The escape sequence begins with a backslash (\ ), but you have to precede this backslash by another backslash when typing in the **echo** command line to remove any special interpretation by the shell as you are entering this command line.

The escape sequences shown on the left here will be replaced by the corresponding ASCII character indicated on the right:

\ \b	Backspace (^H)
\ \f	Form feed (^L)
\ \n	New line (^J)
\ \r	Carriage return (^M)
\ \t	Tab (^I)
\ \ \	Backslash (literal)
\ \nnn	Replace the digits *nnn* with the ASCII character whose octal value is *nnn*, where *nnn* must begin with a zero.

In addition, note that the **echo** program will exit immediately without printing a new line if it encounters the \c escape sequence.

Examples Prepare for these examples as outlined in the introduction to this chapter. Create the link to **wordlist** before you begin your practice with **echo**.

In the simplest use of **echo**, all the arguments on a command line are simply composed of text strings. To demonstrate how text can be printed on your terminal by using the **echo** utility, enter the command line **echo This line is composed of words.**

$ **echo This line is composed of words.**

This line is composed of words.

$ ▓

If you place the same command in an ordinary file and make the file executable, you have a simple shell script:

$ **cat testmessage**

echo This line is composed of words.

$ **chmod u+x testmessage**

$ **testmessage**

This line is composed of words.

$ ▓

Here we named the ordinary file **testmessage**, and we made the file executable through **chmod**.

A command can be used on the **echo** command line if the command is enclosed in backquotes (`` ` ``). This technique is called *command substitution*. All such commands are executed before the **echo** command line itself is executed. To see how this works, enter **echo The date and time is `date`**:

$ **echo The date and time is `date`**

The date and time is Tue Apr 3 13:05:34 PST 1984

$ ▓

The text string argument ("The date and time is") is displayed as typed, while the command surrounded by backquotes (**date**) is actually executed and its standard output merged with the text string to give the final result we have just shown.

Similar to command substitution is the use of **echo** to display the value of a shell variable. For example, enter **echo My home directory is $HOME** and you will see the text "My home directory is" followed by the value of the **HOME** variable, which stores the name of your home directory.

```
$ echo My home directory is $HOME
My home directory is /usr/username
$
```

The pathname for the home directory in our sample file system is of course **/usr/username**.

For a simple example of filename substitution, enter the command **echo ∗**.

```
$ echo *
Mail appeal poem wordlist
$
```

All the filenames in your current directory appear on your screen because the ∗ metacharacter matches any filename string.

For your next example, enter the command line **echo Mail/Username/ Aug15.84/remind?**. Here the **remind?** string will be matched by **remind1** and **remind2** in the **Mail/Username/Aug15.84** directory.

```
$ echo Mail/Username/Aug15.84/remind?
Mail/Username/Aug15.84/remind1  Mail/Username/Aug15.84/remind2
$
```

Consider the case in which no match occurs. The Berkeley version may issue an error message, while the other versions will simply repeat the unsubstituted arguments. For example, if you have a Bell version of **echo**, enter **echo appeal?** to see how the command responds:

```
$ echo appeal?
appeal?
$
```

The Berkeley version, which is built into the C Shell, would issue an error message, such as "echo: No match."

To further illustrate the operation of metacharacters, compare the displays obtained from entering **echo ∗** and **echo \∗**.

```
$ echo *
Mail appeal poem wordlist
$ echo \*
*
$ ▓
```

In the second case, the asterisk acts like any other character (compare this with the results of typing **echo A**) because the backslash removes its special significance to the shell.

All characters enclosed in single quotation marks (except a single quotation mark) are displayed literally. No substitution of any kind is performed inside single quotation marks (contrast this with command substitution via the backquotes). Try this now. Enter **echo '*'**, and observe the display:

```
$ echo '*'
*
$ ▓
```

Double quotation marks can be used like single quotation marks to make **echo** display something literally—except in the case of command substitution and shell variable substitution. If you want to reproduce a command or a shell variable literally, you must use single quotation marks, as shown here:

```
$ echo $HOME
/usr/username
$ echo \$HOME
$HOME
$ echo '$HOME'
$HOME
$ echo "$HOME"
/usr/username
$ ▓
```

If you have access to either the Bell Systems III or V versions, you may enter the remaining examples on line. These versions of **echo** recognize escape sequences in their arguments and replace these by the corresponding ASCII character. For instance, the argument in this next example contains the escape sequence representing a new line character (^J), so when this command line is executed, the text after the new line character will be displayed on the next line.

$ echo This line contains an imbedded \ \n new line.

This line contains an imbedded

  new line.

$

In our final example, the argument for **echo** contains an escape sequence that will be replaced by a ^G (octal value 7). A ^G will ring the terminal bell (if this is available on your system).

$ echo This line rings the terminal bell \ \07

This line rings the terminal bell [RING]

$

Messages The following message applies only to the Berkeley version of **echo**:

echo: No match
> The filename that was abbreviated by filename generation characters (metacharacters or wild cards) cannot be matched to any actual filenames.

tee — Sample a Pipeline

$ **tee** [*option...*] *file...*

Options for All Versions:
- **−i** Ignore the interrupt signal.
- **−a** Append the copy to *file* instead of overwriting.

The **tee** command is a filter program that works like a T connection. **tee** transfers data unchanged from its standard input to its standard output but at the same time diverts a copy of this data into one or more files that you specify on the command line. The most common use for **tee** is to sample data at an intermediate point in a pipeline; that is, **tee** allows you to store the intermediate results in a disk file or to divert them to your terminal for immediate display.

The command line format for diverting a copy of a pipeline data stream into *file* is

$$command1 \mid \textbf{tee} \; file \mid command2$$

By means of this command line, the standard output of *command1* becomes the

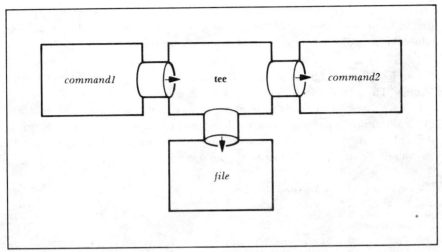

Figure 6-5. *tee creates a T connection in a pipeline*

standard input for **tee**. The standard output of **tee** is then passed on as the standard input of *command2*, and a copy is simultaneously diverted to *file*. Using **tee** in this way is commonly referred to as "pipe fitting," because using this command is like making a T connection in a pipeline, as Figure 6-5 shows. If *file* doesn't already exist, it is created. If *file* does exist, the diverted information is copied to the *file*, overwriting any contents already there.

All versions of **tee** recognize the same two options. You specify the option or options using the following command line format:

command1 | tee [*option...*] *file* | *command2*

Use the append option (−**a**) when you wish to add the diverted data to the end of an existing *file* rather than overwrite its previous contents. Use the interrupt (−**i**) option when it is necessary to ignore the interrupt signal (usually generated by pressing the DEL or RUBOUT key).

If you wish the diverted output to appear on your terminal, specify /**dev**/**tty** as the *file*, since /**dev**/**tty** is the general name for your control terminal. Remember that all physical devices in the UNIX system may be referenced as files.

This command also provides a simple way to create a short text file. Simply type

$ **tee** *file*

and all the text that you type until you enter an end-of-file character on a separate line will be entered into *file*. A copy of what you type is being saved to disk as *file* while the standard output copy appears on your terminal screen.

Examples   Prepare for these examples as discussed in the introduction to this chapter. The **wordlist** is not necessary for this command.

First let's see how to use **tee** to store the intermediate data in a pipeline in a disk file. For example, enter the command line **who | tee who.now | wc −l**, and when the shell prompt returns, enter **cat who.now**. Your results will differ in content but should be similar in format to the following:

```
$ who | tee who.now | wc −l
       4
$ cat who.now
root        console   Oct 31   16:58
username    tty01     Oct 31   15:42
spilchuk    tty02     Oct 31   14:56
username    tty03     Oct 31   10:32
$
```

As you can see, the output of **who** is piped into **tee**, which puts a copy of **who**'s output into the file **who.now**. The results of **who** are also sent to the word count program **wc**. The line option (−l) used with **wc** causes **wc** to report the number of lines produced by **who**, which in our example is "4". Finally, we used **cat** to check the copy of **who**'s output sent to **who.now**.

To display this same intermediate data directly on your terminal without using **cat**, enter **who | tee /dev/tty | wc −l**. Note that result of **tee** is displayed before the output from **wc −l**.

```
$ who | tee /dev/tty | wc −l
root        console   Oct 31   16:58
username    tty01     Oct 31   15:42
spilchuk    tty02     Oct 31   14:56
username    tty03     Oct 31   10:32
       4
$
```

For our next example we use the **tee** utility to divert a copy of the output of the **who** command to a temporary file named **tmp**. The output of the **who** command is then piped into the **wc** to give the line count. Finally, these results are directed to the standard input of a **cat** command. The minus sign (−) after the **cat** command causes **cat** to display its standard input file (the input from the pipe) on the screen (that is, the results of the **wc** command are sent to the screen) followed by the display of the **tmp** file. If you did not include the minus sign, **cat** would not display the input coming from the pipe (its standard input file).

```
$ who | tee tmp | wc −l | cat − tmp
    4
root          console   Oct 31   16:58
username      tty01     Oct 31   15:42
spilchuk      tty02     Oct 31   14:56
username      tty03     Oct 31   10:32
$
```

Finally, let's use **tee** to put characters that you type directly into a disk file. For instance, enter **tee textfile** followed by one or more lines of text. When you are finished, type your end-of-file character (^D by default) as the first entry on the next line. In this way what you type (that is, the standard input of **tee**) is stored in **textfile**:

```
$ tee textfile
This is a line of text.
This is a line of text.
[ ^D ]
$ cat textfile
This is a line of text.
$
```

Messages   The following message applies to all the versions of **tee**:

> **tee: cannot open** *file*
> The file in which you wanted to store the intermediate results already exists and cannot be opened for writing.

Working With Text

The eight UNIX commands described in this section enable you to manipulate text in a variety of ways. You can detect spelling errors in a document, alphabetically sort lists or any other kind of text, or find any patterns of words within a piece of text that you need to find. In addition, you can compare two files to determine their differences and similarities, or you can compare lines in the same file and adjust for the differences. Finally, by encrypting your files, you can ensure that they will not be read by other users, including the superuser.

sort — Sort or Merge Files

$ **sort** [*option...*] [+*pos*] [−*pos*] [−o *filenameout*] [*filename*]

Options for All Versions:

−b	Ignore leading blanks and tabs in comparisons.
−d	Dictionary order: only letters, digits, and blanks count.
−f	Ignore distinction between upper- and lowercase.
−n	Sort on first numeric field. Implies −b option.
−r	Reverse order of sort.
−u	Eliminate duplicate lines in sorted output.
−i	Ignore nonprinting ASCII characters in nonnumeric comparisons.
−t*c*	Specify field separator to be character *c*.
−c	Only check that the input file is already sorted.
−m	Merge the specified files.
−o *filenameout*	Save output in *filenameout* (which can be the same as *filename*).

The **sort** command is a very capable and fairly efficient program for sorting and merging files. The wide range of options and the ability to select key fields precisely makes this an outstanding utility for the UNIX system environment.

A *field* is a collection of adjacent characters that are not whitespace characters (that is, space and tab characters). One field can be separated from the next by whitespace or by other specially designated field separation characters. For example, a personal name can be thought of as having three fields: the first name, middle name, and last name, separated by spaces. The fields are numbered beginning with zero. Thus, a personal name would have field numbers

0	1	2
firstname	middlename	lastname

If **sort** is invoked using the basic command line format

$ sort *filename*...

all lines in *filename* are ordered by treating the entire line as the *key field*. By definition, the *key field* is the portion of the line that is compared for the sorting operation. You may specify a key field less than the entire line by using the command line format

$ sort [+*pos1*] [−*pos2*] *filename*

This limits the sort to a key field beginning with *pos1* and ending just before *pos2*, where *pos1* and *pos2* are field numbers. If *pos2* is omitted, the key field extends from *pos1* to the end of the line. In all cases, each line is ordered as a unit according to these specifications, and the rearranged result appears on the standard output.

The ordering is based on *ASCII collating sequence*. The ASCII sequence for all printing characters is reproduced here:

!"#$%&'( )*+,−./0123456789:;<=>?@

ABCDEFGHIJKLMNOPQRSTUVWXYZ[\ ]^ _

abcdefghijklmnopqrstuvwxyz{|}~

The ordering of any two characters depends on their placement in the ASCII character set. For instance, a capital "A" comes before a lowercase "a"; all digits occur before any letters, and the punctuation characters occur at various places between the digits and letters, as shown.

The corresponding characters in a key field are compared one at a time for ordering. Thus after ordering, "UNIX" would appear before "Unix", which would appear before "unix". Lines are sorted by ordering the contents of the key field; the rest of the line has no effect on the ordering. For example, these lines are sorted using the entire line as the key:

A unix file
The UNIX system
This Unix user

And these are sorted using the second field as the key:

The UNIX system
This Unix user
A unix file

The default ordering may be modified by specifying certain *options* when invoking **sort**. The command line format for using one or more *options* is

$ **sort** [*option*...] [+*pos*] [−*pos*] *filename*

Any whitespace that separates one field from the next is considered part of the second field when ordering occurs. The whitespace would not influence the ordering if *each* field entry contained the *same* number of leading whitespace characters. Generally, this is not the case, so you must specify the blank option (−**b**) to ignore the leading whitespace in the field comparison.

The default ordering scheme does not order numbers by their arithmetic value. Thus a field containing "19" would be placed before "2", "29" before "3", and so forth. Use the −**n** option when sorting on a numeric key field to order by arithmetic value.

Often fields are not separated by spaces or tabs but by some other character that isn't used within the field itself. In this way, the whitespace characters may be included in the field. For example, many UNIX data files are composed of fields separated by colons or commas. These files may be sorted correctly if you use the "tab character" option, −t*c*, where *c* is the field separator character.

You may indicate more than one key field by repeating the +*pos1* and, if necessary, the −*pos2* field numbers on the invocation command line. For example, you could sort our list of personal names by last name (**2**), first name (**0**), and middle name (**1**) like this:

$ **sort** +2 +0 +1 *namelist*

You may also associate different options with different fields by concatenating these options immediately after the field number. For instance,

$ **sort** +2bdf +0b +1bd *namelist*

associates the **bdf** options with the third field (number 2), **b** with the first field (number 0), and **bd** with the second field (number 1).

Each *pos1* and *pos2* may be expressed as *m.n*, where *m* is field number and *n* is the number of characters to skip farther into this field. Each field designator, *m.n*, may be followed by one or more of the invocation options (**b, d, f, i, n,** and **r**). A missing *.n* means **.0** and a missing −*pos2* means the end of the line.

The most general **sort** command line format is

$ **sort** [*option*...] [+*pos*] [−*pos*] [−o *filenameout*] [*filename*...]

which sorts *filename* (or data from the standard input file if *filename* is not specified) and optionally stores the result in *filenameout*. Note that you may specify *filenameout* to be the same as *filename* because the result is only renamed to *filenameout* after the sorting is complete.

Examples Prepare for these examples as described in the introduction to this chapter.

Employ your favorite editor to enter the list of names shown in the next example into the file named **namelist**. Note that there are two spaces between the "R." and "Oates" fields on line 1 and two spaces between "Sue" and "S." fields on line 3. There is only one space between all other fields.

```
$ cat namelist
John R. Oates
Sue A. Oates
Sue S. Oates
Mary A. O'Conner
$
```

The fields in the previous screen are designated left to right as 0 (first name), 1 (middle initial), and 2 (surname). If you don't specify any options, **sort** will order the list using the entire line as the sort key to order the characters in first names, then in the middle initials, and finally in the last names to give the following display:

```
$ sort namelist
John R. Oates
Mary A. O'Conner
Sue S. Oates
Sue A. Oates
$
```

To order such a list by last name, skip the first two fields (**+2**) and use the third field as the key field, as shown:

```
$ sort +2 namelist
John R. Oates
Mary A. O'Conner
Sue S. Oates
Sue A. Oates
$
```

This list was still not sorted correctly, however, since there are an unequal number of blanks before the third field. Add the blank option (**b**) to the field designator (**+2**) in order to ignore the blanks in front of the third field:

$ sort +2b namelist

Mary A. O'Conner

John R. Oates

Sue S. Oates

Sue A. Oates

$

Although this is an improvement, the surname "Oates" should appear before "O'Conner". You may ignore the nonalphabetical character (') by adding the dictionary option (**d**) to the field designator, as shown here:

$ sort +2bd namelist

Mary A. O'Conner

John R. Oates

Sue S. Oates

Sue A. Oates

$

Even though the nonalphabetical character (') in "O'Conner" was ignored, we still didn't get the desired result. The uppercase "C" in "O'Conner" comes before the lowercase "a" in "Oates" (see the preceding ASCII collating list), so we have to add the **−f** option to ignore the upper- and lowercase distinction:

$ sort +2bdf namelist

John R. Oates

Sue S. Oates

Sue A. Oates

Mary A. O'Conner

$

Well, the last names were sorted correctly, but now the first name and middle initials are not. To remedy this, add keys to sort by first name and then middle initial.

$ sort +2bdf +0b +1b namelist

John R. Oates

Sue S. Oates

Sue A. Oates

Mary A. O'Conner

$ ▨

This result is still not correct since "Sue A." should come before "Sue S." even though the blank option was used. You must limit the comparison to the first field by specifying **−1** immediately after **+0b**:

$ sort +2bdf +0b −1 +1b namelist

John R. Oates

Sue A. Oates

Sue S. Oates

Mary A. O'Conner

$ ▨

Now the list is correctly sorted. These last few examples illustrate a useful approach to setting up the sort operation. Create a small sample data file that contains all the difficult and unusual entries from your larger data file. Experiment with the command line options until the small test file can be sorted correctly. Then you should have the correct command line for sorting the larger data file.

Use your editor again to add phone numbers to this list of names. The result is stored in **phonelist**:

$ cat phonelist

John R. Oates	619-642-3228
Sue A. Oates	415-653-6550
Sue S. Oates	415-336-4554
Mary A. O'Conner	212-961-0052

$ ▨

If we sort this file by the same command line that worked previously, the result would not be correct.

```
$ sort +2bdf +0b −1 +1b phonelist
Sue A. Oates            415-653-6550
Sue  S. Oates           415-336-4554
John R.  Oates          619-642-3228
Mary A. O'Conner        212-961-0052
$
```

To sort this list by last name, you must ignore the phone numbers. Add the −3 field delimiter to restrict the first sort key to between fields 2 and 3 so as not to include the phone numbers in the comparison, as shown here:

```
$ sort +2bdf −3 +0b −1 +1b phonelist
John R.  Oates          619-642-3228
Sue A. Oates            415-653-6550
Sue  S. Oates           415-336-4554
Mary A. O'Conner        212-961-0052
$
```

Now let's sort this list by the phone numbers. Skip the first three fields as shown:

```
$ sort +3 phonelist
Sue  S. Oates           415-336-4554
Sue A. Oates            415-653-6550
John R.  Oates          619-642-3228
Mary A. O'Conner        212-961-0052
$
```

Either specify the blank option (b), the numeric option (n), or both with the field designator (+3) to get the correct result. To be on the safe side, we added both options:

```
$ sort +3bn phonelist
Mary A. O'Conner        212-961-0052
Sue  S. Oates           415-336-4554
Sue A. Oates            415-653-6550
John R.  Oates          619-642-3228
$
```

If you wished to skip the area code and sort by the remaining numbers, you could specify the sort key in the format *m.n* as shown:

```
$ sort +3.4bn phonelist
Sue  S. Oates          415-336-4554
John R.  Oates         619-642-3228
Sue A. Oates           415-653-6550
Mary A. O'Conner       212-961-0052
$
```

Alternatively, you could achieve the same result by specifying the field separator to be a dash, and then skipping the first field (from the beginning of the line through the area code).

```
$ sort −t− +1 phonelist
Sue  S. Oates          415-336-4554
John R.  Oates         619-642-3228
Sue A. Oates           415-653-6550
Mary A. O'Conner       212-961-0052
$
```

The −t− option divides each line into three fields: the first field starts at the beginning of each line and extends to the first −; the second field extends from after the first − until the second −, and so on.

This last example shows that there is usually more than one way to set up the **sort** command line to achieve the desired result. With practice you should be able to come up with a minimal set of necessary options.

Enter the following two lists of numbers with an editor. Store the lists in the files with the name indicated by the argument to the appropriate **cat** command in the following screen:

```
$ cat even.numbers
2
8
6
10
4
$ cat odd.numbers
7
```

```
9
1
3
5
$
```

First we shall merge these files using the **m** option. The merge operation combines the contents of the files without sorting them. Enter **sort −mn odd.numbers even.numbers** and observe the result:

```
$ sort −mn odd.numbers even.numbers
2
7
8
6
9
1
3
5
10
4
$
```

Now let's sort each of the number lists before performing a merge and store the result in a file with the same name as the original source file. Follow the output option (−o) with the name of the desired output file. Note that in this case the output file may have the same name as the input file without erasing the contents of the input file. You must also specify the number option (−n) to sort the numbers by numeric value rather than by ASCII collating sequence.

```
$ sort −n odd.numbers −o odd.numbers
$ cat odd.numbers
1
3
5
7
9
$ sort −n even.numbers −o even.numbers
```

$ cat even.numbers

2

4

6

8

10

$ ▓

Now merge the sorted files. Note that you must specify the −n option as well:

$ sort −mn odd.numbers even.numbers

1

2

3

4

5

6

7

8

9

10

$ ▓

Messages Most versions of **sort** report the same messages. Generally these versions ignore unrecognized invocation options.

The following messages apply to all the versions of **sort**:

sort: can't open *file*
The input *file* can't be opened for reading.

sort: can't locate temp
The intermediate temporary work files cannot be created in either /**tmp** or /**usr/tmp**. See your system administrator for assistance.

sort: too many keys
You cannot specify more than ten sort keys.

sort: can check only 1 file
You may only check one file when using the check (−c) option.

sort: can't create *fileout*
The specified output file *fileout* cannot be created for writing. If *fileout* already exists, enable write permission with **chmod**. If *fileout* doesn't exist,

enable search or write permission with **chmod** for the directory that is to contain the output file. If you can't change the permission because you are not the file owner, see your system administrator for assistance.

spell — *Find Spelling Errors*

$ spell [*option*]... [*file*]...

Bell Version 7 and System III Options:

   −**v**   Print derivatives of words listed in the dictionary.
   −**b**   Use the British spelling dictionary for the spelling check.
   −**x**   Print every plausible stem (indicated by =).

Additional Bell System V Option:

   +*local file*   Specify an additional spelling list named *local file*.

The **spell** command is actually a *shell command file*, or shell script, that directs other programs to process the words in a document. Because the script is easy to modify, there are many local variations.

The **spell** command and related utilities provide the user with the basic tools for checking the spelling of words in a document. A 24,000-word, on-line spelling dictionary is used in the spelling check. Most systems maintain a readable form of this work list, which has the pathname **/usr/dict/words** in the Bell Version 7 and Berkeley systems and **/usr/lib/spell/list** in the newer Bell system versions. Some UNIX implementations may not include the readable form of the dictionary since a condensed form of this same list is actually used by **spell**.

The output of the **spell** command will be a list of words that are neither in the dictionary nor derivable from words that are in the dictionary. Certain rules for adding prefixes or suffixes or both are employed to recognize words that may be derived from words in the basic dictionary.

A *stop list* is used to filter out genuine misspellings that are derivable from words in the spelling list. For instance, without a stop list the **spell** program would consider "thier" to be spelled correctly because it could be derived from "thy" (which is in the dictionary) by subtracting the "y" suffix and adding "ier."

The Bell System V version also allows you to specify an additional dictionary named *local file*, which contains a sorted list of words, one per line. The **spell** command will consider any words in *local file* that it encounters in processing the document to be correctly spelled. The original spelling list is also used.

The local file provides an easy way to specify a specialized dictionary containing, for example, proper names in addition to the default spelling list. Other versions of the **spell** command—for instance, the Berkeley version—generally provide a similar capability, but creating and maintaining the specialized dictionary is much more complex in these versions.

Examples Prepare for these examples as discussed in the introduction to this chapter. The **wordlist** is not necessary for this command.

We shall use a short example in this tutorial to save space. However, the principles shown are appropriate for larger documents. The text is contained in a file named **doc** and consists of a single line, "UNIX is thier graat computerrific operating system."

Now run the spelling check by entering **spell doc** and observe the results:

```
$ spell doc
computerrific
graat
thier
$
```

This example shows that the words "computerrific," "graat," and "thier" were considered misspelled. They either did not appear in the spelling dictionary or were not derivable from words in the dictionary.

If you use the −**v** option, all words that are not literally in the spelling list are displayed and words that can be derived are shown along with the rule(s) used to derive them:

```
$ spell −v doc
computerrific
graat
−e+ing operating
thier
$
```

In this last example, "operating" was not literally in the spelling dictionary; however, it may be derived from "operate," which is in the list, by removing the "e" suffix and adding "ing."

You might run a spelling check and decide to place certain words in the dictionary so that they would not be flagged as misspelled in the future. First create a file containing all the misspelled words. We use **doc.errs** for this purpose

```
$ spell doc | tee doc.errs
computerrific
graat
thier
$
```

Then use an editor to delete all genuine misspellings (in this instance, "graat" and "thier"), leaving only the words you wish to install in your own specialized dictionary (in this instance, only the word "computerrific"). Here we will name the specialized dictionary **my_dictionary**, although any valid filename will do.

Now transfer "computerrific" from **doc.errs** to **my_dictionary**. In the following example, we use the Bell System V version of the command, which enables us to specify our personal dictionary on the command line.

```
$ spell +my_dictionary doc
graat
thier
$
```

As a result, **spell** will check not only its own on-line dictionary but also the local dictionary **my_dictionary**. Thus, the screen shows that only "graat" and "thier" are misspelled.

If you are using other versions of **spell**, you may still create your own customized dictionary, but the task is much more involved. For instance, run the spelling check, placing the result in a temporary file by entering **spell doc >doc.errs**. Then make sure **my_dictionary** is sorted, and send the ordered list through a pipe as one argument to the **comm** command, which is set up to display all words in **doc.errs** that aren't in **my_dictionary**:

```
$ spell doc >doc.errs
$ sort my_dictionary | comm -23 doc.errs -
graat
thier
$
```

The output of the **sort** process becomes the second input for **comm**, replacing the dash — argument. The —23 option causes **comm** to output all words in **doc.errs** that aren't in **my_dictionary**, as desired.

On some systems, **spell** will internally log all its output lists (along with your user name, terminal name, and time of login) to the spelling history file. Your system administrator may examine this file from time to time to add some of the more commonly occurring entries to the public dictionary.

The pathname for the history file is generally **/usr/lib/spellhist** for Bell Version 7 and Berkeley systems and **/usr/lib/spell/spellhist** for the newer Bell versions. If you examine the tail end of this file, you should observe a record of your last spelling check transaction. Normally, spelling history files will be quite long, and you would need to use **tail** to examine the end of the file. Here, because our spelling history file is so short, we can simply use **cat.**

```
$ cat /usr/lib/spellhist
graat
thier
username      tty01      Oct   5 19:57
$
```

The last line in the history file is the output of **who** when you specify two arguments, such as **who am i.**

Messages Since the **spell** command is a shell script, error messages can either come from the shell or the individual commands invoked during execution of the shell script. Some of the messages which may arise from the individual UNIX command programs that are involved in **spell**'s operation are listed here:

Deroff: z invalid option
If the shell script does not trap invalid command line options, they will be passed to **deroff**, which is used by the spelling program.
Bad flag for spell: −z
Usage: spell [−v] [−b] [−d hlist] [−s hstop] [−h spellhist]
The Berkeley **spell** script catches invalid options.

grep — Search a File for a Pattern

$ grep [*option* . . .] *pattern* [*file* . . .]

Options for All Versions:

−v	Display all lines except those containing *pattern*.
−c	Report only the number of matching lines.
−l	List only the name(s) of files containing *pattern*.
−n	Precede each line by the line number in the source *file*.
−b	Precede each line by the block number on which it was located.

Additional Bell Version 7 Options:

—h   Suppress display of filename headers in output.

—y   Ignore case distinction.

Additional Bell Systems III and V Options:

—s   Suppress error messages about files that don't exist or cannot be opened for reading.

Additional Berkeley Options:

—i   Ignore case when matching *pattern*.

—w   Have *pattern* match only whole words.

The Berkeley version of **grep** recognizes all the options for other versions except —y (Berkeley uses —i instead).

You will appreciate the usefulness of this command when you have to search one or more files for a pattern of characters. The basic command line format for using **grep** is

$ **grep** *pattern file...*

If *pattern* is in fact contained in the *files* specified on the **grep** command line, the line of text containing that *pattern* is displayed on the standard output.

You can use one or more metacharacters as a shorthand in the pattern argument for **grep**. For instance, you may specify a match at the beginning of a line using (^), or at the end of the line by indicating ($). In fact, you may employ most of the pattern-matching metacharacters in your **grep** pattern argument that you did for **ed**.

For a single file, an editor program could perform the pattern search. However, you have to invoke the editor, read the file into the edit buffer, and then specify the search pattern. The **grep** utility enables you to find the pattern more quickly since you don't have to enter an editor. When you need to search more than one file, **grep** outperforms an editor for the same task.

Use the following general command line format when you employ one or more *options:*

$ **grep** [*option...*] *pattern* [*file...*]

All versions of **grep** recognize a number of options useful for modifying the output. These include the —v option, which displays all lines *except* those containing *pattern*. If you simply need a count of the lines containing the pattern, use the count ($-c$) option. The number option ($-n$) will also display the source file line number of any line containing *pattern*. This number could be used to assist in searching for the desired line with an editor. If more than one file is being examined, you might use the $-l$ option to list the names of *files* containing *pattern* to identify those files that contain the pattern. Other options are used to ignore case distinction when locating the pattern so that either uppercase or lowercase letters in the input will match lowercase letters in the pattern.

If no files are specified with the **grep** command, input text will be taken from the standard input file (keyboard by default) until an end-of-file code (^D, by default) is typed. You may also provide the input text as a data stream from a pipeline. For instance, if you specify the command line

$$\$ \textit{command} \mid \textbf{grep} \textit{ pattern}$$

the text output from *command* will be input to **grep**. All lines in this text containing *pattern* will appear on the standard output of **grep**.

The command name, **grep**, is an acronym for "globally find regular expressions and print." The pattern argument is also known as a *regular expression*.

Examples Prepare for these examples as outlined in the introduction to this chapter. The **wordlist** is not necessary for this command.

For the first example, enter **grep the appeal** to search for all instances of "the" in the file **appeal**:

```
$ grep the appeal
Now is the time
to come to the aid
of their country.
$ ▒
```

Note that the last line matched because "the" is a part of "their". If you want to avoid this, enclose the pattern in single or double quotation marks and include a leading or a trailing blank or both. For instance, enter **grep 'the ' appeal**:

```
$ grep 'the ' appeal
Now is the time
to come to the aid
$ ▒
```

If you are using the Berkeley version, you could specify the word option (−w) to achieve the same effect. In this case the quotation marks and extra whitespace would not be needed.

Use the reverse (−v) option to display all lines that *do not* contain the pattern. Enter **grep −v the appeal** and observe the result:

```
$ grep −v the appeal
for all good citizens
$
```

The number option (−n) displays the line number for the line or lines in the file that contain the pattern. To number the lines that match the pattern, enter **grep −n the appeal**.

```
$ grep −n the appeal
1:Now is the time
3:to come to the aid
4:of their country.
$
```

If only a count of the lines that match the pattern is needed, use the count (−c) option. For instance, enter the command **grep −c the appeal**:

```
$ grep −c the appeal
3
$
```

Sometimes the pattern match may fail because of lower- and uppercase distinctions. To avoid missing such a match, use the −y option with the Bell version or −i with the Berkeley version of **grep**. Then lowercase letters in the pattern will match both lower- and uppercase letters in the input file. To illustrate, use the pattern "now" with and without this option, as shown in the following display:

```
$ grep −y now appeal
Now is the time
$ grep now appeal
$
```

In the first case, there was a match between "now" and "Now" because there was no case distinction with the −y option. In the second case, there was no match since "now" and "Now" are not identical.

Use the list option (−l) when you need to search several files that might contain occurrences of the pattern. In this case only the name of files that contain the indicated pattern are displayed.

As an example, let's say you have several business letters in files named **letter1**, **letter2**, and **letter3**. You need a quick way to determine which of the three letters was sent to Acme Computers. To do this, enter **grep −l "Acme Computers" letter?**. The phrase "Acme Computers" must be enclosed in quotation marks so that **grep** will understand that the two words with the space between them constitute the pattern to be searched for. The filename that **grep** reports is the file where the match occurred and is also the file containing the letter to Acme Computers.

The list option alone does not provide the location within the file or files containing the pattern. Frequently, the number option (−n) is used in conjunction with the list option to pinpoint the line number where the pattern occurs.

Messages   The following messages apply to Bell versions of the **grep** command:

> **grep: illegal option —*option***
> **usage: grep −blcnsv pattern file . . .**
> You specified an unrecognized *option*.

> **RE error**
> You specified an invalid *pattern*.

> **grep: can't open *file***
> The argument *file* cannot be opened for reading.

The following messages apply to the Berkeley version of **grep**:

> **grep: unknown flag**
> You specified an unrecognized option.

> **grep: argument too long**
> Use a shorter argument.

> **grep: RE error**
> **grep: RE botch**
> You specified an invalid *pattern*.

diff—Report the Differences Between Files

> **$ diff** [*option...*] *file1 file2*
>
> Bell Options:
> **−b**   Ignore trailing whitespace and compare other strings of space characters as equal.

—e   Produce a script of **ed** commands that would recreate *file2* from *file1*.

—f   Produce a script in the opposite order (not useful with **ed**).

—h   Use for files of "unlimited" length.

Additional Berkeley Options:

—c[*n*]   Report the change in context. Specify *n* to report *n* lines around each change (default is three lines).

The **diff** utility conveniently reports the differences between two text files on a line-by-line basis. The report is couched in terms of how to change the contents of the first file argument to become the same as the contents of the other file. Note that **diff** itself doesn't change one file into another, but only reports how to make such a transformation.

The text files are compared on a line-by-line basis. This means that even if two lines differ by only one character, the entire line is reported. In this way a report of the differences between two files can be generated quickly.

The general command line format for using **diff** is

$$\text{\$ \textbf{diff} [} option... \text{] } file1 \; file2$$

Specify the blank option (—b) when you wish to ignore trailing whitespace characters (that is, space and tab characters) when comparing the text lines. Strings of space characters will also be ignored. Note that while the —b option may be used with any other **grep** option, all the other **grep** options are mutually exclusive.

Specify the edit (—e) option to obtain a list of the **ed** editor's append, change, and delete commands. These commands, in turn, can be used to create *file2* from *file1*.

On a very large file, you need to employ the —h option. This option actually causes **diff** to invoke another program, usually **/usr/lib/diffh**, to perform the comparisons. This program works best when the differences between the two files are minimal and well separated. A drawback is that the —e and —f options are not available with this program.

The Berkeley version recognizes a context option (—c) to report the changes in context; that is, lines surrounding the change or changes are also output. Normally, up to three surrounding lines are displayed, but this may be changed to *n* lines if you specify this option as —c*n*, where *n* is a decimal integer.

You may use the **diff** utility for economical storage of several versions of a file. Each time you produce a new version, run **diff** between the original and new version and collect the "difference" file. This "diff" file may be used at any time to recreate the latest version of the file from the original. In this way you need only keep several small "diff" files (along with your original) instead of the same number of the larger complete versions of the original file. We will show an example of this feature in the next section.

Examples Prepare for these examples as described in the introduction to this chapter. The **wordlist** is not necessary for this command.

Use your favorite editor and change **appeal** by misspelling citizens as "citozens" and appending "This is the time" and "to get on the UNIX bandwagon." Save the result as **appeal2**.

For our first example, enter **diff appeal appeal2**. The result tells you that line 2 of **appeal** must be changed from "for all good citizens" to "for all good citozens" and that the two lines "This is the time" and "to get on the UNIX bandwagon." must be appended to **appeal** to create **appeal2**.

```
$ diff appeal appeal2
2c2
< for all good citizens
---
> for all good citozens
4a5,6
> This is the time
> to get on the UNIX bandwagon.
$
```

Let's employ the −e option with **diff** to produce a list of **ed** commands that would create **appeal2** from **appeal**, as shown:

```
$ diff −e appeal appeal2 >ed.script
$ cat ed.script
4a
This is the time
to get on the UNIX bandwagon.
.
2c
for all good citozens
.
$
```

Commands to save the changed text and exit the editor must be added to **ed.script** before it may be used as an *editing script*. An editing script is a file we create to contain commands that an editor can later execute. For example, use your text editor and manually append the commands **w appeal3** on one line and **q** on the next, so that when used, **ed.script** will save the result as **appeal3** before exiting. In this example, we show the editor prompt (*) so that you can distinguish text entry mode from command mode more easily.

```
$ ed ed.script
79
P
*$a
w appeal3
q
*.
*w
91
*q
$
```

Now, to actually produce **appeal3** from **appeal**, you may either type in these same **ed** commands from the keyboard or redirect the standard input of **ed** to come from a file containing these commands. We show the last approach in the next example:

```
$ ed appeal <ed.script
75
122
$
```

The display indicates that there were 75 characters read in from **appeal** and 122 characters written out as **appeal3**.

The point of saving the original file **appeal** and any intermediate "difference" files like **ed.script** is that you could create any version of **appeal** you wanted without having to store all the intermediate versions themselves. Even though our example showed the "difference" file to be almost as large as the result (**appeal3**), in practice you will find that the "difference" files are generally smaller than the files they operate on.

Unless you use the blank (−**b**) option, unequal numbers of blanks will also be flagged. The blank option causes trailing whitespace (both space and tab characters) and other strings of blanks to be ignored in **diff**'s comparison. For instance, you could modify **appeal** by inserting extra blanks between some words and save the result on disk as **appeal4**. In our version of **appeal4**, we added enough blanks to justify the right margin, as shown here:

```
$ cat appeal4
    Now is the time
for all good citizens
  to come to the aid
    of their country.
$ ▓
```

Now compare **appeal** and **appeal4** first without and then with the blank option, and observe that both files are considered to be the same (that is, there is no output from **diff**) when the blank option is specified.

```
$ diff appeal appeal4
1c1
< Now is the time
---
> Now  is  the  time
3,4c3,4
< to come to the aid
< of their country.
---
> to come to the aid
> of  their  country.
$ diff −b appeal appeal4
$ ▓
```

If you have access to the Berkeley version, you may display lines around the indicated changes. This feature lets you view the context around the indicated change. For instance, enter the command line **diff −c appeal appeal2**:

```
$ diff −c appeal appeal2
*** appeal      Thu Nov 10 10:49:30 1984
--- appeal2     Thu Nov 10 10:50:01 1984
**************
```

*** 1,4

Now is the time
! for all good citizens
to come to the aid
of their country.

--- 1,5 -----

Now is the time
! for all good citozens
to come to the aid
of their country.
This is the time

****

*** 2,4

for all good citizens
to come to the aid
of their country.

--- 2,6 -----

for all good citozens
to come to the aid
of their country.
+ This is the time
+ to get on the UNIX bandwagon.

$ ▓

The names of the file arguments and their creation dates are first noted. Each change is bordered by asterisks. Lines changed from one file to the other are marked with an exclamation point (!); lines removed from *file1* are denoted by a minus sign (−), and lines added to *file2* are denoted by a plus sign (+).

You should remove the extra files created in this tutorial session by entering **rm appeal? ed.script.**

Messages The following messages apply to the Bell versions of the **diff** command:

diff: arg count
> You must specify two file arguments.

diff: files too big, try −h
The input files are too big to compare; in this case specify the huge (−h) option.

diff: cannot find diffh
The auxiliary program, **/usr/lib/diffh**, which is invoked with the huge option, cannot be executed. See your system administrator.

diff: cannot create /tmp/d*XXXXX*
The temporary work file, **/tmp/d*XXXXX***, cannot be created. The work file is used when one input is the standard input. See your system administrator.

diff: cannot open *filename*
The file argument *filename* cannot be opened for reading.

The following messages apply to the Berkeley version of the command:

diff: *file*: permission denied
You do not have permission to access the *file* argument.

diff: *file*: no such file or directory
The *file* cannot be located.

diff: −*option*: unknown option
The *option* was not recognized by **diff**.

diff: two filename arguments required
You must specify two file arguments.

diff: −h doesn't support −e, −f, −c, or −I
You cannot specify these other options with −h.

diff: ran out of memory
Try the comparison using huge (−h) option.

comm — Display Common Lines in Two Files

```
$ comm [ − [1] [2] [3] ] file1 file2
```

Use the **comm** utility to display lines that are common to two input files as well as lines that are unique to each of the two files. The lines in the two files must have been sorted by some means—for example, by the UNIX **sort** program. One of the two input files may be the standard input file. Thus **comm** can compare a data stream coming from a pipe as **comm**'s standard input with the contents of a disk file.

The lines in the two files are compared one at a time for equality. The lines are considered identical only if *every* character is the same in both lines. In the default case the output from **comm** consists of lines in three columns: lines that are unique to each input file, and lines common to each file.

The most general command line format for using **comm** is

$$\text{\$ \textbf{comm} } [\; - \; [1] \, [2] \, [3] \;] \; \textit{file1 file2}$$

which displays unique and common lines in sorted files *file1* and *file2*. You may replace either *file1* or *file2* with the standard input file, indicated by a −. Use the flags **1**, **2**, or **3** to suppress the display of the corresponding column. Thus, −**123** would display nothing.

Examples   Prepare for these examples as described in the introduction to this chapter. Create the link to **wordlist** before you begin your practice with **comm**.

First let's create two customer lists. Use your favorite editor and add the names from *List A* to the file **customer.A** and those from *List B* to **customer.B**.

List A	List B
Anderson	Barnes
Flemming	Haws
Haws	Smith
Ingold	Thomas
Jones	White
Smith	
Wright	

Note that the two lists are already sorted. Otherwise, you would have to sort each list before using **comm**.

Now you may employ **comm** to see the overlap in the two lists.

```
$ comm customer.A customer.B
Anderson
          Barnes
Flemming
                    Haws
Ingold
Jones
                    Smith
          Thomas
          White
Wright
$ ▓
```

The first column lists lines unique to the first file (*List A*), the second column lines unique to the second file (*List B*), and the third column lines common to both files.

You may replace one of the input disk files for **comm** with the standard input file. For example, let's use **cat** to send the contents of **customer.A** into a pipeline. This data stream is input to **comm** and compared with the contents of **customer.B** to give the same result as in the preceding example.

```
$ cat customer.A I comm − customer.B
Anderson
          Barnes
Flemming
                    Haws
Ingold
Jones
                    Smith
          Thomas
          White
Wright
$ ▓
```

If you wish to restrict the output to names unique to one list or common to both lists, use the appropriate option. For instance, entering **comm** **−23**

customer.A customer.B suppresses listing of columns 2 and 3, leaving column 1 (customers unique to *List A*):

```
$ comm −23 customer.A customer.B
Anderson
Flemming
Ingold
Jones
Wright
$
```

Or to get a list of customers unique to *List B,* enter the following:

```
$ comm −13 customer.A customer.B
Barnes
Thomas
White
$
```

Finally, to have **comm** report which customers are common to both lists, enter this:

```
$ comm −12 customer.A customer.B
Haws
Smith
$
```

The **comm** command is useful for manipulating words, prefixes, roots, and suffixes. As an example, let's create two files, one containing words with the prefix "em" and the other containing words ending in "tion." Use your **wordlist** file and the **grep** pattern-matching program:

```
$ grep '^em' wordlist >em.words
$ grep 'tion$' wordlist >tion.words
$
```

The pattern '^em' is matched by words which begin with "em", and the pattern 'tion$' is matched by words which end in "tion". Since your **wordlist** is already sorted, the files **em.words** and **tion.words** are ready to be processed by **comm**.

To list the words common to both categories, use the **comm** utility as shown here:

```
$ comm −12 em.words tion.words
emotion
$
```

Only the word "emotion" is displayed. The on-line spelling dictionary does not have entries for "emaciation," "emanation," "emigration," or "emulation," for instance.

Messages   The following messages apply to Bell versions of **comm**:

> usage: comm [− [123]] file1 file2
> Either you indicated less than two file arguments or you didn't specify a 1, 2, or 3 as an option.
>
> comm: cannot open *filename*
> The input file *filename* cannot be opened for reading.

These messages apply to the Berkeley version of **comm**:

> comm: arg count
> You specified less than two arguments.
>
> comm: illegal flag
> You didn't specify a 1, 2, or 3 as an option.
>
> comm: cannot open *filename*
> The input file *filename* cannot be opened for reading.

uniq — Remove Adjacent Repeated Lines in a Sorted File

$ uniq [*option...* [+*n*][−*m*]] [*input* [*output*]]

Options for All Versions:

−**u**   Display only the lines *not* repeated in the file named *input*.

−**d**   Display only the lines that are repeated in the file *input*.

−**c**   Precede each line displayed by the number of times it occurs.

−*m*   Ignore the first *m* fields and any blanks before each.

+*n*   Ignore the first *n* characters along with any blanks before each in the comparisons.

The **uniq** program reads an input file (or the standard input, if no input file is named) to compare adjacent lines. In the default case (that is, when no options are entered), the second and succeeding copies of repeated lines are removed. The remainder is written to the output file (or the standard output, if no output file is named). Repeated lines have to be adjacent to be found. Use the **sort** utility to arrange the input file so that all repeated lines will be adjacent. (The **sort** utility is discussed earlier in this chapter.)

The basic command line format for using **uniq** is

$ **uniq** [*option...*] [*input* [*output*]]

This causes removal of repeated adjacent lines in *input* file when copying to *output* file under direction of one or more *options*.

If you specify the −**u** (unique) option, only the lines not repeated in the input are displayed. The −**d** (duplicate) option causes only repeated lines to be displayed. The −**c** (count) option precedes each line with the number of times it occurs in the input file.

You may skip *m* fields and skip *n* characters before the comparison by specifying −*m* or +*n* options or both. (A *field* is defined as a series of nonspace, nontab characters that are separated from one another by spaces and tabs.) Note that you must include the whitespace characters that occur before the field in your count of the number of characters to be skipped in a field. The general command line format to use when specifying fields is

$ **uniq** [*option...* [+*n*] [−*m*]] [*input* [*output*]]

See the discussion of the **sort** command earlier in this chapter for a more complete description for specifying fields within a line of text.

Examples   Prepare for these examples as described in the introduction to this chapter. The **wordlist** is not necessary for this command.

For the following examples, a list of words that appear in **appeal** is required, one word per line. If your system has the **deroff** program, you may easily create such a list by entering **deroff** −w <**appeal** >**appeal2**. If your system doesn't have **deroff**, simply create the word list using your favorite editor and store the result in **appeal2**. The contents of **appeal2** are shown in the following example:

$ **deroff** −w <**appeal** >**appeal2**
$ **cat appeal2**
Now

is
the
time
for
all
good
citizens
to
come
to
the
aid
of
their
country
$

Use the **uniq** program to remove all duplicate words in the file **appeal2** by typing **uniq appeal2**. Note that the repeated words "the" and "to" were not removed. Words must be adjacent in order for **uniq** to remove them. Use the **sort** program to order the contents of **appeal2**. For instance, enter the command line **sort appeal2 | uniq** and note the results:

$ **sort appeal2 | uniq**
Now
aid
all
citizens
come
country
for
good

    is
    of
    the
    their
    time
    to
    $ ▨

To count the number of times the lines were repeated in **appeal2**, enter **sort
appeal2 | uniq −c**:

```
$ sort appeal2 | uniq −c
   1 Now
   1 aid
   1 all
   1 citizens
   1 come
   1 country
   1 for
   1 good
   1 is
   1 of
   2 the
   1 their
   1 time
   2 to
$ ▨
```

The −u option reports all the lines that are not repeated in the original file. To
try this, enter **sort appeal2 | uniq −u**:

```
$ sort appeal2 | uniq −u
Now
aid
all
citizens
come
country
```

```
for
good
is
of
their
time
$ ▮
```

On the other hand, if you wish to report only the lines that were duplicated in the original file, use the −d option. Enter **sort appeal2 | uniq −d**:

```
$ sort appeal2 | uniq −d
the
to
$ ▮
```

If you attempt to use the −c option with either the −u or −d option, you will obtain a report of the repeat count, but both of the other options will be ignored.

If the original file contains more than one field (column) of information, you may wish **uniq** to ignore one or more fields before the comparison for duplicates is made. To illustrate, use an editor and enter the following short list of names in the file named **namelist**.

```
$ cat namelist
John Q. Public
Judy N. Public
James A. Smith
Jean L. Smith
$ ▮
```

First apply the **uniq** command without skipping any fields by entering **uniq namelist**.

```
$ uniq namelist
John Q. Public
Judy N. Public
James A. Smith
Jean L. Smith
$ ▮
```

Note that no lines were removed because the lines are already unique when the entire line is considered.

To ignore the first two fields here (that is, the columns) and any blanks before each entry during the comparison, enter the command line **uniq −2 namelist newlist**. The **uniq** program chooses the first entry from each family as a representative. We also indicated an output file, **newlist**, in which to store the result.

```
$ uniq −2 namelist newlist
$ cat newlist
John Q. Public
James A. Smith
$
```

If you need to skip several more characters in the field (but not the entire field), you should specify an additional option in the form +*n*, where *n* is the number of additional characters to skip. To illustrate, use your editor again and add the following invoice numbers and dates to the end of the appropriate lines, as shown in the next example. Note that there are two tab characters separating field 4 from field 3.

```
$ cat namelist
John Q. Public      Inv.443:Jan10
Judy N. Public      Inv.534:Jan10
James A. Smith      Inv.495:Jan10
Jean L. Smith       Inv.605:Jan11
$
```

Now suppose that you wish to collapse all adjacent entries that were invoiced on the same date and obtain a count for each date. Since the date entry in the last field contains the invoice number as well as the date, you must skip to the last field and ignore the invoice number (which consists of the first eight characters of that field) in order to compare the lines solely on the basis of the date entry.

```
$ uniq −c −3 +8 namelist
   1 John Q. Public      Inv.443:Jan10
   1 Judy N. Public      Inv.534:Jan10
   1 James A. Smith      Inv.495:Jan10
   1 Jean L. Smith       Inv.605:Jan11
$
```

This is not the desired result. With **uniq** you also have to count the space or tab characters before the field in your character count into that field. Since there are two tab characters separating field 4 from the previous field, you need to specify a 10-character jump into field 4. Let's also store the result in the file **invoices**, as follows:

```
$ uniq −c −3 +10 namelist invoices
$ cat invoices
    3 John Q. Public        Inv.443:Jan10
    1 Jean L. Smith         Inv.605:Jan11
$ ▓
```

Before leaving this section, erase the extra files you created. Enter **rm appeal2 invoices *list**.

Messages   The following messages apply to all versions of **uniq**:

cannot open *input*
> The specified input file, named *input*, cannot be opened for reading.

cannot create *output*
> The specified output file, named *output*, cannot be created. Either a write-protected version of *output* already exists or you don't have permission to write in the directory to contain *output*.

Note that **uniq** generates no error messages for incorrectly specified command line options.

crypt — Encode or Decode Information

$ crypt [*key*] [<*filein*] [>*fileout*]
No Options

The **crypt** command is used to encrypt (or encode) and decrypt (or decode) files for security purposes. If you store your data files in encrypted form, no system user, not even the superuser, can read their contents. The UNIX line editors **ed** and **ex/vi** have an encryption mode that is compatible with **crypt**. You can use both programs, the editor to create and edit your data files, and **crypt** to prepare the data files for manipulation by UNIX text-processing utilities, so that the readable form of your text files would never appear on the system disk. We show you how to perform these operations in the "Examples" section of this command.

The basic command line format for invoking **crypt** is

$$\$ \text{ crypt } [\text{ key }]$$

This program requires that you specify an encryption *key* or *password* that **crypt** uses to encode its input text. You may specify *key* as a command line argument when you invoke **crypt**. If you don't specify *key*, **crypt** will prompt you for it after execution begins. Some versions of **ps** allow the entire invocation command line to be viewed by another user. For maximum security you should not specify the *key* on the invocation command line.

You should also select a key that cannot be easily guessed. Use the same guidelines for selecting a **crypt** key as those presented in the section on **passwd**.

Since **crypt** is a filter program, it reads its input data from the standard input file and writes its output on the standard output file. Generally you would have the shell redirect the input for **crypt** to come from one disk file and redirect the output from **crypt** to go to another disk file. Thus, you might employ the following more general command line format when using **crypt**:

$$\$ \text{ crypt } [\text{ key }] [<filein] [>fileout]$$

The **ed** and **ex/vi** editors are editor is the only other standard UNIX system programs that handle encrypted files. You might use the encryption mode of the editor to create and modify a text file, which will be encrypted before it is written to disk.

Otherwise you might employ **crypt** to decode the file, and then pipe the results into some other text programs, and finally encrypt the result again at the end of the pipeline. In this way the time that the document appears unencrypted (in readable form) is minimized.

Although the **crypt** program does not use the most powerful encryption scheme, it is certainly adequate for most purposes. Any cryptanalysis applied to an encrypted file would probably require so much effort, both in human and machine time, that it would not be practical for anyone wishing to tamper with your encrypted files.

Note that the Bell documentation for **crypt** is careful not to guarantee the results of using this program.

Examples Prepare for these examples as discussed in the introduction to this chapter. The **wordlist** is not necessary for this command.

For our first example, let's encode the contents of **poem**. Enter **crypt <poem >poem.secret**, and note that you will be prompted for an encryption key:

```
$ crypt <poem >poem.secret
Enter key: ▓
```

Now enter in your key, a code made up of as many as eight alphabetic characters and digits. Remember your key, since you cannot decrypt your text file without it. Now if you examine **poem.secret** by entering **cat poem.secret**, you should see gibberish characters.

Now try the same example, but this time specify the encryption key as you invoke **crypt** by entering **crypt** *key* **<poem >poem.secret**, and note that the contents of **poem.secret** are the same as when **crypt** prompts you for the encryption key.

To decode **poem.secret**, use the same encryption key and enter **crypt <poem.secret**. After you enter the encryption key, **crypt** should display the original contents of **poem** on the terminal screen (standard output file), as shown:

```
$ crypt <poem.secret
Enter key:
Roses are Red
Violets are Blue
Sugar is Sweet
And so are You.
$ ▓
```

The remainder of this tutorial outlines the steps required (1) to create an encrypted document with the **ed** editor, (2) to use the **crypt** utility to decode the text momentarily in order to pipe it into one or more UNIX system utilities, and (3) to encode the document again for storage in nonreadable form.

First invoke **ed** (or **ex**) to edit the file **poem** using encryption mode by entering **ed −x poem** (or **ex −x poem**). The editor will respond with a prompt like "Key: " or "Enter file encryption key: ".

```
$ ed −x poem
Enter file encryption key: ▓
```

At this point type in a password. For example, type **secret** and press RETURN; you will now be in the editor. To ensure that no one sees your encryption password, it will not be echoed back to your terminal.

Note that you may invoke **ed** and then enter encryption mode by typing **X** from the command mode. You will be prompted for a key as before. The **ex** or **vi** editors won't allow you to enter encryption mode after you invoke it, so you must specify the −x as a command line option when you invoke this editor.

While the editor is in encryption mode, the read (r), edit (e), and write (w) commands will encrypt and decrypt the text with the key you just specified. You work with unencrypted text in the edit buffer.

For instance, enter 1,$p, and you will see the text appear readable as before. The contents of the edit buffer are readable (unencrypted) when the editor is in encryption mode. However, if you write the contents of the buffer to disk, it will be encrypted.

```
$ ed −x poem
Enter file encryption key: 
62
1,$p
Roses are Red
Violets are Blue
Sugar is Sweet
And so are You.
w
62
q
$ cat poem
[ Gibberish ]
$ 
```

You can always use the three editors in encryption mode to read and modify encoded text. You may wish to use other UNIX system commands to manipulate the text without having a copy of the text in decoded form stored on your file system. First decrypt the text with the **crypt** program, pipe it through the desired sequence of utilities, and then encrypt the file again for security storage. Since both the UNIX editors and the **crypt** program use the same encryption algorithm, encrypted data files are interchangeable between these two programs.

Continuing our example, we will use the **sort** program to order the text of **poem** and then store the encoded result as **poem.sort**. Enter the command line shown in the next example. Answer both prompts with the same encryption key.

```
$ (sleep 10;crypt <poem) | sort | crypt >poem.sort
Enter key:
Enter key:
$ 
```

Notice that we delayed the key prompt for one instance of **crypt** since confusion results if they both ask for the key at the same time. We used **sleep** to suspend the execution of the first instance by ten seconds, which should be sufficient time to enter the key for the other instance of **crypt**.

Now invoke **ed**, enter encryption mode, specify the same encryption key, and finally ask to edit **poem.sort**.

```
$ ed
X
Enter file encryption key:
e poem.sort
62
1,$p
And so are You.
Roses are Red
Sugar is Sweet
Violets are Blue
q
$
```

At no time during this process was unencrypted text present on the disk. This means that if another user who has access to your files tries to read your files while you are editing, that user will only encounter undecipherable text.

Messages   The following message applies to all versions of **crypt**:

> **crypt: cannot generate** *key*
> The *key* cannot be encrypted. See your system administrator for assistance.

tr — Translate Characters

> `$ tr [ option... ] string1 [string2]`
>
> Options for All Versions:
> −c   This option complements the contents of *string1;* that is, all characters except those in *string1* are considered.
> −d   This option deletes all the input characters specified in *string1*. Any *string2* is ignored.

> **−s**   This option compresses or squeezes all strings of repeated output characters that are in *string2* into single characters.

Use the **tr** command to convert one character into another character, compress a group of characters into a single character, or delete specified characters. The **tr** command provides a quicker way to substitute one character for another than do the UNIX editors, which, of course, must be entered and exited. The **tr** command acts, in effect, like a stream character editor. With **tr**, furthermore, you can eliminate unwanted control characters that cannot be deleted easily through the UNIX editors.

This command is a filter program that doesn't recognize file arguments. Thus, the input for this command may either be a data stream from a pipeline or the redirected data from a disk file. The output appears on your terminal screen unless it is directed into a pipeline or redirected to a disk file. The **tr** command without any options takes two string arguments, designated *string1* and *string2*. The command line format is

$$\text{\$ } \textbf{tr } \textit{string1 string2}$$

The characters specified in *string2* will be substituted for the corresponding characters in *string1* when the input is copied to the output. For instance, specify

$$\text{\$ } \textbf{tr abc ABC}$$

to translate any occurrences of the lowercase letters *a*, *b*, or *c* in the standard input to their corresponding uppercase value on the standard output.

The general command line format for using **tr** is

$$\text{\$ } \textbf{tr } [\textit{ option...}] \textit{ string1 } [\textit{string2}]$$

All versions recognize the same three options to modify the translation. A delete (−**d**) option causes all input characters that are named in *string1* to be deleted from the output stream. Any *string2* is simply ignored when you indicate the delete option.

The complement option (−**c**) complements the contents of *string1*. In other words, the −**c** option means that **tr** will translate all input characters *except* those in *string1*. The net effect is the generation of the reverse of *string1*. Since *string1* usually names only a few characters, the complement is generally much larger. The printing characters (excluding the control characters) that are the complement of *string1* would be all characters in the ASCII sequence *not* in *string1*.

The squeeze option (−s) is used when you wish to remove repeated sequences of characters. In other words, all characters in *string1* that occur in the input as a repeated sequence will be compressed into only a single character in the output. Frequently the squeeze option is used in conjunction with the complement option to remove characters that would otherwise be duplicated on output.

The Bell Version 7 and Berkeley version recognize a shorthand notation, *a-b*, as indicating a range of characters from *a* to *b* in increasing ASCII order. For the Bell Systems III and V versions, you must enclose the range in square brackets, like [*a-b*]. You must then prevent the square brackets from being interpreted by the shell either by preceding each bracket with a backslash, as in \[*a-b*\], or by enclosing the entire string in single or double quotation marks, as in "[*a-b*]".

In their character-by-character mapping of one string onto another, all versions of **tr** will translate a longer *string1* to a shorter *string2*. The Bell Version 7 and Berkeley version duplicate the last character indicated in *string2* so that the effective length of *string2* equals *string1*.

The Bell Systems III and V versions do not duplicate the last character of *string2* when *string1* is longer. If you do specify translation of a longer *string1* into a shorter *string2*, only the characters in *string2* corresponding to characters in *string1* will be translated. For instance, if you specified the command line

$ **tr** "[0-9]" "[a-d]"

only the numbers 0 through 3 would be translated into *a* through *d*. All the other input characters (4 through 9) would pass through unchanged.

If you are using one of the recent Bell versions and you wish to translate *string1* into a single character that is repeated so *string2* equals the length of *string1*, you can use an expression in the form [*a*∗*n*], which means *n* repetitions of the character *a*. Thus the command line

$ **tr** "[0-9]" "[a∗10]"

would cause all digits in the standard input to be translated to a lowercase *a*. Note that if the first digit of *n* is a zero, then *n* is taken to be an octal value; otherwise, it is considered to be a decimal value. You may omit the *n* and indicate [*a*∗] to represent an arbitrarily large number of *a* characters. Thus, you could have specified the shorter form

$ **tr** "[0-9]" "[a∗]"

to translate all digits to a lowercase *a*.

All versions of **tr** allow you to indicate any ASCII character by typing a backslash followed by one, two, or three octal digits corresponding to its ASCII code. (See Appendix E for a table of ASCII characters and their octal equivalents.) This approach is necessary for specifying nonprinting control characters.

A backslash followed by any other character stands for that character. This notation is useful when you wish to use any individual character that might otherwise be interpreted in a special way by the shell.

This command will not accept the ASCII null character in either *string1* or *string2*. This command always deletes the ASCII null character from the input.

Examples Prepare for these examples as described in the introduction to this chapter. The **wordlist** is not necessary for this command.

In many of the following examples, where we do not redirect input from a file, after you type the command line, the cursor will be poised at the beginning of the next line waiting for further input.

For our first example, enter the command **tr abc ABC** and note that the cursor appears at the beginning of the next line.

$ tr abc ABC

Now continue typing the text shown in the next example and end the line with a RETURN. The system will immediately display the translated input.

$ tr abc ABC
The quick brown fox jumps over the lazy dog.
The quiCk Brown fox jumps over the lAzy dog.

Notice that the cursor is waiting at the beginning of the next line. You can either type more lines to continue the translation process or press your end-of-file code (usually a ^D) to exit **tr**.

If you are using the Bell Version 7 or Berkeley **tr** command, you may convert all lowercase letters (a through z) to the corresponding uppercase value (A through Z) by entering the command **tr a-z A-Z**. Next, input your text, end the line with a RETURN, and exit with your end-of-file code:

```
$ tr a-z A-Z
The quick brown fox jumps over the lazy dog.
THE QUICK BROWN FOX JUMPS OVER THE LAZY DOG.
[ ^D ]
$ ▓
```

The Bell Systems III and V versions require a different invocation command line: namely, **tr** "[a-z]" "[A-Z]".

The **tr** command is a filter program. You may use the shell to redirect its standard input or output or both to be a disk file. For instance, the contents of the file **appeal** may be translated to uppercase and stored in another file (**appeal2**) by entering the command **tr** "[a-z]" "[A-Z]" <appeal >appeal2:

```
$ tr "[a-z]" "[A-Z]" <appeal >appeal2
$ cat appeal2
NOW IS THE TIME
FOR ALL GOOD CITIZENS
TO COME TO THE AID
OF THEIR COUNTRY.
$ ▓
```

Or you might employ **tr** in a pipeline to transform text into uppercase:

```
$ cat appeal | tr a-z A-Z
NOW IS THE TIME
FOR ALL GOOD CITIZENS
TO COME TO THE AID
OF THEIR COUNTRY.
$ ▓
```

Three options modify the action of the **tr** command. The −**d** option deletes characters indicated in *string1* when copying to the output. For example, you may remove all space characters ' ' from the input with the command **tr** −**d** ' '. Here the space character is indicated by the single quotation marks surrounding one space.

```
$ tr −d ' '
```
The quick brown fox jumps over the lazy dog.
Thequickbrownfoxjumpsoverthelazydog.
[^D]
$

Note that it is not appropriate to specify a *string2* here. If you do, it will be ignored.

The squeeze option may be used to replace more than one consecutive occurrence of a specified character by a single character. Here we convert two spaces between words into one space.

```
$ tr −s ' '
```
The quick brown fox jumps over the lazy dog.
The quick brown fox jumps over the lazy dog.
[^D]
$

You could use this same approach to remove multiple blank lines in a file. For instance, you would enter the command line **tr −s ' \012' <input.file** to remove adjacent blank lines from **input.file**. This would be useful for removing the extraneous blank lines produced by **pr** and **nroff**. For example:

```
$ pr poem | tr −s ' \012'
```
Nov 19 18:17 1984 poem Page 1
Roses are Red
Violets are Blue
Sugar is Sweet
And so are You.
$

What happens if *string1* has more characters than *string2*? The Bell Systems III and V versions simply ignore the extra characters. In other words, only the first group of characters in *string1* that correspond to characters in *string2* will be translated. Other characters in *string1* will simply be ignored as shown.

```
$ tr "[a-z]" "[1-9]" <appeal
Now 9s t85 t9m5
6or 111 7oo4 39t9z5ns
to 3om5 to t85 194
o6 t859r 3ountry.
$ ▐
```

Here the first nine letters of the alphabet are replaced, but the rest are left untouched.

In contrast, the Bell Version 7 and Berkeley version will pad *string2* to the length of *string1* by duplicating the last character in *string2*. When you use these versions, the result will be something like the following:

```
$ tr a-z 1-9 <appeal
999 99 985 9995
699 199 7994 39999599
·99 3995 99 985 194
96 98599 3999999.
$ ▐
```

Here all lowercase letters are mapped onto a smaller subset of numerals. The numeral 9 is repeated frequently because, as the last character in *string2*, it is used to pad *string2*, which was quite a bit shorter than *string1*.

You can use the complement option (−c) to specify all characters *except* those in *string1*. Since this usually produces a set of characters larger than *string2*, the Bell Version 7 and Berkeley version automatically pad *string2* to the new length of *string1* by duplicating the last character in *string2*. Since this may produce a confusing display, the −s (squeeze) option is usually concatenated with the complement option. This next example shows how to convert any character that is not a lowercase letter (including new lines) into a space character:

```
$ tr −cs a-z " " <appeal
ow is the time for all good citizens to come to the aid of their country $ ▐
```

· Here we represented the ASCII space character as `" "`, but you could have used `' '`, `'\040'`, or `'\40'` as well.

Another useful application is to convert all nonalphabetic characters into new line characters through the following command line:

tr —cs "[A-Z] [a-z]" "[\012]" <appeal

This will create a list of all the words in **appeal**, one word per line. The 012 is the octal value for the new line character. With such a one-word-per-line list, you could use other UNIX utilities to perform statistical operations or to create a customized dictionary.

The Bell Systems III and V versions require that you pad *string2* explicitly by using the notation [*a*∗] to get the same result as we just got:

$ tr —cs "[a-z]" "[\040∗]" <appeal
ow is the time for all good citizens to come to the aid of their country $ ▓

You could concatenate the complement and delete option to delete all characters except those specified in the first string argument. For example, enter **tr —cd** "[a-z]" <appeal to delete all characters in **appeal** that aren't lowercase letters:

$ tr —cd "[a-z]" <appeal
owisthetimeforallgoodcitizenstocometotheaidoftheircountry $ ▓

Use the **tr** command to solve your character translation requirements for processing data. You may wish to practice on a small test file or line input from the keyboard before applying **tr** to your actual data.

Messages   The following messages apply to the Bell Systems III and V versions of **tr**. The Bell Version 7 and Berkeley version do not produce any error messages.

> **Bad string**
> You didn't specify *string1* or *string2* correctly.

Communication

The UNIX system provides several utilities that enable users to communicate with each other on a given system and between systems. We will discuss two in particular: **mail**, which is used to send messages to a user's *mailfile*, and **write**, which is used to send messages directly between user terminals. In this section, we also explain the UNIX **calendar** program, which is used to provide an engagement calendar reminder service.

mail — Send or Receive Electronic Mail Among Users

> **$ mail** *username...*
>
> **$ mail** [*option...*] [**−f** *file*]
>
> Options for All Versions:
>
> **−p**   Display entire contents of *mailfile* without prompting for instructions; then **mail** exits.
>
> **−q**   Cause **mail** to exit after receiving an interrupt signal without changing the *mailfile*.
>
> **−r**   Reverse order in which **mail** displays messages.
>
> **−f***file*   Use the named *file* as if it were the *mailfile*.

After you sign on to your UNIX system, the system may inform you that you have messages in your *mailfile* by displaying a message like "You have mail" before you see your shell prompt. Some systems are also set up to inform you when new mail has arrived while you are logged on. If new mail arrives, you will see a message like "new mail arrived" after the current command has finished executing.

There are two basic ways to invoke the **mail** command (that is why two format statements are listed in the options box). One way you invoke **mail** is for sending a message to one or more recipients, and the other is for reading the contents of your *mailfile*. To send a message to one or more users (or even to yourself as a reminder) use the following command line format when invoking **mail**:

$ mail *username...*

The **mail** command will store the text you type in a buffer until it reads the end-of-file character (^D is the default). Some versions of **mail** will terminate message entry when you type a line containing only a period followed immediately by a RETURN. The **mail** program then places the message in the proper *mailfile*. A header listing the sender's account name and a postmark (date and time of origination) precedes each message.

The *mailfile* is an ordinary file in which messages sent via **mail** are stored. This file, which is also frequently referred to as the *mailbox*, has the same basename as the recipient's user name. In this discussion of **mail**, we will refer the *mailfile* as

/user/mail/username, but when you execute the examples on-line, you should replace **username** with your actual user name. Note that while the name of the *mailfile* in Bell Systems III and V versions of mail is **usr/mail/username**, this name (pathname) is slightly different in earlier versions of the command (usually **usr/spool/mail/username**).

To read the contents of your *mailfile*, use this command line format when invoking **mail**:

$$\$ \text{ mail } [\text{ option... }] [-f \text{ file }]$$

If no options are specified, the last message in *mailfile* will be displayed first. This order can be reversed with the −**r** option. You can read all your messages at once and then exit to the shell with the −**p** option. With another option, −**q**, you can exit from **mail** without changing the *mailfile* contents when you type the interrupt code. Usually an interrupt only stops what **mail** is doing and returns you to the **mail** program command mode (usually indicated by the **?** prompt). With the −**f** option you may specify an alternate *mailfile* instead of the default, **/usr/mail/username**. This is useful, for instance, when accessing messages from your own mailbox file in your home directory (named **mbox**) for manipulation by **mail**.

Unless the **mail** program was invoked with the −**p** option, after displaying each message **mail** will issue a prompt, usually a **?**, and wait for instructions from the standard input (the keyboard by default). Use one of the commands shown in Table 6-3 after the **mail** prompt appears to direct the disposal of the message, exit **mail**, or perform some other task.

Examples   Let's practice using **mail**. Prepare for these examples as described in the introduction to this chapter, but do not link **wordlist**. In addition, the examples that follow assume the following three messages are in your *mailfile*, **/usr/mail/username**. You should use your favorite editor to add these messages to your *mailfile* so that you can work with the examples in this section. Of course, you should substitute actual account names on your system for **barbm**, **spilchuk**, and **username**.

From barbm Fri Aug 10 10:34 PDT 1984
Dear Becca,
Please call me as soon as possible.

From spilchuk Tue Sep 4 09:56 PDT 1984
Don't forget the meeting Friday at Osento.

From username Fri Sep 7 09:00 PDT 1984
Remember dentist appointment at 10 am Monday.

Table 6-3. *Interactive* **mail** *Commands*

Command	Description
RETURN	Display the next message. The **mail** program exits after printing the last message.
+	Same as RETURN.
d	Delete the last message displayed and go on to the next message, if any.
p	Display the previous message again.
—	Go back to last message and print it again.
s [*file...*]	Save the message by appending to *file*. If no filename is specified, the message will be saved in a file named **mbox** in your home directory.
w [*file...*]	Save the message, without a header (sender's postmark), by appending to *file*. If no filename is given, the message is saved in **mbox** in your home directory.
m [*username...*]	Forward the message to one or more accounts, *username*.
q	Return undeleted messages to *mailfile* and exit **mail** program.
EOT (end-of-text)	Same as **q**. EOT is the name for the ASCII ^D character that is used to signal the end-of-text entry.
x	Place *all* messages back in *mailfile* and exit.
!*commandline*	Invoke a subshell to execute shell *commandline*.
?	Any invalid command character will cause this list of commands for message disposition to be displayed on your terminal.

The **mail** program provides a convenient way to leave yourself a reminder when you next log in. To try this now, simply type **mail**, a space, and your user name, and press RETURN. Now type your message, and when you are finished, type a period as the first and only entry on a new line and press RETURN. Alternatively, you can press the end-of-file character (a ^D by default) to send your message and exit from **mail**.

$ **username**

Remember the meeting this evening.

$

Remember to replace **username** by your actual account name (user name) in all the examples in this section.

If you wish to change your message text before mailing it, you can use an editor to create your message, save the desired result to disk, and then instruct the shell to redirect the standard input for the **mail** program to come from the disk file. This technique is useful when you wish to create a longer document and make any necessary corrections before mailing.

As an example, use an editor to enter the text of the message "Meet with department managers a week from Wednesday." Then save the file as **reminder**. Now send the message to yourself as a reminder:

$ **cat reminder**

Meet with department managers a week from Wednesday.

$ **mail username <reminder**

$

Now log off your system and log on again. You should see a message from the system informing you that "You have mail" (although some systems don't support this feature). To read your mail, simply enter **mail** (the most recent message will be displayed). Every time you press RETURN, the next message will be displayed. The **mail** program exits after displaying the last message in your mail file.

Now invoke **mail** again, and after the first message is displayed, enter ? to read all the options you have for disposing of this message.

$ **mail**

From username Fri Sep 7 12:40 PDT 1984

Meet with department managers a week from Wednesday.

? ?

q	quit
x	exit without changing mail
p	print
s [file]	save (default mbox)
w [file]	same without header

—	print previous
d	delete
+	next (no delete)
m [user]	mail to user
! cmd	execute cmd
? ▓	

All the commands listed here are explained more fully in Table 6-3. Enter **s** to save the message, and **mail** will append the message to a file named **mbox** in your home directory.

Once you have saved the message we just viewed, the next message in *mailfile* will be displayed (you may have to press RETURN first). Forward this message to user **barbm** by entering **m barbm**. (Of course, you should substitute the name of an account on your local UNIX system in place of **barbm**.) The next message in your mailbox will be displayed automatically, as the following example shows:

```
? s
From username Fri Sep 7 12:38 PDT 1984
Remember the meeting this evening.

? m barbm
From username Fri Sep 7 09:00 PDT 1984
Remember dentist appointment at 10am Monday.
? ▓
```

The next message in your mailbox was "Remember dentist appointment at 10am Monday." Display the next message by pressing RETURN. Then delete this message by entering **d**, and the next message will be printed.

Before leaving **mail**, try executing a shell command to examine the contents of **mbox**. For instance, type **!cat mbox**. This verifies that the last message was in fact saved. Then exit mail by entering **q**. Now examine the contents of the *mailfile* for the user you forwarded the message to. Of course, you must have permission to access that user's files (in this case for **/usr/mail/barbm**) to do this.

The following example shows the actions we just described:

```
From spilchuk Tue Sep 4 09:56 PDT 1984
Don't forget the meeting Friday at Osento.
? d
```

From barbm Fri Aug 10 10:34 PDT 1984

Dear Becca,

Please call me as soon as possible.

? !cat mbox

From username Fri Sep 7 12:40 PDT 1984

Meet with department managers a week from Wednesday.

!

? q

$ cat /usr/mail/barbm

>From username Fri Sep 7 12:38 PDT 1984 forwarded by username

Remember the meeting this evening.

$ ▓

Note that the forwarded message has a greater-than sign ($>$) preceding the postmark and the message "forwarded by username", which tells **barbm** the source.

When you first invoke the **mail** command to read your messages, there are a number of options you can specify. If you want to read all the messages in your *mailfile* one after the other without your intervention and then leave **mail**, use the −**p** (print) option:

$ mail −p

From username Fri Sep 7 09:00 PDT 1984

Remember dentist appointment at 10am Monday.

From barbm Fri Aug 10 10:34 PDT 1984

Dear Becca,

Please call me as soon as possible.

$ ▓

To "reverse" the order of the messages so that you read the first message (oldest chronologically) in your *mailfile*, enter **mail** −**r**. You could concatenate this option with the print option to read all your messages, oldest first.

```
$ mail —pr
From barbm Fri Aug 10 10:34 PDT 1984
Dear Becca,
Please call me as soon as possible.

From username Fri Sep 7 09:00 PDT 1984
Remember dentist appointment at 10am Monday.

$
```

As a final example, let's say you are going on vacation and wish to have all your mail forwarded to account **spilchuk**. You would place the directive "Forward to spilchuk" on the first line of your *mailfile* with an editor. Then mail intended for your account would appear in the *mailfile* for **spilchuk**.

```
$ ed /usr/mail/username
172
1i
Forward to spilchuk
.
w
192
q
$
```

The actual number of characters read in and written out to your *mailfile* may differ from what we show here, but the number of characters written out should be 20 more in any case than the number read in.

Now mail yourself a short test message as shown. If you can examine the *mailfile* belonging to account **spilchuk**, you would observe the test message. If you try to read your own mail, you will be informed that your mail is being forwarded:

```
$ mail username
This is a test of forwarding.
.
$ cat /usr/mail/spilchuk
```

From username Fri Sep 7 12:55 PDT 1984
This is a test of forwarding.

$ **mail**
Your mail is being forwarded to spilchuk
and your mailbox contains extra stuff
$ ▓

Note that the message "and your mailbox contains extra stuff" means that there
are messages in *mailfile* in addition to the forwarding directive.

Messages   The following messages may appear when you use the **mail** command
to read your mail.

The error, warning, and informational messages displayed by your version of
mail may not be exactly like those presented here, but the meaning of the messages should be similar.

> **mail: illegal option—*option***
> Here *option* is an invalid invocation option for the **mail** command.
>
> **mail: cannot open /tmp/ma*XXXXX* for writing**
> *XXXXX* would be the actual process number (PID) of the **mail** program
> process. This error message would occur if you didn't have permission to
> write in the **/tmp** directory. Check your access permissions for **/tmp** and
> see your system administrator if you need assistance.
>
> **mail: permission denied**
> Indicates that you don't have read permission for your own *mailfile*. You
> should be able to enable read permission for **/usr/mail/username** with
> **chmod** since you are the owner of your *mailfile*.
>
> **mail: cannot open *mailfile***
> This message could occur if you employed the **−f** (file) option and speci-
> fied a *mailfile* argument that doesn't exist or for which you don't have
> read permission.
>
> **No mail**
> You don't have any messages in your *mailfile* to read.
>
> **Your mail is being forwarded to *username***
> This message occurs if you attempt to read your mail when you are using
> the *forwarding feature*. That is, if your *mailfile* contains "Forward to
> *username*" on the first line, any messages sent to your *mailfile* would have
> been forwarded on to the *mailfile* for *username*.

and your mailbox contains extra stuff
Indicates that your *mailfile* contains messages in addition to the forwarding directive.

mail: /usr/mail/username.lock not creatable after 10 tries
This message indicates that the *lockfile* used when performing critical manipulations of your *mailfile* cannot be created. Use **chmod** to enable write permission for the *lockfile* so you can erase it with **rm**. If you are unsuccessful, see your system administrator for help.

The following error messages may occur while you are using the interactive commands in response to the **?** prompt to dispose of your mail messages:

invalid command
This message might occur if you didn't follow the save, write, or mail (forwarding) instruction by whitespace before the argument to that instruction—for instance, entering **mbarbm** instead of **m barbm**.

mail: cannot append to *file*
Occurs if the file specified as an argument to the save or write instruction could not be appended to (by writing). Enable write permission for *file* with **chmod**.

null name
Occurs in response to giving a "null" user name as an argument for the mail instruction (for instance, entering **m !** in response to the **?** prompt).

usage

q	quit
x	exit without changing mail
p	print
s [file]	save (default mbox)
w [file]	same without header
—	print previous
d	delete
+	next (no delete)
m [user]	mail to user
! cmd	execute cmd

A list of valid instructions for disposing of your messages is displayed whenever you type an invalid instruction.

The following messages may appear when you use the **mail** command to send your mail:

mail: cannot reopen /tmp/ma*XXXXX* for reading
Occurs if there is no read permission for your temporary *mailfile*, /tmp/ma*XXXXX*.

Mail saved in dead.letter

Means that the message you intended to send was saved in the file named **dead.letter** in your current directory. This warning occurs if (1) an interrupt signal is received while you are typing in your message to be sent; (2) the intended recipient for the message is not a valid UNIX system account, or (3) an "unbounded forwarding" error occurs. For (2) check the password file, **/etc/passwd**, for the correct account user name.

mail: cannot create dead.letter

Occurs if you cannot create the file **dead.letter** in your current directory. If **dead.letter** already exists, enable write permission and erase it. Otherwise change to a directory for which you have write permission when using **mail.**

unbounded forwarding

This message occurs if you attempt to forward messages through more than 20 user accounts. Reduce the number of forwarding requests, or check for the accounts having an endless forwarding loop. Such loops can be set up if, for example, account x forwards mail to account y, and account y forwards mail back to account x, and so on.

write — Write to Another User

$ write *username* [*ttyname*]

No Options

The **write** program permits direct communication between two terminals that are currently logged on the same UNIX system. After one system user invokes the **write** program, all lines of text that are typed at that user's keyboard will be sent to the recipient's terminal screen. The recipient UNIX user may also invoke **write** to answer and thus establish a direct two-way on-line communication between the two users.

Before initiating communication with **write,** use the **who** command to see if the person you want to write to is currently on-line. Since a user can be logged in to more than one terminal at a time, you may need to specify the destination terminal name as well. The **who** command also lists the terminal names.

To initiate transmission, use the command line format

$ write *username* [*ttyname*]

Here *username* is the recipient's user account (or login) name. The *ttyname* should be supplied if *username* is logged in more than one terminal. You should not begin the terminal name designation with **/dev/**, since **write** automatically adds this prefix.

The **write** command scans the user accounting file, **/etc/utmp**, for *username*. The **/etc/utmp** file is a publicly readable file that lists all users currently logged on, their terminal names, and time of log on. If *username* cannot be found, **write** issues an error message and exits. If *username* is logged on more than one terminal, **write** gives a warning message and tries to communicate with the terminal that corresponds to the first entry for *username* in **/etc/utmp**. However, if that particular terminal is not being used, the recipient wouldn't know you were trying to communicate. In this case, use the **who** command to find an alternate terminal, or examine a **ps** listing for all system processes to see if a terminal owned by the desired recipient is currently being used.

The recipient will receive a message on his or her screen indicating your attempt to communicate:

Message from *username userttyname*...

The **write** program informs the sender if the message cannot be delivered. However, the sender won't know that the recipient has actually seen and read the message unless the recipient also invokes **write** to communicate back to the original sender.

Interterminal messages cannot be received if the recipient is using a program such as **nroff** or **pr**. These programs temporarily disallow such messages in order to prevent outside influence over the formatted terminal output. Also, the recipient can deny write permission on his or her terminal by using the **mesg** program, as discussed in the next section.

If the recipient wishes to return your communication, he or she needs to invoke **write** specifying your user name and terminal:

$ **write** *username* [*userttyname*]

Messages are sent a line at a time when RETURN is pressed. The Bell Laboratories documentation recommends using the following protocol to prevent messages from crossing and producing confusing displays:

- When you first write to another user, wait for that user to respond before you start to send your message.

- Keep each message line short since the recipient can't see what you type until you press RETURN.

- Each party should end each message with a distinctive signal, such as "o" for "over."

- Each party should use a signal for "over and out" such as "oo" when he or she wishes to terminate the conversation.

To execute a shell command without leaving the **write** program, type the following as the first expression on a line:

!command line

Note that neither the *!command line* nor any output from the command is sent to the user with whom you are communicating. The **write** program will display an ! on a line by itself to let you know that the shell command has finished.

To exit the **write** program and return to the shell, use a ^D. The **write** program will transmit the message "EOF" to the recipient's terminal, indicating that you have exited **write**.

The **write** command will always attempt to communicate with a specified *ttyname* whether or not a valid *username* is specified. Thus, you could communicate with a particular terminal irrespective of the user logged in at that terminal. For instance, entering **write - console** would attempt communication with /dev/console, the system console.

Many UNIX systems allow you to use **stty** to change the way the kernel program processes terminal transmission so that a character can be transmitted to a recipient terminal as soon as it is typed at the sending terminal keyboard. If you don't transmit a character at a time, the entire line is not sent until a RETURN is pressed.

Examples   Prepare for these examples as described in the introduction to this chapter. The **wordlist** is not necessary for this command.

As a first example of using **write**, try writing to yourself. This will help you become familiar with the protocol. To initiate transmission, enter **write username**, substituting your user name for **username**. Then enter a message like the one shown in boldface in the following example:

```
$ write username
Message from username tty01...
I'm writing to myself.
I'm writing to myself.
o
o
```

After invoking the **write** program to write to your own account, you received a message like "Message from username tty01...", telling you that **username** was initiating transmission from terminal tty01. Of course, your *ttyname* will probably be different. On the next line, you typed yourself the message "I'm writing to myself." After pressing RETURN, you saw that the message was received. On the next line, you typed **o** to indicate end of message. The "o" is a voluntary protocol, *not* a signal recognized by **write**.

Execute the shell command to list your directory while still in the **write** program by entering **!ls**.

!ls

Mail

appeal

poem

!

■

After the shell command was executed, an exclamation mark "!" appeared on your terminal screen. Although there is no prompt, you are still in the **write** program. Send yourself a sign-off message and then leave **write** by pressing a ^D.

Time to leave...

Time to leave...

oo

oo

[^D]

EOF

$ ■

Note that the ^D does not appear nor does it introduce a blank line, as shown here. The **write** program sends you an "EOF" message before you return to the shell.

Now try to send a message to another user. Use the **who** command to see if you know anyone currently logged in. Use the **ps** command with the −**a** (Bell Version 7 or Berkeley) or −**e** (Bell Systems III or V) option to learn what process the desired recipient is executing. To avoid confusing that person's screen display, you should choose to write to someone who is using the shell interactively (indicated by "-sh" or "-csh" in the rightmost column of the **ps** output) rather than to someone who is using a program (such as an editor).

For our next example, let's say you wish to send several system users the same message. This message will be created with an editor. First, as a courtesy to prepare each user for receiving a message, use **write** to send a short notice informing them that they are about to receive a message via **write**. This way they won't be distracted when their screen fills with text.

The next example shows a simulation of the one-way communication from account **username** to account **friend**. The arrows are used to indicate cause and effect.

Terminal Display of **username:**		Terminal Display of **friend:**
$ write friend	------>	**Message from username tty01...**
Hi, I'm going to	------>	**Hi, I'm going to**
send you a message.	------>	**send you a message.**
[^D]	------>	**EOF**
$ ▓		▓

Now **username** uses an editor to create the message text and save it as a disk file. The message is sent by instructing the shell to redirect the standard input for **write** to be the file containing the message:

$ **cat message**
Board Meeting tonight.
Please bring minutes
from the last meeting.
$ **write friend <message**
$ ▓

The terminal display for **friend** would appear something like:

$ Message from username tty01...
Board meeting tonight.
Please bring minutes
from the last meeting.
EOF
▓

Let's say that user **friend** wishes to invoke **write** to ask **username** for more information. This next screen shows a simulation of a two-way communication between **username** and **friend**.

Terminal Display of **username:**   Terminal Display of **friend:**

Message from friend tty03...	<------	**$ write username**
write friend	------>	Message from username tty01...
Thanks, what time?	<------	**Thanks, what time?**
o	<------	o
8 o'clock sharp.	------>	8 o'clock sharp.
o	------>	o
Okay, see you there.	<------	**Okay, see you there.**
oo	<------	oo
EOF	<------	**[^D]**
[^D]	------>	EOF
$ ▓		$ ▓

In this example **friend** initiates communication with **username.** This user waits until **username** responds before typing the question. This way **friend** is sure that **username** has seen the message "Message from friend tty03..." and is able to communicate. After each message is exchanged, the voluntary protocol "o" (or "oo") is sent to signal the end of the message (or session). Each user exits **write** by typing a ^D (which doesn't actually appear) and **write** transmits "EOF" to the other user just before exiting.

Messages   The following messages may appear when you have made an error while using any version of the **write** command:

usage: write user [ttyname]
  You must at least specify a *username* argument for **write.**

write: cannot open /etc/utmp
  The user accounting file cannot be read. See your system administrator.

write: cannot find your tty
  The **write** program cannot determine your terminal name. See your system administrator.

username **not logged in**
  The specified recipient, *username,* is not currently logged on. Note that the **write** program doesn't check to see if *username* has an account on your system.

username **logged more than once**
writing to *ttyname*
  The intended recipient is logged on more than one terminal and no *ttyname* was designated when invoking **write.** The **write** program will

attempt to contact *ttyname,* which corresponds to the first entry for *user-name* found in **/etc/utmp.**

write: no such tty
There is no terminal named *ttyname* connected to the system.

write: timeout opening their tty
The recipient's terminal can't be opened for writing with a certain time interval, usually 5 seconds. Wait and try again later.

write: permission denied
The recipient's terminal is write-protected. Try again later or send electronic mail instead.

write: cannot fork — try again
This message occurs if you attempt to execute a shell command from within **write** and the total number of processes would exceed either the system-wide or user-imposed limit.

The following error message is generated by the System V version of this command:

username is logged on more than one place.
You are connected to "*ttyname*".
Other locations are:
ttyname...
The specified recipient *username* is logged on more than once. In this case all alternate terminals are listed for you.

The following informational messages apply to all versions of the **write** command:

Message from *username* ttyname
Indicates that account *username* on *ttyname* is using **write** to initiate communciation with you.

EOF
This message is received by the recipient when the sender exits **write** by issuing an end-of-file, hangup, interrupt, or quit signal.

mesg — Permit or Deny Messages

$ mesg [*option*]

Options for All Versions:
none	Report your terminal write permission.
n	Remove write permission for your terminal.
y	Grant write permission for your terminal.

The **mesg** utility provides a convenient way to prevent other users from writing on your terminal with the **write** command. You may wish to write-protect your terminal when you are editing a document to prevent others from interfering with your screen display.

If you invoke **mesg** without an argument, it displays the status of your terminal's write permission. A response "is y" means your terminal is write-enabled, and "is n" means your terminal is write-protected. Other system users cannot communicate with you by using the **write** command when your terminal is write-protected.

Invoke **mesg** with the argument **n** to forbid message reception and with the argument **y** to reenable message reception. To verify that the write permission was correctly set or reset after changing the permission, invoke **mesg** without an argument and check the terminal status.

Generally your terminal will be write-enabled after you sign on to your UNIX system. If you wish to disable write permission automatically, add the shell command **mesg n** to your shell startup file. See Session 8 in Chapter 4 and the section in Appendix C, "Customizing Your Working Environment," for more information about shell startup files.

Examples Prepare for these examples as described in the introduction to this chapter. The **wordlist** is not necessary for this command.

As a first example for using **mesg**, enter **mesg** to see your terminal's current write permission status. Generally after you log on to your UNIX system, your terminal will be write-enabled.

```
$ mesg
is y
$
```

If for some reason your terminal's write permission is disabled, reenable it before proceeding with this tutorial. Enter **mesg y** and check the status again.

Next, you need to determine your terminal number. You may use the **tty** command to do this by entering **tty**, and the response will be your terminal filename. The terminal number follows the "/**dev**/" string. As a cross-check, enter **who** and you should see the same terminal number associated with your user name. For example, if your terminal number is "tty01", you would observe responses similar to the following, where the ellipses "..." indicate other output from the **who** command.

```
$ tty
/dev/tty01
$ who
...
username tty01 Jul30 10:34
...
$ ▮
```

The UNIX system treats your terminal as a file. The terminal is a special type of file known as a *character device file*. To observe the permission modes for this file directly, simply list the terminal permissions by invoking the **ls** command with the long listing (−l) option. Enter **ls** −l /dev/*ttyname*, where *ttyname* is your current terminal number. Continuing with our example, you should observe a display similar to the following:

```
$ ls −l /dev/tty01
crw——w——w—    1 username    2, 1 Jul 30 10:34
$ ▮
```

The "c" to the left of the permission modes indicates that the file /**dev/tty01** is a character device file. The presence of a "w" character indicates that write permission is enabled for either you (the terminal owner), other users in your group, or all other users. In the preceding example, write permission is enabled for all three classes of users. (More information on file permissions is available in Chapter 3, Session 4.)

Next, write-protect your terminal by entering **mesg n**. Invoke **mesg** without an argument to verify the change:

```
$ mesg n
$ mesg
is n
$ ▮
```

Examine the permission modes again by using the long listing. Enter **ls** −l /dev/*ttyname*. Some "w" characters have been replaced by dashes, indicating that there is no write permission for the "group" and "other" category of system users.

```
$ ls −l /dev/tty01
crw————————    1 username    2, 1 Jul 30 10:35
$ ▮
```

To see how your system enforces the terminal write-protection feature, enter **write username**, replacing *username* with your actual user name, and press RETURN a second time if you need to move the cursor to a new line. An error message will appear on the screen, as it will on any other user's screen who tries to write to you.

$ **write username**
write: permission denied
$ ▮

Finally, before leaving this tutorial, reenable your terminal's write permission by entering **mesg y**.

Messages   The following messages apply to all the versions of **mesg**:

mesg: usage: mesg [−y] [−n]
This indicates that an invalid option was used. Specify a first argument for **mesg**, which begins with either **y** or **n**. Thus you could use, for example, **yes** or **no**, if desired.

mesg: cannot change mode
The **mesg** command cannot change the write permission for your terminal. See your system administrator.

mesg: cannot stat
The **mesg** command cannot determine your terminal's write permission. See your system administrator.

calendar — Create an Engagement Calendar

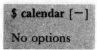

$ **calendar** [−]

No options

The UNIX system provides an engagement calendar reminder service. Whenever you invoke the **calendar** program, the text file containing your appointments and whatever else you choose to put in your calendar will be examined; any lines containing today's and tomorrow's dates will be displayed on your terminal. (The **calendar** command is not the same as the **cal** program, which displays a perpetual calendar.)

The **calendar** program relies on a text file that is named **calendar**. You could create and modify this text file at any time with an editor. The **calendar** command recognizes dates in your **calendar** file that begin with a month name followed by a number for the day of the month. The month name may be either capitalized or not and may be abbreviated as well. Also, the format *mm/dd* is recognized, where *mm* is the month number (ranges from 1 to 12) and *dd* is the day of the month (1 to 28, 30, or 31, as appropriate). Some valid and invalid date formats are listed here:

Valid dates	Invalid dates
November 14	14 November
november 14	14 november
Nov. 14	14 Nov.
nov. 14	14 nov.
nov 14	14 nov
11/14	14/11
11/14/84	84/14/11

The **calendar** command will display lines from the **calendar** file that contain a valid date specification for the current day and the next day. If tomorrow would occur on a weekend, every line containing a date from that weekend as well as the following Monday would be displayed. If a line doesn't contain a date or a valid date, it will not be displayed by the **calendar** command.

You may execute the **calendar** command at any time to examine your engagement calendar. However, the file **calendar** *must* be in the same directory from which you invoked the **calendar** command (that is, in your current directory).

Many UNIX systems will execute the **calendar** command for *all* system accounts if you specify **calendar** with the — argument. Generally this is done during a slack period when the system load is light, since this process consumes a lot of system resources.

You may use the **at** command to execute **calendar** unattended if you wish and then have the output mailed to you. In this way, when you log in the next day, you will have all your current engagement calendar entries in your mailbox.

The **calendar** program is actually a shell script. Since a shell script is easy to modify, you may find that your implementation differs somewhat from our description. However, most implementations should adhere fairly closely to our discussion.

Examples   Prepare for these examples as described in the introduction to this chapter. The **wordlist** is not necessary for this command.

Create a file in your home directory which contains entries like those in the following example:

$ cat calendar
Meeting with Mr. Knapp at 11am. Nov. 14.
Nov. 15 Dentist appointment tomorrow.
Prepare for weekend trip - nov. 16
Take camera, raincoat, N.Cal map.
Group meeting tonight - november 15
11/15 Call about aerobics class.
Call accountant before departure 11/17/84.
Mon, Nov. 19 review manuscript.
$

For the next few examples, consider today's date to be Thursday, November 15, 1984. Enter **calendar** and in a few moments, you should get a display like the following:

calendar
Nov. 15 Dentist appointment tomorrow.
Prepare for weekend trip - nov. 16
Group meeting tonight - november 15
11/15 Call about aerobics class.
$

This result shows lines containing today's (11/15) and tomorrow's (11/16) dates. Note that if a line doesn't contain a valid date specification, it will not be displayed. Thus the line "Take camera, raincoat, N.Cal map." would never be displayed by **calendar** since it doesn't contain a date.

For the next example, consider today's date to be Friday, November 16, 1984:

$ calendar
Prepare for weekend trip - nov. 16
Call accountant before departure 11/17/84.
Mon, Nov. 19 review manuscript.
$

This result shows lines containing today's (11/16), tomorrow's (11/17), and even next Monday's (11/19) dates. If tomorrow's date falls on a weekend, every entry for that weekend and the following Monday will be displayed.

If your system can execute **calendar** — unattended, you will be informed of your engagements by mail when you log in. For example, let's say you just logged in on Friday morning, November 16, 1984. You might see a display like the following:

```
(YOUR UNIX SYSTEM BANNER)
login: username
Password:
(YOUR UNIX SYSTEM MESSAGES)
You have mail.
$ mail
From root Mon Nov 15 04:01:26 1984
Prepare for weekend trip - nov. 16
Call accountant before departure 11/17/84.
Mon, Nov. 19 review manuscript.
?
```

If your system is not set up to run **calendar** periodically, you may use the **at** command to execute **calendar** and mail the results to yourself. For instance, type the commands shown in boldface in the following screen:

```
$ at 0400
calendar | mail username
[ ^D ]
$
```

At 4 A.M. the next morning, **atrun** will execute your memo file, which contains the command **calendar | mail username**. Thus when you log in the next morning, your current reminders will be in your mailfile.

Messages The particular error messages will depend on your system implementation of **calendar**. One common message is as follows:

egrep: can't open calendar
> You don't have a file named **calendar** in your current directory that can be opened for reading.

PART FOUR

APPENDIX **A**

RESOURCES

APPENDIX **B**

SUMMARY OF
UNIX SYSTEM V

APPENDIX **C**

INTERACTING WITH
YOUR UNIX SYSTEM

A RESOURCES FOR USERS OF THE UNIX SYSTEM

When you decide to purchase a UNIX-based system or to enhance your computer by adding the UNIX system, you will be faced with a number of questions about available products. This appendix describes products related to the UNIX system to help you determine which best suit your needs. Of course, this list is not complete, and new manufacturers appear daily. Use this appendix as a general guide only.

The first section of this appendix identifies the range of computers available to you. If you want a relatively inexpensive system, consider the 16-bit microcomputers. You have as many as 100 vendors from which to choose. If you need a larger system, consider the minicomputers and mainframe computers described.

The UNIX system is complicated to maintain. Choose your computer vendors based upon their ability to support the operating system. Some computer companies specialize in systems for many users, while others specialize in computers limited to eight system users. The choice of your computer depends upon your needs.

The manufacturers' addresses and telephone numbers are included in this appendix, along with a description of the company and any areas of specialization.

The second section of this appendix describes a wide variety of applications programs that are available for computers on the UNIX system, and more are being written or converted every month. Not enough business applications packages are available today, but this situation is changing rapidly; the lists that follow will be only a subset of the products available within a year.

Large companies and university personnel wrote many of the programs available for the system. Few were written by hobbyists. For this reason, software based on the UNIX system is more complex and comprehensive than programs written for personal microcomputers. Much of the UNIX software we describe was developed for the PDP-11 computer and is priced higher than most microcomputer programs. The addition of multiuser, multiaccess options with software packages increases the price. A more complicated program has a higher price, both because the system took longer to write and because it requires more support. In general, you will pay more for software based on the UNIX system than for software designed for similar microcomputer applications.

Computer manufacturers also sell applications programs. Some of these programs are generated by the manufacturer, while others have been acquired from outside sources.

Computers That Run UNIX And UNIX-like Operating Systems

Alcyon Corporation
8716 Production Avenue
San Diego, California 92121
(619) 578-0860

Alcyon Corporation is a manufacturer of UNIX workstations and systems software utilizing 68000 microprocessors. Alcyon is the author and supplier of REGULUS, a UNIX-compatible operating system that includes real-time support and commercial applications.

Altos Computer Systems
2641 Orchard Parkway
San Jose, California 95134
(408) 945-6700

The Altos Series 586 and 986 business systems feature multiuser business systems that support five to nine users and have 20- to 84-MB hard disks. The 8086-based systems run the XENIX operating system and C, BASIC, COBOL, Pascal, and FORTRAN Softbol (Dibol II).

Auragen Systems Corporation
2 Executive Drive
Fort Lee, New Jersey 07024
(201) 461-3400 or (800) 847-4276

Auragen offers a fault-tolerant, UNIX-based transaction system consisting of up to 32 clusters. The system runs C, COBOL, FORTRAN, Pascal, and BASIC.

BBN Communications Corporation
70 Fawcett Street
Cambridge, Massachusetts 02238
(617) 497-2800

BBN Communications Corporation manufactures and develops computers, communications products, and applications software. Its hardware systems are time-sharing c/60 and c/70 minicomputers that run UNIX and use the C and FORTRAN programming languages.

Charles River Data Systems, Inc.
983 Concord Street
Framingham, Massachusetts 01701
(617) 655-1800

Charles River Data Systems offers the UNOS operating system, which is written in C, for their 68000-based microcomputers. UNOS is compatible with UNIX, and it includes many extensions. This manufacturer also offers UNIX System V, which has a real-time kernel.

Chromatics, Inc.
2558 Mountain Industrial Boulevard
Tucker, Georgia 30084
(404) 493-7000

The C 7900 computer, based on the 68000 microprocessor, uses Whitesmiths' IDRIS operating system and supports color graphics applications.

Codata Systems Corporation
285 North Wolfe Road
Sunnyvale, California 94086
(408) 735-1744

Codata sells the 3300 system, which is 68000-based, configured with as much as 1 MB of memory and as many as 18 serial ports. Codata runs UNISIS, which is UNIX Version 7 with the Berkeley enhancements.

Computer Automation
Naked Mini Division
8651 Von Karman
Irvine, California 92713
(714) 833-8830

Computer Automation delivers a variety of Naked Mini Series 5 systems that support as many as 28 users. All the Series 5 systems operate under UNIX System III. The Series 5 computers are 8-register, 20-MHz, 16-bit processors that run C, Pascal, COBOL, and FORTRAN 77.

Computer Consoles
97 Humboldt Street
Rochester, New York 14609
(716) 482-5000

This company sells a UNIX-based office automation system called the Office Power System.

Corvus Systems, Inc.
Special Products
2100 Corvus Avenue
San Jose, California 95124
(408) 559-7000

The Corvus Concept+, based on the MC 68000 processor, is a high-performance workstation that can be run in networks. It runs Pascal, FORTRAN 77, BASIC PLUS, RM/COBOL, and C. The system has a 760 $\times$ 540-bit memory-mapped screen. The built-in Omninet local area network is utilized by UNIX System III for advanced kernel-process networking.

Cromemco, Inc.
P.O. Box 7400
Mountain View, California 94039
(415) 964-7400

Cromemco offers UNIX System V on its CS-100 and CS-300 microcomputers.

Cyb Systems
6448 Highway 290 E, Suite D 106
Austin, Texas 78723
(512) 458-3224

The Cyb Multibox family and Network Server family use the MC 68000, MC 68010 and 8088 microprocessor chips. Models are available with 4, 6, 9, or 15 Multibus card cages. Dual operating system models are designed to interface directly with the IBM PC and PC "lookalikes." They can run UNIX Version 7 (Systems III and V), PC-DOS, COS, and MS-DOS, as well as FORTRAN, Pascal, COBOL, BASIC, APL, ADA, C, and Modula-2. Ethernet networking is available on most models.

Data General
Technical Products and Information Systems Division
4400 Computer Drive
Westboro, Massachusetts 01580
(617) 366-8911, ext. 5273

UNX/VS is derived from UNIX System III and is integrated with Data General's proprietary AOS/VS (Advanced Operating System/Virtual Storage). The UNX/VS operating system environment is available for the Eclipse/MV 32-bit computers, which also run COBOL, BASIC, FORTRAN 77, Pascal, PL/1, and C.

Data Resources, Inc.
24 Hartwell Avenue
Lexington, Massachusetts 02173
(617) 863-5100

Data Resources sells a workstation with the UNIX System III that can be networked. The workstation is targeted to financial analysts, strategic planners, and economists. DRILINK is a software package designed for economic financial analysis and planning and utilizes Data Resources' procedures and data sets.

The DRILINK computer is based on the Zilog 8000 microprocessor and includes a hard disk drive. The system can run four graphics terminals, printers, plotters, and communications devices, allowing it to access data from large computers and from the Data Resources central computer facility.

Digital Equipment Corporation
146 Main Street
Maynard, Massachusetts
(617) 897-5111

Digital Equipment Corporation (DEC) manufactures the line of minicomputers on which Bell Laboratories developed UNIX software. Today, more than 30,000 DEC computers run the UNIX operating system. The product lines include the PDP-11, VAX, and MicroVAX. The MicroVAX 1 is compatible with the well-established VAX line. DEC supports and sells a UNIX system called ULTRIX.

Dual Systems Control Corporation
2530 San Pablo Avenue
Berkeley, California 94702
(415) 549-3854

This company targets their 68000-based microcomputer with UNIX System V to scientific research and development, education, and process control applications.

Fortune Systems Corporation
101 Twin Dolphin Drive
Redwood City, California 94065
(415) 595-8444

Fortune sells the 32:16 UNIX-based microcomputer. It has a 68000 microprocessor CPU and comes with 512K of memory. Disk storage ranges from 10 MB to 30 MB. The 32:16 operates in single or multiuser mode.

Fortune sells word processing and accounting packages. Fortune's UNIX system is based on Bell Labs Version 7 and UNIX System III with Berkeley enhancements.

Hewlett-Packard Company
19447 Pruneridge Avenue
Cupertino, California 95014
(408) 825-9111

The HP 9000 Series 500 32-bit computer uses the HP-UX operating system, an HP-enhanced version of UNIX.

Ithaca Intersystems Incorporated
1650 Handshaw Road
Ithaca, New York 14850
(607) 273-2500

Ithaca Intersystems offers a Z8000-based microcomputer with Microsoft's XENIX, an operating system based on the UNIX system.

IBM
2000 N.W. 51st Street
Boca Raton, Florida 33431
(800) 426-3333

IBM offers PC/IX (Personal Computer Interactive Executive), a multitasking, single-user version of the UNIX operating system. It incorporates Version 7, utilities from System III, and a few of the Berkeley enhancements. PC/IX runs on the IBM PC XT and includes only one language, the C compiler; it also includes INED, a full-screen windowing editor. PC/IX was developed by Interactive Systems Corp., but is being distributed by IBM through its branch offices. The telephone number cited here will connect you with an operator who can tell you the number for the branch office nearest you.

Momentum Computer Systems International
2730 Junction Avenue
San Jose, California 95134
(408) 942-0638

This company offers a 68000- or 68010-based computer, the 32E, which runs under Unisoft's UniPlus, and which is configurable for as many as 16 users. Also offered is a cluster workstation, the 32/4, which has a dual 68000 architecture and a high-resolution bit map graphics screen, which runs multiwindowing, Tektronix graphics, and a 4014 graphics emulator.

Morrow Designs
600 McCormick
San Leandro, California 94577
(415) 430-1970

Morrow Designs offers a Z80-based system with their own operating system, Micronix, which is UNIX-based.

Netcom Products, Inc.
430 Toyama Drive
Sunnyvale, California 94089
(408) 744-0721

The Series 1600 Multiprocessor System runs under Microsoft's XENIX.

Onyx Systems, Incorporated
73 East Trimble Road
San Jose, California 95131
(408) 946-6330

Onyx manufactures a Z8000-based computer system with the UNIX operating system. Onyx also sells an integrated UNIX software package for office automation called Onyx Office.

Perkin-Elmer Corporation
Data Systems Group
2 Crescent Place
Oceanport, New Jersey 07757
(800) 631-2154

Perkin-Elmer manufactures a range of minicomputers supported by UNIX System V and a line of microcomputers.

Pixel Computer, Inc.
260 Fordham Road
Wilmington, Massachusetts 01881
(617) 657-8720

The Pixel 80 and 100/AP use the UNIX operating system and have a multiprocessor architecture. The main CPU, a 10-MHz 68000, can access up to 7 megabytes of no-wait state RAM. The systems run Pixel BASIC PLUS, Mumps, RomBASIC, LISP, SMC Thoroughbred BASIC, Level II COBOL, RM/COBOL, SIBOL, APL 68000, FORTRAN 77, C, Pascal, and TeleSoft-ADA.

Plexus Computers, Inc.
3833 North First Street
San Jose, California 95134
(408) 988-1755

Plexus Computers offers a family of powerful UNIX-based microcomputers. The P/35 and P/60 systems enhance the Plexus multiprocessor architecture with a 12.5-MHz MC68000 CPU. These systems feature cache memory, on-board static RAM, and a high-speed memory map. The P/35 supports 16 users, and the P/60 supports 40 users.

For information management and other I/O-intensive applications, Plexus offers the P/25 and P/40 systems. These systems also feature multiprocessor architecture, standard peripheral interfaces, a Multibus I/O bus, and a number of popular languages.

All Plexus systems can be linked in an Ethernet local area network. In addition, they can be networked to other systems, such as the IBM PC and mainframes.

Pyramid Technology Corporation
1295 Charleston Road
Mountain View, California 94043
(415) 965-7200

The Pyramid 90X is a minicomputer with a 32-bit proprietary CPU running under UNIX. Pyramid's UNIX operating system, called OSX, encompasses the commands and utilities from both the 4.2BSD and Bell System V versions. The Pyramid 90X runs C, Pascal, and FORTRAN 77.

Sun Microsystems, Inc.
2550 Garcia Avenue
Mountain View, California 94043
(415) 960-1300

The Sun 2 computers and graphics workstations are based on the Motorola MC68010 processor, have a 32-bit internal architecture, and run UNIX Version 4.2. The SunStations offer 4 MB of main memory and demand-paged virtual memory to support sophisticated applications. Sun's advanced user interface includes a multiwindow screen management package and an optical mouse. The SunStations are designed to be linked via Ethernet.

Tektronix, Inc.
Design Automation Division
P.O. Box 4600 DS 92-635
Beaverton, Oregon 97075
(503) 629-1718

Tektronix sells the TNIX operating system (derived from UNIX Version 7) for DEC computers. TNIX uses the ColorKey graphic user interface and runs Assembler, Pascal, and C.

uniq computer corporation
28 South Water Street
Batavia, Illinois 60510
(312) 879-1566

uniq sells the UNIX operating system on Digital Equipment Corporation hardware as a complete system. The company offers newsletters, software modifications, patches, and other support services. The company also offers consulting services for software development.

Wicat Systems
P.O. Box 539
1875 South State Street
Orem, Utah 94058
(801) 224-6400

Wicat Systems offers a UNIX-based operating system called the System 150, which includes a 10-MB hard-disk drive, 5 1/4-inch floppy backup, two RS-232 serial ports, the Wicat operating systems, and the UNIX Version 7 operating system. The System 150 can support six users. In addition, Wicat has other systems that offer as much as 12 MB of RAM and can support as many as 48 users.

Zilog
1315 Dell Avenue
Campbell, California 95008
(408) 370-8000

Zilog offers a Z8000-based, high-performance, multiuser UNIX system. The machines will support 24 users and include optional disk storage of 520 MB.

Software That Runs Under UNIX

The following lists some of the software available for UNIX systems.

Vendors That Sell UNIX And UNIX-like Operating Systems

Alcyon Corporation
8716 Production Avenue
San Diego, California 92121
(619) 578-0860

Alcyon Corporation is the author and supplier of REGULUS, a UNIX-compatible operating system that includes real-time support and commercial applications.

AT&T Technologies, Inc.
P.O. Box 25000
Greensboro, North Carolina 27420
(800) 828-UNIX; in North Carolina call collect (919) 279-3666

Contact this address for marketing and licensing information on the UNIX system and related products. Inexpensive educational licenses are available from AT&T. Schools, universities, and nonprofit research organizations should also apply to this address for the educational license.

AT&T's latest release of UNIX, UNIX System V, is a multitasking, multiuser operating system designed for use in many computing environments. Older versions of UNIX include UNIX/V7, which runs on the DEC PDP-11/45 and 11/70, and UNIX/32V, which runs on the DEC VAX-11/780.

AT&T also sells software including:

- **PWB/UNIX Programmer's Workbench.** The Programmer's Workbench is a specialized computing facility dedicated to satisfying the needs of developers of computer programs. It improves productivity by efficient specialization of programming tasks. The PWB is an expanded version of the UNIX operating system for DEC PDP series minicomputers.

- **Magic Bench.** MAGIC (Machine Aided Graphics for Illustration and Composition) is an interactive computer graphics software package used for the preparation, editing, production, and storage of line pictorials, diagrams, and other technical documentation.

- **ROFF utility program.** ROFF is a publications formatting program that offers unusual format for stylizing a document.

- **Phototypesetter Version 7 utility program.** Phototypesetter is a typesetting package that includes text formatting and utility mathematical equation processing. The Phototypesetter's language has been designed to be easily learned by people who know neither mathematics nor typesetting.

Interactive Systems Corporation
1212 7th Street
Santa Monica, California 90401
(213) 450-8363

Interactive sells IS/3, an enhanced version of UNIX System III, and has developed a UNIX port for the IBM PC XT. This product, PC/IX, is distributed by IBM.

Microsoft
400 108th Avenue, N.E.
Suite 200
Bellevue, Washington 98004
(206) 454-1315

Microsoft sells and supports the XENIX operating system, a 16-bit microprocessor adaptation of the UNIX system Version 7 and System III. The XENIX system has been configured for the Intel 8086, Zilog Z8000, and Motorola 68000 microprocessors, and is available on several different computer systems.

SMC Software Systems
P.O. Box 6800
1011 Route 22
Bridgewater, New Jersey 08807
(201) 685-9000

SMC Software Systems offers a UNIX System III-like operating system, which is called Thoroughbred UNI-DOL.

Unisoft Corporation
739 Allston Way
Berkeley, California 94710
(415) 644-1230

Unisoft has ported UniPlus, its enhanced version of UNIX System III, to more than seventy-five 68000-based hardware configurations including a port to the Apple LISA. Unisoft also offers several languages, including BASIC PLUS, COBOL, FORTRAN, Pascal, and ADA. Unisoft distributes and supports a variety of software applications including Lex 68, ViewComp, ASM68, and BNET (for networking).

VenturCom
215 First Street
Cambridge, Massachusetts 02142
(617) 661-1230

VenturCom offers VENIX, an operating system based on UNIX System III. VENIX is a real-time operating system, compatible with PDP-11, VAX, and the 8086 microprocessor.

Whitesmiths, Limited
97 Lowell Road
Concord, Massachusetts 01742
(617) 369-8499

Whitesmiths offers IDRIS, a UNIX-like operating system. IDRIS's features lie between Version VI and System V. It is available for PDP-11, 68000, and 8086-based computers.

Mark Williams Company
1430 W. Wrightwood Avenue
Chicago, Illinois 60614
(312) 472-6659

Mark Williams Company sells COHERENT, a UNIX-like operating system. Written in C, COHERENT contains many UNIX system features and is available for the DEC PDP-11, 8086, Z8000, and 68000 microprocessors.

The Wollongong Group
1129 San Antonio Road
Palo Alto, California 94303
(415) 962-9224

Wollongong provides standard and proprietary versions of UNIX, as well as system level products and support services. Wollongong also performs consulting services for end users and other UNIX suppliers.

Wollongong's main products are

- **EUNICE.** A program that allows information transfer between UNIX and VAX environments.
- **IP/TCP.** . A software communication system that employs Department of Defense standard interface software services for VAX/VMS users.
- **PEGASUS.** A system to distribute CPU-intensive terminal management and improve overall system performance.

Applications Programs

The following list shows the wide variety of applications programs that run under UNIX.

Text Processing

Computer Methods, Limited
P.O. Box 709
Chatsworth, California 91311
(213) 844-2000

Computer Methods' products include the XED Word Processing System with Menu Processor and Programmer's Editor; Forms Generation, Data Entry and Edit, and Financial Analysis module; Legal Office and Government Document extensions module; and Document Assembly/Database Merge System. XED offers balance sheet mathematics, block statistical functions with decimal and tab settings, spelling checker, and other capabilities. XED includes a separate programmer's ASCII text editor. A user's shell is also provided as an aid to less experienced UNIX users.

Handle Corporation
P.O. Box 7018
140 Mackinaw Road
Tahoe City, California 95730
(916) 583-7283

This company's products include Handle Writer, Handle Mail Merge, Handle Spell Proofer/Thesaurus, Handle Calc/Math, Handle Automatic Graphics System, and Handle List.

Horizon Software Systems, Inc.
China Basin Building, Suite 4821
185 Berry Street
San Francisco, California 94107
(415) 543-1199

This company offers Horizon Word Processing, a program that is geared toward business, laboratory, and scholastic environments.

Interactive Systems Corporation
1212 7th Street
Santa Monica, California 90401
(213) 450-8363

Interactive Systems offers INword, an enhanced text processor for UNIX, which includes a special terminal, the INtext II, which enhances the operation of the software.

Syntactics Corporation
3333 Bowers Avenue, #145
Santa Clara, California 95051
(408) 727-6400 or (800) 626-6400

CrystalWriter is a UNIX-based word processor and full screen editor. Its features include user-definable keys and on-line help.

Technical Type and Composition
6443 Lardon Road
Salem, Oregon 97303
(503) 371-8655

This company offers phototypesetting programs for the UNIX system. These programs currently support Compugraphic phototypesetters. The programs can work directly from any type of text formatter, including **nroff** or **troff** files, Word-Star, Final Word, and MS Word. The program adds kerning, ligatures, and hyphenation (including a 120K-word dictionary). The company can work from magnetic tape, UNIX or CP/M floppy disks, OCR B text output, or telecommunications.

UniPress Software, Inc.
2025 Lincoln Highway
Edison, New Jersey 08817
(201) 985-8000

EMACS is a full-screen editor available on a wide range of hardware running UNIX. It features multiple windows, search and replace commands, and programming aids such as automatic indenting and parenthesis checking. EMACS also has macros and its own built-in programming language called MLISP.

Accounting and Business Applications

American Business Systems, Inc.
3 Littleton Road
Westford, Massachusetts 01886
(617) 692-2600

American Business Systems markets multiuser business accounting software as well as applications software for retail/point of sale, manufacturing, and medical offices.

Cybernetics, Incorporated
8041 Newman Avenue, Suite 208
Huntington Beach, California 92647
(714) 848-1922

Cybernetics sells accounting packages written in COBOL that operate under UNIX.

Lifeboat Associates
1651 Third Avenue
New York, New York 10128
(212) 860-0300

Lifeboat Associates offers a wide variety of UNIX applications packages including financial packages, system tools, database management, graphics, languages, and telecommunications.

Officesmiths, Inc.
331 Cooper Street
Ottawa, Ontario, Canada K2P 0G5
(613) 235-6749

Officesmiths has two software products for office applications. Officesmith is an applications development system designed for office systems developers building departmental administrative support systems. OfficePolicy is an applications product of the Officesmith, which includes a comprehensive management guide, training courses, and software for policy and procedure systems.

Olympus Software, Inc.
644 Elizabeth Street
Salt Lake City, Utah 84102
(801) 487-4534

Olympus Systems offers a spreadsheet program, UltraCalc, that provides a virtually unlimited worksheet. English names in all commands and formulas, linking of related spreadsheets, automatic consolidation, import/export of data, on-line help, procedure files, color, multiple windows, and a full set of numeric formats are among the features of this spreadsheet program.

Open Systems
430 Oak Grove
Minneapolis, Minnesota 55403
(612) 870-3515

Open Systems offers a set of accounting packages written in RM/COBOL and Business BASIC. Programs include accounts payable, accounts receivable, fixed assets, general ledger, inventory, job cost, payroll, sales order processing, and purchase order processing. The package includes the Open System Report Writer, which allows the user to generate unlimited custom-designed reports and can reformat accounting data for use with all popular spreadsheet, word processing, and graphics software. The applications feature full multiuser capabilities including record and file locking, terminal transaction controls, and multiple printer configurations.

Reliable Data Systems
900 N. San Antonio Road, Suite 201
Los Altos, California 94022
(415) 949-3600

Reliable Data Systems offers a full line of turnkey systems, including general ledger, accounts payable, accounts receivable, inventory management, bill of materials, customer order processing, and purchase order.

Sunburst Software
2696 North University Avenue, Suite 250
Provo, Utah 84604
(801) 374-5223

This company's accounting package includes inventory control, general ledger, accounts receivable, accounts payable, and payroll. In addition, Sunburst Software offers an office management package, which includes a word processor, database manager, and spreadsheet, that permits interaction with each component and the accounting system. Other complete packages for specific types of businesses are also offered.

Unicomp Corporation
1736 E. Sunshine, #202
Springfield, Missouri 65804
(417) 883-6800

The Office Automation System (OAS) includes UniRite word processing, document control and archiving, electronic mail, network communication, communication to other computers, user-to-user communication, user-generated on-line documentation, and spelling checker.

Unicorp Software, Inc.
303 West 42nd Street
New York, New York 10036
(212) 307-6800

Viewcomp is an electronic spreadsheet that features global, column, and row formats, and C-style user-defined macros.

Urban Software Corporation
330 West 42nd Street
New York, New York 10036
(212) 736-4030

Urban Software Corporation is a software house specializing in UNIX-based applications.

Database Management

Britton Lee, Inc.
14600 Winchester Drive
Los Gatos, California 95030
(408) 378-7000

Britton Lee offers the System 500XX series of hardware for data base applications. It implements a B-tree-index RDBUS so that DBMS applications run faster. It runs on any system using the UNIX operating system.

Eaglefield & Nash, Inc.
678 Massachusetts Avenue, #205
Cambridge, Massachusetts 01239
(617) 576-2640

The Firefinch Software Project is a package of file management, statistical analysis, and data entry programs. The software is geared toward medical science and social science applications, as well as applied statistics and data analysis, and has an unlimited dataset size. It is also useful for market research, research and development, and quality control.

Inspiration Systems, Inc.
Production Plaza
Sewickley, Pennsylvania 15143
(412) 771-4000

VERTEX combines a powerful database management system with word processing, spreadsheet, graphics, electronic mail, and data communications in an easy-to-use environment. It also features a data manipulation language, which allows a professional programmer to develop applications. VERTEX supports C and other high-level languages.

Logical Software, Inc.
17 Mount Auburn Street
Cambridge, Massachusetts 02138
(617) 864-0137

Logical Software offers LOGIX, a relational database management system for the UNIX system. LOGIX includes a complete interactive command language, a full screen relation editor, Q programming language/report writer, query compiler, and C interface.

Micro Data Base Systems
Applications Development Products
85 West Algonquin Road, Suite 400
Arlington Heights, Illinois 60005
(312) 981-9200

MDBS III is a database management system that includes hierarchical, relational, and CODASYL network data structures. Its extended network architecture allows modeling, supports full security checking, automatic recovery from crashes, up to 127 simultaneous users, and 4.2 gigabytes of data.

Oracle Corporation
2710 Sand Hill Road
Menlo Park, California 94025
(415) 854-7350

ORACLE is a full-function relational database management system for mainframes, minicomputers, and microcomputers. ORACLE offers a unified, nonprocedural data language, SQL PLUS, for all data entry, inquiry, updating, and control. ORACLE also has an interactive applications facility, an integrated data dictionary, a report writer, and applications development tools.

Pacific Software Manufacturing Company
2608 8th Street
Berkeley, California 94710
(415) 540-5000

Pacific Software offers Sequitur, a relational database management system with integrated word processing for the UNIX system. It includes integral text-editing and report-generation facilities.

Relational Database Systems, Inc.
2471 E. Bayshore Road, Suite 600
Palo Alto, California 94303
(415) 242-1300

Informix is a relational database system featuring menu-driven function selection, interactive query facilities, screen-oriented data entry, dynamic database restructuring, extensive audit trail, and many other features. c-isam is a B+−Tree-based access method that allows programmers to create, manipulate, and retrieve data using indexed files.

Relational Technology, Inc.
2855 Telegraph Avenue
Berkeley, California 94705
(415) 424-1300

This company offers INGRES, a full-function relational database management system. Included with INGRES are an integrated set of forms-based applications development tools for forms management, query update, reports, graphics, and applications development. In addition, INGRES offers distributed access to remote databases across computer networks.

Rhodnius, Inc.
10 St. Mary Street, Suite 602
Toronto, Ontario, Canada M4Y 1P9
(416) 922-1743

Rhodnius offers the Mistress family of DBMS, which includes a query language and a host-language interface.

Communications

Compion Corporation
1101 East University Avenue
Urbana, Illinois 61801
(217) 384-8500

Compion supplies communications software products that meet Department of Defense and international protocol standards.

Communication Solutions, Inc.
992 S. Saratoga-Sunnyvale Road
San Jose, California 95129
(408) 725-1568

Access/SNA is a C-based software package that allows UNIX systems to communicate with IBM mainframe computers using Systems Network Architecture (SNA). It provides both IBM 3270 emulation and IBM 3770 emulation for batch file transfer.

Interactive Systems Corporation
1212 7th Street
Santa Monica, California 90401
(213) 450-8363

Interactive Systems Corporation sells networking, electronic mail, and remote communications programs for UNIX.

Network Research Corporation
1964 Westwood Blvd., Suite 2000
Los Angeles, California 90025
(213) 474-7717

FUSION network software allows the interconnection of different processors and operating systems on the same Ethernet local area network. FUSION provides the user with access to the resources available on a remote machine. FUSION is also able to incorporate LAN hardware from various vendors, including 3Com, Interlan, and Communication Machinery Corporation.

Phone 1, Inc.
461 N. Mulford Road
Rockford, Illinois 61107
(815) 897-8110

Phone 1's products include CLEO-3780 Bisync Communications and CLEO 3270 Emulator. CLEO provides 3274, 3278, and 3287 cluster emulation for the UNIX environment.

SoftTest
555 Goffle Road
Ridgewood, New Jersey 07450
(201) 447-3901

SofGram is an electronic communications manager that guides the user through message creation and transmission via the Telex, TWX, or DDD networks. The system also receives incoming messages and routes them appropriately among users.

Sytek, Inc.
1225 Charleston Road
Mountain View, California 94043
(415) 966-7300

Sytek offers a local network called "LocalNet," a local data communications system that connects "intelligent" and "dumb" terminals. LocalNet provides a data communications interface with the UNIX operating system.

3Com Corporation
1365 Shorebird Way
P.O. Box 7390
Mountain View, California 94039
(415) 961-9602

3Com's UNET software provides Ethernet-compatible communication among computers running the UNIX operating system. UNET transfers files, connects remote terminals, and carries electronic mail.

Winterhalter, Incorporated
3853 Research Park Drive
Ann Arbor, Michigan 48104
(313) 662-2002

Datatalker I allows a microcomputer to communicate to IBM mainframes via 3270 and 3780/2780 bisync.

ZAIAZ Communications, Inc.
2227 Drake Avenue
Huntsville, Alabama 35805
(204) 881-2200

ZAIAZ offers voice mail that runs under UNIX using special hardware.

Utility Software

Graphic Software Systems, Inc.
P.O. Box 673
25117 Southwest Parkway
Wilsonville, Oregon 97070
(503) 682-1606

GSS produces graphics utilities, tools, and applications for the professional user of microcomputer graphics. GSS offers software for the programmer and system or applications builder, as well as the nonprogrammer. Products include GSS-Drivers, GSS-Toolkit, and GSS-Solutions.

Interactive Systems Corporation
1212 7th Street
Santa Monica, California 90401
(213) 450-8363

Interactive Systems Corporation develops, sells, and supports computer software products based upon its own version of the UNIX operating system. These products are used in software development, communications, text processing, and automation of office functions. Among Interactive's offerings is the Advanced Productivity System (APS), which is an integrated set of software tools designed to increase the productivity of professionals working in offices and in software development groups. Interactive also has a user interface for UNIX, called TEN/PLUS.

Nuvatec, Inc.
261 Eisenhower Lane
Lombard, Illinois 60148
(312) 620-4830

Nuvatec offers various UNIX-based cross-development tools. Nuvatec also offers consulting services including custom applications software, UNIX system administration, custom cross-development tools, custom language processors, and language consulting (C, FORTRAN, BASIC, Pascal).

TouchStone Software Corporation
909 Electric Avenue, Suite 207
Seal Beach, California 90740
(213) 598-7746

Menus and Forms Development System provides developers with the means to create and maintain sophisticated user interfaces for custom applications. Features include amplified design of complex screens and actions, password protection, menu integrity checks, user dialogue functions, and a common help facility. The system supports C and assembler.

UNIFY Corporation
1111 Howe Avenue, Suite 580
Sacramento, California 95825
(916) 920-9092

UNIFY is an applications development system that supplies the necessary tools for UNIX users developing and operating information management systems. UNIFY enhances the UNIX capabilities with programming tools, operational utilities, and end-user tools such as database management and a language interface with C.

Languages and Compilers

Digital Research/Language Division
P.O. Box 579
160 Central Avenue
Pacific Grove, California 93950
(408) 649-3896

CBASIC-86 is an implementation of BASIC designed to permit commercial applications to be executed in a UNIX or UNIX-like environment. It supports CBASIC-86 and C language and operates on 8086- and 8088-based UNIX systems. Features include 14-digit decimal arithmetic, random and sequential disk accessing, complete string processing facilities, and enhanced code maintenance.

Human Computing Resources Corporation
10 St. Mary Street
Toronto, Ontario, Canada M4Y 1P9
(416) 922-1937

Human Computing Resources offers HCR/BASIC and HCR/Pascal.

Interactive Systems Corporation
1212 7th Street
Santa Monica, California 90401
(213) 450-8363

Interactive Systems offers FORTRAN, C cross-compilers, and other languages for the UNIX operating system on the PDP-11, VAX, and VAX/VMS systems.

Lattice, Inc.
P.O. Box 3072
Glen Ellyn, Illinois 60138
(312) 858-7950

Lattice offers cross-compilers for the 8086 under UNIX.

Micro Focus
2465 East Bayshore Road, Suite 400
Palo Alto, California 94303
(415) 856-4161

Micro Focus produces Level II COBOL, Animator, Forms-2, and native code generators. The Micro Focus Visual Programming environment includes the only GSA certified Federal High Level COBOL for micros along with a unique source code level, interactive program analysis and debugging tool. In addition, code generators for source as well as native machine code are included.

Oracle Corporation
2710 Sand Hill Road
Menlo Park, California 94025
(415) 854-7350

Oracle Corporation offers a C compiler for the IBM 370, 4300, and Series 30 computers running UNIX.

Ryan-McFarland Corporation
609 Deep Valley Drive
Rolling Hills Estates, California 90274
(213) 541-4828

RM/COBOL is an implementation of ANSI 74 COBOL Standard. Applications written in RM/COBOL can run on the many systems that support the language. RM/FORTRAN is a full implementation of the ANSI 77 FORTRAN standards with extensions optimized for execution speed.

UNIX User Support

The following lists the many types of support available for UNIX users.

Newsletters

InfoPro Systems
P.O. Box 849
Denville, New Jersey 07834
(201) 989-0570

InfoPro Systems publishes a monthly newsletter entitled *UNIQUE: The UNIX System Information Source*. The newsletter is oriented toward both new and experienced users of the UNIX system. *UNIQUE* covers UNIX and UNIX-like computer hardware, software written in C (and other languages that run on UNIX), and related services offered by consulting and educational firms and user groups.

The staff periodically evaluates software and hardware products submitted by manufacturers for this purpose. Coverage includes pricing, technical details, and product analysis. Feature articles, industry news and rumors, and tutorials on UNIX-related subjects are presented. As a matter of editorial policy, commercial advertising is not accepted.

User Groups

Canadian UNIX SIG
c/o Human Computing Resources Corporation
10 St. Mary Street
Toronto, Ontario, Canada M4Y 1P9
(416) 922-1937

This is a Human Computing Resources user group offering a newsletter, software exchanges, and meetings. It is affiliated with DECUS.

USENIX Association
P.O. Box 7
El Cerrito, California 94530
(415) 528-UNIX

The USENIX Association is an organization whose goals are education and information exchange related to the VAX computer and UNIX operating system. The Association sponsors technical meetings twice annually, publishes a newsletter (*;login;*), and coordinates software exchanges among its members.

/usr/group
4655 Old Ironside Drive, Suite 200
Santa Clara, California 95050
(408) 986-8840

/usr/group is dedicated to the promotion of UNIX in the commercial marketplace. It sponsors UniForum, the annual UNIX trade conference and tradeshow, and publishes a monthly newsletter and a products directory of UNIX-compatible software, hardware, and services.

Uni-Ops
P.O. Box 27097
Concord, California 94527-0097
(415) 689-4382

Uni-Ops is a user group for beginners and experienced users of UNIX and related products. Membership in Uni-Ops includes a subscription to its newsletter, *U-NEWS*. The company also offers a mailing list program for the UNIX system and periodic meetings and tutorials.

Educational Materials

User Training Corporation
P.O. Box 970
Soquel, California 95073
(408) 354-6433

User Training Corporation offers a variety of tutorial packages on the UNIX system. Included are courses in the ex and vi editors, UNIX for programmers, and courses on the C language. All tutorials come with tutorial cassettes and a manual.

Seminars

Computer Technology Group
310 South Michigan Avenue
Chicago, Illinois 60604
(312) 986-4000

Computer Technology Group offers a curriculum for end-users, management, and applications staff in the UNIX operating system and the C programming language. Seminars, video tape training, and interactive video courses using a combination of video disk and microcomputers are also available.

Concentric Associates, Inc.
22 Betherwood Avenue
Plainfield, New Jersey 07062
(201) 756-2291

Concentric Associates, Inc., provides custom instruction, courseware licensing, course development, and consulting services for UNIX.

Institute for Advanced Professional Studies
55 Wheeler Street
Cambridge, Massachusetts 02138
(617) 497-2075

The Institute offers a variety of hands-on workshops on programming languages, including C, ADA, COBOL and Pascal, and the UNIX system.

International Technical Seminars
520 Waller Street
San Francisco, California 94117
(415) 621-6415

International Technical Seminars presents courses on advanced UNIX topics such as shell script writing, uucp installation, fast prototyping, and writing device drivers. Its documentation team produces system administration materials for a number of UNIX-oriented manufacturers. Its affiliate, the Independent UNIX

Bookstore, is a major resource for UNIX and C-oriented materials.

Plum Hall, Inc.
One Spruce Avenue
Cardiff, New Jersey 08232
(609) 927-3770

Plum Hall offers training in the UNIX and IDRIS operating systems and C programming. Courses are presented on a regular public schedule as well as in-house.

Structured Methods Incorporated
7 West 18th Street
New York, New York 10011
(212) 741-7720

Structured Methods offers a wide variety of UNIX training courses and C programming courses.

UNIX Consultants

Gnostic Concepts, Inc.
951 Mariners Island Boulevard
San Mateo, California 94404
(415) 345-7400

Gnostic Concepts' Software Information Service is a continuing program of market research on the UNIX operating system. The yearly fee for this service ranges from $8500 to $18,000, depending on depth of coverage, and includes reports, telephone inquiry privileges, and consulting. Gnostic Concepts also offers custom and multiclient market research on the UNIX system and other areas of the electronics industry.

The Perchwell Corporation
56 Cliffside Trail
Denville, New Jersey 07834
(201) 625-1797

The Perchwell Corporation provides management and technical consulting services for firms becoming actively involved with the UNIX operating system. Custom studies, in-house training, technology forecasts, software guidance, and advice on product planning and positioning are made available to companies competing in the UNIX marketplace.

Commercial Time Sharing

B.A.S.I.S.
1700 Shattuck Avenue, Suite 1
Berkeley, California 94709
(415) 841-1800

B.A.S.I.S. is a UNIX time-sharing service bureau, which offers a variety of commercial applications packages, standard UNIX utilities, and communications to other computers. Also available are stand-alone system evaluation and configuration, hardware and software sales, and consulting.

Computer Habitat
2231 Calle de Luna
Santa Clara, California 95050
(408) 986-1972

Computer Habitat offers business, office, or programming facilities for the software development environment.

International Data Services, Inc.
2231 Calle de Luna
Santa Clara, California 95050
(408) 986-1972

International Data Services custom configures UNIX computer systems for advanced research and development in the scientific, engineering, and software development fields. Consulting, networking, time sharing, and UNIX support services are also available.

OCTAL, Inc.
1951 Colony Street
Mountain View, California 94043
(415) 962-8080

OCTAL offers Berkeley 4.2 UNIX on DEC VAX hardware. OCTAL can also provide many forms of output, including laser printing and microfiche.

APPENDIX **B**

SUMMARY OF
UNIX SYSTEM V

In addition to the commands and programs described in Chapter 6, holders of a UNIX software license have many more programs, commands, and languages at their disposal. The following is a list of all the programs supplied with UNIX; the list also notes which programs are included in Bell Version 7 and System III. In addition, this appendix includes a separate list of those programs and commands that are included only in Version 7 or System III.

Software Included With UNIX System V

The following sections give brief descriptions of the many software programs included with UNIX System V.

Basic Software

The following is a list of the basic software.

Operating System

boot   Start the UNIX system. (System III, Version 7 also.)

config   Tailor device-dependent system code to a particular hardware configuration. (System III, Version 7 also.)

unix   The kernel program, which is the resident code on which everything else depends. (System III, Version 7 also.)

User Access Control

login   Sign on as a new user. Verify the password and establish a user's individual and group (project) identity. (System III, Version 7 also.)

newgrp   Change working group (project). (System III, Version 7 also.)

passwd   Change or assign a password. (System III, Version 7 also.)

stlogin   Sign on to the UNIX system using a synchronous terminal line.

su   Temporarily become the superuser or another account user with all the rights and privileges of the new user. May require a password. (System III, Version 7 also.)

Terminal Handling

st   Set various synchronous terminal controls (includes **stload, stcntrl,** and **stprint**).

stty   Set options for terminal characteristics. (System III, Version 7 also.)

tabs   Set tab stops. (System III, Version 7 also).

File Handling

arcv   Convert archive files from PDP-11 to common archive format.

cancel   Cancel requests to an LP line printer.

cat   Concatenate one or more files onto standard output. (System III, Version 7 also.)

cmp   Compare two files and report differences character by character. (System III, Version 7 also.)

convert   Convert VAX and 3B20 object and archive files to common formats.

cp	Copy one file to another or a set of files to a directory. (System III, Version 7 also.)
cprs	Compress an IS25 object file.
csplit	Context split — separate a file into specified sections. (System III also.)
dd	Physical file format translator for exchanging data with foreign systems. (System III, Version 7 also.)
dpr	Print off-line. (System III also.)
line	Read one line of a file. (System III also.)
lp	Send requests to an LP line printer.
lpr	Spool files to the line printer. (System III, Version 7 also.)
pack	Compress a file. (System III also.)
pr	Print files with title, date, and page number on every page. (System III, Version 7 also.)
scat	Concatenate and print files on a synchronous printer.
split	Split a large file into pieces. (System III, Version 7 also.)
sum	Print checksum and block count of a file. (System III, Version 7 also.)
tail	Print last lines, characters, or blocks of a file. (System III, Version 7 also.)
touch	Update the access and modification times of a file. (System III, Version 7 also.)
unpack	Expand a file compressed with **pack**. (System III also.)
vpr	Queue files for printing on Versatec printer. (System III also.)

Directory and Filename Handling

basename	Deliver suffix of pathnames (all directory prefixes removed). (System III also.)
cd	Change working directory. (System III, Version 7 also.)
chgrp	Change group (project) to which a file belongs. (Version 7 also.)
chmod	Change permissions on one or more files. (System III, Version 7 also.)
chown	Change individual owner of one or more files. (System III, Version 7 also.)
dircmp	Compare directory contents. (System III also.)

dirname   Deliver directory prefix of pathname (basename removed).

find   Search the directory hierarchy, finding or acting on every file that meets specified criteria. (System III, Version 7 also.)

ln   Link another name (an *alias*) to an existing file. (System III, Version 7 also.)

mkdir   Make a new directory. (System III, Version 7 also.)

mv   Move a file or files (used for renaming files). (System III, Version 7 also.)

rm   Remove a file. Only the individual name goes away if any other names are linked to the file. (System III, Version 7 also.)

rmdir   Remove an empty directory. (System III, Version 7 also.)

umask   Set the file-creation mode mask. (System III also.)

Program Execution

chroot   Change root directory for a command. (System III also.)

disable   Disable LP printers.

echo   Print remainder of command line after interpretation by shell. (System III, Version 7 also.)

enable   Enable LP printers.

env   Set or display environment for command execution. (System III also.)

expr   Execute string and integer arithmetic computations for evaluating command arguments as expressions. (System III, Version 7 also.)

getopt   Parse options in command lines for shell procedures. (System III also.)

kill   Terminate named processes. (System III, Version 7 also.)

nice   Run a command at low priority, or set the priority of a background program. (System III, Version 7 also.)

nohup   Run a command that is immune to hanging up the terminal. (System III, Version 7 also.)

rsh   The restricted shell. (System III also.)

sh   The shell, or command language interpreter. (System III, Version 7 also.)

sleep   Suspend execution for a specified time. (System III, Version 7 also.)

tee   Pass data between processes and divert a copy into one or more files. (System III, Version 7 also.)

test	Test a shell conditional. (System III, Version 7 also.)
wait	Wait for termination of asynchronously running processes. (System III, Version 7 also.)
xargs	Construct an argument list and execute a command. (System III also.)

Status Inquiries

bfs	Scan big files. (System III also.)
date	Print today's date and time. (System III, Version 7 also.)
du	Print a summary of total space occupied by all files in a hierarchy. (System III, Version 7 also.)
file	Classify (or type) a file. (System III, Version 7 also.)
id	Print the user and group's identification numbers and names. (System III also.)
ipcrm	Remove a message queue, semaphore set, or shared memory identification.
ipcs	Report inter-process communication facilities status.
logname	Get login name. (System III also.)
lpstat	Print LP status information.
ls	List the names of files in one or more directories. (System III, Version 7 also.)
news	Print system news items. (System III also.)
ps	Report process status. (System III, Version 7 also.)
pwd	Print the name of the working directory. (System III, Version 7 also.)
rjestat	Report on the RJE status and interactive status console. (System III also.)
ststat	Report on the status of the synchronous terminal facilities.
tty	Print the name of your terminal. (System III, Version 7 also.)
uname	Print the name of the current UNIX system. (System III also.)
who	Tell who is on the system. (System III, Version 7 also.)

System Maintenance

accept	Allow LP requests.
bcopy	Copy file blocks. (System III also.)

checkall	Check the file system.
clri	Clear an inode. (System III, Version 7 also.)
cpio	Copy file archives. (System III also.)
cron	Execute commands at specified times. (System III, Version 7 also.)
df	Report the number of free disk blocks. (System III, Version 7 also.)
dfsck	Check two different disk drives simultaneously.
errdead	Extract error records from dump.
errdemon	Error-logging daemon.
errpt	Process a report of logged errors.
errstop	Terminate the error-logging daemon.
ff	List file names and statistics for a file system.
filesave	Daily disk-to-disk UNIX file system backup shell script. (System III also.)
finc	Perform an incremental backup.
frec	Recover files from a backup tape created by **finc**.
fsck	Check the file system. (System III also.)
fsdb	Debug the file system. (System III also.)
fuser	Identify processes using a file.
fwtmp	Manipulate login accounting records. (System III also.)
getty	Set terminal type, modes, speed, and characteristics for user login. (System III, Version 7 also.)
grpck	Check the group of files /etc/group. (System III also.)
init	Control process initialization. (System III, Version 7 also.)
install	Install command programs on the system. (System III also.)
killall	Kill all active processes to prepare for system shutdown.
labelit	Provide labels for unmounted backup systems. (System III also.)
link	Exercise link and unlink system calls. (System III also.)
lpadmin	Set up or configure the LP spooling system.
lpmove	Move LP requests.
lpsched	Start the LP request schedules.
lpshut	Stop the LP request schedules.
mkfs	Construct a file system. (System III, Version 7 also.)
mknod	Create a special device file. (System III, Version 7 also.)

mount	Mount the file system. (System III, Version 7 also.)
mvdir	Move a directory. (System III also.)
ncheck	Generate names from i-numbers. (System III, Version 7 also.)
profiler	Give a profile of the operating system. (System III also.)
pwck	Check the password file, /etc/passwd. (System III also.)
reject	Prevent LP requests.
setmnt	Create a mount table. (System III also.)
shutdown	Terminate all processing for shutdown of the system. (System III also.)
stgetty	Monitor the synchronous terminal line for user login.
sync	Flush all I/O buffers. (System III, Version 7 also.)
tapesave	Weekly disk-to-tape UNIX file system backup shell script. (System III also.)
tar	Manage file archives (backups) on magnetic media. (System III, Version 7 also.)
trouble	Log a trouble report.
umount	Dismount the file system. (System III, Version 7 also.)
volcopy	Backup the file systems. (System III also.)
wall	Write a message to all users. (System III, Version 7 also.)
whodo	Find out who is doing what. (System III also.)

Accounting

acct	Request overview of accounting and miscellaneous accounting commands. (System III also.)
acctcms	Request command summary from per-process accounting records. (System III also.)
acctcom	Search and print process accounting files. (System III also.)
acctcon	Perform connect time accounting. (System III also.)
acctmerg	Merge or add total accounting file. (System III also.)
acctprc	Process accounting. (System III also.)
acctsh	Shell procedures for accounting. (System III also.)
runacct	Run daily accounting procedure. (System III also.)
sadp	Get profile of disk access.

sag	Present graph of system activity. (System III also.)
sar	Present report of system activity.
timex	Time a command and report process data and system activity. (System III also.)

Communications

acuset	Connect ACUs and communication lines.
calendar	Run interactive engagement calendar. (System III, Version 7 also.)
ct	Send **getty** to a remote terminal. (System III also.)
cu	Call up another UNIX system. (System III, Version 7 also.)
gather	Gather files for submitting as part of RJE job. (System III also.)
mail	Mail a message to one or more users, or read your mail. (System III, Version 7 also.)
mesg	Inhibit or enable receipt of messages from **write** and **wall**. (System III, Version 7 also.)
net	Execute a command on the PCL network.
nscstat	Query the operation status of the NSC network.
nsctorje	Reroute jobs from the NSC network to RJE.
nusend	Send files to another UNIX system on the NSC network.
send	Submit an RJE job. (System III also.)
uuclean	Clean up the **uucp** spool directory. (System III also.)
uucp	Copy files from one UNIX system to another UNIX system. (System III, Version 7 also.)
uustat	Give **uucp** status. (System III also.)
uusub	Monitor **uucp** network. (System III also.)
uuto	Copy files from one UNIX to another UNIX system. (System III also.)
uux	Execute a command on another UNIX system. (System III, Version 7 also.)
write	Establish terminal communication with another user. (System III, Version 7 also.)

Program Development

adb	Interactive absolute debugger. (System III, Version 7 also.)

ar	Maintain archives and libraries (combines several object files into one). (System III, Version 7 also.)
as	Assembler. (System III, Version 7 also.)
dis	3B20 disassembler.
dump	Dump selected parts of an object file as characters with hexadecimal, octal, or decimal representation.
false	Provide symbolic "false" value. (System III, Version 7 also.)
ld	Combines relocatable object files and inserts required routines from specified library to produce an executable program. (System III, Version 7 also.)
lorder	Find ordering relation for an object library. (System III, Version 7 also.)
machid	Report your processor type.
make	Maintain, update, and regenerate groups of programs. (System III, Version 7 also.)
nl	Filter line numbering. (System III also.)
nm	Print the namelist (symbol table) of an object program. (System III, Version 7 also.)
od	Dump the contents of any file. (System III, Version 7 also.)
prof	Construct a profile of time spent per routine from statistics gathered by time-sampling the execution of a program. (System III, Version 7 also.)
sdb	Interactive symbolic debugger. (System III also.)
size	Report the core requirements of one or more object files. (System III, Version 7 also.)
strip	Remove the relocation and symbol table information from an object file to save space. (System III, Version 7 also.)
time	Run a command and report timing information on it. (System III, Version 7 also.)
true	Provide symbolic "true" value. (System III, Version 7 also.)

UNIX System Documentation

help	Explain system messages. (System III also.)
man	Print part of UNIX manual on your terminal. (System III, Version 7 also.)

Languages

The following lists the programming languages and related utilities supplied with System V.

The C Language

cb	Reformat a C program to make it more readable. (System III, Version 7 also.)
cc	Compile and link edit programs in the C language. (System III, Version 7 also.)
cflow	Generate a C flow graph, charting the external references.
cpp	Preprocessor for the C language. (System III, Version 7 also.)
cxref	Generate a C program cross-reference.
lint	Verify syntax for C programs. (System III, Version 7 also.)
list	Produce C source listing from 3B20S object file.
pcc	Portable C compiler. (System III, Version 7 also.)
regcmp	Regular C expression compiler. (System III also.)
scc	C compiler for stand-alone programs. (System III also.)

FORTRAN

asa	Interpret ASA carriage control characters.
efl	Extended FORTRAN language. (System III also.)
f77	Compiler for ANSI standard FORTRAN 77. (System III, Version 7 also.)
fsplit	Split f77, ratfor, or efl files.
ratfor	Add rational control structure (similar to C) to FORTRAN programs. (System III, Version 7 also.)

Other Algorithmic Languages

bc	A C-like interactive interface to the desk calculator dc. (System III, Version 7 also.)
bs	A compiler/interpreter similar to BASIC and SNOBOL. (System III also.)
dc	Interactive programmable desk calculator. (System III, Version 7 also.)
sno	SNOBOL compiler and interpreter. (System III also.)

Macro Processing

m4   A general-purpose macroprocessor. (System III, Version 7 also.)

Compiler Generators

lex   Generator of lexical analyzers. (System III, Version 7 also.)

yacc   A compiler-writing system. (System III, Version 7 also.)

Source Code Control System (SCCS)

admin   Create and administer SCCS files. (System III also.)

cdc   Change the "delta commentary" of an SCCS delta. (System III also.)

comb   Combine SCCS deltas. (System III also.)

delta   Make a change in an SCCS file. (System III also.)

get   Get a version of an SCCS file. (System III also.)

help   Provide detailed explanation of an SCCS command diagnostic or information about using an SCCS command. (System III also.)

prs   Print an SCCS file. (System III also.)

rmdel   Remove a delta from an SCCS file. (System III also.)

sact   Print current SCCS file-editing activity. (System III also.)

sccsdiff Compare two versions of an SCCS file. (System III also.)

unget   Undo a previous get of an SCCS file. (System III also.)

val   Validate an SCCS file. (System III also.)

what   Identify an SCCS file. (System III also.)

Text Processing

The following programs are used for creating and editing documents and programs.

Document Preparation

crypt   Encrypt and decrypt files for security. (System III, Version 7 also.)

ed   Interactive context editor. (System III, Version 7 also.)

ex   Line-oriented text editor.

makekey	Generate an encryption key. (System III, Version 7 also.)
ptx	Make a permuted (keyword in context) index. (System III, Version 7 also.)
red	Restricted version of the **ed** text editor. (System III also.)
se	Screen editor for video terminals.
spell	Look for spelling errors by comparing each word in a document against a word list. (System III, Version 7 also.)
vi	Screen-oriented text editor.

Document Formatting

checkeq	Check document for **eqn** errors. (System III, Version 7 also.)
checkmm	Check document for **mm** and **eqn** errors. (System III also.)
col	Create columns for **nroff.** (System III, Version 7 also.)
cw	Prepare text using a constant-width font for **troff.** (System III also.)
deroff	Remove all formatting directives from input. (System III, Version 7 also.)
diffmk	Mark all differences between files for **nroff** and **troff.** (System III also.)
eqn	A mathematical typesetting preprocessor for **troff.** (System III, Version 7 also.)
greek	Enable fancy printing on Diablo-mechanism terminals like DASI-300, DASI-450, Tektronix 4014 (System III, Version 7 also), Diablo 1620, and Hewlett-Packard 26xx series. (System III also).
hyphen	Find hyphenated words. (System III also.)
mm	Format documents using the **mm** macros with **nroff.** (System III also.)
mmt	Format documents using the **mm** macros with **troff.** (System III also.)
neqn	A version of **eqn** for **nroff.** (System III, Version 7 also.)
newform	Change the format of a text file.
nroff	Format documents for printing on ASCII terminals. (System III, Version 7 also.)
tbl	A preprocessor for **nroff** and **troff** that translates simple descriptions of table layouts and contents into detailed typesetting instructions. (System III, Version 7 also.)

tc	Simulate Graphic Systems typesetter output on Tektronix 4014 scope. (System III, Version 7 also.)
troff	Advanced typesetting for a Graphic Systems photo-typesetter. (System III, Version 7 also.)

Information Handling

awk	Pattern scanning and processing language. (System III, Version 7 also.)
bdiff	Differential comparator for large files. (System III also.)
comm	Identify unique and common lines in two sorted files. (System III, Version 7 also.)
cut	˙Cut out selected fields of each line of a file. (System III also.)
diff	Report line changes, additions, and deletions necessary to bring two files into agreement. (System III, Version 7 also.)
diff3	Three-way differential file comparator. (System III also.)
grep	Print all lines in a file that contain a specified pattern. (System III, Version 7 also.)
join	Combine two files by joining records that have identical keys. (System III, Version 7 also.)
paste	Merge the same lines of several files, or concatenate subsequent lines of one file. (System III also.)
sdiff	Produce a side-by-side listing of the differences between two files. (System III also.)
sed	Stream-oriented version of **ed**. (System III, Version 7 also.)
sort	Sort or merge ASCII files line by line. (System III, Version 7 also.)
tr	Do one-to-one character translation or deletion according to an arbitrary code. (System III, Version 7 also.)
tsort	Topological sort. (System III, Version 7 also.)
uniq	Collapse successive duplicate lines in a sorted file into one line. (System III, Version 7 also.)
vc	Version control processor. (System III also.)
wc	Count the lines, words (strings separated by blanks), and characters in a file. (System III, Version 7 also.)

Graphics

gdev	Graphics device routines and filters. (System III also.)
ged	Graphics editor. (System III also.)
graph	Prepares a graph from pairs of input numbers. (System III, Version 7 also.)
graphics	Access graphical and numerical commands. (System III also.)
gutil	Graphics utilities. (System III also.)
spline	Provide a smooth curve through a set of points intended for graph. (System III, Version 7 also.)
stat	Statistical network useful with graphics commands. (System III also.)
toc	Graphics table of contents routines. (System III also.)
tplot	Graphics filters. (System III also.)

Novelties, Games, and Miscellaneous Features

arithmetic	A test of number facts. (System III, Version 7 also.)
back	Play backgammon. (System III, **backgammon** in Version 7.)
banner	Print output in large letters. (System III, Version 7 also.)
bj	Play blackjack. (System III, Version 7 also.)
cal	Print a calendar. (System III, Version 7 also.)
chess	Play class D chess. (System III, Version 7 also.)
craps	Play craps. (System III also.)
factor	Factor large integers. (System III, Version 7 also.)
hangman	Play the word-guessing game. (System III, Version 7 also.)
jotto	Play the word game.
maze	Construct random mazes. (System III, Version 7 also.)
moo	Play the number-guessing game. (System III, Version 7 also.)
quiz	Test your knowledge. (System III, Version 7 also.)
reversi	Play the board game. (System III, Version 7 also.)
sky	Print a short quote. (System III also.)
ttt	Play tic-tac-toe. (System III, Version 7 also.)

units	Convert amounts between different scales of measurement. (System III, Version 7 also.)
wump	Play wumpus. (System III, Version 7 also.)

Software Included
With UNIX System III and Version 7 Only

This section gives a brief description of the software that was included with System III or Version 7 but not with System V.

Basic Software

The following is a list of the basic software.

Operating System

mkconf	Tailor device-dependent system code to hardware configuration. (Version 7 only.)

Program Execution

at	Schedule a program to run later. (Version 7 only.)

Status Inquiries

iostat	Print statistics about system I/O activity. (Version 7 only.)
quot	Print summary of file space used. (Version 7 only.)

System Maintenance

restor	Restore parts or all of a dumped file system. (System III and Version 7.)
tp	Manage file archives on magnetic tape or DECtape. (System III and Version 7.)

Accounting

ac	Publish cumulative connect time report. (Version 7 only.)
sa	Publish shell accounting report. (Version 7 only.)

Computer-Aided Instruction (CAI)

learn	A program for interpreting CAI scripts. (Version 7 only.)

Languages

struct	Converts ordinary FORTRAN programs into structured FORTRAN. (Version 7 only.)
bas	An interactive interpreter similar to BASIC. (Version 7 only.)
cref	Make a cross-reference listing of assembler or C programs. (System III only.)
look	Search for lines with specified prefix. (Version 7 only.)

Text Processing

The following programs are used for creating and editing documents and programs.

Document Preparation

look	Search for words in dictionary based on a prefix. (Version 7 only.)
typo	Look for spelling errors by a statistical technique. (System III and Version 7.)

Document Formatting

ms	A standardized manuscript layout (macro) package for use with **nroff** and **troff**. (Version 7 only.)
refer	Fill in bibliographic citations in a document from a data base. (Version 7 only.)
reform	Reformat a text file. (System III only.)
roff	Typesetting program for terminals. (Version 7 only.)

Graphics

plot   A set of filters for printing graphs produced by **graph** and other
            programs on various terminals. (Version 7 only.)

Novelties, Games,
And Miscellaneous Features

backgammon Play the game. (Version 7 only.)

bcd   Converts ASCII files to card-image form. (Version 7 only.)

checkers   Plays class D checkers. (Version 7 only.)

ching   Cast the I Ching. (Version 7 only.)

cubic   Play 4 × 4 × 4 tic-tac-toe. (Version 7 only.)

fish   Play the card-guessing game. (Version 7 only.)

fortune   Present a random "fortune cookie." (Version 7 only.)

C

INTERACTING WITH YOUR UNIX SYSTEM

Appendix C discusses topics related to communicating, or interacting, with your UNIX system. We use the term communicating here in a broad sense. It not only means communication between hardware devices, such as between your terminal and the CPU (Central Processor Unit), but also communication between you and the UNIX software, like your interactions with the UNIX command-level programs.

First you will learn how to set up your terminal for communication with the CPU of the UNIX system. The discussion will be relevant for either a direct terminal connection to the UNIX system or a remote connection using a modem. You will learn how to configure your terminal to match the baud rate, full-duplex mode, parity checking, and several other serial communication parameters.

Many users have microcomputers that they will use for communicating with a time-sharing UNIX system. We address the software requirements for the microcomputer communication program that is needed in order to communicate with the UNIX system.

Then we will describe how you can interact more efficiently with the shell and other UNIX command programs. You learn about environment variables and how to use and tailor them to your needs.

The next major section discusses the general features of the terminal interface to the UNIX system. You will learn about control terminals, more about communication options, use of characters with special interpretation on input, and how to communicate with uppercase terminals.

In the last section we tabulate the most important terminal modes for the Bell Version 7, Berkeley, and Systems III and V terminal controls. You can display or reset these modes with the **stty** program, as described in Chapter 6.

Setting Up to Communicate With Your UNIX System

The basic steps for configuring your terminal and modem for communicating with the CPU of the UNIX system are presented here. The following communication parameters, or communications protocol, must be set correctly whether your terminal is communicating with UNIX by either a direct or modem (dial-up) connection:

- The data transmission speed (also known as the *baud rate*) for your terminal or modem device must match that for the communication line of your UNIX system CPU. If you are using a modem, the baud rate for both your terminal and the modem must be the same. Terminals that are connected directly to the UNIX system typically operate at 9600 baud; whereas modem phone connections generally operate at 300 or 1200 baud. (A 300 baud rate is about 30 characters per second, and 1200 baud is about 120 characters per second.)

- Enable full-duplex mode for your terminal and modem. In full-duplex mode characters typed at the keyboard are sent to the UNIX CPU, but do not appear on the terminal screen until UNIX sends them back (or echoes them) to the terminal. If you use half-duplex mode, you will see double character images since the terminal displays both the character as you type it, and then as it is echoed from UNIX.

- Parity is a simple error-checking scheme that detects if an error has occurred in a transmitted character (data) from one device to another. In general, parity checking is disabled for the communication line between your terminal and UNIX.

- In serial communication, a stop bit is appended to every character that is transmitted to signify the end of the character. Depending upon the installation, there can be one or two stop bits. You should specify only one stop bit unless you are communicating at 110 baud with a Teletype 33 or an equivalent terminal, in which two stop bits are required.

- Use lowercase mode if your terminal device supports it. If not, you can still communicate with your UNIX system, but you must denote capital letters and some special ASCII characters in a special way. See "Using Uppercase Terminals" for a discussion on this technique.

Consult the manual for your terminal or modem to see how to change these communication options. If you are communicating with a microcomputer, most of these communication parameters are set by the communication software. But if you are communicating to UNIX with a direct connect terminal, you may have to reset one or more switches on the back or inside of the terminal.

Communicating Between UNIX and a Microcomputer

You can communicate with a UNIX system from a microcomputer system, but you need to use software on your microcomputer that enables it to act like a communication terminal. The communication software must be able to send characters you type at your keyboard to a serial-communication port on your microcomputer and then onto the remote UNIX system. The communication software must display characters on your microcomputer's screen that it has received from the remote UNIX system. You will need to set up your communication software and communication port to conform to the communication parameters listed in the previous section.

Most microcomputer communication software allows you to send files and receive files from a remote UNIX system. Sending data from your microcomputer to the remote UNIX system is known as *uploading,* and the reverse process is called *downloading.* Now let's discuss downloading and then uploading of data between your microcomputer and a remote UNIX system.

You can receive a file from a remote UNIX system and store it on your microcomputer's disk. But your communication program must be able to store, or buffer, the characters it receives in your microcomputer's memory and then later write them to your system disk. The files from the remote UNIX system are transferred to your microcomputer through the execution of one or more UNIX programs. The basic steps for downloading a text file are

- Request your communication program to begin capturing into its buffer characters that will be received from the remote UNIX system.

- Use a file examination utility, such as **cat** or **pr**, to display the contents of the text file from the UNIX system.

- If your microcomputer's memory buffer is full, but the transmission of the file is not complete, either you or your communication program must send the stop character (usually a ^S) to the remote UNIX system to suspend further transmission.

- The contents of your microcomputer's memory buffer must be written to disk.

- Resume the transmission by sending the start character (usually a ^Q) to the remote UNIX system.

- Continue to download the file until all data has been transferred.

You can upload a file to the remote UNIX system if your communication program can read characters from your microcomputer's disk into a memory buffer and then send the characters one at a time to the microcomputer's communication port. The basic steps for uploading a text file are as follows:

- When you want the remote UNIX system to begin storing the characters that it receives from your microcomputer, enter the shell command line on the remote UNIX system:

$$\text{\$ cat } -\text{u} > \textit{filename}$$

The characters you send from your microcomputer become the standard input of **cat**, and this data is redirected unchanged to the disk file, *filename*. Use the unbuffered option (−**u**) so that if **cat** were terminated because (1) the remote UNIX system went down, (2) you were disconnected, or (3) a accidental interrupt occurred (common on noisy phone connections), all the text you sent would be saved on the UNIX system disk except for the last input line.

- Request your microcomputer's communication program to send the contents of the file on your microcomputer's system disk to the serial communication port.

- You must ensure that the remote UNIX system input buffer doesn't overflow. Some microcomputer communication software can be set so that the next character is not transmitted until the previous character has been echoed from UNIX. This would prevent the overflow problem. Some UNIX systems, however, can transmit a stop character (^S is the default) when its input buffer is nearly full. When the UNIX buffer has been drained sufficiently (because the **cat** program of this example reads enough characters), the UNIX system sends a start character (^Q is the default) to signal that your microcomputer can continue to send characters. Of course, your microcomputer communication program must stop and restart the transmission in response to receiving these UNIX stop and start characters.

- After transmission is complete, close the file on the remote UNIX system by sending the end-of-file code (EOF), which is usually a ^D. Be careful that you don't type more than one ^D or you might be logged off the remote UNIX system.

Customizing Your Working Environment

The *environment* is an area in memory where you can place definitions of shell variables so that they are accessible by any program you run. If you don't place a variable definition in the environment, its value is only known to the shell that defined the variable.

Placing a variable definition in the environment requires two steps. In the first step you define the shell variable; in the second step you place that variable definition in the environment. After a shell variable definition has been placed in the UNIX environment, it is called an environment variable (even though it is still considered a shell variable). Customizing your working environment simply means placing particular shell variable definitions in the environment. By placing shell variables in the environment, you can change the way your programs work.

The shell is the primary program interested in the environment. For instance, the Bourne Shell prompt is stored in the environment variable **PS1**, and the command search path in environment variable **PATH**. A few programs besides the shell do look at the environment. For instance, both **nice** and **nohup** refer to the **PATH** environment variable definition just as the shell does when you specify a command using an incomplete pathname.

Setting Bourne Shell Variables

In Chapter 4, tutorial Session 8, you learned how to define C Shell variables using the **set** command. Then you learned how to display the value of the variable using the **echo** command. In this section you will learn how to define and display the value of Bourne Shell variables. In the next section you will learn how to place Bourne and C Shell variable definitions in the environment.

You can set a variable for the Bourne Shell by using the command line syntax:

$$\$ \ variable\text{-}name = value$$

Here *variablename* is the name of the variable and *value* can either be a string of characters or a number. A shell variable that has a numeric value is treated by the shell as if it were a string value.

The next example shows several variables being defined (named on the left) to the values shown (on the right side of the equal sign).

```
$ count=10
$ user='Becca Thomas'
$ dir1=/lib  dir2=/usr/lib
$ PATH=:/bin:/usr/bin
$ time='date'
$
```

The variable **count** is defined to be "10"; **user** assumes the string value "Becca Thomas". You can define more than one variable on a line, such as **dir1** to be "/lib" and **dir2** to be "/usr/lib". The shell variable **PATH** is set to the value ":/bin:/usr/bin", and **time** takes the value that results from execution of the **date** command. All shell variables that are assigned to a command, like the variable **time**, must have the command surrounded by grave accents. When a whitespace is included in the *value* string, you must surround it with single or double quotation marks.

To display the value of a variable, use the **echo** command and precede each variable with a dollar sign ($). The next screen shows how to display the value of the variables, which we just defined, with the **echo** command:

```
$ echo $count
10
$ echo $user
Becca Thomas
$ echo $dir1
/lib
$ echo $dir2
/usr/lib
$ echo $PATH
:/bin:/usr/bin
$ echo $time
Thu Nov  1 09:32:30 PST 1984
$
```

Although we have just defined **count**, **user**, **dir1**, **dir2**, **PATH**, and **time** as shell variables, they are not environment variables because we have not placed them in the environment. In the next section, we will show you how to place a shell variable that has been set into the environment.

Environment Variables

Environment variables are made available to each program process as it begins execution. The process can elect to examine and use the information stored in the environment variable, or ignore it. Thus environment strings provide a way to pass "global" information to any executing program. An environment variable is simply a shell variable that has been placed in the environment. Placing the variable in the environment, however, differs from shell to shell.

You can add a Bourne Shell variable to the environment by using the **export** command. The command line syntax is simply

$ **export** *variable-name*

Thus defining and setting an environment Bourne Shell variable involves two steps — setting and then exporting the variable. As an example, let's redefine the variable for the shell prompt, **PS1**, and place it in the environment.

$ **PS1="Your wish is my command "; export PS1**

Your wish is my command ▓

We placed both commands on one line by separating them with a semicolon. You can redefine **PS1** to be its original value by entering **PSI='$'; export PS1.**

You can define and add a C Shell variable to the environment in one step by using the built-in **setenv** command. The syntax is simply

% **setenv** *variable-name value*

As an example, let's redefine the C Shell prompt to display the event number. Recall from Chapter 4, tutorial Session 8, that an event is a command in the C Shell history list. The event number is a number that the C Shell gives to each command line that was executed. The new variable definition can be placed in the environment using one command line:

% **setenv prompt ' \!) '**

12) ▓

Notice that you must escape the exclamation point, which will be replaced by the current event number, with a backslash (\ ) so that it won't be interpreted as an event specifier as you enter the command line that redefines the **prompt** variable.

Bourne environment variable names are generally capitalized to distinguish them from ordinary shell variables. Some C Shell environment variables are also capitalized, but others may not be. A few common environment variables used by both the Bourne and C Shells are listed here. Note that you should not use these same names for other quantities to avoid conflict with these reserved names:

HOME

Your *home directory*, the directory where your login shell is initially located after signing on.

PATH

Your *command search path*, which is a list of directories your shell and other commands search to locate programs you invoke unless a full path-name is given.

MAIL

Your *mailfile*, that is, the pathname for the ordinary file where your electronic mail is stored.

TERM

Your *terminal type*.

These environment variables are used by the Bourne Shell only:

IFS

Internal field separators, which are the space, tab, and new line characters by default. These are the characters that separate elements (or words) on the shell command line.

LOGNAME

The user (or login) name of the person who is running the shell process.

PS1

The login Bourne Shell prompt. Default value is "$ ".

PS2

The subshell Bourne Shell prompt. Default value is " >".

TZ

The *time zone* specification, whose value has the format *xxxnzzz*, where *xxx* is the standard local time zone abbreviation, *n* is the difference in hours from Greenwich Mean Time (GMT), and *zzz* is the abbreviation for the daylight savings time zone, if any. For example, **PST8PDT** is for the Pacific time zone (eight hours different from GMT).

This last variable is particular to the C Shell:

USER

The user (or login) name of the person who is running the shell process.

As an example of an environment variable that is referenced by a program other than by a shell, consider the **MORE** environment variable used by the Berkeley **more** program (discussed in Chapter 6). When **more** begins execution it looks in the environment for a variable named **MORE**. If found, the string value is interpreted by **more** as the invocation command line option(s).

For example, let's say you wanted **more** to display the long form of the prompt.

You could do this by invoking **more** with the **−d** option, or you could predefine the variable **MORE** to equal this same option by typing (from the Bourne Shell) **MORE=−d;export MORE**, or (from the C Shell) **setenv MORE −d**. The variable **MORE** is placed in the environment so that its value may be accessed by the **more** program. If **MORE** were simply defined, but not placed in the environment, its value would only be known to the shell that defined it.

Telling UNIX Software Your Terminal Type

In order for programs like **vi**, **more**, and others to control the display on your terminal screen, they must know the characteristics of the terminal you are using. The characteristics for hundreds of terminals are described in a terminal capability database (termcap) with the pathname **/etc/termcap**. This database was developed at U.C. Berkeley in conjunction with the **vi** editor; however, it is used in other applications on the UNIX system.

The Bell System V release contains a similar terminal capability database known as **terminfo**. But this database is not compatible with **termcap**. Each terminal database has its strengths and weaknesses. Most of the UNIX software available today that needs to know about your terminal uses **termcap**. But more and more software will be using **terminfo** for compatibility with Bell System V. We will only be concerned, however, with Berkeley's **termcap** database.

The **termcap** database is a text file made up of several lines for each terminal entry. Each entry for a terminal begins with a *name field* on a separate line. This name field is usually written as a sequence of abbreviated names for the terminal and is separated by vertical bars. Also within this name field is the *terminal type.* The UNIX system can access information about a terminal if it knows the name of the terminal type. Below the name field are lines that consist of colon-separated fields. These fields describe the terminal capabilities and contain the characters that are sent to the terminal in order to control it. We will only be concerned with the name field for this discussion and how to tell UNIX which terminal type you are using. You can learn how to interpret and even make your own custom "termcap" entries by studying the on-line manual entry for the **termcap** database. The manual entry is usually in Section 5, so enter **man 5 termcap** to display it.

To find the entry that matches your terminal, you would scan the **/etc/termcap** file with an editor or the **cat** command. Here is an example using the **termcap** entry for the ADM3A terminal manufactured by Lear-Siegler.

```
la|adm3a|3a|lsi adm3a| \
  :am:bs:cm= \E=%+ %+ :cl=^Z:co#80:li#24:ma=^K^P: \
  ho=^^:nd=^L:up=^K:
```

The items of the name field (first line) are as follows:

- The first item, la, always consists of two characters, the first is a code for the terminal manufacturer and the second is an abbreviation for the model or mode.

- The next item specifies the *terminal type* name. This is the abbreviation you would use when informing UNIX software of the type of terminal you are using. Thus the terminal type name for the Lear-Siegler model ADM3A is adm3a.

- The other entries in the name field represent additional synonyms for the terminal name.

The remaining lines in a given **termcap** entry are abbreviations for describing the terminal capabilities to the UNIX system software. Information — such as the terminal screen size, how to address or move the cursor, and the codes to send to the terminal for adding or deleting lines — would be contained in these entries.

The UNIX system software determines your terminal type name by examining the value of the environment variable **TERM**. Thus after you discover your terminal type in the **terminal** database, you would set the variable **TERM** to be the terminal type for your terminal. After placing the **TERM** variable definition in the environment, it may be referenced by any UNIX program.

To set and place the variable **TERM** in the environment, from the Bourne Shell, enter the commands

$$\text{\$ TERM} = terminal\text{-}type$$

$$\text{\$ export TERM}$$

The first command sets the value of **TERM** to be the *terminaltype,* and the second exports the value of this variable into the environment.

From the C Shell you would set and export the variable with the command line:

$$\% \text{ setenv TERM } terminal\text{-}type$$

The next two examples illustrate setting the **TERM** variable to correspond to the Lear-Siegler ADM3A terminal. The left side shows the commands for the Bourne Shell, and the example on the right shows the command for the C Shell.

```
$ TERM=adm3a               % setenv TERM adm3a
$ export TERM              %
$
```

If you have not defined and placed the **TERM** variable in the environment, you can inform the **ex** or **vi** program of your terminal type after you have invoked either editor by using the editor **set** command. The **set** command is used for setting editor options (see Chapter 4, Sessions 10 and 11) . From within line-editing mode, you would enter:

:**set** **term**=*terminal-type*

The **vi** program will not let you set the terminal type through a temporary escape to line-editing mode from visual mode. You must first enter line-editing mode by typing **Q**, and then use the **set** command.

Setting the User File Creation Mask

As you create a file or directory, it is assigned a pattern of permission modes. (File access permission modes are discussed in Chapter 3, Session 4.) The task of assigning permission modes to a file is given to the **umask** value. When you log on to the system, the **umask** is given an arbitrary value; but you can change this value while you are on the system. Changing the access permission assigned to your files is another way of customizing your working environment.

You can display the **umask** value by entering the shell command **umask**. You can change the value by entering **umask** *value*, where *value* is the desired value in octal.

To determine the **umask** value that you want to reassign to **umask**, first list the desired permissions in symbolic format and then write down the equivalent in binary pattern. Next complement this binary pattern by changing all ones to zeros and all zeros to ones. Finally, write down the octal equivalent of this complemented binary value. The resulting octal number is the desired **umask** value.

For example, let's say the desired pattern is **rwxr—x————**. The **umask** value may be determined as shown:

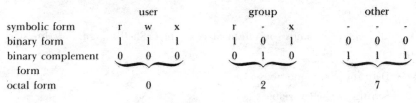

	user			group			other		
symbolic form	r	w	x	r	-	x	-	-	-
binary form	1	1	1	1	0	1	0	0	0
binary complement form	0	0	0	0	1	0	1	1	1
octal form		0			2			7	

umask value = 027

Now if you set your **umask** value to 027 and create a new file, the resulting permissions for a directory would be **rwxr—x———**. For an ordinary file the permission would be **rw—r—————**, since execute permission is generally not enabled when an ordinary file is created.

Shell Start-Up Files

You can manually customize your environment by entering all the commands after you have logged on to the system. Alternatively you could place the same commands in an executable file, known as a *shell start-up* file, and when you log on to the system, the file would automatically be executed.

The shell start-up file has a reserved name that is recognized by your login shell. The Bourne Shell recognizes the name **.profile**, and the Berkeley C Shell recognizes both **.login** and **.cshrc**. The **.profile** and the **.login** start-up files are executed only once and before the shell program issues you a prompt. The C Shell's **.cshrc** file is not only executed when you log on to the system, but also every time you create a subshell. Thus if there is any command that is executed in the **.login** start-up file whose effects will carry over to a subshell, there is no need to include it in the **.cshrc** file.

Commands you might place in your Bourne Shell **.profile** or C Shell **.login** start-up file include:

- Changing the terminal modes with **stty**.
- Resetting the command search path.
- Resetting the shell prompt.
- Setting shell variables.
- Setting shell variables and then placing them in the environment.
- Display the current values of shell and environment variables.
- Display and record your log-on time.
- Display system status information, such as the number of users, who is on the system, all processes currently executing (to see how loaded the system is), and so on.

Additional commands you might place in the C Shell's **.login** or .cshrc start-up file might include:

- Defining command aliases.
- Setting C Shell variables.
- Display the values of all command aliases and the C Shell and environment variables.

• Enabling the history function.

As an example, the following displays the contents of a **.profile** start-up file:

```
$ cat .profile
PATH=:/bin:/usr/bin:/usr/lbin
TERM=kA
export PATH TERM
stty erase '^h' kill '^x' quit '^u' intr '^c'
stty ixon
echo Your login time is 'date'.
echo Currently 'who | wc -l' terminals on-line.
echo The shell variables that are set include:
set
echo The terminal driver is set up for:
stty
$
```

When executed on the Bell System III UNIX by the Bourne Shell, the following result was obtained:

```
(UNIX SYSTEM BANNER)
login: username
Password:
(UNIX SYSTEM MESSAGES)
Your login time is Tue Oct 30 10:13:05 PST 1984.
Currently 4 terminals on-line.
The shell variables that are set include:
HOME=/usr/username
IFS=

LOGNAME=username
PATH=:/bin:/usr/bin:/usr/lbin
PS1=$
PS2=>
SHELL=/bin/sh
TERM=kA
TZ=PST8PDT
```

The terminal driver is set up for:

speed 9600 baud; —parity

intr = ^c; quit = ^u; erase = ^h; kill = ^x

brkint —inpck icrnl onlcr tab3

echo echoe echok

$ ▓

The C Shell also recognizes a file named **.logout** that will execute commands contained within the file after you make the request to sign off your UNIX system. You might place "clean up" commands or a command to record your logout time in this file.

The Bourne Shell doesn't recognize a **.logout** file, but if you place the command **trap '$HOME/.logout' 0** in your **.profile** start-up file, a **.logout** in your home directory will be executed automatically when you log off the system. The file permission mode for **.logout** must be set to executable.

The General Terminal Interface

The UNIX kernel program supports communication with an asynchronous serial device such as a CRT display terminal, a modem, or a serial line printer. This section describes some of the general features of this communication interface (or communication line) provided by the kernel program.

Your Control Terminal

When you log in to your UNIX system, a terminal device file is opened to become the standard input, standard output, and standard error output files for your login shell. This terminal device file is also known as your *control terminal*. Any process that your login shell starts up will be monitored by your control terminal. Taken together, all these processes that are created by the login shell are referred to as a process group, and your login shell process is the *process group leader*.

The device name **/dev/tty** is recognized as a synonym for your control terminal. You can often use **/dev/tty** as a generic name instead of the full pathname for the control terminal (determined by the **tty** command). For instance, you can use **/dev/tty** instead of the name of your control terminal in this example of a pipeline using the **tee** command:

command1 | **tee** **/dev/tty** | *command2*

Here **/dev/tty** is used instead of your terminal device name, which might be **/dev/tty01** — depending on what terminal you are assigned to when you log on to the system.

Assume that you are communicating with UNIX via a dial-up (modem) connection. If your terminal connection is broken because the phone was hung up, the hangup signal generated by the system kernel is sent to all processes in the process group associated with your control terminal. This signal normally causes these processes to terminate unless other arrangements have been made with the **nohup** command.

You may be executing a program that "hangs," that is, there is no response to any keyboard input. If this happens, hang up the telephone and UNIX will generally log you off the system. However, some systems will not lay you off. When you log in again, you can continue your work.

The Input Buffer

You can type characters during any time that you are logged on the system and they will be received by UNIX, even while output from another process is occurring. The characters are stored in an input buffer (generally 256 characters in capacity). The system will store all the characters that you type in the input buffer, unless this input buffer overflows, which is rare. The buffer could overflow, however, if you were sending data faster than the system could handle. If indeed the input buffer overflows, the system discards all the characters in the input buffer without warning.

Special Input Characters

It is necessary for certain ASCII characters to have a special meaning on input. These special ASCII characters are accepted by the terminal device and are processed at the level of the kernel, but are not passed to the command program making the read request. Here are some of these special characters:

intr
   The interrupt character (default rubout or ASCII del) generates an interrupt signal, which is sent to all processes in the process group. An interrupt character will cause each process to terminate unless arrangements have been made by the process to "catch" or ignore this signal.

quit
   The quit character (default ^\ or ASCII fs) generates a quit signal. This signal acts like the interrupt except that if a process is terminated, a copy of the process is written to the current directory with filename **core**.

erase

The erase character (default #, but may have been changed to ^H on some systems) erases the preceding input character. It will not erase beyond the beginning of a line. The beginning of the line may be indicated by a new line, EOF, or EOL character.

kill

The line kill character (default @, but may have been changed to ^X on some systems) erases the entire line. A line may be marked by a new line, EOF, or EOL character. The cursor may or may not be positioned on the next line after typing this character.

eof

The end-of-file character (default ^D or ASCII EOT) is used to generate an end-of-file from a terminal. When received, all the characters waiting to be read are passed to the program making the read request; then the EOF is discarded.

new line

The ASCII line feed (lf character, or ^J) is the usual line delimiter.

return

Generally RETURN is equivalent to the new line character unless —nl mode (explained later) is in effect.

stop

The stop character (default ^S or ASCII dc3) will suspend all terminal output. While suspended, any additional characters are ignored with the exception of ^Q, although some systems will resume output when any key has been pressed.

start

The start character (default ^Q or ASCII dc1) will resume output that has been suspended by a stop character.

You can remove the special interpretation given to the ERASE, KILL, or EOF character by preceding it with the backslash (\ ), which acts as an *escape character*. The backslash character will not be included in the input unless you precede it with another backslash character to remove its special interpretation as an escape character. That is, type \ \ to enter one \.

The STOP and START characters can be used to suspend and resume output to the terminal. This process is known as *flow control*. In general, only the Berkeley **stty** program lets you redefine these flow control characters.

Using Uppercase Terminals

When you log on to the UNIX system, the **getty** process, which monitors your terminal line, will note if you answer the "login:" prompt with uppercase characters. If so, the system assumes you are using a terminal that can produce only uppercase letters and sets your kernel program accordingly. Then all uppercase characters that you type will be translated to their lowercase equivalent by the kernel before they are passed to any UNIX command program. The characters are manipulated as lowercase equivalents within the UNIX system and then are translated back to uppercase upon output for display on your uppercase terminal. You can specify a capital letter on input by preceding the character with a backslash (\ ). On output, the kernel program shows a capital letter by supplying a backslash prefix to the letter.

Many uppercase terminals have a limited character set that cannot generate several ASCII characters. The grave accent (`), tilde (~), vertical bar (|), and left and right braces ({ and }), can be represented by the escape sequences tabulated here.

Sequence To Type	Character To Be Produced
\`	`
\!	|
\^	~
\(	{
\)	}

You can input a character shown under the **Character To Be Produced** column by keying in the corresponding escape sequence shown in the **Sequence To Type** column.

Terminal Mode Settings

In this section, we tabulate the most common and useful terminal mode settings for the different UNIX versions. We first begin by addressing the terminal modes for Bell Version 7, then move on to Bell Systems III and V, and finally the Berkeley version. Within each version, the terminal modes have been divided into six major groups: (1) Control Modes, which allow resetting of the communication options, (2) Input Modes, which affect input character processing, (3) Output Modes, which affect output character processing, (4) Local Modes, which are some miscellaneous modes affecting both terminal input and output, (5) the Combination Modes, if present, which will generally affect several of the five basic terminal modes, and (6) Control Assignments, which enable you to reset or disable recognition of the special input characters. In order to save space, we have condensed those mode settings that have an enable and disable property. For example, the Bell Version 7 has two modes for even parity: **even** and **−even**. A setting of **even** allows even parity, while −even disallows even parity. Even parity will be represented in the table as follows:

> **even** (−**even**)
> Allow (disallow) even parity.

The setting enclosed in the parentheses corresponds to the word that is enclosed in the parentheses in the explanation. If you wanted to allow even parity, you would enter **stty even**; but if you wanted to disallow even parity, you would enter **stty** −**even**.

Bell Version 7 Control Modes:

> **even** (−**even**)
> Allow (disallow) even parity.
> **odd** (−**odd**)
> Allow (disallow) odd parity.
> **hup** (−**hup**)
> Hang up (don't hang up) dataphone on log off.
> **0**
> Hang up phone immediately.
> **50 75 110 134 150 200 300 600 1200 1800 2400 4800 9600**
> Set baud rate.

Bell Version 7 Input Modes:

> **nl**
> Accept only new line characters to end line.
> −**nl**
> Accept new line and return characters to end the line.
> **lcase** (−**lcase**)
> Convert (don't convert) uppercase to lowercase.

Bell Version 7 Output Modes: A suffix of 0 means no delay while a suffix of 3 gives the longest delay.

> **cr0 cr1 cr2 cr3**
> Delay after outputting a carriage return.
> **nl0 nl1 nl2 nl3**
> Delay after a new line.
> **tab0 tab1 tab2 tab3**
> Delay after a tab.

ff0 ff1
Delay after a form feed (^L).

bs0 bs1
Delay after a backspace.

Bell Version 7 Local Modes:

echo (−echo)
Echo (don't echo) typed characters.

Bell Version 7 Combination Modes:

cbreak (−cbreak)
Read each character (each line) as received.

raw (−raw)
Raw (cooked) mode.

ek
Reset erase and kill characters to default values # and @, respectively.

tabs
Preserve tabs.

−tabs
Replace tabs with a space character.

tty33
Set modes appropriate for the Teletype 33.

tty37
Set modes appropriate for the Teletype 37.

vt05
Set modes appropriate for Digital Equipment Corporation VT05.

tn300
Set modes appropriate for General Electric TermiNet 300.

ti700
Set modes appropriate for Texas Instruments Silent 700.

tek
Set modes appropriate for Tektronix 4014.

Bell Version 7 Control Assignments:

erase *c*
Set erase character to *c*.

kill *c*
Set kill character to *c*.

Bell Systems III and V Control Modes:

parenb (−**parenb**)
Enable (disable) parity generation and checking.

parodd (−**parodd**)
Select odd (even) parity. Ignored if −**parenb** mode is set.

cs5 cs6 cs7 cs8
Select number of bits in character size during transmission and reception.
Does not include parity bit (if any). Thus **cs8** is not compatible with
parenb mode.

cstopb (−**cstopb**)
Use two (one) stop bits per character. Two stop bits are customary at 110
baud, one otherwise.

cread (−**cread**)
Enable (disable) the receiver. No characters are received if disabled.

clocal (−**clocal**)
Assume a direct (dial-up) connection without (with) modem control.

0
Hang up the phone immediately.

50 75 110 134 150 300 600 1200 2400 4800 9600 exta extb
Set data communication speed to the baud rate specified.

hupcl (−**hupcl**)
or
hup (−**hup**)
Hang up (do not hang up) modem connection after logging off.

Bell Systems III and V Input Modes:

ignbrk (−**ignbrk**)
Ignore (don't ignore) a break character on input.

brkint (−**brkint**)
Signal (don't signal) interrupt on receiving a break character.

ignpar (−**ignpar**)
Ignore (don't ignore) parity errors.

parmrk (−**parmrk**)
Mark (don't mark) parity errors.

inpck (−**inpck**)
Enable (disable) parity checking on input.

istrip (−**istrip**)
Strip (don't strip) input characters to 7 bits.

inlcr (−**inlcr**)
Convert (don't convert) a new line character to a return character on
input.

igncr (−**igncr**)
Ignore (don't ignore) a return character on input.

icrnl (−**icrnl**)
Convert (don't convert) a return character to a new line character on input.

iuclc (−**iuclc**)
Convert (don't convert) uppercase characters to lowercase equivalent on input.

ixon (−**ixon**)
Enable (disable) start and stop character output control.

ixany (−**ixany**)
Allow any character (only ^Q) to restart output.

ixoff (−**ixoff**)
Request to send (not send) start and stop characters when the input queue is nearly empty or full.

Bell Systems III and V Output Modes:

opost (−**opost**)
Enable (don't enable) output mode processing.

olcuc (−**olcuc**)
Convert (don't convert) lowercase characters to uppercase equivalent on output.

onlcr (−**onlcr**)
Convert (don't convert) a new line to carriage return/line feed pair on output.

ocrnl (−**ocrnl**)
Convert (don't convert) return to new line on output.

onocr (−**onocr**)
Don't (do) output a return at column zero.

onlret (−**onlret**)
The new line character performs (doesn't perform) the return function on the terminal.

ofill (−**ofill**)
Send fill characters (use timing) for delays.

ofdel (−**ofdel**)
Fill characters are ASCII delete (or nul).

For the following, a suffix of 0 means no delay, while a suffix of 3 gives the longest delay.

cr0 cr1 cr2 cr3
Amount of delay after sending a return character.

nl0 nl1
Amount of delay after sending a new line character.

tab0 tab1 tab2
Amount of delay after sending horizontal tab character.

bs0 bs1
Amount of delay after sending a backspace character.

ff0 ff1
Amount of delay after sending form-feed character.

vt0 vt1
Amount of delay after sending vertical tab character.

Bell Systems III and V Local Modes:

isig (−isig)
Enable (disable) the intr and quit character processing.

icanon (−icanon)
Enable (disable) erase and kill character processing.

xcase (−xcase)
Processed (unprocessed) upper- and lowercase presentation.

echo (−echo)
Echo (don't echo) received characters to the terminal.

echoe (−echoe)
Echo (don't echo) the erase character as a backspace, followed by a space, and then a backspace again. This sequence erases the erase character on most CRT terminals.

echok (−echok)
or
lfkc (−lfkc)
Echo (don't echo) new line after kill character.

echonl (−echonl)
Echo (don't echo) the new line character.

noflsh (−noflsh)
Disable (enable) output buffer flushing after a intr or quit character.

Bell Systems III and V Combination Modes:

evenp
parity
Enable even parity with word size of 7 bits (not including the parity bit).

oddp
Enable odd parity with a word size of 7 bits (not including the parity bit).

−parity
−evenp
−oddp
Disable parity and set word size to 8 bits.

raw (−raw or cooked)
Enable (disable) raw input and output. If enabled, there is no erase, kill, intr, quit, EOT character and output post processing.

nl (−nl)
Unset (set) the **icrnl** and **onlcr** mode. In addition, **−nl** unsets the **inlcr**, **igncr**, **ocrnl**, and **onlret** modes.

lcase (−lcase)
or
LCASE (−LCASE)
Set (unset) the **xcase**, **iuclc**, and **olcuc** modes.

tabs
Preserve tabs when printing.

−tabs or tab3
Expand tabs to 8 spaces when printing.

ek
Reset erase and kill character back to defaults # and @.

sane
Reset all modes to some default values. Use ^J instead of RETURN to enter into the computer.

tty33
Set modes appropriate for Teletype 33.

tty37
Set modes appropriate for Teletype 37.

vt05
Set modes appropriate for DEC VT05.

tn300
Set modes appropriate for GE TermiNet 300.

ti700
Set modes appropriate for TI 700.

tek
Set modes appropriate for Tektronix 4014.

Bell Systems III and V Control Assignments:

erase *c*
Set erase character to *c*.

kill *c*
Set line kill character to *c*.

intr *c*
>   Set interrupt character to *c*.

quit *c*
>   Set quit character to *c*.

eof *c*
>   Set end-of-file character to *c*.

eol *c*
>   Set alternate end-of-line character to *c*.

line *i*
>   Set line discipline to *i*, where *i* is an integer from 0 to 127.

Bell System V Mode Enhancements: The Bell System V terminal drive now supports synchronous terminals. This system has added a few local modes for synchronous lines:

stwrap (−stwrap)
>   Disable (enable) truncation of lines longer than 79 characters on a synchronous line.

stflush (−stflush)
>   Enable (disable) output flush on a synchronous line after every write operation.

stappl (−stappl)
>   Use application or block mode (line mode) on a synchronous line.

The original Berkeley UNIX mode has been supplemented by a new version. If you have the old version, you should consult the Bell Version 7 modes since the two are identical.

Berkeley Control Modes:

intrup (−intrup)
>   Send (don't send) the sigtint signal to the control terminal process group whenever an input line is available for reading.

mdmbuf
>   Start and stop output on carrier transitions (not implemented).

−mdmbuf
>   Return error if write to terminal attempted after carrier drops.

nohang (−nohang)
>   Don't (do) send hangup signal to control terminal process group when carrier drops.

tostop (−tostop)
>   Stop (don't stop) background jobs if they attempt terminal output.

Berkeley Input Modes:

decctlq (—decctlq)
Allow only ᐃQ (any character) to restart output after being suspended by stop character. The name is derived from DEC (Digital Equipment Corporation) control. This is the same as —**ixany** (**ixany**) mode in Bell UNIX System's III and IV.

pendin (—pendin)
Input is (isn't) pending after a switch from cbreak to cooked mode and will be reinput when a read becomes pending or more input arrives.

tandem (—tandem)
Request send (not send) start/stop characters when the input queue is nearly empty/full. This is equivalent to Bell "ixoff" mode.

Berkeley Output Modes:

litout (—litout)
Send output characters without (with) post processing.

tilde (—tilde)
Convert (don't convert) tilde to grave accent on output for Hazeltine terminals.

New Berkeley Driver Local Modes:

crtbs (—crtbs)
Echo (don't echo) backspaces on erase characters.

crterase (—crterase)
Echo (don't echo) erase character as backspace then space and then backspace, which erases the erase character on most CRT terminals.

crtkill (—crtkill)
Erase (don't erase) input line after kill.

ctlecho (—ctlecho)
Echo (don't echo) control characters as ^c (and delete as ^?.) In cooked mode EOT (^D) is not echoed.

flusho (—flusho)
Discard (don't discard) output because user pressed ^O (internal state bit).

prterase (—prterase)
Echo (don't echo) erased characters within "\" and "/".

Berkeley Combination Modes:

crt
Set options for a CRT mode **crtbs**, **ctlecho** mode; and, if baud rate is greater than or equal to 1200, enable **crterase** and **crtkill** mode.

Berkeley Control Assignments:

brk *c*
  Set break character to *c*.

dsusp *c*
  Set delayed suspend process character to *c*. (default ^Y.)

eof *c*
  Set end-of-file character (EOF) to *c*.

flush *c*
  Set flush output character to *c*. (default ^O.)

intr *c*
  Set interrupt character to *c*.

lnext *c*
  Set literal next character to *c* (default ^V.)

quit *c*
  Set quit character to *c*.

rprnt *c*
  Set reprint line character to *c* (default ^R.)

start *c*
  Set start character to *c*.

stop *c*
  Set stop character to *c*.

susp *c*
  Set suspend process character to *c*. (default ^Z.)

werase *c*
  Set word erase character to *c*. (default ^W.)

APPENDIX *D*

ESSENTIALS OF SYSTEM ADMINISTRATION

Whether you are the only user of your UNIX system or are responsible for maintaining a multiuser UNIX system, you will need to know the essential procedures for setting up and administering your system. In Appendix D we cover the most important routine maintenance and frequently used system set-up procedures. Among other topics, we will discuss how to safely start and shut down your UNIX system, how to back up your file system, and how to add and delete user accounts.

It is impossible for any book to cover every aspect of setting up and maintaining your UNIX system. In particular, topics that are implementation-dependent (details that vary greatly from system to system) cannot be included in a general discussion. And especially for this reason, there is no substitute for good hardware and system software documentation from your computer hardware and UNIX system software supplier.

615

Overview of System Administration

Exactly what is system administration? In general, any activity involving setup (configuration) and maintenance of your UNIX system. Who should be responsible for system administration? If you are the sole user of your system, you will probably be administering it. On a larger multiuser system, one user is generally selected for this task. A person who is consistent and responsible is the best choice for administrator — not necessarily the best system programmer.

What are the duties of the system administrator? Almost anything involving setting up and maintaining the system — from the regular tasks of system start-up, shutdown, and file system backup, to emergency tasks such as repairing the file system after a system crash, and to less routine tasks like adding and deleting user accounts.

The Superuser Account

The *superuser* account, which has the account name **root**, is a nonrestricting account in that anyone logged on to the system with the superuser account can access all files and perform any task that is within the capabilities of UNIX. Anyone who has access to the supervisor account is considered a *superuser*. The superuser account is usually assigned to the system administrator.

If you are the system administrator, you must be logged on as **root** in order to perform system configuration and maintenance. You should be *very* careful when using the superuser account since there are no system access restrictions for the superuser. For instance, you may change or delete any file or kill any process on the system. Thus you should carefully consider everything you do by taking common sense precautions *before* you do it.

The superuser account is a privileged account. It is a large responsibility to have total power over your UNIX system. Here are a few guidelines to help you safely maintain your system:

* Use superuser privileges as little as possible. *Do not* use this account for your routine work on the system, and *do not* use this account when you are tired or fatigued.

* Be careful when using commands and techniques that could irreparably damage the system. In particular, be especially careful when using utilities like **rm**, **mv**, **cp**, **fsck**, and **clri** (**fsck** and **clri** commands are covered later in this chapter). *Always* use the interactive option (—i) with the **rm**, **mv** and **cp** commands, in order to give yourself another chance in case you make a typing mistake.

• Keep a system log book. Other users may find a log book helpful for solving problems when you are not available.

Most of the command programs used for system maintenance are contained in the /etc directory instead of the usual command directories /bin and /usr/bin. This way, ordinary users are less likely to execute them by mistake. But to be sure, remove execute permission for programs in the /etc directory so that accounts other than **root** cannot execute them.

When using system maintenance commands, you will either need to use the full pathname for the system maintenance command names or add the /etc directory to the command search path for the **root** account. For example, let's modify the command search path (contained in the variable **PATH**) so that /etc is the first directory searched. From the Bourne Shell enter

PATH=/etc:$PATH; export PATH

You could place this command line in the .profile shell start-up file for the **root** account. Note that $PATH is expanded to be the former value of **PATH**, so /etc is effectively prefixed to the former search path.

If you are using the C Shell, enter the command line

set path = (/etc $path)

Notice that you do not need to use the **setenv** command since the C Shell will place the variable in the environment automatically. If you want the /etc prefixed to your **PATH** variable when you log on, include the following command line in your C Shell .login file:

setenv PATH /etc:$PATH

In this appendix we will prefix the /etc directory to the names of commands that reside in this directory. Otherwise we use only the basename for the commands that are found in the conventional /bin and /usr/bin command directories.

Usage Policy

Users frequently ask, "Should I leave the computer system running continuously?" The UNIX system software is designed to run continuously; however, your hardware system may not be. Consult your system manuals or the system supplier if you aren't sure. In general, modern hardware can be run continuously as long as there is adequate ventilation and cooling for the hardware and protection from line voltage surges and outages. You can purchase line voltage stabilizers and filters if power surges are a problem. You can purchase a device containing batteries that will continue to power the system when the main power source is interrupted. Most users of single-user systems shut down their systems when they are done for the day, but systems used by several different people tend to be left running so that they can be accessed at any time. Whether or not you should shut down the system is a policy the users of the system should decide.

Parts of the UNIX File System

It is important that you know the internal structure of the UNIX file system, since many of the following discussions will refer to this topic. So before we go any farther, we will briefly discuss the important components of the file system.

There are three major parts to every file in the UNIX file system. They are:

- The *inode*. Each file in the file system is described by a structure called an inode. They are located in special data blocks (not used for file data) and each 512-byte block can contain as many as eight 64-byte inodes. The inode contains all the data about the file except the *filename* and the actual data contained in the file. Note that the disk addresses (locations on disk) for the file's data blocks are contained in the inode area. The inodes are numbered from 2 (reserved for the root directory, /) through 65,535. This identifying number is known as the *inode number* or the *i-number*.

  Recall that in the tutorial chapters we referred to pointers to the physical file. These pointers are the inode numbers. They actually point to the inode, which in turn points to the disk blocks containing the file data.

- The *data blocks*. The data blocks are located on the disk and contain the actual data of a file. Each block can typically hold 512 characters. Some UNIX implementations (such as Berkeley UNIX) use larger block sizes ranging from 1024 characters and up. Even if the file contains only *one* character, an entire data block must be allocated to hold this single character.

- The *directory*. A directory contains one or more filenames. Each entry in a directory contains one filename and the inode number that points to the inode for the file. Directories also have an inode.

Figure D-1 shows the relationship between the data blocks, the inode, and a directory that references the file. In this figure we show that the directory associates the filename **poem** with the inode for the file (we show 23284 as the inode number for this file). We also show the inode pointing to a data block. The data

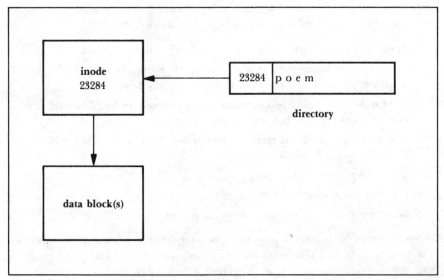

Figure D-1: *The relationship between data blocks, the inode, and a directory entry.*

block contains the actual characters in the file — "Roses are Red", and so on. The file **poem** was used as an example in the tutorial chapters.

Now that the three major parts of the file system have been discussed, we need to mention two other parts important for administration of the file system:

- The *superblock* is a very special block in the file system. It contains global information about the file system such as the file system name, the total size of the file system, the total number of free data blocks and free inodes, and so on.

- The *free-block list* is a chain of blocks that contain the disk address of all the data blocks in the system that are available for use by a file.

Making Your UNIX System Operational

System startup involves several steps that are similar in general procedure from one UNIX system to another. However, the details of each step may vary greatly from system to system. But *before* you plug in your computer system, consult the documentation that comes with it, since the detailed steps of system startup

depend on your particular hardware configuration and system software imple-
mention. The general steps in starting up your system are:

* Apply power, or reset a system that is already running.
* The computer hardware may perform a hardware diagnostic, which is usual-
  ly under direction of a program in ROM (read-only memory).
* Read in bootstrapping programs or use one already in ROM (see the discus-
  sion of bootstrapping below).
* The bootstrap program reads in and starts the UNIX kernel program to
  bring the system up to single-user mode.
* Set the system time-of-day clock.
* Run the file system check program (**fsck**).
* Bring the system up to multiuser (if appropriate).

Some of these steps may be automated depending on the design of your system.
For instance, the first four steps are often performed by a ROM-based program
that begins execution as soon as the power is applied or the system is reset.

The individual steps for system startup are discussed in the following sections.
We detail the bootstrapping procedure, how to set the system clock, how to check
the file system, and the steps involved in initiating multiuser operation.

Bootstrapping the System

The procedure of *bootstrapping* (or simply *booting*) involves reading a copy of
the kernel program into memory from disk or tape and then executing the kernel
program. The details of bootstrapping vary from system to system, so you should
consult the documentation that comes with your system for the proper commands
to enter. We will outline, however, a typical example of bootstrapping.

In general, a bootstrap program in ROM (read-only memory) is executed after
power is applied or the reset switch is pressed on a system that is already running.
The program initializes the hardware — setting up the system console terminal to
communicate with the CPU — and performs hardware diagnostics such as testing
main memory. When these checks are complete, the bootstrap program may
prompt you for further action. Since the procedures, at this point, differ greatly
from system to system, you should consult your documentation for the proper
commands that will load the UNIX system kernel from disk (or tape) into computer memory. You may find your system so automated that it will perform the
entire bootstrapping sequence — from power on to starting up the single-user
shell — without your intervention.

If the kernel of UNIX has been successfully loaded, you should see a shell prompt, which is generally a pound, or number sign (#), to signify that you have *superuser* powers. At this point, the system is operating in single-user mode; that is, you can only access the system from the main terminal or system console (the terminal that you used to bring up the system).

Setting the System Clock

Your next task should be to set the system time-of-day clock. If the system clock has been set, any file that is created or updated will have the correct time and date stamp. Related functions, such as those controlled by the **cron** process, will be executed when they are supposed to be.

You use the **date** command to set the clock. The command line format for setting the clock with the Bell Version 7 or Berkeley **date** command is

$$\text{\# date } [yymmdd]hhmm[.ss]$$

Here *yy* is the last two digits of the year (00-99), the first *mm* is the month number (01-12), *dd* is the day of the month number (01-31), *hh* is the hour (00-23), and the final *mm* is the minute (00-59). When you shut down the system, the current setting of date is preserved on the file system and is later restored to the **date** command upon bringing the system back to life. Thus if the year, month, and day are the same, they may be omitted from the command line. The *ss* is the number of seconds past the minute (00-59) and is optional as well.

As an example, let's assume that you shut down your system over the lunch hour and just brought it up again. The current time is 1:20 P.M. and the date is November 1, 1984. First let's enter the **date** command without any argument to display what the system thinks the current time is.

```
# date
Thu Nov 1 11:48:30 PST 1984
#
```

In this case it is the time when the system was last brought down. Then we use the **date** command to reset the system clock as shown.

```
# date 1320
Thu Nov 1 13:20:01 PST 1984
#
```

Notice that we omitted the leading "841101" since the year, month, and day have not changed since the system was last brought down. The **date** command displays the new date and time after the clock has been set.

The Bell Systems III or V command line format for setting the date and time is slightly different:

date *mmddhhmm[yy]*

Here the first *mm* is the month number, *dd* the day of the month number, *hh* is the hour, and the second *mm* the minute. You have to specify the month and day number with this version of **date**; however, the year (indicated by the two digits *yy*) is optional. Since there is no field for seconds, you must set the clock on the minute.

Here is an example of setting the clock to the same date and time as in the last example using the Bell System III or V version of **date**:

```
#  date 11011320
Thu Nov 1 13:20:01 PST 1984
#
```

Notice that with this version of **date** we specified the current month and day number, but since the year was not changed, it did not have to be indicated on the command line.

Every time the system clock is set or changed, the **date** command records the event in the login history file. An entry in the login history file, designated **/usr/adm/wtmp** or **/etc/wtmp** for Bell System V, would have a vertical bar (|), then the previous time setting followed by an opening brace (|), and finally the new time setting. You can examine this file by entering **who /usr/adm/wtmp** (or **who /etc/wtmp** for System V) to see when the clock setting was last changed. We show an example of examining this file in the "Examples" section of the **who** command in Chapter 6. A record of all system sign-ons is also kept in this file.

Checking the File System

The UNIX file system is fragile and can be easily corrupted if the UNIX system is not properly shut down. Thus you should check the condition of the file system *every time* you bring up the UNIX system. If there is an error in the filing system, it must be repaired immediately before the system is used further; otherwise the error in the file system will spread like a cancer until the entire file system is useless.

If your system multiuser preconditioning shell script file **/etc/rc** (discussed in "Going Multiuser") doesn't run a file system check automatically, you should check the status of the file system while still in single-user mode. The file system check program, **fsck**, is available with most UNIX systems for this purpose. The **fsck** program performs the same functions as the outdated **icheck**, **dcheck**, and **ncheck** programs. But the use of these programs was more complicated, and thus prone to operator error, so the Bell System replaced these utilities with the single **fsck** program.

All file systems should be checked and repaired (also called cleaned) before they are mounted. This way file system corruption will not spread to any mounted file system. This is one reason for performing the **fsck** check while still in single-user mode, since additional file systems are not generally mounted until multiuser operation has commenced. Note that some systems do mount additional file systems in single-user mode.

Operating the fsck Program   The file system check utility is an interactive program that will prompt you for yes or no decisions on whether or not to correct certain error conditions. It is a good idea to run **fsck** one time through, answering no to all queries, in order to assess the scope of any problems before **fsck** repairs any errors. One command line for invoking **fsck** is

> # /etc/fsck [−y] [−n] [*filesystem*]

Here *filesystem* is the name of the file system to be checked. In general, you don't have to supply this argument since **fsck** will obtain the name(s) of the file system(s) to be checked from the ordinary file **/etc/checklist** (Bell) or **/etc/fstab** (Berkeley).

The program will automatically answer "no" to all queries if you invoke **fsck** with the −n option. One reason for this conservative approach would be that if there was a problem with the hardware, and not with the file system, you wouldn't want **fsck** to repair the file system.

Immediately after invoking **fsck** the program enters an initialization phase. If **fsck** cannot get enough memory to store its intermediate results, it may query you to name a file to be used temporarily as a "scratchpad" during the checking procedure. There need be nothing special about the particular name you choose, but you should select a scratch file that is not on the file system being checked.

Here is an example of output from **fsck** if there are no errors:

```
# /etc/fsck
/dev/root

** Phase 1 — Check Blocks and Sizes
** Phase 2 — Check Pathnames
** Phase 3 — Check Connectivity
** Phase 4 — Check Reference Counts
** Phase 5 — Check Free List
414 files 9857 blocks 7560 free
#
```

The program may first print the name of the file system it is about to check, and then it scans that file system several times as shown by the different "Phases." Finally some statistics about the file system are displayed.

A discussion of each phase and some commonly occurring error messages and how to deal with them will follow. You need to study this material closely, as the correct operation of the **fsck** program is *critical* to repairing and maintaining a file system. But before we discuss the phases of **fsck**, you need to know how to clear a corrupted inode.

Many of the **fsck** queries ask you to "CLEAR?" an inode because it is corrupted. If you answer yes, the inode is cleared by writing all zeros into it and the corresponding file is destroyed. Sometimes you can save the data in the file by first copying the file contents to another location in the file system.

In saving a file, first answer **no** when the **fsck** program displays the "CLEAR?" query on a bad inode. The **fsck** program will also display the inode number (indicated by "I=") and the size of the file (indicated by "SIZE="). You should record these figures because you will need them later. Continue with the program, answering **no** to any "CLEAR?" prompt on a inode that you intend to save. The problem with the **fsck** program is that you cannot determine the name of the file from the bad inode, because an inode is just a number. This is where the **ncheck** program comes into play. After returning to the shell, use the **ncheck** program to determine the filename associated with the bad inode. The command line syntax for using **ncheck** is

/etc/ncheck −i *inodenumber... filesystem*

Here *inodenumber* is the inode number of the file that you are searching for, and *filesystem* is the name of the file system you are checking.

If no filename was reported by **ncheck**, the file is unreferenced (by a directory entry), so you can't access it for a backup. If the file is referenced, however, a filename is displayed. You can use a UNIX utility, such as **cat**, to examine the contents of the file. If the data is intact, you should back up the file contents, say with **cp**, to a different file system.

After saving the contents of any bad file, rerun the **fsck** program, but this time answer **yes** to the "CLEAR?" queries. Now we will discuss the five phases of the **fsck** program. After the file system is clean (no errors reported during a **fsck** run) retrieve that file that was saved earlier.

In phase 1, each inode in the file system is checked for its own data integrity and then the disk blocks pointed to by the inode are checked. Some error messages at this stage are possible. If the message "BAD" occurs, the block address in the inode is invalid.

Another common error message is "DUP" (for duplicate). This occurs if a block has already been claimed by another inode. You will not be prompted to remove BAD or DUP blocks until phase 2 or 4. A large number of DUP, and BAD, blocks result from a damaged *indirect block*. An indirect block is a data block that contains addresses of other data blocks for the file.

Other warning messages that may occur during phase 1 are

- "POSSIBLE FILE SIZE ERROR" occurs if the estimated number of blocks for an ordinary file does not agree with the actual number of blocks claimed by the inode.

- "DIRECTORY MISALIGNED" occurs if the size of a directory file is not a multiple of 16 bytes.

If these last two error conditions aren't cleared during the interactive repair in later phases of this program, you should back up the file or directory contents. Manually erase the file (with **rm**) or directory (with **rmdir**), and the corrupted inode will be deallocated. After that run **fsck** again to be sure the file system is now clean.

If any DUP blocks were discovered in phase 1, this error will initialize another scan of the inodes as indicated by the message "Phase 1b—Rescan for More DUPS". If a block that has been claimed by the inode that is being examined has already been tagged as a DUP, the "DUP" warning message is repeated and you will be prompted "CLEAR?". If you answer yes, the inode will be marked for possible removal in a later phase. Another possible error message during phase 1b is "PARTIALLY ALLOCATED INODE". This means that the inode is neither allocated nor unallocated. You should answer yes to the following "CLEAR?" prompt but you may want to back up the associated file before clearing the inode.

In phase 2, **fsck** inspects all directory inodes in the file system. First the inode for the **root** directory is examined. If **fsck** reports it "UNALLOCATED", **fsck** will abort since this means the **root** inode is corrupted. If you get the message "ROOT

INODE NOT DIRECTORY... FIX?" answer yes. If you get a message "DUPS/ BAD IN ROOT INODE CONTINUE?" answer yes, but expect a large number of related file system errors as a result of this last error condition.

Most file system errors can be fixed by **fsck** except for a corrupted superblock or inode. In some cases, even these structures may be repaired by someone who is experienced with the file system.

Continuing with phase 2, the inode (and each block for that inode) corresponding to each directory entry in the file system is examined. Some error conditions that could occur here are

- "OUT OF RANGE" means that the inode number of the directory entry is invalid. If you elect to remove the inode in response to the "REMOVE" prompt, the inode field of the directory entry will show zero.

- "UNALLOCATED" means the inode is possibly unallocated, but it should be allocated since it is referenced by a directory entry. In this case, answer yes to the "REMOVE?" prompt so the directory entry doesn't point to an unallocated inode.

At this point you will be given the opportunity to clear the inodes that had a BAD or DUP block that was discovered during phase 1 or 1b of the check procedure. The **fsck** program may supply you with a filename, or you can use **ncheck** to determine it from the inode number. If the file is of no value to you, answer **yes** to clear the inode. The DUP blocks are frequently shared between a file and the free-block list, so in this case don't clear the inode, but wait for an additional phase 6.

In phase 3 all the allocated inodes are scanned for unreferenced directories, that is, directories where the inode corresponding to the parent directory entry (..) does not exist. In this case you will be prompted to "RECONNECT?" any orphaned directories. If you answer yes, a link from the orphan directory to the special directory /lost+found will be made. The name of the link to the /lost+found directory will be the inode number from the orphan, now newly connected, directory. After the **fsck** program is finished, you can examine the entries in /lost+ found and move them (by renaming with **mv**) to their appropriate place in the file system.

If a /lost+found directory doesn't exist in your file system, you can create it easily if your system has the **mklost+found** shell script. This command creates the /lost+found directory by making a large number of directory entries and then deletes these entries to give a large, but empty, directory. (If you delete an entry (file or directory) within a directory, the size of the directory isn't changed.) If you don't have the **mklost+found** shell script, you could simulate the procedure by entering **mkdir/lost+found** and then **cd /lost+found**. Then enter several **mkdir** commands (using any dummy directory names) and finally remove those same directory entries with **rmdir**.

Phase 4 is concerned with the inode count or *reference count* information that was accumulated in phases 2 and 3. In phase 1 the reference count is first set to the *link count* value stored in the inode. The link count is the number of links (or filename aliases) for that physical file. Then, in phases 2 and 3, the reference count is decremented each time a valid link is found while scanning the file system. So the reference count value should be zero when phase 4 begins.

If the reference count for an inode was actually zero to begin with in phase 1 (indicating a corrupted inode), you may clear the inode at this point. To do so, answer yes to the "CLEAR" query for the unreferenced file "UNREF FILE" or directory "UNREF DIR".

If the reference count for the inode is not zero at the start of phase 4, not all the links were discovered in phases 2 and 3. The **fsck** program distinguishes between two cases at this point: (1) none of the claimed links were discovered, in which case the inode refers to an "orphan" file or directory; (2) not all of the claimed links were discovered, in which case the **fsck** program can correct the link count field in the inode.

In the first case, **fsck** can link the orphaned file or directory to the /**lost+found** directory. You should answer yes to the "RECONNECT?" query to accomplish this. If this linkage operation was not successful, or you decided not to link, then answer yes to the subsequent "CLEAR?" query associated with the next "UNREF FILE" (or "DIR") message.

In the second case, **fsck** will adjust the link count if you answer yes to the "ADJUST?" query that follows the "LINK COUNT FILE" (or "DIR") and "COUNT *X* SHOULD BE *Y*" message.

In the last stage of phase 4, you are given the chance to clear the inodes of unreferenced files and files containing bad or duplicate blocks. Finally, if you get the error message "FREE INODE COUNT WRONG IN SUPERBLK", you should answer yes to the "FIX?" query.

Phase 5 checks the free-block list. Any bad or duplicate blocks in this list are flagged, and later you will get the message "BAD FREE LIST" and be prompted to "SALVAGE?" to which you should answer yes. After you have elected to salvage the free list, a phase 6 is initiated that reconstructs the free block list.

If a file system was corrupted and then fixed, you will get a message like "***** BOOT UNIX (NO SYNC!) *****" just before **fsck** exits. This message means that **fsck** had to modify the file system in order to repair it. To prevent the work done by **fsck** from being "undone," the system should be rebooted *without* performing a **sync** operation (see "Updating the File System" section for more about **sync**). At this point, shut the system down by simply turning off the power, wait several seconds, and then turn on the power (or press the RESET switch, if available) and bootstrap the system again. This is the *only* time you should ever shut down or reset the system without performing a **sync** command first. If there were errors on the last run, you should repeat the **fsck** program until no more errors are reported.

Going Multiuser

If your system is single-user only, you can begin your interactive session with UNIX. Many microcomputer UNIX implementations are single-user systems, but can be upgraded to multiuser. If your system supports multiple users, you should invoke multiuser mode even if you are the only user on the system. This way all necessary system functions will be enabled.

To initiate multiuser mode, you must first log out of the single-user shell. For the Bell Version 7 and Berkeley-derived systems, simply type a ^D. Once you are out of the single-user shell, the **init** program will automatically begin to run. If you are using Bell System III or V, enter **init 2** to initiate multiuser mode and then type a ^D when prompted to do so. All other terminals connected to the system should then display the "login:" prompt.

After you exit your single user shell a process called **init** takes control. This process runs a special shell script with the pathname **/etc/rc** that preconditions the system for multiuser mode. Almost any shell command can be placed in the **/etc/rc** shell script, so you might want to place one or more commands in this file. In general, the commands placed in this file perform (1) housekeeping tasks, such as erasing temporary files and accounting log files used in the last session, and perhaps prompting you for setting the system clock, (2) file system-related tasks, such as running the **fsck** program, and (3) starting up daemon processes, such as the clock daemon (**cron**), the line printer spooler daemon (**lpd**), and so on.

Mounting Additional File Systems   Some UNIX implementations may require you to mount additional file systems after going multiuser. Mounting another file system effectively extends the existing file system tree.

The syntax for using the **mount** command is

/etc/mount *devicename directory*

Here *devicename* is the name of the storage device (a special device filename) that you want the file system to be mounted on. You must look up the device name in your system documentation, since the name depends on your particular UNIX implementation. The *directory* is the name of the directory that the newly mounted system will be assigned to. Of course, *directory* must already exist on the current filing system. If not, use the **mkdir** command to create *directory*.

As an example, let's say you want to mount a file system that has the special device name **/dev/fd00** (for floppy disk 0) onto the existing **/usr** directory. Enter the command shown here:

```
# /etc/mount /dev/fd00 /usr
#
```

Now the new file system is simply an extension of the **/usr** directory. You can then create directories and ordinary files in the **/usr** directory subtree just as you would in any other part of the file system.

User Login Processes   Logging a user on to the UNIX system requires a chain of cooperating program processes. The system administrator should be aware of this process sequence. In many cases, the administrator can diagnose logon problems by examining a **ps** listing for all system processes, paying particular attention to the following processes:

$$\text{init} \longrightarrow \text{getty} \longrightarrow \text{login} \longrightarrow \text{log on program}$$

Each of these processes is responsible for a different step of the logon procedure:

init
This process is the predecessor of all other system processes. All other processes in the system are derived from **init**.

getty
This process is invoked by **init** as the first step in allowing users to log on to the system. It supplies the "login:" prompt and then monitors the terminal line for a logon request. The **getty** process then tries to adapt to the terminal line protocol (baud rate, parity, and so on) to the terminal being used for log on.

login
This process is invoked by **getty** as the second step in the logon sequence. It would prompt the user for a password (if necessary), and if supplied correctly, it invokes the appropriate logon program.

logon program
This is the program that runs immediately after the user logs on. The actual identity of this program is determined by the last field in the password file entry for the account user. Usually a general-purpose shell, such as the Bourne or Berkeley C Shell, is specified (as **/bin/sh** or **/bin/csh**, respectively). But a program such as an editor may be used instead.

Shutting Down Your UNIX System

It is *very important* to shut down your UNIX system properly. Knowing how to shut down the system in all circumstances is the single most important task of the system administrator. If the system is not shut down properly, the damage could be extensive: the UNIX file system or even the system disk could be ruined. But even if the system is shut down improperly by pulling the plug, all may not be lost if you carefully follow the system start-up procedure and repair the file system as outlined previously.

As with the system startup, the system shut-down procedure involves several steps that are similar from one UNIX sytem to another. However, the details of each step may vary greatly from system to system. The general steps are

* Log on as **root** on the system console terminal.
* Warn other users that you are bringing the system down in a few minutes.
* Bring the system back to single-user mode by terminating all processes not associated with the console.
* Update the file system with **sync**.
* Unmount all mounted file systems.
* Perform any scheduled file backup procedure.
* Power off, or press RESET and reboot.

Some of these steps may be automated depending on the design of your system. For instance, your system may have a "shutdown" shell script or program that performs all of the steps outlined here except for turning off the power or pressing RESET for you.

Now let's examine these individual steps more closely.

Going Single User

Log in to the system console as **root** if you have not already done so. The system console is the same terminal that you booted the system up from.

If you are running in multiuser mode, first warn the other users that you are about to bring the system down in a few minutes. You can use the **wall** command for this purpose, since it can broadcast to all on-line terminals simultaneously. The **wall** program generally resides in the /etc directory so you can invoke it by entering /etc/wall. When you're finished entering your message, type an end-of-file code (^D), and your message will appear on all terminals currently logged on. Wait until the other users log off (as seen by the absence of their log-in shell on a

ps listing) and if necessary, write directly to the stubborn users who refuse to log off.

If you are using Bell System III or V UNIX, enter **init 1** to return to single-user mode. Other UNIX versions don't require this step. Next you must terminate all processes except your own shell process with the **kill** command (see Chapter 6 for more on the **kill** command). The **swapper** and **init** processes, however, can't be terminated with **kill**. If your system has a "killall" program that can terminate all other processes, then invoke it. Otherwise list all system processes with **ps** ⁻**ax** (Version 7 and Berkeley) or **ps** ⁻**e** (Systems III and V) and then use **kill** to terminate all processes except your login shell. Finally verify that **kill** has done its job by examining a **ps** listing for all system processes. Terminate any stubborn processes with the **kill** ⁻**9** command.

Updating the File System

The single most important step in shutting down the system is to *properly update the file system* by writing the contents of the computer memory to disk. To update the file system, you use the **sync** command. The **sync** command writes all the appropriate information that is in volatile memory (contents disappear when power is removed) to the disk memory. Simply enter **sync** and wait several seconds until all disk activity stops.

Dismounting Additional File Systems

If you had mounted any additional file systems during the system start-up procedure, this would be a good time to dismount those file systems. (You don't have to dismount a file system when shutting down.) Otherwise simply skip this step.

A file system can't be dismounted if it is "busy," that is, a file on that file system is being accessed. All file systems, other than the root file system, should be quiescent at this point since all other users have logged off and all nonconsole processes have been terminated.

Use the **umount** (*not* spelled **unmount**) command for dismounting the file systems. The syntax is

 # /etc/umount *devicename*

Here *devicename* is the same name you specified when the file system was mounted. You can determine this name by simply typing **/etc/mount** (with no arguments) and **mount** will report all the file systems and the device they are currently mounted on.

Shutting Down in an Emergency

If you don't have time to carry out all the steps of a normal shutdown procedure, you should at the very least enter the **sync** command, and then power down immediately before any more file system activity occurs. The system users may lose some of their work, but at least the file system should be relatively intact when you bring the system back up.

It is also a good idea to have a separate account on the system that only executes the **sync** command as the logon program. This way, any system user can execute the **sync** command by merely logging on to the system. See "The Password and Group Files" (later in this appendix) for a discussion on how to set up such an account.

Creating a New File System

The specifics for creating a file system vary greatly from one system to another, but we can discuss the steps in a general way. Consult your system documentation for the specifics of creating a file system for your particular implementation.

You may have to create a file system when you first set up your UNIX system or if your present file system becomes corrupted beyond repair. But before you can create a file system, the disk that it will reside on must first be formatted.

Formatting a Disk

The first step in constructing a file system is to format the system disk. The disk is a memory storage device that arranges its information in sectors along concentric tracks. In order for the UNIX system to read or write information to the proper sector, the sectors must be organized in a scheme that UNIX can understand; and information about the disk must be stored on the disk itself. The disk-formatting program will arrange and write this important information on the disk. You should be aware that formatting a disk will erase any previous information on the disk.

Disk-formatting programs are designed for a particular disk and disk controller hardware. Thus you need to consult your system documentation on how to format your hard or floppy disks.

Creating a File System With mkfs

After you have formatted the system disks, use the **mkfs** command to create a file system. This command will build all the necessary data structures for the file system — such as the superblock, the inodes, the free block list, and the "empty" data blocks. The basic command line format is

 # /etc/mkfs *name size*

Here *name* is the name of the storage device on which the file system will reside and *size* is the size of the file system measured in blocks. You will need to consult your system documentation for the maximum *size* that you can specify on a particular disk.

Managing Disk Space

The complete Bell UNIX operating system requires a large amount, about 8 to 10 megabytes, of disk space. So most UNIX systems installed on a microcomputer will have a minimum of 10 megabytes of storage. This may seem to be a comfortable amount of storage; however, it won't be long before the storage capacity fills up, especially if there are multiple users on the system. When the disk is full you can no longer use your UNIX system. In general, files accumulate because system users don't remove their unwanted files often enough. Thus sooner or later you will have to decide which files to remove from the system disk.

The system administrator should monitor usage of the system disk and take the necessary steps to avoid running out of disk space. The UNIX system provides several utilities for monitoring disk usage, among them **du**, which we discussed at length in Chapter 6. Another command that monitors the system disk is the **df** command. The **df** (disk free) command, which is generally available on most UNIX systems, is used for determining the number of free disk blocks (and inodes) in the file system. The Bell Version 7 and Berkeley systems provide the **quot** command, which summarizes the block usage currently owned by each system user. You can also use the **find** command with all UNIX versions to locate useless files that are taking up valuable disk space.

Whenever disk space is critically low, the system administrator should inform system users by placing a warning message in the messages-of-the-day file,

/etc/motd. The contents of this file are displayed each time a user logs in to the system. Now let's look at each of the command programs mentioned for managing disk space.

The Disk Free Command—df

The most commonly used program of the group, and one available to all users, is **df**. Simply enter **df** (or **/etc/df** if necessary) and this command will display the number of free disk blocks for all the mounted file systems.

The Bell Version 7 **df** command has no options, but you may limit the report to one or more particular file systems by specifying the *filesystem* that you want to examine:

$$\text{\# df } [\text{ filesystem... }]$$

The Berkeley version recognizes a couple of options and an additional argument:

$$\text{\# df } [-i] [-l] [\text{ filesystem... }] [\text{ filename...}]$$

If you specify the −i option, the number of free inodes is reported. The −l option causes **df** to count all the blocks in the free-block list as a double check. Thus **df** takes a little longer. You can also indicate the desired file system by specifying *filename*, which is the name of a file on the system, instead of having to indicate a *filesystem*, which is the device name. For instance, let's say that **/usr** is the directory to which the file system **/dev/hd01** was mounted. You could request **df** to check the available space on the mounted **/dev/hd01** file system by specifying the directory name **/usr**.

The Bell System III and V versions recognize a different set of options:

$$\text{\# df } [-t] [-f] [\text{ filesystem... }]$$

The number of free inodes is displayed by default. The −t option reports the total number of *allocated* blocks and inodes as well. The −f option causes **df** to count the blocks in the free block list (as did the −l option with the Berkeley version). This version lets you specify *filesystem* in two different ways: either as a device name or as a *mount point*. The mount point is the directory to which the file system is mounted. For instance, in a previous example we mounted the **/dev/hd01** file system onto the **/usr** directory, so **/usr** would be the mount point.

The Disk Quota Command—quot

The Bell Version 7 and Berkeley system provide a convenient utility, **quot**, for summarizing the total number of occupied disk blocks for each system user. The invocation command line syntax is

> **# /etc/quot** [*option...*] [*filesystem*]

where you can change the report format by the appropriate *option*. If no options are indicated, **quot** reports the number of blocks for the files owned by each file system account. For instance, the next example shows a result of running **quot** on a small system with about eight accounts:

```
$ /etc/quot /dev/root
/dev/root:
3624      root
485       adm
122       bin
28        uucp
9         beccat
3         junes
3         johnk
1         billk
$
```

The output consists of two columns. The left-hand column displays the number of blocks occupied by the user; and the right-hand column lists the identity of the user. The report is sorted so that the users with the largest number of blocks owned appear first. This way the "greedy" users stand out.

If you want a count of the number of files for each user, specify the —f option. Running **quot** with the —f on the same system as shown previously will give this result:

```
$ /etc/quot-f/dev/root
/dev/root:
3624      587      root
485       90       adm
122       6        bin
28        1        uucp
```

9	2	beccat
3	4	junes
3	1	johnk
1	1	billk

$ ▨

Here the middle column reports the number of files for each user.

The −c option prints a list of the files in three columns: the left column is the file size in blocks, the middle column is the number of files that have the same block size, and the right column is a cumulative total of blocks. The owners of the files are not listed with this option.

The −n option is generally used to produce a cross-reference listing of all files and their owners. The Bell Labs documentation suggests you use the following command line to accomplish this:

/etc/ncheck *filesystem* | sort +0n | /etc/quot −n *filesystem*

Here **ncheck** will produce a list of all inode numbers for *filesystem*. Those numbers are then sorted in increasing numerical order by **sort**. The sorted output is piped into **quot**, which produces a display listing the owner for each inode number. A sample portion is shown here:

$ /etc/ncheck /dev/rhp0a | sort +0n | /etc/quot −n /dev/rhp0a

/dev/rhp0a:

root	/lost+found/.
root	/tmp/.
operato	/etc/operator/.
bin	/bin/.
root	/dev/.
aps	/arch/ultrix/.
aps	/arch/rp06/.

...

$ ▨

The individual owner for each file is listed on the left. The ellipses (...) stand for the remaining output.

The Find Command—find

The **find** command is available to all users of the system and is a valuable aid for the system administrator. The **find** command is used to locate one or more files that satisfy the criteria that you specify. After each file is located, the command will do one of several different operations on that file: (1) you can request that the full pathname of the file be printed; or (2) you can request that a command operate on this file. The syntax for the **find** command is awkward, but powerful:

 # find *pathname-list...condition-list action-list*

To begin, you need to indicate what directory or directories you want the **find** command to search. You can indicate more than one directory in *pathname-list* if each directory is separated by a space. The **find** command searches each directory, and all of its subdirectories, in an effort to find a file that meets the criteria, or *condition-list*. Now let's discuss how to specify the selection criteria to find one or more files.

If you were interested in managing disk space, you would want to specify a criteria to locate files and directories that are wasting disk space. One such way might be to locate all files that have not been accessed for some time, and thus may no longer be needed. The **find** command has a condition called **−atime** that searches for all files that have not been accessed for a time length that you specify.

All *condition-list* items for the **find** command are tabulated in the following list:

Condition-list:

−name *filename*
Specify the name(s) of the file(s) to be *filename*.

−perm *onum*
Find files with octal permission mode *onum*.

−type *x*
Specify file type to be *x*, where *x* may be

d directory
f ordinary file
c character device file
b block device file
p named pipe (FIFO) (Bell Systems III and V)

−user *uname*
Find file(s) with owner given by user name *uname* (or UID number abbreviation).

−group *gname*
Find file(s) with the group owner name *gname* (or GID number).

−newer *file*
Find the file(s) that have been modified more recently than the argument *file*.

The following conditions have a numerical argument, *n*, that may have one of the following conventions:

n Indicates a decimal integer that is exactly *n*.

−*n* Indicates a decimal integer that is less than *n*.

+*n* Indicates a decimal integer that is greater than *n*.

These conditions are

−size *n*
Find file(s) of size *n* blocks.

−links *n*
Locate file(s) with *n* links to them.

−atime *n*
Find file(s) accessed *n* days ago.

−mtime *n*
Find file(s) modified *n* days ago.

−ctime *n*
Find file(s) created *n* days ago. (Bell Version 7 and Bell Systems III and V only)

The *condition-list* items for **find** can be combined with logical operators to form one large *condition-list*. The logical operations are listed in order of decreasing precedence. You will see how to combine the *condition-list* items using these operators in examples that follow.

- Conditions that are grouped together with parentheses will first be operated on. Parentheses are given special interpretation by the shell and thus must be "protected" or escaped with a backslash as you enter the **find** command line, such as \(and \) .

- Negate or reverse the logical meaning of condition or a parenthetical grouping of conditions by prefixing the *unary* NOT operator, the exclamation mark (!). This operator is interpreted to mean find all files that *do not* meet the specified conditions indicated after this operator.

- Linking together conditions with the logical AND is accomplished by placing the conditions on the same command line.

- Alternate conditions can be specified by using a logical OR operator, the —o option, between the conditions, and then enclosing those conditions in escaped parentheses, \(and \).

Once the **find** command has found the files that you are looking for, an action can be performed on the file. If no *action-list* argument is specified when invoking **find**, no output or action is performed. Here is a list of the possible actions:

Action-list:

—**print**
Display the pathname for file(s) meeting criteria.

—**exec** *command*
Execute the UNIX system *command* on file(s) meeting the *condition-list* criteria. This is the most powerful of the *action-list* commands because it lets the **find** command use any system command.

—**ok** *command*
Execute the UNIX system *command* on file(s) meeting the *condition-list* criteria. This action differs from —**exec** in that before the command is executed on each file, you are queried to reply yes.

—**cpio** *device*
Copy the file(s) meeting the conditions to the special *device* in cpio format (5120 byte records). (Bell Systems III and V only).

Specify the *action-list* argument —**exec** *command* to execute the UNIX system *command* for any files found meeting the criteria in *condition-list*. A pair of braces ({ }) must appear in the place where a file argument for *command* would normally appear. The full pathname of any files located by **find** will then replace the braces and *command* will act on those files one at a time. When the braces are used, the **find** command line must end with a semicolon preceded by a backslash. The command line with —**exec** as the argument for *action-list* is shown here for reference:

find *pathname-list condition-list* —**exec** *command* { } \;

You can request the *action-list* argument —**ok** instead of the —**exec** argument and the **find** program will only execute the *command* argument if you type a y after being prompted with the pathname for the file. This interactive approach is recommended for commands that alter a file permanently, such as **rm**.

Here is an example of **find** that will locate all files that have not been accessed

(−**atime**) for over a month (+**30**) and display their pathnames. Access means the file has been either read or written to.

find / −atime +30 −print

Some of the files that **find** has located may be so small to be of no consequence, so let's add the condition that they be larger than 10 blocks:

find / −atime +30 −size +10 −print

Here we combined the conditions −**atime** +**30** and −**size** +**10** together in a logical AND sense of *and* by including both of them on the **find** command line.

Now remove these files with the interactive action command **ok**:

find / −atime +30 −size +10 −ok rm −f { } \;

Backing Up Your File System

Backing up a file system means to create another copy on a different storage medium that could be used to replace the original copy in case the original was destroyed. As system administrator, you should periodically make copies of the entire file system to prevent a major loss of information in the event of a system failure. In fact, you should back up the entire file system the very first time the computer system is brought up. This backup should be archived away permanently as your "system files archive." After that, you only need to make copies of data files, programs, and commands that have been modified or added since the last system backup. You may find it more convenient, however, to back up a file system rather than backing up individual files.

How often you should back up the file system depends on how much file system activity there is. The more quickly files are created, or changed, the more often you should back up the file system. Once a week should be often enough for a full system backup unless you are running a large facility with hundreds of users.

The first backup method that we will describe is well suited for archiving the entire system. Then we will describe an approach that is more suited for backing up the files that you add or change on a daily basis.

Dumping and Restoring the Entire File System

Each major UNIX release seems to have new utilities for backing up the file system. Instead of documenting the "latest" ones, we show you how to use a few "old tried and true" programs, **dump** and **restor**, that are still in use today.

The entire file system can be conveniently copied from the system disk onto backup media by use of the **dump** utility. Later it can be recovered from the backup media and written to the system disk by means of the related **restor** utility. You can use **dump** and **restor** to back up individual files but the procedure is complex and beyond the scope of this appendix. We will illustrate how to back up individual files with the **tar** utility instead.

The syntax for using **dump** is

/etc/dump [*key*... [*argument*...] *filesystem*]

Here *filesystem* is the name of the file system that is copied to the backup medium.

The *key* may be one or more of the following characters: **0, 1, 2, 3, 4, 5, 6, 7, 8, 9, f, s, u,** and **d.** The numbers specify a *dump level*. We shall only use level zero (**0**) to back up the file system. But specify **u** if you want the current date and time to be recorded in the **/etc/ddate** dump history file after the backup operation is complete. Follow the **f** key with a devicename and a destination device other than the default. If your backup media is magnetic tape, you may have to indicate the **s** or **d** options. You would follow the **s** option with an *argument* that specifies the length of the dump tape, expressed in feet, if it were different from the default (usually 2300 feet). You would follow the **d** option with the recording density of the tape, expressed as BPI (bits per inch), if it were different from the default (1600 BPI).

For our example, we illustrate backing up the entire file system (named **/dev/hd00** for hard disk drive zero) onto one or more floppy disks with device name **/dev/fd00** (for floppy disk drive zero).

```
# /etc/dump 0uf /dev/fd00 /dev/hd00
    date = Mon Jan 2 16:23:02 1984
dump date = the epoch
dumping /dev/hd00 to /dev/fd00
I
II
```

estimated 1620 blocks on 4 volumes(s)

III

IV

change volumes

change volumes

change volumes

DONE

1634 blocks on 4 volume(s)

\#

Here the option **0** specifies a zero level dump (the entire file system is backed up). The **u** option causes the current date and time to be written to the history file, **/etc/ddate**. The **f** key indicates the device file; **/dev/fd00** argument specifies that the destination device is named **/dev/fd00**. The source device name is indicated by the last argument, **/dev/hd00**.

The **dump** command begins by displaying the current date and time. All files that were created after the "dump date" will be dumped, and in this example, the dump date is the "epoch." The term "the epoch" is guaranteed to be earlier than the date stamp of any file on the system, as it is January 1, 1970 at 12:00:01 A.M. (GMT). The remaining messages inform you about the current operating stage of the backup procedure. At each "change volumes" prompt, you should change your backup media, such as change the disk or tape, and then press RETURN to continue. Since the files are backed up onto more than one volume, this backup operation is a *multivolume dump*. Finally, the actual number of blocks that are written during the dump is displayed after the "DONE" message.

You can retrieve a file system with the command

/etc/restor rf *devicename filesystem*

Here *filesystem* is the name of the file system that you want to retrieve; and *devicename* is the name of the device that *filesystem* is stored on. The **f** key is necessary for the *devicename;* and **r** indicates that the entire file system is to be copied (as opposed to a file). Before you use this command, be sure that the destination device contains no files of value since the **restor** command will overwrite any information on the device. After the command **restor** is finally complete, run **fsck** since **restor** doesn't always update the free block list correctly.

Backing Up A File Using tar

The **tar** (for tape archiver) utility program is used to copy files from your file system to a backup medium and then restore them. Even though this command is accessible to everyone, it is only applicable to those who have superuser power.

One advantage of the **tar** program over **dump** and **restor** is that **tar** knows about the UNIX hierarchical directory structure, so files are restored with their original pathnames; but the **tar** program is time consuming.

The command line format for using **tar** is

 # tar *key* [*option...*] [*file...*]

Here *key* is any *one* of the following:

c Create a new backup tape. Old files are overwritten.

u Update a tape; the named *files* are added to the backup media if they are not already present or if they have been modified since they were last written.

r Read from the backup storage device until end-of-file, then append the indicated *files*.

x Extract the names of the files within *file* from the backup media. If you specify a directory, all files and subdirectories of that directory are extracted. If no *file* argument is given, *all* files are extracted from the backup tape. Any existing files with the same pathname will be over-written.

t List the names of the files from the backup tape.

The following keys must be followed by one or more *options* as appropriate:

f *devicename*. Uses *devicename* as the backup device name. If *devicename* is a dash (—), **tar** reads from its standard input or writes to its standard output file as appropriate for *key*. If *devicename* is omitted, **/dev/mt1** is assumed.

v Provides informational messages, such as the name of each file as it is encountered.

m Updates the modification time of the extracted file; otherwise it is not updated.

The term "tape" can mean tape or hard or floppy disks.

We will now show you two examples using the **tar** command. The first example illustrates how to copy files from your system disk to a backup storage device. The last example shows you how to extract files from your backup storage device and restore it to the system disk.

The **tar** command is most effective in making backups of recently modified files when used in conjunction with the **find** command. The **find** command can be used to locate all files that have been modified before a date that you have specified, and the **tar** command will then make the backup. For example, using the **find** command, search the **root** file system (pathname **/**) for all files that have been modified in the last week and then make a copy of each on the device name **/dev/fd00** using the **tar** command. The syntax for this example would be

> # find / −mtime −7 −exec tar uf /dev/fd00 {} \;

You can retrieve a file from the device **/dev/fd00**, as used in our example by specifying the file's full *pathname* using

> # tar xf /dev/fd00 *pathname*

Enabling and Disabling Terminal Lines

You can enable or disable terminal lines that support the system users. If a terminal line is enabled, a user can log on to the system from that terminal; if disabled, logging on is prevented. You will want to disable user logon when you wish to use a terminal line for another purpose, such as sending output to a serial printer. The procedure for enabling and disabling terminal lines is similar for both Bell Version 7 and Berkeley, but is substantially different from both Bell Systems III and V. We describe the procedure for Bell System 7 and Berkeley first.

The Bell Version 7 and Berkeley Procedure

Immediately after executing **/etc/rc** when going multiuser, the **init** process reads a file named **/etc/ttys** to determine which terminal ports (or lines) are to have a **getty** process created for them that will allow users to log in.

The **/etc/ttys** is a text file containing the names of the terminals, one terminal per line. A sample file for supporting five terminals (a system console and four additional terminals) is illustrated.

```
# cat /etc/ttys
12console
12tty0
13tty1
03tty2
05tty3
#
```

The first two numbers are not part of the terminal name.

The first character of each line in the file is either a 0 (zero) or 1 (one). If the line begins with a 0, that entry line is ignored by **init** so the corresponding terminal port is temporarily disabled for user login. An entry of 1 causes **init** to spawn a **getty** process that monitors that terminal line for user login. Thus in our example, terminal lines **/dev/console, /dev/tty0,** and **/dev/tty1** will support user login, whereas **/dev/tty2** and **/dev/tty3** will not.

The second number of each line becomes an argument for the **getty** process. This argument specifies the line speed (baud rate) through which **getty** cycles while monitoring the terminal line (see Table D-1). The **getty** process also displays any UNIX system sign-on banner and the "login:" greeting prompt.

Table D-1: A Correspondence Table for **getty** Arguments and Line Speed(s)

Argument	Line Speed(s)	Usage
0	1200,300,150,110	For a dial-up line used with a variety of terminals.
—	110	For a model 33/35 Teletype.
1	150	For a model 37 Teletype.
2	9600	For most hard-wired CRT display terminals.
3	1200,300	For dialups with Bell 212 Datasets.
4	300	For a hard-wired 300-baud terminal, such as the DECWrtier (LS36).
5	1200,300	For dialups with Bell 103 Datasets.

The **getty** process must match the baud rate of your terminal. If a user attempting to log on depresses the terminal's BREAK key, **getty** will switch its baud rate. Thus a user should keep pressing the BREAK key slowly until he or she sees a recognizable "login:" prompt, signifying the correct baud rate for **getty**.

You would edit the **/etc/ttys** file if you wanted to enable or disable user login or change the line speed(s) used by **getty**. Even though you edited **/etc/ttys** to disable a terminal line that a user is using, the terminal wouldn't be "turned off" until the user logs off.

The Bell Systems III and V Procedure

The Bell Systems III and V **init** process is directed by the contents of a database file, **/etc/inittab**. This file (sometimes called the *init table*) has any number of one-line entries, with each line consisting of four colon-separated fields. The fields of Bell System III version are labeled

state:id:flags:command

Whenever **init** is waked up because a user logs off the system, it checks **/etc/inittab** for instructions. We assume that your system has **/etc/inittab** correctly set up, and we will only be concerned with the contents of the *flags* and *command* fields for enabling and disabling user login.

The *command* field contains the command line used by **init** for invoking **getty** to monitor the terminal line. You can examine this command line to determine the terminal device name corresponding to any **/etc/inittab** entry. The terminal device is an argument to **getty**.

The *flags* field is edited to enable or disable the **getty** process. If the *flags* field only contains the character **c**, the terminal line is enabled for user login; if the characters **tko** are present instead, user login for the associated terminal is disabled. (Use the mnemonic "technical knock out" to remember "tko".)

As an example, the next screen depicts a typical **/etc/inittab** file.

```
$ cat /etc/inittab
1:co:c:/bin/sh </dev/console >/dev/console
2:co:c:/etc/getty console 5
2:01:c:/etc/getty tty01 3
2:02:c:/etc/getty tty02 5
2:03:tko:/etc/getty tty03 5
2:04:tko:/etc/getty tty04 5
$
```

The first line begins with a 1 in the *state* field and indicates a single-user operation mode. The other lines begin with a 2 and are used by **init** to mean multiuser operation.

Looking at the multiuser entries, you can see five terminal lines with *id* fields: co, 01, 02, 03, and 04. These numbers correspond to terminal devices **/dev/console** (the system console), **/dev/tty01**, **/dev/tty02**, **/dev/tty03**, and **/dev/tty04**. The console and terminals 01 and 02 are enabled for logon since the *flags* field entries are "c", whereas terminals 03 and 04 are disabled as their *flags* fields contain "tko". The last field in each line, *command*, is the **getty** command line that is invoked by **init** to initiate the user logon sequence.

In System V the **init** program and the **/etc/inittab** file have been generalized even further. A new database file, **/etc/gettydefs**, has also been added so the system administrator can easily change the correspondence table for **getty**.

The entries for the System V version of **/etc/inittab** are different from those for System III. A typical entry line for a System V version is described as having four fields, but their field names and content of the fields are different:

id:rstate:action:process

For this UNIX version you would edit the contents of the *action* and *process* fields for enabling and disabling user login. As with the System III version, the **getty** invocation *command line* will appear in the *process* field; only it will be passed to the Bourne Shell as

sh −c "**exec** *command line*"

This command line means that you can specify commands other than **getty**; for instance, you might invoke a dedicated graphics demo to run on a terminal. The command lines can also be more complex than for the System III version. For instance, they may include redirection and pipelines.

With the System V version, you can enable user logon by placing the word **respawn** in the *action* field. And you can disable logon if the *action* field contains the word **off**.

The Password and Group Files

You may occasionally need to add or delete user accounts from your UNIX system. In both cases you will need to read and write to the password and perhaps the group file. This is why we need to describe these important data files as a prerequisite to learning how to add or delete a system account.

The password file is the database that describes the accounts on your UNIX system. This file has the pathname **/etc/passwd** and is readable by all system users, but usually only the superuser can change it. The entry for each account consists of a single line that has several (usually seven) colon-separated fields. Generally, the fields contain the following information:

* The *user name*, or login name, consisting of up to 8 characters.
* The *password* is present in encrypted form, which consists of 13 characters from the character set (.), (/), **0 to 9**, **A to Z**, and **a to z**. If this field is blank, no password is requested when signing on to the account. Only the **passwd** command should be used to install a password, although you can remove a password completely with an editor.
* The *user ID* number (**UID**), a unique number that is assigned to the account. This number ranges from 0 (reserved for **root**) to 65,535.
* The *group ID* number (**GID**), a number shared by accounts belonging to the same group. This number ranges from 1 to 65,535.
* A *comment field*. The usage of this field is implementation-dependent, but usually is used for a comment or identifying information. Frequently, the full name of the account user is placed here.
* The *home directory*, which is the initial working directory location after signing on.
* The *login program* pathname. This is the program executed by **login** after signing on. Usually a general-purpose shell, such as the Bourne or C Shell, is specified here. When no login program is specified, a program, usually the Bourne Shell, is used. If a UNIX utility is specified after signing on, the utility is executed and when the program is finished, the user is logged out. A few common examples for such utilities would be **who**, **sync**, **ps**, or an editor.

A typical password file entry is depicted here:

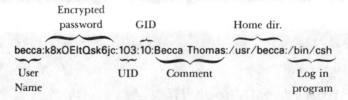

An encrypted form of the password is stored instead of the password itself for security measures. The password file must be readable by all users in order for several of the UNIX utilities, such as **ls** and **find**, to relate the user account name to the user identification number (UID). The password file is usually only writable by its owner (the superuser) to prevent ordinary users from altering this important system file and gaining unauthorized access to system accounts. The superuser must be able to write to the password file in order to add or remove an account from the UNIX system.

An example of a typical password file is given here:

```
# cat /etc/passwd
root:fsvR4s7nd/iDQ:0:1:The System Doctor:/:/bin/csh
daemon::1:1:The Devil Himself:/:
bin:ExGVBv/LEWC.1:2:2:Command Maintenance:/bin:/bin/csh
adm:y.EC0sQ.j0fEw:3:3:Administrative Functions:/usr/adm:
manual:jCWxOA51GCYuo:4:4:Manual Pages:/usr/man:
uucp:POCHBwE/mB51k:5:5:/usr/spool/uucppublic:/usr/lib/uucp/uucico
games::6:7:Play Games:/usr/games:/bin/rsh
sync::7:7:Synchronize File System:/:/bin/sync
username:OB/ZkzYYKMP8fw:100:10:Test Account:/usr/username:/bin/csh
friend:XdJAg131HzUk:101:10:Test Account:/usr/friend:/bin/sh
spilchuk:**NO-LOGIN**:102:20:June Spilchuk:/usr/spilchuk:/bin/csh
becca:k8xOEltQsk6jc:103:20:Becca Thomas:/usr/becca:/bin/csh
#
```

The **games** account (line 7 of the example) is a restricted account in that it uses a restricted shell, **/bin/rsh** (available with Bell Systems III and V), that doesn't allow users to change directories, reset their command search path, use pathnames when specifying command programs, or redirect output to a disk file. These restrictions effectively limit the users who log in as **games** to run the game programs (in **/usr/games**, their home directory).

The **sync** account (line 8) is also a limited access account. When a user logs on to this account, the **sync** command is executed and the user is logged off immediately after this command is completed. The **sync** account is useful for updating the file system in an emergency when logging in to the system and specifying the **sync** command would take too much time.

You should familiarize yourself with the password file on your system. Simply enter **cat /etc/passwd** to view the contents of this important data file. You may notice some accounts with "strange" user names, which are generally located near the beginning of the file. Accounts with names such as **root, daemon, cron, bin, uucp**, and so on are employed for system-related functions, that is, for running and maintaining your UNIX system. The presence and usage of these accounts cannot be discussed in a general way since they differ from system to system.

When you are examining the entries for the ordinary users, note that more than one user may share the same group identification number (GID), which is the fourth field from the left. Each user with the same group identification number belongs to the same group, which we call the *default group*. Each group member can share another member's files if the group access permission is enabled for these files. In our sample password file, we depict accounts **username** and **friend** to be in group 10 and the **spilchuk** and **becca** accounts to be in group 20. So if user **spilchuk** enables group permission for a file, then user **becca** can access that file. This feature provides a simple way for several people working on a common project to access one another's files.

In addition to the default group, users may be assigned to one or more other group associations by means of the group file, **/etc/group**. This file contains entries similar to **/etc/passwd**; however, it only has four fields of information:

- The *group name*, consisting of 8 characters.
- The encrypted *group password*, which usually is not present since most UNIX systems do not provide an easy way to install a password in the group file.
- The *group identification number* (or GID).
- An optional list of comma-separated user account names that are authorized to access files as a group.

An example of a typical group file would be

```
# cat /etc/group
other::1:
bin::2:
adm::3:
manual::4:
uucp::5:
restrict::7:
test::10:becca,spilchuk
docum::20:username,friend
#
```

The group file is generally used for establishing additional group associations in addition to the default groups that were defined in **/etc/passwd**.

It's not necessary to associate a name with a GID, but names are easier to remember than a number; in this example, **/etc/group** has names for group numbers 1 through 7. Additional group associations between accounts can be defined using **/etc/group**. In this example, the groups named **test** and **docum** are used for this purpose. The **test** group, GID 10, already has accounts **username** and **friend** as members by default. That is, both of these accounts were assigned GID 10 in the password file. The **test** entry in **/etc/group** defines two additional accounts as members **becca** and **spilchuk**. Likewise the **docum** group has default members **becca** and **spilchuk** (defined in **/etc/passwd**) and the members, **username** and **friend**, are defined by **/etc/group**.

As we have seen, accounts can belong to the same group by default. Accounts can *potentially* belong to the same group by definition in the group file. However, the **newgrp** command must be used to actually change group association from one group to another.

The **newgrp** command can be used to change your group access to a different group, *groupname*. The command line syntax is

$ **newgrp** *groupname*

The group association can also be changed back to the original default group by using **newgrp** without an argument. As an example, let's say that account **becca** wishes to access files owned by account **username**. These accounts don't belong to the same default group so account **username** cannot access user **becca** files, and vice versa. However, the group file allows user **becca** to change group association temporarily to the group that **username** belongs to. User **becca** would use **newgrp** to accomplish this task, as shown:

```
$ newgrp test
$ 
```

That's all there is to it. Now when user **becca** wishes to return to the default group, only **newgrp** need be entered after the shell prompt.

Adding a User Account

There are several steps involved in adding a new account to a UNIX system: (1) updating the password and perhaps the group file; (2) creating a new home directory; and (3) optionally providing a working environment for the new account.

Actually the first step in adding a new account is to decide on an account name. You can use up to eight letters, digits, and punctuation characters that don't have special meaning to your shell. Generally people use some form of their personal name for their personal account and a functionally descriptive name for other accounts. The author, Rebecca Thomas, likes to use either **becca**, **rathomas**, or **beccat** for her account names.

Editing the Password and Group Files

To create a new account on the password file, first log in as **root**, since only the superuser has permission to write in the password file. Then change to the **/etc** directory to avoid typing full pathnames. The account is stored in the file **/etc/passwd**. Make a copy of this important file before you edit it.

If your system has the **vipw** shell script command, use this for updating the password file. The script ensures that only one user can update the password file at any one time. If you don't have the **vipw** command, enter your favorite editor to edit **/etc/passwd**. As an example, the next screen shows these steps adding a new account, user name **johnk**, using the **ed** editor:

```
# cd /etc
# cp passwd passwd.bak
# ed passwd
791
$p
becca:k8xOEltQsk6jc:103:20:Becca Thomas:/usr/becca:/bin/csh
a
johnk::104:20:John Knapp:/usr/johnk:/bin/sh
.
$p
johnk::104:20:John Knapp:/usr/johnk:/bin/sh
w
835
q
#
```

The password field (second field from left) for **johnk** was left blank since it will be filled by the **passwd** command later. We increased the UID by one over the last entry (from 103 to 104), but we left the GID the same. Thus both the accounts **becca** and **johnk** will be in the same default group (GID = 20). The next field to the right can contain any comment, so we placed the full name of the account user here. The home directory field (second from the right) was patterned after the entry for **becca** since the same parent directory (**/usr**) was used. Finally the Bourne Shell (pathname, **/bin/sh**) was indicated to be the login program.

Now let's add **johnk** to the **test** group in the group file. Since you are still in the **/etc** directory, back up the group file, and then edit it as shown on the next screen:

```
# cp group group.bak
# ed group
108
/test/
test::10:becca,spilchuk
s/$/,johnk/p
test::10:becca,spilchuk,johnk
w
114
q
#
```

We left the second field blank since any password must be installed with a group password command. The Bell and Berkeley UNIX systems do not have such a command; however, some commercial vendors have added it to their system.

Creating a Home Directory

The directory entry in the password file (field number 6) that we created earlier simply names the home directory. Now we need to create the home directory for the new account. First change to the **/usr** directory and from this directory create the new directory **/usr/johnk** with the **mkdir** command. Notice that the home directory basename is the same as the account name. This is a convenience not a necessity.

This new directory is owned by the user who created it — the superuser. You have to change the ownership of the directory to the account user so he or she can change access permissions and do other operations that require file ownership.

There are two commands for changing ownership. The **chown** command is used to change individual ownership of a file. The command syntax is

chown *owner file*

for changing the ownership of *file* to *owner*. The **chgrp** command is used to change the group ownership of a file. The syntax is similar to the **chown** command:

chgrp *group file*

You may specify either *owner* or *group* by name or by number. The following screen shows the process of creating the new directory — and changing the permission of the group and directory — for the new account **johnk**.

```
# cd /usr
# mkdir johnk
# chown johnk johnk
# chgrp docum johnk
# ls −ld johnk
drwxrwxrwx 2 johnk docum 32 Nov 1 12:36 johnk
#
```

Providing a Working Environment

Next you might want to provide the new account with a shell start-up file in the home directory. Recall that the names of these start-up files are **.profile** for the Bourne Shell, or **.login** and **.cshrc** for the C Shell. You could install these files in a couple of different ways, and here we give you two different scenarios. In both cases, we assume that the sample start-up files are present in the **/usr** directory.

If you want the new account user to be able to modify start-up files, make a duplicate of the start-up files (using **cp**) while in the home directory for the new account. Then change the individual and group ownership of these files to the new account as well.

On the other hand, if you don't want the new account user to be able to change the start-up file, link it (using **ln**) to the new home directory and remove any write permission, but leave read permission for the "other" user category. Also retain the original ownership of these files. In this way the shell program of the new account is able to execute the start-up files, but the user cannot alter the start-up file. You can place Bourne Shell start-up commands in the file **/etc/profile** and they will be executed before those in **.profile** for *all* accounts on the system (supported by Bell System III and V).

Deleting a User Account

A user account is not deleted from the system but rather inactivated. This is so any files that were created by that account will not pass in ownership to a new account with the same user identification number (UID). However, the files belonging to the old account should be copied and removed from the system, and then the original copies erased. Also delete the user's home directory.

Removing the Account From the Password And Group Files

The simplest way to inactivate an account involves logging in as **root** and editing the password file entry for the account to place an impossible password in the password field. This is illustrated below for the account we created earlier:

```
# cd /etc
# cp passwd passwd.bak
# ed passwd
835
$p
johnk:O6JqPzZDBVUuw:104:10:John Knapp:/usr/johnk:/bin/sh
s/:.............:/:**NO LOGIN**:/p
johnk:**NO LOGIN**:104:10:John Knapp:/usr/johnk:/bin/sh
w
834
q
#
```

We choose to substitute the string "**NO LOGIN **" for the password; however, you may use any other string that could not be a valid password. But the string "**NOLOGIN **" tells you that **johnk** has been inactivated and so no one can log in to this account.

You can erase the old account name from any entry in the **/etc/group** file. Unlike the password file, a "placeholder name" is not required in the group file.

Removing the Account's Directory

Finally, copy the user's files (if the files are worth saving) and archive them. Then delete all files and remove the home directory (with **rmdir**) for the inactivated account to free up the disk space for other users.

Executing Programs Periodically With cron

The **cron** process executes commands at dates and times specified in the **/usr/lib/crontab** (or "cron" table) file. While the UNIX system is operating, the **cron** process never terminates, so it only needs to be activated once, usually when the system is going multiuser. The **/etc/cron** command, which starts the **cron** process, is specified in the **/etc/rc** preconditioning file. Otherwise you will have to invoke the program explicitly from the console terminal by entering **/etc/cron**.

The contents of the **/usr/lib/crontab** file are read into memory after **cron** starts up, and **cron** examines this copy once a minute and executes any commands that are scheduled to run. If the disk copy of **/usr/lib/crontab** is changed while **cron** is executing, the new copy of **/usr/lib/crontab** will be read into memory. The **cron** process also updates a history log file, **/usr/lib/cronlog**, everytime it performs an action.

The entries in **/usr/lib/crontab** consist of six fields, each separated by spaces or tabs. The first five fields indicate how often to execute the command line that is named in the last field. The first five fields specify the minute $(0-59)$, the hour $(0-23)$, the day of the month $(1-31)$, month of the year $(1-12)$, and day of the week $(0-6$, with $0=$Sunday), respectively. The last field contains the shell command line. The command line can contain redirection, pipes, and even multiple commands, if separated by semicolons.

Each of the first five fields can contain (1) a single number in the range indicated above; (2) two numbers, $m-n$, indicating an inclusive range; such as $1-5$ in *day of week* field to stand for all days in the work week, Monday through Friday; (3) a list of numbers, separated by commas; such as 0,15,30,45 in the *minutes* field to stand for on the hour, quarter past, half past, and quarter to the hour; (4) an asterisk, which means all valid values.

cat /usr/lib/crontab

0 * * * * /bin/date >/dev/console

30 2 * * * /bin/calendar −

30 3 * * * cp /etc/passwd /etc/passwd.bak

30 4 * * * find /tmp /usr/tmp −atime +2 −exec rm −f { } \;

35 4 * * * find /tmp /usr/tmp −type d −mtime +5 −exec rmdir { } \;

0 0 15 * * echo "Time to clean fan filters" | /bin/mail root

0,15,30,45 * * * * /usr/lib/atrun

#

Here is a brief description of what each entry depicted in the example does:

0 * * * * /bin/date >/dev/console
The current date and time are displayed on the system console once every hour on the hour.

30 2 * * * /bin/calendar −
The calendar command is executed for all system users every night at 2:30 A.M.

30 3 * * * cp /etc/passwd /etc/passwd.bak
The password file is backed up every night at 3:30 A.M.

30 4 * * * find /tmp /usr/tmp −atime +2 −exec rm −f { } \;
All files in the temporary directories that haven't been accessed within the last two days are removed every night at 4:30 A.M.

35 4 * * * find /tmp /usr/tmp −type d −mtime +5 −exec rmdir { } \;
All subdirectories of the temporary directories that haven't been changed within the last five days are erased every night at 4:35 A.M.

0 0 15 * * echo "Time to clean fan filters" | /bin/mail root ˙
The message "Time to clean fan filters" will appear in **root**'s mailfile after midnight of the fifteenth day of each calendar month.

0,15,30,45 * * * * /usr/lib/atrun
Execute /usr/lib/atrun on the hour, quarter past, half past, and quarter till for every hour of the day.

E

OCTAL
EQUIVALENTS
OF ASCII

Octal Equivalents of the ASCII Character Set

This table is included in the UNIX system on-line software. To display the table, enter one of the following command lines:

  man 7 ascii
or
  cat /usr/pub/ascii

000 nul	001 soh	002 stx	003 etx	004 eot	005 enq	006 ack	007 bel
010 bs	011 ht	012 nl	013 vt	014 np	015 cr	016 so	017 si
020 dle	021 dc1	022 dc2	023 dc3	024 dc4	025 nak	026 syn	027 etb
030 can	031 em	032 sub	033 esc	034 fs	035 gs	036 rs	037 us
040 sp	041 !	042 "	043 #	044 $	045 %	046 &	047 '
050 (	051)	052 *	053 +	054 ,	055 −	056 .	057 /
060 0	061 1	062 2	063 3	064 4	065 5	066 6	067 7
070 8	071 9	072 :	073 ;	074 <	075 =	076 >	077 ?
100 @	101 A	102 B	103 C	104 D	105 E	106 F	107 G
110 H	111 I	112 J	113 K	114 L	115 M	116 N	117 O
120 P	121 Q	122 R	123 S	124 T	125 U	126 V	127 W
130 X	131 Y	132 Z	133 [	134 \	135]	136 ^	137 _
140 `	141 a	142 b	143 c	144 d	145 e	146 f	147 g
150 h	151 i	152 j	153 k	154 l	155 m	156 n	157 o
160 p	161 q	162 r	163 s	164 t	165 u	166 v	167 w
170 x	171 y	172 z	173 {	174		175 }	176 ~	177 del

Reprinted from UNIX™ *Time-Sharing System: UNIX Programmer's Manual*, Seventh Edition, Volume 1, 1979, with permission from Bell Telephone Laboratories, Incorporated.

QUICK REFERENCE
TO UNIX SYSTEM
COMMANDS

To use this appendix, follow these conventions:

- Type **boldface** text literally.
- Substitute an actual value for *italicized* argument names.
- Optional arguments are in square brackets ([ ]).
- Repeatable arguments are followed by ellipses (...).
- Refer to Chapter 6 for detailed descriptions of each command.

UNIX Commands

at — Execute Commands at a Later Time

$ **at** *time* [*month monthday*] [*dayofweek*] [**week**] [*file*]

Execute commands in *file* (or from standard input, if *file* is omitted) at time and date specified.

cal — Print Calendar

$ **cal** [*month-number*] *year*

Print calendar for entire *year* or *month-number* and *year*.

calendar — Engagement Calendar Reminder Service

$ **calendar** [−]

Remind user of engagements previously entered, or remind all users by mail if "−" is specified.

cat — Concatenate and Print

$ **cat** [*option...*] [*file...*]

Display *file* contents (or standard input if *file* is omitted), or copy the contents of *file1* into *file2*.

Bell Version 7 options:

−	Take input from the standard input file
−u	Don't buffer the output of the **cat** program. This option enables line-by-line transfer from standard input to standard output

Additional Bell Systems III and V option:

−s	Be silent about input files that cannot be accessed for reading

Additional Berkeley options:

−n	Number all the output lines
−b	When used with −n, do not number blank lines
−s	Squeeze multiple adjacent blank lines into a single line
−v	Enable display of nonprinting characters. A CTRL-X is indicated as ^X, and if the next character has its parity bit set, the character is preceded by a M−
−e	When used with −v, mark the end of each line with $
−t	When used with −v, show tabs as ^I

cd — Change Working Directory

$ cd

Return to your home directory.

$ cd *pathname*

Change to another directory by specifying the *pathname* to that directory.

chmod — Change Permission Mode

$ chmod *mode file*...
$ chmod [*who*] *op-code permission file*...

Change the permission modes for files and directories.

comm — Common Lines in Two Files

$ comm [− [1][2][3]] *file1 file2*

Display unique and common lines in sorted files *file1* and *file2* or standard input if "−" is specified. Use flag 1 to suppress lines only from *file1*, 2 to suppress lines only from *file2*, and 3 to suppress lines in both *file1* and *file2*.

cp — Copy a File

$ cp [*option*] *file... target*

Make a copy of *file* and name it *target*. If *target* is a directory, copy *files* to *target* retaining original names.

Berkeley option:

—i   Use an interactive mode in which you are prompted with messages before copying proceeds. This prevents accidental erasure

crypt — Encode/Decode Information

$ crypt [*key*] [<*filein*] [>*fileout*]

Encode or decode using the *key*. If *key* is not specified, **crypt** prompts for it.

date — Display the Current Date and Time

$ date

$ date [+*format*]

Display the current date and time of day using the optional *format* string.

Format String Metacharacters:

%D	Date as MM/DD/YY
%a	Abbreviated weekday (Sun to Sat)
%h	Abbreviated month (Jan to Dec)
%j	Day of the year (001 to 365, or 366 on leap year)
%w	Day of the week (Sunday = 0, Monday = 1)
%m	Month of the year (01 to 12)
%d	Day of the month (01 to 31)
%y	Last two digits of the year
%T	Time as HH:MM:SS
%r	Time as HH:MM:SS (AM/PM)
%H	The hour (00 to 23)
%M	The minute (00 to 59)

%S   The second (00 to 59)

%n   Insert a new line character

%t   Insert a tab character

diff — Report the Differences Between Text Files

$ diff [*option...*] *file1 file2*

Find the differences between *file1* and *file2*.

Bell options:

−b	Ignore trailing whitespace and compare other strings of space characters as equal
−e	Produce a script of **ed** commands that can recreate *file2* from *file1*
−f	Produce a script like the −e option, but in the reverse order (not useful with **ed**)
−h	Use for files of "unlimited" length (−e and −f not available)

Additional Berkeley option:

−c[*n*]	Report the change in context. Specify *n* to report *n* lines around each change (default is three lines)

du — Determine Disk Usage

$ du [*option...*] [*dirname*]

Disk usage for file system beginning with *dirname*.

Options for all versions:

−s	Report only the total number of blocks
−a	Report the size for each ordinary file as well

Note that these options are mutually exclusive.

Additional Bell Systems III and V option:

−r	Report certain error conditions, otherwise ignore

echo — Echo Arguments

$ **echo** [*option*] [*arg...*]

Writes its arguments separated by blanks and ends in new line unless ─**n** option is used.

Bell Version 7 and Berkeley option:
─**n**   Do not terminate output with a new line

Bell Systems III and V escape sequences:
\ \b   Backspace (^H)
\ \f   Form feed (^L)
\ \n   New line (^J)
\ \r   Carriage return (^M)
\ \t   Tab (^I)
\ \ \   Literal backslash (\ )
\ *nnn*   Octal value *nnn* (must start with 0)
\ \c   Don't end with new line

file — Determine File Type

$ **file** [*option...*] *file...*

Classify the type of file.

Bell System III option:
─**f** *filelist*   Classify the list of files contained in *filelist*

Additional Bell System V options:
─**m** *magicfile*   Use the file *magicfile* instead of /**etc**/**magic**
─**c**   Check format of the *magicfile* (or /**etc**/**magic**)

grep — Search a File for a Pattern

$ **grep** [*option...*] *pattern* [*file*] *...*

Find lines in *file* (or standard input, if no *file* is specified) that match *pattern*.

Options for all versions:

—v	Display all lines except those containing *pattern*
—c	Report only the number of matching lines
—l	Only list the name(s) of files containing pattern
—n	Precede each line by the line number in the source file
—b	Precede each line by the block number on which it was located

Additional Bell Version 7 options:

—h	Suppress display of filename headers in output
—y	Ignore case distinction (upper- and lowercase)

Additional Bell Systems III and V option:

—s	Suppress error messages about files that don't exist or cannot be opened for reading

Additional Berkeley options:

—i	Ignore case when matching *pattern*
—w	Only matches whole words in *pattern*

head — Display Beginning of a Text File

$ **head** [*option*] [*file* ...]

Display the initial part of *file*.

Berkeley option:

—*count*	Display the first *count* lines of *file*

kill — Terminate a Process

$ **kill** *pid* ...

$ **kill** —*signo* *pid* ...

$ **kill** —*signame* *pid* ...

Terminate process with PID number *pid* using software termination signal or signal number *signo* or signal name *signame* (Berkeley only).

login — Sign on to Another Account

$ **exec login** [*username*]

Used in Bell Systems III and V.

$ **login** [*username*]

Sign on to the account *username* after logging on to your account. This form of the command is used in Bell Version 7 and Berkeley.

ln — Make Link

$ **ln** *firstname secondname*
$ **ln** *firstname* [*secondname*]

Make link to *firstname*, naming it *secondname*, or with Berkeley only use the last component of *firstname* if *secondname* is omitted.

lpr — Print Files

$ **lpr** [*option...*] *file...*

Put *file* (or input from standard input if no *file* is specified) in line printer queue.

Bell Version 7 and System III options:

−c	Copy *file* to be printed instead of linking
−r	Remove the *file* after placing in queue
−m	Have **mail** inform you when printing is done
−n	Do not inform when printing is complete (default)

Additional Bell System V option:

−f*name*	Use fictitious file *name* for reporting completion by **mail**

ls — List Contents of Directory

$ **ls** [*option...*] [*file...*]

List contents of directory and information on files.

Bell Version 7 options:

−l	List in long format. The entries are sorted by filename, and the permission modes, number of links, file owner, modification date and time, and filename are listed
−t	List in order of last modification time (most recent first)
−a	List all entries, including files whose names begin with dot (.)
−s	Report number of disk blocks occupied by file
−d	List directory file, instead of its contents
−r	Reverse order of sort for listing
−u	List in order of last access time
−c	List in the order of last modification time of the inode instead of the file
−i	Display inode number in first column
−f	Force each argument to be interpreted as a directory. This option turns off recognition of the −l, −t, −s, and −r options, but turns on −a. The contents of ordinary files are displayed incorrectly
−g	Give group ID instead of user ID in long listing

Additional Bell System III options:

−o	List in long format suppressing group name. Normally both user and group names are listed
−g	List in long format suppressing file owner name

Additional Bell System V option

−p	Append slash (/) to name of each directory file

Additional Berkeley options:

−m	Force stream output format, list files across the page, each separated from the next by a comma
−l	Force one-entry-per-line format
−C	Force multicolumn output format
−q	Display nonprinting characters in file names as a question mark (?)
−x	Sort multicolumn output across the page instead of down (default)
−F	Display directories with a trailing slash (/) and executable files with a trailing asterisk (*)
−R	Recursively list all subdirectories

mail — Send or Receive Electronic Mail Among Users

$ mail [*option*...] [−f*file*]

Reads each message in your "mailbox."

Options for all versions:

−p	Display entire contents of *mailfile* without prompting for instructions, then exit
−q	Exit after receiving an interrupt signal without changing the *mailfile*
−r	Reverse order in which messages are displayed
−f*file*	Use the named *file* as if it were the *mailfile*

$ mail *username*...

Sends a message to *username*.

man — Print On-Line UNIX User's Manuals

$ man [*options*] [*section*] *entry*...

Locates and displays the pages of the *UNIX User's Manual* or *UNIX Programmer's Manual*, which are named *entry* in the specified *section*.

Bell Version 7 options:

−t	Phototypeset the section using **troff**
−n	Print on the standard output (terminal screen) using **nroff**
−k	Display the output on a Tektronix 4014 terminal using **troff** and **tc**, which processes **troff** output for phototypesetter simulation on the 4014 graphics terminal
−e	Invoke **neqn** or **eqn**, which are preprocessors for typesetting mathematical equations; −e alone means −te
−w	Display only the pathname of the manual *entry*

Bell Systems III and V options:

−t	Typeset *entry* in normal 8.5 × 11 format
−s	Typeset *entry* in small 6 × 9 format (usable with next 4 options)
−T4014	
−Ttek	Display typeset output on a Tektronix 4014

−Typ	Print typeset output on the Versatec printer
−12	12-pitch (effective only with DASI terminals)
−c	Filter **nroff** output through **col**, which processes multicolumn output
−d	Find *entry* in current directory rather than in the standard directory, /usr/man; you must use complete file name, such as **acct.lm**, with this option
−w	Show only pathnames of *entry* (relative to /usr/man or current directory if −d is also specified)
−y	Use uncompacted version of **man** macros. Generally compacted versions are used to save disk space
other	Other *options* are passed directly to **nroff** or **troff**
Berkeley options:	
none	Display a preformatted manual entry; if not available format the manual page using **nroff**
−	Simulate underlining even if output is not directed to a terminal
−t	Use **vroff** for the Versatec printer
−k *keyword*...	Display manual entry headings containing *keyword*
−f *command name*...	Display a one-line description for *command name*

mesg — Permit or Deny Messages

$ **mesg** [*option*]

Report permission or set nonowner write-protection on terminal.

Options for all versions:

none	Report your terminal write permission
n	Remove write permission for your terminal
y	Grant write permission for your terminal

mkdir — Make a Directory

$ **mkdir** *pathname*...

Create directories in your current directory.

more or *page*—*A File Perusal Program*

$ **more** [*option...*] [*filename...*]
$ **page** [*option...*] [*filename...*]

Displays text from *filename* in controlled increments on a CRT terminal.

Options for all versions:

−*windowsize*	Set display window to *windowsize* lines, where *windowsize* is a decimal integer less than the physical screen size
−c	Clear each screen and begin text display at top of screen. Each screen is erased before displaying the next screen
−d	Display "[Hit space to continue, Rubout to abort]" in addition to the default prompt "—More—". The verbose form may be useful for inexperienced users
−f	Display lines using a logical count. This option is useful for displaying lines which contain nonprinting escape sequences. Otherwise, **more** may consider such lines longer than they actually appear and fold them in the wrong place
−l	Don't pause after a line containing a form feed (^L)
−s	Squeeze multiple adjacent blank lines in the input into one blank line on output display
−u	Suppress generation of escape sequences that perform or simulate underlining on a CRT terminal
+*linenumber*	Start the display at *linenumber*
+/*pattern*	Start display two lines before *pattern*

mv—*Move or Rename Files and Directories*

$ **mv** [*option...*] *file... target*

Move one or more files to the *target* directory.

Berkeley options:

−i	Use interactive mode. Whenever the *target* exists **mv** prompts you with the name of that *target* followed by a question mark. Enter y to initiate that rename operation; otherwise, it is aborted
−f	Override write-protection for *target* and the interactive mode

Interpret all remaining arguments as filenames. This allows filenames that begin with a hyphen

passwd — Change Login Password

$ **passwd** [*username*]

Change or install password for *username* (or your account, if *username* is omitted) for logging on to the UNIX system.

pr — Print File With Pagination

$ **pr** [*option...*] *file...*

Formatted printing of *file...*

Bell Version 7 options:

—*n*	Produces *n*- column output. The column width is automatically decreased as *n* is increased and thus may truncate the columns unless the page width is increased as well
+*n*	Start printing at page *n* skipping the first *n*—1 pages
—h *string*	Replace the filename with *string*. Enclose *string* in single or double quotations if it contains ASCII space or tab characters
—w*n*	Set page width for multicolumn output to *n* columns (default 72 columns)
—l*n*	Set page length to *n* lines (default 66 lines)
—t	Skip printing five-line header and trailer
—s*c*	Separate columns by character *c*, or by a tab if no *c* is indicated (use space characters by default)
—m	Merge and print all the files simultaneously, each in their own column

Additional Bell Systems III and V options:

—a	Display the multicolumn output across instead of down the page (default)
—d	Double space the output

‾e[c] [k]	Replace tabs (or the character *c*) in the input to *k* space characters on output (default k=8)
‾i[c] [k]	Replace *k* successive space characters in input by a tab (or character *c*) on output (default k=8)
‾n[c] [k]	Number lines (integer digits *k*, default k=5), then append a tab (or character *c*)
‾o[k]	Start printing at column *k* (k=0 default)
‾p	Suspend the CRT display at beginning of each page and ring terminal bell if directed to a terminal. Resume display by pressing RETURN
‾r	Suppress error messages about inaccessible input files

Additional Berkeley option:

‾f	Output a form feed instead of blank lines to begin new page. The effective page length remains the same. Generally a form feed does not affect a CRT display terminal; however, it will cause a new page to be ejected with most hardcopy terminals

ps — Get Process Status

$ **ps** [*option...*]

Print information about active processes.

Bell Version 7 options:

none	Display process status information for processes associated with your control terminal
‾a	Display all processes associated with a terminal
‾l	Display in long listing format
‾x	Display information for all system processes

Bell Systems III and V options:

‾e	Display information about every process
‾d	Display information about all processes, except process group leaders
‾a	Display information for all processes, except process group leaders and processes not associated with a terminal
‾t*tlist*	Display information for processes associated with the terminals in the terminal list *tlist*

−p*plist*	Display information for all processes in the process list *plist*
−u*ulist*	Display information for all processes whose user ID or user names are specified in the user list *ulist*
−g*glist*	Display information for all process group leaders specified in *glist*
−l	List the information using the long format
−f	List the information using full format

Berkeley options:

a	Display information about all processes associated with a terminal except process group leaders
g	Display information about all processes associated with a terminal including process group leaders
t*x*	Restrict display to processes associated with terminal name **tty***x*
x	Display information for processes not associated with a terminal
pid...	Restrict display to one or more processes with process identification numbers, *pid*
l	List the information using long format
u	List the information with a user-oriented output
w	Display the output in 132 columns instead of 80
ww	Display the output in wide format
c	Print just the command name instead of the command and its arguments

pwd — *Print Working Directory*

    $ pwd

Display the full pathname of your current directory.

rm — *Remove Files or Directories*

    $ rm [*option*...] *file*...

Remove one or more files.

Options for all versions:

−i	Interactively ask to delete each file. When you combine **−i** with the **−r** option, **rm** asks whether to examine each directory
−f	Force the removal of files for which you do not have permission
−r	Recursively delete the entire contents of the directory as well as the directory file itself

Additional Berkeley option:

−	Treat all arguments following as filenames. This allows removal of files whose names begin with a hyphen

rmdir — Remove a Directory

$ **rmdir** *pathname...*

Removes the directory or directories specified.

sort — Sort or Merge Files

$ **sort** [*option...*] [+*pos*] [−*pos*] [−o *filenameout*] [*filename...*]

Sort lines of *filename* (or standard input, if *filename* is omitted) into *filenameout*.

Options for all versions:

−b	Ignore leading blanks and tabs in comparisons
−d	Sort in dictionary order: only letters, digits, and blanks count
−f	Ignore distinction between upper- and lowercase
−n	Sort on first numeric field,implies **−b** option
−r	Reverse order of sort
−u	Eliminate duplicate lines in sorted output
−i	Ignore nonprinting ASCII characters in nonnumeric comparisons
−t*c*	Specify field separator to be character *c*
−c	Only check that the input file is already sorted
−m	Merge the specified files
−o *filenameout*	Save output in *filenameout*, which can be same as *filename*

spell — *Find Spelling Errors*

$ **spell** [*option*]... [*file*]...

Display words in *file* that are not in the dictionary.

Bell Version 7 and System III options:
−v	Print derivatives of words listed in the dictionary
−b	Use the British spelling dictionary for the spelling check
−x	Print every plausible stem (indicated with an equal sign)

Additional Bell System V option:
+*extradict*	Specify an additional spelling list named *extradict*

stty — *Set Terminal Modes*

$ **stty** [*mode...*]

Set terminal *mode* (or display current settings if *mode* is omitted).

$ **stty** [*option*] [*mode...*]

Report setting of *mode* using options or set *mode*.

Bell Systems III and V options:
−a	Display all of the current mode settings
−g	Display the current mode settings in a format suitable for use as an argument to another **stty** command

Berkeley options:
none	Report the speed of the communication line and the modes that are different from their defaults
all	Display all commonly used mode settings
everything	Display every mode setting

tail — *Deliver the Last Part of a File*

$ **tail** [+ *number* [*unit*]] [*option...*] [*file*]

Copy the *file* (or standard input, if *file* is omitted) to stdout + *number units* from beginning or −*number units* from end.

Options for all versions:
+ [*number*]a   *number* is counted in *units* of lines (default)
+ [*number*]b   *number* is counted in *units* of the disk block size
+ [*number*]c   *number* is counted in *units* of characters

Additional Bell Systems III and V and Berkeley option:
−f   Enables **tail** to follow the growth of *file*

Additional Berkeley Option:
−r   Display lines in reverse order

tee — Sample a Pipeline

$ **tee** [*option...*] *file...*

Divert a copy of data to *file*.

Options for all versions:
−i   Ignore the interrupt signal
−a   Append the copy to *file* instead of overwriting

tr — Translate Characters

$ **tr** [*option...*] *string1 string2*

Translate with substitution or deletion of characters.

Options for all versions:
−c   Consider all characters except those in *string1*
−d   Delete all the input characters specified in *string1* (any *string2* is ignored)
−s   Compress all strings of repeated output characters that are in *string2* into single characters

tty — Get Terminal Name

$ **tty**

Print the pathname of user's terminal.

uniq — Remove Adjacent Repeated Lines in a Sorted File

$ uniq [*option*... [+*n*] [−*m*]] [*input* [*output*]]

Remove repeated adjacent lines in *input* file when copying to *output*.

Options for all versions:

−**u**	Display only the lines that are *not* repeated in the file named *input*
−**d**	Display only the lines that are repeated in the file *input*
−**c**	Precede each line displayed by the number of times it occurs
−**m**	Ignore the first *m* fields and any blanks before each. A field is defined as a series of nonspace, nontab characters, which are separated from one another by spaces and tabs
+**n**	Ignore the first *n* characters along with any blanks before each in the comparisons

wc — Word Count

$ wc [*option*...] *filename*...

Count lines, words, and characters in *filename*.

Bell options:

none	Display the number of lines, words, and characters
−**l**	Display the number of lines
−**w**	Display the number of words
−**c**	Display the number of characters

Additional Berkeley options:

−**p**	Count the number of pages. The default page length is 66 lines but may be reset with the size (−**s**) option
−**t**	Display the time to transmit the file. The default transmission speed is 300 baud (30 characters per second) but may be reset with the baud (−**b**) option
−**b***baud*	Calculate the transmission speed using *baud* baud rate instead of the default
−**s***pagesize*	Calculate the number of pages based on a page size of *pagesize* instead of the default
−**v**	Specify "verbose" output format, which prints a header and includes page count and transmission time

who — *Who is on the System*

$ who [*option...*] [*whofile*]

List on-line user's login name, terminal, and login time.

Option for all versions:

am I   Display who you are logged in as

Bell System V options:

−u   Restrict listing to users currently logged in

−T   Display the state for all logged in users as well (that is, whether someone can write to the terminal)

−l   Display only the terminal lines that are waiting for someone to log in

−b   Display the date and time the system was brought up

−t   Display the last change to the system clock

−a   Turn on all the above options

−s   Display the short form listing, which consists of the user-name, terminal, line, and logon time fields

write — *Write to Another User*

$ write *username* [*ttyname*] [*<file*]

Start interactive conversation with *username* on terminal *ttyname,* or display *file* on the terminal.

G

SELECTED
BIBLIOGRAPHY

This appendix contains a list of publications on topics related to the UNIX system. The list is by no means exhaustive, since new articles and books about UNIX appear almost every day.

The appendix is divided into 16 sections. Each section contains lists of publications about a particular topic: general information, the shell, the C language, or networking. The references in each section are arranged alphabetically by author.

General Information:
Available or On the Way UNIX System Products

Alonso, C. "Sixteen-bit Micros and MUMPS." *MUMPS Users Group Quarterly*, Spring 1982, pp. 49-50.

Azzara, M. "Reporter's Notebook: Marketplace Wheeling & Dealing." *Computer Systems News*, 6 February 1984, pp. 38-42.

Barry, S. "The Fortune 32:16 Business Computer: A Multiuser, Multitasking System that Runs Enhanced UNIX." *BYTE*, May 1983, pp. 82-100.

Bender, E. "AT&T Moves From Phones to Micros." *Micro Marketworld*, 20 February 1984, pp. 42-47.

Blackford, J. "Comdex: The Wheel of Fortune." *Small Business Computers*, January 1984, pp. 10-12.

Chris, R. "Greeting Ma Bell's Baby." *Computer Merchandising*, January 1984, pp. 188-96.

Derfler, F. "Traipsing Through Trendy Territory: Scoping the Field's New Products." *Microcomputing*, June 1983, pp. 19-23.

Duncan, R. "16-bit Software Toolbox." *Dr. Dobb's Journal*, April 1983, p. 79-82.

Dvorak, J. "Western Electric May Market Four Micros." *InfoWorld*, 28 February 1983, pp. 1-4.

Dvorak, J., and P. Freiberger. "Computer Connoisseurs Open Up and Opine on Upcoming Year." *InfoWorld*, 3 January 1983, pp. 31-33.

Fielder, D. "UNIX Users Reunite." *InfoWorld*, 13 April 1981, pp. 12-13.

Fox, T. "Fortune 32:16." *Interface Age*, November 1982, pp. 68-74.

Freiberger, P. "Coming in June: Third-Party Software for Lisa." *InfoWorld*, 28 February 1983.

— — — "Sritek Offers Coprocessors for IBM Personal Computers." *InfoWorld*, 25 April 1983, p. 11.

Kepple, L. "68000 and the Personal Computer." *Micro: The 6502/6809 Journal*, September 1982, pp. 27-29.

Lewis, G. "Western Electric and Chip Makers Ally on UNIX System V Ports." *Mini-Micro Systems*, August 1983, pp. 21-22, 26.

Mace, S. "Micro Source Aims STD-bus Portable at Manufacturers." *InfoWorld*, 12 July 1982, pp. 29-30.

— — — "Monarch 16-bit Computer from Dynabyte Enters the Market." *InfoWorld*, 21 June 1982, p. 5.

— — — "Speech Tech, Mice Draw Crowds at Mini/Micro '82." *InfoWorld*, 11 October 1982, pp. 1-3.

— — — "UNIX Filters Down to Micros: Hardware, Data-Base Manager." *InfoWorld*, 11 October 1982, pp. 1-3.

Markoff, J. "Computers as Big Bad Wolves (Security)." *InfoWorld*, 5 April 1982, p. 28.

——— 'Insight Lets You See Ten Concurrent Tasks on IBM PC Display." *Info-World*, 18 April 1983, p. 3.

Meyer, E. "MULTICS Alumnus Sets the Record Straight on UNIX." *InfoWorld*, 10 May 1982, p. 30.

Milewski, R. "*InfoWorld* Interviews Industry Inquirer (Bob Wickham)." *Info-World*, 16 February 1981, pp. 4-8.

Needle, D. "UNIX Enthusiasts Meet in Cambridge." *InfoWorld*, 11 January 1982, pp. 1-2.

——— "Whitesmiths Hopes New Seal Will Stop Piracy." *InfoWorld*, 25 April 1983, pp. 1-3.

Needle, D., and D. Wise. "UNIX Users: How Does System III Pricing Affect Us?" *InfoWorld*, 11 January 1982, p. 6.

Ohr, S. "1984 Technology Forecast — Personal Computers." *Electronic Design*, 12 January 1984, pp. 184-92+.

Pournelle, J. "Burnouts, Bargains, and Two Sleek Portables." *BYTE*, January 1983, pp. 418-42.

——— "New Machines, Networks, and Sundry Software." *BYTE*, March 1984, pp. 47-50+.

Schindler, M. "Personal Computers: Software." *Electronic Design*, 29 September 1983, pp. 98-110.

Serlin, O. "OEMs Go for Supermicros." *Electronic Engineering Times*, 12 March 1984, pp. 80, 82, 86, 93.

Shea, T. "Other Micro Firms Use Shrunken Sage." *InfoWorld*, 28 March 1983, p. 20.

Sommer, J. "BASIC and Pascal Square Off (Benchmark Tests)." *Kilobaud Micro-computing*, April 1982, pp. 140-43.

Swaine, M. "New 16-bit Computer Runs UNIX Version 7 and FORTH (Dual Systems System 83/)." *InfoWorld*, 15 March 1982, p.

——— "W. Electric Cuts UNIX Prices." *InfoWorld*, 14 December 1981, pp. 1-2.

Veit, S. "News from the Computer Shows." *Popular Electronics*, October 1982, p. 84.

Vose, G.M. "DOS Woes Erode Tandy's Lead." *80 Microcomputing*, September 1982, p. 300.

Willis, R. "The Japan Shows." *BYTE*, March 1984, pp. 336-40+.

——— "Modem Maker Codex Announces New Micro." *InfoWorld*, 21 June 1982, p. 4.

———— "New COSMOS Computers: Supermicros that Run UNIX." *InfoWorld*, 14 March 1983, p. 63.

———— "New Masters Specialization (College Degree in Computer-Based Education)." *Computing Teacher*, December 1982, p. 6.

———— "Reviewing Roles of Hardware, Software Parts in All Computers." *InfoWorld*, 6 December 1982, pp. 108-15.

———— "200 Attend UNIX Conference in SF." *InfoWorld*, 8 February 1982, p. 6.

———— "UNIX Fans Plan Jan. Coast Conference." *InfoWorld*, 6 December 1982, p. 19.

C Language

Clapp, D. "Microsoft C Unveiled." *PC: The Independent Guide to IBM Personal Computers*, October 1983, pp. 503-08.

Derfler, F. "Lattice C Compiler Brings UNIX Closer to Micros." *InfoWorld*, 25 October 1982, pp. 47-48.

Fiedler, D. "The UNIX Tutorial, Part 2: UNIX as an Applications-Programs Base." *BYTE*, September 1983, pp. 257-60, 262+.

Garrett, R. "C Plus (Conclusion)." *Interface Age*, December 1981, pp. 34-38.

Halfant, M. "The UNIX C Compiler in a CP/M Environment." *BYTE*, August 1983, pp. 243-48+.

Jaeschke, R. "The C Spot: A Tutorial on the C Programming Language." *Softalk for the IBM Personal Computer*, January 1984, pp. 83-86.

Joyce, J. "A C Language Primer, Part 2: Tool Building in C." *BYTE*, September 1983, pp. 289-90, 292+.

Schindler, M. "Real-Time Languages Speak to Control Applications." *Electronic Design*, 21 July 1983, pp. 105-12, 114+.

Skjellum, A. "C/UNIX Programmer's Notebook." *Dr. Dobb's Journal*, October 1983, pp. 16-18.

Introduction to the UNIX System And Its Concepts

Darwin, I. "What is UNIX?" *Microsystems*, January/February 1983, pp. 96-97.

Fielder, D. "The UNIX Tutorial, Part 1: An Introduction to Features and Facilities." *BYTE*, August 1983, pp. 186-90+.

Harrar, G. "The UNIX Story." *Computerworld*, 22 August 1983, pp. 1-8.

Hughes, P. "Operating System of the Future (UNIX)." *Kilobaud Microcomputing*, June 1982, pp. 28-31.

Legg, G. "Portable Operating Systems Create Common Program Environment." *EDN*, 29 September 1983, pp. 102-04+.

Leveille, G.R. "1984: The Year of UNIX." *Information Systems News*, 23 January 1984, pp. 54-56.

O'Connor, T. "The UNIX Operating System." *InfoAge*, July/August 1983, pp. 24, 26, 104.

Ritchie, D.M., and K. Thompson. "The UNIX Time-Sharing System." *Communications of the ACM*, January 1983, pp. 84-89.

Santarelli, M.B. "Is UNIX in Your Future?" *Software News*, September 1983, pp. 43-46.

Swaine, M. "Birth and Development of UNIX — Ma Bell's Software Baby." *InfoWorld*, 29 March 1982, p. 11.

——— "16-bit Revolution, Part 2: UNIX Operating System(s)." *InfoWorld*, 15 February 1982, pp. 6-7.

Waite, M., D. Martin, and S. Prata. *UNIX Primer Plus*. Indianapolis, Indiana: Howard W. Sams & Co., Inc., 1983.

Yates, J.L. "Unix and the Standardization of Small Computer Systems." *BYTE*, October 1983, pp. 160-66.

——— "Cover Story: UNIX." *Which Computer*, December 1983, pp. 57-61+.

Yates, J.L., and E. Skrabutenos. "Ma Bell's Favorite DOS." *PC World*, April 1983, pp. 75-79.

The Purposes, Pros, and Cons of the UNIX System

Azzara, M. "Unix Looking to Capture Major Slice of Multiuser Systems Fray." *Computer Systems News*, 17 October 1983, pp. 30, 34-35.

Churchill, R. "UNIX Leads to Greater Flexibility." *Digital Design*, August 1983, pp. 92, 94+.

Fiedler, D. "UNIX the Easy Way." *Computers and Electronics*, September 1983, pp. 43-48+.

Guterl, F. "Technology '84: Microprocessors." *IEEE Spectrum*, January 1984, pp. 50-52.

Krieger, M., and F. Pack. "Unix as an Application Environment." *BYTE*, October 1983, pp. 209-14.

Lewis, G. "Waiting for Unix: Broken Promise or Dream Deferred?" *Electronic Business*, January 1984, pp. 236-37+.

Markoff, J. "Can UNIX Ever Fit Personal Computers?" *InfoWorld*, 26 December 1983, pp. 40-42.

Raleigh, L. "68000 Plus UNIX: It Might Not Fit Today's Market." *ISO World*, 21 March 1983, pp. 33-36.

——— "UNIX is Coming...But Very Slowly." *Micro Marketworld*, 23 January 1984, pp. 27-29.

Rifkin, G. "UNIX Spreads Into the Office." *Computerworld*, 12 October 1983, pp. 61-62, 66.

Skjellum, A. "C/UNIX Programmer's Notebook." *Dr. Dobb's Journal*, December 1983, pp. 14-17.

Thiel, C.T. "Software of the Future." *Infosystems*, September 1983, pp. 40-44.

Operating Systems Like the UNIX System

Boyd, A. "System Notebook: An Introduction to Pipes and Filters." *Softalk for the IBM Personal Computer*, September 1983, pp. 96, 99+.

Chase, T. "UniFLEX (6800 Operating System)." *Kilobaud Microcomputing*, June 1981, pp. 226-28.

Childress, S. "A UNIX-like Operating System for 6809 Microprocessors." *Micro: The 6502/6809 Journal*, June 1983, pp. 46-48.

———. "A UNIX-like Operating System for 6809 Microprocessors: Part II." *Micro: The 6502/6809 Journal*, July 1983, pp. 85-91.

Crawford, B. "The Not-So-BASIC 2.0." *Personal Computer Age*, May 1983, pp. 38, 42-44.

Creane, J. "MS-DOS 2.0: Pipes, Filters, Paths, and Redirections." *Personal Computer Age*, May 1983, pp. 28-37.

Downard, D. "Dynamic Uno: The New 64K CoCo." *Rainbow*, September 1983, pp. 236-240.

Esak, J. "The Zoology of XENIX." *Two/Sixteen Magazine*, November/December 1983, pp. 24-28.

Favitta, M. "Software Review: Unica and XM-80." *Dr. Dobb's Journal,* April 1983, pp. 83-85.

Fiedler, D. "InterSystems DPS-8000 and Coherent." *MicroSystems,* January/ February 1983, pp. 46-50.

———. "UNIX Facilities on CP/M: MicroShell." *MicroSystems,* January/ February 1983, pp. 51-58.

Freiberger, P. "Sage Computer Technology Announces Low-Cost 68000 System." *InfoWorld,* 8 February 1982, p. 3.

———. "What's Mine is Yours: Multiuse Software." *InfoWorld,* 8 June 1981, pp. 7-8.

Gill, P.J. "IBM's Unix Entry Hailed as 'Legitimizing' System." *Information Systems News,* 23 January 1984, pp. 51-56.

Hall, D.E. "Computer System Isolates Faults." *Computer Design,* November 1983, pp. 241-44+.

Hunter, B.N. "A Review of Microshell—A UNIX-Like Utility." *Lifelines: The Software Magazine,* April 1983, pp. 17-21.

Kern, C. "Microshell and Unica: Unix-style Enhancements for CP/M." *BYTE,* December 1982, pp. 206-20.

———. "More Unix-Style Software Tools for CP/M." *BYTE,* October 1983, pp. 428-32+.

Markoff, J. "$99 UNIX-like Operating System." *InfoWorld,* 20 June 1983, pp. 1-2.

———. "Xerox's Smalltalk Lauded by Strategic." *InfoWorld,* 29 March 1982, pp. 1-2.

Miller, A. "MicroShell: UNIX Features for CP/M." *Interface Age,* July 1982, pp. 114-17.

Miller, H. "2.00: The Path to UNIX." *PC World,* April 1983, pp. 42-47.

Morris, J. "The Powerful Tools of QNX." *PC: The Independent Guide to IBM Personal Computers,* April 1983, pp. 269-97.

Naylor, C. "Implementing Minicomputer Capabilities in a Desktop Microcomputer, Multiple Users, Xenix and Local Area Networks Characterize the Altos 586." *BYTE,* June 1983, pp. 138-46.

Needle, D. "Look-alikes Crowd Bell's 'True' UNIX in 16-bit Micro Market." *InfoWorld,* 29 March 1982, pp. 12-13.

Norton, P. "It Takes 2.0 to Tango." *Personal Computer Age,* May 1983, pp. 20-22, 24-25.

Phillips, C. "16-bit Operating Systems Standards and MS-DOS." *Microprocessors and Microsystems,* October 1983, pp. 369-73.

Raleigh, L. "Fortune Systems: Shaking Out a Firm Foundation." *ISO World*, 27 June 1983, pp. 29-32.

Reitz, R. "Small-VOS and Small-Tools." *Microsystems*, January/February 1983, pp. 66-69.

Shea, T. "MicroSoft Pushes XENIX as 16-bit Micro Standard." *InfoWorld*, 2 May 1983, pp. 24-26.

―――. "Powerful 16-bit from NBI Works in Cluster or as a Stand-Alone." *InfoWorld*, 30 May 1983, pp. 1-2.

Skjellum, A. "UNICA: A UNIX-like Utility System for CP/M." *Microsystems*, January/February 1983, pp. 59-65.

Swaine, M. "Cromemco Reveals Details of New 16-bit Systems." *InfoWorld*, 5 April 1982, p. 1.

Ursino, M. "Introduction to the XENIX Operating System." *Microsystems*, January/February 1983, pp. 36-41.

―――. "Pick Operating System." *InfoWorld*, 13 April 1981, p. 9.

Comparisons of Operating Systems

Blaisdell, M. "The Great OS Debate." *Microcomputing*, February 1983, pp. 58-64.

Boss, R.W. "Operating Systems for Multi-User/Tasking Micros." *Software Review*, June 1983, pp. 78-83.

Boyd, A., P. Good, and S. Veit. "User's Guide to Operating Systems." *Personal Computing*, May 1981, pp. 27-32.

Brousell, D.R. "MS-DOS, CP/M, Unix Battle for Domination in Market Demanding Multi-Tasking, Multi-User Capability." *Electronic News*, 26 September 1983, pp. 1, 54-55+.

Cashin, J. "SuperMicros Take On Minis." *Small Systems World*, June 1983, pp. 23-27.

Celko, J. "Which Operating Systems Will Be Tomorrow's Winners?" *Computer Dealer*, November 1983, pp. 272-274+.

Darwin, I.F. "The UNIX File." *Microsystems*, March 1983, pp. 22-26+.

Falcoff, B. "Operating Systems Under the Microscope." *Personal Computing*, July 1982, pp. 97-103.

Fertig, R.T. "On Top Today, Toppled Tomorrow." *Computer Decisions*, March 1984, pp. 63-65.

Fiedler, D. "The Unix Tutorial, Part 3: Unix in the Microcomputer Marketplace." *BYTE*, October 1983, pp. 132-38+.

Foster, S. "Broadening Your Personal Computer's Horizons." *Computer Decisions*, January 1984, pp. 146-58.

Fox, J. "Unraveling the Mysteries of Micro Operating Systems." *Computerworld*, 14 December 1983, pp. 50-53.

Greenberg, R. "UNIX Operating System and the XENIX Standard Operating Environment." *BYTE*, June 1981, pp. 248-64.

Hogan, T. "Should CP/M Be the Standard?" *InfoWorld*, 17 August 1983, p. 14.

Horwitt, E., and A.E. Smith. "The Invisible Office Manager." *Business Computer Systems*, March 1983, pp. 69-82.

King, L. "IBM Seeks UNIX on 4300, Pick System Also Eyed." *Information Systems News*, 16 May 1983, p. 12.

Libes, D. "UNIX and CP/M." *Microsystems*, January/February 1983, pp. 26-43.

Morgan, C. "New 16-bit Operating Systems, or, The Search for Benutzerfreundlichkeit." *BYTE*, June 1981, pp. 6-10.

Schenot, R. "What Portable Operating Systems Promise." *Small Systems World*, January 1984, pp. 28-32+.

Suydam, W. "Microcomputer Operating System Wars." *Hardcopy*, January 1984, pp. 70-76.

Truax, P., L. Burstein, and J. Nitzberg. "Generic Operating Systems: Unix or Pick?" *Technology in Focus*, Fall 1983, pp. 8-12.

Valigra, L. "Intel Teams Up with Microsoft, Pushes Hardware/Software for UNIX OEMs." *Mini-Micro Systems*, January 1983, pp. 23-25.

Xenakis, J.J. "The Operating System Circus." *Computer Update*, November/December 1983, pp. 40-45.

———. "Computer OPS." *Which Computer*, June 1983, pp. 131-33.

———. "A Feverish Race in Operating Systems." *Business Week*, 21 February 1983, pp. 96-98.

———. "Microsoft/Lifeboat Battle Cry (PC-DOS as 16-bit Standard)." *PC: The Independent Guide to IBM Personal Computers*, June 1982, pp. 159-61.

———. "PICK vs UNIX." *Which Computer*, January 1984, pp. 149-53.

———. "Try These Generic Products: Operating Systems Software." *Modern Office Procedures*, March 1983, pp. 78, 80+.

Implementation

Appalaraju, R. "High-End mPs Challenge Mainframes." *Digital Design,* October 1983, pp. 98-102+.

Blackett, R.K. "UNIX-based System Runs Real-Time Applications." *Mini-Micro Systems,* May 1983, pp. 249-52.

Emmett, R. "News in Perspective: Tracking the P.C. Strategy." *Datamation,* August 1983, pp. 48-50.

Jalics, P.J., and T.S. Heines. "Transporting a Portable Operating System: UNIX to an IBM Minicomputer." *Communications of the ACM,* December 1983, pp. 1066-72.

Karshmer, A.I., D.J. Depree, and J. Phelan. "The New Mexico State University Ring-Star System: A Distributed UNIX Environment." *Software—Practice & Experience,* December 1983, pp. 1157-68.

Killmon, P. "Superminis: Changing Direction for the Future." *Computer Design,* November 1983, pp. 167-70+.

Lewis, G. "Pyramid Builds UNIX Supermini with Reduced-Instruction-Set Architecture." *Mini-Micro Systems,* August 1983, pp. 17-20.

Libes, D. "UNIX on Microcomputers: A Hands Off Summary of UNIX Implementations." *Microsystems,* January/February 1983, pp. 42-44.

Tilson, M. "Moving Unix to New Machines." *BYTE,* October 1983, pp. 266-72+.

The Shell

Bourne, S.R. "The Unix Shell." *BYTE,* October 1983, pp. 187-92+.

Foley, M.J. "Software Strategy: Wang Plays the UNIX Shell Game." *Electronic Business,* January 1984, pp. 223-24+.

Files and Data Bases

Eagleson, R. "New Database Software Part 9: INFORMIX." *Small Systems World,* February 1983, pp. 30-33.

Jegado, M. "Recoverability Aspects of a Distributed File System." *Software—Practice & Experience,* January 1983, pp. 33-44.

Joyce, J. "A Tour Through the Unix File System." *BYTE*, October 1983, pp. 170-76+.

Wilson, W.E. "UNIX to CP/M: Floppy Disk File Conversion." *Dr. Dobb's Journal*, October 1983, pp. 20-24+.

Networking

Drohan, R., R. Paulson, D. West, and F. Yee. "Work Station Merges Hardware, Software Design." *Electronic Design*, 15 September 1983, pp. 115-21+.

Emerson, S.L. "Usenet: A Bulletin Board for Unix Users." *BYTE*, October 1983, pp. 219-25+.

Groff, J.R. "Modified UNIX System Tames Network Architecture." *Electronics*, 22 September 1983, pp. 159-63.

Joy, W. "Berkeley 4.2 Gives UNIX Operating System Network Support." *Electronics*, 28 July 1983, pp. 114-18.

van Tilborg, A.M., and L.D. Wittie. "Operating Systems for the Micronet Network Computer." *IEEE Micro*, March/April 1983, pp. 38-47.

———. "Software and Services." *Computerworld*, 30 January 1984, pp. 50-52, 54-56.

———. "'Super Test Set' to Give Users a Fast Fix on the Right Carrier." *Data Communications*, August 1983, pp. 41, 44+.

Software Tools

Cherry, L.L., and N.H. Macdonald. "The Unix Writer's Workbench Software." *BYTE*, October 1983, pp. 241-46+.

Kavuru, S. "Modular Architecture." *BYTE*, June 1983, pp. 194-99+.

Loveluck, J.M. "The PERQ Workstation and the Distributed Computing Equipment." *Software World*, January/March 1983, pp. 2-14.

Markoff, J. "Micro Software in Mini World." *InfoWorld*, 1 February 1982, pp. 1-2.

———. "Sequitur System Available for the Fortune System 32:16." *InfoWorld*, 15 November 1982, p. 9.

Scherrer, D.K., P.H. Sherrer, T.H. Strong, and S.J. Penny. "The Software Tools: UNIX Capabilities on Non-UNIX Systems." *BYTE*, November 1983, pp. 430-36+.

Schindler, M. "1984 Technology Forecast—Engineering Software." *Electronic Design*, 12 January 1984, pp. 150-58+.

Skjellum, A. "Expanded Wildcards Under UNIX." *Dr. Dobb's Journal*, November 1982, pp. 12-16.

Swaine, M. "Scientific Software for UNIX System." *InfoWorld*, 14 February 1983, pp. 34-35.

Thomas, R. "What is a Software Tool?" *BYTE*, August 1983, pp. 222-26+.

———. "Software is Striving to Solve Problems of Standardization, Portability, and User-Friendliness." *Electronics*, 6 October 1983, pp. 141-49.

———. "UNIX Software List Update." *InfoWorld*, 13 April 1981, p. 13.

Text Processing

Joy, W. *An Introduction to Display Editing with Vi.* Berkeley, California: Computing Science Division of the University of California at Berkeley.

Mace, S. "Horizon Introduces Easy-to-Use Word Processor to Run on UNIX." *InfoWorld*, 3 January 1983, pp. 10-11.

Markoff, J. "Sequitur Relational System Hopes to Lead, Not Follow." *InfoWorld*, 23 November 1981, p. 5.

———. "T/Maker II Offers Apples and Oranges." *InfoWorld*, 4 October 1982, p. 13.

Tuthill, B. "Typesetting on the Unix System." *BYTE*, October 1983, pp. 253-58+.

———. "Sphinx and Analyst." *Which Computer*, December 1983, pp. 137-39.

Graphics

Ciarcia, S. "Plotting with the TRS-80 / Matter of Environment / Feasibility Study." *BYTE*, March 1982, pp. 445-46.

Clark, J.H., and T. Davis. "Work Station Unites Real-time Graphics with Unix, Ethernet." *Electronics*, 20 October 1983, pp. 113-19.

Landy, M.S., V. Cohen, and G. Sperling. "HIPS: A UNIX-Based Image Processing System." *Computer Vision, Graphics & Image Processing*, March 1984, pp. 331-47.

Communications

Blair, G., J. Mariani, and W. Shepherd. "A Practical Extension to UNIX for Interprocess Communication." *Software — Practice & Experience,* January 1983, pp. 45-58.

Hayes, P.J., and P.A. Szekely. "Graceful Interaction Through the COUSIN Command Interface." *International Journal of Man-Machine Studies,* September 1983, pp. 285-306.

Jackson, P. "UNIX Variant Opens a Path to Managing Multiprocessor Systems." *Electronics,* 28 July 1983, pp. 118-24.

Other Applications

Alpert, D., D. Carberry, M. Yamamura, and P. Mak. "32-Bit Processor Chip Integrates Major System Functions." *Electronics,* 14 July 1983, pp. 113-19.

Gale, L. "Work Station Performs at the Superminicomputer Level." *Electronics,* 8 September 1983, pp. 119-23.

Glazer, S. "Enhanced Version of Bell Labs' UNIX Serves Fault-Tolerant Multiprocessor System." *Electronics,* 3 November 1983, pp. 145-49.

Lawson, L. "Develop VLSI Test Software Quickly." *Computer Design,* November 1983, pp. 133-38+.

Lee, H. "Terminal Program Serves TRS-80 Computer." *Electronics,* 17 November 1983, pp. 152-55.

Manuel, T. "Western Europe Looks to Parallel Processing for Future Computers." *Electronics,* 16 June 1983, pp. 111-13.

Rushby, J., and B. Randell. "A Distributed Secure System." *Computer,* July 1983, pp. 55-67.

Wallace, J.J. "DMERT Crash Resistant File Systems." *Software — Practice & Experience,* April 1983, pp. 385-87.

Watson, J. "Using Unix for Pascal Programmers." *Journal of PASCAL and ADA,* January 1983, pp. 22-25.

TRADEMARKS

The italicized names are trademarked products of the corresponding companies, with registered trademarks noted with an ®.

Access/SNA	Communication Solution, Inc.
ace	Relational Database Systems, Inc.
Apple® DOS	Apple Computer, Inc.
Apple® II	Apple Computer, Inc.
ASM 68	Unisoft Systems
C5001	Onyx Systems, Inc.
CBASIC-86	Digital Research
C-isam	Relational Database Systems, Inc.
CLEO-3780 Bisynchronous Communications	Phone 1, Inc.
CLEO-3270 Emulator	Phone 1, Inc.
COHERENT®	Mark Williams Company
ColorKey+	Tektronix, Inc.
CP/M®	Digital Research
CP/M-86®	Digital Research
CrystalWriter	Syntactics Corporation
Datatalker I	Winterhalter, Inc.
EMACS	UniPress Software, Inc.
EUNICE	The Wollongong Group
fine-it!	Relational Database Systems, Inc.
Forms-2	Micro Focus, Inc.
FUSION	Network Research Corporation
Handle Business Graphics	Handle Corporation
Handle Calc	Handle Corporation
Handle List	Handle Corporation

Handle Spell	Handle Corporation
Handle Writer	Handle Corporation
Horizon Word Processing®	Horizon Software Systems, Inc.
IBM®	International Business Machines, Inc.
IBM® 370	International Business Machines, Inc.
IDRIS®	Whitesmiths, Ltd.
informix®	Relational Database Systems, Inc.
INGRES	Relational Technology, Inc.
Lear-Siegler ADM3A terminal	Lear-Siegler, Inc.
Level II Animator	Micro Focus, Inc.
Level II COBOL	Micro Focus, Inc.
Lisa	Apple Computer, Inc.
Local Net®	Sytek, Inc.
LOGIX	Logical Software, Inc.
MDBS III	Micro Data Base Systems, Inc.
Menus and Forms Development System	Schmidt Associates
Mistress	Rhodnius, Inc.
MLISP	UniPress Software, Inc.
MP/M	Digital Research
MS-DOS®	Microsoft Corporation
Officesmith	Officesmiths, Inc.
OPEN SYSTEMS	Open Systems, Inc.
ORACLE®	Oracle Corp.
Pascal/2	Ithaca Intersystems, Inc.
PEGASUS®	The Wollongong Group
perform	Relational Database Systems, Inc.
Sequitur	The Community Memory Project
SofGram	SofTest, Inc.
SQL Plus	Oracle Group
Tandy System 16	Radio Shack, a Division of the Tandy Corp.
Telex	The Telex Corporation
Texas Instruments® Silent 700 printer	Texas Instruments, Inc.
Thoroughbred Software	SMC Software Systems
TNIX	Tektronix, Inc.
TWX	Western Union Telegraph Company

UltraCalc	Olympus Software
UNET	3Com Corporation
Unify®	Unify Corporation
UNOS	Charles River Data Systems
UniPlus+	UniSoft Systems
VENIX®	VenturCom
ViewComp	UniCorp Software
VisiCalc®	VisiCorp.
Wang®	Wang Labs, Inc.
WordStar®	MicroPro International Corporation
XENIX®	Microsoft Corporation
Zeus	OSM Computer Corporation

INDEX